ARCO

MASTER THE

GRE®

2006

ARCO

MASTER THE

GRE®

2006

Thomas H. Martinson

THOMSON

PETERSON'S

Australia • Canada • Mexico • Singapore • Spain • United Kingdom • United States

About Thomson Peterson's

With revenues of US$7.8 billion, The Thomson Corporation (www.thomson.com) is a leading global provider of integrated information solutions for business, education, and professional customers. Its Learning businesses and brands (www.thomsonlearning.com) serve the needs of individuals, learning institutions, and corporations with products and services for both traditional and distributed learning.

Peterson's, part of The Thomson Corporation, is one of the nation's most respected providers of lifelong learning online resources, software, reference guides, and books. The Education Supersite[SM] at www.petersons.com—the Internet's most heavily traveled education resource—has searchable databases and interactive tools for contacting U.S.-accredited institutions and programs. In addition, Peterson's serves more than 105 million education consumers annually.

For more information, contact Peterson's, 2000 Lenox Drive, Lawrenceville, NJ 08648; 800-338-3282; or find us on the World Wide Web at: www.petersons.com/about.

Editor: Joe Krasowski; Production Editor: Bret Bollman; Manufacturing Manager: Ray Golaszewski; Composition Manager: Melissa Ignatowski; CD Producer: Carol Aickley; CD Quality Assurance: Jeff Pagano

ISSN: International Standard Serial Number information available upon request.

ISBN: 0-7689-1927-4

Printed in the United States of America

10 9 8 7 6 5 4 3 2   07 06 05

Thirteenth edition

Contents

Contents

PART IV: GRE MATH QUESTIONS

PART V: GRE ANALYTICAL WRITING

PART VI: FIVE PRACTICE TESTS

APPENDICES

Before You Begin

HOW TO USE THIS BOOK

Taking the GRE is a skill. It shares some things in common with other endeavors such as competing in athletics. It requires discipline and practice to succeed. These are skills that can be improved through coaching, but ultimately improvement also requires practice. This book gives you both by including the following:

- "The Top 10 Ways to Raise Your Score" gives you a preview of some of the critical strategies you'll learn. "Track Your Progress" is where you'll record your scores on the diagnostic and practice tests as you work through the book.

- **Part I** provides essential general information about the GRE.

- **Part II** is a full-length diagnostic test. It can show you where your skills are strong—and where they need some shoring up.

- **Parts III through V** are the coaching program. They analyze each question type, give you powerful strategies for attacking the test on its own terms, and provide a full-scale review of GRE mathematics.

- **Part VI** contains five full-length sample GREs followed by a detailed analysis of each question. The detailed analysis is very important in helping you learn from your mistakes.

- The **Appendices** offer a GRE Word List and some helpful information on financing your way through graduate school.

ARCO Master the GRE is published with a CD. The CD is designed to help you practice what you have learned using state-of-the-art computer-adaptive software. It includes 3 CATs (computer-adaptive tests) and access to the Private Tutor Lecture Series. The lecture series is conducted by author Tom Martinson and offers valuable strategies designed to help you achieve your score goal. Lecture topics include:

- Analyzing Arguments
- Data Sufficiency
- Problem Solving
- Reading Comprehension
- Sentence Correction

The Top 10 Ways to Raise Your Score

When it comes to taking the GRE, some test-taking skills will do you more good than others. There are concepts you can learn, techniques you can follow, and tricks you can use that will help you to do your very best. Here's our pick for the top 10 ways to raise your score:

1. **Create a study plan and follow it.** The right GRE study plan will help you get the most out of this book in whatever time you have.

2. **Don't get stuck on any one question.** Since you have to answer questions in order to keep moving, you can't afford to spend too much time on any one problem.

3. **Learn the directions in advance.** If you already know the directions, you won't have to waste your precious test time reading them. You'll be able to jump right in and start answering questions as soon as the test clock starts.

4. **In sentence completions, look for clue words.** These words will reveal the meaning of the sentence and point you in the right direction.

5. **In analogy questions, a sentence can make the connection.** Analogies are about word relationships. The best way to figure out the relationship is to summarize it in a sentence.

6. **In reading comprehension, read for structure, not details.** When you read GRE passages, don't let the details bog you down. Most of the questions will ask about the structure of the passage rather than specific facts. If you need the facts, they're always there in the passage. This is particularly important because you'll probably have to scroll to read the entire passage.

7. **If a problem-solving math question stumps you, work backward from the answers.** The right answer has to be one of the five choices. Since the choices are arranged in size order, starting with (C) results in the fewest calculations.

8. **In quantitative comparisons, consider all possibilities.** Think what would happen if you plugged in 1, 0, a fraction, or a negative number for x in the expressions you're comparing.

9. **If math questions refer to a graph, avoid doing a lengthy calculation and save valuable time by estimating.**

10. **For the Analytical Writing Measure,** use the ARCO "templates" to craft essays that satisfy the criteria that the GRE graders are trained to look for.

Track Your Progress

For each exam:

1. Enter the number of questions that you answered *correctly* in each part (Verbal and Math) in the appropriate rows. (Ignore incorrect responses.)

2. To keep track of your progress in each of the content areas, enter the number of items of each type that you answered correctly into the appropriate row.

   Enter your overall (3-digit) score for each part (Verbal and Math) using the table provided on page 8.

Note: Exercise caution in interpreting the data. Because a book-based exam cannot simulate in every respect a computer-based exam, results tend to be volatile. Do not place much emphasis on small differences in performance.

GRE SCORE TRACKER

	Diagnostic Test	Practice Test 1	Practice Test 2	Practice Test 3	Practice Test 4	Practice Test 5
Verbal Total						
Antonyms						
Sentence Completions						
Reading Comp.						
Verbal Score						
Math Total						
Problem Solving						
Quantitative Comparison						
Graphs						
Math Score						

OTHER TITLES IN SERIES

ARCO Master the GMAT®

ARCO The Master Series LSAT

OTHER RECOMMENDED TITLES

Peterson's MBA Programs

ARCO 30 Days to the GMAT®

ARCO GMAT® Answers to the Real Essay Questions

Petersons.com/publishing

Check out our Web site at www.petersons.com/publishing to see if there is any new information regarding the test and any revisions or corrections to the content of this book. We've made sure the information in this book is accurate and up-to-date; however, the test format or content may have changed since the time of publication.

About the Author

Professor Thomas H. Martinson is widely acknowledged to be America's leading authority on test preparation. Educated at Harvard University with an advanced degree and twelve years of postgraduate research, Professor Martinson has published more than three dozen books on test preparation. He is routinely invited to lecture on test preparation and related topics at top colleges and universities throughout the United States and abroad.

ARCO Master the GRE is published with a CD. You will be able to practice what you have learned using state-of-the-art computer adaptive software. The software was created by Cambridge Educational Services, 2720 River Road, Ste. 36, Des Plaines, IL 60018.

PART I

GRE BASICS

All About the GRE

chapter 1

OVERVIEW

- **What is the GRE?**
- **What is the CAT?**
- **How do you register for the GRE?**
- **What kinds of questions are on the test?**
- **What is a GRE study plan?**
- **What is the best study plan for you?**
- **How is the test scored?**
- **How can you tell if your work is paying off?**
- **Can you predict your GRE score?**
- **What smart test-takers know**
- **Summing it up**

WHAT IS THE GRE?

The letters GRE stand for Graduate Record Examination—a standardized exam given at various locations in the United States and around the world. You'll be taking what is called the GRE CAT (which stands for Computer Adaptive Test). It's a computer-based exam given year-round at universities and learning centers. You'll need to register for the test and make an appointment for your testing session. (See "How Do You Register for the GRE?" on page 4.)

The GRE testing program includes a General Test as well as Subject Tests in disciplines such as Biology, Mathematics, and Psychology. This book is devoted to the GRE General Test, the most widely used of the GREs. For the purpose of simplicity, from here on in this book the term GRE will be used to refer to the General Test.

WHAT IS THE CAT?

CAT exams are the wave of the future for all types of exams, and the GRE is no exception. In previous years, the GRE was a paper-based exam, but now, the GRE is mostly computerized.

The GRE CAT differs from a paper-based exam in that a computer program chooses problems based on a candidate's responses to previous questions. Thus,

NOTE

Spend some quality time with a CAT. Practicing with a CAT on a computer is an essential part of preparing for the GRE. The CD in this book includes a CAT with an algorithm to construct exam versions to test your abilities.

the CAT is "adaptive" or "interactive." Candidates taking a paper-based test are presented with a range of questions (including easy, moderately difficult, and difficult items). A CAT selects questions according to each candidate's ability.

During a CAT, the computer controls the order in which test items appear, basing its selection on the candidate's responses to earlier items. Because the CAT is interactive, it uses fewer items and takes less time to administer than the paper-based version.

At the risk of oversimplifying, the testing procedure can be described as follows. The computer has access to a large number of test items classified according to question type (graphs, antonyms, reading comprehension, and so on) and arranged in order of difficulty. At the outset, the computer presents you with a couple of "seed" questions, items of average level of difficulty. If you answer those successfully, the program selects for the next question an item of greater difficulty; if you do not answer the "seed" questions correctly, the program lowers the level of difficulty. This process is repeated, with the program continuing to adjust the level of difficulty of questions, until you have provided all the answers that the computer needs to calculate your score.

The Analytical Writing Measure is an exception to this general rule. The AWM is an essay section. You'll have 45 minutes to write an essay answer to an "issue" topic and 30 minutes to write an essay answer to an "argument" topic. These essays are then graded by trained readers rather than by computer.

HOW DO YOU REGISTER FOR THE GRE?

TIP

Get the latest GRE information on the Web. You can get up-to-the-minute GRE information on the World Wide Web. The address is www.gre.org.

One way you can register to take the exam is through the GRE Bulletin, which includes registration forms. You can obtain the GRE Bulletin from your Career Placement Office or by writing to:

Graduate Record Examinations Program
P.O. Box 6000
Princeton, NJ 08541-6000

The CAT is given at hundreds of Sylvan Technology Centers, ETS Field Service offices, and other designated test sites worldwide. To schedule an appointment to take the CAT, call the test center or (800) GRE-CALL during regular business hours. If you are paying for the test by credit card, you can make the appointment and arrange for payment over the telephone. Otherwise, you will need to submit the registration form by mail and wait two to four weeks for authorization to schedule a test appointment.

WHAT KINDS OF QUESTIONS ARE ON THE TEST?

The GRE includes verbal and mathematics sections in multiple-choice format plus the essay part. Here's a test description:

Verbal Questions

- **Sentence Completions.** Sentence completion questions ask you to choose a word or words that fill in the blanks in a given sentence.

- **Analogies.** Analogy questions present a pair of words that have some logical relationship. Then the choices present other pairs of words. You have to choose the pair that has the same kind of relationship as the first pair.

- **Reading Comprehension.** Reading comprehension questions relate to a passage that is provided for you to read. The passage can be about almost anything, and the questions about it test how well you understood the passage and the information in it.

- **Antonyms.** Antonym questions present a single vocabulary word. You must pick the answer choice that is most nearly opposite in meaning to the given word.

Mathematics Questions

- **Quantitative Comparisons.** Quantitative comparison questions test your skills in comparing information and in estimating. You'll see two quantities, one in Column A and one in Column B. The task is to compare the two quantities and decide if one is greater than the other, if they are equal, or if no comparison is possible.

- **Problem Solving.** Problem-solving questions present multiple-choice problems in arithmetic, basic algebra, and elementary geometry. The task is to solve the problems and choose the correct answer from among five answer choices.

- **Graphs.** Graph questions present mathematical information in pictorial form. Each graph is followed by questions about it.

Analytical Writing Measure

- **Issue Topic.** The 45-minute "Present Your Perspective on an Issue" prompt asks you to take a position on a topic of general interest and to then develop your opinion from any perspective that you choose.

- **Argument Topic.** The 30-minute "Analyze an Argument" topic requires you to critique an argument by assessing the reasonableness of its assumptions, the validity of its logic, and the reliability of its conclusion.

TIP

Because of the CAT function, the first few questions count more than the last few. Take a little extra time at the beginning to make sure you get those all-important questions right.

NOTE

The CAT is offered year-round, and you can see your scores immediately upon completing the test. Just make sure you schedule far enough in advance for your official score reports to get to your targeted schools along with the other parts of your applications.

Your testing session will last from $2\frac{1}{2}$ to 4 hours, depending on whether you are selected to receive one or more pretest or research sections:

Section	Number of Items	Time
Warm-Up	—	—
Analytical Writing	1 Issue Prompt*	45 min.
	1 Argument Prompt	30 min.
Math	28	45 min.
Verbal	30	30 min.
Pretest**	Variable	Variable
Research***	Variable	Variable

*For the Issue part, you'll be given two prompts and will choose one to write on.

**A pretest section contains questions that are being validated for use on future exams. A pretest section can be either verbal or math and can appear at any time after the Analytical Writing part. A pretest section will not be identified as such, but the items in a pretest section will not affect your scores.

***A research section contains items being tested for possible future use. A research section will be identified as "research" and always comes after all other parts of the test.

The Math Section, Verbal Section, and pretest section (if your test includes one of these) can be presented in any order; however, Analytical Writing is always first.

Since a "Pretest" section is not identified for you, you should answer all questions as though they are vital to your score.

WHAT IS A GRE STUDY PLAN?

As you can tell, this book contains a lot of information about the GRE, and you'll probably want to work with the CD and with the Web-based resources provided by Peterson's. So, you'll need a plan for getting through it all.

The right study plan will help you manage your time so that you get the most out of this book and the other resources, whether you have three months, three weeks, or only a few days to prepare. It will help you work efficiently and keep you from getting stressed out.

WHAT IS THE BEST STUDY PLAN FOR YOU?

To decide on your study plan, answer these two questions: (1) How long do you have until the test? (2) How much time can you devote to GRE study?

Here are some suggestions to make your job easier. If you are starting early and the GRE is two or three months away, you can do it all. You can study from beginning to end, you can use the CAT on the CD, you can take advantage of the valuable Private Tutor classes

NOTE

Why does the GRE use scaled scores? Scaled scores allow the test-makers to account for differences from one version of the GRE to another. Using scaled scores ensures that a score of, say, 430 on one GRE is equivalent to 430 on another.

on the CD, and you can visit the Author's Edge at www.petersons.com/authorsedge/gre to get even more study materials and help. If the GRE is a month or less away and you need a more concentrated course, take the Diagnostic Test and tailor your study plan to your areas of weakness, and cover those parts of the book that will be of most value to you.

HOW IS THE TEST SCORED?

Your score is based on a combination of the number of questions you answered correctly and the difficulty level of the questions answered. You get more credit for answering a harder question than you get for answering an easier one. There is no deduction for wrong answers; in fact, you will be penalized for any question left unanswered when time runs out. The scoring scale runs from 200 (the minimum) to 800 (the maximum). Your score report for the multiple-choice parts will include two different scores—one for verbal and one for math. It will also include a percentile ranking for each section.

Your essay responses on the Analytical Writing Measure (AWM) will be scored by a team of readers on a scale of 1 (the minimum) to 6 (the maximum). Two graders will read the essays, and each will assign scores. If there is more than a one-point differential between the two graders' scores (which, according to ETS, rarely happens), a third reader will be called in as an arbiter to determine the final score. Your final AWM score will be a single score for both essays, reported on the 1 to 6 scale in half-point intervals.

HOW CAN YOU TELL IF YOUR WORK IS PAYING OFF?

Again, no matter how much time you have to prepare, you should start by taking the Diagnostic Test found in Part II. After you score it, you'll be able to see where you need to concentrate your efforts.

The next step is to see how you do with the exercises at the end of each chapter in Part III (Verbal), Part IV (Math), and Part V (Analytical Writing). Compare your scores on the Verbal and Math parts to your results on the Diagnostic Test. Have you improved? Where do you still need work? Also, monitor your improvement on the essay portion to make sure that your answers are getting stronger.

When you're ready, take the Practice Tests found in Part VI. These are like the tests you'll take in terms of content, number of questions, and time limit. You should try to simulate test conditions as nearly as you can. After you score a Practice Test, make another comparison to the chapter exercises and to the Diagnostic Test. This will show you how your work is paying off.

CAN YOU PREDICT YOUR GRE SCORE?

The use of computer-adaptive testing technology makes it difficult to predict your actual GRE score based on your performance on a paper-and-pencil practice test. We have tried, however, to develop a scoring table that provides a general idea of your performance at this point in your preparation. To predict your score on the practice tests in this book, count the correct answers in each section and find that number in the left column of the charts below. The corresponding number in the right column represents an approximation of your GRE test score. You can use the *Track Your Progress* chart on page xiii, to keep a record of your progress.

MATH SUBSCORE (C = CORRECT, S = SCORE)

C	S	C	S	C	S	C	S	C	S
28	800	22	650	16	500	10	350	4	200
27	780	21	630	15	480	9	330	3	200
26	750	20	600	14	450	8	300	2	200
25	730	19	580	13	430	7	280	1	200
24	700	18	550	12	400	6	250	0	200
23	680	17	530	11	380	5	230		

VERBAL SUBSCORE (C = CORRECT, S = SCORE)

C	S	C	S	C	S	C	S	C	S
30	800	23	620	16	450	9	270	3	200
29	770	22	600	15	420	8	250	2	200
28	750	21	570	14	400	7	220	1	200
27	720	20	550	13	370	6	200	0	200
26	700	19	520	12	350	5	200		
25	670	18	500	11	320	4	200		
24	650	17	470	10	300				

Note: Remember that the Analytical Writing Measure will be scored by trained readers, so it is not possible for you to give yourself a score on that part.

WHAT SMART TEST-TAKERS KNOW

YOU HAVE TO BEAT THE CLOCK.

Many years ago, there was a program on television called *Beat the Clock*. Contestants were given silly things to do within a certain time limit. For example, a contestant might be asked to stack 100 paper cups on top of each other in 30 seconds—while blindfolded! On the television studio wall was a large clock with a single hand so contestants could keep track of the passing time. The GRE is a lot like this, but without the blindfold.

Your computer screen keeps track of the time and the number of questions you've answered on the exam. Use the information to stay on track. (If you find the timer function distracting, then you can suppress it; but it will reappear automatically at the five-minute mark and won't go away.)

THE GRE TAKES CONCENTRATION.

The GRE is an arduous task. There is no way that you can maintain your concentration through both of the sections. There will be times when your attention begins to flag. Learn to recognize this. For example, if you find that you are reading and rereading the same line without understanding it, sit back in your chair, close your eyes, take a deep breath or two (or rub your eyes or whatever), and then get back to work.

THE ANSWERS ARE ALL THERE IN FRONT OF YOU.

The multiple-choice format gives you a real advantage. The correct answer is always right there on the monitor screen. To be sure, it's surrounded by wrong choices, but it may be possible to eliminate one or more of those other choices as non-answers. Look at the following reading comprehension question:

> The author argues that the evidence supporting the new theory is
> - **(A)** hypothetical
> - **(B)** biased
> - **(C)** empirical
> - **(D)** speculative
> - **(E)** fragmentary

You might think that it is impossible to make any progress on a reading comprehension question without the reading selection, but you can eliminate three of the five answers in this question as non-answers. Study the question stem. We can infer that the author of the selection has at least implicitly passed judgment on the evidence supporting the new theory. What kind of judgment might someone make about the evidence adduced to support a theory? (A), (C), and (D) all seem extremely unlikely. As for (A), while the theory is itself a hypothesis, the evidence supporting the theory would not be hypothetical. As for (C), evidence is empirical by definition. So it is unlikely that anyone would argue "This evidence is empirical." And (D) can be eliminated for the same reason as (A).

TIP

The on-screen toolbar features a clock icon that keeps track of the passing time. You can suppress the function by clicking on the icon and reactivate it by clicking a second time. An additional status feature keeps track of the number of questions answered and remaining in the section.

TIP

Play the odds. If you can eliminate one answer choice, your guess has a 25 percent chance of being right. Eliminate two choices, and you have a $33\frac{1}{3}$ percent chance. Eliminate three choices, and you have a 50 percent chance of guessing correctly.

Admittedly, this leaves you with a choice of (B) or (E), a choice that depends on the content of the reading selection; but at least you have a 50-50 chance of getting the question correct—even without reading the selection.

BIORHYTHMS COUNT.

We all have biorhythms. Some of us are morning people, some afternoon. Schedule your appointment for the GRE for a time when you are likely to be at your peak.

IF YOU ARE A "COMPUTER DUMMY," YOU SHOULD BUY, BEG, BORROW, OR RENT ONE.

Now, first of all, you are not a "complete dummy" even if you have never used a computer. You've certainly seen them in a bank, or a grocery store, or at a friend's home, so you have some idea of what one looks like and what it is supposed to do. But there is a big difference between knowing what a car looks like and knowing how to drive one. If you have to, go down to your local office service or computer store and buy an hour or two of time on a computer and take the CD that came with this book with you. A technical support rep will help you load it onto the computer so you can practice taking a CAT.

IT'S WORTH SPENDING TIME ON THE TUTORIALS.

The computerized version of the GRE begins with these tutorials:

- How to Use a Mouse
- How to Select an Answer
- How to Use the Testing Tools
- How to Scroll

The program forces you to work through these tutorials, and you should pay careful attention to the directions. If you have never before worked with a mouse and a scroll bar, stay in the appropriate tutorials until you are comfortable with the mechanics of the computer. Time spent on the tutorials is not taken away from your time on the testing sections. And even if you are already "computer literate" and don't need to practice those techniques, you should nonetheless pay careful attention to the idiosyncrasies of the CAT program, e.g., how to indicate an answer, how to change an answer, how to move forward and backward, and what the various screen icons mean.

SCROLLING IS THE ONLY WAY TO SEE ALL OF SOME QUESTIONS.

In many computer programs, when a body of text is too long to be displayed in its entirety on the screen, you have the option of "scrolling" through the text. You can scroll up or down. The scroll function removes the top (or bottom) line and moves the other lines of text up (or down) one line on the screen, adding the next (or preceding) line of text. Your first experience with the scroll function may be a bit frustrating because it can be very sensitive. If you have the opportunity to play with a computer in advance of the test, you should also test a program that manipulates text, e.g., a word processing program. Pay particular attention to the scrolling feature.

YOU HAVE TO DISMISS THE DIRECTIONS.

When you begin a new section or question type, the directions for that part will appear. But they don't time out. So your first order of business is to get rid of them from the screen: Point and click on the "Dismiss Directions" box.

YOU HAVE TO CONFIRM YOUR ANSWER CHOICES.

You select your choice by directing the pointer to an oval and clicking. This illuminates the oval, indicating that you have selected the associated answer choice. Then you click on the "Arrow" button. But that's not the last step. You still have to confirm your choice using the "Confirm" button on the toolbar.

This is both a good and a bad feature of the program. On the one hand, it reduces the risk that you'll make a silly mistake because you have to confirm your choice. On the other hand, you could wind up wasting a lot of time if you forget to confirm your choice. If you don't confirm, the machine acts as though you're still working and sits there patiently waiting for additional input.

YOU SHOULD ANSWER EVERY QUESTION.

Because on the CAT you'll be penalized for any questions left unanswered when time runs out, the best strategy is to answer every question in a section. The screen display will tell you how many questions you have yet to answer, so you can pace yourself to make sure you complete the section.

YOU MUST ANSWER QUESTIONS IN THE ORDER PRESENTED.

While the "adaptive" aspect of the CAT should have no effect on your preparation, it has a great effect on your approach to the exam itself. On a CAT exam, you MUST ANSWER THE QUESTIONS IN THE ORDER PRESENTED. Since the exam adapts itself in response to your answers, you cannot skip and later return to any questions. And, you cannot rethink and change your answer at a later time. You cannot seek out and answer the easier question styles first. In other words, you must do the best you can to answer each question. Choose the answer that you have determined is best, or guess if necessary, confirm your choice, and move on to the next question.

THE FIRST HALF OF A SECTION IS WHERE THE POINTS ARE.

On the CAT, how well you do on the first half of each section plays a very big part in determining your final score. That's because the first half of each section is where the computer program that moves you up and down the ladder of difficulty does the major part of its work. If you do well early in the test, the computer will give you harder questions—and those questions are worth more points. So work carefully through the first half of each section. If you find that time is running out, you can always pick up the pace in the second half.

TIP

"Dismiss" the directions. The on-screen directions do not disappear automatically. Instead, you have to "dismiss" them by clicking on the "Dismiss Directions" box. Do this immediately so you can get started on the test.

ALERT!

Don't spin your wheels. Don't spend too much time on any one question. Give it some thought, take your best shot, and move along.

GUESSING IS PART OF THE GAME.

On the CAT there will be two times when you'll have to guess. First, any time you have no idea of how to solve a problem, you'll have to choose an answer just to move on to the next question. Second, if time is running out, it will be worth your while to guess at the answers to any remaining questions—there's always the chance that you'll guess right, and you'll be penalized if you leave questions unanswered.

DECIDE WHETHER TO KEYBOARD OR WRITE YOUR ESSAY RESPONSES.

You will be given the option of keyboarding your responses to the essay prompts or writing them out by hand. Some people are not comfortable with the keyboard. If you are one of them, then you may be better off writing your responses by hand. If you decide to use the keyboard, you should be aware that the editing program you'll be using is fairly primitive. It will only have the basic functions: type, undo, cut, and paste. It will not have spell check or a grammar check function.

SUMMING IT UP

- The computer chooses CAT problems based on your answers to previous questions.

- The multiple-choice parts of the GRE test verbal and math reasoning skills.

- Tailor your study plan based on the amount of time you have to prepare prior to your test.

- Use the scoring table to predict your actual GRE score.

- If you know the directions in advance, you won't have to waste time reading them.

- On the multiple-choice parts of the GRE, the answers are all right in front of you. One of the choices has to be right.

- You must answer every question on the CAT portion of the test before the time expires. If you don't know the answer, eliminate obviously wrong choices and make an educated guess.

GRE Questions—
A First Look

chapter 2

OVERVIEW

- How does the GRE test verbal reasoning?
- How does the GRE test mathematical reasoning?
- How does the GRE test analytical writing?
- Summing it up

This chapter will describe each question type in turn and show you samples. Learning the question types in advance is the best way to prepare for the GRE. That way, you'll know what to expect and won't have any unpleasant surprises on test day.

HOW DOES THE GRE TEST VERBAL REASONING?

The GRE tests your verbal reasoning ability with these four question types:

- Sentence completions
- Analogies
- Reading comprehension
- Antonyms

The verbal section includes 5 to 7 sentence completions, 6 to 8 analogies, 7 to 9 antonyms, and 9 or so reading comprehension questions.

Sentence Completions

Sentence completions consist of a sentence, a part or parts of which have been omitted, followed by five letter choices that are possible substitutions for the omitted parts of the sentence. The idea is to select the choice that best completes the sentence.

Here are the directions for sentence completions and a sample question:

> **Directions:** The question below contains one or more blank spaces, each blank indicating that something has been omitted. Each sentence is followed by five (5) words or sets of words. Read and determine the general sense of each sentence. Then choose the word, or set of words that, when inserted in the sentence, best fits the meaning of the sentence.

Her desire for —— soon became apparent when she adamantly refused to answer questions about her identity or mission.
- **(A)** assistance
- **(B)** anonymity
- **(C)** success
- **(D)** publicity
- **(E)** recognition

The correct answer is (B). The logic of the sentence requires that the missing element indicate a desire for something that can be achieved only by refusing to give information. If you don't give any information about your identity or your activities, you hope to ensure that you remain anonymous.

Analogies

A GRE analogy consists of one capitalized word pair followed by five answer choices (also word pairs). The idea is to select from among the choices a word pair that expresses a relationship similar to that expressed by the capitalized word pair.

Here are the directions for analogies and a sample question:

> **Directions:** In the following question, you are given a related pair of words or phrases in capital letters. Each capitalized pair is followed by five (5) pairs of words or phrases. Choose the pair that best expresses a relationship similar to that expressed by the original pair.

MINISTER : PULPIT ::
- **(A)** doctor : patient
- **(B)** student : teacher
- **(C)** mechanic : engine
- **(D)** programmer : logic
- **(E)** judge : bench

The correct answer is (E). The PULPIT is the place where the MINISTER does his or her job, and the bench is the place where the judge does her or his job.

Reading Comprehension

Reading comprehension questions, as the name implies, test your ability to understand the substance and logical structure of a written selection. The GRE uses reading passages of various lengths, ranging from 200 to 550 words. The questions ask about the main point of the passage, about what the author specifically states, about what can be logically inferred from the passage, and about the author's attitude or tone. Here are the directions for reading comprehension questions and an example of a shorter reading passage. (The passage is followed by only two questions, rather than the usual three or four.)

> **Directions:** The passage below is followed by questions based on its content. Choose the best answer to each question.

The international software market represents a significant business opportunity for U.S. microcomputer software companies, but illegal copying of programs is limiting the growth of sales abroad. If not dealt with quickly, international piracy of
(5) software could become one of the most serious trade problems faced by the United States.

Software piracy is already the biggest barrier to U.S. software companies entering foreign markets. One reason is that software is extremely easy and inexpensive to duplicate com-
(10) pared to the cost of developing and marketing the software. The actual cost of duplicating a software program, which may have a retail value of $400 or more, can be as little as a dollar or two—the main component being the cost of the CD-ROM. The cost of counterfeiting software is substantially less than the cost of
(15) duplicating watches, books, or blue jeans. Given that the difference between the true value of the original and the cost of the counterfeit is so great for software, international piracy has become big business. Unfortunately, many foreign governments view software piracy as an industry in and of itself and
(20) look the other way.

U.S. firms stand to lose millions of dollars in new business, and diminished U.S. sales not only harm individual firms but also adversely affect the entire U.S. economy.

In this passage, the author's primary purpose is to

(A) criticize foreign governments for stealing U.S. computer secrets

(B) describe the economic hazards software piracy poses to the United States

(C) demand that software pirates immediately cease their illegal operations

(D) present a comprehensive proposal to counteract the effects of international software piracy

(E) disparage the attempts of the U.S. government to control software piracy

The correct answer is (B). This question, typical of the GRE, asks about the main point of the selection. (A) is incorrect. Though the author implies criticism of foreign governments, their mistake, so far as we are told, is not stealing secrets but tacitly allowing the operation of a software black market. (C) is incorrect since this is not the main point of the selection. You can infer that the author would approve of such a demand, but issuing the demand is not the main point of the selection you just read. (D) can be eliminated for a similar reason. Though the author might elsewhere offer a specific proposal, there is no such proposal in the selection you just read. (E) also is wrong since no such attempts are ever discussed. Finally, notice how well (B) does describe the main issue. The author's concern is to identify a problem and to discuss its causes.

The author's attitude toward international software piracy can best be described as

   (A) concern

   (B) rage

   (C) disinterest

   (D) pride

   (E) condescension

The correct answer is (A). This question asks about the tone of the passage, and *concern* very neatly captures that tone. You can eliminate (B) as an overstatement. Though the author condemns the piracy, the tone is not so violent as to qualify as *rage*. (C) must surely be incorrect since the author does express concern and, therefore, cannot be disinterested.

Antonyms

An antonym item consists of a single, capitalized word followed by five answer choices. The basic idea is to pick the answer that has the meaning that is most nearly opposite that of the capitalized word.

Here are the directions for antonyms and a sample question:

> **Directions:** Each of the following questions consists of a word printed in capital letters, followed by five (5) words or phrases. Choose the word or phrase that is most nearly opposite in meaning to the word in capital letters. Be sure to consider all the choices before deciding which one is best.

WAIVE :

- **(A)** repeat
- **(B)** conclude
- **(C)** insist upon
- **(D)** improve on
- **(E)** peruse

The correct answer is (C). To WAIVE means to forgo or to relinquish. A fairly precise opposite is *insist upon*.

HOW DOES THE GRE TEST MATHEMATICAL REASONING?

The GRE tests mathematical reasoning ability with these three question types:

- Problem solving
- Quantitative comparisons
- Graphs

The math sections test your knowledge of arithmetic, basic algebra, elementary geometry, and common charts and graphs.

The math section includes 9 to 11 problem-solving items, 13 to 15 data-sufficiency items, and 4 or so graph items.

Problem Solving

If you have taken any other standardized exams that included math questions (such as the SAT), then you have probably already seen examples of problem-solving questions. These are your typical word problem questions. Here are the directions for problem-solving questions and three sample questions:

NOTE

Do you need to know college-level math to do well on the GRE? No, you do not need to know college-level math. The GRE math sections test only the basic math concepts you learned in high school.

Betty left home with $60 in her wallet. She spent $\frac{1}{3}$ of that amount at the supermarket, and she spent $\frac{1}{2}$ of what remained at the drugstore. If Betty made no other expenditures, how much money did she have when she returned home?

(A) $10

(B) $15

(C) $20

(D) $40

(E) $50

The correct answer is (C). Betty spent $\frac{1}{3}$ of $60, or $20, at the supermarket, leaving her with $40. Of the $40, she spent $\frac{1}{2}$, or $20, at the drugstore, leaving her with $20 when she returned home.

If $2x + 3y = 8$ and $y = 2x$, then what is the value of x?

(A) −6

(B) −4

(C) 0

(D) 1

(E) 4

The correct answer is (D). To answer the question, you need to solve for x. Since $y = 2x$, you can substitute $2x$ for y in the first equation:

$$2x + 3(2x) = 8$$

Multiply: $\quad 2x + 6x = 8$

Add: $\qquad\qquad 8x = 8$

Divide: $\qquad\qquad x = 1$

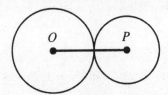

In the figure above, circle O and circle P are tangent to each other. If the circle with center O has a diameter of 8 and the circle with center P has a diameter of 6, what is the length of $\overline{OP}$?

   (A) 7

   (B) 10

   (C) 14

   (D) 20

   (E) 28

The correct answer is (A). $\overline{OP}$ is made up of the radius of circle O and the radius of circle P. To find the length of $\overline{OP}$, you need to know the lengths of the two radii. Since the length of the radius is one half that of the diameter, the radius of circle O is $\frac{1}{2}$ (8) or 4, and the radius of circle P is $\frac{1}{2}$ (6) or 3. So the length of $\overline{OP}$ is $3 + 4 = 7$.

Quantitative Comparisons

Quantitative comparisons are presented in an unusual format with special instructions. Without trying to understand all of the subtleties of the type, you can get the general idea of quantitative comparisons by reading the directions and studying the sample questions that follow.

> **Directions:** For each of the following questions, select the best of the answer choices. For quantitative comparison questions, two quantities are given, one in Column A and one in Column B. Compare the two quantities and choose
>
> **(A)** if the quantity in Column A is greater
> **(B)** if the quantity in Column B is greater
> **(C)** if the two quantities are equal
> **(D)** if the relationship cannot be determined from the information given
>
> Information applying to both columns is centered between the columns and above the quantities in columns A and B. Symbols that appear in both columns represent the same idea or quantity in each column.

Column A	Column B
$6 - \dfrac{4}{2}$	$5 - \dfrac{4}{4}$

The correct answer is (C). Column A is just $6 - 2 = 4$, and Column B is $5 - 1 = 4$. Both columns have the value of 4, so they are equal.

Column A   **Column B**

$x + 1$ $x - 1$

The correct answer is (A). Whatever the value of x, the expression $x + 1$ is one more than x, and the expression $x - 1$ is one less than x. So no matter what the value of x, Column A is 2 larger than Column B.

TIP

Column A   **Column B**

The right answer must always be true. In quantitative comparisons, answer (A), (B), or (C) can be correct only if it is true in every case. If not, the answer must be (D).

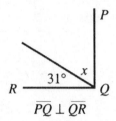

$PQ \perp QR$

x 60

The correct answer is (B). $\overline{PQ}$ is perpendicular to $\overline{QR}$, so $\angle PQR$ is a 90-degree angle. Since one of the two angles making up the right angle is 31 degrees, the other must be 59 degrees. So $x = 59$, and Column B (which is 60) is larger.

Column A   **Column B**

The price of a sweater   The price of a coat
that is marked 25% off   that is marked 20% off

The correct answer is (D). You are asked to compare the prices of the two articles. Although you know the percent discount taken on each, you have no way of knowing the actual cost of the item. Since the comparison cannot be made on the basis of what is given, the correct choice is (D).

Graphs

Graph questions are like problem-solving items except that the information to be used in solving the problem is presented in pictorial form. Here are some sample graph questions:

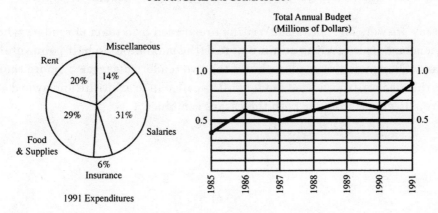

**HILLTOP DAY SCHOOL
FINANCIAL INFORMATION**

The total annual budget for Hilltop Day School increased by what percent from 1985 to 1991?

- **(A)** 4%
- **(B)** 8%
- **(C)** 50%
- **(D)** 125%
- **(E)** 200%

The correct answer is (D). The operating budget increased from $0.4 million in 1985 to $0.9 million in 1991—an increase of $0.5 million. Expressed as a percentage increase: $\frac{0.5}{0.4} \times 100 = 1.25 \times 100 = 125\%$

How much money did Hilltop Day School spend for rent in 1991?

- **(A)** $180,000
- **(B)** $225,000
- **(C)** $240,000
- **(D)** $800,000
- **(E)** $2,000,000

The correct answer is (A). From the graph on the right, we learn that the total budget for 1991 was $0.9 million. The graph on the left breaks down the budget for 1991. It shows that 20% of the 1991 budget went for rent: 20% of $0.9 million = $180,000.

HOW DOES THE GRE TEST ANALYTICAL WRITING?

Analytical Writing consists of two essay questions. One of the questions is called the "issue" question. The "issue" prompt asks you to take a position on a general topic and then to develop ideas that support your position. You'll have 45 minutes to respond to the "issue" prompt. The second topic is an "argument" prompt. You'll be given an argument and asked to analyze it by examining its assumptions, looking at its logic, and testing its conclusion. You'll have 30 minutes to write your essay response to the "argument" topic.

Your essay answers on Analytical Writing are graded by a team of readers who will score them on a scale of 1 (the minimum) to 6 (the maximum) in half-point intervals. The team will include two readers: but if the two readers disagree by more than one point, a third, more experienced reader will be called in to arbitrate and award a final score. You'll get one score for both the essays combined.

SUMMING IT UP

- The GRE uses sentence completions, analogies, reading comprehension, and antonyms to test verbal reasoning ability.

- The GRE uses problem solving, quantitative comparisons, and graphs to test mathematical reasoning ability.

- The Analytical Writing section consists of two essay questions. Your essays are graded by a team of readers. Make sure you know how to write essays that satisfy the criteria that readers look for.

PART II

DIAGNOSING STRENGTHS AND WEAKNESSES

CHAPTER 3   Practice Test 1: Diagnostic

PRACTICE TEST 1: DIAGNOSTIC ANSWER SHEET

Directions: Answer each question in the test and indicate your response by filling in the oval of your choice. In order to simulate the testing experience of the CAT, you should answer the questions in the order presented, entering a choice for each one before going on to the next. Once you have entered your choice, you may NOT return to that problem or to any problems presented earlier. When time has expired or you have entered your choice for the last item in a section, you are finished with that section. You may not return to problems earlier in the section or to earlier sections.

Verbal Section

1. Ⓐ Ⓑ Ⓒ Ⓓ Ⓔ   7. Ⓐ Ⓑ Ⓒ Ⓓ Ⓔ   13. Ⓐ Ⓑ Ⓒ Ⓓ Ⓔ   19. Ⓐ Ⓑ Ⓒ Ⓓ Ⓔ   25. Ⓐ Ⓑ Ⓒ Ⓓ Ⓔ

2. Ⓐ Ⓑ Ⓒ Ⓓ Ⓔ   8. Ⓐ Ⓑ Ⓒ Ⓓ Ⓔ   14. Ⓐ Ⓑ Ⓒ Ⓓ Ⓔ   20. Ⓐ Ⓑ Ⓒ Ⓓ Ⓔ   26. Ⓐ Ⓑ Ⓒ Ⓓ Ⓔ

3. Ⓐ Ⓑ Ⓒ Ⓓ Ⓔ   9. Ⓐ Ⓑ Ⓒ Ⓓ Ⓔ   15. Ⓐ Ⓑ Ⓒ Ⓓ Ⓔ   21. Ⓐ Ⓑ Ⓒ Ⓓ Ⓔ   27. Ⓐ Ⓑ Ⓒ Ⓓ Ⓔ

4. Ⓐ Ⓑ Ⓒ Ⓓ Ⓔ   10. Ⓐ Ⓑ Ⓒ Ⓓ Ⓔ   16. Ⓐ Ⓑ Ⓒ Ⓓ Ⓔ   22. Ⓐ Ⓑ Ⓒ Ⓓ Ⓔ   28. Ⓐ Ⓑ Ⓒ Ⓓ Ⓔ

5. Ⓐ Ⓑ Ⓒ Ⓓ Ⓔ   11. Ⓐ Ⓑ Ⓒ Ⓓ Ⓔ   17. Ⓐ Ⓑ Ⓒ Ⓓ Ⓔ   23. Ⓐ Ⓑ Ⓒ Ⓓ Ⓔ   29. Ⓐ Ⓑ Ⓒ Ⓓ Ⓔ

6. Ⓐ Ⓑ Ⓒ Ⓓ Ⓔ   12. Ⓐ Ⓑ Ⓒ Ⓓ Ⓔ   18. Ⓐ Ⓑ Ⓒ Ⓓ Ⓔ   24. Ⓐ Ⓑ Ⓒ Ⓓ Ⓔ   30. Ⓐ Ⓑ Ⓒ Ⓓ Ⓔ

Math Section

1. Ⓐ Ⓑ Ⓒ Ⓓ Ⓔ   7. Ⓐ Ⓑ Ⓒ Ⓓ Ⓔ   13. Ⓐ Ⓑ Ⓒ Ⓓ Ⓔ   19. Ⓐ Ⓑ Ⓒ Ⓓ Ⓔ   25. Ⓐ Ⓑ Ⓒ Ⓓ Ⓔ

2. Ⓐ Ⓑ Ⓒ Ⓓ Ⓔ   8. Ⓐ Ⓑ Ⓒ Ⓓ Ⓔ   14. Ⓐ Ⓑ Ⓒ Ⓓ Ⓔ   20. Ⓐ Ⓑ Ⓒ Ⓓ Ⓔ   26. Ⓐ Ⓑ Ⓒ Ⓓ Ⓔ

3. Ⓐ Ⓑ Ⓒ Ⓓ Ⓔ   9. Ⓐ Ⓑ Ⓒ Ⓓ Ⓔ   15. Ⓐ Ⓑ Ⓒ Ⓓ Ⓔ   21. Ⓐ Ⓑ Ⓒ Ⓓ Ⓔ   27. Ⓐ Ⓑ Ⓒ Ⓓ Ⓔ

4. Ⓐ Ⓑ Ⓒ Ⓓ Ⓔ   10. Ⓐ Ⓑ Ⓒ Ⓓ Ⓔ   16. Ⓐ Ⓑ Ⓒ Ⓓ Ⓔ   22. Ⓐ Ⓑ Ⓒ Ⓓ Ⓔ   28. Ⓐ Ⓑ Ⓒ Ⓓ Ⓔ

5. Ⓐ Ⓑ Ⓒ Ⓓ Ⓔ   11. Ⓐ Ⓑ Ⓒ Ⓓ Ⓔ   17. Ⓐ Ⓑ Ⓒ Ⓓ Ⓔ   23. Ⓐ Ⓑ Ⓒ Ⓓ Ⓔ

6. Ⓐ Ⓑ Ⓒ Ⓓ Ⓔ   12. Ⓐ Ⓑ Ⓒ Ⓓ Ⓔ   18. Ⓐ Ⓑ Ⓒ Ⓓ Ⓔ   24. Ⓐ Ⓑ Ⓒ Ⓓ Ⓔ

Analytical Writing—Issue Topic

_____

_____

_____

_____

_____

_____

_____

_____

_____

_____

_____

_____

_____

_____

_____

_____

_____

_____

_____

_____

_____

_____

_____

_____

_____

_____

_____

_____

Analytical Writing—Argument Topic

_____

_____

_____

_____

_____

_____

_____

_____

_____

_____

_____

_____

_____

_____

_____

_____

_____

_____

_____

_____

_____

_____

_____

_____

_____

_____

_____

_____

_____

_____

_____

_____

_____

_____

_____

_____

_____

_____

_____

_____

_____

_____

_____

_____

_____

_____

_____

_____

_____

_____

_____

_____

_____

_____

Practice Test 1: Diagnostic

ANALYTICAL WRITING

Issue Topic • 45 Minutes
Present Your Perspective on an Issue

In this part, two topics appear as brief quotations. Each states, either explicitly or implicitly, an issue of broad interest. You are to choose one of the two topics. You will then use the remainder of the 45 minutes to write an essay in which you take a position on the issue.

You may agree with the quotation, disagree with it, or challenge the statement in any way, so long as the ideas that you present are clearly relevant to the topic. You should provide reasons and examples to support your position. In doing so, you may want to draw on your reading of various sources, your personal experience and observations, or your academic studies.

It is a good idea to begin by reading the topic carefully. Then you should decide what position you want to take, after which you will probably want to outline your answer before you begin to write. Your essay will be graded on how well you:

- Assess the implications of the issue, including various complexities implicit in the topic
- Organize, develop, and express your thoughts on the issue
- Provide supporting reasons and examples
- Demonstrate your mastery of the elements of standard written English

You should leave yourself sufficient time to read what you have written and to make any revisions to your essay that you think are needed.

For this exercise, you may choose to use an editing program on a computer (word processing) or write your response by hand using the space provided.

On the CAT, timing for this part begins when you click on the "Dismiss the Directions" icon.

ISSUE TOPIC

Choose <u>one</u> of the following two topics to write on.

> "The university of today is a kind of service industry. In order to operate successfully, the administration and faculty need to be responsive to the desires of the students who are the paying customers."

> "It is frequently advisable for those in positions of authority in government to withhold information from the general public."

Argument Topic • 30 Minutes
Analyze an Argument

In this part, you will be given an argument and have 30 minutes within which to write a critique of the argument. Your essay must address the argument given.

You are to <u>analyze</u> the reasoning of the argument. You should consider whether any of its assumptions are questionable and whether the evidence presented supports the conclusion. You might also discuss what changes in the line of reasoning or additional evidence would strengthen or weaken the conclusion.

Importantly, you are **NOT** being asked to state your own views on the underlying subject.

It is a good idea to begin by reading the argument carefully. Then you should evaluate the argument and consider what response you want to make, after which you will probably want to outline your answer before you begin to write.

Your essay response will be graded on how well you:

- Identify and analyze the important elements of the argument
- Organize, develop, and state your analysis
- Support your analysis with relevant reasons and examples
- Demonstrate your mastery of the elements of standard written English

You should leave yourself sufficient time to read what you have written and to make any revisions to your essay that you think are needed.

For this exercise, you may choose to use an editing program on a computer (word processing) or write your response by hand using the space provided.

On the CAT, timing for this part begins when you click on the "Dismiss the Directions" icon.

ARGUMENT TOPIC

The following editorial appeared in the Herbert Falls *Post-Star* newspaper:

> "One of the most important reasons for the decline in the number of visitors to the downtown Herbert Falls area is the presence of teen-aged skateboarders. Pedestrians are few and far between, and the graffiti and litter are widespread. Fully 80% of business owners surveyed recently responded that they favored putting limitations on the use of the mall by skateboards. Clearly, then, banning the use of skateboards on the mall will reverse the decline in business in the downtown area."

VERBAL SECTION

30 Questions • 30 Minutes

> **Directions:** Each of the questions below contains one or more blank spaces, each blank indicating that something has been omitted. Each sentence is followed by five (5) words or sets of words. Read and determine the general sense of each sentence. Then choose the word, or set of words that, when inserted in the sentence, best fits the meaning of the sentence.

1. —— and piety seem to have been two qualities almost universally shared by the original settlers of the Northeast who faced the almost —— problems of the weather and disease.

   (A) Candor . . insignificant
   (B) Veracity . . understandable
   (C) Cowardice . . enduring
   (D) Avarice . . threatening
   (E) Fortitude . . insurmountable

2. A —— review of the recent performance of La Bohème called the production grotesque and the conducting of the orchestra ——.

   (A) glowing . . benign
   (B) scathing . . pedestrian
   (C) laudatory . . heretical
   (D) premeditated . . prejudicial
   (E) concentrated . . munificent

3. The young soloist broke a string in the middle of the performance of the Tchaikovsky Violin Concerto and motioned to the concertmaster to hand over his own violin so that she might —— her performance, demonstrating —— rare in one so young.

   (A) interrupt . . confidence
   (B) continue . . aplomb
   (C) rehearse . . stage presence
   (D) illuminate . . perseverity
   (E) renew . . elegance

> **Directions:** In each of the following questions, you are given a related pair of words or phrases in capital letters. Each capitalized pair is followed by five (5) pairs of words or phrases. Choose the pair that best expresses a relationship similar to that expressed by the original pair.

4. TRAP : GAME ::
   - **(A)** novel : author
   - **(B)** net : fish
   - **(C)** leash : dog
   - **(D)** wall : house
   - **(E)** curtain : window

5. MANSARD : ROOF ::
   - **(A)** ice : igloo
   - **(B)** spine : book
   - **(C)** closet : hallway
   - **(D)** dormer : window
   - **(E)** tent : military

6. PASTOR : CONGREGATION ::
   - **(A)** shepherd : flock
   - **(B)** teacher : faculty
   - **(C)** chef : restaurant
   - **(D)** clerk : market
   - **(E)** painter : canvas

diagnostic test

Directions: The passage below is followed by questions based on its content. Choose the best answer to each question.

War has escaped the battlefield and now can, with modern guidance systems on missiles, touch virtually every square yard of the earth's surface. War has also
(5) lost most of its utility in achieving the traditional goals of conflict. Control of territory carries with it the obligation to provide subject peoples certain administrative, health, education, and other so-
(10) cial services; such obligations far outweigh the benefits of control. If the ruled population is ethnically or racially different from the rulers, tensions and chronic unrest often exist, which further
(15) reduce the benefits and increase the costs of domination. Large populations no longer necessarily enhance state power and, in the absence of high levels of economic development, can impose
(20) severe burdens on food supply, jobs, and the broad range of services expected of modern governments. The noneconomic security reasons for the control of territory have been progressively under-
(25) mined by the advances of modern technology. The benefits of forcing another nation to surrender its wealth are vastly outweighed by the benefits of persuading that nation to produce and exchange

(30) goods and services. In brief, imperialism no longer pays.

Making war has been one of the most persistent of human activities in the eighty centuries since men and women settled in
(35) cities and thereby became "civilized," but the modernization of the past eighty years has fundamentally changed the role and function of war. In premodernized societies, successful warfare brought significant
(40) material rewards, the most obvious of which were the stored wealth of the defeated. Equally important was human labor—control over people as slaves or levies for the victor's army, and there was the
(45) productive capacity—agricultural lands and mines. Successful warfare also produced psychic benefits. The removal or destruction of a threat brought a sense of security, and power gained over others
(50) created pride and national self-esteem.

War was accepted in the premodernized society as a part of the human condition, a mechanism of change, and an unavoidable, even noble, aspect of life. The ex-
(55) citement and drama of war made it a vital part of literature and legends.

7. According to the passage, leaders of pre-modernized society considered war to be

    (A) a valid tool of national policy

    (B) an immoral act of aggression

    (C) economically wasteful and socially unfeasible

    (D) restricted in scope to military participants

    (E) necessary to spur development of unoccupied lands

8. The author most likely places the word *civilized* in quotation marks (line 35) in order to

    (A) show dissatisfaction at not having found a better word

    (B) acknowledge that the word was borrowed from another source

    (C) express irony that war should be a part of civilization

    (D) impress upon the reader the tragedy of war

    (E) raise a question about the value of war in modernized society

9. The author mentions all of the following as possible reasons for going to war in a premodernized society EXCEPT

    (A) possibility of material gain

    (B) total annihilation of the enemy and destruction of enemy territory

    (C) potential for increasing the security of the nation

    (D) desire to capture productive farming lands

    (E) need for workers to fill certain jobs

Directions: Each of the following questions consists of a word printed in capital letters, followed by five (5) words or phrases. Choose the word or phrase that is most nearly opposite in meaning to the word in capital letters. Be sure to consider all the choices before deciding which one is best.

10. RESIDENT :

    (A) factual

    (B) constrained

    (C) transitory

    (D) lofty

    (E) merciful

11. PROLIFIC :

    (A) worthless

    (B) barren

    (C) practical

    (D) baleful

    (E) youthful

12. LAMBAST :

    (A) deny

    (B) understand

    (C) praise

    (D) imagine

    (E) flatten

13. COURT :

    (A) reject

    (B) uncover

    (C) infect

    (D) subject

    (E) elect

Directions: The passage below is followed by questions based on its content. Choose the best answer to each question.

There is extraordinary exposure in the United States to the risks of injury and death from motor vehicle accidents. More than 80 percent of all households own
(5) passenger cars or light trucks and each of these is driven an average of more than 11,000 miles each year. Almost one half of fatally injured drivers have a blood alcohol concentration (BAC) of 0.1
(10) percent or higher. For the average adult, over five ounces of 80 proof spirits would have to be consumed over a short period of time to attain these levels. A third of drivers who have been drinking, but
(15) fewer than 4 percent of all drivers, demonstrate these levels. Although less than 1 percent of drivers with BACs of 0.1 percent or more are involved in fatal crashes, the probability of their involve-
(20) ment is 27 times higher than for those without alcohol in their blood.

There are a number of different approaches to reducing injuries in which intoxication plays a role. Based on the
(25) observation that excessive consumption correlates with the total alcohol consumption of a country's population, it has been suggested that higher taxes on alcohol would reduce both. While the
(30) heaviest drinkers would be taxed the most, anyone who drinks at all would be penalized by this approach.

To make drinking and driving a criminal offense is an approach directed only
(35) at intoxicated drivers. In some states, the law empowers police to request breath tests of drivers cited for any traffic offense and elevated BAC can be the basis for arrest. The National Highway
(40) Traffic Safety Administration estimates, however, that even with increased arrests, there are about 700 violations for every arrest. At this level there is little evidence that laws serve as deterrents to
(45) driving while intoxicated. In Britain, motor vehicle fatalities fell 25 percent immediately following implementation of the Road Safety Act in 1967. As the

British increasingly recognized that they
(50) could drink and not be stopped, the effectiveness declined, although in the ensuing three years the fatality rate seldom reached that observed in the seven years prior to the Act.

(55) Whether penalties for driving with a high BAC or excessive taxation on consumption of alcoholic beverages will deter the excessive drinker responsible for most fatalities is unclear. In part, the
(60) answer depends on the extent to which those with high BACs involved in crashes are capable of controlling their intake in response to economic or penal threat. Therapeutic programs that range from
(65) individual and group counseling and psychotherapy to chemotherapy constitute another approach, but they have not diminished the proportion of accidents in which alcohol was a factor. In the few
(70) controlled trials that have been reported, there is little evidence that rehabilitation programs for those repeatedly arrested for drunken behavior have reduced either the recidivism or crash
(75) rates. Thus far, there is no firm evidence that Alcohol Safety Action Project supported programs, in which rehabilitation measures are requested by the court, have decreased recidivism or crash in-
(80) volvement for clients exposed to them, although knowledge and attitudes have improved. One thing is clear, however; unless we deal with automobile and highway safety and reduce accidents in which
(85) alcoholic intoxication plays a role, many will continue to die.

14. The author is primarily concerned with

 (A) interpreting the results of surveys on traffic fatalities

 (B) reviewing the effectiveness of attempts to curb drunk driving

 (C) suggesting reasons for the prevalence of drunk driving in the United States

 (D) analyzing the causes of the large number of annual traffic fatalities

 (E) making an international comparison of the U.S. and Britain

15. It can be inferred that the 1967 Road Safety Act in Britain

 (A) changed an existing law to lower the BAC level which defined driving while intoxicated

 (B) made it illegal to drive while intoxicated

 (C) increased the number of drunk driving arrests

 (D) placed a tax on the sale of alcoholic drinks

 (E) required drivers convicted under the law to undergo rehabilitation therapy

16. The author implies that a BAC of 0.1 percent

 (A) is unreasonably high as a definition of intoxication for purposes of driving

 (B) penalizes the moderate drinker while allowing the heavy drinker to consume without limit

 (C) will operate as an effective deterrent to over 90 percent of the people who might drink and drive

 (D) is well below the BAC of most drivers who are involved in fatal collisions

 (E) proves that a driver has consumed five ounces of 80 proof spirits over a short time

17. With which of the following statements about making driving while intoxicated a criminal offense versus increasing taxes on alcohol consumption would the author most likely agree?

 (A) Making driving while intoxicated a criminal offense is preferable to increased taxes on alcohol because the former is aimed only at those who abuse alcohol by driving while intoxicated.

 (B) Increased taxation on alcohol consumption is likely to be more effective in reducing traffic fatalities because taxation covers all consumers and not just those who drive.

 (C) Increased taxation on alcohol will constitute less of an interference with personal liberty because of the necessity of blood alcohol tests to determine BACs in drivers suspected of intoxication.

 (D) Since neither increased taxation nor enforcement of criminal laws against drunk drivers is likely to have any significant impact, neither measure is warranted.

 (E) Because arrests of intoxicated drivers have proved to be expensive and administratively cumbersome, increased taxation on alcohol is the most promising means of reducing traffic fatalities.

18. The author cites the British example in order to

(A) show that the problem of drunk driving is worse in Britain than in the U.S.

(B) prove that stricter enforcement of laws against intoxicated drivers would reduce traffic deaths

(C) prove that a slight increase in the number of arrests of intoxicated drivers will not deter drunk driving

(D) suggest that taxation of alcohol consumption may be more effective than criminal laws

(E) demonstrate the need to lower BAC levels in states that have laws against drunk driving

19. Which of the following, if true, most weakens the author's statement that the effectiveness of proposals to stop the intoxicated driver depends, in part, on the extent to which the high BAC driver can control his or her intake?

(A) Even if the heavy drinker cannot control intake, criminal laws against driving while intoxicated can deter him or her from driving while intoxicated.

(B) Rehabilitation programs aimed at drivers convicted of driving while intoxicated have not significantly reduced traffic fatalities.

(C) Many traffic fatalities are caused by factors unrelated to the excessive consumption of alcohol by the driver involved.

(D) Even though severe penalties may not deter the intoxicated driver, these laws will punish him or her for the harm caused by driving while intoxicated.

(E) Some sort of therapy may be effective in helping the problem drinker to control the intake of alcohol, thereby keeping him or her off the road.

Directions: In each of the following questions, you are given a related pair of words or phrases in capital letters. Each capitalized pair is followed by five (5) pairs of words or phrases. Choose the pair that best expresses a relationship similar to that expressed by the original pair.

20. ODE : POEM ::

(A) character : novel

(B) brick : building

(C) ballad : song

(D) street : intersection

(E) museum : painting

21. TENACITY : WEAK ::

(A) apathy : caring

(B) pity : strong

(C) immorality : wrong

(D) frequency : known

(E) control : expensive

22. CURATOR : PAINTING ::

(A) jailer : sheriff

(B) treasurer : secretary

(C) archivist : manuscript

(D) general : army

(E) machinist : metal

23. CREPUSCULE : TWILIGHT ::

(A) week : calendar

(B) temperature : climate

(C) dawn : daybreak

(D) radiation : sun

(E) commutation : voyage

Directions: Each of the questions below contains one or more blank spaces, each blank indicating that something has been omitted. Each sentence is followed by five (5) words or sets of words. Read and determine the general sense of each sentence. Then choose the word, or set of words that, when inserted in the sentence, best fits the meaning of the sentence.

24. The Supreme Court, in striking down the state law, ruled the statute had been enacted in an atmosphere charged with religious convictions that had —— the lawmaking process, a —— of the Constitutional provision requiring the separation of church and state.

    (A) written . . bastion

    (B) influenced . . harbinger

    (C) infected . . violation

    (D) repealed . . fulfillment

    (E) sanctified . . union ✗

25. Because customers believe that there is a direct correlation between price and value, software manufacturers continue to —— their prices at —— rate.

    (A) raise . . an astonishing

    (B) inflate . . a moderate ✗

    (C) advertise . . a rapid ✗

    (D) control . . an acceptable

    (E) determine . . a shared ✗

26. The—— performance of the Rachmaninoff Piano Concerto in D Minor, one of the most difficult modern compositions for the piano, —— the audience and earned the pianist a standing ovation.

    (A) virtuoso . . thrilled

    (B) excellent . . offended ✗

    (C) miserable . . excited ✗

    (D) mediocre . . incited

    (E) masterful . . disappointed ✗

Directions: Each of the following questions consists of a word printed in capital letters, followed by five (5) words or phrases. Choose the word or phrase that is most nearly opposite in meaning to the word in capital letters. Be sure to consider all the choices before deciding which one is best.

27. FORGE :
    (A) continue
    (B) dissolve
    (C) quiet
    (D) invite
    (E) prevent

28. MOTILE :
    (A) confused
    (B) frightened
    (C) immobile
    (D) willing
    (E) nervous

29. LACHRYMOSE :
    (A) sacred
    (B) unknowable
    (C) miraculous
    (D) humble
    (E) joyful

30. QUIESCENCE :
    (A) calamity
    (B) timidity
    (C) persistence
    (D) frenzy
    (E) eternity

MATH SECTION

28 Questions • 45 Minutes

Numbers: All numbers used are real numbers.

Figures: The position of points, angles, regions, and so forth are in the order shown. Figures are assumed to lie in a plane unless otherwise indicated. Figures are drawn as accurately as possible for problem-solving questions, unless otherwise indicated. Figures are NOT drawn to scale for quantitative analysis problem, unless otherwise indicated. You should solve the problems by using your knowledge of mathematics and not by estimating sizes by sight or measurement.

Lines: Assume that lines shown as straight are indeed straight.

Directions: For each of the following questions, select the best of the answer choices. For quantitative comparison questions, two quantities are given, one in Column A and one in Column B. Compare the two quantities and choose

(A) if the quantity in Column A is greater
(B) if the quantity in Column B is greater
(C) if the two quantities are equal
(D) if the relationship cannot be determined from the information given

Information applying to both columns is centered between the columns and above the quantities in columns A and B. Symbols that appear in both columns represent the same idea or quantity in each column.

	Column A	**Column B**
1.	$5 - \frac{6}{6}$	$5 - \frac{4}{4}$

x is 4 more than y

2.	x	y

The price of a book increased
from \$7.95 to \$8.95.

3.	The percent increase in the price of the book	12%

$M + 2$ is the average (arithmetic mean)
of x and y.

4.	$\dfrac{x+y}{2}$	M
5.	$(x+y)(x-y)$	$x^2 - y^2$

---

6. $5^2 + 12^2 =$

(A) 13^2

(B) 17^2

(C) 20^2

(D) 144^2

(E) 169^2

7. A salesperson works 50 weeks each year and makes an average (arithmetic mean) of 100 sales per week. If each sale is worth an average (arithmetic mean) of $1,000, then what is the total value of sales made by the salesperson in a year?

(A) $50,000

(B) $100,000

(C) $500,000

(D) $1,000,000

(E) $5,000,000

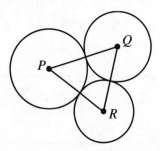

8. In the figure above, the three circles are tangent to each other at the points shown. If circle P has a diameter of 10, circle Q has a diameter of 8, and circle R has a diameter of 6, then what is the perimeter of triangle PQR?

(A) 24

(B) 18

(C) 12

(D) 9

(E) 6

9. If $x = 1$ and $y = -2$, then $\dfrac{x^2 - xy}{y} =$

(A) -3

(B) -2

(C) $-\dfrac{3}{2}$

(D) 2

(E) 3

10. Which of the following numbers does NOT satisfy the inequality $5x - 2 < 3x - 1$?

(A) 1

(B) 0

(C) -1

(D) -2

(E) -3

Directions: For each of the following questions, select the best of the answer choices. For quantitative comparison questions, two quantities are given, one in Column A and one in Column B. Compare the two quantities and choose

(A) if the quantity in Column A is greater
(B) if the quantity in Column B is greater
(C) if the two quantities are equal
(D) if the relationship cannot be determined from the information given

Information applying to both columns is centered between the columns and above the quantities in columns A and B. Symbols that appear in both columns represent the same idea or quantity in each column.

Column A	**Column B**

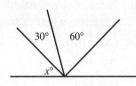 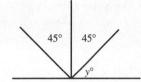

11. x y

The population of City X decreased by
5 percent while the population of City
Y decreased by 7.5 percent

12. The loss of population   The loss of population
by City X   by City Y

The perimeter of square $PQRS$ is $12\sqrt{3}$.

13. length of side $\overline{PQ}$ $3\sqrt{3}$

---

14. $\left(\dfrac{3}{7}\times\dfrac{101}{104}\right)+\left(\dfrac{3}{7}\times\dfrac{4}{104}\right)$ $\dfrac{3}{7}$

Point P has coordinates $(-2,2)$;
point Q has coordinates $(2,0)$.

15. 4   The distance from P to Q

Directions: For each of the following questions, select the best of the answer choices given.

16. If x is an even integer and y is an odd integer, then which of the following is an even integer?

    (A) $x^2 + y$

    (B) $x^2 - y$

    (C) $(x^2)(y)$

    (D) $x + y$

    (E) $x - y$

17. If $pq \neq 0$ and $p = \frac{1}{3}q$, then the ratio of p to $3q$ is

    (A) 9:1

    (B) 3:1

    (C) 1:1

    (D) 1:3

    (E) 1:9

18. If a certain chemical costs $50 for 30 gallons, then how many gallons of the chemical can be purchased for $625?

    (A) 12.5

    (B) 24

    (C) 325

    (D) 375

    (E) 425

19. Which of the following can be expressed as the sum of three consecutive integers?

    (A) 17

    (B) 23

    (C) 25

    (D) 30

    (E) 40

20. If the areas of the three different sized faces of a rectangular solid are 6, 8, and 12, then what is the volume of the solid?

    (A) 576

    (B) 288

    (C) 144

    (D) 48

    (E) 24

Directions: For each of the following questions, select the best of the answer choices given.

QUESTIONS 21–24 ARE BASED ON THE GRAPHS BELOW.

SELECTED MOTOR VEHICLE REGISTRATION DATA
FOR TWO CITIES (BY MANUFACTURER)

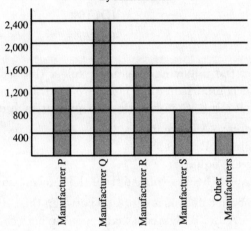

Number of Vehicles Registered in City Y
By Manufacturer

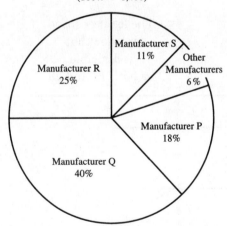

Distribution of Motor Vehicles Registered
in City X According to Manufacturer
(100% = 8,400)

Number of Vehicles Registered in City X Manufactured by Other Manufacturers	
Manufacturer T	212
Manufacturer U	210
Manufacturer V	250

21. In City X, how many of the registered motor vehicles were manufactured by Manufacturer Q?

(A) 1,512

(B) 1,600

(C) 2,400

(D) 3,360

(E) 6,000

22. How many more of the motor vehicles registered in City Y were manufactured by Manufacturer R than were manufactured by Manufacturer P?

(A) 400

(B) 688

(C) 800

(D) 1,200

(E) 1,688

23. Of the following, which is the closest approximation to the percentage of motor vehicles registered in City X that were manufactured by Manufacturer V?

(A) 45%

(B) 37%

(C) 8%

(D) 3%

(E) 1%

24. In City Y, the number of motor vehicles registered that were manufactured by Manufacturer R accounted for what percentage of all motor vehicles registered in City Y?

(A) 4%

(B) 8%

(C) 12.5%

(D) 16%

(E) 25%

Directions: For each of the following questions, select the best of the answer choices. For quantitative comparison questions, two quantities are given, one in Column A and one in Column B. Compare the two quantities and choose

(A) if the quantity in Column A is greater

(B) if the quantity in Column B is greater

(C) if the two quantities are equal

(D) if the relationship cannot be determined from the information given

Information applying to both columns is centered between the columns and above the quantities in columns A and B. Symbols that appear in both columns represent the same idea or quantity in each column.

Column A	Column B
25. The least positive integer that is divisible by both 18 and 24	The least positive integer that is divisible by both 18 and 28

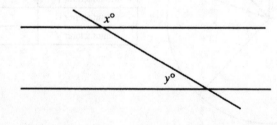

26.	x	y

For all real numbers P and Q,
$$P * Q = P + Q - PQ.$$

27.	$4 * 1$	$4 * 2$

$j > 0, k > 0, m < 0$

28.	$(3j)(3k)(3m)$	$3(j)(k)(m)$

ANSWER KEY AND EXPLANATIONS

Analytical Writing
Issue Topics
Topic 1

As you read the following sample response, try to judge for yourself how well it meets the criteria that will be applied by graders:

Category	Below Avg.	Avg.	Above Avg.
Analysis of the Topic			
Organization and Development			
Use of Reasons and Examples			
Use of Standard Written English			
OVERALL SCORE*			

*Below Average = 1–2; Average = 3–4; Above Average = 5–6

SAMPLE RESPONSE AND COMMENTARY TO ISSUE TOPIC 1

Note: The sample answers contain spelling and grammatical errors. This is done to simulate a first draft written under time pressure.

> The university of today is basically a service industry. The students are like paying customers, which makes the administration management and the faculty the sales force.
>
> You can't run a successful business unless you satisfying your customers. As they say, "The customer is always rite." So what is it that students want? They want a good education but they want the eduction to be relevant. They don't want to take courses that won't help them in their careers, so they should take classes in practical things like accounting and marketing.
>
> This means that the requirements for graduation should be very flexible. For example, a student who is going into business should take business courses. For that student, a course in English or sociology is not really going to be helpful.
>
> And the faculty should teach accordingly. A course in business should be about business today and not about the history of business. The lectures should be given that will tell the students what they need to know to succeeds.

COMMENTARY

This essay is pretty much devoid of any structure. The author does begin by agreeing with the topic, but then the development of the analogy between the university and business seems weak: why are faculty a sales force? Then the essay doesn't really develop the points it mentions. For example, what is the distinction between a "good education" (paragraph two) and "practical things," and how would a university balance those competing considerations? In addition, the use of examples is weak. While "business" and "English" are, in a manner of speaking, examples, the examples are not discussed in sufficient enough detail to make them meaningful. The writer might have chosen, say, to contrast a course in Chaucer with a business-writing course in the English department. Finally, the language is not particularly robust, e.g., "The customer is always rite [sic]" is trite and superficial. This essay would probably earn at best a score of 2.

Topic 2

As you read the following sample response, try to judge for yourself how well it meets the criteria that will be applied by graders:

Category	Below Avg.	Avg.	Above Avg.
Analysis			
Organization and Development			
Use of Reasons and Examples			
Use of Standard Written English			
OVERALL SCORE*			

*Below Average = 1–2; Average = 3–4; Above Average = 5–6

SAMPLE RESPONSE AND COMMENTARY TO ISSUE TOPIC 2

Note: The sample answers contain spelling and grammatical errors. This is done to simulate a first draft written under time pressure.

While there may be instances when a government is justified in withholding vital information from the general public, it surely cannot be said that it is "frequently" adviseable to do so. Times of national crisis when the nation's security is implicated may require discretion on the part of our leaders, but it is doubtful whether these occur with great frequence. Additionally, by withholding key information, leaders undermine the right of people to make choices for themselves. Moreover, allowing leaders to make the decisions on when and what to withhold raised the question of "Who will police the police?"

First, it must be allowed that there are times when national security or even less important considereations demand that the public not be fully informed. Consider, for example, the implications of the Manhattan project, one of the most closely guarded secrets in history. It would be foolish to suggest that the U.S. government should have revealed to the public, and therefore the enemy, that it was even working an atomic bomb. And it is unthinkable that it should have provided regular "updates" in the form of news releases on the various technical problems and their solutions.

Even more mundane issues, however, require discretion. A mayor, for example, may be in daily contact with her police commissioner about the progress on a criminal case, say a high-profile serial killer. And the mayor may have details of the investigation that the public would like to hear. Obviously, however, releasing such information might jeopardize the investigation and put the public at greater risk.

What is important about the examples of the Manhattan project and the serial killer is that these are highly unusual occurrences. They don't prove that leaders are "frequently" entitled to withhold information.

Additionally, information about government affairs is made public because it is the public's business. The "people's right to know" is not just some abstract philosophical doctrine. Rather, it reflects the judgment that people should, within reason, make their own decisions, collectively by voting or individually by life-choices. Suppose, for example, that the governor of a state knew of a government health survey that showed increased incidence of cancer near smelting plants. Obviously, that information might adversely affect business, but it would be wrong to suppress the study because those people affected are entitled to the information that makes their own life-choices meaningful, say a decision to relocated.

Finally, as previous paragraph suggests, it is not reasonable to expect that government officials will always act altruistically. Elected leaders are politicians. That's niether bad nor good but a fact. So there is always the temptation to withhold potentially damaging facts. For that reason alone, we should insist that full disclosure be the general rule and discretionary suppression the rare exception.

COMMENTARY

This writer disagrees with the quotation and says so explicitly in the first sentence. The first paragraph then briefly states three reasons for the position. Each of those reasons is developed in some detail, and there are transitions and paragraph signals to help the reader follow the development of the essay. Finally, the essay restates the writer's conclusion in the final sentence—but at a higher level. There the author concludes that the third reason alone would be enough to reject the position stated in the topic. The essay makes good use of examples, particularly the mention of the Manhattan Project; and it is well-written with only a few errors. One criticism might be that the author could have found better language than "police the police," which is somewhat trite and not exactly the point being made in the final paragraph. Overall, the essay is well-reasoned and strongly written, and would probably earn a score of 5 or 6.

Argument Topic

As you read the following sample response, try to judge for yourself how well it meets the criteria that will be applied by graders:

Category	Below Avg.	Avg.	Above Avg.
Analysis			
Organization and Development			
Use of Reasons and Examples			
Use of Standard Written English			
OVERALL SCORE*			

*Below Average = 1–2; Average = 3–4; Above Average = 5–6

SAMPLE RESPONSE AND COMMENTARY FOR THE ARGUMENT TOPIC

Note: The sample answers contain spelling and grammatical errors. This is done to simulate a first draft written under time pressure.

The argument, on first reading, has some appeal. After all, the spectre of hormone-driven teens careening madly about on skateboards at high speeds performing all manner of reckless maneuvers that frighten off law-abiding adults (and paying customers) and then littering and defacing property as well is a pretty gruesome picture from a business point of view. It would be easy to understand why the downtown area merchants might favor some sort of direct action. On closer reading, however, the reasons given really do not support the conclusion that banning skateboards from the mall will reverse the decline in business.

First, consider the point of view of the business community. The topic states that 80% of merchants "surveyed" favor some from of action, but that is not the same thing as saying that 80% of "all" merchants want action. It would be useful to know how comprehensive the survey was, and it is important that 20% of the merchants surveyed don't favor action at all. Then, the evidence that 80% of the merchants surveyed favor "some limitations" on skateboards does not necessarily support a total ban. It would be important to know whether their use could be limited in time and/or locations as an alternative to a total ban.

Second, the argument fails to establash a clear connection between the decline in business and the presence of the skateboards. In fact, it doesn't even say that the litter and grafitti are problems created by the teens. Perhaps, like so many other cities, the downtown area of Herbert Falls in losing business to the large suburban malls where there are upscale "anchor" stores, cleaner environments, and ample parking.

Finally, a total ban on skateboarder might actually negatively impact business. Where does that litter come from? If it is fastfood wrappers, that strongly suggests that they skateboarders are, in fact, patronizing businesses. Of course, litter and graffiti are not pleasant and should be cleaned up, but it might be better for the merchants to do that themselves.

In the final analysis, the argument proposes a simple solution for what seems like a simple problem. But the deterioration of downtown areas are rarely simple and usually involve a lot factors. The business decline probably won't be reversed by addressing one isolated problem.

COMMENTARY

This response starts off by clearly coming to grips with the argument. And, in the first paragraph, it uses some fairly nice language that is calculated to engage the reader's attention, but it seems to lose steam toward the end. On the other hand, it does address the argument in three specific ways. It effectively challenges the survey evidence by carefully distinguishing what the survey seems to say from what it actually says. The essay also points out that a causal connection has yet to be proved, thus casting doubt on the conclusion of the argument. And the response ends by arguing that some unmentioned factors might prevent achievement of the goal of reversing the business decline and even wind up by contributing to further decline. All in all, this response should earn a 4 or even a 5.

Verbal Section

1.	E	7.	A	13.	A	19.	A	25.	A
2.	B	8.	C	14.	B	20.	C	26.	A
3.	B	9.	B	15.	B	21.	A	27.	B
4.	B	10.	C	16.	A	22.	C	28.	C
5.	D	11.	B	17.	A	23.	C	29.	E
6.	A	12.	C	18.	C	24.	C	30.	D

1. **The correct answer is (E).** The keys here are the parallelisms or continuations required by each blank. For the first substitution you need something that is parallel to *piety*, another virtue. On this ground you can eliminate both (C) and (D). Then, in the second blank you will need an adjective describing serious problems such as weather and disease, and only (E) does this.

2. **The correct answer is (B).** The key to this question is the parallel or continuation set up by the structure of the entire sentence. It is possible that the sentence can be completed in one of two ways. Either the review was good, in which case the adjective completing the second blank must suggest something positive, or the review was bad, and the second element must also suggest something negative. If the review labeled the production *grotesque*, it must have been a negative review as suggested by answer choice (B).

3. **The correct answer is (B).** There are two ways of attacking this question. First, the initial substitution must make sense in terms of the situation described. It is possible to eliminate (A), (C), and (D) on this basis. For example, since the violinist is already performing, it makes no sense to say that she is rehearsing her performance. You might make an argument for *renew* in choice (E), but you can eliminate (E) on the ground that it fails to carry through the continuation indicated by the action.

4. **The correct answer is (B).** The part of speech of *trap* is ambiguous. It might be either a verb or a noun. The issue is settled, however, by consulting choice (A). There the first element is *novel*, a word that cannot be a verb. So we formulate the relationship as a "TRAP is used to catch GAME." So, too, a net is used to catch fish. Notice also the "echo" relationship. Both activities are very similar—hunting and fishing.

5. **The correct answer is (D).** The relationship is that of example to category. A MANSARD is a type of ROOF, and a dormer is a type of window. Further, there is a confirming "echo": Both are architectural features.

6. **The correct answer is (A).** The PASTOR is charged with the care of the CONGREGATION just as the *shepherd* is charged with the care of the *flock*. And there is the interesting and very powerful "echo" between pastor and shepherd and congregation and flock.

7. **The correct answer is (A).** The passage describes the attitude of premodernized society toward war as accepted, even noble, and certainly necessary. Coupled with the goals of war in premodernized societies, we can infer that leaders of premodernized society regarded war as a valid policy tool. On this ground we select (A), eliminating (B) and (C). As for (D), although this can be inferred to have been a feature of war in premodernized society, (D) does not respond to the question: What did the leaders

think of war, that is, what was their attitude? (E) can be eliminated on the same ground and also because that "necessity" for war was not that described in (E).

8. **The correct answer is (C).** The author is discussing war, a seemingly uncivilized activity. Yet the author argues that war, at least in premodernized times, was the necessary result of certain economic and social forces. The use of the term *civilized* is ironic. Under other circumstances, the explanations offered by (A) and (B) might be plausible, but there is nothing in this text to support either of them. (D), too, might under other circumstances be a reason for placing the word in quotation marks, but it does not appear that this author is attempting to affect the reader's emotions; the passage is too detached and scientific for that. Finally, (E) does articulate one of the author's objectives, but this is not the reason for putting the one word in quotations. The explanation for that is something more specific than an overall idea of the passage.

9. **The correct answer is (B).** This is an explicit idea question, and (A), (C), (D), and (E) are all mentioned at various points in the passage as reasons for going to war; (B), however, is not explicitly mentioned. Indeed, the author states that control and exploitation, not *annihilation* and *destruction*, were goals.

10. **The correct answer is (C).** The part of speech of the stem word is ambiguous, but that issue is settled by choice (A), which is an adjective. Something that is RESIDENT lives in a particular area or, more figuratively, belongs to a particular institution in a permanent fashion. So a good opposite would be *transitory*.

11. **The correct answer is (B).** PROLIFIC means "producing in great quantity," so a good opposite would be *barren*, which means "unable to produce at all."

12. **The correct answer is (C).** To LAMBAST is to heap criticism upon, to scold, or to denounce severely. So a good opposite would be to *praise*.

13. **The correct answer is (A).** The part of speech of the stem word is ambiguous. It might be a verb or it might be a noun. The issue is settled by choice (A). Here COURT is a verb. As a verb, to court means to solicit or to try to get. So a possible opposite is to *reject*.

14. **The correct answer is (B).** This is a main idea question. The author first states that a large number of auto traffic fatalities can be attributed to drivers who are intoxicated and then reviews two approaches to controlling this problem, taxation and drunk driving laws. Neither is very successful. The author finally notes that therapy may be useful, though the extent of its value has not yet been proved. (B) describes this development fairly well. (A) can be eliminated since any conclusions drawn by the author from studies on drunk driving are used for the larger objective described in (B). (C) is incorrect since, aside from suggesting possible ways to reduce the extent of the problem, the author never treats the causes of drunk driving. (D) is incorrect for the same reason. Finally, (E) is incorrect, because the comparison between the U.S. and Britain is only a small part of the passage.

15. **The correct answer is (B).** This is an inference question. In the third paragraph, the author discusses the effect of drunk driving laws and states that after the implementation of the Road Safety Act in Britain, motor vehicle fatalities fell considerably. On this basis, we infer that the RSA was a law aimed at drunk driving. We can eliminate (D) and (E) on this ground. (C) can be eliminated as not warranted on the basis of this information. It is not clear whether the num-

ber of arrests increased. Equally consistent with the passage is the conclusion that the number of arrests dropped because people were no longer driving while intoxicated. (C) is incorrect for a further reason, the justification for (B). (B) and (A) are fairly close since both describe the RSA as a law aimed at drunk driving. But the last sentence of the third paragraph calls for (B) over (A). As people learned that they would not get caught for drunk driving, the law became less effective. This suggests that the RSA made drunk driving illegal, not that it lowered the BAC required for conviction. This makes sense of the sentence " . . . they could drink and not be stopped." If (A) were correct, this sentence would have to read " . . . they could drink the same amount and not be convicted."

16. **The correct answer is (A).** This is an inference question. In the first paragraph, the author states that for a person to attain a BAC of 0.1 percent, he or she would need to drink over five ounces of 80 proof spirits over a short period of time. The author is trying to impress on us that that is a considerable quantity of alcohol for most people to drink. (A) explains why the author makes this comment. (B) is incorrect and confuses the first paragraph with the second paragraph. (C) is incorrect since the point of the example is that the BAC is so high most people will not exceed it. This is not to say, however, that people will not drink and drive because of laws establishing maximum BAC levels. Rather, they can continue to drink and drive because the law allows them a considerable margin in the level of BAC. (D) is a misreading of that first paragraph. Of all the very drunk drivers (BAC in excess of 0.1), only 1 percent are involved in accidents. But this does not say that most drivers involved in fatal collisions have BAC levels in excess of 0.1 percent, and that is what (D) says. As for

(E), the author never states that the only way to attain a BAC of 0.1 percent is to drink five ounces of 80 proof spirits in a short time; there may be other ways of becoming intoxicated.

17. **The correct answer is (A).** This is an application question. In the second paragraph, the author states that increased taxation on alcohol would tax the heaviest drinkers most, but notes that this would also penalize the moderate and light drinker. In other words, the remedy is not sufficiently focused on the problem. Then, in the third paragraph, the author notes that drunk driving laws are aimed at the specific problem drivers. We can infer from this discussion that the author would likely advocate drunk driving laws over taxation for the reasons just given. This reasoning is presented in answer (A). (B) is incorrect for the reasons just given and for the further reason that the passage never suggests that taxation is likely to be more effective in solving the problem. The author never really evaluates the effectiveness of taxation in reducing drunk driving. (C) is incorrect for the reason given in support of (A) and for the further reason that the author never raises the issue of personal liberty in conjunction with the BAC test. (D) can be eliminated because the author does not discount the effectiveness of anti-drunk driving measures entirely. Even the British example gives some support to the conclusion that such laws have an effect. (E) is incorrect, for the author never mentions the expense or administrative feasibility of BAC tests.

18. **The correct answer is (C).** This is a question about the logical structure of the passage. In paragraph 3, the author notes that stricter enforcement of laws against drunk driving may result in a few more arrests; but a few more arrests are not likely to have much impact on the problem because the number of arrests is

small compared to those who do not get caught. As a consequence, people will continue to drink and drive. The author supports this with the British experience. Once people realize that the chances of being caught are relatively small, they will drink and drive. This is the conclusion of answer (C). (A) is incorrect since the passage does not support the conclusion that the problem is any worse or any better in one country or the other. (B) is incorrect since this is the conclusion the author is arguing against. (D) is wrong because the author is not discussing the effectiveness of taxation in paragraph 3. (E) is a statement the author would likely accept, but that is not the reason for introducing the British example. So answer (E) is true but nonresponsive.

19. **The correct answer is (A).** This is an application question that asks us to examine the logical structure of the argument. In the fourth paragraph, the author argues that the effectiveness of deterrents to drunk driving will depend upon the ability of the drinker to control consumption. But drunk driving has two aspects: being drunk and driving. The author assumes that drunk driving is a function of drinking only. Otherwise, the author would not suggest that control on consumption is necessary as opposed to helpful. (A) attacks this assumption by pointing out that it is possible to drink to excess without driving. It is possible that stiff penalties could be effective deterrents to drunk driving if not to drinking to excess. (B) is incorrect because the author makes this point, so this choice does not weaken the argument. (C) is incorrect since the author is concerned only with the problem of fatalities caused by drunk driving. (D) can be eliminated since the author is concerned with eliminating fatalities caused by drunk driving, not with whether the drunk driver ought to be punished. (E) is not a strong

attack on the argument since the author does leave open the question of the value of therapy in combating drunk driving.

20. **The correct answer is (C).** The relationship is that of example to general type. An ODE is a kind of POEM, and a *ballad* is a kind of *song*. And again there is an "echo," for there is a kinship between poem and song.

21. **The correct answer is (A).** The relationship here is one of opposition. Someone who displays TENACITY is not WEAK, just as one who displays *apathy* is not *caring*.

22. **The correct answer is (C).** The CURATOR is in charge of caring for PAINTINGS, and the *archivist* has the same relationship to *manuscripts*. And there is an "echo" of kinship between the curator and the archivist and between paintings and manuscripts.

23. **The correct answer is (C).** CREPUSCULE means TWILIGHT, so the stem words are synonyms, just as *dawn* and *daybreak* are synonyms. And you will notice the "echo" between twilight and daybreak.

24. **The correct answer is (C).** There are two points of attack here. First, you need a word to parallel the idea of a charged atmosphere. What happened to the law? It was *infected* with religious overtones. Second, you need a parallel to this. As a consequence, what did the law do to the required separation of state and church? It *violated* it—and this was the reason the law was struck down.

25. **The correct answer is (A).** You should almost be able to complete the sentence even without looking at the choices. Since there is a perceived correlation between price and value, you would expect that sellers would raise prices. This suggests either (A) or (B) as the correct choice. (B), however, fails to carry through the paral-

lel. Given the correlation, the price increase would not be moderate but very great.

26. **The correct answer is (A).** Parallelism or continuation is the key here. Notice that we must use adjectives with positive overtones—the audience gave the performance a standing ovation. So we can eliminate (C) on the basis of the first element. And we eliminate (B) and (E) on the basis of the second substitution. (A) is the only choice to carry through the positive notion.

27. **The correct answer is (B).** To FORGE has the literal meaning of shaping metal. The more figurative meaning is to create or to shape anything. For example, to forge a union means to create that unity. So a good opposite would be to "uncreate" or *dissolve*.

28. **The correct answer is (C).** MOTILE means "having the power of motion or able to move," so a good opposite is *immobile*.

29. **The correct answer is (E).** LACHRYMOSE means "tearful" or "sad," so a good opposite is *joyful*.

30. **The correct answer is (D).** QUIESCENCE refers to a state of quiet or rest. A good opposite would be one referring to a state of motion, even violent motion, such as *frenzy*.

Math Section

1.	C	7.	E	13.	C	19.	D	25.	B
2.	A	8.	A	14.	A	20.	E	26.	D
3.	A	9.	C	15.	B	21.	D	27.	A
4.	A	10.	A	16.	C	22.	A	28.	B
5.	C	11.	D	17.	E	23.	D		
6.	A	12.	D	18.	D	24.	E		

1. **The correct answer is (C).** With a problem that indicates a very simple manipulation, as this one does, the easiest way to arrive at a comparison is often just to do the operation. In this case, Column A is $5 - 1 = 4$, and Column B is $5 - 1 = 4$.

2. **The correct answer is (A).** A question like this just tests your understanding of the centered statement. If x is 4 more than y, then x must be greater than y. So Column A is greater than Column B.

3. **The correct answer is (A).** Contrast this question with question 1. Notice that the manipulation here would be more difficult. To find the percent increase you would create a fraction with the change as the numerator and the original amount as the denominator:

$$\frac{\text{change}}{\text{original amount}} = \frac{\$1.00}{\$7.95}$$

But rewriting this fraction as a decimal and then as a percent is tiresome. Instead of actually performing the calculation, you should look for an alternative way of making the comparison. In this case, you are asked to compare $\frac{1}{7.95}$ to 12%. $\frac{1}{7.95}$ is very close to $\frac{1}{8}$ (slightly more, since 7.95 is less than 8, and the less the denominator the greater the value of the fraction). And $\frac{1}{8}$ is exactly $12\frac{1}{2}$%. So $\frac{1}{7.95}$ must be more than $12\frac{1}{2}$%, and that is enough to justify the conclusion that Column A is greater than Column B.

4. **The correct answer is (A).** Since $M + 2$ is the average of x and y, $\frac{(x+y)}{2} = M + 2$. This means that Column A could be rewritten as $M + 2$. Since Column B is M and Column A is 2 more than M, Column A must be greater.

5. **The correct answer is (C).** With a question of this type, a good strategy is to do the indicated algebraic manipulation. If we do the multiplication indicated in Column A, we have $(x + y)(x - y) = x^2 + xy - xy - y^2 = x^2 - y^2$. The two expressions are equivalent, so the two columns are equal.

6. **The correct answer is (A).** One way of attacking a question like this with easily performed operations is to do the arithmetic: $5^2 = 25$, $12^2 = 144$, and $25 + 144 = 169$. Then look for an equivalent answer choice: $13^2 = 169$. Alternatively, you might have remembered that one set of "magic" Pythagorean numbers is 5, 12, 13, that is, a triangle with sides of 5, 12, 13 is a right triangle, so $5^2 + 12^2 = 13^2$.

7. **The correct answer is (E).** This is essentially a bookkeeping problem, and all you need to do is multiply the numbers to find the total value of sales: 50 weeks × 100 sales per week = 5,000 sales; 5,000 sales × $1,000 per sale = $5,000,000.

8. **The correct answer is (A).** Given the diameter of a circle, we know the radius, since the radius is just half the diameter:

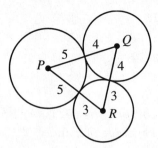

So the perimeter of the triangle formed by the radii of the circles is 24.

9. **The correct answer is (C).** With a question of this type, the best approach is to substitute the values provided into the expression:

$$\frac{x^2 - xy}{y} = \frac{1^2 - (1)(-2)}{-2} = \frac{1 - (-2)}{-2} = \frac{3}{-2} = -\frac{3}{2}$$

10. **The correct answer is (A).** Here we suggest that you manipulate the inequality until you have a single x on one side:

$$5x - 2 < 3x - 1$$

Subtract $3x$ from both sides: $2x - 2 < -1$

Add 2 to both sides: $2x < 1$

Divide both sides by 2: $x < \frac{1}{2}$

So x is less than $\frac{1}{2}$, which means that 1 is not a possible value of x.

11. **The correct answer is (D).** Remember that quantitative comparison figures are not necessarily drawn to scale. Because of that, we cannot make a comparison based upon measuring. Moreover, since the size of the unlabeled angles is unknown, we cannot deduce any conclusion about the size of angles x and y.

12. **The correct answer is (D).** Remember that "percent" means "per 100," and it is just a convenient ratio to work with. But because it is only a ratio, percent itself gives you no information about the actual numbers involved. Although City Y

experienced a greater *percentage* decrease than City X, we cannot reach any conclusion about the actual number of persons involved.

13. **The correct answer is (C).** A square has four equal sides, so its perimeter is just 4 times the length of one side. Conversely, the perimeter divided by 4 gives you the length of each side. In this case, the perimeter is $12\sqrt{3}$, so the length of each of the four sides is $12\sqrt{3} \div 4 = 3\sqrt{3}$.

14. **The correct answer is (A).** Here is another question with a difficult manipulation, so we look for another way to make the comparison. Here it is possible to factor out $\frac{3}{7}$ from both terms of the left-hand expression, yielding $\frac{3}{7}\left(\frac{101}{104} + \frac{4}{104}\right)$ which is equal to $\left(\frac{3}{7}\right)\left(\frac{105}{104}\right)$. At this point a comparison is possible. Since $\frac{105}{104}$ is greater than 1, $\frac{3}{7} \times \frac{105}{104}$ must be slightly greater than $\frac{3}{7}$, so Column A must be greater than Column B.

15. **The correct answer is (B).** Since no drawing is provided, you might find it easiest to reach a comparison by sketching the coordinate system:

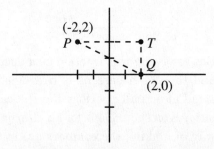

You could now find the distance from P to Q by using the Pythagorean Theorem: $PT^2 + TQ^2 = PQ^2$. There is no need to work out the actual length, however, because you can make your comparison with an approximation. Notice that the length of $\overline{PT}$ is 4. This means that $\overline{PQ}$, which is the hypotenuse of the right triangle, is longer than 4, so Column B must be greater.

16. **The correct answer is (C).** To answer this question, you might try substituting values for x and y, or you might just think generally about the properties of the numbers they describe. As for (A), if x is even, then x^2, which is x times x, must also be even; but since y is an odd number, the entire expression is odd. As for (B), x^2 is even, and since y, an odd number, is subtracted from x, the result must also be an odd number. As for (D) and (E), an even number plus or minus an odd number is odd. (C) is the correct choice, for x^2 is even, and an even number multiplied by an odd number generates an even result.

17. **The correct answer is (E).** Here we might manipulate the equation that is given. Since $p = \frac{1}{3}q$, you can set up a direct proportion:

$$\frac{p}{q} = \frac{1}{3}$$

$$\left(\frac{1}{3}\right)\frac{p}{q} = \frac{1}{3}\left(\frac{1}{3}\right)$$

$$\frac{p}{3q} = \frac{1}{9}$$

So 1:9 is the correct response.

18. **The correct answer is (D).** A direct proportion will easily solve the problem. Since the cost remains constant, the more chemical purchased the greater the cost, and vice versa:

$$\frac{\$50}{30} = \frac{\$625}{x}$$

Cross-multiply: $50x = 18,750$

Divide by 50: $x = 375$

19. **The correct answer is (D).** The best way to the solution here might be just to try various combinations. For example, for 17 you might try $4 + 5 + 6$, which is 15, and then $5 + 6 + 7$, which is 18. So there is no set of three consecutive integers that will do the trick. When you get to (D), you will find that $9 + 10 + 11 = 30$.

For the mathematically inclined, you can express the sum of three consecutive integers as follows: Let x be the first of the three integers; the second integer is one more, or $x + 1$; and the third is one more than that, or $x + 2$. So the sum of any three consecutive integers is $x + x + 1 + x + 2 = 3x + 3$. For a number to be the sum of three consecutive integers, it must be 3 more than some other number that is divisible by 3. Or, in other words, for a number to be the sum of three consecutive integers, if you subtract 3 from it, what is left will be divisible by 3. Of the available choices, only the number 30 fits this description.

20. **The correct answer is (E).** The information given can be rendered in equation form. Let x, y, and z represent the three sides, x being the shortest and z being the longest. Given the information about the area of the faces: $xy = 6$, $xz = 8$, and $yz = 12$. Now treat these as simultaneous equations. Since $xy = 6$, $x = \frac{6}{y}$. Substitute this value for x in the second equation, and you have $z\left(\frac{6}{y}\right) = 8$, so $z = 8\left(\frac{y}{6}\right) = \left(\frac{4y}{3}\right)$. Now put this value for z in the third equation: $y\left(\frac{4y}{3}\right)$, so $4y^2 = 36$, $y^2 = 9$, and $y = +3$ or -3. Since we are dealing with distances, y cannot be negative, so $y = +3$. From here on in, the solution is easy. If $y = 3$, then $x = 2$; and if $x = 2$, then $z = 4$. So the three sides are 2, 3, and 4, and the volume of the solid is $2 \times 3 \times 4 = 24$.

21. **The correct answer is (D).** The pie chart shows the distribution of motor vehicles in City X according to their manufacturer: 40% were manufactured by Q. Since the total number of motor vehicles registered is 8,400, the number registered that were manufactured by Q is 40% of 8,400 = 3,360.

22. **The correct answer is (A).** This question is based on the information for City Y, which is given in the bar graph. Consulting that portion of the chart, we find that there were 1,600 motor vehicles registered in City Y manufactured by R and 1,200 manufactured by P: $1,600 - 1,200 = 400$. So there were 400 more vehicles manufactured by R registered in City Y.

23. **The correct answer is (D).** Notice that this question specifically asks for an approximation. If you look at the small table that summarizes the information for City X and manufacturers T, U, and V, you will see that each of those manufacturers accounted for approximately the same number of registrations. The three together accounted for 8% of all City X registrations, as shown in the pie chart. This means that Manufacturer V accounted for about $\frac{1}{3}$ of the 8%, or about 3%, so (D) is the best approximation.

24. **The correct answer is (E).** To answer this question, you will first need the total number of registrations in City Y. Adding the various values we have $1,200 + 2,400 + 1,600 + 800 + 400 = 6,400$, of which 1,600 were from Manufacturer R. And $\frac{1,600}{6,400} = \frac{1}{4} = 25\%$.

25. **The correct answer is (B).** One way to make the comparison is to find the greatest common factor for each of the pairs. 18 and 24 have a common factor of 6: $6 \times 3 = 18$ and $6 \times 4 = 24$. Since the least number evenly divisible by both 3 and 4 is $3 \times 4 = 12$, the least number divisible by 18 and 24 is $6 \times 12 = 72$. On the other side, 18 and 28 have a common factor of 2: $2 \times 9 = 18$ and $2 \times 14 = 28$, the least number divisible by both 9 and 14 is $9 \times 14 = 126$, so the least number evenly divisible by both 18 and 28 is $2 \times 126 = 252$. Thus, Column B is greater. Alternatively, you might have realized that since 18 is not a factor of either 24 or 28, it's "easier" to find a number divisible by 18 and 24 than by 18 and 28. By easier we mean that if you kept trying number after number, you would get to the one divisible by 18 and 24 before you got to the one divisible by 18 and 28.

26. **The correct answer is (D).** Remember that figures are not necessarily drawn to scale. You cannot conclude, without further information, that the two lines in the figure are parallel to each other. Without that information, you should not attempt to arrive at any conclusion regarding the relative sizes of x and y.

27. **The correct answer is (A).** This question defines a certain operation "*". All you need to do is substitute the numbers provided in the two columns into the definition. Since $P * Q = P + Q - PQ$, to find $4 * 1$, you substitute 4 for P and 1 for Q: $4 + 1 - (4)(1) = 1$. To find $4 * 2$, substitute 4 for P and 2 for Q: $4 + 2 - (4)(2) = -2$. You can see that Column A is greater.

28. **The correct answer is (B).** You might find it useful to perform the algebraic operations indicated: $(3j)(3k)(3m) = 9jkm$ and $3(j)(k)(m) = 3jkm$. But that alone does not answer the question. You need to consider the centered information. Notice that j and k are positive while m is negative. This means that both columns are negative numbers (positive $\times$ positive $\times$ negative yields a negative number). Consequently, Column A is even less than Column B since it is 9 times that negative number rather than 3 times that negative number.

PART III

GRE VERBAL QUESTIONS

Sentence Completions

OVERVIEW

- **What are sentence completions?**
- **How do you answer sentence completions?**
- **What smart test-takers know**
- **Summing it up**

WHAT ARE SENTENCE COMPLETIONS?

The basic idea of a sentence completion is to "fill in the blank." The question type is a sort of hybrid, consisting of reading comprehension, word usage, and vocabulary. The question type is designed on the premise that it is possible to understand the gist of something even without hearing (or reading) every single word.

A little experiment will show you that this is true. Imagine that you are sitting in a lecture hall, listening to a professor, and someone sitting near you keeps rattling papers so you miss some words:

> Tensions between the United States and Great Britain —— even after the end of the War of 1812. One important —— in Anglo-American relations during the nineteenth century was their —— for one another, rather stronger on the side of the United States. "Twisting the lion's tail" was a favorite American political pastime, vestiges of which were still —— even in the early part of the twentieth ——.

Even though you are missing some words, you should still be able to make sense of the lecture. In essence, based on the logic of the sentences, you are "automatically" filling in the blanks. There are several words that might be used to fill each blank such as:

> Tensions between the United States and Great Britain *continued* even after the end of the War of 1812. One important *factor* in Anglo-American relations during the nineteenth century was their *antipathy* for one another, rather stronger on the side of the United States. "Twisting the lion's tail" was a favorite American political pastime, vestiges of which were still *evident* even in the early part of the twentieth *century*.

chapter 4

Of course, these words are not the only possible substitutions, but they will serve to show the general idea of a sentence completion. This technique is the basic strategy for attacking sentence completions. The Verbal portion of the exam will contain 5 to 7 sentence completions.

GRE Sentence Completions

TIP

Don't let sentence completions hold you up. You can't afford to spend more than a minute on one.

Here are the directions for GRE sentence completions, together with a sample question and its explanation.

Anatomy of Sentence Completions

> **Directions:** The question below contains one or more blank spaces, each blank indicating that something has been omitted. Each sentence is followed by five (5) words or sets of words. Read and determine the general sense of each sentence. Then choose the word, or set of words that, when inserted in the sentence, best fits the meaning of the sentence.

When Great Britain declared war on Germany in 1914, many people expected Lloyd George to resign because his —— tendencies made him an unsuitable leader during a time of conflict.

- **(A)** conservative
- **(B)** ambitious
- **(C)** pacifist
- **(D)** unfazed
- **(E)** precocious

Familiarize yourself with the directions now. That way, on your test, you'll be able to dismiss them immediately with a click of the mouse and get right to work. The idea is to find an answer choice that makes sense when substituted in the sentence.

This sentence completion item has only one blank. Some sentence completion items have two blanks.

The correct answer is (C). *Unsuitable* sets up a contrast between *conflict* and an opposite. Word clues are very important in sentence completions, so pay careful attention to words that amplify or reverse a thought.

HOW DO YOU ANSWER SENTENCE COMPLETIONS?

Here's a simple five-step plan that can help you fill in all the blanks.

Sentence Completions: Getting It Right

1 Read the sentence through for meaning.

2 Try to anticipate the missing word or words.

3 Scan the choices to find one that matches your guess. If it's there, click it, confirm it, and go on.

4 If your guess was not there, test choices to find the one that works best.

5 Test your selection by plugging it into the blank to see if it "sounds right."

Now let's try out these steps on three GRE-type sentence completions.

> There is no —— for the United States to sign the treaty since there is every reason to believe no other nation intends to honor its provisions.
>
> **(A)** arrangement
>
> **(B)** continuation
>
> **(C)** incentive
>
> **(D)** procedure
>
> **(E)** importance

1 Read the sentence.

2 You should be able to anticipate that an appropriate completion would be something like *reason*.

3 Scan the choices. Choice (C), *incentive*, is close to *reason* and makes sense in the sentence, so choose it and move on.

> Even though he is a leading authority on the French Revolution, the chairperson of the department is a —— speaker whose lectures on even the most exciting aspect of that historical period cause students to yawn and fidget.
>
> **(A)** sublime
>
> **(B)** confident
>
> **(C)** lackluster
>
> **(D)** honest
>
> **(E)** meritorious

1 Read the sentence.

2 You should be able to anticipate that the answer might be a word like *dull* or *boring*.

3 *Dull* and *boring* are not in the answer choices, so look for the closest match. *Lackluster*, choice (C), is a good synonym and is the correct answer.

NOTE

What if more than one answer seems to make sense? Remember that there is only one correct answer. Make your best guess based on the full meaning of the sentence.

The chairperson, who is a specialist in French history, is a —— speaker whose lectures on the French Revolution completely —— students.

    (A) lackluster . . entertain

    (B) moving . . alienate

    (C) dull . . absorb

    (D) forceful . . require

    (E) scintillating . . enthrall

1 Read the sentence.

2 In this case, you can't anticipate a likely answer without checking the answer choices, since a variety of completions could be correct.

3 Since you can't anticipate an answer, you must go on to step 4.

4 Test choices to find one that works:

Choice (A) is wrong: A *lackluster* speaker is not likely to *entertain* students.

Choice (B) is wrong: A *moving* speaker is not likely to *alienate* students.

Choice (C) is wrong: A *dull* speaker is not likely to *absorb* students.

Choice (D) is wrong: It makes no sense that a *forceful* speaker would *require* students.

Choice (E) is correct: A *scintillating* speaker is very likely to *enthrall* students.

WHAT SMART TEST-TAKERS KNOW

SOME BLANKS PRACTICALLY FILL IN THEMSELVES.

If you read the sentence carefully, you're likely to come up with the right answer on your own. Even if the word you guess isn't exactly right, you can often spot a synonym among the answer choices. Click it, confirm it, and go on; you've saved precious time that you can use to make sure you answer all of the questions in the section.

CLUE WORDS CAN TELL YOU WHERE THE SENTENCE IS GOING.

If you can't come up with the missing word immediately, look for clue words in the sentence. Clue words can reveal the logical structure of the sentence. Is it continuing along one line of thought? If so, you're looking for a word that supports that thought. Is it changing direction in midstream? Then you're looking for a word that indicates a contrast between the thoughts expressed in the sentence.

SOME BLANKS CONTINUE OR AMPLIFY A THOUGHT IN THE SENTENCE.

Often the blank must be filled by a word that will make one part of the sentence parallel to another part by continuing a thought or amplifying a thought. Here is an example:

The conductor's choice of tempo seemed entirely ——, so that each successive movement of the piece seemed to have no necessary connection to what had come before.

   (A) musical

   (B) believable

   (C) arbitrary

   (D) subtle

   (E) cautious

The correct answer is (C). The logical clue is the parallel that is required. What comes after the comma is intended to clarify or amplify what is contained in the blank. Which of the five choices has a meaning related to *no necessary connection*? Only (C), *arbitrary*, has such a meaning.

After a period of protracted disuse, a muscle will atrophy, —— both its strength and the ability to perform its former function.

   (A) regaining

   (B) sustaining

   (C) losing

   (D) insuring

   (E) aligning

The correct answer is (C). The logical structure requires a continuation of the idea of *atrophy*.

SOME BLANKS REVERSE A THOUGHT IN THE SENTENCE.

Sometimes the substitution must be the reverse of some other thought in the sentence. In such cases, the substitution must create a phrase that contrasts with some other element in the sentence. Look at these examples:

Although the conditions in which she chooses to live suggest that she is miserly, her contributions to charities show that she is ——.

   (A) stingy

   (B) thrifty

   (C) frugal

   (D) intolerant

   (E) generous

The correct answer is (E). *Although* signals a thought-reverser. The idea that comes after the comma must contrast with the idea that comes before the comma. Only (E) sets up the needed contrast: *miserly* vs. *generous*.

TIP

Some words signal blanks that continue a thought:

and

also

consequently

as a result

thus

hence

so

for example

TIP

Some words signal blanks that reverse a thought:

but

yet

although

on the other hand

in contrast

however

nevertheless

There are many dialects of English with radically different pronunciations of the same word, but the spelling of these words is ——.

    (A) inconstant

    (B) uniform

    (C) shortened

    (D) contemplated

    (E) abbreviated

The correct answer is (B). The *but* introduces a thought-reverser. The phrase completed by the substitution must create a contrast with the idea of difference expressed in the first clause. (B) does this nicely, contrasting *uniform* with *different*.

IN SOME SENTENCES, ONE BLANK CONTINUES A THOUGHT AND ANOTHER REVERSES ONE.

The report issued by the committee was completely ——, extolling in great detail the plan's strengths but failing to mention its ——.

    (A) comprehensive . . proposal

    (B) unbiased . . weaknesses

    (C) one-sided . . shortcomings

    (D) printed . . good points

    (E) skewed . . defenders

The correct answer is (C). The logical structure of this sentence cannot be described as either a thought-reverser or a thought-continuer, for there are elements of both. First, the phrase following the comma, taken in isolation, expresses a contrast. The second blank must be filled by a word that is somehow the opposite of *strengths*. Both (B) and (C) will provide the needed contrast. Second, the phrase following the comma, taken as a whole, is a continuer of the thought expressed before the comma. So the first blank must be filled by a word that describes something that covers only the good, not the bad. *One-sided* will do the trick.

The quarterback's injury was very painful but not ——, and he managed to —— the game in spite of it.

    (A) serious . . interrupt

    (B) incapacitating . . finish

    (C) harmful . . abandon

    (D) conclusive . . enter

    (E) excruciating . . concede

The correct answer is (B). The first blank must complete the contrast set up by *but not*. Only (A), (B), and (E) are possible choices on this basis. Then, the *in spite of* sets up a contrast between what comes before the comma and what follows. Only (B) provides the needed thought reversal.

THE RIGHT ANSWER ALWAYS CREATES A MEANINGFUL ENGLISH PHRASE.

Eliminate all choices that would not result in an idiomatic construction.

> The plot of the movie was extremely complicated and included many minor characters —— to the central events.
>
> **(A)** momentous
>
> **(B)** tangential
>
> **(C)** contemporary
>
> **(D)** essential
>
> **(E)** impervious

The correct answer is (B). Two of the choices can be eliminated because they would not create a meaningful phrase:

(A) . . . momentous to . . . (WRONG!)
(C) . . . contemporary to . . . (WRONG!)

Then you would use the logic of the sentence to settle on (B). The blank must continue the idea of *minor characters*, and (B) does this. The characters were only *tangential* to the main plot.

> The governor's intolerance of —— among his aides was intensified by his insistence upon total —— from all.
>
> **(A)** dissent . . loyalty
>
> **(B)** dishonesty . . imagination
>
> **(C)** flattery . . communication
>
> **(D)** compliance . . commitment
>
> **(E)** insight . . familiarity

The correct answer is (A). You can eliminate (D) and (E) on the basis of their first elements:

(D) . . . intolerance of compliance . . . (WRONG!)
(E) . . . intolerance of insight . . . (WRONG!)

It is almost impossible to construct an English sentence using these phrases. (And if you can come up with some bizarre sentence using them, that only proves the point. Such a sentence would not appear on the GRE.) You can eliminate (B) and (C) because the second substitution would not be idiomatic:

(B) . . . total imagination . . . (WRONG!)
(C) . . . total communication . . . (WRONG!)

ELIMINATING GIBBERISH ANSWERS IMPROVES YOUR GUESSING ODDS.

Eliminating answer choices that result in gibberish will improve your chances of guessing correctly.

Know the most common sentence completion types.
1. Continuing a thought
2. Reversing a thought

XXXXX XXXXX XXXXXXXX XXX X XXXXXXXXXX XX XXXXXXX, XXX XXXXXXX XXXX XXX XXXXXXX XXXXX —— our existing resources.

(A) squander

(B) conserve

(C) belie

(D) eliminate

(E) deny

The sentence above has been concealed from you to put you in the same position you would find yourself in if you were not able to penetrate the logic of a sentence. Still, you can eliminate some choices by tossing out the gibberish. Which of the following phrases are most likely to appear in an English sentence?

(A)   . . . squander our existing resources.

(B)   . . . conserve our existing resources.

(C)   . . . belie our existing resources.

(D)   . . . eliminate our existing resources.

(E)   . . . deny our existing resources

Choices (A) and (B) are the most likely candidates, and this is a good basis for an educated guess.

TWO BLANKS ARE BETTER THAN ONE.

When there are two blanks in a sentence completion, you have two ways to eliminate answer choices. You can start with either blank to eliminate choices that don't work. So pick the one that's easier for you. If you can eliminate just one of the words in a two-word answer choice, the whole choice won't work so you can toss it out and go on.

EXERCISE 1

10 Questions • 10 Minutes

Directions: Each of the questions below contains one or more blank spaces, each blank indicating that something has been omitted. Each sentence is followed by five (5) words or sets of words. Read and determine the general sense of each sentence. Then choose the word, or set of words that, when inserted in the sentence, best fits the meaning of the sentence.

1. Although his work was often —— and ——, he was promoted anyway, simply because he had been with the company longer than anyone else.

   (A) forceful . . extraneous
   (B) negligent . . creative
   (C) incomplete . . imprecise
   (D) predictable . . careful
   (E) expeditious . . concise

2. Her acceptance speech was ——, eliciting thunderous applause at several points.

   (A) tedious
   (B) well-received
   (C) cowardly
   (D) uninteresting
   (E) poorly-written

3. Shopping malls account for 60 percent of the retail business done in the United States because they are controlled environments, which —— concerns about the weather.

   (A) eliminate
   (B) necessitate
   (C) foster
   (D) justify
   (E) maintain

4. An oppressive ——, and not the festive mood one might have expected, characterized the mood of the gathering.

   (A) senility
   (B) capriciousness
   (C) inanity
   (D) solemnity
   (E) hysteria

5. In order to —— museums and legitimate investors and to facilitate the —— of pilfered artifacts, art magazines often publish photographs of stolen archaeological treasures.

   (A) perpetuate . . return
   (B) protect . . recovery
   (C) encourage . . excavation
   (D) undermine . . discovery
   (E) confuse . . repossession

6. Despite some bad reviews, Horowitz's stature was not ——, and his fans and critics in Tokyo were unanimous in expressing their —— his unique talent.

   (A) distilled . . kinship with
   (B) embellished . . ignorance of
   (C) criticized . . disdain for
   (D) diminished . . appreciation of
   (E) convincing . . concern for

7. Though the concert had been enjoyable, it was overly —— and the three encores seemed ——.

    (A) extensive . . curtailed
    (B) protracted . . gratuitous
    (C) inaudible . . superfluous
    (D) sublime . . fortuitous
    (E) contracted . . lengthy

8. Peter, —— by the repeated rejections of his novel, —— to submit his manuscript to other publishers.

    (A) encouraged . . declined
    (B) elated . . planned
    (C) undaunted . . continued
    (D) inspired . . complied
    (E) undeterred . . refused

9. All —— artists must struggle with the conflict between —— their own talent and knowledge that very few are great enough to succeed.

    (A) great . . neglect of
    (B) aspiring . . faith in
    (C) ambitious . . indifference to
    (D) prophetic . . dissolution of
    (E) serious . . disregard of

10. The judge, after ruling that the article had unjustly —— the reputation of the architect, ordered the magazine to —— its libelous statements in print.

    (A) praised . . communicate
    (B) injured . . retract
    (C) sullied . . publicize
    (D) damaged . . disseminate
    (E) extolled . . produce

EXERCISE 2

5 Questions • 5 Minutes

Directions: Each of the questions below contains one or more blank spaces, each blank indicating that something has been omitted. Each sentence is followed by five (5) words or sets of words. Read and determine the general sense of each sentence. Then choose the word, or set of words that, when inserted in the sentence, best fits the meaning of the sentence.

1. Although the language was —— and considered to be inferior to standard English, Robert Burns wrote his love poetry in the language of the Scots.

    (A) interpreted

    (B) belittled

    (C) distinguished

    (D) appreciated

    (E) elevated

2. Given the Secretary of State's —— the President's foreign policies, he has no choice but to resign.

    (A) reliance upon

    (B) antipathy toward

    (C) pretense of

    (D) support for

    (E) concurrence with

3. In order to —— the deadline for submitting the research paper, the student tried to —— additional time from the professor.

    (A) extend . . wheedle

    (B) accelerate . . obtain

    (C) postpone . . forego

    (D) sustain . . imagine

    (E) conceal . . procure

4. Joyce's novel *Finnegans' Wake* continues to —— critics, including those who find it incomprehensible and call it ——.

    (A) appall . . genial

    (B) enthrall . . nonsensical

    (C) baffle . . transparent

    (D) bore . . compelling

    (E) entertain . . monotonous

5. Jazz is an American art form that is now —— in Europe through the determined efforts of —— in France, Scandinavia, and Germany.

    (A) foundering . . governments

    (B) diminishing . . musicians

    (C) appreciated . . opponents

    (D) waning . . novices

    (E) flourishing . . expatriates

ANSWER KEY AND EXPLANATIONS

Exercise 1

| 1. | C | 3. | A | 5. | B | 7. | B | 9. | B |
| 2. | B | 4. | D | 6. | D | 8. | C | 10. | B |

1. **The correct answer is (C).** The *although* sets up a contrast between the idea of a promotion and the quality of the person's work. So the work must be bad, even though the person was promoted. Additionally, the two blanks must themselves be parallel, since both describe the poor quality of work.

2. **The correct answer is (B).** The key to this item is a thought-extender; what follows the comma must extend or amplify what comes before it. So your thinking should be "the speech was *something,* and that got applause." You might anticipate several completions with positive overtones such as *brilliant, magnificent,* or *persuasive.* None of these appears as an answer choice, so you should match your anticipated response to the best actual choice available. Only choice (B) has the positive overtones you need to complete the parallel between the quality of the speech and the applause.

3. **The correct answer is (A).** The blank is a thought-extender that explains the result of a controlled environment. What would be the result of a controlled environment? You would not need to worry about the weather.

4. **The correct answer is (D).** The *not,* a thought-reverser, introduces a contrast. The blank must be a word that means the opposite of "a festive mood."

5. **The correct answer is (B).** The logical structure here requires a thought-extender. The information that comes before the comma must explain why art magazines publish photos of stolen prop-

erty. Additionally, the two blanks must create a parallel. Publishing the photos must do roughly the same thing for museums and legitimate investors that it does for stolen property. In this case, the result must be good. The museums and investors are protected and the stolen property is recovered.

6. **The correct answer is (D).** In this sentence, *despite* introduces a contrast, but notice there is a *not* in the sentence. The blank will actually complete a parallel to bad reviews: Bad reviews but *not* something negative. On this basis, you can eliminate (A), (B), and (E). Then, you should see that the second blank must continue the idea expressed in the first. Only (D) accomplishes this.

7. **The correct answer is (B).** The *though* sets up a contrast. The concert was enjoyable, but it suffers from some defect. You can eliminate (D) since to be *sublime* is not a defect. Additionally, the two blanks themselves are parallel, for they complete similar thoughts. (A) and (E) contain words opposite in meaning, so they must be wrong. And the words in (C) are unrelated, so they cannot provide the needed contrast.

8. **The correct answer is (C).** There are several ways to analyze this item. First, you might see that the overall structure is that of a thought-extender. The first blank must complete a phrase set off by commas that explains why Peter does what he does. Also, the word in the first blank must describe an emotional reaction that is an appropriate response to

rejection. On this ground you can surely eliminate (A), (B), and (D), since it is not logical for anyone to be *encouraged, elated,* or *inspired* by rejection. (C) and (E) are both possible reactions to rejection, but (E) does not provide the overall logical continuity we need.

9. **The correct answer is (B).** The sentence sets up a contrast between the artists' view of their own talent and the knowledge that few will succeed. You can eliminate choices (A), (C), and (E) because they fail to provide a contrast. It would not be surprising that an artist who *neglected,* or *was indifferent to,* or *disregarded* his or her talent would not succeed. And you can eliminate choice (D) on the grounds that the phrase *dissolution of talent* is not meaningful.

10. **The correct answer is (B).** There are several ways of analyzing this item. First, the overall structure is that of a thought-extender. The second blank must explain the results or consequence of the first blank. Additionally, you can rely on key words such as *unjustly* and *libelous* to learn that the action of the magazine was wrong. On this basis you can eliminate (A) and (E) since there is nothing wrong with *praising* or *extolling.* Then, you should eliminate (C) and (D) because they do not explain the natural consequences of the judge's ruling. (B), however, does the job. The judge ruled that the article had wrongly *injured* the architect's reputation, so the magazine was ordered to make amends by *retracting* what it had printed.

Exercise 2

1. B	2. B	3. A	4. B	5. E

1. **The correct answer is (B).** The most obvious logical clue to be found here is the parallel between the blank and the *inferior*. You must find something that has similar negative overtones; and, of the five choices, only (B) will provide the parallel.

2. **The correct answer is (B).** Again, we need a parallel. What is the cause of the Secretary's resignation? It cannot be the fact that the Secretary is in favor of the President's policies, so you can eliminate (D) and (E). Then, you can eliminate (A) and (C) because they do not make meaningful statements. (B), however, does provide the reason you are looking for. Since the Secretary is in disagreement with the President, he will resign.

3. **The correct answer is (A).** We need a thought-extender. The second blank must give the student's reason for doing what is mentioned in the first part of the sentence. Test each choice to see if it does just that. (A) is the only choice that works. The student needs to *extend* the deadline, so he *wheedles* some extra time. (B) and (C) make the opposite statement. (D) and (E) create phrases that are not idiomatic English.

4. **The correct answer is (B).** The key to this item is the parallel setup between *incomprehensible* and the second blank. The second element of the correct choice must be a word like *incomprehensible*.

5. **The correct answer is (E).** You can eliminate (A) by "going to pieces." Although a musical style might be famous, or unknown, or fading out of memory, you would not be likely to say that it is *foundering*. Remember that even eliminating one choice allows you to make an educated guess! Beyond that, the second substitution must extend the idea of the first: The music is doing something thanks to the determined efforts of someone. Given the phrase *determined efforts*, you can eliminate (B) and (D), since *diminishing* and *waning* are not things accomplished by determined efforts. And you can eliminate (C) since *opponents* do not create an appreciation for the things they oppose. Finally, notice how well (E) works. The sentence states that jazz is an American art form *flourishing* in Europe. How is that possible? Because of the efforts of American *expatriates*.

SUMMING IT UP

- Follow these steps when solving sentence completion questions:

  1. Read the entire sentence before trying to complete it. This will help you fully understand its meaning.

  2. Try to anticipate the missing word or words.

  3. Scan the choices to find one that matches your guess. If it's there, mark it and move on.

  4. If your guess is not listed, test the choices to find the one that works best.

  5. Test your selection by plugging it into the blank to see if it "sounds right."

- Clue words can tell you where the sentence is going in terms of meaning.

- Some blanks continue or amplify a thought in the sentence; others reverse a thought.

Analogies

chapter 5

OVERVIEW

- **What is an analogy?**
- **How do you answer analogy questions?**
- **What smart test-takers know**
- **Summing it up**

WHAT IS AN ANALOGY?

GRE analogies are all about relationships. They test your ability to see a relationship between two words and to recognize a similar relationship between two other words. The key to analogy success is being able to express the relationship between the words in a pair.

GRE Analogy Questions

You will have 6 to 8 analogies in the verbal part of your GRE (out of a total of 30 questions that will also include sentence completions, antonyms, and reading comprehension).

Question Format

A GRE analogy reads like a mathematical proportion. Colons and double colons are a shorthand way of expressing the relationship. Each analogy starts with a capitalized word pair, which is followed by five other word pairs in lowercase letters. The task is to find the answer choice pair that expresses a relationship similar to that of the capitalized word pair. When you've solved a typical analogy, you can read it like this:

ACTOR : CAST :: singer : chorus

ACTOR *is to* CAST *as* singer *is to* chorus

Here are the directions for GRE analogy questions, together with a sample question and its explanation.

Anatomy of an Analogy

Directions: In each of the following questions, you are given a related pair of words or phrases in capital letters. Each capitalized pair is followed by five (5) pairs of words or phrases. Choose the pair that best expresses a relationship similar to that expressed by the original pair.

ANALGESIC : PAIN ::
- **(A)** expenses : audit
- **(B)** truss : suspension
- **(C)** durability : hardware
- **(D)** improvisation : jazz
- **(E)** lubricant : friction

Now that you've read the directions, you won't need to read them again. Instead, you'll recognize analogy items by their format (two capitalized words separated by a colon) and know to look for the similar pair. Click the "Dismiss directions" box immediately.

The capitalized words always express a conceptual relationship, and you'll be able to summarize the relationship in a sentence: An ANALGESIC lessens PAIN.

(A) expresses a wrong relationship: An *audit* is an examination of *expenses* and other financial matters. This is in no way similar to the conceptual relationship between the capitalized words.

(B) expresses a conceptual relationship: the *function* of a truss is to provide *suspension*. But this is not the same relationship that connects the capitalized words.

(C) also expresses a wrong relationship: *durability* is characteristic of *hardware*. But *analgesic* is not characteristic of *pain*.

(D), too, expresses a wrong relationship: *improvisation* is a characteristic of *jazz*.

(E) is the correct response: a *lubricant* lessens *friction*.

HOW DO YOU ANSWER ANALOGY QUESTIONS?

To solve GRE analogies, follow these five steps.

Analogies: Getting It Right

1 Figure out how the capitalized words are related.

2 Create a sentence that expresses that connection.

3 Test the choices with your sentence and eliminate the ones that don't work.

4 If you're left with more than one answer—or no answer at all—go back and refine your sentence.

5 Choose the best answer. If none of the choices fits exactly, choose the one that works best.

Now let's try out these five steps on a typical GRE analogy question.

CONDEMNATION : DISAPPROVAL ::

    (A) ignorance : patience

    (B) optimism : insight

    (C) blasphemy : irreverence

    (D) sorrow : intention

    (E) longing : hostility

1 By definition, the relationship is one of "defining characteristic." This is the most common analogy relationship on the GRE.

2 A sentence that expresses this connection is "DISAPPROVAL is the defining characteristic of CONDEMNATION."

3 Test the choices with the sentence. (C) works perfectly: "*Irreverence* is the defining characteristic of *blasphemy*." There is no need to go back and refine the sentence, so skip to step 5 and mark your answer.

Other examples of the "defining characteristic" pattern include:

FLUIDITY : LIQUID

HEROISM : EPIC

AGGRESSION : BELLICOSITY

HUMOR : COMEDIAN

RIDICULE : BURLESQUE

FAME : CELEBRITY

POVERTY : MONK

MISCHIEVOUSNESS : IMP

Now use the five-step plan to solve the following examples.

LOYALTY : TRAITOR ::

   (A) truthfulness : liar

   (B) hope : optimist

   (C) diligence : worker

   (D) understanding : sage

   (E) longevity : crone

The correct answer is (A). This is the mirror image of the analogy connection just discussed. This time the relationship is "lack of something is the defining characteristic."

Other examples of this pattern are:

MATURITY : YOUTHFULNESS
WORDS : TACITURN
MEMORY : AMNESIA
MOVEMENT : PARALYSIS
FRICTION : LUBRICATION
PREMEDITATION : IMPULSE
ENERGY : LETHARGY
NOURISHMENT : STARVATION

MUMBLE : SPEAK ::

   (A) adorn : denude

   (B) inflame : damage

   (C) delimit : expand

   (D) plagiarize : write

   (E) convert : preach

The correct answer is (D). MUMBLING is a spurious (or defective) form of SPEAKING, and *plagiarizing* is a spurious (or defective) form of *writing*.

Here are some more word pairs that fit this analogy pattern:

BRAVADO : COURAGE
QUACK : PHYSICIAN
POACHER : HUNTER
MINCE : WALK
SIMPER : SMILE
ALCHEMY : SCIENCE
EMBEZZLE : WITHDRAW
MALINGERING : ILLNESS
EXTORT : CHARGE

TOSS : HURL ::
  - **(A)** speak : shout
  - **(B)** forget : learn
  - **(C)** consider : formulate
  - **(D)** sense : flourish
  - **(E)** prepare : emit

The correct answer is (A). The relationship is one of degree. To HURL and TOSS are similar actions but one is more violent than the other; similarly, to *shout* and to *speak* are similar, but one is more violent than the other.

Here are some other word pairs that fit this analogy form:

DRIZZLE : POUR
COOL : FRIGID
DISAPPROVED : CONDEMNED
JOG : SPRINT
MERCHANT : MAGNATE
DEFEAT : ROUT
PARTY : ORGY
GIGGLE : LAUGH
TIFF : BATTLE
PROTEST : REVOLUTION

NOTE : SCALE ::
  - **(A)** musician : instrument
  - **(B)** conductor : orchestra
  - **(C)** letter : alphabet
  - **(D)** book : cover
  - **(E)** singer : music

The correct answer is (C). A NOTE is a part of a SCALE, and a *letter* is a part of the *alphabet*.

Here are some other word pairs that fit this pattern:

PAGE : BOOK
CLIMAX : DRAMA
COLOR : SPECTRUM
VOLUME : LIBRARY
VERSE : SONG
LEG : JOURNEY
VERDICT : TRIAL
WICK : CANDLE
NOON : DAY

BALLAD : SONG ::
- **(A)** credit : movie
- **(B)** shutter : darkness
- **(C)** novel : chapter
- **(D)** portrait : painting
- **(E)** melody : rhythm

The correct answer is (D). A BALLAD is a type of SONG, and a *portrait* is a type of *painting*.

Here are some more word pairs that fit this pattern:

CARDIOLOGIST : PHYSICIAN
TIGER : CARNIVORE
BEER : BEVERAGE
SOPRANO : VOCALIST
SYNCOPATION : RHYTHM
THYME : SPICE
MONARCHY : GOVERNMENT
MEASLES : DISEASE
PROTESTANTISM : RELIGION
COURAGE : VIRTUE

REHEARSAL : PERFORMANCE ::
- **(A)** entrapment : game
- **(B)** engagement : marriage
- **(C)** applause : audience
- **(D)** antidote : illness
- **(E)** satisfaction : appetite

The correct answer is (B). A REHEARSAL precedes a PERFORMANCE, and an *engagement* precedes a *marriage*.

Here are other word pairs that fit this pattern. Notice that some are related as a matter of logical sequence, while others form a causal sequence.

TADPOLE : FROG
TUMBLE : FALL
SWELL : BURST
CONVICT : SENTENCE
INFECTION : ILLNESS
PROSELYTIZE : CONVERT
CROUCH : SPRING
SALUTATION : FAREWELL
CLIMAX : DENOUEMENT

NOTE

What if none of the answer pairs seems exactly right? Remember: The directions tell you to choose the best answer. The correct answer won't necessarily be a perfect fit, but it will work better than the other choices.

RETIREMENT : SERVICE ::

(A) employment : salary

(B) arrangement : flowers

(C) contract : agreement

(D) graduation : studies

(E) exchange : communication

The correct answer is (D). RETIREMENT signifies the end of SERVICE, and *graduation* signifies the end of *studies*.

Here are some other word pairs that fit this pattern:

RECESS : TRIAL
DISMISSAL : EMPLOYMENT
RELAPSE : RECOVERY
INCARCERATION : RELEASE
LUNCH BREAK : WORKDAY
DIVORCE : MARRIAGE
LAYOVER : JOURNEY
INTERMISSION : PERFORMANCE
DIGRESSION : SPEECH

SCALPEL : SURGEON ::

(A) pen : reader

(B) bow : violinist

(C) bed : patient

(D) pistol : angler

(E) auto : soldier

The correct answer is (B). The SCALPEL is the tool commonly associated with the SURGEON, and the *bow* is the tool commonly associated with the *violinist*.

Here are some further examples:

TROWEL : BRICKLAYER
PALLET : PAINTER
FILTER : PURIFICATION
NEEDLE : SEW
PADDLE : CANOE
TACK : JOCKEY
TELESCOPE : ASTRONOMER
KNIFE : WHITTLE

UMPIRE : PLAYING FIELD ::

(A) carpenter : cabinet

(B) plumber : wrench

(C) judge : courtroom

(D) player : locker

(E) farmer : city

TIP

Use analogies as a time-saver. Analogies are short questions. If you can do them quickly, you will have more time to spend on lengthier reading questions.

The correct answer is (C). The UMPIRE is found on the PLAYING FIELD, and the *judge* is found in the *courtroom*.

Here are some further examples:

WATER : RESERVOIR
PROFESSOR : CLASSROOM
COFFEE : MUG
SAILOR : SHIP
ROUSTABOUT : CIRCUS
HORSE : STABLE
PAINTING : MUSEUM
FARMER : FIELD
CHEF : KITCHEN
DOCTOR : HOSPITAL

YAWN : BOREDOM ::

(A) smile : hatred

(B) blink : nausea

(C) sigh : hope

(D) grimace : joy

(E) wince : pain

The correct answer is (E). A YAWN is a sign of BOREDOM, and a *wince* is a sign of *pain*.

Here are some other word pairs that fit this pattern:

GRIMACE : PAIN
FIDGET : RESTLESSNESS
SNARL : ANGER
PURR : CONTENTMENT
STRUT : VANITY
GLOAT : SELF-SATISFACTION
SIGH : RELIEF
HISS : DISAPPROVAL
APPLAUSE : APPROBATION
SNEER : CONTEMPT

WHAT SMART TEST-TAKERS KNOW

A SENTENCE CAN MAKE THE CONNECTION.

SCRIBBLE : WRITE ::
- **(A)** inform : supply
- **(B)** mutter : listen
- **(C)** nuzzle : feel
- **(D)** ramble : play
- **(E)** stagger : walk

Summarize each analogy relationship with a sentence. In this case, *scribbling* is a bad kind of *writing*. Use the same sentence to test connections between the words in the answer choices. When you find one that works, you've found your answer.

(A) *Informing* is a bad kind of *supplying*. (WRONG!)
(B) *Muttering* is a bad kind of *listening*. (WRONG!)
(C) *Nuzzling* is a bad kind of *feeling*. (WRONG!)
(D) *Rambling* is a bad kind of *playing*. (WRONG!)
(E) *Staggering* is a bad kind of *walking*. (CORRECT!)

IT PAYS TO KNOW THE MOST COMMON GRE ANALOGY CATEGORIES.

The vast majority of GRE analogies fall into one of several recognizable categories. Knowing what they are and looking for them as you tackle each problem will make your job much easier. Here are the most common GRE analogy categories:

① **"Part of the definition of" analogies**
GENEROSITY : PHILANTHROPIST
GENEROSITY is part of the definition of a PHILANTHROPIST.

② **"Lack of something is part of the definition" analogies**
POVERTY : FUNDS
Part of the definition of POVERTY is a lack of FUNDS.

③ **"This is a spurious form of that" analogies**
STUMBLE : WALK
STUMBLING is a spurious form of WALKING.

④ **"Degree" analogies**
BREEZE : GALE
A GALE is more powerful than a BREEZE.

⑤ **"Part to whole" analogies**
MOVEMENT : SONATA
A MOVEMENT is a part of a SONATA.

TIP

Know the most common analogy connections:
1. Part of the definition of
2. Lack of something is part of the definition
3. Spurious form
4. Degree
5. Part to whole
6. Type of
7. Sequence
8. Interruption
9. Tool of
10. A Place for
11. Sign of

6 **"Type of" analogies**

SWORD : WEAPON

A SWORD is a type of WEAPON.

7 **"Sequence" analogies**

FOREWORD : APPENDIX

In books, a FOREWORD precedes the APPENDIX.

8 **"Interruption" analogies**

LANDING : FLIGHT

LANDING marks an interruption of, or an ending to, a FLIGHT.

9 **"Tool" analogies**

PAINTBRUSH : ARTIST

A PAINTBRUSH is a tool used by an ARTIST.

10 **"A place for/where" analogies**

WITNESS : COURTROOM

A COURTROOM is the place for a WITNESS.

11 **"Sign of" analogies**

GRIMACE : PAIN

A GRIMACE is a sign of PAIN.

THE MORE PRECISE YOUR SENTENCE, THE BETTER.

You cannot expect to solve every GRE analogy by simply plugging in the list of common analogy types. Use the common categories as a starting point, but be prepared to refine the relationship by making your sentence more precise. Consider this example:

GRAIN : SILO ::
- **(A)** pilot : plane
- **(B)** judge : courtroom
- **(C)** water : reservoir
- **(D)** clock : time
- **(E)** automobile : highway

If you apply the "place where" idea without thinking, here is what happens.

A SILO is a place where you would find GRAIN.

- (A) A *plane* is a place where you would find a *pilot*.
- (B) A *courtroom* is a place where you would find a *judge*.
- (C) A *reservoir* is a place where you would find *water*.
- (D) A *clock* is a place where you would find *time*.
- (E) A *highway* is a place where you would find *automobiles*.

You can eliminate (D), but that still leaves you with four possible answers. Now is the time to go back and make your original sentence fit better. How can you express the relationship between silo and grain more precisely?

A *silo* is a place where *grain* is stored.

(A)   A *plane* is a place where a *pilot* is stored.

(B)   A *courtroom* is a place where a *judge* is stored.

(C)   A *reservoir* is a place where *water* is stored.

(E)   A *highway* is a place where *automobiles* are stored.

Now it's easy to see that the correct answer is (C).

ANALOGIES WORK ONLY IF THERE'S A CLEAR-CUT CONNECTION.

An analogy depends upon a necessary connection between pairs of words based on the meaning of the words. This clear-cut connection must exist for both the original capitalized word pair and the correct answer choice. That means you can eliminate any answer choice for which you cannot describe a necessary relationship between the words. For example, the pair "career : descriptive" could not possibly be a correct answer choice to a GRE analogy because the words do not exhibit a clear-cut connection. (Check this out by trying to make up a sentence that describes the connection between these words.)

You can use the "clear-cut connection" test to rule out answer choices even when you don't know one of the capitalized words.

XXXXXX : XXXXXXX ::
    (A)   note : scale
    (B)   ocean : merchandise
    (C)   expert : automobile
    (D)   victory : farmland
    (E)   teacher : classroom

You don't know what the capitalized words are in this analogy, but you can still eliminate choices (B), (C), and (D). There is no clear-cut connection between the words of those choices. (The actual analogy above is LETTER : ALPHABET :: note : scale.)

SOME ANALOGIES WORK BETTER WHEN YOU TURN THEM AROUND.

Sometimes the capitalized words fall easily into a sentence that expresses their relationship—and sometimes they don't. If you're having trouble making up a sentence that relates the two words, be prepared to shift gears. Try reversing the order of the original word pair. Let's see how this technique works on the following analogy.

ALERT!

Non-answers are traps. Two words that have no logical connection can never be the answer to an analogy question. Here are two examples of non-answers:
typewriter : ant
gruesome : pavement

ICE : GLACIER ::

    (A)   train : trestle

    (B)   sand : dune

    (C)   path : forest

    (D)   feather : bird

    (E)   ocean : ship

If you can't come up with a sentence relating ICE to GLACIER, try relating GLACIER to ICE:

A *glacier* is made up of *ice*.

Here's the only catch: If you reverse the order of the capitalized words, you must also reverse the order of the words in each answer choice. So when you apply your sentence to the answer choices, this is how you'll have to do it:

(A)   A *trestle* is made up of a *train*.

(B)   A *dune* is made up of *sand*.

(C)   A *forest* is made up of a *path*.

(D)   A *bird* is made up of a *feather*.

(E)   A *ship* is made up of an *ocean*.

Clearly (B) exhibits the same relationship as the original pair.

YOU CAN LEARN A LOT FROM THE ANSWER CHOICES.

Many words have different meanings depending upon whether they are used as nouns, verbs, or adjectives. If you are not sure how one of the capitalized words is being used, just check the answer choices. In GRE analogies, all the answer choices will have the same grammatical structure as the capitalized word pair. That means if the answer choices are noun : noun, the capitalized pair will be NOUN : NOUN. On the other hand, if the answer choices are adjective : noun, then the capitalized pair will be ADJECTIVE : NOUN.

EXERCISE 1

10 Questions • 8 Minutes

Directions: In each of the following questions, you are given a related pair of words or phrases in capital letters. Each capitalized pair is followed by five (5) pairs of words or phrases. Choose the pair that best expresses a relationship similar to that expressed by the original pair.

1. HEAR : INAUDIBLE ::
   - (A) touch : intangible
   - (B) mumble : praiseworthy
   - (C) spend : wealthy
   - (D) prepare : ready
   - (E) enjoy : illegal

2. GARGOYLE : GROTESQUE ::
   - (A) magician : elegant
   - (B) boulevard : serene
   - (C) government : amicable
   - (D) miser : affectionate
   - (E) philanthropist : benevolent

3. EXTINGUISHED : RELIT ::
   - (A) completed : discouraged
   - (B) announced : publicized
   - (C) collapsed : rebuilt
   - (D) evicted : purchased
   - (E) imagined : denied

4. VACUUM : AIR ::
   - (A) invitation : host
   - (B) vacancy : occupant
   - (C) love : passion
   - (D) literacy : writing
   - (E) bait : trap

5. BLAME : SCAPEGOAT ::
   - (A) explain : answer
   - (B) convict : punishment
   - (C) lionize : hero
   - (D) appreciate : art
   - (E) relate : secret

6. LIBEL : DEFAMATORY ::
   - (A) praise : laudatory
   - (B) option : selective
   - (C) value : sparse
   - (D) insult : apologetic
   - (E) struggle : victorious

7. ANNEX : BUILDING ::
   - (A) bedroom : apartment
   - (B) fountain : park
   - (C) epilogue : novel
   - (D) dining car : train
   - (E) memory : computer

8. BOOK : TOME ::
   - (A) page : binding
   - (B) plot : character
   - (C) omission : diligence
   - (D) library : borrower
   - (E) story : saga

9. GREGARIOUSNESS : SOCIABILITY ::
   - (A) courageousness : fearfulness
   - (B) reliability : esteem
   - (C) forgetfulness : memorability
   - (D) affability : friendliness
   - (E) gullibility : believability

10. HARBINGER : BEGINNING ::
    - (A) ordain : decree
    - (B) herald : advent
    - (C) amend : correction
    - (D) emancipate : freedom
    - (E) commiserate : news

EXERCISE 2

5 Questions • 4 Minutes

Directions: In each of the following questions, you are given a related pair of words or phrases in capital letters. Each capitalized pair is followed by five (5) pairs of words or phrases. Choose the pair that best expresses a relationship similar to that expressed by the original pair.

1. FOREST : TREES ::
   (A) fleet : ships
   (B) lumber : wood
   (C) rose : thorns
   (D) shelf : books
   (E) camera : film

2. RAMPART : FORTRESS ::
   (A) bicycle : wheel
   (B) river : lake
   (C) cage : animal
   (D) ladder : roof
   (E) fence : house

3. SCYTHE : REAPING ::
   (A) screws : turning
   (B) crops : planting
   (C) lights : reading
   (D) shears : cutting
   (E) saws : gluing

4. MOISTEN : DRENCH ::
   (A) pump : replenish
   (B) chill : freeze
   (C) deny : pretend
   (D) dance : rejoice
   (E) announce : suppress

5. MAVERICK : STRAY ::
   (A) hermit : recluse
   (B) expert : ignorance
   (C) trickster : payment
   (D) miser : money
   (E) rumor : truth

ANSWER KEY AND EXPLANATIONS

Exercise 1

| 1. | A | 3. | C | 5. | C | 7. | C | 9. | D |
| 2. | E | 4. | B | 6. | A | 8. | E | 10. | B |

1. **The correct answer is (A).** The defining characteristic of something that is INAUDIBLE is that it cannot be HEARD, and the defining characteristic of something that is *intangible* is that it cannot be *touched*. Additionally, you can eliminate (B), (C), and (E) as non-answers.

2. **The correct answer is (E).** Being GROTESQUE is a defining characteristic of a GARGOYLE, and being *benevolent* is a defining characteristic of a *philanthropist*.

3. **The correct answer is (C).** RELIGHTING follows EXTINGUISHING, and *rebuilding* follows *collapse*. This is an analogy based on sequence. You can eliminate (A), (D), and (E) as non-answers. (B) is a possible analogy, but it does not fit the sequence pattern.

4. **The correct answer is (B).** Lack of AIR is a defining characteristic of a VACUUM, and lack of an *occupant* is a defining characteristic of a *vacancy*. The other choices are possible analogies, but they do not fit the "lack of" pattern.

5. **The correct answer is (C).** BLAME is a defining characteristic of a SCAPEGOAT, and *lionize* is a defining characteristic of a *hero*. You can eliminate (A), (D), and (E) as non-answers. Further, (B) does not fit the "defining characteristic" pattern.

6. **The correct answer is (A).** DEFAMATORY is a defining characteristic of what it is to LIBEL, and *laudatory* is a defining characteristic of what it is to *praise*. The remaining choices are so weak that they are non-answers.

7. **The correct answer is (C).** This analogy does not fit any of our standard patterns.

An ANNEX is not really a part of a BUILDING, but something added to an already existing building. Similarly, an *epilogue* is a section or comment added to a play or a *novel*. Perhaps it best fits as a sequence. An ANNEX comes after the original BUILDING, and an *epilogue* comes after the original *novel*. You can eliminate (A), for a *bedroom* is part of, not added to, an *apartment*. And for the same reason you can eliminate (D) and (E). Finally, (B) qualifies as a non-answer. A *fountain* is not necessarily found in a *park*, and a *park* does not necessarily contain a *fountain*.

8. **The correct answer is (E).** A TOME is a large BOOK, and a *saga* is a lengthy *story*. The analogy is one of degree, but to see this you have to be attentive to the precise meaning of TOME. This is what makes the analogy difficult. A TOME is not merely a BOOK; it is a large BOOK. (C) can be eliminated as a non-answer, and the others must be incorrect since they do not fit the pattern for degree.

9. **The correct answer is (D).** SOCIABILITY is a defining characteristic of GREGARIOUSNESS, and *friendliness* is a defining characteristic of *affability*.

10. **The correct answer is (B).** To HARBINGER is to announce the BEGINNING of something, and to *herald* is to announce the *advent* of something. This is a difficult analogy because of the HARBINGER, and it is made more difficult because HARBINGER is used as a verb. (It is usually used as a noun: "The robin is a harbinger of spring.") But even if you do not know the meaning of the key word in this analogy, you should be able to eliminate (E) as a non-answer.

Exercise 2

| 1. | A | 2. | E | 3. | D | 4. | B | 5. | A |

1. **The correct answer is (A).** A TREE is a part of the FOREST, and a *ship* is part of the *fleet*. Once we change the word order, the fairly common "is part of" pattern becomes evident. You might, however, need to refine your sentence to eliminate some of the other choices. You might try: a FOREST is a group of TREES, and a *fleet* is a group of *ships*.

2. **The correct answer is (E).** This is a fairly odd analogy. It doesn't fit any of the patterns. It is based on a physical similarity. A RAMPART is an embankment encircling a FORTRESS, and a *fence* encircles a *house*. Occasionally, the GRE will have analogies based on physical similarities, e.g., FRAME : PICTURE :: envelope : letter. (The FRAME surrounds the PICTURE, and the *envelope* surrounds the *letter*.) You could have eliminated both (B) and (D) as non-answers.

3. **The correct answer is (D).** SCYTHE is a tool for REAPING, and *shears* are a tool for *cutting*. Choices (A), (C), and (E) are non-answers, and (B) does not fit the tool pattern.

4. **The correct answer is (B).** To DRENCH is to do more than just MOISTEN, and to *freeze* is to do more than just *chill*. This analogy is based upon a relationship of degree. You can eliminate (A), (C), and (D) as non-answers; and (E), though a possible analogy, does not fit the pattern we are looking for.

5. **The correct answer is (A).** A defining characteristic of a MAVERICK is that he is a STRAY, and a defining characteristic of a *hermit* is that he is a *recluse*. You can easily eliminate (C) as a non-answer. And (B) and (E) fail because they are based upon the "is a lack of" pattern. What about (D)? It is the love of *money*, or greed, that is the defining characteristic of a *miser*. Had (D) read *miser : greed*, it would have been better. Since we can improve (D), we know it is not the best choice as it originally stands.

SUMMING IT UP

- Follow these steps when solving analogy questions:
    1. Determine how the capitalized words are related.
    2. Create a sentence that expresses that connection.
    3. Test the choices with your sentence and eliminate the ones that don't work.
    4. If you're left with more than one answer—or no answer at all—go back and refine your sentence.
    5. Choose the best answer. If none of the choices fits exactly, choose the one that works best.
- The most common GRE analogy types are:
    1. Part of the definition of
    2. Lack of something is part of the definition
    3. This is a spurious form of that
    4. Degree
    5. Part to whole
    6. Type of
    7. Sequence
    8. Interruption
    9. Tool of
    10. A place for
    11. Sign of

Reading Comprehension

OVERVIEW

- **What is reading comprehension?**
- **How do you answer reading comprehension questions?**
- **What smart test-takers know**
- **Summing it up**

WHAT IS READING COMPREHENSION?

GRE reading comprehension is a test of your ability to read and understand unfamiliar materials and to answer questions about them. You will be presented with passages of varying lengths drawn from a variety of subject areas, including both the humanities and the sciences. The questions will ask you to analyze what is stated in the passage and to identify underlying assumptions and implications.

Question Format

Reading comprehension questions follow the standard multiple-choice format with five answer choices each. All of the questions fall into one of the following six categories:

1. The main idea of the passage
2. Specific details mentioned in the passage
3. The author's attitude or tone
4. The logical structure of the passage
5. Further inferences that might be drawn from the text
6. Application of the ideas in the text to new situations

Here are the directions for GRE reading comprehension, along with some sample questions and explanations.

chapter 6

Anatomy of a Reading Comprehension Passage

Directions: The passage below is followed by questions based upon its content. Choose the best answer to each question.

Instead of casting aside traditional values, the Meiji Restoration of 1868 dismantled feudalism and modernized the country while preserving certain traditions as the foundations for a modern Japan. The oldest tradition and basis of the entire
(5) Japanese value system was respect for and even worship of the Emperor. During the early centuries of Japanese history, the Shinto cult in which the imperial family traced its ancestry to the Sun Goddess became the people's sustaining faith. Although later subordinated to imported Buddhism and Confu-
(10) cianism, Shintoism was perpetuated in Ise and Izumo until the Meiji modernizers established it as a quasi-state religion.

Another enduring tradition was the hierarchical system of social relations based on feudalism and reinforced by Neo-Confucianism, which had been the official ideology of the pre-
(15) modern world. Confucianism prescribed a pattern of ethical conduct between groups of people within a fixed hierarchy. Four of the five Confucian relationships were vertical, requiring loyalty and obedience from the inferior toward the superior. Only the relationship between friend and friend was horizontal,
(20) and even there the emphasis was on reciprocal duties.

The author is primarily concerned with

  (A) providing a history of the rise of feudalism in Japan

  (B) identifying the influences of Confucianism on Japanese society

  (C) speculating on the probable development of Japanese society

  (D) developing a history of religion in Japan

  (E) describing some important features of the Meiji Restoration

The directions are deceptively simple: Read the selection; answer the questions. There's a lot more to Reading Comprehension than just "read and answer." Since the directions are not helpful, be sure to dismiss them as quickly as possible when they appear.

Typically, reading passages discuss an unfamiliar topic—such as the Meiji Restoration. The first sentence here summarizes the main point of this selection. This is fairly common. Also typical is a lot of supporting detail, only some of which will be the basis for a question.

Most passages discuss competing theories or different factors that contribute to the events being discussed. Here you have more detail. While it's relevant to the author's argument, it may not be important in so far as your answering of the questions is concerned.

The part of the question leading to the choices is called the "stem." The question stem here asks about the central theme of the selection.

The correct answer is (E). The right answer to a "main idea" question has to describe the overall development of the selection.

> The passage mentions all of the following as being elements of Japanese society EXCEPT
> **(A)** obedience to authority
> **(B)** sense of duty
> **(C)** respect for the Emperor
> **(D)** concern for education
> **(E)** loyalty to one's superior

This question stem asks about details that are explicitly stated in the passage. The "EXCEPT" indicates that four of the five choices are mentioned in the selection. The one that is NOT mentioned is the right choice.

The correct answer is (D). Concern for education is not mentioned.

> It can be inferred from the passage that those who led Japan into the modern age were concerned primarily with
> **(A)** maintaining a stable society
> **(B)** building a new industrial base
> **(C)** expanding the nation's territory
> **(D)** gaining new adherents of Confucianism
> **(E)** creating a new middle class

This question stem asks about an idea that is not explicitly stated in the selection but can be inferred from what is stated. Inference questions are usually of above-average difficulty.

The correct answer is (A). Preserving the old traditions was a primary concern of the architects of the Meiji Restoration.

HOW DO YOU ANSWER READING COMPREHENSION QUESTIONS?

To answer reading comprehension questions, follow these three steps:

Reading Comprehension: Getting It Right

❶ Preview key sentences.

❷ Read for structure; ignore details.

❸ Do a mental wrap-up.

Now let's look at this process in more detail.

❶ **Preview key sentences.** The first sentence of a paragraph is often the topic sentence. It will give you an overview of the paragraph. Previewing the first sentence of each paragraph will give you a general sense of the logical structure of the passage. You should also preview the very last sentence of the passage because it often contains the main conclusion of the passage. On the computer-based test, you can view key sentences by scrolling through the passage.

❷ **Read for structure; ignore details.** This is an open-book test, so you do not have to memorize anything. Additionally, most of the questions ask about the *structure* of the passage rather than specific facts. As you read, consciously ask yourself "What is the main point of the passage?" and "Why is the author introducing this idea?"

Your academic training has taught you to read for details because you know that you will be tested on them. However, do *not* dwell on the particulars during the test. In the first place, there are not likely to be many questions about details. And in the second place, this is an open-book test, so you can refer to the passage.

❸ **Do a mental wrap-up.** Before moving on to the questions, pause for just a few seconds and review in your mind what you have just read. Try to summarize in your own words the main point of the selection (think up a title for the passage) and to see in your mind's eye an outline of the passage.

Now let's look at a sample reading comprehension passage and questions about it. As you read the explanations, think about how the solution process applies.

Directions: The passage below is followed by questions based on its content. Choose the best answer to each question.

A fundamental principle of pharmacology is that all drugs have multiple actions. Actions that are desirable in the treatment of disease are considered therapeutic, while those that are undesirable or pose risks to the patient are called "effects." Adverse
(5) drug effects range from the trivial, e.g., nausea or dry mouth, to the serious, e.g., massive gastrointestinal bleeding or thromboembolism; and some drugs can be lethal. Therefore, an effective system for the detection of adverse drug effects is an important component of the health care system of any advanced
(10) nation. Much of the research conducted on new drugs aims at

identifying the conditions of use that maximize beneficial effects and minimize the risk of adverse effects. The intent of drug
labeling is to reflect this body of knowledge accurately so that
physicians can properly prescribe the drug; or, if it is to be sold
(15) without prescription, so that consumers can properly use the
drug.

The current system of drug investigation in the United
States has proved very useful and accurate in identifying the
common side effects associated with new prescription drugs. By
(20) the time a new drug is approved by the Food and Drug Administration, its side effects are usually well described in the
package insert for physicians. The investigational process,
however, cannot be counted on to detect all adverse effects
because of the relatively small number of patients involved in
(25) premarketing studies and the relatively short duration of the
studies. Animal toxicology studies are, of course, done prior to
marketing in an attempt to identify any potential for toxicity,
but negative results do not guarantee the safety of a drug in
humans, as evidenced by such well known examples as the birth
(30) deformities due to thalidomide.

This recognition prompted the establishment in many countries of programs to which physicians report adverse drug
effects. The United States and other countries also send reports
to an international program operated by the World Health
(35) Organization. These programs, however, are voluntary reporting programs and are intended to serve a limited goal: alerting
a government or private agency to adverse drug effects detected
by physicians in the course of practice. Other approaches must
be used to confirm suspected drug reactions and to estimate
(40) incidence rates. These other approaches include conducting
retrospective control studies; for example, the studies associat-
ing endometrial cancer with estrogen use, and systematic
monitoring of hospitalized patients to determine the incidence
of acute common side effects, as typified by the Boston Collabo-
(45) rative Drug Surveillance Program.

Thus, the overall drug surveillance system of the United
States is composed of a set of information bases, special studies,
and monitoring programs, each contributing in its own way to
our knowledge about marketed drugs. The system is decentral-
(50) ized among a number of governmental units and is not administered as a coordinated function. Still, it would be inappropriate
at this time to attempt to unite all of the disparate elements into
a comprehensive surveillance program. Instead, the challenge
is to improve each segment of the system and to take advantage
(55) of new computer strategies to improve coordination and communication.

*In the first paragraph, the author announces a "fundamental principle" of pharma-
cology. The paragraph then goes on to contrast "desirable" and "adverse" drug
effects. The author emphasizes the need for an effective system of making this
information available to doctors.*

In the second paragraph, the author says that the current system of drug investigation is useful and accurate. But then the author goes on to identify some weaknesses in the system.

In the third paragraph, the author claims that the system has been improved by establishing programs that keep records of reports by doctors of adverse drug consequences. But, the author notes, these reporting programs are not perfect.

In the final paragraph, the author summarizes by saying that the system is a composite one with many different aspects. And the last sentence summarizes the conclusion of the passage.

The author is primarily concerned with discussing

(A) methods for testing the effects of new drugs on humans

(B) the importance of having accurate information about the effects of drugs

(C) procedures for determining the long-term effects of new drugs

(D) attempts to curb the abuse of prescription drugs

(E) the difference between the therapeutic and nontherapeutic actions of drugs

The correct answer is (B). This is a main idea question. (B) correctly describes the overall point of the passage. The author starts by stating that all drugs have both good and bad effects, and that correct use of a drug requires balancing the effects. For such a balancing to take place, it is essential to have good information about how the drugs work. Some of this can be obtained prior to approval of the drug, but some information will not become available until the drug has been in use for years.

(A) is incorrect, for the different methods for testing drugs are mentioned only as a part of the development just described. The author is not concerned with talking about how drugs are tested but about why it is important that they be tested. (C) is incorrect for the same reason. As for (E), this is the starting point for the discussion—not the main point of the discussion. Finally, the idea of drug abuse, (D), is not part of the passage at all.

The author implies that a drug with adverse side effects

(A) will not be approved for use by consumers without a doctor's prescription

(B) must wait for approval until lengthy studies prove the effects are not permanent

(C) should be used only if its therapeutic value outweighs its adverse effects

(D) should be withdrawn from the marketplace pending a government investigation

(E) could be used in foreign countries even though it is not approved for use in the United States

TIP

The main idea of the passage is critical. Every GRE reading comprehension passage is organized around a main idea. All else is supporting argument and detail. If you can say in your own words what that idea is, you are halfway home to answering most of the questions.

TIP

Most details are irrelevant. With all the different types of questions that are asked, there can't be many devoted solely to details. Therefore, most of the details are not important.

The correct answer is (C). This is an inference question, so the correct answer is (C). In the first paragraph, the author states that all drugs have effects and that these effects range from the unimportant to the very important. One purpose of drug labeling is to ensure that physicians (and ultimately consumers) are aware of these effects. We can infer, therefore, that drugs with side effects are used—provided the gain is worth the risks. And this is what (C) says.

(A) seems to be contradicted by the passage. One purpose of labeling, according to the author, is to let consumers of nonprescription drugs know of possible side effects of those drugs. As for (B) and (D), the analysis in the preceding paragraph clearly shows that drugs are approved for use and are used even though they have unwanted side effects. Finally, there is nothing in the passage to support the conclusion expressed in (E).

Which of the following can be inferred from the passage?
- **(A)** Drugs with serious side effects are never approved for distribution.
- **(B)** A centralized drug oversight function would improve public health.
- **(C)** Most physicians are not aware that prescription drugs have side effects.
- **(D)** Some rare adverse drug effects are not discovered during the limited testing.
- **(E)** Consumers are seldom unable to understand directions for proper use of a drug.

The correct answer is (D). This is an inference question, and the correct answer is (D). Although this conclusion is not stated in so many words, the author does say that some effects are not uncovered because of the short duration of the studies. We may therefore infer that some effects do not manifest themselves for a long period.

The author introduces the example of thalidomide (lines 28–29) to show that some
- **(A)** drugs do not have the same actions in humans that they do in animals
- **(B)** drug testing procedures are ignored by careless laboratory workers
- **(C)** drugs have no therapeutic value for humans
- **(D)** drugs have adverse side effects as well as beneficial actions
- **(E)** drugs are prescribed by physicians who have not read the manufacturer's recommendations

The correct answer is (A). This is a logical structure question, and the correct answer is (A). The example is introduced in lines 28–29 where the author is discussing animal studies. The author says that the fact that a drug shows no dangerous effects in animals does not necessarily mean that it will not adversely affect humans and then gives the example. Thus, the example proves that a drug does not necessarily work in humans the same way it does in animals.

The author of the passage regards current drug investigation procedures as

(A) important but generally ineffectual

(B) lackadaisical and generally in need of improvement

(C) necessary and generally effective

(D) comprehensive but generally unnecessary

(E) superfluous but generally harmless

The correct answer is (C). This is an author's attitude question, and the correct answer is (C). We have already determined that the author regards drug investigation procedures as necessary, so we can eliminate (D) and (E). And at various points in the passage the author speaks of the current mechanism for gathering information as effective. For example, the author states that unwanted side effects are usually described in detail in the pamphlets distributed to physicians and also mentions that there is an entire discipline devoted to this area, so you can eliminate (A) and (B).

It can be inferred that the estrogen study mentioned in lines 40–42

(A) uncovered long-term side effects of a drug that had already been approved for sale by the Food and Drug Administration

(B) discovered potential side effects of a drug that was still awaiting approval for sale by the Food and Drug Administration

(C) revealed possible new applications of a drug that had previously been approved for a different treatment

(D) is an example of a study that could be more efficiently conducted by a centralized authority than by volunteer reporting

(E) proved that the use of the drug estrogen was not associated with side effects such as thromboembolism

The correct answer is (A). This is an inference question, and the correct answer is (A). The key to this question is the word *retrospective*. This tells you that the control study mentioned was done after the drug was already in use. (B) is incorrect because although the study uncovered harmful side effects, according to the passage, the drug was already in use. (C) is incorrect because the paragraph in which this study is mentioned deals with methods of reporting adverse drug effects, not new applications for drugs. (D) is incorrect first because the author does not mention the efficiency of the study and because the author is not in favor of a centralized authority. In fact, in the last paragraph the author says that it would be inappropriate at this time to attempt to unite all of the disparate elements into a comprehensive surveillance program. Finally, (E) is incorrect because although thromboembolism is mentioned in the passage as one of the possible harmful side

ALERT!

"So what" answers are traps. Test writers love to include something actually mentioned in the passage as a wrong answer. People look at the answer and think "Yes, that is in the passage, so it must be right." But it can be in the passage and still not be an answer to the question asked.

effects of drugs, it is not mentioned in connection with estrogen. The use of estrogen is mentioned in connection with endometrial cancer.

The author is most probably leading up to a discussion of some suggestions about how to

(A) centralize authority for drug surveillance in the United States

(B) centralize authority for drug surveillance among international agencies

(C) better coordinate the sharing of information among the drug surveillance agencies

(D) eliminate the availability and sale of certain drugs now on the market

(E) improve drug testing procedures to detect dangerous effects before drugs are approved

The correct answer is (C). This is an application question, and the correct answer is (C). In the last paragraph, the author suggests that uniting disparate elements into a comprehensive surveillance program is inappropriate at this time. This eliminates choices (A) and (B). The author suggests, however, that improvements are possible in each segment of the system and urges reliance on computers to improve coordination and communication, so (C) is the correct answer. (D) is wrong because although the author might advocate the elimination of the availability of certain drugs, that is not what the passage is leading up to. As for (E), although the author acknowledges that preapproval studies are not infallible, this notion is too narrow in scope to be the next logical topic for discussion.

The author relies on which of the following in developing the passage?

(A) Statistics

(B) Analogy

(C) Examples

(D) Authority

(E) Rhetorical questions

The correct answer is (C). This is a logical structure question, and the correct answer is (C). The author frequently illustrates the argument's points by using examples. In the first paragraph, there are examples of side effects. In the second paragraph, there is an example of side effects not detected by animal studies, and in the third, the Boston Collaborative Drug Surveillance Program is an example. The author does not, however, use statistics (no numbers in this passage), does not use an analogy (no "this is like that"), does not mention an authority (citing an example is not the same as appealing to an authority), and doesn't use rhetorical questions.

WHAT SMART TEST-TAKERS KNOW

READING COMPREHENSION QUESTIONS CALL FOR DIFFERENT LEVELS OF UNDERSTANDING.

According to the test-writers, good reading involves three levels of understanding and evaluation. First, you must be able to grasp the overall idea or main point of the selection along with its general organization. Second, you must be able to subject the specific details to greater scrutiny and explain what something means and why it was introduced. Finally, you should be able to evaluate what the author has written, determining what further conclusions might be drawn and judging whether the argument is good or bad. This sequence dictates the strategy you should follow in reading the selection.

DETAILS CAN BOG YOU DOWN.

If a part of a passage gets too detailed, just skip it. Bracket it mentally. You do not need to have a full understanding of every single detail to appreciate the organization of the passage and to answer some, perhaps even all, of the questions.

THE GRE USES SIX—AND ONLY SIX—TYPES OF READING COMPREHENSION QUESTIONS.

Identify the type of question asked, and you are halfway home to finding the correct answer.

1 Main idea questions ask about the central theme or main point of the passage.

2 Specific detail questions ask about details included by the author to support or to develop the main theme.

3 Inference questions ask about ideas that are not explicitly stated in the selection but are strongly implied.

4 Logical structure questions ask about the organization or the overall development of the passage.

5 Application questions ask you to take what you have learned from the passage and apply it to a new situation.

6 Attitude or tone questions ask you to identify the overall tone of the passage or the author's attitude toward something discussed in the passage.

For each of the six question types, there are special clues in the answer choices that help you tell right ones from wrong ones.

ALERT!

"Categorical" answers are traps. Common sense says that categorical statements that use "all," "always," and "never" are more likely to be proved wrong than statements that use "some," "sometimes," and "seldom." The test-writers know this and use categorical statements as wrong answers.

IN MAIN IDEA QUESTIONS, THE "GOLDILOCKS PRINCIPLE" APPLIES.

On a main idea question, choose an answer that refers to all of the important elements of the passage without going beyond the scope of the passage. The correct answer to a main idea question will summarize the main point of the passage. The wrong answers are too broad or too narrow. Some will be too broad and attribute too much to the passage. Others will be too narrow and focus on one small element of the selection, thereby ignoring the overall point.

IN SOME MAIN IDEA QUESTIONS, THE ANSWER LIES IN THE FIRST WORD OF EACH CHOICE.

Some main idea questions are phrased as sentence completions. With a main idea question in sentence completion form, the first word of each choice may be all you need to pick the answer. Here's an example:

> The author's primary purpose is to
> - **(A)** argue for . . .
> - **(B)** criticize . . .
> - **(C)** describe . . .
> - **(D)** persuade . . .
> - **(E)** denounce . . .

The correct answer is (C). Note that the first word in each choice describes the passage differently. If the selection were neutral in tone, providing nothing more than a description of some phenomenon, you could safely eliminate (A), (B), (D), and (E).

IN SPECIFIC DETAIL QUESTIONS, LOCATOR WORDS POINT THE WAY.

A detail question basically asks "What did the author say?" So, the correct answer to a detail question will be found right there in the passage. And there will be a word or phrase in the question stem to direct you to the appropriate part of the passage. Just find the relevant information and answer the question.

IN SPECIFIC DETAIL QUESTIONS, "SO WHAT" ANSWERS ARE WRONG.

Often wrong answer choices look like right ones because they refer to specific points in the passage. The point is right there in the passage, but it is not an answer to the question asked. So your reaction to such answer choices should be "Yes, this is mentioned, but so what?"

ALERT!

Your academic training is hazardous to your test-taking health. In college, you are rewarded for memorizing details. The GRE penalizes for this. This is an open-book test. Do not waste time trying to understand insignificant points.

IN SPECIFIC DETAIL QUESTIONS, "WAY OUT" ANSWERS ARE WRONG.

Wrong answers can also refer to things never mentioned in the selection. On a detail question, eliminate answer choices referring to something not mentioned in the passage or anything going beyond the scope of the passage. One way the test-writers have of preparing wrong answers is to mention things related to the general topic of the selection but not specifically discussed there. An answer to an explicit question will appear in the selection.

IN SPECIFIC DETAIL QUESTIONS, THOUGHT-REVERSERS TURN A QUESTION INSIDE-OUT.

Sometimes the test-writer will use a thought-reverser. For example:

The author mentions all of the following EXCEPT

Sometimes a detail question uses a thought-reverser. In that case, it is asking for what is not mentioned in the selection. Out of the five choices, four will actually appear in the selection. The fifth, and wrong, choice will not.

INFERENCE QUESTIONS CALL FOR A FURTHER CONCLUSION.

An inference question should not require a long chain of deductive reasoning. It is usually a one-step inference. For example, the selection might make a statement to the effect that "X only occurs in the presence of Y." The question might ask, "In the absence of Y, what result should be expected?" The correct answer would be: "X does not occur."

LOGICAL STRUCTURE QUESTIONS ARE ALL ABOUT ORGANIZATION.

Some logical structure questions ask about the overall structure of the passage. The correct answer to this kind of question should describe in general terms the overall development of the selection.

Another kind of logical structure question asks about the logical function of specific details. For this kind of question, find the appropriate reference and determine why the author introduced the detail at just that point.

APPLICATION QUESTIONS ARE THE TOUGHEST, AND YOU MAY HAVE TO JUST GUESS.

Application questions are the most abstract and therefore the most difficult kind of question. There is no "silver bullet" for this type of question, and you may find that it is better to make a guess and just move on.

FOR ATTITUDE/TONE QUESTIONS, THE ANSWER CHOICES RUN A GAMUT.

Attitude or tone questions often have answer choices that run a gamut of judgments or emotions, from negative to positive. On this kind of question, try to create a continuum of the answer choices and locate the author's attitude or tone on that continuum. Here's an example:

The tone of the passage is best described as one of
- **(A)** outrage
- **(B)** approval
- **(C)** objectivity
- **(D)** alarm
- **(E)** enthusiasm

Arrange these attitudes in a line, from the most negative to the most positive:

(–) . . outrage . . alarm . . objectivity . . approval . . enthusiasm . . (+)

EXERCISE 1

14 Questions • 20 Minutes

Directions: The passages below are followed by questions based on their content. Choose the best answer to each question.

The mental health movement in the United States began with a period of considerable enlightenment. Dorothea Dix was shocked to find the mentally ill
(5) in jails and almshouses and crusaded for the establishment of asylums in which people could receive humane care in hospital-like environments and treatment which might help restore them to
(10) sanity. By the mid 1800s, 20 states had established asylums, but during the late 1800s and early 1900s, in the face of economic depression, legislatures were unable to appropriate sufficient funds
(15) for decent care. Asylums became overcrowded and prison-like. Additionally, patients were more resistant to treatment than the pioneers in the mental health field had anticipated, and secu-
(20) rity and restraints were needed to protect patients and others. Mental institutions became frightening and depressing places in which the rights of patients were all but forgotten.
(25)   These conditions continued until after World War II. At that time, new treatments were discovered for some major mental illnesses theretofore considered untreatable (penicillin for syphilis of the
(30) brain and insulin treatment for schizophrenia and depressions), and a succession of books, motion pictures, and newspaper exposés called attention to the plight of the mentally ill. Improve-
(35) ments were made, and Dr. David Vail's Humane Practices Program became a beacon for today. But changes were slow in coming until the early 1960s. At that time, the Civil Rights movement led
(40) lawyers to investigate America's prisons, which were disproportionately populated by blacks, and they in turn followed prisoners into the only institutions that

were worse than the prisons—the hospi-
(45) tals for the criminally insane. The prisons were filled with angry young men who, encouraged by legal support, were quick to demand their rights. The hospitals for the criminally insane, by con-
(50) trast, were populated with people who were considered "crazy" and who were often kept obediently in their place through the use of severe bodily restraints and large doses of major tran-
(55) quilizers. The young cadre of public interest lawyers liked their role in the mental hospitals. The lawyers found a population that was both passive and easy to champion. These were, after all,
(60) people who, unlike criminals, had done nothing wrong. And in many states, they were being kept in horrendous institutions, an injustice, which once exposed, was bound to shock the public and, par-
(65) ticularly, the judicial conscience. Patients' rights groups successfully encouraged reform by lobbying in state legislatures.
    Judicial interventions have had some
(70) definite positive effects, but there is growing awareness that courts cannot provide the standards and the review mechanisms that assure good patient care. The details of providing day-to-day
(75) care simply cannot be mandated by a court, so it is time to take from the courts the responsibility for delivery of mental health care and assurance of patient rights and return it to the state mental
(80) health administrators to whom the mandate was originally given. Though it is a difficult task, administrators must make rules and standards to provide the training and surveillance that will assure
(85) that treatment is given and patient rights are respected.

1. The main purpose of the passage is to
    (A) discuss the influence of Dorothea Dix on the mental health movement
    (B) provide a historical perspective on problems of mental health care
    (C) increase public awareness of the plight of the mentally ill
    (D) shock the reader with vivid descriptions of asylums
    (E) describe the invention of new treatments for mental illness

2. According to the passage, all of the following contributed to the deterioration of the asylum system EXCEPT a(n)
    (A) scarcity of public funds to maintain the asylums
    (B) influx of more patients than the system was designed to handle
    (C) lack of effective treatments for many mental illnesses
    (D) need to employ restraints to maintain order and ensure safety
    (E) waning interest in patient rights on the part of lawyers

3. It can be inferred from the passage that which of the following factors contributed to post-war reform of state mental institutions?
    (A) Increased funding provided by state legislatures to rehabilitate asylums
    (B) Availability of drugs to sedate and otherwise render passive mental patients
    (C) Discovery of effective treatments for illnesses previously considered untreatable
    (D) Realization that some criminal behavior is attributable to mental illness
    (E) Advances in penology that de-emphasized the value of incarceration

4. The author's attitude toward people who are patients in state institutions can best be described as
    (A) inflexible and insensitive
    (B) detached and neutral
    (C) understanding and sympathetic
    (D) enthusiastic and supportive
    (E) uncaring and unemotional

5. The passage provides information that would help answer all of the following questions EXCEPT
    (A) Who are some people who have had an important influence on the public health movement in the United States?
    (B) What were some of the mental illnesses that were considered untreatable until the 1950s?
    (C) What were some of the new treatments for mental illness that were adopted in the 1950s?
    (D) What were some of the most important legal cases that contributed to the new concern for patients' rights?
    (E) What effect did the Civil Rights movement have on the rights of prisoners?

exercises

6. It can be inferred from the passage that, had the Civil Rights movement not prompted an investigation of prison conditions,

   (A) states would never have established asylums for the mentally ill

   (B) new treatments for major mental illness would have likely remained untested

   (C) the Civil Rights movement in America would have been politically ineffective

   (D) conditions in mental hospitals might have escaped judicial scrutiny

   (E) many mentally ill prisoners would have been transferred from hospitals back to prisons

7. The tone of the final paragraph can best be described as

   (A) stridently contentious

   (B) overly emotional

   (C) cleverly deceptive

   (D) cautiously optimistic

   (E) fiercely independent

The beginning of what was to become the United States was characterized by inconsistencies in the values and behavior of its population, inconsistencies that (5) were reflected by its spokesmen, who took conflicting stances in many areas; but on the subject of race, the conflicts were particularly vivid. The idea that the Caucasian race and European civili- (10) zation were superior was well entrenched in the culture of the colonists at the very time that the "egalitarian" republic was founded. Voluminous historical evidence indicates that, in the mind of the aver- (15) age colonist, the African was a heathen, he was black, and he was different in crucial philosophical ways. As time progressed, he was also increasingly captive, adding to the conception of deviance. (20) The African, therefore, could be justifiably (and even philanthropically) treated as property according to the reasoning of slavetraders and slaveholders.

Although slaves were treated as ob- (25) jects, bountiful evidence suggests that they did not view themselves similarly. There are many published autobiographies of slaves; African-American scholars are beginning to know enough about (30) West African culture to appreciate the existential climate in which the early captives were raised and which therefore could not be totally destroyed by the enslavement experience. This was a cli- (35) mate that defined individuality in collective terms. Individuals were members of a tribe, within which they had prescribed roles determined by the history of their family within the tribe. Indi- (40) viduals were inherently a part of the natural elements on which they depended, and they were actively related to those tribal members who once lived and to those not yet born.

(45) The colonial plantation system which was established and into which Africans were thrust did virtually eliminate tribal affiliations. Individuals were separated from kin; interrelationships among kin (50) kept together were often transient because of sales. A new identification with those slaves working and living together in a given place could satisfy what was undoubtedly a natural tendency to be a (55) member of a group. New family units became the most important attachments of individual slaves. Thus, as the system of slavery was gradually institutionalized, West African affiliation tendencies (60) adapted to it.

This exceedingly complex dual influence is still reflected in black community life, and the double consciousness of black Americans is the major characteristic of (65) African-American mentality. DuBois articulated this divided consciousness as follows:

"The history of the American Negro is the history of this strife—this longing to (70) attain self-conscious manhood, to merge his double self into a better and truer self. In this merging, he wishes neither of the older selves to be best."

Several black political movements have (75) looked upon this duality as destructively conflictual and have variously urged its reconciliation. Thus, the integrationists and the black nationalists, to be crudely general, have both been concerned with (80) resolving the conflict, but in opposite directions.

8. Which of the following would be the most appropriate title for the passage?

    (A) "The History of Black People in the United States"

    (B) "West African Tribal Relations"

    (C) "The Origin of Modern African-American Consciousness"

    (D) "Slavery: A Democratic Anomaly"

    (E) "The Legacy of Slavery: A Modern Nation Divided"

9. The author makes all of the following points about Africans who were forcibly brought to America EXCEPT

   (A) they did not regard themselves as the objects of someone else's ownership

   (B) they formed new groups to replace the tribal associations that had been destroyed

   (C) the cultural forms brought from Africa were never completely eradicated by the enslavement experience

   (D) new affective relationships evolved to replace those made ineffectual by the practice of slavery

   (E) they brought with them a sense of intertribal unity in which all were regarded as members of the same group

10. Which of the following can be inferred about the viewpoint expressed in the second paragraph of the passage?

    (A) It is a reinterpretation of slave life based on new research done by African-American scholars.

    (B) It is based entirely on recently published descriptions of slave life written by slaves themselves.

    (C) It is biased and overly sympathetic to the views of white, colonial slaveholders.

    (D) It is highly speculative and supported by little actual historical evidence.

    (E) It is supported by descriptions of slave life written by early Americans who actually owned slaves.

11. The author puts the word *egalitarian* in line 12 in quotation marks to

    (A) emphasize his admiration for the early Americans

    (B) ridicule the idea of democracy

    (C) remind the reader of the principles of the new nation

    (D) underscore the fact that equality did not extend to everyone

    (E) express his surprise that slavery could have existed in America

12. The tone of the passage could best be described as

    (A) informed and anecdotal

    (B) critical and argumentative

    (C) impassioned and angry

    (D) analytical and objective

    (E) caustic and humorous

13. It can be inferred that which of the following pairs are the two elements of the "dual influence" mentioned at lines 62–63?

    (A) Slavery and West African culture

    (B) Tribal affiliations in West Africa and family affiliations in West Africa

    (C) A sense of individuality and a sense of tribal identification

    (D) The history of West Africa and modern black political movements

    (E) Integrationism and black nationalism

14. The author's argument logically depends upon which of the following assumptions?

    (A) The duality that characterizes the consciousness of modern Black Americans is so deeply rooted that it cannot be eliminated by political action.

    (B) African captives who were brought to North America had learned a basic orientation toward the world that remained with them.

    (C) At the time of the beginning of the United States, white Americans were not aware of the contradiction between the notion of equality and the institution of slavery.

    (D) The influence of the slavery experience on the West Africans was more powerful than the memory of West African attitudes.

    (E) Black Americans today are knowledgeable about the world view that was dominant in West Africa at the time slavery began in America.

EXERCISE 2

7 Questions • 10 Minutes

> **Directions:** The passage below is followed by questions based on its content. Choose the best answer to each question.

In the summer of 999, Leif Erikson voyaged to Norway and spent the following winter with King Olaf Tryggvason. Substantially the same account is given by
(5) both the Saga of Eric the Red and the Flat Island Book. The latter says nothing about Leif's return voyage to Greenland, but according to the former it was during this return voyage that
(10) Leif discovered America. The Flat Island Book, however, tells of another and earlier landfall by Biarni, the son of a prominent man named Heriulf, and makes that the inspiration for the voy-
(15) age to the new land by Leif. In brief, like Leif, Biarni and his companions sight three countries in succession before reaching Greenland, and to come upon each new land takes 1 "doegr" more than
(20) the last until Biarni comes to land directly in front of his father's house in the last-mentioned country.

This narrative has been rejected by most later writers, and they may be
(25) justified. Possibly, Biarni was a companion of Leif when he voyaged from Norway to Greenland via America, or it may be that the entire tale is but a garbled account of that voyage and Biarni an-
(30) other name for Leif. It should be noted, however, that the stories of Leif's visit to King Olaf and Biarni's to that king's predecessor are in the same narrative in the Flat Island Book, so there is less
(35) likelihood of duplication than if they were from different sources. Also, Biarni landed on none of the lands he passed, but Leif apparently landed on one, for he brought back specimens of wheat, vines,
(40) and timber. Nor is there any good reason to believe that the first land visited by Biarni was Wineland. The first land was "level and covered with woods," and

"there were small hillocks upon it." Of
(45) forests, later writers do not emphasize them particularly in connection with Wineland, though they are often noted incidentally; and of hills, the Saga says of Wineland only that "wherever there
(50) was hilly ground, there were vines."

Additionally, if the two narratives were taken from the same source we should expect a closer resemblance of Helluland. The Saga says of it: "They found there
(55) hellus (large flat stones)." According to the Biarni narrative, however, "this land was high and mountainous." The intervals of 1, 2, 3, and 4 "doegr" in both narratives are suggestive, but mythic
(60) formulas of this kind may be introduced into narratives without altogether destroying their historicity. It is also held against the Biarni narrative that its hero is made to come upon the coast of
(65) Greenland exactly in front of his father's home. But it should be recalled that Heriulfsness lay below two high mountains which served as landmarks for navigators.
(70) I would give up Biarni more readily were it not that the story of Leif's voyage contained in the supposedly more reliable Saga is almost as amazing. But Leif's voyage across the entire width of
(75) the North Atlantic is said to be "probable" because it is incorporated into the narrative of a preferred authority, while Biarni's is "improbable" or even "impossible" because the document containing
(80) it has been condemned.

1. The author's primary concern is to demonstrate that

   (A) Leif Erikson did not visit America

   (B) Biarni might have visited America before Leif Erikson

   (C) Biarni did not visit Wineland

   (D) Leif Erikson visited Wineland first

   (E) Leif Erikson was the same person as Biarni

2. The author specifically defines which of the following terms?

   (A) Flat Island Book

   (B) Helluland

   (C) Heriulfsness

   (D) doegr

   (E) hellus

3. According to the passage, Wineland was characterized by all of the following EXCEPT

   (A) forests

   (B) hills

   (C) mountains

   (D) vines

   (E) hilly ground

4. It can be inferred from the passage that scholars who doubt the authenticity of the Biarni narrative make all of the following objections EXCEPT

   (A) Biarni might have accompanied Leif Erikson on the voyage to America, and that is why a separate, erroneous narrative was invented

   (B) the similarity of the voyages described in the Saga and in the Flat Island Book indicates that there was only one voyage, not two voyages

   (C) it seems very improbable that a ship, having sailed from America to Greenland, could have found its way to a precise point on the coast of Greenland

   (D) the historicity of the Saga of Eric the Red is well-documented, while the historicity of the Flat Island Book is very doubtful

   (E) both the Saga of Eric the Red and the Flat Island Book make use of mythical formulas, so it is probable that they were written by the same person

5. The author mentions the two high mountains in order to show that it is

   (A) reasonable for Biarni to land precisely at his father's home

   (B) possible to sail from Norway to Greenland without modern navigational equipment

   (C) likely that Biarni landed on America at least 100 years before Leif Erikson

   (D) probable that Leif Erikson followed the same course as Biarni

   (E) questionable whether Biarni required the same length of time to complete his voyage as Leif Erikson

6. All of the following are mentioned as similarities between Leif Erikson's voyage and Biarni's voyage EXCEPT

   (A) both visited Norway

   (B) on the return voyage, both visited three different lands

   (C) both returned to Greenland

   (D) both visited Wineland

   (E) both visited Helluland

7. It can be inferred that the author regards the historicity of the Biarni narrative as

   (A) conclusively proved

   (B) almost conclusively proved

   (C) possibly true

   (D) highly unlikely

   (E) conclusively disproved

exercises

ANSWER KEY AND EXPLANATIONS

Exercise 1

1. B	4. C	7. D	10. A	13. A
2. E	5. D	8. C	11. D	14. B
3. C	6. D	9. E	12. D	

1. **The correct answer is (B).** This is a main idea question, and by now the drill for answering such questions should be familiar to you. The passage does summarize the history of mental health care in the United States, so (B) is a good choice.

   You can eliminate (D) on the basis of the word *shock*. There are no vivid images, and there is nothing in the passage that would shock a reader. You can eliminate (C) for a similar reason. Although a side effect of the selection may be to make some readers aware of a problem, the primary purpose of the passage is to describe, not to *increase awareness*.

   Finally, (A) and (E) violate that part of the main idea rule which states that the correct answer cannot be too narrow. Both (A) and (E) refer to interesting points made by the author, but neither is the main theme of the selection.

2. **The correct answer is (E).** This is a specific detail question—with a thought-reverser. Four of the five ideas are mentioned in the selection; one—the correct answer—is not. The information you need is in the first paragraph. There, the author mentions that, due to economic conditions, public funding for the asylums dried up, the asylums became overcrowded, mental illness was less susceptible to treatment than had been hoped, and administrators found it necessary to use restraints and similar measures. The correct answer, (E), is not mentioned in this paragraph. The discussion of lawyers and patients' rights—

   and this is typical of wrong answers to this type of question—is found in a different part of the selection, here the second paragraph.

3. **The correct answer is (C).** This is an implied idea question: Which of the statements can be logically deduced from the selection? We need to focus on the second paragraph, since the question asks about the causes of postwar reform. There the author mentions in passing that new treatments had been discovered. When coupled with the point made in the first paragraph about the lack of treatment for some conditions, this strongly implies that the new treatments made reform more likely. Now look at the wrong answers. (A) can be eliminated because the asylums were not *rehabilitated*. (B) is wrong because powerful drugs were part of the problem. (D) and (E) simply have no support in the text.

4. **The correct answer is (C).** This is a tone question, and the drill for tone questions should be familiar by now. Here it is possible to arrange all five choices to create a spectrum of attitudes ranging from positive to negative:

   MOST POSITIVE
   enthusiastic and supportive
   understanding and sympathetic
   detached and neutral
   uncaring and unemotional
   inflexible and insensitive
   MOST NEGATIVE

   Start by dividing the range in the middle. Does the passage tend toward the negative or positive direction? The author's attitude inclines more to the positive side. The passage speaks of the "plight" of the patient, a term that would not be used by someone who was detached, or uncaring, or insensitive.

Now the question is one of degree. How positive is the tone? Although the attitude toward patients might be described as either *sympathetic* or *supportive*, *understanding* is a better description than *enthusiastic*. The author seems to understand the position of the patient, but he is not a cheerleader for the patient.

5. **The correct answer is (D).** This is a specific detail question. You will find information in the passage that would be useful in answering four of the five questions. As for (A), two names, Dorothea Dix and Dr. David Vail, are mentioned in the passage. As for (B) and (C), help for answering these questions can be found in the second sentence of the second paragraph. And as for (E), an answer to this question is contained later in the second paragraph. (D), however, cannot be answered on the basis of the passage, for no specific case names are included.

6. **The correct answer is (D).** This is an implied idea question. The author states that civil rights lawyers who represented black prisoners were drawn naturally into representing patients in mental hospitals. In other words, X caused Y. The question stem asks us to assume that X did not occur, and on that basis we can infer that Y might not have occurred. This is choice (D).

    (A) is incorrect, for the cause of the establishment of the asylum system was Dorothea Dix's crusade. (B) is incorrect, for the passage does not state that judicial activism resulted in the discovery of any new treatments (even though it may have resulted in better treatment). (C) goes far beyond the scope of the passage. We cannot conclude that a failure in the area of prison reform would have meant complete failure of the Civil Rights movements. Finally, as for (E), nothing in the passage suggests that judicial activism resulted in the transfer of prisoners to hospitals, so a lack of judicial activism would not necessarily have this effect.

7. **The correct answer is (D).** This is an author's attitude question that focuses on the final paragraph. There the author makes a specific proposal, which, he acknowledges, will require effort to implement. Since the author made the proposal, he must be optimistic about its chance for success. And since he acknowledges that it will not be easy, we can call the author cautious as well.

    As for (A) and (B), though the author does make an argument in that paragraph, he does so in rather neutral terms. The paragraph is not contentious or strident or emotional. As for (C), there is nothing in the selection to suggest that the author is attempting to mislead the reader. You may or may not agree with the author's suggestion in that last paragraph, but there is no warrant for the conclusion that he is trying to fool you. Finally, as for (E), although the author evidently does his own thinking, the tone of the final paragraph cannot be described in these terms.

8. **The correct answer is (C).** Here we have a main idea question presented in the format "Name that passage." We'll go down the list of choices, eliminating those that are too narrow or too broad.

    We eliminate (A) because it is too broad. Most of the discussion focuses on an early period of this country's history, even though there is the one paragraph that points out the modern implications of this history. This hardly constitutes an entire history of black people in the United States. Next, we eliminate (B) because it is too narrow. Though the discussion of

West African tribal relations is an important element of the passage, it is not the main theme. The correct answer must be a title that also includes reference to the implications of these cultural elements.

(C) gives us what we are looking for. The passage contrasts white attitudes toward slaves with the attitudes the Africans held about themselves and then shows what implications this cultural history has for modern black Americans. You can eliminate (D), since the main theme of the passage is not really the relationship between slavery and democracy. The anomaly of slavery in a supposedly egalitarian society is only a small part of the discussion. Finally, (E) has the merit of using the phrase *legacy of slavery*, which is an important element in the discussion. But the division mentioned in the final paragraph is a division of consciousness—not the division of a nation.

9. **The correct answer is (E).** This is a specific detail question. You will find the ideas expressed by (A) through (D) specifically mentioned in the second paragraph. (E), however, is contradicted by the passage. The author states that West Africans felt a *tribal* unity, not an *intertribal* unity.

10. **The correct answer is (A).** This is an implied idea question. It's difficult because you have to pick up on the key phrase *African-American scholars are beginning to know* in the second paragraph; but the question stem doesn't tell you that is the key to the question.

That phrase implies that something new has been learned that has prompted scholars to change their ideas about the experience of slavery. In other words, the scholars have rejected the traditional view of what Africans thought of slavery. So we infer that the position outlined in the last two paragraphs is a new interpretation, and (A) correctly describes this.

(B) is incorrect since the author mentions evidence other than the published autobiographies. And in any case, it is the information about West African culture that has been newly discovered, not the autobiographies. (C) is incorrect since the second paragraph doesn't even deal with the attitudes of the white slaveholders.

Next, given that the author cites two sources in support of his interpretation (autobiographies and new research), we can eliminate (D). Finally, (E) is incorrect since the paragraphs in question do not discuss the attitudes of those who owned slaves.

11. **The correct answer is (D).** This is a logical structure question. Why does the author place the term *egalitarian* in quotation marks? The term appears in the first paragraph, where the author is discussing the contradictions in early American attitudes. They are particularly evident in the area of race. These *egalitarian* thinkers believed that they were superior to the Africans.

The author places the term in quotation marks to indicate that he thinks the early white Americans were not really egalitarian. This surely eliminates (A) and (C). (B), however, overstates the case. The author is not implying that democracy, as a concept, is indefensible—only that the early American thinkers did not do a very good job of implementing the idea. Additionally, you can eliminate (E) because the passage does not express surprise. It treats slavery as an historical fact.

12. **The correct answer is (D).** This is a tone question using answer choices with two words. On the basis of first words, we can eliminate both (C) and (E). Although the topic is obviously of interest to the author, the treatment does not qualify as *impassioned*. Further, though the

author's use of quotation marks to surround the word egalitarian might qualify as irony or even sarcasm, the overall tone of the passage is not *caustic*.

Next, using the second words, we eliminate (A) and (B). The author does not tell stories, so the tone cannot be *anecdotal*. Finally, the tone is not *argumentative*. Though the passage develops logically and has the form of a logical argument, it cannot be described as argumentative. Argumentative means contentious and aggressive.

13. **The correct answer is (A).** This is an implied idea question. In the final paragraph, the author refers to the *dual influence* but does not name those influences. Given the context, however, we may conclude that the two influences are slavery and the elements of West African culture that survived. (B) is, therefore, only partially correct. West African culture is only one of the two influences. (C) is a dichotomy mentioned in the selection but it is not the one to which the author is referring in the final paragraph. (D) is only partially correct. The elements of West African culture constitute one of the two influences, but *modern black political movements* could not be one of the origins mentioned by the author (though it is an outcome of the dual influences). Finally, as for (E), the author does mention these two contrasting movements, but they are a reflection of the duality, not the origin of the duality.

14. **The correct answer is (B).** Although this question uses the word *logically*, it is an implied idea question rather than a logical structure question. The question asks you to identify one of the choices as being a hidden premise of the argument. (B) is essential to the argument. For the argument regarding the West African influences to go through, it must be assumed that the West Africans had learned a world view that survived their being uprooted and transported to America. Without that critical assumption, the argument about the influence of West African culture fails.

(A) is not necessary to the author's argument. The author tries to prove the existence of such a duality, but he does not make any suggestion about how it might be eliminated. (C) is incorrect for the author merely states that there was such a contradiction. Whether white Americans were aware of the inconsistency in their behavior and beliefs is irrelevant. (D) is incorrect because the author merely states that there was the "dual" influence. He does not suggest that one or the other was more important in shaping the structure of modern black American consciousness. Finally, as for (E), though the author must assume that West African culture did survive in some form, he need not assume that black Americans today are still familiar with the elements of West African culture during the time of slavery. The legacy of that culture can survive even without conscious knowledge of its elements.

Exercise 2

1.	B	3.	C	5.	A	7.	C
2.	E	4.	E	6.	D		

1. **The correct answer is (B).** This is a main idea question. The author offers several reasons for the conclusion that the Biarni narrative does not describe the same series of events described by the Saga. And if he can pull this off, then he can claim that Biarni visited America before Leif Erikson did. This is summarized by (B).

    (A) misinterprets the author's strategy. The author doesn't need to prove that Leif Erikson did not visit America, only that Biarni did so before him. (C) is too narrow. It is true that the author wants to show that the two voyages are to some extent dissimilar, and that is why he tries to prove that Biarni did not visit Wineland. But this is a small part of the overall development. As for (D), as was just noted, the author only needs to argue that Biarni did not visit the same three lands later visited by Leif Erikson. Finally, (E) would be fatal to the author's argument, so this is a point he wishes to disprove.

2. **The correct answer is (E).** This is a specific detail question. The author explicitly defines hellus as meaning large flat stones. While you may infer meanings for the other terms ("doegr" must be a measure of time and "Heriulfsness" apparently was named for Biarni's father), the author does not specifically define those terms.

3. **The correct answer is (C).** This is a specific detail question. The material you need is contained in the second paragraph. There the author states that Wineland is described as having forests or woods as well as hills and hilly ground and, of course, its vines. The mention of mountains comes in the next paragraph and applies to a different place altogether.

4. **The correct answer is (E).** This is an implied idea question. The author doesn't give us a list of the objections to the historicity of the Biarni narrative, but we can infer what some of those objections must be from the refutations of them offered in the selection. As for (A), in the second paragraph, the author acknowledges that Biarni might have been a companion of Leif Erikson's and that the narrative of Biarni might be a garbled tale of that adventure. We can infer, therefore, that the objectors try to explain away the "other voyage" in this way. As for (B), since the author spends so much effort in attempting to prove that the two voyages did not include exactly the same countries, we can infer that the objectors use the similarity between the two as proof that there was but one voyage. As for (C), in the third paragraph, the author argues that it is not unreasonable to believe that Biarni could sail directly to his father's house since the house was situated by a known navigational landmark. And as for (D), the author specifically attributes this objection to them in the closing sentences.

    (E), however, is not an objection that would undermine the historicity of the narrative of Biarni. An objector would insist that the sequence of "doegr" suggests that the two voyages were the same one. The author of this selection points out, however, that this sequence was probably not historically accurate in the first place but was included as a kind of literary device, like the number three or seven in fairy tales. If the author of our selection is correct, then the similarity of the sequence of "doegr" is not surprising. If it is true that a story like this generally contains such a literary device, then the fact that both stories contain such a device doesn't prove that they are based on the same incidents.

5. **The correct answer is (A).** This is a logical detail question. As noted above, one of the objections to the Biarni narrative is that it would have been difficult for Biarni to navigate so accurately. But the author points out that the location of Heriulf's house was clearly indicated by mountains. So the author mentions the mountains to prove that Biarni could have found the location.

6. **The correct answer is (D).** This is a specific detail question, with a thought-reverser. Four of the five ideas are specifically stated in the selection. (A), (B), and (C) are mentioned in the first paragraph, and (E) is mentioned in the third. But the author is at pains to prove that Biarni did not visit Wineland as the first of his three lands.

7. **The correct answer is (C).** This is an author's attitude question. The answer choices are already neatly arranged for us on a spectrum. The best choice is (C). The author gives several arguments for the historicity of the narrative. So we can eliminate (D) and (E). On the other hand, the author does not claim to have proved his case conclusively. In fact, in the first sentence of the second paragraph, he admits that the objectors *may be justified*. And in the final paragraph, the phrasing *I should be willing to give up* ... strongly suggests that the author does not regard the issue as settled.

SUMMING IT UP

- Follow these steps when solving reading comprehension questions:
    1. Preview key sentences.
    2. Read for structure; ignore details.
    3. Do a mental wrap-up.

- The GRE uses six reading comprehension question types:
    1. Main Idea
    2. Specific Detail
    3. Inference
    4. Logical Structure
    5. Application
    6. Author's Attitude or Tone

Antonyms

OVERVIEW

- **What is an antonym?**
- **How do you answer antonym questions?**
- **What smart test-takers know**
- **Summing it up**

WHAT IS AN ANTONYM?

The basic idea of a GRE antonym question is to find an opposite for a word. Antonym items are first and foremost a test of vocabulary.

This is both good and bad news. First the bad news: If you have no idea of the meaning of the given word, there's not much you can do. That's the bad news; now the good news. When you don't know the meaning of an antonym, don't waste a lot of time trying to figure it out. In other words, once you recognize that you are out of ammunition, just click a random guess, confirm it, and move on to the next item.

GRE Antonym Questions

Each GRE antonym starts with a capitalized word, which is followed by five words or phrases in lowercase letters. The task is to find the word or phrase that is most nearly opposite in meaning to the capitalized word.

chapter 7

Anatomy of Antonym Questions

> **Directions:** Each of the following questions consists of a word printed in capital letters, followed by five (5) words or phrases. Choose the word or phrase that is most nearly opposite in meaning to the word in capital letters. Be sure to consider all the choices before deciding which one is best.

TRANSIENT :
- **(A)** urgent
- **(B)** youthful
- **(C)** original
- **(D)** eternal
- **(E)** unfaithful

ACARPOUS :
- **(A)** assiduous
- **(B)** poignant
- **(C)** fecund
- **(D)** reticent
- **(E)** prolix

The directions just say "pick the opposite," so don't bother with them again. On the test, dismiss them and start answering questions. It's true that some antonyms are fairly subtle, so you do want to read all of the choices before confirming your selection.

In question 1, the word in caps is the one you have to find the opposite of. The best answer is (D). TRANSIENT means temporary or passing, so a good opposite would be *eternal*.

In question 2, the best answer is (C); but unless you know that ACARPOUS means infertile and that *fecund* means fertile, there's not much you can do with the question except guess. This way you will free up time for other questions in the section. The bad news is not quite as bad as it sounds. You will recognize most of the words.

HOW DO YOU ANSWER ANTONYM QUESTIONS?

Here's a simple five-step plan that can help you answer GRE antonym questions.

Antonyms: Getting It Right

1 Define the capitalized word.

2 Think of a meaning that is opposite to this word.

3 Read all the answer choices. Eliminate those that do not relate to the meaning you thought of. If only one choice remains, mark it and go on.

4 If more than one choice remains, go back and refine your thinking about the capitalized word.

5 Pick the answer choice that is most nearly opposite to the capitalized word.

Now let's try out these steps on some typical GRE antonym questions.

SQUANDER :
  (A) whisper
  (B) conserve
  (C) import
  (D) deny
  (E) quarrel

1 The capitalized word means "to waste."

2 The opposite of "to waste" is "to save."

3 Looking at all the answer choices, the only one that comes close to meaning "save" is *conserve*. Mark it and go.

TEDIOUS :
  (A) unlimited
  (B) confined
  (C) enthralling
  (D) appetizing
  (E) illuminating

1 The capitalized word means "boring" or "tiresome."

2 The opposite of "boring" would be something like *exciting* or *interesting*.

3 Looking at all the answer choices, you can immediately eliminate (A), (B), and (E) as having nothing to do with excitement. But that leaves (C), *enthralling,* and (D), *appetizing.*

4 Of the two remaining choices, *enthralling,* which means "captivating" or "fascinating," is more nearly opposite in meaning to TEDIOUS than *appetizing,* which means "savory" or "delicious."

5 Mark (C), *enthralling,* as the correct choice.

Antonym questions primarily test vocabulary. Appendix A presents a GRE Word List that offers a good indication of the vocabulary level tested on the GRE.

WHAT SMART TEST-TAKERS KNOW

ANTONYM QUESTIONS OFTEN TEST UNUSUAL MEANINGS OF A WORD THAT YOU KNOW.

Sometimes the test-writer selects a word you are likely to be familiar with, but sets up the question to test a meaning you do not ordinarily associate with the word. Here is an example:

PRECIPITOUS :
- **(A)** pleasantly sweet
- **(B)** overly ambitious
- **(C)** agreeably situated
- **(D)** publicly known
- **(E)** gently sloping

The correct answer is (E). We most often use the word PRECIPITOUS to mean *rash* or *foolhardy,* but its central meaning is related to *precipice,* a sharp drop-off.

AMPLIFY :
- **(A)** announce
- **(B)** entertain
- **(C)** simplify
- **(D)** covet
- **(E)** require

The correct answer is (C). One common meaning of the word AMPLIFY is "to make louder," for example, amplified sound. But the word means generally "to increase," "to enlarge," or "to make fuller." Thus it can be used to mean "to describe something in increased detail." The best available opposite, therefore, is (C), *simplify*.

YOU CAN LEARN A LOT FROM THE ANSWER CHOICES.

Words can have different meanings based upon their part of speech. If you are uncertain about the part of speech of the capitalized word, just check the answer choices. If they're all verbs, for example, so is the capitalized word. Here's an example:

COUNTENANCE :
- **(A)** procure
- **(B)** insist
- **(C)** disapprove
- **(D)** forego
- **(E)** interpret

TIP

Eliminate non-answers. One simple way to eliminate answer choices is to toss out any words that don't have opposite meanings.

The correct answer is (C). The word COUNTENANCE can be either a noun (meaning "face") or a verb (meaning "to approve of"). Which meaning is intended? The answer choices are unequivocally verbs, which means the capitalized word must also be a verb. So the capitalized word means "approve of," and (C) is the best opposite.

IT IS OKAY TO PLAY AROUND WITH A WORD.

If it helps to solve the problem, you can alter the part of speech of the capitalized word and answer choices in your own mind. Sometimes an antonym will use a word you know but as a part of speech that is unfamiliar to you. Here is an example:

SUBLIMITY :
- **(A)** erosion
- **(B)** baseness
- **(C)** conciseness
- **(D)** insistence
- **(E)** partiality

The correct answer is (B). You may know the word SUBLIMITY better as the adjective *sublime,* meaning "lofty, high, or noble." So you may find it easier to think about the antonym by changing *sublimity* to the more familiar form *sublime.* As you think about each answer choice, you would then change it in your mind to an adjective. *Baseness,* therefore, would become *base*; and *base* is an opposite of *sublime.*

YOU CAN USE WORD CONNOTATIONS TO ELIMINATE ANSWER CHOICES.

Even if you don't know the exact meaning of a word, you may have a vague recollection of the context in which you first encountered it. So you may know whether the word has positive overtones or negative ones. This recollection may be sufficient to get a correct answer. Here's an example:

RAFFISH :
- **(A)** grotesque
- **(B)** delinquent
- **(C)** uncaring
- **(D)** noble
- **(E)** evil

The correct answer is (D). Let's assume that you do not know that RAFFISH means "low, vulgar, and base." And let's further assume, however, that you have a vague knowledge of the word. You've seen it used to describe a character who is dishonest and not trustworthy. So even though you don't know the exact meaning of the word, you know that it has negative overtones. Since you are looking for the opposite of a word with negative overtones, you would eliminate every answer

TIP

Parts of speech. It is okay to play around with the part of speech of a word if that helps to answer the question.

choice with negative overtones. As it turns out, this strategy works perfectly with this antonym; only one word is left. *Noble* is the only word with positive overtones.

YOU CAN UNLOCK WORD MEANINGS BY TAKING THE WORD APART.

Even when you encounter a word for the first time, you may be able to ascertain its meaning from its parts. Here's an example:

COGNOSCITIVE :
- **(A)** courageous
- **(B)** expensive
- **(C)** unconscious
- **(D)** redundant
- **(E)** immature

The correct answer is (C). This is a very unusual word, but you can probably figure out its meaning by looking at its root *cog-* . This is the same root found in words such as *cognition* and *recognize*, and it has to do with knowledge. So we infer that COGNOSCITIVE has something to do with awareness, and (C) looks like a good opposite. A word of caution, however: Don't spend too much time trying to decipher the meaning of a word. Remember that each antonym counts for only one point. Therefore, guess and go on.

EXERCISE 1

10 Questions • 5 Minutes

Directions: Each of the following questions consists of a word printed in capital letters, followed by five (5) words or phrases. Choose the word or phrase that is most nearly opposite in meaning to the word in capital letters. Be sure to consider all the choices before deciding which one is best.

1. LOUTISH :
   (A) boisterous
   (B) provocative
   (C) calamitous
   (D) sophisticated
   (E) insightful

2. ENIGMATIC :
   (A) talkative
   (B) oppressed
   (C) easily understood
   (D) easily avoided
   (E) very common

3. RECALCITRANT :
   (A) polished
   (B) feckless
   (C) yielding
   (D) somber
   (E) miserly

4. MITIGATE :
   (A) intensify
   (B) defend
   (C) mire
   (D) frequent
   (E) coax

5. TREPIDATION :
   (A) contempt
   (B) restlessness
   (C) rancor
   (D) vigilance
   (E) courage

6. PRECIPITOUS :
   (A) well-planned
   (B) gargantuan
   (C) prolific
   (D) short-lived
   (E) extremely hostile

7. PROCLIVITY :
   (A) prodigality
   (B) avoidance
   (C) credence
   (D) calumny
   (E) inception

8. TENUOUS :
   (A) unseemly
   (B) inherited
   (C) substantial
   (D) forlorn
   (E) awkward

9. SALIENT :
   (A) concealed
   (B) inclined
   (C) stagnant
   (D) blameworthy
   (E) omnipotent

10. ENERVATE :
    (A) invigorate
    (B) contemplate
    (C) necessitate
    (D) evaluate
    (E) elucidate

EXERCISE 2

5 Questions • 3 Minutes

Directions: Each of the following questions consists of a word printed in capital letters, followed by five (5) words or phrases. Choose the word or phrase that is most nearly opposite in meaning to the word in capital letters. Be sure to consider all the choices before deciding which one is best.

1. SPURIOUS :
   (A) malignant
   (B) authentic
   (C) incumbent
   (D) gracious
   (E) speculative

2. OPAQUE :
   (A) feverish
   (B) monstrous
   (C) inclined
   (D) resolved
   (E) transparent

3. NEFARIOUS :
   (A) virtuous
   (B) pedestrian
   (C) resourceful
   (D) sordid
   (E) potent

4. INDEFATIGABLE :
   (A) redolent
   (B) exhausted
   (C) famished
   (D) regrettable
   (E) ignorant

5. PLETHORA :
   (A) piety
   (B) agility
   (C) paucity
   (D) chagrin
   (E) harmony

ANSWER KEY

Exercise 1

1.	D	3.	C	5.	E	7.	B	9.	A
2.	C	4.	A	6.	A	8.	C	10.	A

Exercise 2

1.	B	2.	E	3.	A	4.	B	5.	C

SUMMING IT UP

- Follow these steps when solving antonym questions:

   1. Define the capitalized word.

   2. Think of a meaning that is opposite to this word.

   3. Read all the answer choices. Eliminate those that do not relate to the meaning you thought of. If only one choice remains, mark it and move on.

   4. If more than one choice remains, go back and refine your thinking about the capitalized word.

   5. Pick the answer choice that is most nearly opposite to the capitalized word.

PART IV

GRE MATH QUESTIONS

Problem Solving

OVERVIEW

- **What is problem solving?**
- **How do you answer problem-solving questions?**
- **What smart test-takers know**
- **Summing it up**

WHAT IS PROBLEM SOLVING?

Problem-solving questions are your ordinary, garden-variety math questions—the kind you saw on the SAT. The questions test your mastery of basic mathematical skills and your ability to solve problems using arithmetic, elementary algebra, and geometry. Some problems are strictly math questions, such as solving for the value of a variable; the rest will be presented as real-life word problems that require a mathematical solution.

If your basic math skills need work, you'll find plenty of practice here, in Part IV. This section provides a complete review of arithmetic, algebra, and geometry, along with exercises to build your skills.

GRE Problem-solving Questions

Problem-solving questions are interspersed with quantitative comparisons in the scored math section. You'll have 9 to 11 problem-solving questions.

Here are the directions for GRE problem-solving questions and four sample questions together with their explanations.

Anatomy of Problem-Solving Questions

Directions: For each of the following questions, select the best of the answer choices given.

1. $0.2 \times 0.005 =$
    - **(A)** 0.0001
    - **(B)** 0.001
    - **(C)** 0.01
    - **(D)** 0.1
    - **(E)** 1.0

2. If $x + 5 = 8$, then $2x - 1 =$
    - **(A)** 25
    - **(B)** 12
    - **(C)** 5
    - **(D)** 4
    - **(E)** 0

3. Joe works two part-time jobs. One week Joe worked 8 hours at one job, earning $150, and 4.5 hours at the other job, earning $90. What were his average hourly earnings for the week?
    - **(A)** $8
    - **(B)** $9.60
    - **(C)** $16
    - **(D)** $19.20
    - **(E)** $32

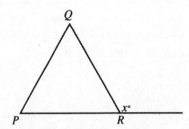

4. In the figure above, $PQ = QR = PR$. What is the value of x?
    - **(A)** 30°
    - **(B)** 45°
    - **(C)** 60°
    - **(D)** 90°
    - **(E)** 120°

You really don't need the directions at all. Problem solving is your standard-issue, multiple-choice math question.

Question 1 is a simple manipulation problem. Manipulation problems, as the name implies, test your knowledge of arithmetic or algebraic manipulations. The correct answer is (B). The item tests whether or not you remember how to keep track of the decimal point in multiplication.

Question 2, a manipulation problem, tests algebra. The correct answer is (C). Since $x + 5 = 8$, $x = 3$. Then substitute 3 for x in the expression $2x - 1$: $2(3) - 1 = 5$.

Question 3 is a practical word problem. Practical word problems go beyond simple manipulations. They require that you use your knowledge of manipulations in practical situations. The correct choice is (D). To find Joe's average hourly earnings, divide the total earnings by the number of hours worked: $\frac{150+90}{8+4.5} = \frac{240}{12.5} = 19.20$.

Question 4 is obviously a geometry problem. Equally obvious, geometry problems involve the use of basic principles of geometry. The correct answer is (E). This is an equilateral triangle (one having three equal sides), and equilateral triangles also have three equal angles, each 60 degrees. Then $\overline{PR}$, as extended, forms a straight line. So $x + 60° = 180°$, and $x = 120°$.

HOW DO YOU ANSWER PROBLEM-SOLVING QUESTIONS?

Here's a simple, four-step plan that can help you answer GRE problem-solving questions.

Problem-Solving: Getting It Right

1 Read the question carefully.

2 Before solving the problem, check the answers.

3 Eliminate choices that are completely off the radar screen.

4 For complex questions, break down the problem.

NOTE

Does the GRE test college math? No. All of the topics tested in GRE math questions are covered in high school math.

Now let's examine each of these steps in more detail.

❶ Read the question carefully. Some GRE problems are fairly simple, but others are more complex, particularly practical word problems and more difficult geometry problems. The more complex the question, the easier it is to misread and set off down a wrong track. The importance of this point is illustrated by the following very difficult practical word problem.

> The people eating in a certain cafeteria are either faculty members or students, and the number of faculty members is 15 percent of the total number of people in the cafeteria. After some of the students leave, the total number of persons remaining in the cafeteria is 50 percent of the original total. The number of students who left is what fractional part of the original number of students?
>
> **(A)** $\dfrac{17}{20}$
>
> **(B)** $\dfrac{10}{17}$
>
> **(C)** $\dfrac{1}{2}$
>
> **(D)** $\dfrac{1}{4}$
>
> **(E)** $\dfrac{7}{20}$

The correct answer is (B). Let T be the total number of people originally in the cafeteria. Faculty account for 15 percent of T, or $.15T$, and students account for the remaining 85 percent of T, or $.85T$. Then some students leave, reducing the total number of people in the cafeteria to half of what it was originally, or $.5T$. The number of faculty, however, does not change. So the difference between $.5T$ and $.15T$ must be students: $.5T - .15T = .35T$. But this is not yet the answer to the question. The question asks "The number of students who left is what fraction of the original number of students?" Originally there were $.85T$ students; now there are only $.35T$ students, so $.50T$ students left. Now, to complete the solution we set up a fraction: $\left(\frac{.50T}{.85T} = \frac{10}{17}\right)$.

By this point, you can appreciate that there are several ways to misread the question. Someone might just put $.35T$ over $.85T\left(\frac{.35T}{.85T} = \frac{7}{17}\right)$ and choose (D). But this answers the question "The remaining students are what fraction of the original number of students?" That is not the question asked.

Someone might also put $.35T$ over $T\left(\frac{.35T}{T} = \frac{7}{20}\right)$ and select (E). But this too answers a different question: "The number of students who remain is what fractional part of the original number of people in the cafeteria?"

There are probably hundreds of other ways to misread the question, but it would be a shame to know how to answer the question and still miss it just because you did not read the question carefully.

② **Before solving the problem, check the answers.** As you tackle each problem, start by looking at the answer choices. That way you'll know what form your own solution should take. For example, are the choices all in miles per hour? If so, that's the form your answer must take. Are they all decimals? If so, your solution should be a decimal, not a fraction or a radical.

③ **Eliminate choices that are completely off the radar screen.** The answer choices are generally arranged in a logical order.

> X xxx xxxxxxx xxxx xxxxxxxxxxxx xxxxxxx xxxxxxxxxx xxxx xxxxxxxxxxx xxxx xxxxxxx xxxxxxxxxxx?
> - **(A)** 3200
> - **(B)** 4800
> - **(C)** 12,000
> - **(D)** 16,000
> - **(E)** 20,000

Notice that the choices in this dummy question are arranged from least to greatest. Occasionally, choices are arranged from greatest to least. And in algebra questions, the choices are arranged logically according to powers and coefficients of variables.

In addition, the wrong choices are not just picked at random. They are usually written to correspond to possible mistakes (misreadings, etc.). This actually helps you. To illustrate this, here is an actual question to go with the dummy answers.

> In a certain population, 40 percent of all people have biological characteristic X; the others do not. If 8000 people have characteristic X, how many people do not have X?
> - **(A)** 3200
> - **(B)** 4800
> - **(C)** 12,000
> - **(D)** 16,000
> - **(E)** 20,000

The correct answer is (C). You can arrive at this conclusion by setting up a proportion:

$$\frac{\text{Percent with X}}{\text{Number with X}} = \frac{\text{Percent without X}}{\text{Number without X}}$$

Supplying the appropriate numbers:

$$\frac{40\%}{8000} = \frac{60\%}{x}$$

Cross-multiply: $.40x = .60(8000)$

Solve for x: $x = 12,000$

TIP

Look for shortcuts. GRE problem-solving questions test your math reasoning, not your ability to make endless calculations. If you find yourself mired in calculations, you probably missed a shortcut that would have made your work easier.

TIP

The answers line up by size. The quantities in GRE problem-solving answer choices either go from larger to smaller or the other way around. Remember that when you're trying to eliminate or test answers.

You can avoid even this little bit of work. A little common sense, when applied to the answer choices, would have eliminated all but (C). In the first place, 40 percent of the people have X, so more people don't have X. If 8000 people have X, the correct choice has to be greater than 8000. This eliminates both (A) and (B). Next, we reason that if the correct answer were (D), 16,000, then only about $\frac{1}{3}$ of the people would have X. But we know 40 percent have X. This allows us to eliminate (D) and also (E).

④ **For complex questions, break down the problems.** Some practical word problems are fairly complex, and it is easy to get lost. You'll fare better if you break the solution process into separate steps. First, formulate a statement of what is needed; second, find the numbers you need; and third, perform the required calculation.

> The enrollments at College X and College Y both grew by 8 percent from 1980 to 1985. If the enrollment at College X grew by 800 and the enrollment at College Y grew by 840, the enrollment at College Y was how much greater than the enrollment at College X in 1985?

> **(A)** 400
>
> **(B)** 460
>
> **(C)** 500
>
> **(D)** 540
>
> **(E)** 580

The correct answer is (D). But the solution is a good deal more involved than the one needed for the preceding problem, so proceed step by step.

First, isolate the simple question that must be answered:

> The enrollments at College X and College Y both grew by 8 percent from 1980 to 1985. If the enrollment at College X grew by 800 and the enrollment at College Y grew by 840, <u>the enrollment at College Y was how much greater than the enrollment at College X in 1985?</u>

This can be summarized as follows:

College Y in 1985 − College X in 1985

So you know you must find the enrollments at both colleges in 1985. How can you do that? The numbers are there in the question; you just have to figure out how to use them. Take College Y first. You know that enrollments grew by 840 and that this represents an increase of 8%. These numbers will allow you to find the enrollment in 1980:

$$8\% \text{ of 1980 Total} = 840$$

$$0.08 \times T = 840$$

Solve for T: $\qquad\qquad\qquad\qquad T = 10{,}500$

This was the enrollment at College Y in 1980, but you need to know the enrollment at College Y in 1985. To do that, just add the increase:

$$1980 + \text{Increase} = 1985$$

$$10,500 + 840 = 11,340$$

Now do the same thing for College X:

$$8\% \text{ of 1980 Total} = 800$$

$$0.08 \times T = 800$$

$$T = 10,000$$

$$1980 + \text{Increase} = 1985$$

$$10,000 + 800 = 10,800$$

Now you have the numbers you were looking for. Substitute them back into your original solution statement:

$$\text{College Y in 1985} - \text{College X in 1985} = \text{Final Answer}$$

$$11,340 - 10,800 = 540$$

This is not the only way of reaching the correct solution, but it is the one most people would be likely to use. It does illustrate nicely what you should do when you encounter a complex practical word problem.

Now let's look at some more problem-solving questions and their solutions. As you read the solutions, think about how the four-step process would help you find the answers.

Manipulation Problems

Here are five typical GRE manipulation problems.

$0.04 \times 0.25 =$
- **(A)** 0.0001
- **(B)** 0.001
- **(C)** 0.01
- **(D)** 0.1
- **(E)** 1.0

Your approach to a manipulation problem like this one depends upon the degree of difficulty of the manipulation.

The correct answer is (C). The manipulation is very simple, so you should just do the indicated multiplication (keeping careful track of the decimal).

$$\frac{2}{3} \times \frac{3}{4} \times \frac{4}{5} \times \frac{5}{6} \times \frac{6}{7} \times \frac{7}{8} =$$

(A) $\dfrac{2}{33}$

(B) $\dfrac{1}{4}$

(C) $\dfrac{3}{8}$

(D) $\dfrac{1}{2}$

(E) $\dfrac{27}{33}$

The correct answer is (B). If the problem seems too difficult, look for a way to simplify things. The test-writers have no interest in determining whether you can do "donkey" math. If a manipulation problem looks to be too difficult, then there is a trick to be discovered. Given enough time, you could work the problem out by multiplying all the numerators, multiplying all the denominators, and then reducing. But the very fact that this would be time consuming should prompt you to look for an alternative. Try dividing out common terms:

$$\frac{2}{\cancel{3}} \times \frac{\cancel{3}}{\cancel{4}} \times \frac{\cancel{4}}{\cancel{5}} \times \frac{\cancel{5}}{\cancel{6}} \times \frac{\cancel{6}}{\cancel{7}} \times \frac{\cancel{7}}{8} = \frac{2}{8} = \frac{1}{4}$$

$(27 \times 34) - (33 \times 27) =$

(A) -1

(B) 1

(C) 27

(D) 33

(E) 918

The correct answer is (C). This time you can simplify matters by factoring:

$$(27 \times 34) - (33 \times 27) = 27(34 - 33) = 27(1) = 27$$

If $3x - 5 = x + 11$, then $x =$

   (A) 16

   (B) 8

   (C) 3

   (D) 2

   (E) 1

The correct answer is (B). If a problem consists of an equation with just one variable, the solution is almost certainly to solve for the unknown, whether it be x or some other variable. The appropriate method is to solve for x:

$$3x - 5 = x + 11$$

Combine terms:$\qquad\qquad 2x = 16$

Solve for x:$\qquad\qquad\quad x = 8$

If $x + y = 8$ and $2x - y = 10$, then $x =$

   (A) 16

   (B) 8

   (C) 6

   (D) 4

   (E) 2

The correct answer is (C). If a problem presents two equations with two variables, the best strategy is almost certainly to treat them as a system of simultaneous equations. First, isolate y from the first equation:

$$x + y = 8$$

So:$\qquad\qquad\qquad y = 8 - x$

Next, substitute $8 - x$ into the second equation in place of y:

$$2x - (8 - x) = 10$$

Combine terms:$\qquad\qquad 3x = 18$

Solve for x:$\qquad\qquad\quad x = 6$

NOTE

What do you do with a complex word problem? Break it down into easy-to-handle steps. Compare what you are asked for with what you are given, and build a mental bridge between the two before you start doing math. (Tip: This works for complex graph questions also.)

Practical Word Problems

Here is a typical GRE word problem:

> $2000 is deposited into a savings account that earns interest at the rate of 10 percent per year, compounded semiannually. How much money will there be in the account at the end of one year?
>
> **(A)** $2105
>
> **(B)** $2200
>
> **(C)** $2205
>
> **(D)** $2400
>
> **(E)** $2600

The correct answer is (C). For complex word problems, break the problem down into smaller parts. First determine what you need to calculate and set up a mathematical expression.

This problem is asking you to calculate the total amount of money in the account at the end of the year. That means you must find the interest earned and add it to the original amount. First, calculate the interest earned during the first six months. To do this, you need to know that the formula for calculating interest is:

$$\text{Principal} \times \text{Rate} \times \text{Time} = \text{Interest Earned}$$

First Six Months:

Principal	×	Rate	×	Time	=	Interest Earned
$2000	×	10%	×	0.5	=	$100

This $100 is then paid into the account. The new balance is $2100. Now you would calculate the interest earned during the second six months.

Second Six Months:

Principal	×	Rate	×	Time	=	Interest Earned
$2100	×	10%	×	0.5	=	$105

This is then paid into the account. So the final balance is:

$$\$2100 + \$105 = \$2205$$

WHAT SMART TEST-TAKERS KNOW

IT'S SMART TO TEST ANSWER CHOICES.

The GRE is a multiple-choice test, so the correct answer is staring you in the face. Take advantage of this. Solve problems by plugging in the answer choices until you find the one that works.

$5^3 \times 9 =$

   (A) 5×27

   (B) 15×9

   (C) $15 \times 15 \times 5$

   (D) 25×27

   (E) 125×27

The correct choice is (C). You learn this by testing each choice to see which one is equivalent to $5^3 \times 9$. The expression $5^3 \times 9 = (5 \times 5 \times 5)\,(3 \times 3) = 15 \times 15 \times 5$.

WHEN TESTING ANSWER CHOICES, IT'S SMART TO START WITH (C).

Remember, the answer is right there in front of you. If you test all the choices, you'll find the right one. However, the smart place to start is with choice (C). Why? Because the quantities in the choices are always arranged in order, either from smallest to largest or the other way around. If you start with (C) and it's too large, you'll only have to concentrate on the two smaller choices. That eliminates three of the five choices right away. Here's how this works:

A car dealer who gives a customer a 20 percent discount on the list price of a car still realizes a net profit of 25 percent of cost. If the dealer's cost is $4800, what is the usual list price of the car?

   (A) $6000

   (B) $6180

   (C) $7200

   (D) $7500

   (E) $8001

You know that one of these five choices must be correct, so all you have to do is test each one until you find the correct one. Start with (C).

If the usual list price is $7200, what will be the actual selling price after the 20% discount?

Usual List Price − 20% of Usual List Price = Final Selling Price

$7200 − 20% of $7200 = Final Selling Price

$7200 − $1440 = $5760

On that assumption, the dealer's profit would be:

Final Selling Price − Cost = Profit
$5760 − $4800 = $960

Is that a profit of 25%?

$\frac{\$960}{\$4800}$ is less than $\frac{1}{4}$ and so less than 25%. This proves that (C) is wrong.

Now you need to test another choice, logically either (B) or (D). But which one? Apply a little reasoning to the situation. Assuming a usual cost of $7200, the numbers worked out to a profit that was too small. Therefore, we need a larger price to generate a larger profit. So try (D).

$7500 − (.20)($7500) = $6000

If the final selling price is $6000, that means a profit for the dealer of $1200. And $\frac{\$1200}{\$4800}$ = 25%. So (D) must be the correct answer.

Now suppose instead that you had this set of answer choices:

(A) $4000

(B) $6000

(C) $6180

(D) $7200

(E) $7500

In this case, you test (C) first and learn that it is incorrect. Then you go to (D) as above. Again, another wrong choice. Does this mean you have to do a third calculation? No! Since the choices are arranged in order, once you have eliminated (C) and (D), you know that (E) must be correct.

YOU CAN ASSUME NUMBER VALUES FOR UNKNOWNS.

Often it is easier to work with numbers than with unknowns. Therefore, when you are faced with a problem like the one below, in which some numbers are presented as variables, try substituting real numbers for each variable.

At a certain printing plant, each of m machines prints 6 newspapers every s seconds. If all machines work together but independently without interruption, how many minutes will it take to print an entire run of 18,000 newspapers?

(A) $\dfrac{180s}{m}$

(B) $\dfrac{50s}{m}$

(C) $50ms$

(D) $\dfrac{ms}{50}$

(E) $\dfrac{300m}{s}$

Since the information is given algebraically, the letters could stand for any numbers (so long as you don't divide by 0). Pick some values for m and s and see which answer choice works. Start with easy numbers. For purpose of discussion, assume that the plant has 2 machines, so $m = 2$. Also assume that $s = 1$, that is, that each machine produces 6 newspapers each second. On this assumption, each machine prints 360 papers per minute; and with two such machines working, the plant capacity is 720 papers per minute. To find how long it will take the plant to do the work, divide 18,000 by 720:

$$\frac{18,000}{720} = 25 \text{ minutes}$$

On the assumption that $m = 2$ and $s = 1$, the correct formula should produce the number 25. Test the choices:

(A) $\dfrac{180s}{m} = \dfrac{180(1)}{720}$ is not equal to 25 (WRONG!)

(B) $\dfrac{50s}{m} = \dfrac{50(1)}{2}$ is equal to 25 (CORRECT!)

(C) $50ms = 50(2)(1)$ is not equal to 25 (WRONG!)

(D) $\dfrac{ms}{50} = \dfrac{(2)(1)}{50}$ is not equal to 25 (WRONG!)

(E) $\dfrac{300m}{s} = \dfrac{300(2)}{(1)}$ is not equal to 25 (WRONG!)

WHEN NO NUMBERS OR VARIABLES ARE SUPPLIED, YOU CAN PICK YOUR OWN.

When no numbers or variables are supplied, you may find it easier to solve the problem if you assign numerical values to the given information. Pick numbers that are easy to work with.

> If the value of a piece of property decreases by 10 percent while the tax rate on the property increases by 10 percent, what is the effect on the taxes?
>
> **(A)** Taxes increase by 10 percent.
>
> **(B)** Taxes increase by 1 percent.
>
> **(C)** There is no change in taxes.
>
> **(D)** Taxes decrease by 1 percent.
>
> **(E)** Taxes decrease by 10 percent.

The correct answer is (D). Since no numbers are supplied, you are free to supply your own. Assume the piece of property has a value of $1000, and assume further that the original tax rate is 10%. On the basis of those assumptions, the tax bill is originally 10% of $1000 or $100. Now make the specified adjustments. The value of the property drops by 10%, from $1000 to $900, but the tax rate goes up by 10%, from 10% to 11%. The new tax bill is 11% of $900, or $99. The original tax bill was $100; the new tax bill is $99; the net result is a decrease of $1 out of $100, or a 1% decrease.

YOU HAVE TO BE CAREFUL OF YOUR UNITS OF MEASURE.

Practical word problems often require you to work with units of measure. Sometimes several different units are involved, so be sure that your answer is expressed in the unit that's asked for.

> A certain copy machine produces 13 copies every 10 seconds. If the machine operates without interruption, how many copies will it produce in an hour?
>
> **(A)** 78
>
> **(B)** 468
>
> **(C)** 1800
>
> **(D)** 2808
>
> **(E)** 4680

NOTE

Will I have to know how to convert units of measure? No. Measurements in problem-solving questions may be given in either English or metric units, but you don't have to know how to convert from one system to the other or from one unit of measure to another. If you need such information, it will be given to you.

The correct answer is (E). The question stem gives information about copies per 10 seconds, but you must answer in terms of copies per hour. To solve the problem, first convert copies per 10 seconds to copies per minute. This can be done with a proportion:

$$\frac{13 \text{ copies}}{10 \text{ seconds}} = \frac{x \text{ copies}}{60 \text{ seconds}}$$

Solve by cross-multiplication: $13 \times 60 = 10x$

Solve for x: $x = 78$

The correct answer, however, is not 78. A machine that produces 78 copies per minute produces 60 times that in an hour: $60 \times 78 = 4680$.

THOUGHT-REVERSERS CHANGE THE TERMS.

A thought-reverser is any word, such as *not, except,* or *but,* that turns a question inside-out. It will determine the solution you're looking for, so you'll need to keep it clearly in mind as you make your calculations.

A survey of 100 persons revealed that 72 of them had eaten at restaurant *P* and that 52 of them had eaten at restaurant *Q*. Which of the following could not be the number of persons in the surveyed group who had eaten at both *P* and *Q*?

(A) 20

(B) 24

(C) 30

(D) 50

(E) 52

The correct answer is (A). Since there are only 100 people in the group, some of them must have eaten at both *P* and *Q*. The combined responses for *P* and *Q* equal 124, and $124 - 100 = 24$. So 24 is the smallest possible number of people who could have eaten at both *P* and *Q*. (The largest possible number would be 52, which is possible if all of those who ate at *Q* had also eaten at *P*.) Thus far we have been concentrating on the question stem, but the answer choices also deserve special mention.

A picture can help. In problem-solving questions, draw a diagram if none is supplied. A diagram is a great way to organize information. Mark it up with the information you're given, and you'll have a better idea of what you're looking for.

MOST PROBLEM-SOLVING FIGURES ARE DRAWN TO SCALE.

Most of the problem-solving figures are drawn as accurately as possible. (*Note:* This is not true of quantitative comparisons.) If a figure is not drawn to scale, it will include the warning: "Note: Figure not drawn to scale."

Unless you are told that a problem-solving figure is not drawn to scale, you may assume that angles and other geometric relationships are as shown. You may also assume that, for example, what looks like a right triangle is a right triangle even if you can't support your assumption with a formal geometric theorem.

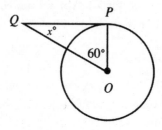

In the figure above, what is the measure of angle x?

  (A)   15°

  (B)   30°

  (C)   45°

  (D)   60°

  (E)   90°

The correct answer is (B). To solve the problem, you need to know that angle P is a right angle. Then you have a triangle whose angles measure 60°, 90°, and x. Since there are 180 degrees in a triangle, x must be 30°.

You probably did realize that angle P must be a right angle and not just by looking at it and seeing that it seems to be 90 degrees. Rather your mind's eye probably told you that for some reason or other, angle P had to be 90 degrees.

In fact, angle P must be 90 degrees. PQ is a tangent, and PO is a radius. A tangent intersects a radius at a 90-degree angle. But you do not need to know the "official" justification to answer correctly. Just trust your spatial intuition.

YOU CAN USE MEASURES OF SIMPLE FIGURES TO FIND MEASURES OF MORE COMPLEX ONES.

Many geometry problems involve complex figures. You can often calculate their measures by breaking them up into simpler figures.

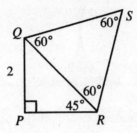

In the figure above, what is the perimeter of triangle QRS?

   (A) 12

   (B) $6\sqrt{2}$

   (C) 6

   (D) $3\sqrt{2}$

   (E) $2\sqrt{2}$

The correct answer is (B). The trick is to see that $\overline{QR}$ is not only a side of triangle PQR, but is also a side of triangle QRS. Further, triangle QRS is an equilateral triangle, so if you can find the length of one side, you know the length of the other sides as well.

How can you find the length of $\overline{QR}$? Triangle PQR is a 45-45-90 triangle. Since QP is 2, PR is also 2. Now you know two legs of the right triangle, and you can use the Pythagorean Theorem to find the hypotenuse:

$$QP^2 + PR^2 = QR^2$$

So: $2^2 + 2^2 = QR^2$

$$4 + 4 = QR^2$$

$$QR^2 = 8$$

$$QR = \sqrt{8}$$

$$QR = 2\sqrt{2}$$

Each of the three sides of triangle QRS is equal to $2\sqrt{2}$, so the perimeter of triangle $QRS = 3 \times 2\sqrt{2} = 6\sqrt{2}$.

YOU CAN MEASURE IRREGULAR SHADED AREAS BY RELATING THEM TO FIGURES WITH REGULAR SHAPES.

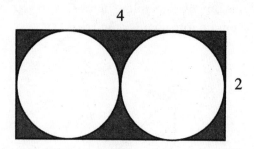

What is the area of the shaded portion of the figure above?

(A) $8 - 8\pi$

(B) $8 - 4\pi$

(C) $8 - 2\pi$

(D) $8 - \pi$

(E) π

The correct answer is (C). The shaded area is what's left over if you take the area of the two circles away from the area of the rectangle:

$$\text{Rectangle} - \text{Two Circles} = \text{Shaded Area}$$

First, the area of the rectangle is just $2 \times 4 = 8$. Then, the diameter of the circles is equal to the width of the rectangle. So the diameter of the circles is 2, and the radius is 1. The formula for the area of a circle is πr^2, so each circle has an area of $\pi(1^2) = \pi$. Now we know the area of the shaded part of the diagram:

$$8 - 2(\pi) = 8 - 2\pi$$

BECAUSE A PROBLEM-SOLVING FIGURE IS DRAWN TO SCALE, YOU CAN ESTIMATE MEASURES.

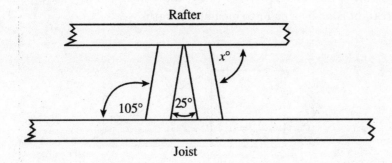

The figure above shows a cross section of a building. If the rafter is parallel to the joist, what is the measure of angle x?

(A) 45°

(B) 60°

(C) 80°

(D) 90°

(E) 105°

The correct answer is (C). You can get that without a calculation. Look at the size of x. It is not quite a right angle, so you can eliminate both (D) and (E). Is it as small as 60 degrees? No, so you eliminate (B) and (A) as well. This means that (C) must be the correct answer.

BECAUSE A PROBLEM-SOLVING FIGURE IS DRAWN TO SCALE, YOU CAN MEASURE LENGTHS.

Unless it is specified that a figure is not drawn to scale, you can use a pencil or other available straight edge as a ruler to measure lengths.

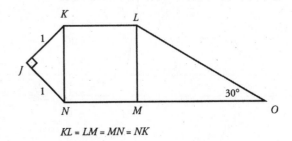

$KL = LM = MN = NK$

In the figure above, what is the length of $\overline{LO}$?

   (A) 2

   (B) $2\sqrt{2}$

   (C) $2\sqrt{3}$

   (D) 4

   (E) $4\sqrt{2}$

The correct answer is (B).

Take a piece of scratch paper (you'll be given some at the beginning of the test) and mark the length of $\overline{JK}$. The distance is 1. Now measure that distance against $\overline{LO}$.

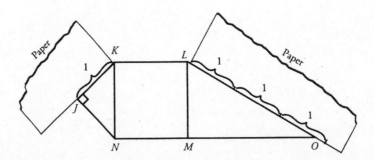

It appears to have a measurement slightly more than 2.5; make it about 2.8. Which answer is closest? The best approximation for $\sqrt{2}$ is 1.4, so (B) is 2(1.4) = 2.8.

EXERCISE 1

10 Questions • 10 Minutes

Directions: For each of the following questions, select the best of the answer choices given.

1. If $\frac{3}{4}x = 1$, then $\frac{2}{3}x =$

   (A) $\frac{1}{3}$

   (B) $\frac{1}{2}$

   (C) $\frac{2}{3}$

   (D) $\frac{8}{9}$

   (E) 2

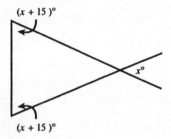

2. In the figure above, $x =$
   (A) 20°
   (B) 35°
   (C) 50°
   (D) 65°
   (E) 90°

3. If $x = \frac{y}{7}$ and $7x = 12$, then $y =$
   (A) 3
   (B) 5
   (C) 7
   (D) 12
   (E) 72

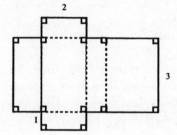

4. A rectangular box with a top is created by folding the figure above along the dotted lines. What is the volume of the box in cubic units?
   (A) 6
   (B) 9
   (C) 12
   (D) 18
   (E) 24

5. What is the difference of the areas of two squares with sides of 5 and 4, respectively?
   (A) 3
   (B) 4
   (C) 9
   (D) 16
   (E) 41

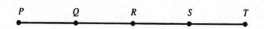

6. If the spaces between the lettered points in the figure above are all equal, then $\frac{PT}{2} - \frac{QS}{2}$ is equal to which of the following?

   (A) $PS - QR$

   (B) $QR - QS$

   (C) PR

   (D) QT

   (E) ST

7. Exactly three years before the year in which Anna was born, the year was $1980 - x$. In terms of x, on Anna's twentieth birthday, the year will be

   (A) $1977 + x$

   (B) $1997 + x$

   (C) $2003 - x$

   (D) $2003 + x$

   (E) $2006 + x$

8. If $x = k + \frac{1}{2} = \frac{k+3}{2}$, then $x =$

   (A) $\frac{1}{3}$

   (B) $\frac{1}{2}$

   (C) 1

   (D) 2

   (E) $\frac{5}{2}$

9. For how many 3-digit whole numbers is the sum of the digits equal to 3?

   (A) 4

   (B) 5

   (C) 6

   (D) 7

   (E) 8

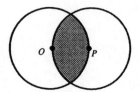

10. In the figure above, if the radius of the circles is 1, what is the perimeter of the shaded part of the figure?

    (A) $\frac{1}{6}\pi$

    (B) $\frac{2}{3}\pi$

    (C) $\frac{4}{3}\pi$

    (D) $\frac{3}{2}\pi$

    (E) Cannot be determined from the information given.

EXERCISE 2

5 Questions • 5 Minutes

> **Directions:** For each of the following questions, select the best of the answer choices given.

1. If $7 - x = 0$, then $10 - x =$
   - (A) -3
   - (B) 0
   - (C) 3
   - (D) 7
   - (E) 10

2. A triangle with sides of 4, 6, and 8 has the same perimeter as an equilateral triangle with sides of length
   - (A) 2
   - (B) $\dfrac{3}{2}$
   - (C) 3
   - (D) 6
   - (E) 8

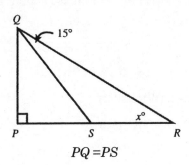

$PQ = PS$

3. In the figure above, $x =$
   - (A) $15°$
   - (B) $30°$
   - (C) $40°$
   - (D) $60°$
   - (E) $75°$

4. If x and y are negative numbers, which of the following is negative?
   - (A) xy
   - (B) $(xy)^2$
   - (C) $(x - y)^2$
   - (D) $x + y$
   - (E) $\dfrac{x}{y}$

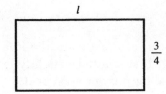

5. If the area of the rectangle shown above is equal to 1, then $l =$
   - (A) $\dfrac{4}{9}$
   - (B) 1
   - (C) $\dfrac{4}{3}$
   - (D) $\dfrac{9}{4}$
   - (E) Cannot be determined from the information given.

ANSWER KEY AND EXPLANATIONS

Exercise 1

1. D	3. D	5. C	7. C	9. C
2. C	4. A	6. E	8. E	10. C

1. **The correct answer is (D).** Solve for x. $\frac{3}{4}x = 1$, so $x = \frac{4}{3}$. Then substitute this for x in the expression $\frac{2}{3}x$. $\frac{2}{3}\left(\frac{4}{3}\right) = \frac{8}{9}$.

2. **The correct answer is (C).** Since the unlabeled angle inside the triangle is equal to x:

$$(x + 15)° + (x + 15)° + x = 180°$$

$$3x + 30° = 180°$$

$$3x = 150°$$

$$x = 50°$$

   You can also estimate the size of the angle. It seems to be slightly less than 60°, so the answer must be (C).

3. **The correct answer is (D).** Treat the two equations as simultaneous equations. You can substitute $\frac{y}{7}$ for x in the second equation. $7\left(\frac{y}{7}\right) = 12$, so $y = 12$.

4. **The correct answer is (A).** The box when assembled looks like this:

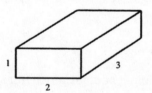

   Its volume is $1 \times 2 \times 3 = 6$.

5. **The correct answer is (C).** The question asks for:

   (Area of square with side 5) minus (area of square with side 4) = $(5 \times 5) - (4 \times 4) = 25 - 16 = 9$.

6. **The correct answer is (E).** $\frac{PT}{2}$ is $\frac{1}{2}$ the length of the entire segment. QS is $\frac{1}{2}$ the length of the segment, and $\frac{QS}{2}$ is $\frac{1}{4}$ of the segment. So $\frac{PT}{2} - \frac{QS}{2}$ is $\frac{1}{2}$ of the segment minus $\frac{1}{4}$ of the segment, which is $\frac{1}{4}$ of the length of the segment. Only (E) is $\frac{1}{4}$ the length of the segment.

   You can also assign numbers to the lengths. Assume that each segment is equal to 1. Then PT is 4, and $\frac{PT}{2} = 2$. And QS is 2, and $\frac{QS}{2} = 1$. Finally, $2 - 1 = 1$. So the correct answer choice should have a length of 1.

   (A) $3 - 1 = 2$ (WRONG!)

   (B) $1 - 2 = -1$ (WRONG!)

   (C) 2 (WRONG!)

   (D) 3 (WRONG!)

   (E) 1 (CORRECT!)

7. **The correct answer is (C).** Create a formula. Anna was born three years after $1980 - x$, so she was born in $1980 - x + 3$. Twenty years later the year will be $1980 - x + 3 + 20 = 2003 - x$.

   You can also substitute numbers. Assume $x = 1$. And then assume Anna was born three years after $1980 - 1 = 1979$, so she was born in 1982. So she will turn 20 in 2002. Substituting 1 for x in each of the answer choices:

   (A) $1977 + 1 = 1978$ (WRONG!)

   (B) $1997 + 1 = 1998$ (WRONG!)

   (C) $2003 - 1 = 2002$ (CORRECT!)

   (D) $2003 + 1 = 2004$ (WRONG!)

   (E) $2006 + 1 = 2007$ (WRONG!)

8. **The correct answer is (E).** You really have two equations:

   $$x = k + \tfrac{1}{2} \text{ and } k + \tfrac{1}{2} = \tfrac{k+3}{2}$$

   Solve for k:

   $$k + \frac{1}{2} = \frac{k+3}{2}$$
   $$2\left(k + \frac{1}{2}\right) = k + 3$$
   $$2k + 1 = k + 3$$
   $$k = 2$$

   Now substitute 2 for k:

   $$x = k + \tfrac{1}{2} = 2 + \tfrac{1}{2} = \tfrac{5}{2}$$

   You can also try testing the choices, but the process is tedious. For example, assume that $x = 1$. On that assumption, the first equation gives the value of k as $\frac{1}{2}$, but when $\frac{1}{2}$ is substituted for k in the second equation, the statement is false. So (C) is incorrect. (E), however, does work. If $x = \frac{5}{2}$, then the value of k in the first equation is 2. And substituting 2 for both ks in the second equation produces a true statement.

9. **The correct answer is (C).** They are 102, 111, 120, 201, 210, and 300. The solution is mostly a matter of mental brute force, just counting the possibilities. But that's not too much to do. The only digits that can be used are 0, 1, 2, and 3. You don't have to worry about numbers using digits of 4 or more (4 is already more than 3).

10. **The correct answer is (C).** The solution depends on seeing the following:

    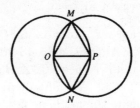

    The triangles are equilateral ($\overline{OM}$, $\overline{ON}$, $\overline{PM}$, and $\overline{PN}$ are equal and all radii), and $\angle MON$ and $\angle MPN$ are both 120°. So each arc is 120°, or $\frac{1}{3}$ of the circle. Since the radius of the circle is 1, the circumference of each circle is $2\pi(1) = 2\pi$. Therefore, each arc is $\frac{1}{3}$ of 2π, or $\frac{2}{3}\pi$. Together, they total $\frac{2}{3}\pi + \frac{2}{3}\pi = \frac{4}{3}\pi$.

    This problem can also be attacked by "guesstimation." Each arc looks to be $\frac{1}{3}$ of the circle. Use that assumption and you will select (C).

Exercise 2

1.	C	2.	D	3.	B	4.	D	5.	C

1. **The correct answer is (C).** Solve for x: $7 - x = 0$, so $7 = x$. Then substitute 7 for x in the expression $10 - x$: $10 - 7 = 3$.

2. **The correct answer is (D).** A triangle with sides of 4, 6, and 8 has a perimeter of $4 + 6 + 8 = 18$. An equilateral triangle with the same perimeter would have a side of $18 \div 3 = 6$.

3. **The correct answer is (B).** Since $PQ = PS$, $\triangle PQS$ is a 45-45-90 triangle. $\angle PQR$ is $45° + 15° = 60°$. And $x = 180° - 90° - 60° = 30°$. You should also be able to estimate the angle as 30°.

4. **The correct answer is (D).** Since x and y are negative, both (A) and (E) must be positive. As for (B) and (C), so long as neither x nor y is zero, those expressions must be positive. (Any number other than zero squared gives a positive result.) (D), however, is negative, since it represents the sum of two negative numbers. And you can also test the choices with numbers.

5. **The correct answer is (C).** Just use the formula for the area of a rectangle: $l \times \frac{3}{4} = 1$, so $l = \frac{4}{3}$. You can also test choices until you find one that works in the area formula, but you should be able to solve a simple equation like this without needing to substitute.

SUMMING IT UP

- Follow these steps when working through problem solving questions:

    1. Read the question carefully.

    2. Before solving the problem, check the answers.

    3. Eliminate choices that are completely off the radar screen.

    4. For complex questions, break down the problem.

- Solve problems by testing answer choices.

- Solve problems by substituting real numbers for variables.

- Remember that most figures are drawn to scale.

Quantitative Comparison

OVERVIEW

- **What is quantitative comparison?**
- **How do you solve quantitative comparison questions?**
- **What smart test-takers know**
- **Summing it up**

WHAT IS QUANTITATIVE COMPARISON?

For this type of question, you must compare two quantities, one shown in Column A and one shown in Column B. You must decide if one quantity is greater than the other, if the two quantities are the same, or if the relationship between the quantities cannot be determined from the information given.

For each question, you are given four answer choices:

       (A) if the quantity in Column A is the greater

       (B) if the quantity in Column B is the greater

       (C) if the two quantities are equal

       (D) if the relationship cannot be determined from the information given

Note: Since the computer processes your mouse clicks, the answer choices that appear on the monitor screen won't have letters. But for ease of reference in this book, we'll continue to refer to the letters.

GRE Quantitative Comparison Questions

Quantitative comparisons are interspersed with regular problem-solving questions and graphs in the math section. You'll get 13 to 15 quantitative comparison questions.

Quantitative comparisons cover the same mix of arithmetic, algebra, and geometry that appears in the regular problem-solving questions.

chapter 9

Here are the directions for GRE quantitative comparison questions, together with some sample questions and explanations.

Anatomy of Quantitative Comparisons

Directions: For each of the following questions two quantities are given, one in Column A and one in Column B. Compare the two quantities and choose

(A) if the quantity in Column A is greater
(B) if the quantity in Column B is greater
(C) if the two quantities are equal
(D) if the relationship cannot be determined from the information given

Common Information: In any question, information applying to both columns is centered between the columns and above the quantities in columns A and B. Any symbol that appears in both columns represents the same idea or quantity in both columns.

	Column A	Column B
1.	$\frac{1}{2}+\frac{1}{2}$	$\frac{1}{2}\times\frac{1}{2}$
2.	Twice the area of a circle with a radius of 1	Area of a circle with a radius of 2
3.	$\dfrac{6x+6y}{x+y}$	6
4.	x^2	x^3

You'll recognize quantitative comparison questions on the test by the Column A/ Column B layout. So just dismiss the directions and get right to work.

The answer ovals on your CAT monitor screen won't have letters, so just think:

First oval: A is greater. Second oval: B is greater. Third oval: A and B are equal. Fourth oval: Cannot be determined.

Centered information is often an equation, a geometry figure, or a verbal description such as "R is a square room."

You can't trust the figures in quantitative comparisons. You can trust the sequence and relationships, but you can't rely on the apparent magnitudes. An angle that looks to be 90° may not be; a line segment that looks longer than another line segment may not be; and a region that appears to be equal in area to another may not be. So use your knowledge of math instead.

The correct answer to question 1 is (A). Column A has the value 1 while Column B has the value $\frac{1}{4}$.

The correct answer to question 2 is (B). The value of Column A is 2π, and the value of Column B is 4π.

The correct answer to question 3 is (C). Simplify first by factoring and then by dividing: $6x + 6y = 6(x+y)$. Then you can divide the $x+y$ in both the numerator and the denominator of Column A, leaving just 6.

The correct answer to question 4 is (D). The variable x could be positive, negative, or even zero. Consequently, it cannot be determined which of the two quantities is larger.

HOW DO YOU SOLVE QUANTITATIVE COMPARISON QUESTIONS?

Here's a simple, five-step plan to help you solve GRE quantitative comparison questions:

Quantitative Comparisons: Getting It Right

1 Memorize the sequence of the answer choices.

2 For each question, read the centered information.

3 Compare the quantity in Column A to the quantity in Column B.

4 Do only as much work as is needed to make the comparison.

5 Choose your answer.

Now let's look at these steps in more detail.

1 **Memorize the sequence of the answer choices, but don't learn the rest of the directions.** This will save you time because you won't need to refer to them for every question.

2 **For each question, read the centered information.** Remember that the centered information governs the entire problem.

3 **Compare the quantity in Column A to the quantity in Column B.** Even though there are two quantities in each question, deal with one at a time. See how each quantity relates to the centered information.

TIP

Memorize the directions. The directions are very intuitive. Just keep this simple key in mind.

First answer choice oval = A is greater.

Second answer choice oval = B is greater.

Third answer choice oval = Columns are equal.

Fourth answer choice oval = Determination impossible.

④ **Do only as much work as is needed to make the comparison.** Simplify mathematical expressions. You shouldn't have to do involved calculations to get the answer. If you're calculating endlessly, you've probably missed the mathematical principle the question is asking about. Consider all possibilities for any unknowns. Think what would happen if special numbers such as 0, negative numbers, or fractions were put into play.

⑤ **Choose the appropriate answer oval by clicking on it with the mouse and then confirm.**

Now let's look at some additional sample quantitative comparison questions. As you read each explanation, think of how the five-step solution process applies.

Column A	Column B
$5 \times 6 \times 7 \times 8$	$5 + 6 + 7 + 8$

The correct answer is (A). Column A is 1680 while Column B is 26.

Column A	Column B
$\dfrac{1}{7} - \dfrac{1}{8}$	$\dfrac{1}{8}$

The correct answer is (B). $\dfrac{1}{7} - \dfrac{1}{8} = \dfrac{1}{56}$. $\dfrac{1}{8}$ is greater than $\dfrac{1}{56}$.

Column A	Column B
3429	$3(10^3) + 4(10^2)$ $+ 2(10^1) + 9(10^0)$

The correct answer is (C):

$$3(10^3) = 3(1000) = 3{,}000$$
$$4(10^2) = 4(100) = 400$$
$$2(10^1) = 2(10) = 20$$
$$9(10^0) = 9(1) = +\ \ 9$$
$$= 3{,}429$$

The two quantities are the same.

Column A	Column B
The product of three numbers between 3 and 4	The product of four numbers between 2 and 3

The correct answer is (D). You don't know the value of any of the numbers. If the three numbers in Column A are almost 4, then Column A could be almost as great as 64. On the other hand, the least it could be is almost 27. As for Column B, if those four numbers are almost as great as 3, then Column B could be almost 81. On the other hand, since the least they might be is 2, the least Column B could be is almost 16.

Column A	Column B

The price of a pound of cheese increased from $2.00 to $2.50.

The percent increase in the price of cheese	25%

The correct answer is (C). Remember that the centered information applies to both columns. The percent increase in the price of cheese is 25%.

Column A	Column B
$(x)(x)(x)(x)(x)$	x^5

The correct answer is (C). $(x)(x)(x)(x)(x) = x^5$. Remember that according to the directions, any symbol that appears in both columns represents the same idea or quantity in both columns. So the x on the left means the same thing as the x on the right, and the two expressions are the same.

WHAT SMART TEST-TAKERS KNOW

A COMPARISON IS FOREVER.

In quantitative comparisons, the first answer choice (A) is correct only if the quantity is always greater than that in Column B. The reverse is true of the second oval (B); it must always be greater than the information in Column A. If you choose the third oval (C), it means that the two quantities are *always* equal. The condition must hold true regardless of what number you plug in for a variable.

QUANTITATIVE COMPARISONS ARE NOT ABOUT CALCULATING.

If you find yourself calculating up a storm on a quantitative comparison, you've probably missed the boat. There's sure to be a simpler, shorter way to solve the problem. Find a way to reduce the amount of actual math you need to do. Take a look at these examples.

Column A	Column B
$31 \times 32 \times 33$ $\times 34 \times 35$	$32 \times 33 \times 34$ $\times 35 \times 36$

You don't have to do any calculations to get the answer. You would be comparing the product of five consecutive integers, but notice that the integers in Column B are greater. Therefore, the product of those numbers would be greater than Column A. So, the correct answer is (B) and you didn't have to multiply a thing.

ALERT!

Long calculations are a tip-off that something's wrong. If a quantitative comparison seems to require a calculator, you are not looking at it correctly. Try to find a shortcut such as simplification.

Column A	Column B

The formula for the volume of a right circular cylinder is $V = \pi r^2 h$

The volume of a right circular cylinder with $r = 3$ and $h = 6$	The volume of a right circular cylinder with $r = 6$ and $h = 3$

You might think that for this question you absolutely have to do the complete calculations to find the volume of each cylinder. But you don't! Take a look at how simply this problem can be solved.

Volume $A = \pi(3^2)(6) = (3.14)(3)(3)(6)$

Volume $B = \pi(6^2)(3) = (3.14)(6)(6)(3)$

Since you're doing the same operation for both formulas—multiplying by 3.14—that can be eliminated. So the problem then shifts to the other factors: Which is larger, $(3^2)(6)$ or $(6^2)(3)$? At this point you should be able to see that the second one is greater. If you still need to take it another step, multiply $(3^2)(6) = (9)(6) = 54$ and then $(6^2)(3) = (36)(3)$. You don't have to finish because you can see that $(36)(3)$ is greater than 54.

IF THE MATH IS NOT DIFFICULT, YOU SHOULD DO IT.

Column A	Column B
$10,000,001 + 0.009$	$10,000,002 - 0.00199$

The correct answer is (B). The indicated addition and subtraction is not that difficult, so you won't lose much time doing it. Instead of trying to find an elegant logical solution to the comparison, use the crude method of adding and subtracting.

Column A	Column B
$(x^3)(x^2)(x^7)$	$(x^3)^4$

The correct answer is (C). Again, you should just do the operations that are indicated. Column A becomes x^{12}; so too does Column B.

WHEN THE CENTERED INFORMATION CONTAINS UNKNOWNS, YOU SHOULD SOLVE FOR THE UNKNOWNS.

Column A	Column B
$3x = 12$	$4y = 20$
x	y

The correct answer is (B). You need values for x and y, so solve for both.

IT PAYS TO SIMPLIFY.

Simplify complex arithmetic or algebraic expressions before trying to make a comparison.

Column A	Column B
$\dfrac{2,000,000}{200,000}$	$\dfrac{1,000}{100}$

The correct answer is (C). Simplify the comparison by dividing, and you wind up comparing $\frac{20}{2}$, which is 10, with $\frac{10}{1}$, which is also 10.

YOU CAN SIMPLIFY BY ADDING OR SUBTRACTING THE SAME VALUE IN EACH COLUMN.

Column A	Column B
$4x + 5$	$3x + 6$

The correct answer is (D). At first, however, you may not be able to see that the relationship is indeterminate. Start by subtracting 5 from both sides of the comparison. The result is:

Column A	Column B
$4x$	$3x + 1$

Now subtract $3x$ from both sides:

Column A	Column B
x	1

In this form, the comparison is fairly easy. Since you have no information about x, the answer must be (D).

TIP

Use the "good-enough" principle. Do only so much work as you have to to make the comparison. Once you know that one column is greater than the other, enter the answer. You do not have to find out how much greater.

YOU CAN SIMPLIFY BY MULTIPLYING OR DIVIDING EACH COLUMN BY THE SAME POSITIVE NUMBER.

Here's another example, in which the quantities in both columns can be simplified by dividing.

Column A	Column B
$9^{99} - 9^{98}$	9^{98}

The correct answer is (A). Divide both sides by 9^{98}:

$\dfrac{9^{99} - 9^{98}}{9^{98}}$	$\dfrac{9^{98}}{9^{98}}$
$9^1 - 9^0$	9^0
$9 - 1$	1
8	1

This proves that Column A is greater. (It doesn't prove how much greater since dividing changed the ratio between the two quantities, but we are only interested in which is greater—not how much greater.)

WARNING! DO NOT SIMPLIFY BY MULTIPLICATION OR DIVISION UNLESS YOU KNOW THE QUANTITY YOU ARE USING IS POSITIVE.

Column A	Column B
$3x$	$4x$

The correct answer is (D). But watch what happens if you try to divide both quantities by x:

$\dfrac{3x}{x} = 3$	$\dfrac{4x}{x} = 4$

This move is wrong since you do not know for certain that x is positive. As a result, you arrive at the erroneous conclusion that Column B is greater. You can prove this by trying a couple of different values for x. If x is a number like 2 or 5, it is true that Column B is greater. But if x is a negative number, then Column A is greater. Or if x is zero, the columns are equal. This technique only works when you know for certain that the term you are dividing or multiplying by is positive.

YOU HAVE TO CONSIDER ALL THE POSSIBILITIES.

When there are unknowns in the quantities being compared, you have to remember to consider all possibilities for what those unknowns might be. For example, an unknown might be 1, 0, a fraction, or a negative number. In each of these cases, the number has special properties that will affect your calculations.

ALERT!

Variables are shifty. Unless otherwise restricted, a variable can be positive, negative, or even zero.

AN UNKNOWN MIGHT BE ZERO.

Zero has special properties that come into play when you plug it in for an unknown.

Column A	**Column B**
	$x > 0, y > 0, z = 0$	
$3z(2x + 5y)$	$3x(2z + 5y)$

If $z = 0$, then $3z = 0$ and the product of Column A is 0. In Column B, though, $2z = 0$, so it comes out of the comparison. The product will be $(3x)(5y)$, which will be a positive number. This means that (B) is the correct answer choice.

Column A	**Column B**
	$x < 0, y > 0, z = 0$	
$3z(2x + 5y)$	$3x(2z + 5y)$

Again, the product of Column A is 0, because $3z$ still equals 0. The change comes in Column B. Because x is less than 0, $3x$ will be negative and $5y$ will be positive, so the product will be a negative number. This time, (A) is the correct answer.

AN UNKNOWN MIGHT BE A NEGATIVE NUMBER.

Column A	**Column B**
	$3x = 4y$	
x	y

Don't think that (A) is the correct answer, even though if x and y are positive, x is greater than y. What if x and y are negative, as in $3(-4) = 4(-3)$; then y is greater than x. And if x and y are both zero, both columns are equal. Since you have no way of knowing what the values are, the correct answer is (D).

AN UNKNOWN MIGHT BE A FRACTION.

Column A	**Column B**
	$x > 0$ and $x \neq 1$	
x^2	x

The correct answer to this comparison is (D). If x is greater than 1, then x^2 is greater than x. But if x^2 is between 0 and 1—a fraction—then x^2 is less than x.

PROPER FRACTIONS CAN PLAY TRICKS.

Remember that a proper fraction raised to a power is less than the fraction itself.

Column A	Column B
$\dfrac{27}{41}$	$\left(\dfrac{27}{41}\right)^{15}$

If you keep the math principle in mind, you don't even have to think about doing these calculations. Since each successive multiplication would result in a smaller value, Column A will always be greater than Column B, so your answer is (A).

IN QUANTITATIVE COMPARISONS, FIGURES ARE NOT NECESSARILY DRAWN TO SCALE.

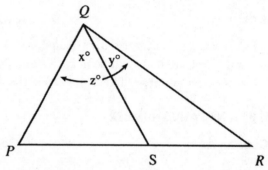

	Column A	Column B
1.	PS	PR
2.	PS	SR
3.	x	z
4.	x	y

Figures in quantitative comparison questions are not necessarily drawn to scale. This is very important. Although you can rely upon the arrangement of points, angles, lines, etc., you cannot trust the apparent magnitude of geometrical quantities.

The answer to question 1 is (B). Since point S lies between P and R, the entire length of $\overline{PR}$ must be longer than that part which is $\overline{PS}$.

The answer to question 2 is (D). You are not entitled to assume anything about the location of point S—other than that it is on $\overline{PR}$ somewhere between P and R. Thus, although it looks like $\overline{PS}$ is longer than $\overline{SR}$, you cannot determine that as a matter of mathematics.

The answer to question 3 is (B). m$\angle z$ is equal to $x + y$, so the entire measure of angle z must be greater than just that part labeled x.

The answer to question 4 is (D). The relative size of angles x and y is determined by the location of point S. Again, although S lies somewhere between P and R, its exact location cannot be mathematically determined. So the relative sizes of x and y remain an unknown.

PLUGGING IN NUMBERS CAN HELP.

If you're stuck on a comparison with unknowns, try substituting numbers. Choose the numbers at random and plug them into the equations. Do this with three different substitutions and see if there is any consistent result. It's not a guarantee, but it's definitely worth a shot.

STRATEGIC GUESSING CAN RAISE YOUR SCORE.

When all else fails, call up your guessing skills. Here's how you can tip the scales in your favor, even if it's only a little bit.

- If a comparison involves only numbers without any unknowns, chances are that you'll be able to figure out the quantities and make a comparison. So in this situation, don't guess (D).
- If the comparison does contain an unknown or a figure, as a last resort guess (D).

Quantitative comparisons can be your friend. Almost half the math questions on the GRE are quantitative comparisons. That means that knowing how to handle them can give a major boost to your score.

EXERCISE 1

15 Questions • 12 Minutes

> **Directions:** For each of the following questions two quantities are given, one in Column A and one in Column B. Compare the two quantities and choose
>
> **(A)** if the quantity in Column A is greater
> **(B)** if the quantity in Column B is greater
> **(C)** if the two quantities are equal
> **(D)** if the relationship cannot be determined from the information given
>
> *Common Information:* In any question, information applying to both columns is centered between the columns and above the quantities in columns A and B. Any symbol that appears in both columns represents the same idea or quantity in both columns.

	Column A	**Column B**
1.	$\sqrt{9+16}$	7

$$7n = 7$$

	Column A	**Column B**
2.	$\dfrac{7}{n}$	$\dfrac{n}{7}$
3.	$\left(\dfrac{1}{2}\right)^{11}$	$\left(-\dfrac{1}{2}\right)^{11}$

The digit 3 in the numeral 123,456 represents 3×10^{n}

	Column A	**Column B**
4.	n	5
5.	The greatest prime number less than 29	23

Mary has $5 less than Sam,
and Mark has half as much money as Sam.

	Column A	**Column B**
6.	Amount of money that Mary has	Amount of money that Mark has

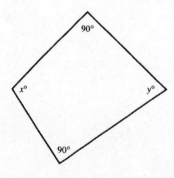

	Column A	**Column B**
7.	x	y

Column A	**Column B**

8. $\dfrac{0.125}{4}$ | $\dfrac{0.25}{8}$

$$xy = 25$$

9. x | y

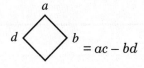

10. yz | xz

x and y are positive integers and $x < y$

11. $\dfrac{x}{y}$ | $\sqrt{\dfrac{x}{y}}$

$$x + y \neq 0$$

12. $\dfrac{5x + 5y}{x + y}$ | 5

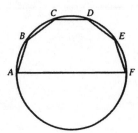

$$\begin{array}{c} a \\ d \diamondsuit b \\ c \end{array} = ac - bd$$

(for all non-zero numbers a, b, c, d)

13. $\begin{array}{c} 4 \\ 1 \diamondsuit 3 \\ 2 \end{array}$ | 4

14. $\begin{array}{c} x \\ y \diamondsuit y \\ x \end{array}$ | $(x + y)(x - y)$

$\overline{AF}$ is the diameter of the circle.
$$\overline{AF} = 2$$

15. Area of polygon A, B, C, D, E, F | $\dfrac{\pi}{2}$

EXERCISE 2

8 Questions • 8 Minutes

Directions: For each of the following questions two quantities are given, one in Column A and one in Column B. Compare the two quantities and choose

(A) if the quantity in Column A is greater
(B) if the quantity in Column B is greater
(C) if the two quantities are equal
(D) if the relationship cannot be determined from the information given

Common Information: In any question, information applying to both columns is centered between the columns and above the quantities in columns A and B. Any symbol that appears in both columns represents the same idea or quantity in both columns.

	Column A	Column B
1.	$5 \times (6 \times 7) \times 8$	$8 \times (5 \times 6) \times 7$

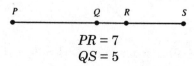

$$PR = 7$$
$$QS = 5$$

2.	QR	2

The weight of package x is more than twice the weights of packages y and z combined.

3.	The weight of package z	$\dfrac{1}{3}$ the weight of package x

$$x + y > 3$$

4.	$\dfrac{x + y}{3}$	$\dfrac{3}{x + y}$

$$a + 2b = 3$$
$$a - 2b = 3$$

5.	a	b

<u>Column A</u>   <u>Column B</u>

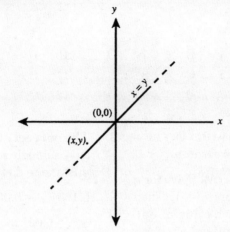

6. x y

7.   Volume of a rectangular solid   Volume of a rectangular solid
          with sides of lengths   with sides of lengths
      $\frac{1}{2}, \frac{1}{3}$, and $\frac{1}{6}$ $\frac{1}{6}, \frac{1}{6}$, and 1

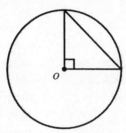

O is the center of the circle.
The area of the triangle is 4.

8.   Radius of the circle   4

ANSWER KEY AND EXPLANATIONS

Exercise 1

1.	B	4.	B	7.	D	10.	D	13.	A
2.	A	5.	C	8.	C	11.	B	14.	C
3.	A	6.	D	9.	D	12.	C	15.	B

1. **The correct answer is (B).** $\sqrt{9+16} = \sqrt{25} = 5$. So Column B is greater.

2. **The correct answer is (A).** Solve for n in the centered equation: $n = 1$. Then substitute 1 for n in each column. Column A is $\frac{7}{1} = 7$; Column B is $\frac{1}{7}$.

3. **The correct answer is (A).** Column A is a positive number (a positive number raised to any power is positive). Column B is a negative number (a negative number raised to an odd power is negative).

4. **The correct answer is (B).** The digit 3 in 123,456 is the thousands digit. It represents 3,000, which is equal to 3×10^3. So $n = 3$.

5. **The correct answer is (C).** 23 is the greatest prime number less than 29. (24, 25, 26, 27, and 28 are not primes.)

6. **The correct answer is (D).** You have enough information to conclude that both Mary and Mark have less money than Sam, but you don't have enough information to draw a conclusion about how much each has.

   If you need to, you can assume some numbers. If Sam has $20, then Mary has $15 and Mark has $10. Eliminate (B) and (C). If Sam has $10, then Mary has $5 and Mark also has $5. Eliminate (A) as well. So the correct choice is (D).

7. **The correct answer is (D).** Since the figure is a quadrilateral, the measures of the four interior angles total 360°. So, $x + y = 180°$, but you cannot draw any conclusions about the size of x or the size of y.

8. **The correct answer is (C).** The math is easy enough so that it would not be a mistake to do the division:

   $0.125 \div 4 = 0.03125$ and

   $\frac{0.25}{8} = 0.03125$.

   Division, however, is not the most elegant solution. Since 4 and 8 are positive numbers, you can multiply both sides of the comparison by both 4 and 8. Column A becomes 8(0.125) and Column B becomes 4(0.25). These operations are easier than division: $8(0.125) = 1$ and $4(0.25) = 1$.

   You can avoid the math altogether by reasoning that the numerator in the fraction in Column A is half the numerator of the fraction in Column B, and the denominator in Column A is half the denominator in Column B. So, the two fractions are equivalent, as are $\frac{1}{2}$ and $\frac{4}{8}$.

9. **The correct answer is (D).** x and y might be 5 and 5. But they might also be 1 and 25 or –1 and –25.

10. **The correct answer is (D).** Don't make the mistake of dividing both sides of the comparison by z. You can't be sure that z is positive.

    The relationship is indeterminate because you don't know the signs of the numbers. If y and z are both negative, while x is positive, then yz is positive and xz is negative (and Column A is greater). If y is negative but x and z are positive, then yz is negative and xz is positive (and Column B is greater). If z happens to be zero, then yz and xz are equal.

11. **The correct answer is (B).** There are several ways to attack this comparison. The most sophisticated is to reason that since $x < y$ (and both are positive integers), $\frac{x}{y}$ is a fraction. Moreover, the square root of a fraction is larger than the fraction itself. (For example, $\sqrt{\frac{1}{4}} = \frac{1}{2}$, and $\frac{1}{2} > \frac{1}{4}$.)

You can also grind out a solution by manipulating both sides of the comparison. Start by squaring both sides. Column A becomes $\frac{x^2}{y^2}$ and Column B becomes $\frac{x}{y}$. Since x and y are both positive, you can then divide both sides by x and multiply both sides by y. Column A becomes $\frac{x}{y}$ and Column B becomes 1. At this point, you should be able to see that $\frac{x}{y}$ is less than 1. If you still are not sure, multiply both sides by y again. Column A becomes simply x and Column B simply y. The centered information states specifically that $x < y$. Finally, you could substitute some numbers.

12. **The correct answer is (C).** Factor the expression in Column A: $5x + 5y = 5(x + y)$. Then $\frac{x+y}{x+y} = 1$, so Column A is just 5. Of course, if you didn't see the possibility of factoring, you could substitute a few simple numbers. The fact that one or two substitutions show the columns to be equal is not proof that the correct answer is (C), but substitution allows you to eliminate (A) and (B) and strongly guess that the answer is (C) rather than (D).

13. **The correct answer is (A).** Do the indicated operations. $(4)(2) - (3)(1) = 8 - 3 = 5$. So Column A is greater.

14. **The correct answer is (C).** Set up the operation: $(x)(x) - (y)(y) = x^2 - y^2$. By now, you should recognize that this can be factored:

$$x^2 - y^2 = (x + y)(x - y)$$

So the two columns are equal.

15. **The correct answer is (B).** The "good enough" principle is the key to this comparison. First, since the circle has a diameter of 2, it has a radius of 1 and an area of $\pi(1^2) = \pi$. Whatever the area of the polygon really is, it is less than that of the semicircle. So the area of the polygon is less than $\frac{\pi}{2}$.

Exercise 2

1.	C	3.	D	5.	A	7.	C
2.	D	4.	A	6.	B	8.	B

1.   **The correct answer is (C).** There is no need even to do the multiplication. Since the order of multiplication is irrelevant, the two columns are equal.

2.   **The correct answer is (D).** Use the technique of distorting the figure:

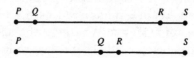

3.   **The correct answer is (D).** No information is supplied about the actual weights of the packages. Assume some numbers. If $x = 100$, $y = 1$, and $z = 1$, then $\frac{1}{3}x > z$. If $x = 100$, $y = 1$, and $z = 48$, then $\frac{1}{3}x < z$.

4.   **The correct answer is (A).** You can simplify across the comparison. Multiply both sides by 3 and both sides by $(x + y)$ (you know $x + y$ is positive). Column A becomes $(x + y)^2$ and Column B becomes 3^2. Take the square root of both sides. Column A becomes $x + y$; Column B becomes 3. Since $x + y > 3$, Column A is larger.

You can reason to the same conclusion. Since $x + y$ is greater than 3, Column A is greater than $\frac{3}{3}$, while Column B is less than $\frac{3}{3}$. In other words, Column A is greater than 1 and Column B is a fraction.

5.   **The correct answer is (A).** Solve the centered equations by adding them together. $2a = 6$, so $a = 3$. Thus, b must be zero.

6.   **The correct answer is (B).** Since the point (x,y) is above the line $x = y$, the absolute value of x is greater than the absolute value of y. But both coordinates are negative. So x is less than y. For example, (x,y) might be $(-3, -2)$.

7.   **The correct answer is (C).** The calculations are simple, so do them. $\frac{1}{2} \times \frac{1}{3} \times \frac{1}{6} = \frac{1}{36}$ and $\frac{1}{6} \times \frac{1}{6} \times 1 = \frac{1}{36}$. The volumes are equal.

8.   **The correct answer is (B).** The two sides of the triangle that form a right angle can be treated as altitude and base. Since they are both radii of the circle, they are equal. Using r to represent their length:

$$\frac{1}{2}(r)(r) = 4$$
$$r^2 = 8$$
$$r = 2\sqrt{2}$$

SUMMING IT UP

- Follow these steps when solving quantitative comparison problems:

    1. Memorize the answer choices.

    2. Read the centered information for each question.

    3. Only do as much work as needed to make the comparison.

- Quantitative comparisons are not about calculating. If you find yourself performing a long calculation, you've probably missed an important math principle in the problem.

- Consider all the possibilities for unknowns, including 1, 0, fractions, and negative integers.

- Remember that figures are not necessarily drawn to scale.

Graphs

chapter 10

OVERVIEW

- **What is a graph?**
- **How do you solve graph questions?**
- **What smart test-takers know**
- **Summing it up**

WHAT IS A GRAPH?

A graph is really just a picture of some numbers. Graphs are useful because you can literally see "at a glance" various comparisons and trends.

Learning to read graphs is not that difficult once you understand the fundamental premise underlying all graphs: "One picture is worth a thousand words."

GRE Graph Questions

Graph questions form a separate set within the mathematics section because the questions are based on the graph. Graph questions are interspersed with problem-solving questions and quantitative comparisons in the scored math section.

The information on which graph questions are based may be presented in several different formats:

- Table or chart
- Bar graph
- Line graph
- Pie chart

The directions for GRE graph questions are the same as the directions for regular problem-solving questions. They look like this:

> **Directions:** For each of the following questions, select the best of the answer choices given.

Now let's look at some typical GRE graph questions.

Anatomy of Graph Questions

Directions: For each of the following questions, select the best of the answer choices given.

QUESTIONS 1 AND 2 REFER TO THE FOLLOWING GRAPH.

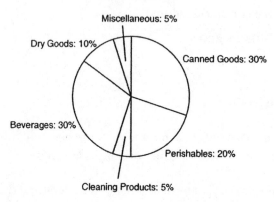

Store Inventory
(Total = $10,000)

The dollar value of the Store Inventory of canned goods and perishables combined is:

(A) $1000

(B) $1500

(C) $2500

(D) $5000

(E) $6000

The correct answer is (D). Together, canned goods and perishables account for 50% of the inventory, and 50% of $10,000 is $5000.

The dollar value of the beverages is how much greater than the dollar value of the dry goods?

(A) $500

(B) $750

(C) $2000

(D) $2500

(E) $5000

This is a simple pie chart. The size of each "slice" corresponds to the numerical value of the sector—in this case, the dollar value of that part of the store's inventory.

The correct answer is (C). Beverages account for $3000 and dry goods for $1000. So the difference is $2000.

HOW DO YOU SOLVE GRAPH QUESTIONS?

Here's a simple three-step process to help you solve GRE graph questions:

Graphs: Getting It Right

1 Determine what kind of graph you have.

2 Read all the labels.

3 Answer the questions.

Now let's look at these steps in more detail.

1 **Determine what kind of graph you have.** Different graphs give different types of information in different forms. The GRE can include bar graphs, pie charts, line graphs, and simple charts.

2 **Read all the labels.** Graphs may have a title, legends, and different kinds of accompanying information. Often the key to a question is some clarifying remark contained in an inset or a footnote.

3 **Answer the questions.** Make sure that you estimate and approximate whenever possible.

Now let's look at some additional sample graph questions. As you read the answers, consider how the three-step solution process applies.

BUDGET OF COUNTRY X (IN MILLIONS OF DOLLARS)

	1991	1992	1993	1994	1995
Domestic	$200	$300	$400	$500	$600
Military	$400	$400	$300	$250	$500
Debt	$300	$250	$350	$400	$400

What was the total budget of Country X in 1995?

(A) $1.5 million

(B) $15 million

(C) $1 billion

(D) $1.5 billion

(E) $15 billion

The correct answer is (D). The total for 1995 is $600 + $500 + $400 = $1500 million, which is equal to $1.5 billion.

NOTE

How does "graph math" differ? It does not. All of the questions based on a graph are solved using the same basic math principles used to answer other problem-solving questions.

NOTE

How important are graphs? Historically, graphs have accounted for the smallest portion of the math part of the exam.

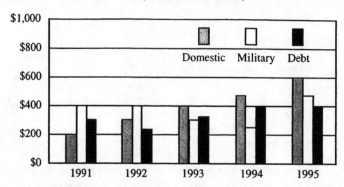

For Country X, domestic expenditures in 1995 were how much greater than domestic expenditures in 1993?

(A) $20 million

(B) $100 million

(C) $200 million

(D) $250 million

(E) $500 million

The correct answer is (C). For 1995, domestic expenditures were $600 million and in 1993 they were $400 million.

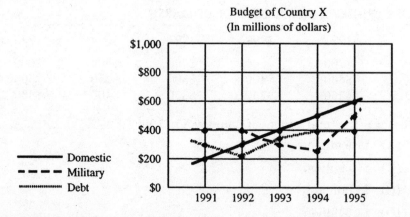

The percent increase in military spending by Country X from 1994 to 1995 was approximately

(A) 10%

(B) 50%

(C) 100%

(D) 150%

(E) 200%

The correct answer is (C). In 1994, military spending was approximately $250 million; in 1995 approximately $500 million.

ALERT!

Percents can be a trap. Remember that percents are different from absolute quantities. In graph questions, you often have to convert from one to the other.

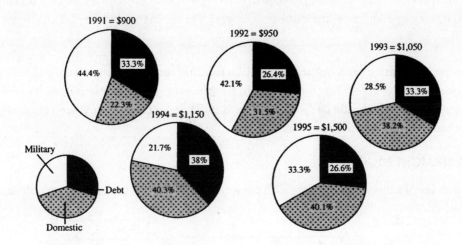

Budget of Country X
(In millions of dollars)

In which year did debt account for the greatest percentage of the budget of Country X?

(A) 1991

(B) 1992

(C) 1993

(D) 1994

(E) 1995

The correct answer is (D).

WHAT SMART TEST-TAKERS KNOW

READ THE GRAPH FIRST.

Take an overview of the graph to make sure that you understand its important features, but do not try to memorize any details. The graph is there for you to refer to when you need it.

To a certain extent, graph questions are like reading comprehension questions: Some test the most general level of understanding, while others test subtle points. Your first reading of the graph should be for its main points. Then you can go back for details if you need them.

USE A STRAIGHT EDGE.

TIP

Read all graph labels carefully. Before you try to answer a question, make sure that you understand the important features of the graph.

Use the edge of a piece of paper (scratch paper or even a pencil) to make the graph easier to read.

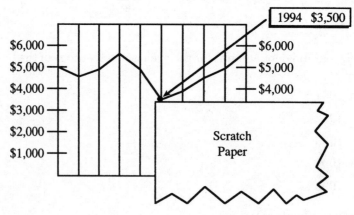

"GUESSTIMATE."

ALERT!

Units can be a trap. Make sure that you correctly identify the units used in the graph, e.g., thousands of dollars or millions of dollars.

What was the ratio of 1994 to 1995?

(A) $\frac{1}{5}$

(B) $\frac{2}{5}$

(C) $\frac{1}{2}$

(D) $\frac{2}{3}$

(E) $\frac{3}{4}$

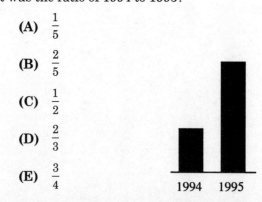

The correct answer is (B). You should be able to "guesstimate" this answer. The length of bar on the left is more than $\frac{1}{5}$ but less than $\frac{1}{2}$ the length of the bar that is on the right.

EXERCISE 1

5 Questions • 5 Minutes

> **Directions:** For each of the following questions, select the best of the answer choices given.

QUESTIONS 1–5 REFER TO THE FOLLOWING GRAPH.

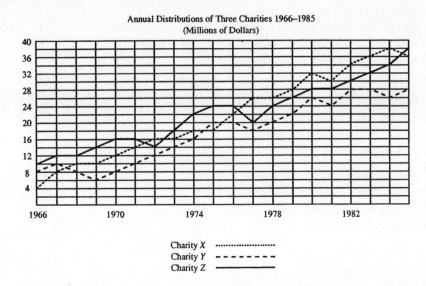

Annual Distributions of Three Charities 1966–1985
(Millions of Dollars)

Charity X ················
Charity Y − − − − − −
Charity Z ——————

1. For how many years was the annual distribution of Charity X greater than those of both Charity Y and Charity Z?

   (A) 4

   (B) 9

   (C) 11

   (D) 14

   (E) 15

2. From 1971 to 1982, by how many millions of dollars did the annual distribution by Charity Z increase?

   (A) 8

   (B) 12

   (C) 14

   (D) 16

   (E) 18

3. From 1970 to 1981, by what percent did the annual distribution by Charity X increase?

   (A) 100%

   (B) 150%

   (C) 200%

   (D) 250%

   (E) 300%

4. In 1977, what were the combined annual distributions of Charity X and Charity Z (in millions of dollars)?

   (A) 38

   (B) 44

   (C) 46

   (D) 52

   (E) 64

5. Which of the following statements can be inferred from the information given?

    (A) For each year after the first year shown, annual distributions by Charity Y failed to increase in exactly four years.

    (B) In 1977, annual distributions for exactly one of the charities fell while those of the other two charities increased.

    (C) For the entire time period shown, total combined annual disbursements for the three charities increased by 900%.

    (D) For the years 1978 and 1979 combined, Charity X accounted for more than $\frac{1}{3}$ of all money distributed by the three charities combined.

    (E) For the entire time period shown, there were exactly two years in which annual distributions declined for all three charities.

EXERCISE 2

3 Questions • 3 Minutes

Directions: For each of the following questions, select the best of the answer choices given.

QUESTIONS 1–3 REFER TO THE FOLLOWING GRAPH.

NUMBER OF VISITORS TO HOTEL CONVENTION CENTER K

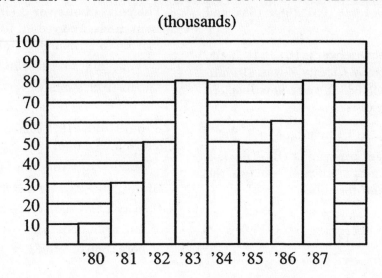

1. For the period shown, what was the amount of the greatest increase in the number of visitors from one year to the next?

   (A) 10,000

   (B) 20,000

   (C) 30,000

   (D) 70,000

   (E) 80,000

2. For the period 1982 to 1986 inclusive, what was the average (arithmetic mean) number of visitors per year?

   (A) 48,000

   (B) 56,000

   (C) 59,250

   (D) 75,000

   (E) 84,000

3. In which of the years from 1981 to 1985 did the number of visitors change by the greatest percent over the previous year?

   (A) 1981

   (B) 1982

   (C) 1983

   (D) 1984

   (E) 1985

ANSWER KEY AND EXPLANATIONS

Exercise 1

| 1. | B | 2. | C | 3. | B | 4. | C | 5. | D |

1. **The correct answer is (B).** This is purely a graph-reading question. In nine years, the annual distribution of Charity X exceeded the distributions of both Charity Y and Charity Z: 1972, 1977, 1978, 1979, 1980, 1981, 1982, 1983, and 1984.

2. **The correct answer is (C).** In 1971, the distribution by Charity Z was $16 million, and in 1982 it was $30 million. So the difference is:

$$30 - 16 = \$14 \text{ million}$$

3. **The correct answer is (B).** This is a percent change question, so use the "change-over" formula:

$$\frac{1981-1970}{1970} = \frac{30-12}{12} = \frac{18}{12} = \frac{3}{2} = 150\%$$

4. **The correct answer is (C).** Find the data you need and add:

Charity X in 1977 + Charity Z in 1977 = $26 + 20 = \$46$ million

5. **The correct answer is (D).** This statement can be inferred. In 1978, the three charities distributed a total of:

$$26 + 20 + 24 = 70$$

And in 1979, a total of:

$$28 + 22 + 26 = 76$$

So in 1978 and 1979 combined, the three distributed a total of:

$$70 + 76 = 146$$

Of this, $26 + 28 = 54$ was distributed by Charity X. So Charity X accounted for $\frac{54}{146}$ of all distributions in the two years, which is more than one third.

Exercise 2

| 1. | C | 2. | B | 3. | A |

1. **The correct answer is (C).** Here, you should rely on the fact that the figure is drawn to scale. Look for the greatest distance between two adjacent bars (provided the bar to the right is longer, since we are looking for the greatest *increase*). The greatest difference is between the bar for 1982 and that for 1983. It's a simple matter to do the subtraction:

    $$80,000 - 50,000 = 30,000$$

    Or you could also use the edge of a sheet of paper. Measure the difference between the two bars and compare that difference against the scale.

2. **The correct answer is (B).** This item asks you to calculate an average. Just make sure you get the right years. Since the scale indicates thousands of visitors, you can work with the units in the scale and later add the "thousands":

    $$\frac{50+80+50+40+60}{5} = \frac{280}{5} = 56$$

    This means that the average number of visitors each year for that particular period was 56,000.

3. **The correct answer is (A).** This item asks about percent change, and for percent change you can use the "change-over" formula. The largest percent increase occurred from 1980 to 1981:

    $$\frac{30-10}{10} = \frac{20}{10} = 2 = 200\%$$

    At this point, keep in mind two points about questions that ask you to find the largest percent change. First, the answer to such a question is not likely to be the change that shows the largest difference in absolute terms. Here, for example, the largest increase in the number of visitors occurred between 1982 and 1983, a change of 30,000, but that was a percent increase of only:

    $$\frac{80-50}{50} = \frac{30}{50} = 60\%$$

    The point of asking such a question is to determine whether you understand the difference between a change in absolute terms and relative change.

    Second, since percent change is a relative change—relative to the initial quantity—given the same change in absolute terms, the smaller the initial quantity, the larger the relative change. For example, think about what a change of ten units means for various starting points. For a starting point of 1, an increase of 10 units is an increase of 1000 percent. For a starting point of 10, an increase of 10 units is an increase of 100 percent. For a starting point of 100, an increase of 10 units is an increase of 10 percent, and so on.

SUMMING IT UP

- Follow these steps when solving graph problems:

    1. First determine what kind of graph you are looking at.

    2. Read all the labels.

    3. Answer the questions.

GRE Math Review

In order to solve a mathematical problem, it is essential to know the mathematical meaning of the words used. There are many expressions that have the same meaning in mathematics. These expressions may indicate a relationship between quantities or an operation (addition, subtraction, multiplication, division) to be performed. This chapter will help you to recognize some of the mathematical synonyms commonly found in word problems.

EXPRESSIONS

Equality

The following expressions all indicate that two quantities are equal (=):

is equal to
is the same as
the result is
yields
gives

Also, the word "is" is often used to mean "equals," as in "8 *is* 5 more than 3," which translates to "8 = 5 + 3."

Addition

The following expressions all indicate that the numbers A and B are to be added:

$A + B$	$2 + 3$
the sum of A and B	the sum of 2 and 3
the total of A and B	the total of 2 and 3
A added to B	2 added to 3
A increased by B	2 increased by 3
A more than B	2 more than 3
A greater than B	2 greater than 3

chapter 11

Subtraction

The following expressions all indicate that the number B is to be subtracted from the number A:

$A - B$	$10 - 3$
A minus B	10 minus 3
A less B	10 less 3
the difference of A and B	the difference of 10 and 3
from A subtract B	from 10 subtract 3
A take away B	10 take away 3
A decreased by B	10 decreased by 3
A diminished by B	10 diminished by 3
B is subtracted from A	3 is subtracted from 10
B less than A	3 less than 10

Multiplication

If the numbers A and B are to be multiplied ($A \times B$), the following expressions may be used:

$A \times B$	2×3
A multiplied by B	2 multiplied by 3
the product of A and B	the product of 2 and 3

The parts of a multiplication problem are indicated in the example below:

$$
\begin{array}{rl}
15 & \text{(multiplicand)} \\
\times\,10 & \text{(multiplier)} \\
\hline
150 & \text{(product)}
\end{array}
$$

Other ways of indicating multiplication are:

Parentheses: $A \times B = (A)(B)$

Dots: $A \times B = A \cdot B$

In algebra, letters next to each other: $A \times B = AB$

A **coefficient** is a number by which to multiply a variable, such as in $3B$, where 3 is the coefficient.

Inequalities

When two numbers are not necessarily equal to each other, this idea can be expressed by using the "greater than" symbol (>) or the "less than" symbol (<). The wider part of the wedge is always toward the greater number.

$A > B$	$A < B$
A is greater than B	A is less than B
$A \geq B$	$A \leq B$
A is greater than or equal to B	A is less than or equal to B

An **integer** can be defined informally as a whole number, either positive or negative, including zero, e.g., +5, −10, 0, +30, −62, etc.

A **prime number** can be defined informally as a whole number (positive only) with exactly two factors, namely itself and 1, e.g., 1, 2, 3, 5, 7, 11, 13, 17, 19, etc.

Division

Division of the numbers A and B (in the order $A \div B$) may be indicated in the following ways. (See also the discussion of fractions.)

$A \div B$	$14 \div 2$
A divided by B	14 divided by 2
the quotient of A and B	the quotient of 14 and 2

The parts of a division problem are indicated in the example below:

$$5\tfrac{1}{7} \text{ (quotient)}$$
$$\text{(divisor) } 7\overline{)36} \text{ (dividend)}$$
$$\underline{35}$$
$$1 \text{ (remainder)}$$

Factors and Divisors

The relationship $A \times B = C$, for any whole numbers A, B, and C, may be expressed as:

$A \times B = C$	$2 \times 3 = 6$
A and B are factors of C	2 and 3 are factors of 6
A and B are divisors of C	2 and 3 are divisors of 6
C is divisible by A and by B	6 is divisible by 2 and by 3
C is a multiple of A and of B	6 is a multiple of 2 and of 3

Symbols

Common symbols used on the exam are*:

$\neq$	is not equal to
$>$	is greater than ($3 > 2$)
$<$	is less than ($2 < 3$)
$\geq$	is greater than or equal to
$\leq$	is less than or equal to
: and ::	is to; the ratio to (see also section on ratios)
$\sqrt{\ }$	radical sign—used without a number, it indicates the square root of ($\sqrt{9} = 3$) or with an index above the sign to indicate the root to be taken if the root is not a square root ($\sqrt[3]{8} = 2$) (see also section on powers and roots)
$\lvert x \rvert$	absolute value of (in this case x) (see section on basic properties of numbers, item 6)

* *Geometric symbols are reviewed in the section on geometry.*

BASIC PROPERTIES OF NUMBERS

1. A number greater than zero is called a **positive number.**

2. A number less than zero is called a **negative number.**

3. When a negative number is added to another number, this is the same as subtracting the equivalent positive number.

   Example: $2 + (-1) = 2 - 1 = 1$

4. When two numbers of the same sign are multiplied together, the result is a positive number.

   Example: $2 \times 2 = 4$

   Example: $(-2)(-3) = +6$

5. When two numbers of different signs are multiplied together, the result is a negative number.

   Example: $(+5)(-10) = -50$

   Example: $(-6)(+8) = -48$

6. The **absolute value** of a number is the equivalent positive value.

   Example: $|+2| = +2$

   Example: $|-3| = +3$

7. An **even number** is an integer that is divisible by two. Zero would be considered an even number for practical purposes.

8. An **odd number** is an integer that is not an even number.

9. An even number times any integer will yield an even number.

10. An odd number times an odd number will yield an odd number.

11. Two even numbers or two odd numbers added together will yield an even number.

12. An odd number added to an even number will yield an odd number.

FRACTIONS

Fractions and Mixed Numbers

1. A **fraction** is part of a unit.

   a. A fraction has a **numerator** and a **denominator.**

   Example: In the fraction $\frac{3}{4}$, 3 is the numerator and 4 is the denominator.

   b. In any fraction, the numerator is being divided by the denominator.

   Example: The fraction $\frac{2}{7}$ indicates that 2 is being divided by 7.

   c. The whole quantity 1 may be expressed by a fraction in which the numerator and denominator are the same number.

   Example: If the problem involves $\frac{1}{8}$ of a quantity, then the whole quantity is $\frac{8}{8}$, or 1.

2. A **mixed number** is an integer together with a fraction such as $2\frac{3}{5}$, $7\frac{7}{8}$, etc. The integer is the integral part, and the fraction is the fractional part.

3. An **improper fraction** is one in which the numerator is equal to or greater than the denominator, such as $\frac{19}{6}$, $\frac{25}{4}$, or $\frac{10}{10}$.

4. To rename a mixed number as an improper fraction:

    a. Multiply the denominator of the fraction by the integer.

    b. Add the numerator to this product.

    c. Place this sum over the denominator of the fraction.

    Illustration: Rename $3\frac{4}{7}$ as an improper fraction.

    SOLUTION: $\qquad 7 \times 3 = 21$

    $$21 + 4 = 25$$

    $$3\frac{4}{7} = \frac{25}{7}$$

    Answer: $\dfrac{25}{7}$

5. To rename an improper fraction as a mixed number:

    a. Divide the numerator by the denominator. The quotient, disregarding the remainder, is the integral part of the mixed number.

    b. Place the remainder, if any, over the denominator. This is the fractional part of the mixed number.

    Illustration: Rename $\frac{36}{13}$ as a mixed number.

    SOLUTION: $\qquad 13\overline{)36}$ with quotient 2

    $$\underline{26}$$

    $$10 \text{ (remainder)}$$

    $$\frac{36}{13} = 2\frac{10}{13}$$

    Answer: $2\dfrac{10}{13}$

6. The numerator and denominator of a fraction may be changed, without affecting the value of the fraction, by multiplying both by the same number.

    Example: The value of the fraction $\frac{2}{3}$ will not be altered if the numerator and the denominator are multiplied by 2, to result in $\frac{4}{6}$.

7. The numerator and the denominator of a fraction may be changed, without affecting the value of the fraction, by dividing both by the same number. This process is called **simplifying the fraction.** A fraction that has been simplified as much as possible is said to be in **simplest form.**

    Example: The value of the fraction $\frac{3}{12}$ will not be altered if the numerator and denominator are divided by 3, to result in $\frac{1}{4}$.

    Example: If $\frac{6}{30}$ is simplified to simplest form (by dividing both numerator and denominator by 6), the result is $\frac{1}{5}$.

8. As a final answer to an exam question, it may be necessary to:

    a. simplify a fraction to simplest form

    b. rename an improper fraction as a mixed number

    c. rename a mixed number as an improper fraction

Addition of Fractions

9. Fractions cannot be added unless the denominators are all the same.

    a. If the denominators are the same, add all the numerators and place this sum over the common denominator. In the case of mixed numbers, follow the above rule for the fractions and then add the integers.

    Example: The sum of $2\frac{3}{8} + 3\frac{1}{8} + \frac{3}{8} = 5\frac{7}{8}$.

    b. If the denominators are not the same, the fractions, in order to be added, must be converted to ones having the same denominator. The least common denominator is often the most convenient common denominator to find, but any common denominator will work. You can divide out the extra numbers after the addition.

10. The **least common denominator** (henceforth called the **L.C.D.**) is the least number that can be divided evenly by all the given denominators. If no two of the given denominators can be divided by the same number, then the L.C.D. is the product of all the denominators.

    Example: The L.C.D. of $\frac{1}{2}$, $\frac{1}{3}$, and $\frac{1}{5}$ is $2 \times 3 \times 5 = 30$.

11. To find the L.C.D. when two or more of the given denominators can be divided by the same number:

    a. Write the denominators across the page, leaving plenty of space between the numbers, as illustrated below.

    b. Select the least number (other than 1) by which one or more of the denominators can be divided evenly

    c. Divide each of the denominators by this number and write the answer directly below the dividend. Those numbers that cannot be divided evenly should be carried down to the next line.

    d. Moving down to the line of numbers you just wrote, repeat this division process until there are no longer any denominators that can be divided evenly by any number other than 1.

    e. Multiply together all the divisors to find the L.C.D.

Illustration: Find the L.C.D. of $\frac{1}{5}$, $\frac{1}{7}$, $\frac{1}{10}$, and $\frac{1}{14}$.

SOLUTION:

$$
\begin{array}{r|cccc}
2 & 5 & 7 & 10 & 14 \\
\hline
5 & 5 & 7 & 5 & 7 \\
\hline
7 & 1 & 7 & 1 & 7 \\
\hline
 & 1 & 1 & 1 & 1
\end{array}
$$

$$7 \times 5 \times 2 = 70$$

Answer: The L.C.D. is 70.

12. To add fractions having different denominators:

    a. Find the L.C.D. of the denominators.

    b. Rename each fraction as an equivalent fraction having the L.C.D. as its denominator.

    c. When all of the fractions have the same denominator, they may be added, as in the example following item 9a.

Illustration: Add $\frac{1}{4}$, $\frac{3}{10}$, and $\frac{2}{5}$.

SOLUTION: Find the L.C.D.:

$$
\begin{array}{r|ccc}
2 & 4 & 10 & 5 \\
\hline
5 & 2 & 5 & 5 \\
\hline
2 & 2 & 1 & 1 \\
\hline
 & 1 & 1 & 1
\end{array}
$$

L.C.D. $= 2 \times 5 \times 2 = 20$

$$
\begin{aligned}
\frac{1}{4} &= \frac{5}{20} \\
\frac{3}{10} &= \frac{6}{20} \\
+\frac{2}{5} &= +\frac{8}{20} \\
\hline
 & \frac{19}{20}
\end{aligned}
$$

Answer: $\frac{19}{20}$

13. To add mixed numbers in which the fractions have different denominators, add the fractions by following the rules in item 12 above, then add the integers.

Illustration: Add $2\frac{5}{7}$, $5\frac{1}{2}$, and 8.

SOLUTION: L.C.D. = 14

$$2\frac{5}{7} = 2\frac{10}{14}$$
$$5\frac{1}{2} = 5\frac{7}{14}$$
$$\underline{+8 = +\ 8\ \ \ }$$
$$15\frac{17}{14} = 16\frac{3}{14}$$

Answer: $16\frac{3}{14}$

Subtraction of Fractions

14. a. Unlike addition, which may involve adding more than two numbers at the same time, subtraction involves only two numbers.

    b. In subtraction, as in addition, the denominators must be the same.

15. To subtract fractions:

    a. Find the L.C.D.

    b. Rename both fractions so that each has the L.C.D. as the denominator.

    c. Subtract the numerator of the second fraction from the numerator of the first, and place this difference over the L.C.D.

    d. Simplify, if possible.

Illustration: Find the difference of $\frac{5}{8}$ and $\frac{1}{4}$.

SOLUTION: L.C.D. = 8

$$\frac{5}{8} = \frac{5}{8}$$
$$\underline{-\frac{1}{4} = -\frac{2}{8}}$$
$$\frac{3}{8}$$

Answer: $\frac{3}{8}$

16. To subtract mixed numbers:

    a. It may be necessary to "borrow," so that the fractional part of the first term is greater than the fractional part of the second term.

    b. Subtract the fractional parts of the mixed numbers and simplify.

    c. Subtract the integers.

Illustration: Subtract $16\frac{4}{5}$ from $29\frac{1}{3}$.

SOLUTION: L.C.D. = 15

$$29\frac{1}{3} = 29\frac{5}{15}$$
$$-16\frac{4}{5} = -16\frac{12}{15}$$

Note that $\frac{5}{15}$ is less than $\frac{12}{15}$. Borrow 1 from 29, and rename as $\frac{15}{15}$.

$$29\frac{5}{15} = 28\frac{20}{15}$$
$$-16\frac{12}{15} = -16\frac{12}{15}$$
$$\overline{\phantom{-16\frac{12}{15} = }12\frac{8}{15}}$$

Answer: $12\frac{8}{15}$

Multiplication of Fractions

17. a. To be multiplied, fractions need not have the same denominators.

    b. A whole number can be thought of as having a denominator of $1 : 3 = \frac{3}{1}$.

18. To multiply fractions:

    a. Rename the mixed numbers, if any, as improper fractions.

    b. Multiply all the numerators, and place this product over the product of the denominators.

    c. Simplify, if possible.

Illustration: Multiply $\frac{2}{3} \times 2\frac{4}{7} \times \frac{5}{9}$.

SOLUTION:
$$2\frac{4}{7} = \frac{18}{7}$$
$$\frac{2}{3} \times \frac{18}{7} \times \frac{5}{9} = \frac{180}{189}$$
$$= \frac{20}{21}$$

Answer: $\frac{20}{21}$

19. a. **Dividing common factors** is a method to facilitate multiplication. To divide common factors means to divide a numerator and a denominator by the same number in a multiplication problem.

    Example: In the problem $\frac{4}{7} \times \frac{5}{6}$, the numerator 4 and the denominator 6 may be divided by 2.

    $$\frac{\overset{2}{\cancel{4}}}{7} \times \frac{5}{\underset{3}{\cancel{6}}} = \frac{10}{21}$$

    b. With fractions (and percentages), the word "of" is often used to mean "multiply."

    Example: $\frac{1}{2}$ of $\frac{1}{2} = \frac{1}{2} \times \frac{1}{2} = \frac{1}{4}$

20. To multiply a whole number by a mixed number:

    a. Multiply the whole number by the fractional part of the mixed number.

    b. Multiply the whole number by the integral part of the mixed number.

    c. Add both products.

    Illustration: Multiply $23\frac{3}{4}$ by 95.

    SOLUTION:

    $$\frac{95}{1} \times \frac{3}{4} = \frac{285}{4}$$
    $$= 71\frac{1}{4}$$
    $$95 \times 23 = 2185$$
    $$2185 + 71\frac{1}{4} = 2256\frac{1}{4}$$

    Answer: $2256\frac{1}{4}$

Division of Fractions

21. The **reciprocal** of a fraction is that fraction inverted.

    a. When a fraction is inverted, the numerator becomes the denominator and the denominator becomes the numerator.

    Example: The reciprocal of $\frac{3}{8}$ is $\frac{8}{3}$.

    Example: The reciprocal of $\frac{1}{3}$ is $\frac{3}{1}$, or simply 3.

    b. Since every whole number has the denominator 1 understood, the reciprocal of a whole number is a fraction having 1 as the numerator and the number itself as the denominator.

    Example: The reciprocal of 5 (expressed fractionally as $\frac{5}{1}$) is $\frac{1}{5}$.

22. To divide fractions:

    a. Rename all the mixed numbers, if any, as improper fractions.

    b. Multiply by the reciprocal of the second fraction.

    c. Simplify, if possible.

    Illustration: Divide $\frac{2}{3}$ by $2\frac{1}{4}$.

    SOLUTION:
    $$2\frac{1}{4} = \frac{9}{4}$$
    $$\frac{2}{3} \div \frac{9}{4} = \frac{2}{3} \times \frac{4}{9}$$
    $$= \frac{8}{27}$$

    Answer: $\frac{8}{27}$

23. A **complex fraction** is one that has a fraction as the numerator, or as the denominator, or as both.

    Example: $\dfrac{\frac{2}{3}}{5}$ is a complex fraction.

24. To simplify a complex fraction:

    a. Divide the numerator by the denominator.

    b. Simplify, if possible.

    Illustration: Simplify $\dfrac{\frac{3}{7}}{\frac{5}{14}}$.

    SOLUTION:
    $$\frac{3}{7} \div \frac{5}{14} = \frac{3}{7} \times \frac{14}{5} = \frac{42}{35}$$
    $$= \frac{6}{5}$$
    $$= 1\frac{1}{5}$$

    Answer: $1\frac{1}{5}$

Comparing Fractions

25. If two fractions have the same denominator, the one having the greater numerator is the greater fraction.

    Example: $\frac{3}{7}$ is greater than $\frac{2}{7}$.

26. If two fractions have the same numerator, the one having the least denominator is the lesser fraction.

    Example: $\frac{5}{12}$ is less than $\frac{5}{11}$.

27. To compare two fractions having different numerators and different denominators:

    a. Rename the fractions as equivalent fractions having their L.C.D. as their new denominator.

    b. Compare, as in the example following item 25, for the greatest numerator.

    Illustration: Compare $\frac{4}{7}$ and $\frac{5}{8}$.

    SOLUTION: L.C.D. $= 7 \times 8 = 56$

    $$\frac{4}{7} = \frac{32}{56}$$
    $$\frac{5}{8} = \frac{35}{56}$$

    Answer: Since $\frac{35}{56}$ is greater than $\frac{32}{56}$, $\frac{5}{8}$ is greater than $\frac{4}{7}$.

    Note: Actually, any common denominator will work, not only the L.C.D.

28. To compare two fractions, multiply the denominator of the left fraction by the numerator of the right fraction and write the result above the right fraction. Then multiply the denominator of the right fraction by the numerator of the left fraction and write the result over the left fraction. If the number over the left fraction is greater than the number over the right fraction, the left fraction is greater. If the number over the right fraction is greater, the right fraction is greater. If the numbers over the two fractions are equal, the fractions are equal.

    Illustration: Compare $\frac{5}{7}$ and $\frac{3}{4}$.

    SOLUTION: 20   21

    $$\frac{5}{7} \bowtie \frac{3}{4}$$

    $$3 \times 7 = 21$$
    $$4 \times 5 = 20$$
    $$20 < 21$$

    Answer: $\frac{5}{7} < \frac{3}{4}$. This method will only determine which fraction is greater. It cannot be used to tell you the size of the difference.

Fraction Problems

29. Most fraction problems can be arranged in the form: "What fraction of a number is another number?" This form contains three important parts:

    - The fractional part
    - The number following "of"
    - The number following "is"

    a. If the fraction and the "of" number are given, multiply them to find the "is" number.

    Illustration: What is $\frac{3}{4}$ of 20?

    SOLUTION: Write the question as "$\frac{3}{4}$ of 20 is what number?" Then multiply the fraction $\frac{3}{4}$ by the "of" number, 20:

    $$\frac{3}{1\cancel{4}} \times \cancel{20}^{5} = 15$$

    Answer: 15

    b. If the fractional part and the "is" number are given, divide the "is" number by the fraction to find the "of" number.

    Illustration: $\frac{4}{5}$ of what number is 40?

    SOLUTION: To find the "of" number, divide 40 by $\frac{4}{5}$:

    $$40 \div \frac{4}{5} = \frac{\cancel{40}^{10}}{1} \times \frac{5}{\cancel{4}_{1}} = 50$$

    Answer: 50

    c. To find the fractional part when the other two numbers are known, divide the "is" number by the "of" number.

    Illustration: What part of 12 is 9?

    SOLUTION: $9 \div 12 = \dfrac{9}{12} = \dfrac{3}{4}$

    Answer: $\dfrac{3}{4}$

Practice Problems Involving Fractions

1. Simplify $\frac{60}{108}$ to simplest form.

   (A) $\frac{1}{48}$

   (B) $\frac{1}{3}$

   (C) $\frac{1}{9}$

   (D) $\frac{5}{9}$

   (E) $\frac{15}{59}$

2. Rename $\frac{27}{7}$ as a mixed number.

   (A) $2\frac{1}{7}$

   (B) $3\frac{6}{7}$

   (C) $6\frac{1}{3}$

   (D) $7\frac{1}{2}$

   (E) $8\frac{1}{7}$

3. Rename $4\frac{2}{3}$ as an improper fraction.

   (A) $\frac{10}{3}$

   (B) $\frac{11}{3}$

   (C) $\frac{14}{3}$

   (D) $\frac{24}{3}$

   (E) $\frac{42}{3}$

4. Find the L.C.D. of $\frac{1}{6}$, $\frac{1}{10}$, $\frac{1}{18}$, and $\frac{1}{21}$.

   (A) 160
   (B) 330
   (C) 630
   (D) 890
   (E) 1260

5. Add $16\frac{3}{8}$, $4\frac{4}{5}$, $12\frac{3}{4}$, and $23\frac{5}{6}$.

   (A) $57\frac{91}{120}$

   (B) $57\frac{1}{4}$

   (C) 58

   (D) 59

   (E) $59\frac{91}{120}$

6. Subtract $27\frac{5}{14}$ from $43\frac{1}{6}$.

   (A) 15

   (B) $15\frac{5}{84}$

   (C) $15\frac{8}{21}$

   (D) $15\frac{15}{20}$

   (E) $15\frac{17}{21}$

7. Multiply $17\frac{5}{8}$ by 128.

   (A) 2256
   (B) 2305
   (C) 2356
   (D) 2368
   (E) 2394

8. Divide $1\frac{2}{3}$ by $1\frac{1}{9}$.

   (A) $\frac{2}{3}$

   (B) $1\frac{1}{2}$

   (C) $1\frac{23}{27}$

   (D) 4

   (E) 6

9. What is the value of $12\frac{1}{6} - 2\frac{3}{8} - 7\frac{2}{3} + 19\frac{3}{4}$?

   (A) 21

   (B) $21\frac{7}{8}$

   (C) $21\frac{1}{8}$

   (D) 22

   (E) $22\frac{7}{8}$

10. Simplify the complex fraction $\dfrac{\frac{4}{9}}{\frac{2}{5}}$.

    (A) $\dfrac{1}{2}$

    (B) $\dfrac{9}{10}$

    (C) $\dfrac{2}{5}$

    (D) 1

    (E) $1\frac{1}{9}$

11. Which fraction is greatest?

    (A) $\dfrac{9}{16}$

    (B) $\dfrac{7}{10}$

    (C) $\dfrac{5}{8}$

    (D) $\dfrac{4}{5}$

    (E) $\dfrac{1}{2}$

12. One brass rod measures $3\frac{5}{16}$ inches long and another brass rod measures $2\frac{3}{4}$ inches long. Together their length is

    (A) $6\frac{9}{16}$ in.

    (B) $6\frac{1}{16}$ in.

    (C) $5\frac{1}{2}$ in.

    (D) $5\frac{1}{16}$ in.

    (E) $5\frac{1}{32}$ in.

13. The number of half-pound packages of tea that can be weighed out of a box that holds $10\frac{1}{2}$ lb. of tea is

    (A) 5

    (B) $10\frac{1}{2}$

    (C) 11

    (D) $20\frac{1}{2}$

    (E) 21

14. If each bag of tokens weighs $5\frac{3}{4}$ pounds, how many pounds do 3 bags weigh?

    (A) $7\frac{1}{4}$

    (B) $15\frac{3}{4}$

    (C) $16\frac{1}{2}$

    (D) $17\frac{1}{4}$

    (E) $17\frac{1}{2}$

15. During one week, a man traveled $3\frac{1}{2}$, $1\frac{1}{4}$, $1\frac{1}{6}$, and $2\frac{3}{8}$ miles. The next week he traveled $\frac{1}{4}$, $\frac{3}{8}$, $\frac{9}{16}$, $3\frac{1}{16}$, $2\frac{5}{8}$, and $3\frac{3}{16}$ miles. How many more miles did he travel the second week than the first week?

(A) $1\frac{37}{48}$

(B) $1\frac{1}{2}$

(C) $1\frac{3}{4}$

(D) 1

(E) $\frac{47}{48}$

16. A certain type of board is sold only in lengths of multiples of 2 feet. The shortest board sold is 6 feet and the longest is 24 feet. A builder needs a large quantity of this type of board in $5\frac{1}{2}$-foot lengths. For minimum waste the lengths to be ordered should be

(A) 6 ft.

(B) 12 ft.

(C) 22 ft.

(D) 24 ft.

(E) 26 ft.

17. A man spent $\frac{15}{16}$ of his entire fortune on buying a car for $7500. How much money did he possess?

(A) $6000

(B) $6500

(C) $7000

(D) $8000

(E) $8500

18. The population of a town was 54,000 in the last census. It has increased $\frac{2}{3}$ since then. Its present population is

(A) 18,000

(B) 36,000

(C) 72,000

(D) 90,000

(E) 108,000

19. If $\frac{1}{3}$ of the liquid contents of a can evaporates on the first day and $\frac{3}{4}$ of the remainder evaporates on the second day, the fractional part of the original contents remaining at the close of the second day is

(A) $\frac{5}{12}$

(B) $\frac{7}{12}$

(C) $\frac{1}{6}$

(D) $\frac{1}{2}$

(E) $\frac{4}{7}$

20. A car is run until the gas tank is $\frac{1}{8}$ full. The tank is then filled to capacity by putting in 14 gallons. The capacity of the gas tank of the car is

(A) 14 gal.

(B) 15 gal.

(C) 16 gal.

(D) 17 gal.

(E) 18 gal.

Problem Solutions—Fractions

1. D	5. A	9. B	13. E	17. D
2. B	6. E	10. E	14. D	18. D
3. C	7. A	11. D	15. A	19. C
4. C	8. B	12. B	16. C	20. C

1. **The correct answer is (D).** Divide the numerator and denominator by 12:

$$\frac{60 \div 12}{108 \div 12} = \frac{5}{9}$$

One alternate method (there are several) is to divide the numerator and denominator by 6 and then by 2:

$$\frac{60 \div 6}{108 \div 6} = \frac{10}{18}$$

$$\frac{10 \div 2}{18 \div 2} = \frac{5}{9}$$

2. **The correct answer is (B).** Divide the numerator (27) by the denominator (7):

$$7 \overline{)27}$$
$$\underline{21}$$
$$6 \text{ (remainder)}$$

$$\frac{27}{7} = 3\frac{6}{7}$$

3. **The correct answer is (C).**

$$4 \times 3 = 12$$
$$12 + 2 = 14$$
$$4\frac{2}{3} = \frac{14}{3}$$

4. **The correct answer is (C).**

$2\,\overline{)\;6\quad 10\quad 18\quad 21}$ (2 is a divisor of 6, 10, and 18)

$3\,\overline{)\;3\quad 5\quad 9\quad 21}$ (3 is a divisor of 3, 9, and 21)

$3\,\overline{)\;1\quad 5\quad 3\quad 7}$ (3 is a divisor of 3)

$5\,\overline{)\;1\quad 5\quad 1\quad 7}$ (5 is a divisor of 5)

$7\,\overline{)\;1\quad 1\quad 1\quad 7}$ (7 is a divisor of 7)

$\;1\quad 1\quad 1\quad 1$

L.C.D. $= 2 \times 3 \times 3 \times 5 \times 7 = 630$

5. **The correct answer is (A).**

L.C.D. = 120

$$16\frac{3}{8} = 16\frac{45}{120}$$
$$4\frac{4}{5} = 4\frac{96}{120}$$
$$12\frac{3}{4} = 12\frac{90}{120}$$
$$+23\frac{5}{6} = +23\frac{100}{120}$$
$$55\frac{331}{120} = 57\frac{91}{120}$$

6. **The correct answer is (E).**

L.C.D. = 42

$$43\frac{1}{6} = 43\frac{7}{42} = 42\frac{49}{42}$$
$$-27\frac{5}{14} = -27\frac{15}{42} = -27\frac{15}{42}$$
$$15\frac{34}{42} = 15\frac{17}{21}$$

7. **The correct answer is (A).**

$$17\frac{5}{8} = \frac{141}{8}$$

$$\frac{141}{\cancel{8}_1} \times \frac{\overset{16}{\cancel{128}}}{1} = 2256$$

8. **The correct answer is (B).**

$$1\frac{2}{3} \div 1\frac{1}{9} = \frac{5}{3} \div \frac{10}{9}$$

$$= \frac{\cancel{5}^1}{\cancel{3}_1} \times \frac{\cancel{9}^3}{\cancel{10}_2}$$

$$= \frac{3}{2} = 1\frac{1}{2}$$

9. **The correct answer is (B).**

L.C.D. = 24

$$12\frac{1}{6} = 12\frac{4}{24} = 11\frac{28}{24}$$

$$-2\frac{3}{8} = -2\frac{9}{24} = -2\frac{9}{24}$$

$$9\frac{19}{24} = 9\frac{19}{24}$$

$$-7\frac{2}{3} = -7\frac{16}{24}$$

$$2\frac{3}{24} = 2\frac{3}{24}$$

$$+19\frac{3}{4} = +19\frac{18}{24}$$

$$21\frac{21}{24}$$

$$21\frac{21}{24} = 21\frac{7}{8}$$

10. **The correct answer is (E).** To simplify a complex fraction, divide the numerator by the denominator:

$$\frac{4}{9} \div \frac{2}{5} = \frac{\cancel{4}^2}{9} \times \frac{5}{\cancel{2}_1}$$

$$= \frac{10}{9}$$

$$= 1\frac{1}{9}$$

11. **The correct answer is (D).** Write all of the fractions with the same denominator. L.C.D. = 80

$$\frac{9}{16} = \frac{45}{80}$$

$$\frac{7}{10} = \frac{56}{80}$$

$$\frac{5}{8} = \frac{50}{80}$$

$$\frac{4}{5} = \frac{64}{80}$$

$$\frac{1}{2} = \frac{40}{80}$$

12. **The correct answer is (B).**

$$3\frac{5}{16} = 3\frac{5}{16}$$

$$+2\frac{3}{4} = +2\frac{12}{16}$$

$$5\frac{17}{16}$$

$$= 6\frac{1}{16}$$

13. **The correct answer is (E).**

$$10\frac{1}{2} \div \frac{1}{2} = \frac{21}{2} \div \frac{1}{2}$$

$$= \frac{21}{2} \times \frac{2}{1}$$

$$= 21$$

14. **The correct answer is (D).**

$$5\frac{3}{4} \times 3 = \frac{23}{4} \times \frac{3}{1}$$

$$= \frac{69}{4}$$

$$= 17\frac{1}{4}$$

15. **The correct answer is (A).** First week:

L.C.D. = 24

$$3\frac{1}{2} = 3\frac{12}{24} \text{ miles}$$
$$1\frac{1}{4} = 1\frac{6}{24}$$
$$1\frac{1}{6} = 1\frac{4}{24}$$
$$+2\frac{3}{8} = +2\frac{9}{24}$$
$$\overline{7\frac{31}{24}} = 8\frac{7}{24} \text{ miles}$$

Second week:

L.C.D. = 16

$$\frac{1}{4} = \frac{4}{16} \text{ miles}$$
$$\frac{3}{8} = \frac{6}{16}$$
$$\frac{9}{16} = \frac{9}{16}$$
$$3\frac{1}{16} = 3\frac{1}{16}$$
$$2\frac{5}{8} = 2\frac{10}{16}$$
$$+3\frac{3}{16} = +3\frac{3}{16}$$
$$\overline{8\frac{33}{16}} = 10\frac{1}{16} \text{ miles}$$

L.C.D. = 48

$$10\frac{1}{16} = 9\frac{51}{48} \text{ miles second week}$$
$$-8\frac{7}{24} = -8\frac{14}{48} \text{ miles first week}$$
$$\overline{1\frac{37}{48}} \text{ more miles traveled}$$

16. **The correct answer is (C).** Consider each choice:

Each 6-ft. board yields one $5\frac{1}{2}$-ft. board with $\frac{1}{2}$ ft. waste.

Each 12-ft. board yields two $5\frac{1}{2}$-ft. boards with 1 ft. waste ($2 \times 5\frac{1}{2} = 11$; $12 - 11 = 1$ ft. waste).

Each 22 ft. board may be divided into four $5\frac{1}{2}$-ft. boards with no waste ($4 \times 5\frac{1}{2} = 22$ exactly).

Each 24-ft. board yields four $5\frac{1}{2}$-ft. boards with 2 ft. waste ($4 \times 5\frac{1}{2} = 22$; $24 - 22 = 2$ ft. waste).

17. **The correct answer is (D).** $\frac{15}{16}$ of his fortune is $7,500.

Therefore, his fortune $= 7,500 \div \frac{15}{16}$

$$= \frac{\overset{500}{\cancel{7,500}}}{1} \times \frac{16}{\underset{1}{\cancel{15}}}$$

$$= 8000$$

18. **The correct answer is (D).** $\frac{2}{3}$ of $54,000 =$ increase

$$\text{Increase} = \frac{2}{\underset{1}{\cancel{3}}} \times \overset{18,000}{\cancel{54,000}}$$

$$= 36,000$$

Present population $= 54,000 + 36,000$

$$= 90,000$$

19. The correct answer is (C).

First day: $\frac{1}{3}$ evaporates

$\frac{2}{3}$ remains

Second day: $\frac{3}{4}$ of $\frac{2}{3}$ evaporates

$\frac{1}{4}$ of $\frac{2}{3}$ remains

The amount remaining is $\frac{1}{\overset{}{\underset{2}{4}}} \times \frac{\overset{1}{2}}{3} = \frac{1}{6}$

of original contents.

20. The correct answer is (C). $\frac{7}{8}$ of capacity = 14 gal.

Therefore, capacity = $14 \div \frac{7}{8}$

$= \frac{\overset{2}{14}}{1} \times \frac{8}{\underset{1}{7}}$

$= 16$ gal.

DECIMALS

1. A **decimal,** which is a number with a decimal point (.), is actually a fraction, the denominator of which is understood to be 10 or some power of 10.

   a. The number of digits, or places, after a decimal point determines which power of 10 the denominator is. If there is one digit, the denominator is understood to be 10; if there are two digits, the denominator is understood to be 100, etc.

   Example: $.3 = \frac{3}{10}$; $.57 = \frac{57}{100}$; $.643 = \frac{643}{1000}$.

   b. The addition of zeros after a decimal point does not change the value of the decimal. The zeros may be removed without changing the value of the decimal.

   Example: .7 = .70 = .700, and vice versa: .700 = .70 = .7.

   c. Since a decimal point is understood to exist after any whole number, the addition of any number of zeros after such a decimal point does not change the value of the number.

   Example: 2 = 2.0 = 2.00 = 2.000.

Addition of Decimals

2. Decimals are added in the same way that whole numbers are added, with the provision that the decimal points must be kept in a vertical line, one under the other. This determines the place of the decimal point in the answer.

   Illustration: Add 2.31, .037, 4, and 5.0017.

   SOLUTION:
   $$
   \begin{array}{r}
   2.3100 \\
   .0370 \\
   4.0000 \\
   +\,5.0017 \\
   \hline
   11.3487
   \end{array}
   $$

   Answer: 11.3487

Subtraction of Decimals

3. Decimals are subtracted in the same way that whole numbers are subtracted, with the provision that, as in addition, the decimal points must be kept in a vertical line, one under the other. This determines the place of the decimal point in the answer.

   Illustration: Subtract 4.0037 from 15.3.

   SOLUTION:
   $$
   \begin{array}{r}
   15.3000 \\
   -\,4.0037 \\
   \hline
   11.2963
   \end{array}
   $$

   Answer: 11.2963

Multiplication of Decimals

4. Decimals are multiplied in the same way that whole numbers are multiplied.

    a. The number of decimal places in the product equals the sum of the decimal places in the multiplicand and in the multiplier.

    b. If there are fewer places in the product than this sum, then a sufficient number of zeros must be added in front of the product to equal the number of places required, and a decimal point is written in front of the zeros.

    Illustration: Multiply 2.372 by .012.

    SOLUTION:
    $$\begin{array}{r} 2.372 \\ \times\ .012 \\ \hline 4744 \\ 2372 \\ \hline .028464 \end{array}$$

    Answer: .028464

5. A decimal can be multiplied by a power of 10 by moving the decimal point to the *right* as many places as indicated by the power. If multiplied by 10, the decimal point is moved one place to the right; if multiplied by 100, the decimal point is moved two places to the right, etc.

    Example: .235 × 10   =   2.35

    .235 × 100   =   23.5

    .235 × 1000 = 235

Division of Decimals

6. There are four types of division involving decimals:

    - When the dividend only is a decimal
    - When the divisor only is a decimal
    - When both are decimals
    - When neither dividend nor divisor is a decimal

    a. When the dividend only is a decimal, the division is the same as that of whole numbers, except that a decimal point must be placed in the quotient exactly above that in the dividend.

Illustration: Divide 12.864 by 32.

SOLUTION:
$$
\begin{array}{r}
.402 \\
32\overline{)12.864} \\
\underline{12\ 8} \\
64 \\
\underline{64}
\end{array}
$$

Answer: .402

    b. When the divisor only is a decimal, the decimal point in the divisor is omitted and as many zeros are placed to the right of the dividend as there were decimal places in the divisor.

Illustration: Divide 211,327 by 6.817.

SOLUTION:

$$6.817\overline{)211327}$$

(3 decimal places)

$$
= 6817\overline{)211327000} \quad \begin{array}{r} 31000 \end{array}
$$
$$
\begin{array}{r}
\underline{20451} \\
6817 \\
\underline{6817}
\end{array}
$$

Answer: 31,000

c. When both divisor and dividend are decimals, the decimal point in the divisor is omitted and the decimal point in the dividend must be moved to the right as many decimal places as there were in the divisor. If there are not enough places in the dividend, zeros must be added to make up the difference.

Illustration: Divide 2.62 by .131.

SOLUTION: $.131\overline{)2.62} = 131\overline{)2620}$

$$\begin{array}{r} 20 \\ 131\overline{)2620} \\ \underline{262} \end{array}$$

Answer: 20

d. In instances when neither the divisor nor the dividend is a decimal, a problem may still involve decimals. This occurs in two cases: when the dividend is a lesser number than the divisor, and when it is required to work out a division to a certain number of decimal places. In either case, write in a decimal point after the dividend, add as many zeros as necessary, and place a decimal point in the quotient above that in the dividend.

Illustration: Divide 7 by 50.

SOLUTION:
$$\begin{array}{r} .14 \\ 50\overline{)7.00} \\ \underline{5\,0} \\ 2\,00 \\ \underline{2\,00} \end{array}$$

Answer: .14

Illustration: What is 155 divided by 40, carried out to 3 decimal places?

SOLUTION:
$$\begin{array}{r} 3.875 \\ 40\overline{)155.000} \\ \underline{120} \\ 350 \\ \underline{320} \\ 300 \\ \underline{280} \\ 200 \end{array}$$

Answer: 3.875

7. A decimal can be divided by a power of 10 by moving the decimal to the *left* as many places as indicated by the power. If divided by 10, the decimal point is moved one place to the left; if divided by 100, the decimal point is moved two places to the left, etc. If there are not enough places, add zeros in front of the number to make up the difference and add a decimal point.

    Example: .4 divided by 10   = .04

                   .4 divided by 100 = .004

Rounding Decimals

8. To round a number to a given decimal place:

    a. Locate the given place.

    b. If the digit to the right is less than 5, omit all digits following the given place.

    c. If the digit to the right is 5 or more, raise the given place by 1 and omit all digits following the given place.

    Examples: 4.27 = 4.3 to the nearest tenth

                   .71345 = .713 to the nearest thousandth

9. In problems involving money, answers are usually rounded to the nearest cent.

Renaming of Fractions as Decimals

10. A fraction can be renamed as a decimal by dividing the numerator by the denominator and working out the division to as many decimal places as required.

    Illustration: Rename $\frac{5}{11}$ as a decimal of 2 places.

    $$\text{SOLUTION:} \qquad \frac{5}{11} = 11\overline{)5.00}$$

    $$
    \begin{array}{r}
    .45 \\
    \underline{44} \\
    60 \\
    \underline{55} \\
    5
    \end{array}
    $$

    Answer: .45

11. To simplify fractions containing a decimal in either the numerator or the denominator, or in both, divide the numerator by the denominator.

Illustration: What is the value of $\frac{2.34}{.6}$?

SOLUTION:
$$\frac{2.34}{.6} = .6\overline{)2.34} = 6\overline{)23.4} \quad \begin{array}{r} 3.9 \\ \underline{18} \\ 54 \\ \underline{54} \end{array}$$

Answer: 3.9

Renaming of Decimals as Fractions

12. Since a decimal point indicates a number having a denominator that is a power of 10, a decimal number can be expressed as a fraction, the numerator of which is the number itself and the denominator of which is the power indicated by the number of decimal places in the decimal number.

Examples: $.3 = \frac{3}{10}$ $\qquad$ $.47 = \frac{47}{100}$

13. When to rename decimals as fractions:

a. When dealing with whole numbers, do not rename the decimal.

Example: In the problem $12 \times .14$, it is better to keep the decimal:

$$12 \times .14 = 1.68$$

b. When dealing with fractions, rename the decimal as a fraction.

Example: In the problem $\frac{3}{5} \times .17$, it is better to change the decimal to a fraction:

$$\frac{3}{5} \times .17 = \frac{3}{5} \times \frac{17}{100} = \frac{51}{500}$$

14. Because decimal equivalents of fractions are often used, it is helpful to be familiar with the most common equivalences:

$\frac{1}{2} = .5$ $\qquad$ $\frac{1}{3} = .3333$

$\frac{1}{4} = .25$ $\qquad$ $\frac{2}{3} = .6667$

$\frac{3}{4} = .75$ $\qquad$ $\frac{1}{6} = .1667$

$\frac{1}{5} = .2$ $\qquad$ $\frac{1}{7} = .1429$

$\frac{1}{8} = .125$ $\qquad$ $\frac{1}{9} = .1111$

$\frac{1}{16} = .0625$ $\qquad$ $\frac{1}{12} = .0833$

Note that the left column contains exact values. The values in the right column have been rounded to the nearest ten-thousandth.

Practice Problems Involving Decimals

1. Add 37.03, 11.5627, 3.4005, 3423, and 1.141. _____

2. Subtract 4.64324 from 7. _____

3. Multiply 27.34 by 16.943. _____

4. What is 19.6 divided by 3.2, carried out to 3 decimal places? _____

5. What is $\frac{5}{11}$ in decimal form (to the nearest hundredth)? _____

6. What is 0.64 in fraction form? _____

7. What is the difference between $\frac{3}{5}$ and $\frac{9}{8}$ expressed decimally? _____

8. A boy saved up $4.56 the first month, $3.82 the second month, and $5.06 the third month. How much did he save altogether? _____

9. The diameter of a certain rod is required to be $1.51 \pm .015$ inches. The rod's diameter must be between _____ and _____.

10. After an employer figures out an employee's salary of $190.57, he deducts $3.05 for social security and $5.68 for pension. What is the amount of the check after these deductions? _____

11. If the outer radius of a metal pipe is 2.84 inches and the inner radius is 1.94 inches, the thickness of the metal is _____

12. A boy earns $20.56 on Monday, $32.90 on Tuesday, and $20.78 on Wednesday. He spends half of all that he earned during the three days. How much does he have left?

   _____

13. The total cost of $3\frac{1}{2}$ pounds of meat at $1.69 a pound and 20 lemons at $.60 a dozen will be _____.

14. A reel of cable weighs 1279 lbs. If the empty reel weighs 285 lbs and the cable weighs 7.1 lbs per foot, the number of feet of cable on the reel is _____.

15. 345 fasteners at $4.15 per hundred will cost _____.

Problem Solutions—Decimals

1. **The correct answer is 3476.1342.**
    Line up all the decimal points one
    under the other. Then add:

    $$\begin{array}{r} 37.03 \\ 11.5627 \\ 3.4005 \\ 3423.0000 \\ +\quad 1.141 \\ \hline 3476.1342 \end{array}$$

2. **The correct answer is 2.35676.** Add
    a decimal point and five zeros to the 7.
    Then subtract:

    $$\begin{array}{r} 7.00000 \\ -4.64324 \\ \hline 2.35676 \end{array}$$

3. **The correct answer is 463.22162.**
    Since there are two decimal places
    in the multiplicand and three deci-
    mal places in the multiplier, there
    will be $2 + 3 = 5$ decimal places in the
    product.

    $$\begin{array}{r} 27.34 \\ \times\ 16.943 \\ \hline 8202 \\ 10936 \\ 24606 \\ 16404 \\ 2734 \\ \hline 463.22162 \end{array}$$

4. **The correct answer is 6.125.** Omit
    the decimal point in the divisor by
    moving it one place to the right. Move
    the decimal point in the dividend one
    place to the right and add three zeros
    in order to carry your answer out to
    three decimal places, as instructed in
    the problem.

    $$\begin{array}{r} 6.125 \\ 3.2\overline{)19.6.000} \\ 19\ 2 \\ \hline 40 \\ 32 \\ \hline 80 \\ 64 \\ \hline 160 \\ 160 \\ \hline \end{array}$$

5. **The correct answer is 0.45 to the
    nearest hundredth.** To rename a
    fraction as a decimal, divide the
    numerator by the denominator:

    $$\begin{array}{r} .454 \\ 11\overline{)5.000} \\ 4\ 4 \\ \hline 60 \\ 55 \\ \hline 50 \\ 44 \\ \hline 6 \end{array}$$

6. **The correct answer is $\frac{16}{25}$.** To re-
    name a decimal as a fraction, divide
    by the power of 10 indicated by the
    number of decimal places.

    $$64 \div 100 = \frac{64}{100} = \frac{16}{25}$$

7. **The correct answer is 0.525.** Rename each fraction as a decimal and subtract to find the difference:

$$\frac{9}{8} = 1.125 \qquad \frac{3}{5} = .60$$

$$\begin{array}{r} 1.125 \\ -\,0.60 \\ \hline 0.525 \end{array}$$

8. **The correct answer is $13.44.** Add the savings for each month:

$$\begin{array}{r} \$4.56 \\ 3.82 \\ +\,5.06 \\ \hline \$13.44 \end{array}$$

9. **The rod may have a diameter of 1.495 inches to 1.525 inches inclusive.**

$$\begin{array}{cc} 1.510 & 1.510 \\ +\,.015 & -\,.015 \\ \hline 1.525 & 1.495 \end{array}$$

10. **The correct answer is $181.84.** Add to find total deductions:

$$\begin{array}{r} \$3.05 \\ +\,5.68 \\ \hline \$8.73 \end{array}$$

Subtract total deductions from salary to find amount of check:

$$\begin{array}{r} \$190.57 \\ -\,8.73 \\ \hline \$181.84 \end{array}$$

11. **The correct answer is .90 in.** Outer radius minus inner radius equals thickness of metal:

$$\begin{array}{r} 2.84 \\ -\,1.94 \\ \hline .90 \end{array}$$

12. **The correct answer is $37.12.** Add daily earnings to find total earnings:

$$\begin{array}{r} \$20.56 \\ 32.90 \\ +\,20.78 \\ \hline \$74.24 \end{array}$$

Divide total earnings by 2 to find out what he has left:

$$\begin{array}{r} \$37.12 \\ 2)\overline{\$74.24} \end{array}$$

13. **The correct answer is $6.92.** Find cost of $3\frac{1}{2}$ pounds of meat:

$$\begin{array}{r} \$1.69 \\ \times\ 3.5 \\ \hline 845 \\ 507 \\ \hline \$5.915 \end{array}$$

$5.915 = $5.92 to the nearest cent

Find cost of 20 lemons:

$.60 ÷ 12 = $.05 (for 1 lemon)

$.05 × 20 = $1.00 (for 20 lemons)

Add cost of meat and cost of lemons:

$$\begin{array}{r} \$5.92 \\ +\,1.00 \\ \hline \$6.92 \end{array}$$

14. **The correct answer is 140.** Subtract weight of empty reel from total weight to find weight of cable:

$$1279 \text{ lbs}$$
$$- 285 \text{ lbs}$$
$$994 \text{ lbs}$$

Each foot of cable weighs 7.1 lbs. Therefore, to find the number of feet of cable on the reel, divide 994 by 7.1:

```
        14 0.
7.1.) 994.0.
       71
      284
      284
        0
```

15. **The correct answer is $14.32.** Each fastener costs:

$4.15 ÷ 100 = $.0415

345 fasteners cost:

```
      345
  ×  .0415
     1275
      345
    1380
   14.3175
```

PERCENTS

1. The **percent symbol** (%) means "parts out of a hundred." Thus a percent is really a fraction—25% is twenty-five parts out of a hundred, or $\frac{25}{100}$, which simplifies to $\frac{1}{4}$, or one part out of four. Some problems involve expressing a fraction or a decimal as a percent. In other problems it is necessary to express a percent as a fraction or decimal in order to perform the calculations efficiently. When you have a percent (or decimal) that renames as a common fraction (25% = .25 = $\frac{1}{4}$), it is usually best to do any multiplying or dividing by first renaming the percent or decimal as the common fraction, since the numbers are usually smaller and will work better. For adding and subtracting, percentages and decimals are often easier.

2. To rename a whole number or a decimal as a percent:

   a. Multiply the number by 100.

   b. Affix a % sign.

   Illustration: Rename 3 as a percent.

   SOLUTION: $3 \times 100 = 300$
   $$3 = 300\%$$

   Answer: 300%

   Illustration: Rename .67 as a percent.

   SOLUTION: $.67 \times 100 = 67$
   $$.67 = 67\%$$

   Answer: 67%

3. To rename a fraction or a mixed number as a percent:

   a. Multiply the fraction or mixed number by 100.

   b. Simplify, if possible.

   c. Affix a % sign.

   Illustration: Rename $\frac{1}{7}$ as a percent.

   SOLUTION: $\frac{1}{7} \times 100 = \frac{100}{7}$
   $$= 14\frac{2}{7}$$
   $$\frac{1}{7} = 14\frac{2}{7}$$

   Answer: $14\frac{2}{7}\%$

   Illustration: Rename $4\frac{2}{3}$ as a percent.

   SOLUTION: $4\frac{2}{3} \times 100 = \frac{14}{3} \times 100 = \frac{1400}{3}$
   $$= 466\frac{2}{3}$$
   $$4\frac{2}{3} = 466\frac{2}{3}\%$$

   Answer: $466\frac{2}{3}\%$

4. To remove a % sign attached to a decimal, divide the decimal by 100. If necessary, the resulting decimal may then be renamed as a fraction.

   Illustration: Rename .5% as a decimal and as a fraction.

   SOLUTION: $.5\% = .5 \div 100 = .005$

   $$.005 = \frac{5}{1000} = \frac{1}{200}$$

   Answer: $.5\% = .005$

   $$.5\% = \frac{1}{200}$$

5. To remove a % sign attached to a fraction or mixed number, divide the fraction or mixed number by 100, and simplify, if possible. If necessary, the resulting fraction may then be renamed as a decimal.

   Illustration: Rename $\frac{3}{4}$% as a fraction and as a decimal.

   SOLUTION: $\frac{3}{4}\% = \frac{3}{4} \div 100 = \frac{3}{4} \times \frac{1}{100} = \frac{3}{400}$

   $$\frac{3}{400} = 400\overline{)3.0000}^{.0075}$$

   Answer: $\frac{3}{4}\% = \frac{3}{400}$

   $$\frac{3}{4}\% = .0075$$

6. Some fraction-percent equivalents are used so frequently that it is helpful to be familiar with them:

$\frac{1}{25} = 4\%$	$\frac{1}{5} = 20\%$
$\frac{1}{20} = 5\%$	$\frac{1}{4} = 25\%$
$\frac{1}{12} = 8\frac{1}{3}\%$	$\frac{1}{3} = 33\frac{1}{3}\%$
$\frac{1}{10} = 10\%$	$\frac{1}{2} = 50\%$
$\frac{1}{8} = 12\frac{1}{2}\%$	$\frac{2}{3} = 66\frac{2}{3}\%$
$\frac{1}{6} = 16\frac{2}{3}\%$	$\frac{3}{4} = 75\%$

Solving Percent Problems

7. Most percent problems involve three quantities:
   - The rate, *R*, which is followed by a % sign.
   - The base, *B*, which follows the word "of."
   - The amount of percentage, *P*, which usually follows the word "is."

   a. If the rate *(R)* and the base *(B)* are known, then the percentage $(P) = R \times B$.

   Illustration: Find 15% of 50.

   SOLUTION: Rate = 15%

   Base = 50

   $$P = R \times B$$
   $$P = 15\% \times 50$$
   $$= .15 \times 50$$
   $$= 7.5$$

   Answer: 15% of 50 is 7.5.

   b. If the rate *(R)* and the percentage *(P)* are known, then the base $(B) = \frac{P}{R}$.

   Illustration: 7% of what number is 35?

   SOLUTION: Rate = 7%

   Percentage = 35

   $$B = \frac{P}{R}$$
   $$B = \frac{35}{7\%}$$
   $$= 35 \div .07$$
   $$= 500$$

   Answer: 7% of 500 is 35.

   c. If the percentage *(P)* and the base *(B)* are known, the rate $(R) = \frac{P}{B}$.

   Illustration: There are 96 men in a group of 150 people. What percent of the group is men?

   SOLUTION: Base = 150

   Percentage = 96

   $$\text{Rate} = \frac{96}{150}$$
   $$= .64$$
   $$= 64\%$$

   Answer: 64% of the group are men.

Illustration: In a tank holding 20 gallons of solution, 1 gallon is alcohol. What is the strength of the solution in percent?

SOLUTION: Percentage (amount) = 1 gallon

$$\text{Base} = 20 \text{ gallons}$$

$$\text{Rate} = \frac{1}{20}$$
$$= .05$$
$$= 5\%$$

Answer: The solution is 5% alcohol.

8. In a percent problem, the whole is 100%.

   Example: If a problem involves 10% of a quantity, the rest of the quantity is 90%.

   Example: If a quantity has been increased by 5%, the new amount is 105% of the original quantity.

   Example: If a quantity has been decreased by 15%, the new amount is 85% of the original quantity.

9. Percent change, percent increase, and percent decrease are special types of percent problems in which the difficulty is in making sure to use the right numbers to calculate the percent. The full formula is:

$$\frac{(\text{New Amount}) - (\text{Original Amount})}{(\text{Original Amount})} \times 100 = \text{Percent Change}$$

   Where the new amount is less than the original amount, the number in the numerator will be a negative number and the result will be a **percent decrease.** When a percent decrease is asked for, the negative sign is omitted. Where the new amount is greater than the original amount, the percent change is positive and is called a **percent increase.**

   The percent of increase or decrease is found by putting the amount of increase or decrease over the original amount and renaming this fraction as a percent by multiplying by 100.

   Illustration: The number of automobiles sold by the Cadcoln Dealership increased from 300 one year to 400 the following year. What was the percent of increase?

   SOLUTION: There was an increase of 100, which must be compared to the original 300.

$$\frac{100}{300} = \frac{1}{3} = 33\frac{1}{3}\%$$

   Answer: $33\frac{1}{3}\%$

Practice Problems Involving Percents

1. 10% written as a decimal is
   (A) 1.0
   (B) 0.1
   (C) 0.01
   (D) 0.010
   (E) 0.001

2. What is 5.37% in fraction form?
   (A) $\dfrac{537}{10,000}$
   (B) $\dfrac{537}{1,000}$
   (C) $5\dfrac{37}{10,000}$
   (D) $5\dfrac{37}{100}$
   (E) $\dfrac{537}{10}$

3. What percent is $\frac{3}{4}$ of $\frac{5}{6}$?
   (A) 60%
   (B) 75%
   (C) 80%
   (D) 90%
   (E) 111%

4. What percent is 14 of 24?
   (A) $62\dfrac{1}{4}\%$
   (B) $58\dfrac{1}{3}\%$
   (C) $41\dfrac{2}{3}\%$
   (D) $33\dfrac{3}{5}\%$
   (E) 14%

5. 200% of 800 equals
   (A) 4
   (B) 16
   (C) 200
   (D) 800
   (E) 1600

6. If John must have a mark of 80% to pass a test of 35 items, the number of items he may miss and still pass the test is
   (A) 7
   (B) 8
   (C) 11
   (D) 28
   (E) 35

7. The regular price of a TV set that sold for $118.80 at a 20% reduction sale is
   (A) $158.60
   (B) $148.50
   (C) $138.84
   (D) $95.04
   (E) $29.70

8. A circle graph of a budget shows the expenditure of 26.2% for housing, 28.4% for food, 12% for clothing, 12.7% for taxes, and the balance for miscellaneous items. The percent for miscellaneous items is
   (A) 79.3
   (B) 70.3
   (C) 68.5
   (D) 29.7
   (E) 20.7

9. Two dozen shuttlecocks and four bad-minton rackets are to be purchased for a playground. The shuttlecocks are priced at $.35 each and the rackets at $2.75 each. The playground receives a discount of 30% from these prices. The total cost of this equipment is

    (A) $7.29

    (B) $11.43

    (C) $13.58

    (D) $18.60

    (E) $19.40

10. A piece of wood weighing 10 ounces is found to have a weight of 8 ounces after drying. The moisture content was

    (A) 80%

    (B) 40%

    (C) $33\frac{1}{3}$%

    (D) 25%

    (E) 20%

11. A bag contains 800 coins. Of these, 10 percent are dimes, 30 percent are nick-els, and the rest are quarters. The amount of money in the bag is

    (A) less than $150

    (B) between $150 and $300

    (C) between $301 and $450

    (D) between $451 and $800

    (E) more than $800

12. Six quarts of a 20% solution of alcohol in water are mixed with 4 quarts of a 60% solution of alcohol in water. The alcoholic strength of the mixture is

    (A) 80%

    (B) 40%

    (C) 36%

    (D) $33\frac{1}{3}$%

    (E) 10%

13. A man insures 80% of his property and pays a $2\frac{1}{2}$% premium amounting to $348. What is the total value of his property?

    (A) $19,000

    (B) $18,400

    (C) $18,000

    (D) $17,400

    (E) $13,920

14. A clerk divided his 35-hour workweek as follows: $\frac{1}{5}$ of his time was spent in sorting mail; $\frac{1}{2}$ of his time in filing letters; and $\frac{1}{7}$ of his time in reception work. The rest of his time was devoted to messenger work. The percent of time spent on messenger work by the clerk during the week was most nearly

    (A) 6%

    (B) 10%

    (C) 14%

    (D) 16%

    (E) 20%

15. In a school in which 40% of the en-rolled students are boys, 80% of the boys are present on a certain day. If 1152 boys are present, the total school enrollment is

    (A) 1440

    (B) 2880

    (C) 3600

    (D) 5400

    (E) 5760

16. Mrs. Morris receives a salary raise from $25,000 to $27,500. Find the per-cent of increase.

    (A) 9

    (B) 10

    (C) $12\frac{1}{2}$

    (D) 15

    (E) 90

17. The population of Stormville has increased from 80,000 to 100,000 in the last twenty years. Find the percent of increase.

    (A) 10
    (B) 20
    (C) 25
    (D) 60
    (E) 80

18. The value of Super Company Stock dropped from $25 a share to $21 a share. Find the percent of decrease.

    (A) 4
    (B) 8
    (C) 12
    (D) 16
    (E) 20

19. The Rubins bought their home for $30,000 and sold it for $60,000. What was the percent of increase?

    (A) 300
    (B) 200
    (C) 150
    (D) 100
    (E) 50

20. During the pre-holiday rush, Martin's Department Store increased its sales staff from 150 to 200 people. By what percent must it now decrease its sales staff to return to the usual number of salespeople?

    (A) 20
    (B) 25
    (C) $33\frac{1}{3}$
    (D) 40
    (E) 75

Problem Solutions—Percents

1.	B	5.	E	9.	C	13.	D	17.	C
2.	A	6.	A	10.	E	14.	D	18.	D
3.	D	7.	B	11.	A	15.	C	19.	D
4.	B	8.	E	12.	C	16.	B	20.	B

1. **The correct answer is (B).**

    $10\% = .10 = 0.1$

2. **The correct answer is (A).**

    $5.37\% = .0537 = \dfrac{537}{10,000}$

3. **The correct answer is (D).**

    Base (number following "of ") $= \dfrac{5}{6}$

    Percentage (number following "is") $= \dfrac{3}{4}$

    $\text{Rate} = \dfrac{\text{Percentage}}{\text{Base}}$

    $= \text{Percentage} \div \text{Base}$

    $\text{Rate} = \dfrac{3}{4} \div \dfrac{5}{6}$

    $= \dfrac{3}{\underset{2}{\cancel{4}}} \times \dfrac{\overset{3}{\cancel{6}}}{5}$

    $= \dfrac{9}{10} = .9 = 90\%$

4. **The correct answer is (B).**

    Base (number following "of ") $= 24$
    Percentage (number following "is") $= 14$

    Rate $=$ Percentage $\div$ Base

    Rate $= 14 \div 24$

    $= .58\dfrac{1}{3}$

    $= 58\dfrac{1}{3}\%$

5. **The correct answer is (E).**

    $200\% \text{ of } 800 = 2.00 \times 800$

    $= 1600$

6. **The correct answer is (A).** He must answer 80% of 35 correctly. Therefore, he may miss 20% of 35.

    $20\% \text{ of } 35 = .20 \times 35$

    $= 7$

7. **The correct answer is (B).** Since $118.80 represents a 20% reduction, $118.80 = 80% of the regular price.

    Regular price $= \dfrac{\$118.80}{80\%}$

    $= \$118.80 \div .80$

    $= \$148.50$

8. **The correct answer is (E).** All the items in a circle graph total 100%. Add the figures given for housing, food, clothing, and taxes:

    $\begin{array}{r} 26.2\% \\ 28.4\% \\ 12\ \ \% \\ +12.7\% \\ \hline 79.3\% \end{array}$

    Subtract this total from 100% to find the percent for miscellaneous items:

    $\begin{array}{r} 100.0\% \\ -79.3\% \\ \hline 20.7\% \end{array}$

9. **The correct answer is (C).**

Price of shuttlecocks $= 24 \times \$.35 = \$8.40$

Price of rackets $= 4 \times \$2.75 = \underline{\$11.00}$

Total price $= \$19.40$

Discount is 30% $100\% - 30\% = 70\%$

Actual cost $= 70\%$ of $\$19.40$

$= .70 \times \$19.40$

$= \$13.58$

10. **The correct answer is (E).** Subtract weight of wood after drying from original weight of wood to find amount of moisture in wood:

$$
\begin{array}{r}
10 \\
-8 \\
\hline
2
\end{array}
$$ ounces of moisture in wood

Moisture content $= \frac{2 \text{ ounces}}{10 \text{ ounces}} = .2 = 20\%$

11. **The correct answer is (A).** Find the number of each kind of coin:

10% of 800 = $.10 \times 800 = 80$ dimes

30% of 800 = $.30 \times 800 = 240$ nickels

60% of 800 = $.60 \times 800 = 480$ quarters

Find the value of the coins:

$$
\begin{array}{rll}
80 \text{ dimes} = & 80 \times .10 = & \$\ 8 \\
240 \text{ nickels} = & 240 \times .05 = & 12 \\
480 \text{ quarters} = & 480 \times .25 = & \underline{120} \\
& \text{Total} & \$140
\end{array}
$$

12. **The correct answer is (C).**

First solution contains 20% of 6 quarts of alcohol.

Alcohol content $= .20 \times 6$

$= 1.2$ quarts

Second solution contains 60% of 4 quarts of alcohol.

Alcohol content $= .60 \times 4$

$= 2.4$ quarts

Mixture contains: $1.2 + 2.4 = 3.6$ quarts alcohol

$6 + 4 = 10$ quarts liquid

Alcoholic strength of mixture:

$$\frac{3.6}{10} = 36\%$$

13. **The correct answer is (D).**

$2\frac{1}{2}\%$ of insured value $= \$348$

Insured value $= \dfrac{348}{2\frac{1}{2}\%}$

$= 348 \div .025$

$= 13,920$

$\$13,920$ is 80% of total value

Total value $= \dfrac{\$13,920}{80\%}$

$= \$13,920 \div .80$

$= \$17,400$

14. The correct answer is (D), 16%.

$\frac{1}{5} \times 35 = \quad 7$ hr. sorting mail

$\frac{1}{2} \times 35 = \quad 17\frac{1}{2}$ hr. filing

$\frac{1}{7} \times 35 = \quad 5$ hr. reception

$\qquad 29\frac{1}{2}$ hr. accounted for

$35 - 29\frac{1}{2} = 5\frac{1}{2}$ hr. left for messenger
work

% spent on messenger work:

$= \dfrac{5\frac{1}{2}}{35}$

$= 5\frac{1}{2} \div 35$

$= \dfrac{11}{2} \times \dfrac{1}{35}$

$= \dfrac{11}{70}$

$= .1571$

$= 15.71\%$,

which is most nearly 16%.

15. The correct answer is (C).

80% of the boys $\quad = 1152$

Number of boys $\quad = \dfrac{1152}{80\%}$

$\qquad\qquad\qquad = 1152 \div .80$

$\qquad\qquad\qquad = 1440$

40% of students $\quad = 1440$

Total number of students $= \dfrac{1440}{40\%}$

$\qquad\qquad\qquad\qquad = 1440 \div .40$

$\qquad\qquad\qquad\qquad = 3600$

16. The correct answer is (B).

Amount of increase = $2500

Percent of increase $= \dfrac{\text{amount of increase}}{\text{original}}$

$\dfrac{25\cancel{00}}{25,0\cancel{00}} = \dfrac{1}{10} = 10\%$

17. The correct answer is (C).

Amount of increase = 20,000

Percent of increase =

$\dfrac{20,000}{80,000} = \dfrac{1}{4} = 25\%$

18. The correct answer is (D).

Amount of decrease = $4

Percent of decrease $= \dfrac{4}{25} = \dfrac{16}{100} = 16\%$

19. The correct answer is (D).

Amount of increase = $30,000

Percent of increase =

$\dfrac{30,000}{30,000} = 1 = 100\%$

20. The correct answer is (B).

Amount of decrease = 50

Percent of decrease $= \dfrac{50}{200} = \dfrac{1}{4} = 25\%$

SHORTCUTS IN MULTIPLICATION AND DIVISION

There are several shortcuts for simplifying multiplication and division. Following the description of each shortcut, practice problems are provided.

Dropping Final Zeros

1. a. A zero in a whole number is considered a "final zero" if it appears in the units column or if all columns to its right are filled with zeros. A final zero may be omitted in certain kinds of problems.

    b. In decimal numbers, a zero appearing in the extreme right column may be dropped with no effect on the solution of a problem.

2. In multiplying whole numbers, the final zero(s) may be dropped during computation and simply transferred to the answer.

Examples:

$$
\begin{array}{r} 2310 \\ \times\ 150 \\ \hline 1155 \\ 231 \\ \hline 346500 \end{array}
\qquad
\begin{array}{r} 129 \\ \times\ 210 \\ \hline 129 \\ 258 \\ \hline 27090 \end{array}
\qquad
\begin{array}{r} 1760 \\ \times\ 205 \\ \hline 880 \\ 352 \\ \hline 360800 \end{array}
$$

Practice Problems Involving Dropping Final Zeros

Solve the following multiplication problems, dropping the final zeros during computation.

1. $\begin{array}{r} 230 \\ \times\ 12 \\ \hline \end{array}$

2. $\begin{array}{r} 175 \\ \times\ 130 \\ \hline \end{array}$

3. $\begin{array}{r} 203 \\ \times\ 14 \\ \hline \end{array}$

4. $\begin{array}{r} 621 \\ \times\ 140 \\ \hline \end{array}$

5. $\begin{array}{r} 430 \\ \times\ 360 \\ \hline \end{array}$

6. $\begin{array}{r} 132 \\ \times\ 310 \\ \hline \end{array}$

7. $\begin{array}{r} 350 \\ \times\ 24 \\ \hline \end{array}$

8. $\begin{array}{r} 520 \\ \times\ 410 \\ \hline \end{array}$

9. $\begin{array}{r} 634 \\ \times\ 120 \\ \hline \end{array}$

10. $\begin{array}{r} 431 \\ \times\ 230 \\ \hline \end{array}$

Problem Solutions—Dropping Final Zeros

1.   230
   × 12
     46
     23
   2760

2.   175
   × 130
    525
    175
   22750

3.   203
   × 14
    812
    203
   2842
   (no final zeros)

4.   621
   × 140
   2484
    621
   86940

5.   430
   × 360
    258
    129
   154800

6.   132
   × 310
    132
    396
   40920

7.   350
   × 24
    140
     70
   8400

8.   520
   × 410
     52
    208
   213200

9.   634
   × 120
   1268
    634
   76080

10.   431
    × 230
    1293
     862
    99130

Multiplying Whole Numbers by Decimals

3. In multiplying a whole number by a decimal number, if there are one or more final zeros in the multiplicand, move the decimal point in the multiplier to the right the same number of places as there are final zeros in the multiplicand. Then cross out the final zero(s) in the multiplicand.

Examples:

$$\begin{array}{r} 27500 \\ \times\ .15 \\ \hline \end{array} \quad = \quad \begin{array}{r} 275 \\ \times\ 15 \\ \hline \end{array}$$

$$\begin{array}{r} 1250 \\ \times\ .345 \\ \hline \end{array} \quad = \quad \begin{array}{r} 125 \\ \times\ 3.45 \\ \hline \end{array}$$

Practice Problems Involving Multiplying Whole Numbers by Decimals

Rewrite the following problems, dropping the final zeros and moving decimal points the appropriate number of spaces. Then compute the answers.

1. $\begin{array}{r} 2400 \\ \times\ .02 \\ \hline \end{array}$

2. $\begin{array}{r} 620 \\ \times\ .04 \\ \hline \end{array}$

3. $\begin{array}{r} 800 \\ \times\ .005 \\ \hline \end{array}$

4. $\begin{array}{r} 600 \\ \times\ .002 \\ \hline \end{array}$

5. $\begin{array}{r} 340 \\ \times\ .08 \\ \hline \end{array}$

6. $\begin{array}{r} 480 \\ \times\ .4 \\ \hline \end{array}$

7. $\begin{array}{r} 400 \\ \times\ .04 \\ \hline \end{array}$

8. $\begin{array}{r} 5300 \\ \times\ .5 \\ \hline \end{array}$

9. $\begin{array}{r} 930 \\ \times\ .3 \\ \hline \end{array}$

10. $\begin{array}{r} 9000 \\ \times\ .001 \\ \hline \end{array}$

Problem Solutions—Multiplying Whole Numbers by Decimals

The rewritten problems are shown, along with the answers.

1.	24 × 2 48	**6.**	48 × 4 192
2.	62 × .4 24.8	**7.**	4 × 4 16
3.	8 × .5 4.0	**8.**	530 × 5 2650
4.	6 × .2 1.2	**9.**	93 × 3 279
5.	34 × .8 27.2	**10.**	9 × 1 9

Dividing by Whole Numbers

4. a. When there are final zeros in the divisor but no final zeros in the dividend, move the decimal point in the dividend to the left as many places as there are final zeros in the divisor, then omit the final zeros.

Example: $2700.\overline{)37523.}\, = 27.\overline{)375.23}$

   b. When there are fewer final zeros in the divisor than there are in the dividend, drop the same number of final zeros from the dividend as there are final zeros in the divisor.

Example: $250.\overline{)45300.}\, = 25.\overline{)4530.}$

   c. When there are more final zeros in the divisor than there are in the dividend, move the decimal point in the dividend to the left as many places as there are final zeros in the divisor; then omit the final zeros.

Example: $2300.\overline{)690.}\, = 23.\overline{)6.9}$

   d. When there are no final zeros in the divisor, no zeros can be dropped in the dividend.

Example: $23.\overline{)690.}\, = 23.\overline{)690.}$

Practice Problems Involving Dividing by Whole Numbers

Rewrite the following problems, dropping the final zeros and moving the decimal points the appropriate number of places. Then compute the quotients.

1. $600.\overline{)72.}$ 6. $700.\overline{)84.}$ 11. $800.\overline{)96.}$

2. $310.\overline{)6200.}$ 7. $90.\overline{)8100.}$ 12. $650.\overline{)1300.}$

3. $7600.\overline{)1520.}$ 8. $8100.\overline{)1620.}$ 13. $5500.\overline{)110.}$

4. $46.\overline{)920.}$ 9. $25.\overline{)5250.}$ 14. $36.\overline{)720.}$

5. $11.0\overline{)220.}$ 10. $41.0\overline{)820.}$ 15. $87.0\overline{)1740.}$

Rewritten Practice Problems

1. $6.\overline{).72}$ 6. $7.\overline{).84}$ 11. $8.\overline{).96}$

2. $31.\overline{)620.}$ 7. $9.\overline{)810.}$ 12. $65.\overline{)130.}$

3. $76.\overline{)15.2}$ 8. $81.\overline{)16.2}$ 13. $55.\overline{)1.1}$

4. $46.\overline{)920.}$ 9. $25.\overline{)5250.}$ 14. $36.\overline{)720.}$

5. $11.\overline{)220.}$ 10. $41.\overline{)820.}$ 15. $87.\overline{)1740.}$

Problem Solutions—Dividing by Whole Numbers

1.
$$6.\overline{)\,.72}^{\,.12}$$

5.
$$11.\overline{)\,220.}^{\,20}$$
$$\underline{22}$$
$$00$$

9.
$$25.\overline{)\,5250.}^{\,210}$$
$$\underline{50}$$
$$25$$
$$\underline{25}$$
$$00$$

13.
$$55.\overline{)\,1.10}^{\,.02}$$
$$\underline{1\,10}$$
$$00$$

2.
$$31.\overline{)\,620.}^{\,20}$$
$$\underline{62}$$
$$00$$

6.
$$7.\overline{)\,.84}^{\,.12}$$

10.
$$41.\overline{)\,820.}^{\,20}$$
$$\underline{82}$$
$$00$$

14.
$$36.\overline{)\,720.}^{\,20}$$
$$\underline{72}$$
$$00$$

3.
$$76.\overline{)\,15.2}^{\,.2}$$
$$\underline{15\,2}$$
$$0\,0$$

7.
$$9.\overline{)\,810.}^{\,90}$$
$$\underline{81}$$
$$00$$

11.
$$8.\overline{)\,.96}^{\,.12}$$

15.
$$87.\overline{)\,1740.}^{\,20}$$
$$\underline{174}$$
$$00$$

4.
$$46.\overline{)\,920.}^{\,20}$$
$$\underline{92}$$
$$00$$

8.
$$81.\overline{)\,16.2}^{\,.2}$$
$$\underline{16.2}$$
$$00$$

12.
$$65.\overline{)\,130.}^{\,2}$$
$$\underline{130}$$
$$0$$

Division by Multiplication

5. Instead of dividing by a particular number, the same answer is obtained by multiplying by the equivalent multiplier.

To find the equivalent multiplier of a given divisor, divide 1 by the divisor.

Example: The equivalent multiplier of $12\frac{1}{2}$ is $1 \div 12\frac{1}{2}$ or .08. The division problem $100 \div 12\frac{1}{2}$ may be more easily solved as the multiplication problem $100 \times .08$. The answer will be the same. This can be helpful when you are estimating answers.

Common divisors and their equivalent multipliers are shown below:

Divisor	Equivalent Multiplier
$11\frac{1}{9}$	.09
$12\frac{1}{2}$	.08
$14\frac{2}{7}$	.07
$16\frac{2}{3}$	.06
20	.05
25	.04
$33\frac{1}{3}$	.03
50	.02

6. A divisor may be multiplied or divided by any power of 10, and the only change in its equivalent multiplier will be in the placement of the decimal point, as may be seen in the following table:

Divisor	*Equivalent Multiplier*
.025	40.
.25	4.
2.5	.4
25.	.04
250.	.004
2500.	.0004

Practice Problems Involving Division by Multiplication

Rewrite and solve each of the following problems by using equivalent multipliers. Drop the final zeros where appropriate.

1. $100 \div 16\frac{2}{3} =$

2. $200 \div 25 =$

3. $300 \div 33\frac{1}{3} =$

4. $250 \div 50 =$

5. $80 \div 12\frac{1}{2} =$

6. $800 \div 14\frac{2}{7} =$

7. $620 \div 20 =$

8. $500 \div 11\frac{1}{9} =$

9. $420 \div 16\frac{2}{3} =$

10. $1200 \div 33\frac{1}{3} =$

11. $955 \div 50 =$

12. $900 \div 33\frac{1}{3} =$

13. $275 \div 12\frac{1}{2} =$

14. $625 \div 25 =$

15. $244 \div 20 =$

16. $350 \div 16\frac{2}{3} =$

17. $400 \div 33\frac{1}{3} =$

18. $375 \div 25 =$

19. $460 \div 20 =$

20. $250 \div 12\frac{1}{2} =$

Problem Solutions—Division by Multiplication

1. $100 \times .06 = 1 \times 6 = 6$
2. $200 \times .04 = 2 \times 4 = 8$
3. $300 \times .03 = 3 \times 3 = 9$
4. $250 \times .02 = 25 \times .2 = 5$
5. $80 \times .08 = 8 \times .8 = 6.4$
6. $800 \times .07 = 8 \times 7 = 56$
7. $620 \times .05 = 62 \times .5 = 31$
8. $500 \times .09 = 5 \times 9 = 45$
9. $420 \times .06 = 42 \times .6 = 25.2$
10. $1200 \times .03 = 12 \times 3 = 36$
11. $955 \times .02 = 19.1$
12. $900 \times .03 = 9 \times 3 = 27$
13. $275 \times .08 = 22$
14. $625 \times .04 = 25$
15. $244 \times .05 = 12.2$
16. $350 \times .06 = 35 \times .6 = 21$
17. $400 \times .03 = 4 \times 3 = 12$
18. $375 \times .04 = 15$
19. $460 \times .05 = 46 \times .5 = 23$
20. $250 \times .08 = 25 \times .8 = 20$

Multiplication by Division

7. Just as some division problems are made easier by changing them to equivalent multiplication problems, certain multiplication problems are made easier by changing them to equivalent division problems. The same answer is obtained by dividing by the equivalent divisor.

To find the equivalent divisor of a given multiplier, divide 1 by the multiplier.

Common multipliers and their equivalent divisors are shown below:

Multiplier	*Equivalent Divisor*
$11\frac{1}{9}$	.09
$12\frac{1}{2}$	.08
$14\frac{2}{7}$	.07
$16\frac{2}{3}$	.06
20	.05
25	.04
$33\frac{1}{3}$	.03
50	.02

Notice that the multiplier-equivalent divisor pairs are the same as the divisor-equivalent multiplier pairs given earlier.

Practice Problems Involving Multiplication by Division

Rewrite and solve each of the following problems by using division. Drop the final zeros where appropriate.

1. $77 \times 14\frac{2}{7} =$

2. $81 \times 11\frac{1}{9} =$

3. $475 \times 20 =$

4. $42 \times 50 =$

5. $36 \times 33\frac{1}{3} =$

6. $96 \times 12\frac{1}{2} =$

7. $126 \times 16\frac{2}{3} =$

8. $48 \times 25 =$

9. $33 \times 33\frac{1}{3} =$

10. $84 \times 14\frac{2}{7} =$

11. $99 \times 11\frac{1}{9} =$

12. $126 \times 33\frac{1}{3} =$

13. $168 \times 12\frac{1}{2} =$

14. $654 \times 16\frac{2}{3} =$

15. $154 \times 14\frac{2}{7} =$

16. $5250 \times 50 =$

17. $324 \times 25 =$

18. $625 \times 20 =$

19. $198 \times 11\frac{1}{9} =$

20. $224 \times 14\frac{2}{7} =$

Problem Solutions—Multiplication by Division

1. $.07\overline{)77.} = 7\overline{)7700.}^{1100.}$

2. $.09\overline{)81.} = 9\overline{)8100.}^{900.}$

3. $.05\overline{)475.} = 5\overline{)47500.}^{9500.}$

4. $.02\overline{)42.} = 2\overline{)4200.}^{2100.}$

5. $.03\overline{)36.} = 3\overline{)3600.}^{1200.}$

6. $.08\overline{)96.} = 8\overline{)9600.}^{1200.}$

7. $.06\overline{)126.} = 6\overline{)12600.}^{2100.}$

8. $.04\overline{)48.} = 4\overline{)4800.}^{1200.}$

9. $.03\overline{)33.} = 3\overline{)3300.}^{1100.}$

10. $.07\overline{)84.} = 7\overline{)8400.}^{1200.}$

11. $.09\overline{)99.} = 9\overline{)9900.}^{1100.}$

12. $.03\overline{)126.} = 3\overline{)12600.}^{4200.}$

13. $.08\overline{)168.} = 8\overline{)16800.}^{2100.}$

14. $.06\overline{)654.} = 6\overline{)65400.}^{10900.}$

15. $.07\overline{)154.} = 7\overline{)15400.}^{2200.}$

16. $.02\overline{)5250.} = 2\overline{)525000.}^{262500.}$

17. $.04\overline{)324.} = 4\overline{)32400.}^{8100.}$

18. $.05\overline{)625.} = 5\overline{)62500.}^{12500.}$

19. $.09\overline{)198.} = 9\overline{)19800.}^{2200.}$

20. $.07\overline{)224} = 7\overline{)22400.}^{3200.}$

AVERAGES

1. a. The term **average** can technically refer to a variety of mathematical ideas, but on the test it refers to the **arithmetic mean.** It is found by adding the numbers given and then dividing this sum by the number of items being averaged.

    Illustration: Find the arithmetic mean of 2, 8, 5, 9, 6, and 12.

    SOLUTION: There are 6 numbers.

    $$\text{Arithmetic mean } = \frac{2+8+5+9+6+12}{6}$$
    $$= \frac{42}{6}$$
    $$= 7$$

    Answer: The arithmetic mean is 7.

    b. If a problem calls for simply the average or the mean, it is referring to the arithmetic mean.

2. If a group of numbers is arranged in order, the middle number is called the **median.** If there is no single middle number (this occurs when there is an even number of items), the median is found by computing the arithmetic mean of the two middle numbers.

    Example: The median of 6, 8, 10, 12, 14, and 16 is the arithmetic mean of 10 and 12.

    $$\frac{10+12}{2} = \frac{22}{2} = 11$$

3. The **mode** of a group of numbers is the number that appears most often.

    Example: The mode of 10, 5, 7, 9, 12, 5, 10, 5, and 9 is 5.

4. When some numbers among terms to be averaged occur more than once, they must be given the appropriate weight. For example, if a student received four grades of 80 and one of 90, his average would not be the average of 80 and 90, but rather the average of 80, 80, 80, 80, and 90.

    To obtain the average of quantities that are weighted:

    a. Set up a table listing the quantities, their respective weights, and their respective values.

    b. Multiply the value of each quantity by its respective weight.

    c. Add up these products.

    d. Add up the weights.

    e. Divide the sum of the products by the sum of the weights.

Illustration: Assume that the weights for the following subjects are: English 3, History 2, Mathematics 2, Foreign Languages 2, and Art 1. What would be the average of a student whose marks are: English 80, History 85, Algebra 84, Spanish 82, and Art 90?

SOLUTION:

Subject	Weight	Mark
English	3	80
History	2	85
Algebra	2	84
Spanish	2	82
Art	1	90

Subject		
English	3 × 80 =	240
History	2 × 85 =	170
Algebra	2 × 84 =	168
Spanish	2 × 82 =	164
Art	1 × 90 =	90
		832

Sum of the weights: $3 + 2 + 2 + 2 + 1 = 10$

$$832 \div 10 = 83.2$$

Answer: Average = 83.2

Note: On the test, you might go directly to a list of the weighted amounts, here totaling 832, and divide by the number of weights; or you might set up a single equation.

Illustration: Mr. Martin drove for 6 hours at an average rate of 50 miles per hour and for 2 hours at an average rate of 60 miles per hour. Find his average rate for the entire trip.

SOLUTION: $\dfrac{6(50) + 2(60)}{8} = \dfrac{300 + 120}{8} = \dfrac{420}{8} = 52\frac{1}{2}$

Answer: $52\frac{1}{2}$

Since he drove many more hours at 50 miles per hour than at 60 miles per hour, his average rate should be closer to 50 than to 60, which it is. In general, average rate can always be found by dividing the total distance covered by the total time spent traveling.

Practice Problems Involving Averages

1. The arithmetic mean of 73.8, 92.2, 64.7, 43.8, 56.5, and 46.4 is
   (A) 60.6
   (B) 62.9
   (C) 64.48
   (D) 75.48
   (E) 82.9

2. The median of the numbers 8, 5, 7, 5, 9, 9, 1, 8, 10, 5, and 10 is
   (A) 5
   (B) 7
   (C) 8
   (D) 9
   (E) 10

3. The mode of the numbers 16, 15, 17, 12, 15, 15, 18, 19, and 18 is
   (A) 15
   (B) 16
   (C) 17
   (D) 18
   (E) 19

4. A clerk filed 73 forms on Monday, 85 forms on Tuesday, 54 on Wednesday, 92 on Thursday, and 66 on Friday. What was the average number of forms filed per day?
   (A) 60
   (B) 72
   (C) 74
   (D) 92
   (E) 370

5. The grades received on a test by twenty students were: 100, 55, 75, 80, 65, 65, 85, 90, 80, 45, 40, 50, 85, 85, 85, 80, 80, 70, 65, and 60. The average of these grades is
   (A) 70
   (B) 72
   (C) 77
   (D) 80
   (E) 100

6. A buyer purchased 75 six-inch rulers costing 15¢ each, 100 one-foot rulers costing 30¢ each, and 50 one-yard rulers costing 72¢ each. What was the average price per ruler?
   (A) $26\frac{1}{8}$ ¢
   (B) $34\frac{1}{3}$ ¢
   (C) 39¢
   (D) 42¢
   (E) $77\frac{1}{4}$ ¢

7. What is the average of a student who received 90 in English, 84 in algebra, 75 in French, and 76 in music, if the subjects have the following weights: English 4, algebra 3, French 3, and music 1?
   (A) 81
   (B) $81\frac{1}{2}$
   (C) 82
   (D) $82\frac{1}{2}$
   (E) 83

QUESTIONS 8–10 REFER TO THE FOLLOWING INFORMATION.

A census shows that on a certain block the number of children in each family is 3, 4, 4, 0, 1, 2, 0, 2, and 2, respectively.

8. Find the average number of children per family.
   - (A) 4
   - (B) $3\frac{1}{2}$
   - (C) 3
   - (D) 2
   - (E) $1\frac{1}{2}$

9. Find the median number of children.
   - (A) 1
   - (B) 2
   - (C) 3
   - (D) 4
   - (E) 5

10. Find the mode of the number of children.
   - (A) 0
   - (B) 1
   - (C) 2
   - (D) 3
   - (E) 4

Problem Solutions—Averages

1.	**B**	3.	A	5.	**B**	7.	E	9.	**B**
2.	**C**	4.	C	6.	**B**	8.	D	10.	**C**

1. **The correct answer is (B).** Find the sum of the values:

    $73.8 + 92.2 + 64.7 + 43.8 + 56.5 + 46.4$
    $= 377.4$

    There are 6 values.

    Arithmetic mean $= \frac{377.4}{6} = 62.9$

2. **The correct answer is (C).** Arrange the numbers in order:

    1, 5, 5, 5, 7, 8, 8, 9, 9, 10, 10

    The middle number, or median, is 8.

3. **The correct answer is (A).** The mode is that number appearing most frequently. The number 15 appears three times.

4. **The correct answer is (C).**

    Average $= \frac{73 + 85 + 54 + 92 + 66}{5}$
    $= \frac{370}{5}$
    $= 74$

5. **The correct answer is (B).**

    Sum of the grades = 1440.
    $\frac{1440}{20} = 72$

6. **The correct answer is (B).**

    $75 \times 15¢ = 1125¢$
    $100 \times 30¢ = 3000¢$
    $\underline{50 \times 72¢ = 3600¢}$
    225   7725¢

    $\frac{7725¢}{225} = 34\frac{1}{3}¢$

7. **The correct answer is (E).**

Subject	Grade	Weight
English	90	4
Algebra	84	3
French	75	3
Music	76	1

    $(90 \times 4) + (84 \times 3) + (75 \times 3) + (76 \times 1) =$

    $360 + 252 + 225 + 76 = 913$

    Weight $= 4 + 3 + 3 + 1 = 11$

    $913 \div 11 = 83$ average

8. **The correct answer is (D).**

    Average $= \frac{3 + 4 + 4 + 0 + 1 + 2 + 0 + 2 + 2}{9}$
    $= \frac{18}{9}$
    $= 2$

9. **The correct answer is (B).** Arrange the numbers in order:

    0, 0, 1, 2, 2, 2, 3, 4, 4

    Of the 9 numbers, the fifth (middle) number is 2.

10. **The correct answer is (C).** The number appearing most often is 2.

RATIO AND PROPORTION

Ratio

1. A **ratio** expresses the relationship between two (or more) quantities in terms of numbers. The mark used to indicate a ratio is the colon (:) and is read "to."

    Example: The ratio 2:3 is read "2 to 3."

2. A ratio also represents division. Therefore, any ratio of two terms may be written as a fraction, and any fraction may be written as a ratio.

    Example: $3{:}4 = \dfrac{3}{4}$

    $\dfrac{5}{6} = 5{:}6$

3. To simplify any complicated ratio of two terms containing fractions, decimals, or percents:

    a. Divide the first term by the second.

    b. Write as a fraction in simplest form.

    c. Write the fraction as a ratio.

    Illustration: Simplify the ratio $\dfrac{5}{6} : \dfrac{7}{8}$.

    SOLUTION: $\dfrac{5}{6} \div \dfrac{7}{8} = \dfrac{5}{6} \times \dfrac{8}{7} = \dfrac{40}{42} = \dfrac{20}{21}$

    $\dfrac{20}{21} = 20:21$

    Answer: 20:21

4. To solve problems in which the ratio is given:

    a. Add the terms in the ratio.

    b. Divide the total amount that is to be put into a ratio by this sum.

    c. Multiply each term in the ratio by this quotient.

    Illustration: The sum of $360 is to be divided among three people according to the ratio 3:4:5. How much does each one receive?

    SOLUTION: $3 + 4 + 5 = 12$

    $\$360 \div 12 = \$30$

    $\$30 \times 3 = \$90$

    $\$30 \times 4 = \$120$

    $\$30 \times 5 = \$150$

    Answer: The money is divided thusly: $90, $120, $150.

Proportion

5. a. A **proportion** indicates the equality of two ratios.

    Example: 2:4 = 5:10 is a proportion. This is read "2 is to 4 as 5 is to 10."

    b. In a proportion, the two outside terms are called the **extremes,** and the two inside terms are called the **means.**

    Example: In the proportion 2:4 = 5:10, 2 and 10 are the extremes, and 4 and 5 are the means.

    c. Proportions are often written in fractional form.

    Example: The proportion 2:4 = 5:10 may be written $\frac{2}{4} = \frac{5}{10}$.

    d. In any proportion, the product of the means equals the product of the extremes. If the proportion is a fractional form, the products may be found by cross-multiplication.

    Example: In $\frac{2}{4} = \frac{5}{10}$, $4 \times 5 = 2 \times 10$.

    e. The product of the extremes divided by one mean equals the other mean; the product of the means divided by one extreme equals the other extreme.

6. Many problems in which three terms are given and one term is unknown can be solved by using proportions. To solve such problems:

    a. Formulate the proportion very carefully according to the facts given. (If any term is misplaced, the solution will be incorrect.) Any symbol may be written in place of the missing term.

    b. Determine by inspection whether the means or the extremes are known. Multiply the pair that has both terms given.

    c. Divide this product by the third term given to find the unknown term.

    Illustration: The scale on a map shows that 2 cm represents 30 miles of actual length. What is the actual length of a road that is represented by 7 cm on the map?

    SOLUTION: The map lengths and the actual lengths are in proportion—that is, they have equal ratios. If m stands for the unknown length, the proportion is:

    $$\frac{2}{7} = \frac{30}{m}$$

    As the proportion is written, m is an extreme and is equal to the product of the means, divided by the other extreme:

    $$m = \frac{7 \times 30}{2}$$
    $$m = \frac{210}{2}$$
    $$m = 105$$

    Answer: 7 cm on the map represents 105 miles.

Illustration: If a money bag containing 500 nickels weighs 6 pounds, how much will a money bag containing 1600 nickels weigh?

SOLUTION: The weights of the bags and the number of coins in them are proportional. Suppose w represents the unknown weight. Then

$$\frac{6}{w} = \frac{500}{1600}$$

The unknown is a mean and is equal to the product of the extremes, divided by the other mean:

$$w = \frac{6 \times 1600}{500}$$
$$w = 19.2$$

Answer: A bag containing 1600 nickels weighs 19.2 pounds.

Practice Problems Involving Ratio and Proportion

1. The ratio of 24 to 64 is
   (A) 1:64
   (B) 1:24
   (C) 20:100
   (D) 24:100
   (E) 3:8

2. The Baltimore Ravens won 8 games and lost 3. The ratio of games won to games played is
   (A) 11:8
   (B) 8:3
   (C) 8:11
   (D) 3:8
   (E) 3:11

3. The ratio of $\frac{1}{4}$ to $\frac{3}{5}$ is
   (A) 1 to 3
   (B) 3 to 20
   (C) 5 to 12
   (D) 3 to 4
   (E) 5 to 4

4. If there are 16 boys and 12 girls in a class, the ratio of the number of girls to the number of children in the class is
   (A) 3 to 4
   (B) 3 to 7
   (C) 4 to 7
   (D) 4 to 3
   (E) 7 to 4

5. 259 is to 37 as
   (A) 5 is to 1
   (B) 63 is to 441
   (C) 84 is to 12
   (D) 130 is to 19
   (E) 25 is to 4

6. 2 dozen cans of dog food at the rate of 3 cans for $1.45 would cost
   (A) $10.05
   (B) $10.20
   (C) $11.20
   (D) $11.60
   (E) $11.75

7. A snapshot measures $2\frac{1}{2}$ inches by $1\frac{7}{8}$ inches. It is to be enlarged so that the longer dimension will be 4 inches. The length of the enlarged shorter dimension will be
   (A) $2\frac{1}{2}$ in.
   (B) 3 in.
   (C) $3\frac{3}{8}$ in.
   (D) 4 in.
   (E) 5 in.

8. Men's white handkerchiefs cost $2.29 for 3. The cost per dozen handkerchiefs is
   (A) $27.48
   (B) $13.74
   (C) $9.16
   (D) $6.87
   (E) $4.58

9. A certain pole casts a shadow 24 feet long. At the same time another pole 3 feet high casts a shadow 4 feet long. How high is the first pole, given that the heights and shadows are in proportion?
   (A) 18 ft.
   (B) 19 ft.
   (C) 20 ft.
   (D) 21 ft.
   (E) 24 ft.

10. The actual length represented by $3\frac{1}{2}$ inches on a drawing having a scale of $\frac{1}{8}$ inch to the foot is

    (A) 3.5 ft.

    (B) 7 ft.

    (C) 21 ft.

    (D) 28 ft.

    (E) 120 ft.

11. Aluminum bronze consists of copper and aluminum, usually in the ratio of 10:1 by weight. If an object made of this alloy weighs 77 lb., how many pounds of aluminum does it contain?

    (A) 0.7 pounds

    (B) 7.0 pounds

    (C) 7.7 pounds

    (D) 70.7 pounds

    (E) 77.0 pounds

12. It costs 31 cents a square foot to lay vinyl flooring. To lay 180 square feet of flooring, it will cost

    (A) $16.20

    (B) $18.60

    (C) $55.80

    (D) $62

    (E) $180

13. If a per diem worker earns $352 in 16 days, the amount that he will earn in 117 days is most nearly

    (A) $3050

    (B) $2575

    (C) $2285

    (D) $2080

    (E) $1170

14. Assuming that on a blueprint $\frac{1}{8}$ inch equals 12 inches of actual length, the actual length in inches of a steel bar represented on the blueprint by a line $3\frac{3}{4}$ inches long is

    (A) $3\frac{3}{4}$ inches

    (B) 30 inches

    (C) 36 inches

    (D) 360 inches

    (E) 450 inches

15. A, B, and C invested $9,000, $7,000, and $6,000, respectively. Their profits were to be divided according to the ratio of their investment. If B uses his share of the firm's profit of $825 to pay a personal debt of $230, how much will he have left?

    (A) $30.50

    (B) $32.50

    (C) $34.50

    (D) $36.50

    (E) $37.50

Problem Solutions—Ratio and Proportion

1.	E	4.	B	7.	B	10.	D	13.	B
2.	C	5.	C	8.	C	11.	B	14.	D
3.	C	6.	D	9.	A	12.	C	15.	B

1. **The correct answer is (E).** The ratio 24 to 64 may be written 24:64 or $\frac{24}{64}$. In fraction form, the ratio can be simplified:

$$\frac{24}{64} = \frac{3}{8} = \text{ or } 3{:}8$$

2. **The correct answer is (C).** The number of games played was $3 + 8 = 11$. The ratio of games won to games played is 8:11.

3. **The correct answer is (C).**

$$\frac{1}{4} : \frac{3}{5} = \frac{1}{4} \div \frac{3}{5}$$
$$= \frac{1}{4} \times \frac{5}{3}$$
$$= \frac{5}{12}$$
$$= 5{:}12$$

4. **The correct answer is (B).** There are $16 + 12 = 28$ children in the class. The ratio of number of girls to number of children is 12:28.

$$\frac{12}{28} = \frac{3}{7}$$

5. **The correct answer is (C).** The ratio $\frac{259}{37}$ simplifies by 37 to $\frac{7}{1}$. The ratio $\frac{84}{12}$ also simplifies to $\frac{7}{1}$. Therefore, $\frac{259}{37} = \frac{84}{12}$ is a proportion.

6. **The correct answer is (D).** The number of cans is proportional to the price. Let p represent the unknown price:

Then
$$\frac{3}{24} = \frac{1.45}{p}$$
$$p = \frac{1.45 \times 24}{3}$$
$$p = \frac{34.80}{3}$$
$$= \$11.60$$

7. **The correct answer is (B).** Let s represent the unknown shorter dimension:

$$\frac{2\frac{1}{2}}{4} = \frac{1\frac{7}{8}}{s}$$
$$s = \frac{4 \times 1\frac{7}{8}}{2\frac{1}{2}}$$
$$= \frac{\overset{1}{\cancel{4}} \times \frac{15}{\underset{2}{\cancel{8}}}}{2\frac{1}{2}}$$
$$= \frac{15}{2} \div 2\frac{1}{2}$$
$$= \frac{15}{2} \div \frac{5}{2}$$
$$= \frac{15}{2} \times \frac{2}{5} = \frac{15}{5} = 3$$

8. **The correct answer is (C).** If p is the cost per dozen (12):

$$\frac{3}{12} = \frac{2.29}{p}$$
$$p = \frac{\overset{4}{\cancel{12}} \times 2.29}{\underset{1}{\cancel{3}}}$$
$$p = 9.16$$

9. **The correct answer is (A).** If f is the height of the first pole, the proportion is:

$$\frac{f}{24} = \frac{3}{4}$$

$$f = \frac{\overset{6}{\cancel{24}} \times 3}{\cancel{4}_1}$$

$$= 18$$

10. **The correct answer is (D).** If y is the unknown length:

$$\frac{3\frac{1}{2}}{\frac{1}{8}} = \frac{y}{1}$$

$$y = \frac{3\frac{1}{2} \times 1}{\frac{1}{8}}$$

$$= 3\frac{1}{2} \div \frac{1}{8}$$

$$= \frac{7}{\cancel{2}_1} \times \frac{\overset{4}{\cancel{8}}}{1}$$

$$= 28$$

11. **The correct answer is (B).** Since only two parts of a proportion are known (77 is total weight), the problem must be solved by the ratio method. The ratio 10:1 means that if the alloy were separated into equal parts, 10 of those parts would be copper and 1 would be aluminum, for a total of $10 + 1 = 11$ parts.

$77 \div 11 = 7$ lb. per part

The alloy has 1 part aluminum.

$7 \times 1 = 7$ lb. aluminum

12. **The correct answer is (C).** The cost (c) is proportional to the number of square feet.

$$\frac{\$.31}{c} = \frac{1}{180}$$

$$c = \frac{\$.31 \times 180}{1}$$

$$= \$55.80$$

13. **The correct answer is (B).** The amount earned is proportional to the number of days worked. If a is the unknown amount:

$$\frac{\$352}{a} = \frac{16}{117}$$

$$a = \frac{\$352 \times 117}{16}$$

$$a = \$2574$$

14. **The correct answer is (D).** If n is the unknown length:

$$\frac{\frac{1}{8}}{3\frac{3}{4}} = \frac{12}{n}$$

$$n = \frac{12 \times 3\frac{3}{4}}{\frac{1}{8}}$$

$$= \frac{\overset{3}{\cancel{12}} \times \frac{15}{\cancel{4}_1}}{\frac{1}{8}}$$

$$= 45 \div \frac{1}{8}$$

$$= 45 \times \frac{8}{1}$$

$$= 360$$

15. **The correct answer is (B).** The ratio of investment is:

9,000:7,000:6,000 or 9:7:6

$9 + 7 + 6 = 22$

$\$825 \div 22 = \$37.50$ each share of profit

$7 \times \$37.50 = \$262.50$, B's share of profit

$$
\begin{aligned}
&\$\ 262.50 \\
&\underline{-230.00} \\
&\$\ 32.50, \text{ amount B has left}
\end{aligned}
$$

POWERS AND ROOTS

1. The numbers that are multiplied to give a product are called the **factors** of the product.

    Example: In $2 \times 3 = 6$, 2 and 3 are factors.

2. If the factors are the same, an **exponent** may be used to indicate the number of times the factor appears.

    Example: In $3 \times 3 = 3^2$, the number 3 appears as a factor twice, as is indicated by the exponent 2.

3. When a product is written in exponential form, the number the exponent refers to is called the **base.** The product itself is called the **power.**

    Example: In 2^5, the number 2 is the base and 5 is the exponent.

    $2^5 = 2 \times 2 \times 2 \times 2 \times 2 = 32$, so 32 is the power.

4. a. If the exponent used is 2, we say that the base has been **squared,** or raised to the second power.

    Example: 6^2 is read "six squared" or "six to the second power."

    b. If the exponent used is 3, we say that the base has been **cubed,** or raised to the third power.

    Example: 5^3 is read "five cubed" or "five to the third power."

    c. If the exponent is 4, we say that the base has been raised to the fourth power. If the exponent is 5, we say that the base has been raised to the fifth power, etc.

    Example: 2^8 is read "two to the eighth power."

5. A number that is the product of a whole number squared is called a **perfect square.**

    Example: 25 is a perfect square because $25 = 5^2$.

6. a. If a number has exactly two equal factors, each factor is called the **square root** of the number.

    Example: $9 = 3 \times 3$; therefore, 3 is the square root of 9.

    b. The symbol $\sqrt{}$ is used to indicate square root.

    Example: $\sqrt{9} = 3$ means that the square root of 9 is 3, or $3 \times 3 = 9$.

    c. In principle, all numbers have a square root. Although many square roots cannot be calculated exactly, they can be found to whatever degree of accuracy is needed (see item 8). Thus, the square root of 10, $\sqrt{10}$, is *by definition* the number that equals 10 when it is squared: $\sqrt{10} \times \sqrt{10} = 10$.

    d. If a number has exactly three equal factors, each factor is called a **cube root.** The symbol $\sqrt[3]{}$ is used to indicate a cube root.

    Example: $8 = 2 \times 2 \times 2$; thus $2 = \sqrt[3]{8}$

    e. In general, the *nth* root is indicated as $\sqrt[n]{}$.

7. The square root of the most common perfect squares may be found by using the following table, or by trial and error; that is, by finding the number that, when squared, yields the given perfect square.

Number	Perfect Square	Number	Perfect Square
1	1	10	100
2	4	11	121
3	9	12	144
4	16	13	169
5	25	14	196
6	36	15	225
7	49	20	400
8	64	25	625
9	81	30	900

Example: To find $\sqrt{81}$, note that 81 is the perfect square of 9, or $9^2 = 81$. Therefore, $\sqrt{81} = 9$.

8. On the GRE you will only rarely have to find the square root of a number that is not a perfect square. The two most common square roots you will have to deal with are $\sqrt{2}$, which equals approximately 1.4, and $\sqrt{3}$, which equals approximately 1.7. Most times you will not have to rename these square roots as their equivalents since the answer choices will be in terms of the square roots, e.g., (A) $4\sqrt{3}$, etc.

9. When more complex items are raised to powers, the same basic rules apply.

   a. To find the power of some multiplied item, find the power of each multiplicand and multiply those powers together.

   Example: $(4x)^2 = (4x)(4x) = (4)(4)(x)(x) = (4)^2 (x)^2 = 16x^2$

   Example: $(2xy)^4 = (2)^4(x)^4(y)^4 = 16x^4y^4$

   b. To find the power of some divided item or fraction, find the power of each part of the fraction and then divide in the manner of the original fraction.

   Example: $\left(\dfrac{2}{x}\right)^2 = \left(\dfrac{2}{x}\right)\left(\dfrac{2}{x}\right) = \left(\dfrac{4}{x^2}\right)$

   c. To find the result when two powers of the same base are multiplied together, *add* the exponents. You add the exponents because you are adding to the length of the string of the same base all being multiplied together.

   Example: $(x^2)(x^3) = (x)(x) \cdot (x)(x)(x) = xxxxx = x^{2+3} = x^5$

   Example: $2^a \cdot 2^b = 2^{(a+b)}$

   d. To find the result when a power is raised to an exponent, *multiply* the exponents. You multiply the exponents together because you are multiplying the length of the string of the same base all being multiplied together.

   Example: $(x^2)^3 = (x^2)(x^2)(x^2) = xxxxxx = x^{(2 \cdot 3)} = x^6$

e. When a power is divided by another power of the same base, the result is found by subtracting the exponent in the denominator (bottom) from the exponent in the numerator (top).

Example: $\dfrac{x^3}{x^2} = \dfrac{xxx}{xx} = x^{(3-2)} = x^1 = x$

Note: Any base to the first power, x^1, equals the base.

Example: $\dfrac{x^9}{x^6} = x^{(9-6)} = x^3$

Example: $\dfrac{x^2}{x^2} = \dfrac{xx}{xx} = x^{(2-2)} = x^0 = 1$

Note: Any base to the "zero-th" power, x^0, equals 1.

Example: $\dfrac{x^3}{x^4} = \dfrac{xxx}{xxxx} = \dfrac{1}{x} = x^{(3-4)} = x^{-1}$

f. A **negative exponent** is a reciprocal, as discussed in the earlier section on fractions.

Example: $z^{-3} = \left(\dfrac{z}{1}\right)^{-3} = \left(\dfrac{1}{z}\right)^{+3} = \dfrac{1^3}{z^3} = \dfrac{1}{z^3}$

Example: $(3p)^{-2} = \dfrac{1}{(3p)^{+2}} = \dfrac{1}{9p^2}$

Example: $\left(r^{-3}\right)^{-6} = \dfrac{1}{\left(r^{-3}\right)^{+6}} = \dfrac{1}{\left(\frac{1}{r^3}\right)^6} = \dfrac{1}{\frac{1}{r^{18}}}$

$$= (1)\left(\dfrac{r^{18}}{1}\right) = r^{18}$$

or $\left(r^{-3}\right)^{-6} = r^{(-3 \times -6)} = r^{+18}$

10. Some problems require that different powers be grouped together. Depending on the relationships, they can be grouped by doing the processes explained in item 9 in the reverse direction.

Example: $9x^2 = 3^2 \cdot x^2 = (3x)^2$

Example: $\dfrac{81}{y^2} = \dfrac{9^2}{y^2} = \left(\dfrac{9}{y}\right)^2$

Example: $m^{12} = (m^5)(m^7)$ or $(m^{10})(m^2)$, etc.

Example: $z^{24} = (z^6)^4$ or $(z^8)^3$, etc.

11. The conditions under which radicals can be added or subtracted are much the same as the conditions for variables in an algebraic expression. The radicals act as a label, or unit, and must therefore be exactly the same. In adding or subtracting, we add or subtract the coefficients, or rational parts, and carry the radical along as a label, which does not change.

Example: $\sqrt{2} + \sqrt{3}$ cannot be added

$\sqrt{2} + 3\sqrt{2}$ can be added

$4\sqrt{2} + 5\sqrt{2} = 9\sqrt{2}$

Often, when radicals to be added or subtracted are not the same, simplification of one or more radicals will make them the same. To simplify a radical, we remove any perfect square factors from underneath the radical sign.

Example: $\sqrt{12} = \sqrt{4}\,\sqrt{3} = 2\sqrt{3}$

$\sqrt{27} = \sqrt{9}\,\sqrt{3} = 3\sqrt{3}$

So, if we wish to add $\sqrt{12} + \sqrt{27}$, we must first simplify each one. Adding the simplified radicals gives a sum of $5\sqrt{3}$.

Illustration: $\sqrt{125} + \sqrt{20} - \sqrt{500}$

SOLUTION: $\sqrt{25}\,\sqrt{5} + \sqrt{4}\,\sqrt{5} - \sqrt{100}\,\sqrt{5} =$

$5\sqrt{5} + 2\sqrt{5} - 10\sqrt{5} = -3\sqrt{5}$

Answer: $-3\sqrt{5}$

12. In multiplication and division we again treat the radicals as we would variables in an algebraic expression. They are factors and must be treated as such.

Example: $(\sqrt{2})(\sqrt{3}) = \sqrt{(2)\,(3)} = \sqrt{6}$

Example: $4\sqrt{2} \cdot 5\sqrt{3} = 20 \cdot \sqrt{6}$

Example: $(3\sqrt{2})^2 = 3\sqrt{2} \cdot 3\sqrt{2} = 9 \cdot 2 = 18$

Example: $\dfrac{\sqrt{8}}{\sqrt{2}} = \sqrt{4} = 2$

Example: $\dfrac{10\sqrt{20}}{\sqrt{4}} = \dfrac{\overset{5}{\cancel{10}}\,\sqrt{20}}{\underset{1}{\cancel{2}}} = 5\sqrt{20} = 5\sqrt{4}\sqrt{5} = 10\sqrt{5}$

Example: $\sqrt{2}(\sqrt{8} + \sqrt{18}) = \sqrt{16} + \sqrt{36} = 4 + 6 = 10$

13. In simplifying radicals that contain several terms under the radical sign, we must combine terms before taking the square root.

Example: $\sqrt{16+9} = \sqrt{25} = 5$

Note: It is not true that $\sqrt{16+9} = \sqrt{16} + \sqrt{9}$, which would be $4 + 3$, or 7.

Example: $\sqrt{\dfrac{x^2}{16} - \dfrac{x^2}{25}} = \sqrt{\dfrac{25x^2 - 16x^2}{400}} = \sqrt{\dfrac{9x^2}{400}} = \dfrac{3|x|}{20}$

Practice Problems Involving Powers and Roots

1. Combine: $4\sqrt{27} - 2\sqrt{48} + \sqrt{147}$
   - (A) $27\sqrt{3}$
   - (B) $-3\sqrt{3}$
   - (C) $9\sqrt{3}$
   - (D) $10\sqrt{3}$
   - (E) $11\sqrt{3}$

2. Combine: $\sqrt{80} + \sqrt{45} - \sqrt{20}$
   - (A) $9\sqrt{5}$
   - (B) $5\sqrt{5}$
   - (C) $-\sqrt{5}$
   - (D) $3\sqrt{5}$
   - (E) $-2\sqrt{5}$

3. Combine: $6\sqrt{5} + 3\sqrt{2} - 4\sqrt{5} + \sqrt{2}$
   - (A) 8
   - (B) $2\sqrt{5} + 3\sqrt{2}$
   - (C) $2\sqrt{5} + 4\sqrt{2}$
   - (D) $5\sqrt{7}$
   - (E) 5

4. Combine: $\frac{1}{2}\sqrt{180} + \frac{1}{3}\sqrt{45} - \frac{2}{5}\sqrt{20}$
   - (A) $3\sqrt{10} + \sqrt{15} + 2\sqrt{2}$
   - (B) $\frac{16}{5}\sqrt{5}$
   - (C) $\sqrt{97}$
   - (D) $\frac{24}{5}\sqrt{5}$
   - (E) None of these

5. Combine: $5\sqrt{mn} - 3\sqrt{mn} - 2\sqrt{mn}$
   - (A) 0
   - (B) 1
   - (C) $\sqrt{mn}$
   - (D) mn
   - (E) $-\sqrt{mn}$

6. Multiply and simplify: $2\sqrt{18} \cdot 6\sqrt{2}$
   - (A) 72
   - (B) 48
   - (C) $12\sqrt{6}$
   - (D) $8\sqrt{6}$
   - (E) 36

7. Find: $(3\sqrt{3})^3$
   - (A) $27\sqrt{3}$
   - (B) $81\sqrt{3}$
   - (C) 81
   - (D) $9\sqrt{3}$
   - (E) 243

8. Multiply and simplify: $\frac{1}{2}\sqrt{2}\left(\sqrt{6} + \frac{1}{2}\sqrt{2}\right)$
   - (A) $\sqrt{3} + \frac{1}{2}$
   - (B) $\frac{1}{2}\sqrt{3}$
   - (C) $\sqrt{6} + 1$
   - (D) $\sqrt{6} + \frac{1}{2}$
   - (E) $\sqrt{6} + 2$

9. Divide and simplify: $\frac{\sqrt{32b^3}}{\sqrt{8b}}$
   - (A) $2\sqrt{b}$
   - (B) $\sqrt{2b}$
   - (C) $2b$
   - (D) $\sqrt{2b^2}$
   - (E) $b\sqrt{2b}$

10. Divide and simplify: $\frac{15\sqrt{96}}{5\sqrt{2}}$
    - (A) $7\sqrt{3}$
    - (B) $7\sqrt{12}$
    - (C) $11\sqrt{3}$
    - (D) $12\sqrt{3}$
    - (E) $40\sqrt{3}$

11. Simplify: $\sqrt{\frac{x^2}{9} + \frac{x^2}{16}}$

    (A) $\dfrac{25x^2}{144}$

    (B) $\dfrac{5|x|}{12}$

    (C) $\dfrac{5x^2}{12}$

    (D) $\dfrac{|x|}{7}$

    (E) $\dfrac{7|x|}{12}$

12. Simplify: $\sqrt{36y^2 + 64x^2}$

    (A) $6y + 8x$

    (B) $10xy$

    (C) $6y^2 + 8x^2$

    (D) $10x^2y^2$

    (E) $2\sqrt{9y^2 + 16x^2}$

13. Simplify: $\sqrt{\frac{x^2}{64} - \frac{x^2}{100}}$

    (A) $\dfrac{x}{40}$

    (B) $-\dfrac{x}{2}$

    (C) $\dfrac{x}{2}$

    (D) $\dfrac{3|x|}{40}$

    (E) $\dfrac{3x}{80}$

14. Simplify: $\sqrt{\frac{y^2}{2} - \frac{y^2}{18}}$

    (A) $\dfrac{2|y|}{3}$

    (B) $\dfrac{|y|\sqrt{5}}{3}$

    (C) $\dfrac{10|y|}{3}$

    (D) $\dfrac{|y|\sqrt{3}}{6}$

    (E) It cannot be simplified.

15. $\sqrt{a^2 + b^2}$ is equal to

    (A) $a + b$
    (B) $a - b$
    (C) $\sqrt{a^2} + \sqrt{b^2}$
    (D) $(a + b)(a - b)$
    (E) None of these

16. Which of the following square roots can be found exactly?

    (A) $\sqrt{.4}$

    (B) $\sqrt{.9}$

    (C) $\sqrt{.09}$

    (D) $\sqrt{.02}$

    (E) $\sqrt{.025}$

Problem Solutions—Powers and Roots

1.	E	5.	A	9.	C	13.	D
2.	B	6.	A	10.	D	14.	A
3.	C	7.	B	11.	B	15.	E
4.	B	8.	A	12.	E	16.	C

1. **The correct answer is (E).**

$$4\sqrt{27} = 4\sqrt{9}\sqrt{3} = 12\sqrt{3}$$
$$2\sqrt{48} = 2\sqrt{16}\sqrt{3} = 8\sqrt{3}$$
$$\sqrt{147} = \sqrt{49}\sqrt{3} = 7\sqrt{3}$$
$$12\sqrt{3} - 8\sqrt{3} + 7\sqrt{3} = 11\sqrt{3}$$

2. **The correct answer is (B).**

$$\sqrt{80} = \sqrt{16}\sqrt{5} = 4\sqrt{5}$$
$$\sqrt{45} = \sqrt{9}\sqrt{5} = 3\sqrt{5}$$
$$\sqrt{20} = \sqrt{4}\sqrt{5} = 2\sqrt{5}$$
$$4\sqrt{5} + 3\sqrt{5} - 2\sqrt{5} = 5\sqrt{5}$$

3. **The correct answer is (C).** Only terms with the same radical may be combined.

$$6\sqrt{5} - 4\sqrt{5} = 2\sqrt{5}$$
$$3\sqrt{2} + \sqrt{2} = 4\sqrt{2}$$

Therefore, we have $2\sqrt{5} + 4\sqrt{2}$.

4. **The correct answer is (B).**

$$\frac{1}{2}\sqrt{80} = \frac{1}{2}\sqrt{36}\sqrt{5} = 3\sqrt{5}$$
$$\frac{1}{3}\sqrt{45} = \frac{1}{3}\sqrt{9}\sqrt{5} = \sqrt{5}$$
$$\frac{2}{5}\sqrt{20} = \frac{2}{5}\sqrt{4}\sqrt{5} = \frac{4}{5}\sqrt{5}$$
$$3\sqrt{5} + \sqrt{5} - \frac{4}{5}\sqrt{5} = 4\sqrt{5} - \frac{4}{5}\sqrt{5}$$
$$= 3\frac{1}{5}\sqrt{5} = \frac{16}{5}\sqrt{5}$$

5. **The correct answer is (A).**

$$5\sqrt{mn} - 5\sqrt{mn} = 0$$

6. **The correct answer is (A).**

$$2\sqrt{18} \cdot 6\sqrt{2} = 12\sqrt{36} = 12 \cdot 6 = 72$$

7. **The correct answer is (B).**

$$3\sqrt{3} \cdot 3\sqrt{3} \cdot 3\sqrt{3} = 27(3\sqrt{3}) = 81\sqrt{3}$$

8. **The correct answer is (A).** Using the distributive law, we have

$$\frac{1}{2}\sqrt{12} + \frac{1}{4} \cdot 2 = \frac{1}{2}\sqrt{4}\sqrt{3} + \frac{1}{2} = \sqrt{3} + \frac{1}{2}$$

9. **The correct answer is (C).** Dividing the numbers in the radical sign, we have $\sqrt{4b^2} = 2b$.

10. **The correct answer is (D).**

$$3\sqrt{48} = 3\sqrt{16}\sqrt{3} = 12\sqrt{3}$$

11. **The correct answer is (B).**

$$\sqrt{\frac{16x^2 + 9x^2}{144}} = \sqrt{\frac{25x^2}{144}} = \frac{5|x|}{12}$$

12. **The correct answer is (E).** The terms cannot be combined, and it is not possible to take the square root of separated terms.

Factor out a 4.

$$\sqrt{4}\sqrt{9y^2 + 16x^2} = 2\sqrt{9y^2 + 16x^2}$$

13. **The correct answer is (D).**

$$\sqrt{\frac{100x^2 - 64x^2}{6400}} = \sqrt{\frac{36x^2}{6400}} = \frac{6|x|}{80} = \frac{3|x|}{40}$$

14. **The correct answer is (A).**

$$\sqrt{\frac{18y^2 - 2y^2}{36}} = \sqrt{\frac{16y^2}{36}} = \frac{4|y|}{6} = \frac{2|y|}{3}$$

15. **The correct answer is (E).** It is not possible to find the square root of separate terms.

16. **The correct answer is (C).** In order to take the square root of a decimal, it must have an even number of decimal places so that its square root will have exactly half as many. In addition to this, the digits must form a perfect square ($\sqrt{.09} = .3$).

ALGEBRAIC FRACTIONS

1. In simplifying algebraic fractions, we must divide the numerator and denominator by the same factor, just as we do in arithmetic. We can never cancel terms, as this would be adding or subtracting the same number from the numerator and denominator, which changes the value of the fraction. When we simplify $\frac{6}{8}$ to $\frac{3}{4}$, we are really saying that $\frac{6}{8} = \frac{2 \cdot 3}{2 \cdot 4}$ and then dividing numerator and denominator by 2. We do not say $\frac{6}{8} = \frac{3+3}{3+5}$ and then say $\frac{6}{8} = \frac{3}{5}$. This is faulty reasoning in algebra as well. If we have $\frac{6t}{8t}$, we can divide numerator and denominator by $2t$, giving $\frac{3}{4}$ as an answer. However, if we have $\frac{6+t}{8+t}$, we can do no more, as there is no factor that divides into the *entire* numerator as well as the *entire* denominator. Canceling terms is one of the most frequent student errors. Don't get caught! Be careful!

   Illustration: Simplify $\frac{3x^2+6x}{4x^3+8x^2}$ to its simplest form.

   SOLUTION: Factoring the numerator and denominator, we have $\frac{3x(x+2)}{4x^2(x+2)}$. The factors common to both numerator and denominator are x and $(x + 2)$. Dividing these out, we arrive at $\frac{3}{4x}$.

   Answer: $\frac{3}{4x}$

2. In adding or subtracting fractions, we must work with a common denominator and the same shortcuts we used in arithmetic.

   Illustration: Find the sum of $\frac{1}{a}$ and $\frac{1}{b}$.

   SOLUTION: Remember to add the two cross-products and put the sum over the denominator product.

   Answer: $\frac{b+a}{ab}$

   Illustration: Add: $\frac{2n}{3} + \frac{3n}{2}$

   SOLUTION: $\frac{4n+9n}{6} = \frac{13n}{6}$

   Answer: $\frac{13n}{6}$

3. In multiplying or dividing fractions, we may divide a factor common to any numerator and any denominator. Always remember in division to multiply by the reciprocal of the fraction following the division sign. Where exponents are involved, they are added in multiplication and subtracted in division.

    Illustration: Find the product of $\frac{a^3}{b^2}$ and $\frac{b^3}{a^2}$.

    SOLUTION: We divide a^2 into the first numerator and second denominator, giving $\frac{a}{b^2} \cdot \frac{b^3}{1}$. Then we divide b^2 into the first denominator and second numerator, giving $\frac{a}{1} \frac{b}{1}$. Finally, we multiply the resulting fractions, giving an answer of ab.

    Answer: ab

    Illustration: Divide $\frac{6x^2y}{5}$ by $2x^3$.

    SOLUTION: $\frac{6x^2y}{5} \cdot \frac{1}{2x^3}$. Divide the first numerator and second denominator by $2x^2$, giving $\frac{3y}{5} \cdot \frac{1}{x}$. Multiplying the resulting fractions, we get $\frac{3y}{5x}$.

    Answer: $\dfrac{3y}{5x}$

4. Complex algebraic fractions are simplified by the same methods used in arithmetic. Multiply *each term* of the complex fraction by the least quantity that will eliminate the fraction within the fraction.

    Illustration: $\dfrac{\frac{1}{a} + \frac{1}{b}}{ab}$

    SOLUTION: We must multiply *each term* by ab, giving $\frac{b+a}{a^2b^2}$. Since no simplification beyond this is possible, $\frac{b+a}{a^2b^2}$ is our final answer. Remember *never* to divide terms unless they apply to the entire numerator or the entire denominator.

    Answer: $\dfrac{b+a}{a^2b^2}$

Practice Problems Involving Algebraic Fractions

1. Find the sum of $\frac{n}{6} + \frac{2n}{5}$.

   (A) $\dfrac{13n}{30}$

   (B) $17n$

   (C) $\dfrac{3n}{30}$

   (D) $\dfrac{17n}{30}$

   (E) $\dfrac{3n}{11}$

2. Combine into a single fraction: $1 - \frac{x}{y}$

   (A) $\dfrac{1-x}{y}$

   (B) $\dfrac{y-x}{y}$

   (C) $\dfrac{x-y}{y}$

   (D) $\dfrac{1-x}{1-y}$

   (E) $\dfrac{y-x}{xy}$

3. Divide $\frac{x-y}{x+y}$ by $\frac{y-x}{y+x}$.

   (A) 1

   (B) -1

   (C) $\dfrac{(x-y)^2}{(x+y)^2}$

   (D) $-\dfrac{(x-y)^2}{(x+y)^2}$

   (E) 0

4. Simplify: $\dfrac{1 + \frac{1}{x}}{\frac{y}{x}}$

   (A) $\dfrac{x+1}{y}$

   (B) $\dfrac{x+1}{x}$

   (C) $\dfrac{x+1}{xy}$

   (D) $\dfrac{x^2+1}{xy}$

   (E) $\dfrac{y+1}{y}$

5. Find an expression equivalent to $\left(\dfrac{2x^2}{y}\right)^3$.

   (A) $\dfrac{8x^5}{3y}$

   (B) $\dfrac{6x^6}{y^3}$

   (C) $\dfrac{6x^5}{y^3}$

   (D) $\dfrac{8x^5}{y^3}$

   (E) $\dfrac{8x^6}{y^3}$

6. Simplify: $\dfrac{\frac{1}{x} + \frac{1}{y}}{3}$

   (A) $\dfrac{3x+3y}{xy}$

   (B) $\dfrac{3xy}{x+y}$

   (C) $\dfrac{xy}{3}$

   (D) $\dfrac{y+x}{3xy}$

   (E) $\dfrac{y+x}{3}$

7. $\frac{1}{a} + \frac{1}{b} = 7$ and $\frac{1}{a} - \frac{1}{b} = 3$. Find $\frac{1}{a^2} - \frac{1}{b^2}$.

   (A) 21

   (B) 10

   (C) 7

   (D) 4

   (E) 3

Problem Solutions—Algebraic Fractions

1. D	3. B	5. E	7. A
2. B	4. A	6. D	

1. **The correct answer is (D).**

$$\frac{n}{6} + \frac{2n}{5} = \frac{5n + 12n}{30} = \frac{17n}{30}$$

2. **The correct answer is (B).**

$$\frac{1}{1} - \frac{x}{y} = \frac{y - x}{y}$$

3. **The correct answer is (B).**

$$\frac{x - y}{x + y} \cdot \frac{y + x}{y - x}$$

   Since addition is commutative, we may divide $x + y$ with $y + x$, as they are the same quantity. However, subtraction is not commutative, so we may not divide $x - y$ with $y - x$, as they are *not* the same quantity. We can change the form of $y - x$ by factoring out a $- 1$. Thus, $y - x = (-1)(x - y)$. In this form, we can divide $x - y$, leaving an answer of $\frac{1}{-1}$, or -1.

4. **The correct answer is (A).** Multiply every term in the fraction by x, giving $\frac{x+1}{y}$.

5. **The correct answer is (E).**

$$\frac{2x^2}{y} \cdot \frac{2x^2}{y} \cdot \frac{2x^2}{y} = \frac{8x^6}{y^3}$$

6. **The correct answer is (D).** Multiply every term of the fraction by xy, giving $\frac{y+x}{3xy}$.

7. **The correct answer is (A).**

   $\frac{1}{a^2} - \frac{1}{b^2}$ is equivalent to $\left(\frac{1}{a} + \frac{1}{b}\right)\left(\frac{1}{a} - \frac{1}{b}\right)$.

   We therefore multiply 7 by 3 for an answer of 21.

PROBLEM SOLVING IN ALGEBRA

1. In solving verbal problems, the most important technique is to read accurately. Be sure you understand clearly what you are asked to find. Then try to evaluate the problem in commonsense terms; use this to eliminate answer choices.

    Example: If two people are working together, their combined speed is greater than either one, but not more than twice as fast as the faster one.

    Example: The total number of the correct answers cannot be greater than the total number of answers. Thus, if x questions are asked and you are to determine from other information how many correct answers there were, they cannot come to $2x$.

2. The next step, when common sense alone is not enough, is to translate the problem into algebra. Keep it as simple as possible.

    Example: 24 is what percent of 12?

    Translation: $24 = x\% \cdot 12$

    $$\text{or } 24 = x\frac{1}{100} \cdot 12$$

    $$\text{or } 24 = \frac{x}{100} \cdot \frac{12}{1}$$

    Divide both sides by 12.

    $$2 = \frac{x}{100}$$

    Multiply both sides by 100.

    $$200 = x$$

3. Be alert for the "hidden equation." This is some necessary information so obvious in the stated situation that the question assumes that you know it.

    Example: Boys plus girls = total class.

    Example: Imported wine plus domestic wine = all wine.

    Example: The wall and floor, or the shadow and the building, make a right angle (thus permitting use of the Pythagorean Theorem).

4. Always remember that a variable (letter) can have any value whatsoever within the terms of the problem. Keep the possibility of fractional and negative values constantly in mind.

5. **Manipulating Equations.** You can perform any mathematical function you think helpful to one side of the equation, *provided* you do precisely the same thing to the other side of the equation. You can also substitute one side of an equality for the other in another equation.

6. **Manipulating Inequalities.** You can add to or subtract from both sides of an inequality without changing the direction of the inequality.

    Example: $8 > 5$

    $$8 + 10 > 5 + 10$$

    $$18 > 15$$

    Example: $3x > y + z$

    $$3x + 5 > y + z + 5$$

You can also multiply or divide both sides of the inequality by any POSITIVE number without changing the direction of the inequality.

Example: $12 > 4$

$3(12) > 3(4)$

$36 > 12$

Example: $x > y$

$3x > 3y$

If you multiply or divide an inequality by a NEGATIVE number, you REVERSE the direction of the inequality.

Example: $4 > 3$

$(-2)(4) < (-2)(3)$

$-8 < -6$

Example: $x^2y > z^2x$

$-3(x^2y) < -3(z^2x)$

7. **Solving Equations.** The first step is to determine what quantity or variable you wish to isolate. Solving an equation for x means getting x on one side of the equal sign and everything else on the other.

    Example: $5x + 3 = y$

      Subtract 3.

$5x = y - 3$

      Divide by 5.

$$x = \frac{y - 3}{5}$$

8. If there are two variables in an equation, it may be helpful to put all expressions containing one variable on one side and all the others on the other.

9. Expressing x in terms of y means having an equation with x alone on one side and some expression of y on the other, such as $x = 4y^2 + 3y + 4$.

We will review some of the frequently encountered types of algebra problems, although not every problem you may get will fall into one of these categories. However, thoroughly familiarizing yourself with the types of problems that follow will help you to translate and solve all kinds of verbal problems.

Coin Problems

In solving coin problems, it is best to change the value of all monies involved to cents before writing an equation. Thus, the number of nickels must be multiplied by 5 to give their value in cents; dimes must be multiplied by 10; quarters by 25; half-dollars by 50; and dollars by 100.

Illustration: Richard has $3.50 consisting of nickels and dimes. If he has 5 more dimes than nickels, how many dimes does he have?

SOLUTION:

$$\text{Let } x = \text{the number of nickels}$$
$$x + 5 = \text{the number of dimes}$$
$$5x = \text{the value of the nickels in cents}$$
$$10x + 50 = \text{the value of the dimes in cents}$$
$$350 = \text{the value of the money he has in cents}$$
$$5x + 10x + 50 = 350$$
$$15x = 300$$
$$x = 20$$

Answer: He has 20 nickels and 25 dimes.

In a problem such as this, you can be sure that 20 would be among the multiple-choice answers. You must be sure to read carefully what you are asked to find and then continue until you have found the quantity sought.

Consecutive Integer Problems

Consecutive integers are one apart and can be represented by $x, x + 1, x + 2$, etc. Consecutive even or odd integers are two apart and can be represented by $x, x + 2, x + 4$, etc.

Illustration: Three consecutive odd integers have a sum of 33. Find the average of these integers.

SOLUTION: Represent the integers as x, $x + 2$, and $x + 4$. Write an equation indicating the sum is 33.

$$3x + 6 = 33$$
$$3x = 27$$
$$x = 9$$

The integers are 9, 11, and 13. In the case of evenly spaced numbers such as these, the average is the middle number, 11. Since the sum of the three numbers was given originally, all we really had to do was to divide this sum by 3 to find the average, without ever knowing what the numbers were.

Answer: 11

Age Problems

Problems of this type usually involve a comparison of ages at the present time, several years from now, or several years ago. A person's age x years from now is found by adding x to his present age. A person's age x years ago is found by subtracting x from his present age.

Illustration: Michelle was 12 years old y years ago. Represent her age b years from now.

SOLUTION: Her present age is $12 + y$. In b years, her age will be $12 + y + b$.

Answer: $12 + y + b$

Interest Problems

The annual amount of interest paid on an investment is found by multiplying the amount of principal invested by the rate (percent) of interest paid.

$$\text{Principal} \cdot \text{Rate} = \text{Interest income}$$

Illustration: Mr. Strauss invests $4,000, part at 6% and part at 7%. His income from these investments in one year is $250. Find the amount invested at 7%.

SOLUTION: Represent each investment.

Let x = the amount invested at 7%. Always try to let x represent what you are looking for.

$$4000 - x = \text{the amount invested at 6\%}$$
$$.07x = \text{the income from the 7\% investment}$$
$$.06(4000 - x) = \text{the income from the 6\% investment}$$
$$.07x + .06(4000 - x) = 250$$
$$7x + 6(4000 - x) = 25000$$
$$7x + 24000 - 6x = 25000$$
$$x = 1000$$

Answer: He invested $1,000 at 7%.

Mixture

There are two kinds of mixture problems with which you could be familiar. These problems are rare, so this is best regarded as an extra-credit section and not given top priority. The first is sometimes referred to as dry mixture, in which we mix dry ingredients of different values, such as nuts or coffee. Also solved by the same method are problems such as those dealing with tickets at different prices. In solving this type of problem, it is best to organize the data in a chart of three rows and three columns labeled as illustrated in the following problem.

Illustration: A dealer wishes to mix 20 pounds of nuts selling for 45 cents per pound with some more expensive nuts selling for 60 cents per pound, to make a mixture that will sell for 50 cents per pound. How many pounds of the more expensive nuts should he use?

SOLUTION:

	No. of lbs.	×	Price/lb.	=	Total Value
Original	20		.45		.45(20)
Added	x		.60		.60(x)
Mixture	20 + x		.50		.50(20 + x)

The value of the original nuts plus the value of the added nuts must equal the value of the mixture. Almost all mixture problems require an equation that comes from adding the final column.

$$.45(20) + .60(x) = .50(20 + x)$$

Multiply by 100 to remove decimals.

$$45(20) + 60(x) = 50(20 + x)$$
$$900 + 60x = 1000 + 50x$$
$$10x = 100$$
$$x = 10$$

Answer: He should use 10 lbs. of 60-cent nuts.

In solving the second type, or chemical, mixture problem, we are dealing with percents rather than prices, and amounts instead of value.

Illustration: How much water must be added to 20 gallons of solution that is 30% alcohol to dilute it to a solution that is only 25% alcohol?

SOLUTION:

	No. of gals.	×	% alcohol	=	Amt. alcohol
Original	20		.30		.30(20)
Added	x		0		0
Mixture	20 + x		.25		.25(20 + x)

Note that the percent of alcohol in water is 0. Had we added pure alcohol to strengthen the solution, the percent would have been 100. The equation again comes from the last column. The amount of alcohol added (none in this case) plus the amount we had to start with must equal the amount of alcohol in the new solution.

$$.30(20) = .25(20 + x)$$
$$30(20) = 25(20 + x)$$
$$600 = 500 + 25x$$
$$100 = 25x$$
$$x = 4$$

Answer: 4 gallons

Motion Problems

The fundamental relationship in all motion problems is that Rate · Time = Distance. The problems at the level of this examination usually derive their equation from a relationship concerning distance. Most problems fall into one of three types.

Motion in opposite directions. When two objects traveling at the same speed start at the same time and move in opposite directions, or when two objects start at points at a given distance apart and move toward each other until they meet, then the distance the second travels will equal one half the total distance covered.

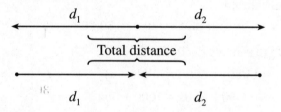

In either of the above cases, $d_1 + d_2 =$ Total distance.

Motion in the same direction. This type of problem is sometimes called the "catch-up" problem. Two objects leave the same place at different times and different rates, but one "catches up" to the other. In such a case, the two distances must be equal.

Round trip. In this type of problem, the rate going is usually different from the rate returning. The times are also different. But if we go somewhere and then return to the starting point, the distances must be the same.

To solve any motion problem, it is helpful to organize the data in a box with columns for rate, time, and distance. A separate line should be used for each moving object. Remember that if the rate is given in *miles per hour,* the time must be in *hours* and the distance in *miles*.

Illustration: Two cars leave a restaurant at 1 p.m., with one car traveling east at 60 miles per hour and the other west at 40 miles per hour along a straight highway. At what time will they be 350 miles apart?

SOLUTION:

	Rate	×	Time	=	Distance
Eastbound	60		x		$60x$
Westbound	40		x		$40x$

Notice that the time is unknown, since we must discover the number of hours traveled. However, since the cars start at the same time and stop when they are 350 miles apart, their times are the same.

$$60x + 40x = 350$$
$$100x = 350$$
$$x = 3\frac{1}{2}$$

Answer: In $3\frac{1}{2}$ hours, it will be 4:30 p.m.

Illustration: Gloria leaves home for school, riding her bicycle at a rate of 12 mph. Twenty minutes after she leaves, her mother sees Gloria's English paper on her bed and leaves to take it to her. If her mother drives at 36 mph, how far must she drive before she reaches Gloria?

SOLUTION:

	Rate	×	Time	=	Distance
Gloria	12		x		$12x$
Mother	36		$x - \dfrac{1}{3}$		$36(x - \dfrac{1}{3})$

Notice that 20 minutes has been changed to $\frac{1}{3}$ of an hour. In this problem the times are not equal, but the distances are.

$$12x = 36(x - \frac{1}{3})$$
$$12x = 36x - 12$$
$$12 = 24x$$
$$x = \frac{1}{2}$$

Answer: If Gloria rode for $\frac{1}{2}$ hour at 12 mph, the distance covered was 6 miles.

Illustration: Judy leaves home at 11 a.m. and rides to Mary's house to return her bicycle. She travels at 12 miles per hour and arrives at 11:30 a.m. She turns right around and walks home. How fast does she walk if she returns home at 1 p.m.?

SOLUTION:

	Rate ×	Time	= Distance
Going	12	$\frac{1}{2}$	6
Return	x	$1\frac{1}{2}$	$\frac{3}{2}x$

The distances are equal.

$$6 = \frac{3}{2}x$$

$$12 = 3x$$

$$x = 4$$

Answer: She walked at 4 mph.

Work Problems

In most work problems, a complete job is broken into several parts, each representing a fractional part of the entire job. For each fractional part, which represents the portion completed by one man, one machine, one pipe, etc., the numerator should represent the time actually spent working, while the denominator should represent the total time needed to do the entire job alone. The sum of all the individual fractions should be 1.

Illustration: John can wax his car in 3 hours. Jim can do the same job in 5 hours. How long will it take them if they work together?

SOLUTION: If multiple-choice answers are given, you should realize that the correct answer must be smaller than the shortest time given, for no matter how slow a helper may be, he does do part of the job and therefore it will be completed in less time.

$$\frac{\text{Time spent}}{\text{Total time needed to do job alone}} \qquad \overset{\text{John}}{\frac{x}{3}} \quad + \quad \overset{\text{Jim}}{\frac{x}{5}} \quad = \quad 1$$

Multiply by 15 to eliminate fractions.

$$5x + 3x = 15$$

$$8x = 15$$

$$x = 1\frac{7}{8} \text{ hours}$$

1. In general, you need as many equations as you have unknowns in order to get a unique numerical solution.

2. The two methods for coping with two or more equations are called **substitution** and **simultaneous.** They overlap. You have used both many times.

Substitution. Whenever one unknown equals something, you can substitute that something for it.

Example: $2x + 3y = 14$ $\Big\}$ given
$x = 2y$

Substitute $2y$ for x in the first equation.

$$2(2y) + 3y = 14$$
$$4y + 3y = 14$$

Add up the ys; divide by 7.

$$7y = 14$$
$$y = 2$$

Substitute for y in the second equation.

$$x = 2(2)$$
$$x = 4$$

Simultaneous. Sometimes adding or subtracting whole equations is shorter.

Example: $5x + 3y = 13$
$2x + 3y = 7$

Subtract the second equation from the first equation.

$$5x + 3y = 13$$
$$\underline{- [2x + 3y = 7]}$$
$$[5x - 2x] + [3y - 3y] = [13 - 7]$$
$$3x = 6$$

Divide by 3.

$$x = 2$$
$$y = 1 \text{ by substitution}$$

Practice Problems Involving Algebra Problem-Solving

1. Sue and Nancy wish to buy a gift for a friend. They combine their money and find they have $4.00, consisting of quarters, dimes, and nickels. If they have 35 coins and the number of quarters is half the number of nickels, how many quarters do they have?

   (A) 3 quarters

   (B) 5 quarters

   (C) 6 quarters

   (D) 10 quarters

   (E) 20 quarters

2. Three times the first of three consecutive odd integers is 3 more than twice the third. Find the third integer.

   (A) 15

   (B) 13

   (C) 11

   (D) 9

   (E) 7

3. Robert is 15 years older than his brother Stan. However, y years ago Robert was twice as old as Stan. If Stan is now b years old and $b > y$, find the value of $b - y$.

   (A) 13

   (B) 14

   (C) 15

   (D) 16

   (E) 17

4. How many ounces of pure acid must be added to 20 ounces of a solution that is 5% acid to strengthen it to a solution that is 24% acid?

   (A) $2\frac{1}{2}$ ounces

   (B) 5 ounces

   (C) 6 ounces

   (D) $7\frac{1}{2}$ ounces

   (E) 10 ounces

5. A dealer mixes a lbs. of nuts worth b cents per pound with c lbs. of nuts worth d cents per pound. At what price should he sell a pound of the mixture if he wishes to make a profit of 10 cents per pound?

   (A) $\dfrac{ab+cd}{a+c} + 10$

   (B) $\dfrac{ab+cd}{a+c} + .10$

   (C) $\dfrac{b+d}{a+c} + 10$

   (D) $\dfrac{b+d}{a+c} + .10$

   (E) $\dfrac{b+d+10}{a+c}$

6. Barbara invests $2,400 in the Security National Bank at 5%. How much additional money must she invest at 8% so that the total annual income will be equal to 6% of her entire investment?

   (A) $3600

   (B) $3000

   (C) $2400

   (D) $1200

   (E) $1000

7. Frank left Austin to drive to Boxville at 6:15 p.m. and arrived at 11:45 P.M. If he averaged 30 miles per hour and stopped one hour for dinner, how far is Boxville from Austin?

   (A) 120 miles

   (B) 135 miles

   (C) 150 miles

   (D) 165 miles

   (E) 180 miles

8. A plane traveling 600 miles per hour is 30 miles from Kennedy Airport at 4:58 p.m. At what time will it arrive at the airport?

   (A) 5:00 p.m.

   (B) 5:01 p.m.

   (C) 5:02 p.m.

   (D) 5:03 p.m.

   (E) 5:20 p.m.

9. Mr. Bridges can wash his car in 15 minutes, while his son Dave takes twice as long to do the same job. If they work together, how many minutes will the job take them?

   (A) 5 minutes

   (B) $7\frac{1}{2}$ minutes

   (C) 10 minutes

   (D) $22\frac{1}{2}$ minutes

   (E) 30 minutes

10. The value of a fraction is $\frac{2}{5}$. If the numerator is decreased by 2 and the denominator increased by 1, the resulting fraction is equivalent to $\frac{1}{4}$. Find the numerator of the original fraction.

    (A) 3

    (B) 4

    (C) 6

    (D) 10

    (E) 15

Problem Solutions—Algebra Problem-Solving

| 1. | D | 3. | C | 5. | A | 7. | B | 9. | C |
| 2. | A | 4. | B | 6. | D | 8. | B | 10. | C |

1. **The correct answer is (D).**

    Let x = number of quarters

    $2x$ = number of nickels

    $35 - 3x$ = number of dimes

    Write all money values in cents.

    $25(x) + 5(2x) + 10(35 - 3x) = 400$

    $\qquad 25x + 10x + 350 - 30x = 400$

    $\qquad\qquad\qquad\qquad 5x = 50$

    $\qquad\qquad\qquad\qquad\ x = 10$

2. **The correct answer is (A).**

    Let x = first integer

    $x + 2$ = second integer

    $x + 4$ = third integer

    $\qquad 3(x) = 3 + 2(x + 4)$

    $\qquad 3x = 3 + 2x + 8$

    $\qquad x = +11$

    The third integer is 15.

3. **The correct answer is (C).**

    b = Stan's age now

    $b + 15$ = Robert's age now

    $b - y$ = Stan's age y years ago

    $b + 15 - y$ = Robert's age y years ago

    $\qquad b + 15 - y = 2(b - y)$

    $\qquad b + 15 - y = 2b - 2y$

    $\qquad\quad 15 = b - y$

4. **The correct answer is (B).**

	No. of oz. ×	% acid ÷ 100 =	Amt. acid
Original	20	.05	1
Added	x	1.00	x
Mixture	$20 + x$	.24	.24(20+x)

    $1 + x = .24(20 + x)$. Multiply by 100 to eliminate the decimal.

    $\qquad 100 + 100x = 480 + 24x$

    $\qquad\qquad 76x = 380$

    $\qquad\qquad\ x = 5$

5. **The correct answer is (A).** The a lbs. of nuts are worth a total of ab cents. The c lbs. of nuts are worth a total of cd cents. The value of the mixture is $ab + cd$ cents. Since there are $a + c$ pounds, each pound is worth $\frac{ab+cd}{a+c}$ cents.

    Since the dealer wants to add 10 cents to each pound for profit, and the value of each pound is in cents, we add 10 to the value of each pound.

6. **The correct answer is (D).** If Barbara invests x additional dollars at 8%, her total investment will amount to $2400 + x$ dollars.

    $\qquad .05(2400) + .08(x) = .06(2400 + x)$

    $\qquad 5(2400) + 8(x) = 6(2400 + x)$

    $\qquad 12,000 + 8x = 14400 + 6x$

    $\qquad\qquad 2x = 2400$

    $\qquad\qquad\ x = 1200$

7. **The correct answer is (B).** Total time elapsed is $5\frac{1}{2}$ hours. However, 1 hour was used for dinner. Therefore, Frank drove at 30 mph for $4\frac{1}{2}$ hours, covering 135 miles.

8. **The correct answer is (B).**

   Time $= \frac{\text{Distance}}{\text{Rate}} = \frac{30}{600} = \frac{1}{20}$ hour, or 3 minutes.

9. **The correct answer is (C).** Dave takes 30 minutes to wash the car alone.

$$\frac{x}{15} + \frac{x}{30} = 1$$

$$2x + x = 30$$

$$3x = 30$$

$$x = 10$$

10. **The correct answer is (C).**

    Let $2x =$ original numerator

    $5x =$ original denominator

$$\frac{2x-2}{5x+1} = \frac{1}{4} \quad \text{Cross-multiply}$$

$$8x - 8 = 5x + 1$$

$$3x = 9$$

$$x = 3$$

    Original numerator is 2(3), or 6.

POLYNOMIAL MULTIPLICATION AND FACTORING

1. A polynomial is any expression with two or more terms, such as $2x + y$ or $3z + 9m^2$.

2. A single term multiplied by another expression must multiply *every* term in the second expression.

    Example: $4(x + y + 2z) = 4x + 4y + 8z$

3. The same holds true for division.

    Example: $\dfrac{(a+b+3c)}{3} = \dfrac{a}{3} + \dfrac{b}{3} + \dfrac{3c}{3} = \dfrac{a}{3} + \dfrac{b}{3} + c$

4. The FOIL method should be used when multiplying two binomials together.

    Example: $(x + y)(x + y)$

    First $(x + y)(x + y) = x^2$

    Outer $(x + y)(x + y) = xy$

    Inner $(x + y)(x + y) = xy$

    Last $(x + y)(x + y) = y^2$

    $(x + y)(x + y) = x^2 + 2xy + y^2$

5. You should know these three equivalencies by heart for the GRE.

    $(x + y)^2 = (x + y)(x + y) = x^2 + 2xy + y^2$

    $(x - y)^2 = (x - y)(x - y) = x^2 - 2xy + y^2$

    $(x + y)(x - y) = x^2 - y^2$

    Work all three out with the FOIL method.

    The x or y could stand for a variable, a number, or an expression.

    Example: $(m + 3)^2 = m^2 + 2 \cdot 3 \cdot m + 3^2 = m^2 + 6m + 9$

    Example: $(2k - p)^2 = (2k)^2 - 2 \cdot 2k \cdot p + p^2$

    $= 4k^2 - 4kp + p^2$

6. You will not need much factoring on the exam. Most of what you do need was covered in the preceding points—if you just reverse the process of multiplication.

    Example: $3x + 6xy = 3x\,(1 + 2y)$

    Example: $2xyz + 4xy = 2xy(z + 2)$

7. One special situation (called a quadratic equation) occurs when an algebraic multiplication equals zero. Since zero can only be achieved in multiplication by multiplying by zero itself, one of the factors must be zero.

   Example: $(x + 1)(x + 2) = 0$

   Therefore, either $x + 1 = 0$, $x = -1$

   or $x + 2 = 0$, $x = -2$.

   In such a situation you simply have to live with two possible answers. This uncertainty may be important in quantitative comparison questions.

8. You may also need to factor to achieve a quadratic format.

   Example: $x^2 + 2x + 1 = 0$

   $(x + 1)(x + 1) = 0$

   Thus, $x + 1 = 0$

   $x = -1$ since both factors are the same.

GEOMETRY

Symbols

The most common symbols used in GRE geometry problems are listed below. The concepts behind the symbols will be explained in this section.

Angles

$\angle$ or $\measuredangle$ angle ($\angle C$ = angle C or $\measuredangle C$ = angle C)

$\llcorner$ right angle (90°)

Lines

$\perp$ perpendicular, at right angles to

$\parallel$ parallel (line B $\parallel$ line C)

$\overline{BD}$ line segment BD

Circles

$\odot$ circle

$\overarc{AC}$ arc AC

Angles

1. a. An **angle** is the figure formed by two lines meeting at a point.

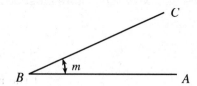

   b. The point B is the **vertex** of the angle and the lines BA and BC are the **sides** of the angle.

2. There are three common ways of naming an angle:

   a. By a small letter or figure written within the angle, as $\angle m$.

   b. By a capital letter at its vertex, as $\angle B$.

   c. By three capital letters, the middle letter being the vertex letter, as $\angle ABC$.

3. a. When two straight lines intersect (cut each other), four angles are formed. If these four angles are equal, each angle is a **right angle** and contains 90°. The symbol ⌐ is used to indicate a right angle.

   Example

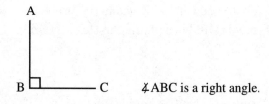

∡ABC is a right angle.

   b. An angle whose measure is less than the measure of a right angle is an **acute angle**.

   c. If the two sides of an angle extend in opposite directions forming a straight line, the angle is a **straight angle** and contains 180°.

   d. An angle whose measure is greater than the measure of a right angle (90°) and less than the measure of a straight angle (180°) is an **obtuse angle**.

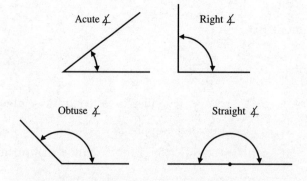

4. a. Two angles are **complementary** if the sum of their measures is 90°.

    b. To find the complement of an angle, subtract the measures of the given angle from 90°.

    Example: The complement of 60° is 90° − 60° = 30°.

5. a. Two angles are **supplementary** if the sum of their measures is 180°.

    b. To find the supplement of an angle, subtract the measure of the given angle from 180°.

    Example: The supplement of 60° is 180° − 60° = 120°.

Lines

6. a. Two lines are **perpendicular** to each other if they meet to form a right angle. The symbol ⊥ is used to indicate that the lines are perpendicular.

    Example: $\angle ABC$ is a right angle. Therefore, $\overline{AB} \perp \overline{BC}$.

    b. Lines that do not meet no matter how far they are extended are called **parallel lines.** Parallel lines are always the same perpendicular distance from each other. The symbol ∥ is used to indicate that two lines are parallel.

    Example: $\overline{AB} \parallel \overline{CD}$

Triangles

7. A **triangle** is a closed, three-sided figure. The figures below are all triangles.

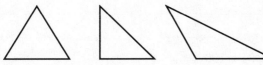

8. a. The sum of the measure of the three angles of a triangle is 180°.

    b. To find the measure of an angle of a triangle when you are given the measures of the other two angles, add the given measures and subtract their sum from 180°.

    Illustration: The measures of two angles of a triangle are 60° and 40°. Find the measure of the third angle.

    SOLUTION: 60° + 40° = 100°

    180° − 100° = 80°

    Answer: The third angle is 80°.

9. a. A triangle that has two congruent sides is called an **isosceles triangle.**

    b. In an isosceles triangle, the angles opposite the equal sides are also congruent.

10. a. A triangle that has all three sides congruent is called an **equilateral triangle.**

    b. The measure of each angle of an equilateral triangle is 60°.

11. a. A triangle that has a right angle is called a **right triangle.**

    b. In a right triangle, the two acute angles are complementary.

    c. In a right triangle, the side opposite the right angle is called the **hypotenuse** and is the longest side. The other two sides are called **legs.**

    Example: $\overline{AC}$ is the hypotenuse.

    $\overline{AB}$ and $\overline{BC}$ are the legs.

12. The **Pythagorean Theorem** states that in a right triangle the square of the hypotenuse equals the sum of the squares of the legs. In the triangle above, this would be expressed as $AB^2 + BC^2 = AC^2$. The simplest whole number example is $3^2 + 4^2 = 5^2$.

13. a. To find the hypotenuse of a right triangle when given the legs:

    1. Square each leg.

    2. Add the squares.

    3. Extract the square root of this sum.

    Illustration: In a right triangle the legs are 6 inches and 8 inches. Find the hypotenuse.

    SOLUTION: $6^2 = 36$ $8^2 = 64$

    $36 + 64 = 100$

    $\sqrt{100} = 10$

    Answer: The hypotenuse is 10 inches.

    b. To find a leg when given the other leg and the hypotenuse of a right triangle:

    1. Square the hypotenuse and the given leg.

    2. Subtract the square of the leg from the square of the hypotenuse.

    3. Extract the square root of this difference.

    Illustration: One leg of a right triangle is 12 feet and the hypotenuse is 20 feet. Find the other leg.

    SOLUTION: $12^2 = 144$ $20^2 = 400$

    $400 - 144 = 256$

    $\sqrt{256} = 16$

    Answer: The other leg is 16 feet.

14. Within a given triangle, the greatest side is opposite the greatest angle; the least side is opposite the least angle; and congruent sides are opposite congruent angles.

Quadrilaterals

15. a. A **quadrilateral** is a closed, four-sided figure in two dimensions. Common quadrilaterals are the **parallelogram, rectangle,** and **square.**

    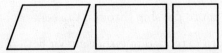

    b. The sum of the measures of the four angles of a quadrilateral is 360°.

16. a. A **parallelogram** is a quadrilateral in which both pairs of opposite sides are parallel.

    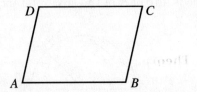

    b. Opposite sides of a parallelogram are also congruent.

    c. Opposite angles of a parallelogram are congruent.

17. A **rectangle** has all of the properties of a parallelogram. In addition, all four of its angles are right angles.

18. A **square** is a rectangle having the additional property that all four of its sides are congruent.

Circles

19. A **circle** is a closed plane curve, all points of which are equidistant from a point within called the **center.**

20. a. A **complete circle** contains 360°.

    b. A **semicircle** contains 180°.

    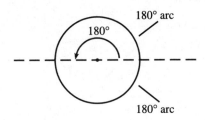

21. a. A **chord** is a line segment connecting any two points on the circle.

   b. A **radius** of a circle is a line segment connecting the center with any point on the circle.

   c. A **diameter** is a chord passing through the center of the circle.

   d. A **secant** is a chord extended in either one or both directions.

   e. A **tangent** is a line touching a circle at one and only one point.

   f. The **circumference** is the length of the curved line bounding the circle.

   g. An **arc** of a circle is any part of the circumference.

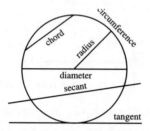

Note: The terms *secant* and *chord* are rarely used on the test.

22. a. A **central angle,** as ∠AOB in the next figure, is an angle whose vertex is the center of the circle and whose sides are radii. A central angle is equal to, or has the same number of degrees as, its intercepted arc.

   b. An **inscribed angle,** as ∠MNP, is an angle whose vertex is on the circle and whose sides are chords. An inscribed angle has half the number of degrees of its intercepted arc. ∠MNP intercepts arc MP and has half the degrees of arc MP.

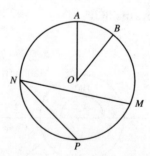

Perimeter

23. The **perimeter** of a two-dimensional figure is the distance around the figure.

Example: The perimeter of the figure above is $9 + 8 + 4 + 3 + 5 = 29$.

24. a. The perimeter of a triangle is found by adding all of its sides.

    Example: If the sides of a triangle are 4, 5, and 7, its perimeter is $4 + 5 + 7 = 16$.

    b. If the perimeter and two sides of a triangle are given, the third side is found by adding the two given sides and subtracting this sum from the perimeter.

    Illustration: Two sides of a triangle are 12 and 15, and the perimeter is 37. Find the other side.

    SOLUTION: $12 + 15 = 27$

    $37 - 27 = 10$

    Answer: The third side is 10.

25. The perimeter of a rectangle equals twice the sum of the length and the width. The formula is $P = 2(l + w)$.

    Example: The perimeter of a rectangle whose length is 7 feet and width is 3 feet equals $2 \times 10 = 20$ feet.

26. The perimeter of a square equals one side multiplied by 4. The formula is $P = 4s$.

    Example: The perimeter of a square, one side of which is 5 feet, is 4×5 feet $= 20$ feet.

27. a. The circumference of a circle is equal to the product of the diameter multiplied by π. The formula is $C = \pi d$.

    b. The number π (pi) is approximately equal to $\frac{22}{7}$, or 3.14 (3.1416 for greater accuracy). A problem will usually state which value to use; otherwise, express the answer in terms of "pi," π.

    Example: The circumference of a circle whose diameter is 4 inches $= 4\pi$ inches; or, if it is stated that $\pi = \frac{22}{7}$, the circumference is $4 \times \frac{22}{7} = \frac{88}{7} = 12\frac{4}{7}$ inches.

    c. Since the diameter is twice the radius, the circumference equals twice the radius multiplied by π. The formula is $C = 2\pi r$.

    Example: If the radius of a circle is 3 inches, then the circumference $= 6\pi$ inches.

    d. The diameter of a circle equals the circumference divided by π.

Example: If the circumference of a circle is 11 inches, then, assuming $\pi = \frac{22}{7}$,

$$\text{diameter } = 11 \div \frac{22}{7} \text{ inches}$$

$$= \overset{1}{\cancel{11}} \times \frac{7}{\underset{2}{\cancel{22}}} \text{ inches}$$

$$= \frac{7}{2} \text{ inches, or } 3\frac{1}{2} \text{ inches}$$

Area

28. a. In a figure of two dimensions, the total space within the figure is called the **area.**

     b. Area is expressed in square units, such as square inches, square centimeters, and square miles.

     c. In computing area, all dimensions must be expressed in the same units.

29. The area of a square is equal to the square of the length of any side. The formula is $A = s^2$.

Example: The area of a square, one side of which is 6 inches, is $6 \times 6 = 36$ square inches.

30. a. The area of a rectangle equals the product of the length and width. The length is any side; the width is the side next to the length. The formula is $A = l \times w$.

Example: If the length of a rectangle is 6 feet and its width 4 feet, then the area is $6 \times 4 = 24$ square feet.

     b. If given the area of a rectangle and one dimension, divide the area by the given dimension to find the other dimension.

Example: If the area of a rectangle is 48 square feet and one dimension is 4 feet, then the other dimension is $48 \div 4 = 12$ feet.

31. a. The altitude, or height, of a parallelogram is a line drawn from a vertex perpendicular to the opposite side, or base.

Example: $\overline{DE}$ is the height.

         $\overline{AB}$ is the base.

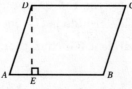

     b. The area of a parallelogram is equal to the product of its base and its height: $A = b \times h$.

Example: If the base of a parallelogram is 10 centimeters and its height is 5 centimeters, its area is $5 \times 10 = 50$ square centimeters.

c. If given one of these dimensions and the area, divide the area by the given dimension to find the base or the height of a parallelogram.

Example: If the area of a parallelogram is 40 square inches and its height is 8 inches, its base is $40 \div 8 = 5$ inches.

32. a. The altitude, or height, of a triangle is a line drawn from a vertex perpendicular to the opposite side, called the base. Each triangle has three sets of altitudes and bases.

b. The area of a triangle is equal to one half the product of the base and the altitude: $A = \frac{1}{2} b \times a$.

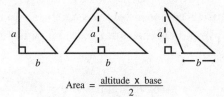

$$\text{Area} = \frac{\text{altitude} \times \text{base}}{2}$$

Example: The area of a triangle having a height of 5 inches and a base of 4 inches is $\frac{1}{2} \times 5 \times 4 = \frac{1}{2} \times 20 = 10$ square inches.

c. In a right triangle, one leg may be considered the height and the other leg the base. Therefore, the area of a right triangle is equal to one half the product of the legs.

Example: The legs of a right triangle are 3 and 4. Its area is $\frac{1}{2} \times 3 \times 4 = 6$ square units.

33. a. The area of a circle is equal to the radius squared, multiplied by π: $A = \pi r^2$.

Example: If the radius of a circle is 6 inches, then the area $= 36\pi$ square inches.

b. To find the radius of a circle given the area, divide the area by π and find the square root of the quotient.

Example: Find the radius of a circle of area 100π.

$$\frac{100\pi}{\pi} = 100$$

$$\sqrt{100} = 10 = \text{radius}$$

34. Some figures are composed of several geometric shapes. To find the area of such a figure it is necessary to find the area of each of its parts.

    Illustration: Find the area of the following figure:

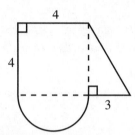

    SOLUTION: The figure is composed of three parts: a square of side 4, a semicircle of diameter 4 (the lower side of the square), and a right triangle with legs 3 and 4 (the right side of the square).

$$\text{Area of square} = 4^2 = 16$$

$$\text{Area of triangle} = \frac{1}{2} \times 3 \times 4 = 6$$

$$\text{Area of semicircle is } \frac{1}{2} \text{ area of circle} = \frac{1}{2}\pi r^2$$

$$\text{Radius} = \frac{1}{2} \times 4 = 2$$

$$\text{Area} = \frac{1}{2}\pi r^2$$

$$= \frac{1}{2} \times \pi \times 2^2$$

$$= 2\pi$$

Answer: Total area $= 16 + 6 + 2\pi = 22 + 2\pi$.

Three-Dimensional Figures

35. a. In a three-dimensional figure, the total space contained within the figure is called the **volume;** it is expressed in **cubic units.**

    b. The total outside surface is called the **surface area;** it is expressed in **square units.**

    c. In computing volume and surface area, all dimensions must be expressed in the same units.

36. a. A **rectangular solid** is a figure of three dimensions having six rectangular faces meeting each other at right angles. The three dimensions are length, width, and height.

    The figure below is a rectangular solid: l is the length, w is the width, and h is the height.

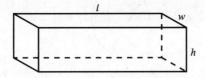

    b. The volume of a rectangular solid is the product of the length, width, and height: $V = l \times w \times h$.

    Example: The volume of a rectangular solid whose length is 6 feet, width 3 feet, and height 4 feet is $6 \times 3 \times 4 = 72$ cubic feet.

37. a. A **cube** is a rectangular solid whose edges are equal. The figure below is a cube; the length, width, and height are all equal to e.

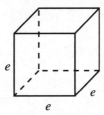

    b. The volume of a cube is equal to the edge cubed: $V = e^3$.

    Example: The volume of a cube whose height is 6 inches equals $6^3 = 6 \times 6 \times 6 = 216$ cubic inches.

    c. The surface area of a cube is equal to the area of any side multiplied by 6.

    Example: The surface area of a cube whose length is 5 inches $= 5^2 \times 6 = 25 \times 6 = 150$ square inches.

38. The volume of a circular cylinder is equal to the product of π, the radius squared, and the height.

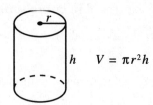

Example: A circular cylinder has a radius of 7 inches and a height of $\frac{1}{2}$ inch. Using $\pi = \frac{22}{7}$, its volume is $\frac{22}{7} \times 7 \times 7 \times \frac{1}{2} = 77$ cubic inches.

39. The volume of a **sphere** is equal to $\frac{4}{3}$ the product of π and the radius cubed.

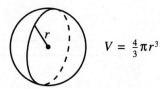

Example: If the radius of a sphere is 3 cm, its volume in terms of π is $\frac{4}{3} \times \pi \times 3 \text{ cm} \times 3 \text{ cm} \times 3 \text{ cm} = 36 \pi \text{ cm}^3$

Practice Problems Involving Geometry

1. If the perimeter of a rectangle is 68 yards and the width is 48 feet, the length is
   (A) 10 yd.
   (B) 18 yd.
   (C) 20 ft.
   (D) 46 ft.
   (E) 56 ft.

2. The total length of fencing needed to enclose a rectangular area 46 feet by 34 feet is
   (A) 26 yd. 1 ft.
   (B) $26\frac{2}{3}$ yd.
   (C) 48 yds.
   (D) 52 yd. 2 ft.
   (E) $53\frac{1}{3}$ yd.

3. An umbrella 50" long can lie on the bottom of a trunk whose length and width are, respectively,
   (A) 26", 30"
   (B) 31", 31"
   (C) 34", 36"
   (D) 40", 21"
   (E) 40", 30"

4. A road runs 1200 ft. from A to B, and then makes a right angle going to C, a distance of 500 ft. A new road is being built directly from A to C. How much shorter will the new road be?
   (A) 400 ft.
   (B) 609 ft.
   (C) 850 ft.
   (D) 1000 ft.
   (E) 1300 ft.

5. A certain triangle has sides that are, respectively, 6 inches, 8 inches, and 10 inches long. A rectangle equal in area to that of the triangle has a width of 3 inches. The perimeter of the rectangle, expressed in inches, is
   (A) 11 inches
   (B) 16 inches
   (C) 22 inches
   (D) 24 inches
   (E) 30 inches

6. A ladder 65 feet long is leaning against the wall. Its lower end is 25 feet away from the wall. How much farther away will it be if the upper end is moved down 8 feet?
   (A) 60 ft.
   (B) 52 ft.
   (C) 14 ft.
   (D) 10 ft.
   (E) 8 ft.

7. A rectangular bin 4 feet long, 3 feet wide, and 2 feet high is solidly packed with bricks whose dimensions are 8 inches, 4 inches, and 2 inches. The number of bricks in the bin is
   (A) 54 bricks
   (B) 320 bricks
   (C) 648 bricks
   (D) 848 bricks
   (E) None of these

8. If the cost of digging a trench is $2.12 a cubic yard, what would be the cost of digging a trench 2 yards by 5 yards by 4 yards?
   (A) $21.20
   (B) $40
   (C) $64
   (D) $84.80
   (E) $104.80

9. A piece of wire is shaped to enclose a square, whose area is 121 square inches. It is then reshaped to enclose a rectangle whose length is 13 inches. The area of the rectangle, in square inches, is

   (A) 64 sq. in.

   (B) 96 sq. in.

   (C) 117 sq. in.

   (D) 144 sq. in.

   (E) 234 sq. in.

10. The area of a 2-foot-wide walk around a garden that is 30 feet long and 20 feet wide is

   (A) 104 sq. ft.

   (B) 216 sq. ft.

   (C) 680 sq. ft.

   (D) 704 sq. ft.

   (E) 1416 sq. ft.

11. The area of a circle is 49π. Find its circumference, in terms of π.

   (A) 14π

   (B) 28π

   (C) 49π

   (D) 98π

   (E) 147π

12. In 2 hours, the minute hand of a clock rotates through an angle of

   (A) 90°

   (B) 180°

   (C) 360°

   (D) 720°

   (E) 1080°

13. A box is 12 inches in width, 16 inches in length, and 6 inches in height. How many square inches of paper would be required to cover it on all sides?

   (A) 192 sq. in.

   (B) 360 sq. in.

   (C) 720 sq. in.

   (D) 900 sq. in.

   (E) 1440 sq. in.

14. If the volume of a cube is 64 cubic inches, the sum of its edges is

   (A) 48 in.

   (B) 32 in.

   (C) 24 in.

   (D) 16 in.

   (E) 12 in.

Problem Solutions—Geometry

1.	B	4.	A	7.	C	10.	B	13.	C
2.	E	5.	C	8.	D	11.	A	14.	A
3.	E	6.	C	9.	C	12.	D		

1. **The correct answer is (B).**

Perimeter = 68 yards

Each width = 48 feet = 16 yards

Both widths = 16 yd. + 16 yd. = 32 yd.

Perimeter = sum of all sides

Remaining two sides must total 68 − 32 = 36 yards.

Since the remaining two sides are equal, they are each 36 ÷ 2 = 18 yards.

2. **The correct answer is (E).**

Perimeter = 2(46 + 34) feet

= 2 × 80 feet

= 160 feet

160 feet = 160 ÷ 3 yards

= $53\frac{1}{3}$ yards

3. **The correct answer is (E).** The umbrella would be the hypotenuse of a right triangle whose legs are the dimensions of the trunk.

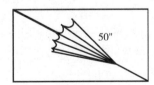

The Pythagorean Theorem states that in a right triangle, the square of the hypotenuse equals the sum of the squares of the legs. Therefore, the sum of the dimensions of the trunk squared must at least equal the length of the umbrella squared, which is 50^2, or 2500.

The only set of dimensions filling this condition is (E):

$$40^2 + 30^2 = 1600 + 900 = 2500$$

4. **The correct answer is (A).** The new road is the hypotenuse of a right triangle, whose legs are the old road.

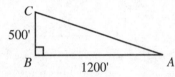

$AC^2 = AB^2 + BC^2$

$AC = \sqrt{500^2 + 1200^2}$

$= \sqrt{250,000 + 1,440,000}$

$= \sqrt{1,690,000}$

$= 1300$ feet

Old road = 1200 + 500 feet

= 1700 feet

New road = 1300 feet

Difference = 400 feet

5. **The correct answer is (C).** Since $6^2 + 8^2 = 10^2$ (36 + 64 = 100), the triangle is a right triangle. The area of the triangle is $\frac{1}{2} \times 6 \times 8 = 24$ square inches. Therefore, the area of the rectangle is 24 square inches.

If the width of the rectangle is 3 inches, the length is $24 \div 3 = 8$ inches. Then the perimeter of the rectangle is $2(3 + 8) = 2 \times 11 = 22$ inches.

6. **The correct answer is (C).** The ladder forms a right triangle with the wall and the ground.

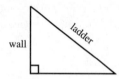

First, find the height that the ladder reaches when the lower end of the ladder is 25 feet from the wall:

$$65^2 = 4225$$
$$25^2 = 625$$
$$65^2 - 25^2 = 3600$$
$$\sqrt{3600} = 60$$

The ladder reaches 60 feet up the wall when its lower end is 25 feet from the wall.

If the upper end is moved down 8 feet, the ladder will reach a height of $60 - 8 = 52$ feet.

The new triangle formed has a hypotenuse of 65 feet and one leg of 52 feet. Find the other leg:

$$65^2 = 4225$$
$$52^2 = 2704$$
$$65^2 - 52^2 = 1521$$
$$\sqrt{1521} = 39$$

The lower end of the ladder is now 39 feet from the wall. This is $39 - 25 = 14$ feet farther than it was before.

7. **The correct answer is (C).** Convert the dimensions of the bin to inches:

4 feet = 48 inches

3 feet = 36 inches

2 feet = 24 inches

Volume of bin = 48 in. × 36 in. × 24 in.

= 41,472 cubic inches

Volume of
each brick = 8 in. × 4 in. × 2 in.

= 64 cubic inches

41,472 ÷ 64 = 648 bricks

8. **The correct answer is (D).** The trench contains:

2 yd. × 5 yd. × 4 yd. = 40 cubic yards

40 × \$2.12 = \$84.80

9. **The correct answer is (C).** Find the dimensions of the square: If the area of the square is 121 square inches, each side is $\sqrt{121} = 11$ inches, and the perimeter is $4 \times 11 = 44$ inches.

Next, find the dimensions of the rectangle: The perimeter of the rectangle is the same as the perimeter of the square, since the same length of wire is used to enclose either figure. Therefore, the perimeter of the rectangle is 44 inches. If the two lengths are each 13 inches, their total is 26 inches, and 44 − 26 inches, or 18 inches, remain for the two widths. Each width is equal to $18 \div 2 = 9$ inches.

The area of a rectangle with length 13 in. and width 9 in. is:

13 × 9 = 117 sq. in.

10. The correct answer is (B).

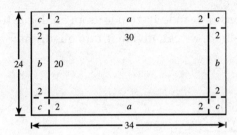

The walk consists of:

a. 2 rectangles of length 30 feet and width 2 feet.

Area of each
    rectangle = 2 × 30 = 60 sq. ft.

Area of both rectangles = 120 sq. ft.

b. 2 rectangles of length 20 feet and width 2 feet.

Area of each = 2 × 20 = 40 sq. ft.

Area of both = 80 sq. ft.

c. 4 squares, each having sides measuring 2 feet.

Area of each square = 2^2 = 4 sq. ft.

Area of 4 squares = 16 sq. ft.

Total area of walk = 120 + 80 + 16

$\qquad\qquad\qquad$ = 216 sq. ft.

Alternate solution:

Area of walk = Area of large rectangle
– area of small rectangle

= 34 × 24 – 30 × 20

= 816 – 600

= 216 sq. ft.

11. The correct answer is (A). If the area of a circle is 49π, its radius is $\sqrt{49}$ = 7. Then, the circumference is equal to 2 × 7 × π = 14π.

12. The correct answer is (D). In one hour, the minute hand rotates through 360°. In two hours, it rotates through 2 × 360° = 720°.

13. The correct answer is (C). Find the area of each surface:

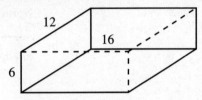

Area of top = 12 × 16 = 192 sq. in.

Area of bottom = 12 × 16 = 192 sq. in.

Area of front = 6 × 16 = 96 sq. in.

Area of back = 6 × 16 = 96 sq. in.

Area of right side = 6 × 12 = 72 sq. in.

Area of left side = 6 × 12 = 72 sq. in.

Total surface area = 720 sq. in.

14. The correct answer is (A). For a cube, $V = e^3$. If the volume is 64 cubic inches, each edge is $\sqrt[3]{64}$ = 4 inches.

A cube has 12 edges. If each edge is 4 inches, the sum of the edges is 4 × 12 = 48 inches.

COORDINATE GEOMETRY

Perhaps the easiest way to understand the coordinate axis system is as an analogue to the points of the compass. If we take a plot of land, we can divide it into quadrants:

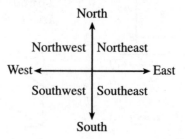

Now, if we add measuring units along each of the directional axes, we can actually describe any location on this piece of land by two numbers. For example, point P is located at 4 units East and 5 units North. Point Q is located at 4 units West and 5 units North. Point R is located at 4 units West and 2 units South. And Point T is located at 3 units East and 4 units South.

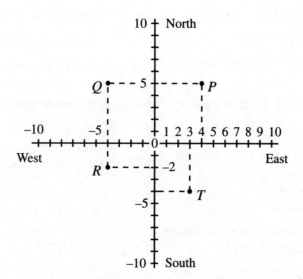

The coordinate system used in coordinate geometry differs from our map of a plot of land in two respects. First, it uses x- and y-axes divided into negative and positive regions.

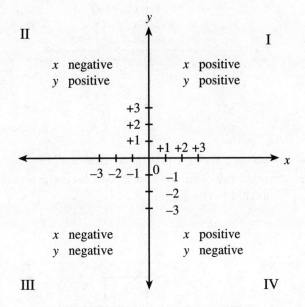

It is easy to see that Quadrant I corresponds to our Northeast quarter, and in it the measurements on both the x- and y-axes are positive. Quadrant II corresponds to our Northwest quarter, and in it the measurements on the x-axis are negative and the measurements on the y-axis are positive. Quadrant III corresponds to the Southwest quarter, and in it both the x-axis measurements and the y-axis measurements are negative. Finally, Quadrant IV corresponds to our Southeast quarter, and there the x-values are positive while the y-values are negative.

Second, mathematicians adopt a convention called **ordered pairs** to eliminate the necessity of specifying each time whether one is referring to the x-axis or the y-axis. An ordered pair of coordinates has the general form (a,b). The first element always refers to the x-value (distance left or right of the *origin,* or intersection, of the axes) while the second element gives the y-value (distance up or down from the origin).

To make this a bit more concrete, let us *plot* some examples of ordered pairs, that is, find their locations in the system: Let us start with the point (3,2). We begin by moving to the positive 3 value on the x-axis. Then from there we move up two units on the y-axis.

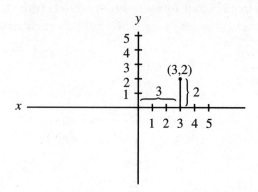

An alternative way of speaking about this is to say that the point (3,2) is located at the intersection of a line drawn through the *x*-value 3 parallel to the *y*-axis and a line drawn through the *y*-value 2 parallel to the *x*-axis.

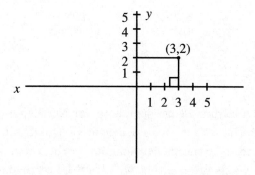

Both methods locate the same point. Let us now use the ordered pairs (−3,2), (−2,−3) and (3,−2):

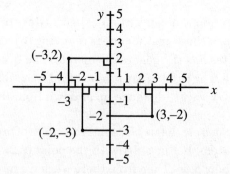

One important use of the coordinate axis system is that it can be used to draw a picture of an equation. For example, we know that the equation *x* = *y* has an infinite number of solutions:

x	1	2	3	5	0	−3	−5	etc.
y	1	2	3	5	0	−3	−5	etc.

We can plot these pairs of x and y on the axis system:

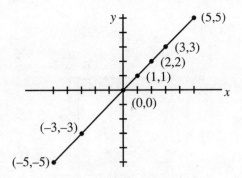

We can now see that a complete picture of the equation $x = y$ is a straight line including all the real numbers such that x is equal to y.

Similarly, we might graph the equation $y = 2x$:

x	-4	-2	-1	0	1	2	4
y	-8	-4	-2	0	2	4	8

After entering these points on the graph, we can complete the picture:

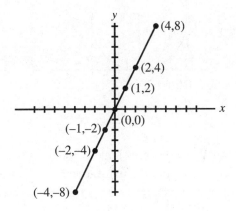

It too is a straight line, but it rises at a more rapid rate than does $x = y$.

A final use one might have for the coordinate system on the GRE is in graphing geometric figures:

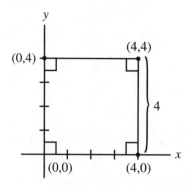

In this case we have a square whose vertices are (0,0), (4,0), (4,4), and (0,4). Each side of the square must be equal to 4 since each side is four units long (and parallel to either the *x*- or *y*-axis). Since all coordinates can be viewed as the perpendicular intersection of two lines, it is possible to measure distances in the system by using some simple theorems.

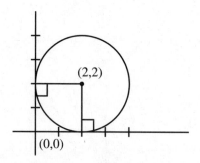

Illustration: What is the area of the circle?

SOLUTION: In order to solve this problem, we need to know the radius of the circle. The center of the circle is located at the intersection of $x = 2$ and $y = 2$, or the point (2,2). So we know the radius is 2 units long and the area is 4π.

Answer: 4π

Illustration: What is the length of $\overline{PQ}$?

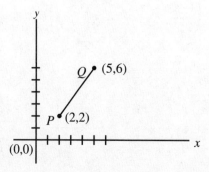

SOLUTION: We can find the length of *PQ* by constructing a triangle:

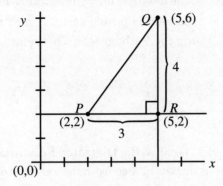

Now, we see that $\overline{QR}$ runs from (5,6) to (5,2) and so it must be 4 units long. We see that $\overline{PR}$ runs from (2,2) to (5,2) so it is 3 units long. We then use the Pythagorean Theorem to determine that $\overline{PQ}$, which is the hypotenuse of our triangle, is 5 units long.

Answer: 5 units

It is actually possible to generalize on this example. Let us take any two points on the graph *P* and *Q*. (For simplicity's sake we will confine the discussion to the First Quadrant, but the method is generally applicable, that is, will work in all quadrants and even with lines covering two or more quadrants.) Now let us assign the value (x_1, y_1) to *P* and (x_2, y_2) to *Q*.

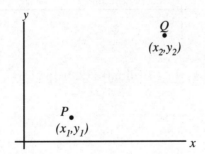

Then, following our method above, we construct a triangle so that we can use the Pythagorean Theorem:

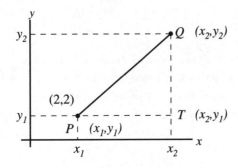

Point T now has the coordinates (x_2, y_1). Side $\overline{PT}$ will be $x_2 - x_1$ units long (the y-coordinate does not change, so the length is only the distance moved on the x-axis), and $\overline{QT}$ will be $y_2 - y_1$ (again, the distance is purely vertical, moving up from y_1 to y_2, with no change in the x-value). Using the Pythagorean Theorem:

$$PQ^2 = PT^2 + QT^2$$
$$PQ^2 = (x_2 - x_1)^2 + (y_2 - y_1)^2$$
$$PQ = \sqrt{(x_2 - x_1)^2 + (y_2 - y_1)^2}$$

And we have just derived what is called the **Distance Formula.** We can find the length of any straight line segment drawn in a coordinate axis system (that is, the distance between two points in the system) using this formula.

Illustration: What is the distance between P and Q?

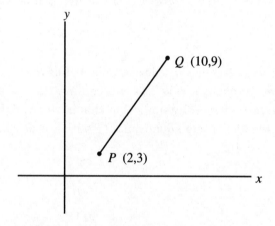

SOLUTION: Point P has the coordinates $(2,3)$ and Q the coordinates $(10,9)$. Using the formula:

$$PQ = \sqrt{(10 - 2)^2 + (9 - 3)^2}$$
$$PQ = \sqrt{8^2 + 6^2}$$
$$PQ = \sqrt{64 + 36}$$
$$PQ = \sqrt{100}$$
$$PQ = 10$$

Answer: 10

For those students who find the Distance Formula a bit too technical, be reassured that the Pythagorean Theorem (which is more familiar) will work just as well on the GRE. In fact, as a general rule, any time one is asked to calculate a distance that does not move parallel to one of the axes, the proper attack is to use the Pythagorean Theorem.

Practice Problems Involving Coordinate Geometry

1. $\overline{AB}$ is the diameter of a circle whose center is O. If the coordinates of A are (2,6) and the coordinates of B are (6,2), find the coordinates of O.

    (A) (4,4)
    (B) (4,–4)
    (C) (2,–2)
    (D) (0,0)
    (E) (2,2)

2. $\overline{AB}$ is the diameter of a circle whose center is O. If the coordinates of O are (2,1) and the coordinates of B are (4,6), find the coordinates of A.

    (A) $(3,3\frac{1}{2})$

    (B) $(1,2\frac{1}{2})$

    (C) (0,–4)

    (D) $(2\frac{1}{2},1)$

    (E) $(-1,-2\frac{1}{2})$

3. Find the distance from the point whose coordinates are (4,3) to the point whose coordinates are (8,6).

    (A) $\sqrt{7}$
    (B) 5
    (C) $\sqrt{67}$
    (D) 15
    (E) 25

4. The vertices of a triangle are (2,1), (2,5), and (5,1). The area of the triangle is

    (A) 12
    (B) 10
    (C) 8
    (D) 6
    (E) 5

5. The area of a circle whose center is at (0,0) is 16π. The circle passes through each of the following points EXCEPT

    (A) (4,4)
    (B) (0,4)
    (C) (4,0)
    (D) (–4,0)
    (E) (0,–4)

Problem Solutions—Coordinate Geometry

1. A   2. C   3. B   4. D   5. A

1. **The correct answer is (A).** Find the midpoint of $\overline{AB}$ by averaging the x-coordinates and averaging the y-coordinates.

$$\left(\frac{6+2}{2}, \frac{2+6}{2}\right) = (4,4)$$

2. **The correct answer is (C).** O is the midpoint of $\overline{AB}$.

$$\frac{x+4}{2} = 2 \qquad x+4=4 \quad x=0$$

$$\frac{y+6}{2} = 1 \qquad y+6=2 \quad y=-4$$

A is the point $(0,-4)$

3. **The correct answer is (B).**

$$d = \sqrt{(8-4)^2 + (6-3)^2}$$
$$= \sqrt{4^2 + 3^2}$$
$$= \sqrt{16+9}$$
$$= \sqrt{25}$$
$$= 5$$

4. **The correct answer is (D).** Sketch the triangle and you will see it is a right triangle with legs of 4 and 3.

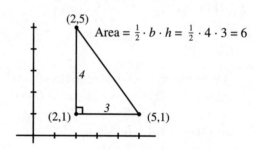

$$\text{Area} = \tfrac{1}{2} \cdot b \cdot h = \tfrac{1}{2} \cdot 4 \cdot 3 = 6$$

5. **The correct answer is (A).**

Area of a circle $= \pi r^2$

$\pi r^2 = 16\pi \quad r = 4$

Points B, C, D, and E are all 4 units from the origin. Point A is not.

PART V

GRE ANALYTICAL WRITING

CHAPTER 12 Analytical Writing

Analytical Writing

OVERVIEW

- **What is GRE Analytical Writing?**
- **How do you handle GRE Analytical Writing?**
- **What smart test-takers know**
- **What smart test-takers know NOT to do**
- **Summing it up**

WHAT IS GRE ANALYTICAL WRITING?

Analytical Writing requires you to respond to two essay topics (called *prompts*). One of the prompts will be an *issue* topic and the other an *argument* topic. The time limit for the issue topic is 45 minutes, and the time limit for the argument topic is 30 minutes. You can produce your responses either by using the word processing function of the computer at the testing center or by writing them out by hand. The essays are then assigned to readers who score them.

Analytical Writing was added as a required section because the GRE Board has been concerned about deficiencies in the writing skills evidenced by graduate students. The goal is to help admissions officers and advisers evaluate a student's ability and needs. It can be used as another tool in the admission process and as a guidance tool to direct students who need special help in developing writing skills into appropriate programs.

GRE Analytical Writing
Anatomy of Analytical Writing

ISSUE TOPIC

Issue Task: Present Your Perspective on an Issue

Time: 45 minutes

You have 45 minutes to plan and write an essay that presents your views on an assigned topic.

The topic is summarized in a brief quotation that states or suggests a position. You can accept, reject, or modify the position. Support your views with reasons and examples drawn from your experience, observation, reading, or study.

chapter 12

Trained graders will score your response, taking into account how well you:

- Understand the complexities and ramifications of the issue
- Organize, develop, and express your ideas
- Employ the elements of Standard Written English

You may wish to spend a few minutes thinking about your response before you begin writing and leave time to reread what you have written in order to make any revisions you think necessary.

Here is a sample issue topic:

> "Despite the occurrence of natural disasters and human tragedies, often on a large scale, the human condition continues to improve materially, spiritually, ethically, and culturally."

The task is to express your point of view. So you have a lot of flexibility in deciding what to say.

You must write on the assigned topic. An essay on any other topic is classified as "off topic" and given an automatic zero for a grade. You will be given two topics; you'll choose one to write on.

The "issue" topic is a quote that expresses the speaker's opinion. When you give your own point of view, you can agree or disagree with the speaker or even agree somewhat and disagree somewhat. You don't need any special knowledge to answer; instead, you should draw from your own experience and study.

Your essay is graded "holistically," taking into account many factors. These are discussed in greater detail below.

Outline your essay before you begin to write. And make sure that you leave some time for proofreading.

Remember: This is the speaker's position. You can agree that things are getting better; you can disagree and say that things are getting worse; you can qualify the position by saying that it's a little of both and only time will tell; or you can take any other position that you can defend.

ARGUMENT TOPIC

Argument Task: Analyze an Argument

Time: 30 minutes

You have 30 minutes to plan and write an essay that presents your views on an assigned topic. Consider the logic of the argument and the soundness of its conclusion.

Trained graders will score your response, taking into account how well you:

- Identify and analyze the structure of the argument
- Organize, develop, and express your ideas
- Employ the elements of standard written English

You may wish to spend a few minutes thinking about your response before you begin writing and leave time to reread what you have written in order to make any revisions you think necessary.

Read the following argument and discuss whether it is well-reasoned. You are *not* being asked to agree or disagree with the conclusion of the argument; you are being asked to analyze the reasoning in the argument. Consider what, if any, assumptions the argument makes and whether they are justified; what evidence is offered for the conclusion and whether it is reliable; and any other factors or information that would strengthen or weaken the argument.

> "Recently, it was reported in the news media that a school bus returning from a field trip overturned on a highway and rolled down an embankment, seriously injuring several students who were tossed from their seats. Common sense says that these children would not have been injured if they had been wearing seat belts. Therefore, the federal government should require all school buses to have seat belts for passengers."

The task is to analyze the argument. Assess the strengths and weaknesses of the reasons given for the conclusion.

Analyze the argument by assessing the conclusion and considering whether the reasons given support the conclusion. You must write on the assigned topic. An essay on any other topic is classified as "off topic" and given an automatic zero for a grade.

Your essay is graded "holistically," taking into account many factors. These are discussed in greater detail below.

Outline your essay before you begin to write. And make sure that you leave some time for proofreading.

The task is not to say what you believe but to comment on how well the speaker's reasons support the conclusion. Good points to make include:

1 *The argument makes assumptions without proof.*

2 *The evidence is not reliable.*

3 *The conclusion does not follow from the evidence.*

4 *The argument fails to consider some important points.*

The conclusion of this argument is: Seat belts should be required on school buses. You should not take a position. But you might raise the following points:

1 *Is this a frequent occurrence?*

2 *Would the children have been injured anyway?*

3 *Can the driver make the children wear the seat belts?*

4 *Was excessive speed or some other controllable factor the cause of the accident?*

Both Analytical Writing essays are graded substantially according to the same criteria (setting aside for the moment the fact that the two prompts require somewhat different approaches). So it is a good idea to know what counts and what does not count in the grading system. Essays are graded on content, organization, and mechanics. Contrast the following descriptions of an "Outstanding" essay (a "6" on the scale of 0 to 6) and a "Seriously Flawed" essay (a "2"):

OUTSTANDING (6)

An essay that presents a cogent analysis. An outstanding essay:

- States and develops a position with reasons and illustrations
- Is focused and clearly well organized
- Expresses ideas clearly and effectively
- Uses language fluently with a variety of sentence structures and rich vocabulary
- Demonstrates superior facility with the conventions of Standard Written English (grammar, usage, mechanics) but may have minor flaws

SERIOUSLY FLAWED (2)

An essay that shows serious weakness in analytical writing. A seriously flawed essay:

- Is unclear or seriously limited in presenting or developing ideas
- Provides few, if any, relevant examples
- Is disorganized
- Contains numerous errors in grammar, usage, or mechanics that interfere with understanding the essay

The most important elements of these contrasting descriptions can be summarized in a table that will help you better see what's required for a good essay score:

	Outstanding (6 out of a possible 6)	Seriously Flawed (2 out of a possible 6)
Content	Insightful Reasons Persuasive Examples	Unclear Position Few Examples
Organization	Well-Focused Well-Organized	Unfocused Disorganized
Execution	Substantially correct with only minor flaws	Numerous errors in grammar, usage, or mechanics

So writing a good essay means doing three things well: generating interesting content, organizing the ideas, and presenting the ideas effectively. We'll look more closely at each of these three aspects in "What Smart Test-Takers Know" later on.

HOW DO YOU HANDLE GRE ANALYTICAL WRITING?

Here is a simple, four-step plan to help you succeed.

GRE Analytical Writing: Getting It Right

1 Read the topic and decide what position or positions you'll take.

2 Outline your thinking using the scratch paper that is provided.

3 Produce your essay either by keyboarding or writing.

4 Proofread your essay.

Now let's try out these steps on the "argument" topic given earlier.

1 **Read the topic and decide what position or positions you'll take.**

You want to generate three or four ideas that critique the *structure* of the argument:

- The proof of the harm is anecdotal.

- There is no evidence that seat belts will be effective.

- The money could be better spent on driver training or other safety equipment such as better brakes.

2 **Outline your thinking using the scratch paper that is provided.**

I. There is no real proof of a serious problem.

    A. The evidence is anecdotal: one example but no statistics.

    B. "Common sense" may be wrong that seat belts would have prevented all or most of the injuries. More information is needed.

II. There is no evidence that seat belts will be effective.

    A. Perhaps other equally serious injuries would have occurred.

    B. Is it reasonable to believe that children will wear the belts or that a bus driver has the authority to enforce such a rule?

TIP

Perhaps the most important thing that the readers will be looking for is organization. If you create an outline and follow it, you are already halfway home.

III. The proposal may not be cost effective.

    A.   It would be necessary to analyze the cost of installing seat belts in all school buses.

    B.   Perhaps the money could be spent better elsewhere, for example, on more driver training.

❸ Produce your essay either by keyboarding or writing.

Write your essay using your outline. Importantly, you can use the main headings in your outline as topic sentences for your paragraphs and your subheads as main sentences within each paragraph. Be sure to add some further detail, e.g., children of school age are notoriously difficult to discipline, particularly in a "free-for-all" situation at the end of the school day.

❹ Proofread your essay.

In the next section, you will find a checklist of the errors most commonly made by test-takers and tips on how to avoid them.

WHAT SMART TEST-TAKERS KNOW

Smart test-takers know that the grading system for the analytical writing emphasizes three elements: content, organization, and execution. Let's look at what you can do to maximize your performance on each of the yardsticks.

What Smart Test-Takers Know About Content

CONTENT IS THE KEY.

While organization, presentation, and grammar are important, content (or what you have to say) is the most important thing. So, no matter how elegant the prose and how well organized the presentation, an essay devoid of content will not receive a top score.

The directions for the analytical writing and the descriptions of the grading criteria make it clear that the expected content or approach will be different for the two types of topics.

ISSUES CAN BE ANALYZED IN SEVERAL DIFFERENT WAYS.

While content is important, there is no single, uniquely correct approach to the Issue topic. The directions for the analytical writing are quite clear in explaining that you are welcome to agree with the topic, disagree with the topic, partly agree and partly disagree with the topic, and even quarrel with the topic.

NOTE

If you are given a choice of two Issue topics, which one should you choose? Ask first whether you have a strong opinion about one topic or the other; if you do, choose that one. If not, ask yourself which one you know more about, and choose that one. Otherwise, quickly make a list of points that you could make about each, and then choose the one about which you have the most to say.

Consider a Sample Issue Topic

"The new technology that has been introduced into education in grades K through 12 such as the Web, computers, and television, has little real benefit and more often than not serves only to distract both teachers and students from the real task of learning."

There are basically four different approaches you might take with this topic. First, you might agree with the statement. If you want to take this approach, you might jot down some ideas as a guide or an outline:

I agree with the topic.

I.   The Web doesn't teach well

    A. Time is wasted searching for relevant information

    B. Many sites are not truly authoritative

    C. The treatment of topics is superficial

II. Computers are overrated

    A. Programs use bells and whistles instead of content

    B. Much software is too difficult to use

III. Television is a waste

    A. The programming is all but worthless

    B. Television is in any event a passive medium

Or you might want to disagree with the topic:

I disagree with the topic.

I.   The Web has a lot to teach

    A. Students have access to much more than in their school library

    B. Students learn to assess the value of the information they find

    C. Electronic research is the wave of the future

II. Computers are excellent teaching tools

    A. Programmed learning is a valuable tool

    B. Teacher time is freed up for more one-on-one attention

    C. Computer literacy is essential

III. Television is a proven medium

    A. Students feel comfortable with it

    B. Travelogues, science, etc., are available

ALERT!

Regardless of whether you agree with the topic, disagree with it, agree in part and disagree in part, or question the terms of the statement, you must make your chosen approach your position.

TIP

The analytical writing exercises in this book include sample answers—both good and bad—with commentary. If you need more practice, the list of topics available is published at the GRE Web site: www.gre.org. Unfortunately, the GRE does not provide sample answers or commentary.

Or you might want to combine those two approaches:

The Web and computers are useful but television is not.

I.   The Web has a lot to teach

    A. Students have access to much more than in their school library

    B. Students learn to assess the value of the information they find

    C. Electronic research is the wave of the future

II. Computers are excellent teaching tools

    A. Programmed learning is a valuable tool

    B. Teacher time is freed up for more one-on-one attention

    C. Computer literacy is essential

III. Television is a waste

    A. The programming is all but worthless

    B. Television is in any event a passive medium

Finally, if none of those approaches appeals to you, you can always "object" to the topic. That is, you can argue that its terms have not been adequately defined or that it is an oversimplification of a complex problem. For example:

The topic is an oversimplification.

I.   The Web offers many different sites

    A. Gaming, chat rooms, and movie trailers are not educational

    B. The Library of Congress' "Thomas" site is educational

II. Computers are tools with different uses

    A. Video games are usually not educational

    B. Programmed learning is educational

III. Television can be good or bad

    A. Cartoons are not educational

    B. The History Channel is educational

At their core, these four approaches are not really radically different. Instead, they are different analytical tools that can be used to stimulate thought and generate ideas that can then be organized into an essay response to the topic. Most important, whichever approach you take, remember that you are expected to take a position on the topic—even if that position is that the wording of the topic really doesn't admit a position. (That is still a definite position.)

ARGUMENTS HAVE WEAKNESSES.

Argument topics are different from issue topics. Argument topics present a situation and a proposed plan of action. An Argument topic always has a structure such as "We should do this because it would accomplish so and so." Unlike your answer to the issue topic in which you are supposed to state your own position, your answer to the argument topic should not say whether you think the plan is ultimately a good or bad idea, but only whether the reasons given in the topic for the plan make sense.

Arguments have weaknesses. This statement is both a tautology and a powerful test-taking strategy. First, taken in a purely formal sense, the statement is simply descriptive of the nature of inductive arguments. Except for deductive arguments (such as "All men are mortal, Socrates is a man, therefore Socrates is mortal"), real-life or inductive arguments (unlike death and taxes) are never certain. The evidence, no matter how powerful or comprehensive, cannot guarantee that the objective will be attained. After all, the best laid plans of mice and men and so on. So, it is always possible to raise objections to any proposed action and therefore to the argument topic of the GRE. Second, in a more concrete sense, the argument topics are written with built-in weaknesses. The topics are drafted so that there are weaknesses in the reasoning that you can exploit in your essay.

First, in a purely formal sense, an argument consists of a set of statements, one of which sets forth the conclusion. The other statements are the premises of the argument. The premises in the argument topic can also be referred to as the evidence for the conclusion.

A very powerful attack on any argument is to point out that it rests upon a hidden or suppressed premise. Suppose, for example, that an argument topic reads:

> "The Midtown Clothing Store should expand its line of men's wear because the Male Outfitter, a men's shop three blocks away, is going out of business."

This argument depends upon some very important suppressed premises such as: the Male Outfitter has a significant number of customers; the customers from Male Outfitter won't go to another, unnamed store; the customers from Male Outfitter will come to Midtown and buy merchandise.

Another way of thinking about this same point is to ask:

> Are there hidden or unanticipated factors that may intervene to prevent the result from being achieved?

Looking at it from this perspective, you would point out that there may be several factors overlooked by the argument topic above: Male Outfitter may be going out of business because there simply aren't any customers (so there won't be any new customers at Midtown); perhaps a new competitor opened on the other side of Male Outfitter and this drove Male Outfitter out of business (and maybe those customers won't switch to Midtown); or maybe the economy is in a recession, and men are just not buying clothes. And you can probably think of other "intervening factors" as well.

NOTE

Effective questions to ask of any argument topic:

- Have factors or conditions been overlooked?
- Is there another reasonable alternative?
- What are the monetary and nonmonetary costs?
- Does the evidence support the conclusion?

A second question to ask of any argument topic is:

> Even assuming the proposal would achieve an advantage, can the same advantage be achieved in some other, more efficient manner?

Sometimes, the result may be achievable in a less drastic way. For example, rather than expand its line of men's wear, Midtown might keep the same line expecting that the additional customers (should they come) will buy from existing stock. Or, if the question is a matter of inventory, then perhaps some additional inventory control (such as restocking more frequently) will enable Midtown to meet any additional demand.

Finally, you should also ask:

> Would the cost of the proposal (both monetary and nonmonetary) exceed the claimed benefit?

Here, you might suggest that an additional line would require additional investment in inventory, and that entails a risk. Or you could note that, so far as is stated, there is no evidence that Midtown has the floor space for expanded inventory and that any investment in expanding the store would be risky. Or, you might ask whether Midtown has the sales force to cover an expanded line and point out that if the sales staff is overextended, customers will be dissatisfied and this would likely affect Midtown's existing reputation in a negative manner.

You may recognize all of this language as derivative of a standard "cost-benefit" analysis—applied to the exercise at hand. The logic behind these three questions is that the proposal should be adopted only if there is good reason to believe the advantage will be obtained, that it cannot be obtained in some other way, and that the cost (using that term very broadly to include nonmonetary costs) will not outweigh the expected benefit.

In addition to these formal considerations, every argument topic is written with built-in weaknesses for you to find. Here is one of the test-writer's favorites:

> "We should switch to the new Acme Inventory Control System. When our competitor switched last year, their profits increased 30%."

Setting aside the point that the statement doesn't prove a causal connection (maybe profits increased because the economy turned around), you should always be ready to attack a percent: percent increase says nothing about absolute numbers. An increase from a profit of $1.00 to $1.30 (total for the whole company) is still a 30% increase. Now, of course, if the increase were from $1 million to $1.3 million, that might be significant; but based on a percentage increase alone, without additional information, you probably would not want to conclude that switching to a different inventory control system would be a wizard idea.

Another thing to watch for in the wording of the argument topic is the descriptive terms used. For example, building on the example of Midtown used above:

> "A market survey done by Jones Consulting indicates that we can expect an increase of 25% in gross sales. Therefore, an expansion at this time would be profitable."

In addition to the other issues that we've discussed, here you might point out that an increase in gross sales does not necessarily translate into an increase in profits. And you might even question the qualifications of "Jones Consulting" and insist that it would be important to see the methodology of the study. Again, you'll notice that these features are built in the wording of the topic. The people who drafted the topic are well aware of the fact that the statement contains weaknesses; they want you to find and expose those weaknesses.

YOU SHOULD ORGANIZE YOUR ESSAY BY USING THE "THREE MAIN POINTS" APPROACH.

This "three main points" approach results in a five-paragraph essay:

- Paragraph 1: Introduction
- Paragraph 2: First point
- Paragraph 3: Second point
- Paragraph 4: Third point
- Paragraph 5: Conclusion

YOU SHOULD BEGIN BY CLEARLY STATING A POSITION.

One of the features of the "outstanding" essay is that it states a clear position. This is absolutely essential for the "issue" topic where you are expected to voice your own opinion. But it is true of the "argument" topic as well, even though your conclusion may be more formalistic, e.g,. "The reasons given in support of the plan to require seat belts do not support the conclusion that the plan would be beneficial."

YOU SHOULD BEGIN EACH PARAGRAPH WITH A TOPIC SENTENCE.

You know what you want to say; your reader does not. That's why good writers use topic sentences. Let the first sentence of each paragraph announce to the reader what aspect of the topic will be discussed in that paragraph. For example:

> First, the limited evidence in the argument doesn't support so broad a conclusion as a law requiring seat belts in all school buses.

YOU SHOULD USE TRANSITIONAL WORDS AND PHRASES.

Even though you announce your paragraph topic in the first sentence, you still need to help the reader follow the details of the development. If you want to make two points of equal importance, then signal the transition from the first to the second with words such as "Additionally," "Furthermore," and "Moreover." Here's an example:

First, the limited evidence in the argument doesn't support so broad a conclusion as a law requiring seat belts in all school buses. The speaker cites a single example of an accident involving a school bus. Without statistical evidence on the number of such accidents each year and the types of injuries sustained, it would be unwise to reach a broad public policy conclusion. Additionally, even the brief description of the accident does not cite the cause. Perhaps it was driver inattention, weather, or a careless motorist in another vehicle; these are all factors that can and should be addressed in different ways.

YOU SHOULD MAKE SURE THAT EACH SENTENCE EXPRESSES ONE MAIN THOUGHT.

You've been taught since the first day of school to begin your sentences with a capital letter and to end them with a period (or question mark or exclamation point). Why? These are signals to the reader that a thought begins (the capital letter) and ends (the period). For this convention to be useful, you have to follow it. Make sure that you develop only one main idea in each sentence.

YOU SHOULD PROOFREAD YOUR ESSAY USING A CHECKLIST OF COMMON ERRORS.

The criteria for grading the analytical writing essays include grammar and usage. The readers are specifically told that good essays must demonstrate facility with the conventions of Standard Written English. This doesn't mean that a single misplaced comma or wrong pronoun automatically results in a bad grade, but it should be clear that poor execution will undermine an otherwise strong essay. So you want to make certain that your essay is as free as possible from mistakes. As you proofread your essay, read each sentence individually and consciously ask the following questions:

Does this sentence have a main verb?

Every sentence must have a main verb. If a sentence doesn't, you need to add one. Here is an example:

> Seat belts in school buses, which are almost always part of the
> original equipment of passenger cars.

There is no main verb in this sentence. The subject of the sentence seems to be *seat belts in school buses*, and there is a dependent clause or thought introduced by *which*; but there is no main verb. So it's not clear what the sentence means to say. However, a way of eliminating the grammatical mistake would be:

> Seat belts, which are almost always part of the original equipment of passenger cars, are not required in school buses.

Does this sentence come to a point?

A real danger with an exercise like the writing assessment is writing sentences that seem to go on without stopping. As the name implies, a run-on sentence does just that. Here is an example:

> Initially, industry leaders were skeptical of seat belts, afterwards it occurred to them that saving lives might also save them money.

This sentence contains two independent clauses that are not properly joined. The portion of this sentence before the comma is an independent clause (which means a clause that can act as a sentence all by itself), and the portion of the sentence after the comma is also an independent clause. A comma by itself is not sufficient to separate two independent clauses; rather, a coordinating conjunction like *and, but, yet, for, or,* or *nor* must be used between the comma and the second independent clause. The sentence can be improved in the following way:

> Initially, industry leaders were skeptical of seat belts, but it later occurred to them that saving lives might also save them money.

Does the verb in this sentence agree with its subject?

It is a hard and fast rule of English grammar that verbs have to agree with their subjects. The following sentence violates this rule:

> Often times, injuries sustained in a motor vehicle accident is aggravated by the failure of the passenger in the vehicle to observe simple safety precautions other than wearing a seat belt.

The subject in this sentence is *injuries*, a plural noun, so you need the plural verb *are* rather than the singular *is*:

> Often times, injuries sustained in a motor vehicle accident are aggravated by the failure of the passenger in the vehicle to observe simple safety precautions other than wearing a seat belt.

The problem of subject-verb agreement is made more difficult anytime that you put modifiers between the subject and the verb. You probably wouldn't miss:

> Injuries is aggravated . . .

But you could easily miss:

> Injuries that are caused by the failure to install and require the use of seat belts is . . .

So in your proofreading, point your finger at the subject and at the verb and, in your mind, juxtapose the two to make sure that they agree.

Does each pronoun have a referent (antecedent)?

A pronoun must always substitute for another word. The following sentence is incorrect because the pronoun *which* doesn't have a referent:

> Not equipping large vehicles with seat belts, which is common practice in the manufacture of buses of all types, is not likely to increase the severity of injuries.

The *which* seems to refer to something, but try to find a word that it substitutes for, and you won't be able to. The sentence needs to be rewritten so that *which* has a referent:

> The failure to equip large vehicles with seat belts, which is common practice in the manufacture of buses of all types, is not likely to increase the severity of injuries.

If the sentence uses a series of elements, are the elements presented in the same form? (Are the elements parallel?)

When you write a series of elements into a sentence, those elements must have the same form, e.g., shooting skeet, playing tennis, and climbing mountains. (All three use the parallel *-ing* form.) The following sentence fails in this respect:

> Seat belts are the best way to reduce the severity of injuries, save lives, and, in general, minimizing the danger of riding in a bus.

The three elements *reduce*, *save*, and *minimizing* are a parallel series, so they should have parallel forms:

> Seat belts are the best way to reduce the severity of injuries, save lives, and, in general, minimize the danger of riding in a bus.

Using a series such as this will boost your score on the "variety of sentences" meter, but a mistake in parallelism will just create an offset in the category of mechanics.

Does each sentence say what it means to say? (Have you avoided misplaced modifiers?)

When you were in school, you probably heard a lot about the notorious "dangling modifier." (And maybe the concept was even defined for you.) You don't need to worry about whether or not a modifier is dangling if you just make certain that all of your modifiers are logically placed, and that usually means placed close to what they modify. Here's an example of a sentence with a misplaced modifier:

> Properly installed as original equipment, bus passengers will enjoy an additional safety margin if they are securely belted in during the trip.

The introductory modifier *properly installed* sounds as though it is intended to modify the element of the sentence closest to it, which would be *bus passengers*. But the sentence clearly does not mean to say that the passengers should be installed on the bus as original equipment. Here's what the sentence really means to say:

> Properly installed as original equipment, seat belts offer bus passengers an additional safety margin if the passengers are securely belted in during the trip.

Is each sentence properly punctuated?

Punctuation is one of those topics that strikes fear into the hearts of most students—like "factoring" in algebra. But for purposes of writing your response to the GRE Writing Assessment, this should not be a grave concern for two reasons. First, since you are doing the writing, you control the structure of your sentence and therefore the punctuation that is needed. If you are in doubt as to how to punctuate a sentence, just change the sentence to avoid the problem. Second, you can let your "ear" be your guide. Punctuation marks are like signals on a car. Just as signals like turn indicators and brake lights help other drivers know what you're doing, punctuation marks let your reader know what you're up to. You should be able to read your sentences to yourself, pausing at each comma and coming to a full stop at a period, to determine whether you've punctuated correctly. If your reading sounds correct to you, then it is what you meant to say and is probably correct. Here is an example of a sentence that is not properly punctuated:

> Retrofitting school buses with seat belts, would probably not be a cost effective measure considering the small number of accidents involving schools buses each year.

If you read this to yourself, you should wonder why there ought to be a pause between *belts* and *would*. And there should not be, so eliminate the comma there. In general, so long as you maintain tight control of the other elements of writing and don't try to create overly elaborate structures, punctuation should not be a major problem.

WRITE IT CORRECTLY.

You probably don't have time to do a full-scale review of English grammar, but you should try to make a place in your preparation schedule for some grammar review. While the exercises that follow do not present a question format found on the GRE, they will give you practice in spotting common errors. The exercises are not scored, but you will find complete explanations following the questions.

WHAT SMART TEST-TAKERS KNOW <u>NOT</u> TO DO

YOU SHOULD NEVER WRITE ABOUT A TOPIC OTHER THAN THE ONES YOU ARE GIVEN.

The directions are very clear on this issue, and the readers are specifically instructed to assign a grade of zero (the lowest possible) to any response that is written on a different topic.

The prompts are specifically designed to provide you with an opportunity to write. To work, then, they must be topics that are accessible to everyone. For this reason, the topics do not presuppose any special knowledge.

YOU SHOULD NOT TRY TO MAKE THE SUBJECT OF THE PROMPT MORE IMPORTANT THAN IT IS.

Many candidates imagine that their essays will be considerably improved if they make clear to the reader that they feel passionately about the topic or that they consider the topic to be of very grave concern. Unfortunately, extreme passion or grave concern is usually simply out of place—even when the topic is one of great importance.

YOU SHOULD NOT TRY TO DO TOO MUCH.

Half or three quarters of an hour may seem like a lot of time, but it's not. By the time you read the topic, think about the issue or the argument, formulate some ideas, create an outline, and generate your response, you'll probably be running out of time—wishing that you had more time for the proofreading phase. So, in this case, more is not necessarily better. It is preferable to write a shorter essay that is complete than to aspire to write a *magnum opus* only to run out of time with the project only barely started.

EXERCISE 1*

25 Questions • 25 Minutes

Directions: Each item in this exercise is a sentence, a part or all of which has been underlined. The underlined part contains an error. Choose the best way of rewriting the sentence.

1. A graduate degree, <u>which requires an enormous investment of time and money, do not guarantee success as there is so much competition.</u>

   (A) which requires an enormous investment of time and money, does not guarantee success since there is so much competition

   (B) requiring an enormous investment of time and money, without guarantee because there is so much competition

   (C) requires an enormous investment of time and money, and it cannot guarantee success because there is so much competition

   (D) requires that an enormous investment of time and money be made and success cannot be guaranteed due to the competition

2. <u>It was believed that a thorough knowledge of Latin would not only enable students to read the classics, also enabling them to think clearly and precisely.</u>

   (A) It had been believed that a thorough knowledge of Latin would not only enable students to read the classics but rather enable them to think clearly and precisely.

   (B) It was believed that a thorough knowledge of Latin would not only enable students to read the classics but also enabling them to think clearly and precisely.

   (C) It used to be believed that a thorough knowledge of Latin would enable a student to be able to read the classics but also enable them to think clearly and precisely.

   (D) It was believed that a thorough knowledge of Latin would enable students not only to read the classics, but also to think clearly and precisely.

3. Most adolescents struggle to be free <u>both of parental domination but also from peer pressure.</u>

   (A) both of parental domination and also from peer pressure too.

   (B) both of parental domination and also of peer pressure too.

   (C) both of parental domination and of peer pressure.

   (D) of parental domination and their peer pressure as well.

* *This exercise is for grammar review only. It does not represent a GRE question type.*

4. The president of the block association tried to convince her neighbors <u>they should join forces to prevent crime in the neighborhood rather than continuing to be victimized.</u>

    (A) that they should join forces to prevent crime in the neighborhood rather than continue to be victimized

    (B) about joining forces to prevent crime in the neighborhood instead of continuing to be victimized

    (C) for the joining of forces to prevent crime in the neighborhood rather than continue to be victimized

    (D) to join forces to prevent crime in the neighborhood rather than continuing to be victimized

5. <u>Although he is as gifted as, if not more gifted than, many of his colleagues, he is extremely modest with his poetry is unpublished.</u>

    (A) Although he is as gifted, if not more gifted, than many of his colleagues, he is extremely modest with his poetry remaining unpublished.

    (B) Although he is as gifted as, if not more gifted than, many of his colleagues, he is extremely modest and will not publish his poetry.

    (C) Despite his being gifted, if not more gifted than his colleagues, he is extremely modest and will not publish his poetry.

    (D) Being as gifted as, or more gifted than, many of his colleagues, he is extremely modest and his poetry is unpublished.

6. Although the manager agreed to a more flexible work schedule, <u>he said it had to be posted on the bulletin board so that both management and labor knows what everyone is</u> assigned to do.

    (A) he said that it must be posted on the bulletin board so that both management and labor will know what everyone is

    (B) he said that they would have to post the assignments on the bulletin board so that management and labor knew what everyone was

    (C) he said that the schedule would have to be posted on the bulletin board so that both management and labor would know what everyone was

    (D) saying that the schedule had to be posted on the bulletin board so that both management and labor would know what everyone had been

7. With just several quick strokes of the pen, <u>the monkeys were drawn by the artist, capturing their antics.</u>

    (A) the artist sketched the monkeys, capturing their antics

    (B) the artist captured the antics of the monkeys, sketching them

    (C) the artist sketched the monkeys and also capturing their antics

    (D) the monkeys and their antics were sketched by the artist

8. <u>Primarily accomplished through the use of the electron microscope,</u> researchers have recently vastly increased their knowledge of the process of cell division.

    (A) Through the competent use of advanced electron microscopy,

    (B) Primarily through the use of electron microscopy,

    (C) In a large sense through the use of the electron microscope,

    (D) In the main, particularly through the use of electron microscopes,

9. Though garlic is often associated with Italian cuisine, it is actually the use of oregano <u>which most distinguishes the Italians from the French</u>.

   (A) which primarily distinguishes Italians from Frenchmen

   (B) which generally serves to distinguish an Italian from a French

   (C) which is a major distinction between great cuisines

   (D) which most distinguishes Italian cookery from French

10. While controversy rages over whether the sign language taught to some great apes is truly human-like speech, there is no similar dispute that our powers of communication <u>are greater by far than that of any other animal</u>.

    (A) are far greater than that of any other animal

    (B) are greater by far than any other animal

    (C) are far greater than those of any other animal

    (D) have been far greater than those of other animals

11. Despite the money that has been invested by industry in the attempt to persuade Americans that highly processed foods are the best foods, the populace stubbornly clings to the belief that such foods <u>are neither particularly healthy or tasty</u>.

    (A) are neither particularly healthful nor tasty

    (B) are not particularly health or tasty

    (C) are not particularly healthful or tasteful

    (D) are not very healthy nor tasty

12. Before adopting such a plan for all schools, we would first want to see evidence <u>that they would improve the reading skills</u> of the students enrolled in the new classes.

    (A) that it would improve the reading skills

    (B) that improvement of reading skill

    (C) of its improving the reading skills

    (D) of improved reading skills

13. The closing of small, inexpensive hospitals while large expensive hospitals remain open <u>seems a luxury that we can no longer afford in order to maintain them</u>.

    (A) seems to emphasize luxury over economy, which we can no longer afford

    (B) seems to be a waste of valuable resources

    (C) seems a luxury we can no longer afford

    (D) seems too luxurious to be any longer affordable

14. The ancient question of the exact difference between plants and animals, which was so complicated with the discovery of microscopic members of both groups, was somewhat side-stepped with the establishment of a third phylum, the Protista, <u>reserved just for them</u>.

    (A) consisting only of them

    (B) inhabited only by them

    (C) which includes all microscopic life

    (D) which would have included all microscopic plants and animals

15. <u>The Lake Manyara Park in Tanzania affords the visitor with unequalled opportunities to photograph lions playing in trees without the aid of telephoto lenses.</u>

   (A) The Lake Manyara Park in Tanzania permits the visitor unequalled opportunities to photograph lions playing in trees without the aid of telephoto lenses.

   (B) The Lake Manyara Park in Tanzania gives the visitor the unequalled opportunity to photograph lions playing in trees without telephoto lenses.

   (C) The visitor to the Lake Manyara Park in Tanzania has the unequalled opportunity to photograph lions playing in trees without the aid of telephoto lenses.

   (D) Even without the aid of telephoto lenses, the visitor to Tanzania's Lake Manyara Park has an unequalled opportunity to photograph lions playing in trees.

16. During the Renaissance, other painters <u>were so influenced by da Vinci's work that ignoring</u> their own training and tried to imitate him directly.

   (A) were influenced by da Vinci's work to such an extent that they were to ignore

   (B) were so influenced with da Vinci as to ignore

   (C) were so influenced by da Vinci that they had to ignore

   (D) were so influenced by da Vinci that they ignored

17. Most members of the trade union rejected the mayor's demand <u>returning</u> to work.

   (A) that they were returning

   (B) that return

   (C) to return

   (D) to returning

18. <u>The players were often punished by the referee's lack of alertness who penalized</u> all those who were involved in fighting, regardless of who had instigated it.

   (A) The referee's lack of alertness often caused him to penalize

   (B) The players were punished by the lack of alertness of the referee who penalized often

   (C) Lacking alertness, the referee's choice was to penalize often

   (D) His lack of alertness to brutality often caused the referee to penalize

19. The Police Department <u>not only was responsible</u> for maintaining order in the metropolitan area but also for rebuilding the bonds among the various ethnic groups.

   (A) was responsible not only

   (B) was not only responsible

   (C) was responsible only not

   (D) was not responsible only

20. <u>In comparison with the literature created by the ancient Greeks, today's Greeks have written nothing worth describing.</u>

   (A) In comparison with the literature created by the ancient Greeks, the literature of today's Greeks are containing nothing worth describing.

   (B) Compared to that of the ancient Greeks, today's Greeks have written nothing worth describing.

   (C) Compared to that of the ancient Greeks, the literature of today's Greeks is not worth describing.

   (D) Compared to the ancient Greek's literature, today's Greeks have written nothing worth describing.

21. <u>Steve, along with his brothers, are</u> going to make a large real estate investment.

    (A) Steve, along with his brothers, is

    (B) Steve, in addition to his brothers, are

    (C) Steve, as well as his brothers, are

    (D) Steve and his brothers is

22. During the war, when it <u>looked as if the German army was going to cross</u> into France, English mercenaries joined the French to resist the assault.

    (A) looked like the German army was going to cross

    (B) looked like the German army would have crossed

    (C) appearances were that the German army would be crossing

    (D) appeared that the German army would cross

23. In stating the argument that the President does not care about the poor, a prominent Democrat <u>inferred that Republicans have never been concerned about it</u>.

    (A) inferred that Republicans have never been concerned about the poor

    (B) implied that Republicans have never been concerned about the poor

    (C) inferred that Republicans have never been concerned about them

    (D) implied that Republicans have never been concerned about it

24. Many travelers state unequivocally <u>that the streets in Paris are more beautiful than any other city</u>.

    (A) that the streets in Paris are more beautiful than in any city

    (B) that Paris streets are more beautiful than any other city

    (C) that, unlike any other city, Paris streets are more beautiful

    (D) that the streets of Paris are more beautiful than the streets of any other city

25. The mayor's <u>media advisor, as well as his three top aides, are</u> traveling with him on a tour of European capital cities.

    (A) media advisor, also his three top aides, are

    (B) media advisor, as well as his three top aides, is

    (C) media advisor, along with his three top aides, are

    (D) media advisor, all in the company of his three top aides, is

EXERCISE 2*

15 Questions • 15 Minutes

> **Directions:** Each item in this exercise is a sentence, a part or all of which has been underlined. The underlined part contains an error. Choose the best way of rewriting the sentence.

1. Lawyers and doctors <u>alike both agree that something should be done about the rise in medical malpractice suits which are on the increase</u>.

    (A) alike agree that something should be done about the rise in medical malpractice suits

    (B) both agree that something should be done about the increasing rise in medical malpractice suits

    (C) agree that something should be done about the rise in medical malpractice suits, which are increasing

    (D) agree that something should be done about the rise in the number of medical malpractice suits

2. The obviously bitter actress stated that <u>if the director would have known what he was doing, the play would have run</u> for more than one night.

    (A) had the director known what he was doing, the play would have run

    (B) if the director had known what he was doing, they would run

    (C) had the director known what he was doing, they would run

    (D) if the director knew what he was doing, they would have run

3. Dr. Smith's findings that emotions affect blood pressure <u>is different from those</u> published by Dr. Loeb.

    (A) are different from those

    (B) are different than those

    (C) is different than those

    (D) are different from that

4. <u>Entering professional tennis as a talented but shy and awkward teenager, for the eight years that Steffi Graf was</u> the dominant force on the women's circuit, a powerful and consistent player.

    (A) Entered into professional tennis as a talented but shy and awkward teenager, Steffi Graf was for eight years

    (B) Steffi Graf entered professional tennis as a talented yet shy and awkward teenager but was for eight years

    (C) For eight years, having entered professional tennis as a talented yet shy and awkward teenager, Steffi Graf was

    (D) Having entered professional tennis for eight years as a teenager who was talented yet shy and awkward, Steffi Graf was

---

* *This exercise is for grammar review only. It does not represent a GRE question type.*

5. The political masters of the health care system have not listened to professional health planners because it <u>has not been profitable for them to do that thing</u>.

   (A) has been unprofitable for them to do it

   (B) has not been profitable for them to do so

   (C) being unprofitable for them to do it

   (D) doing so had not been profitable for them

6. The director of the Miss America pageant continues to maintain that the judges' ultimate choice is based less on the physical appearance of the contestant <u>as on</u> her intelligence, talent, and personality.

   (A) and more on

   (B) than on

   (C) but more on

   (D) than

7. <u>The reason why the boxing commission refused to grant a license to the fighter was because it concluded</u> he could not pass the required physical exam.

   (A) The boxing commission's refusal to grant a license to the fighter was because it concluded

   (B) The boxing commission refused to grant a license to the fighter because it concluded

   (C) The reason the boxing commission refused to grant a license was because it concluded

   (D) The boxing commission refused to grant a license, the reason being that it concluded

8. The court order <u>that transit workers return to their job were</u> generally ignored.

   (A) that transit workers return to their job was

   (B) that transit workers return to their jobs was

   (C) for each transit worker to return to work were

   (D) that each transit worker returns to work was

9. Having been ordered by the judge to resume alimony payments, Ms. Jones <u>was still not allowed by it</u> to see her children on weekends.

   (A) still had not been allowed by it

   (B) still was not to be allowed

   (C) was still not allowed

   (D) was not to be allowed by it

10. The police officers throughout the department <u>was so distrustful of the new commissioner that they refused</u> to carry out his orders.

   (A) were so distrustful of the new commissioner that they refused

   (B) were distrustful of the new commissioner to such an extent that they were to refuse

   (C) was so distrustful of the new commissioner that they had to refuse

   (D) was as distrustful of the new commissioner that they refused

11. <u>To consider a diagnosis on the basis of inadequate or misleading evidence is neglecting</u> years of specialized medical training.

 (A) To consider a diagnosis on the basis of inadequate or misleading evidence is to neglect

 (B) In considering a diagnosis on the basis of inadequate or misleading evidence is neglecting

 (C) Considering a diagnosis on the basis of inadequate or misleading evidence is to neglect

 (D) Considering a diagnosis on the basis of inadequate or misleading evidence amounts to neglecting

12. The recent discovery of Tutankhamen's tomb by Egyptologists has provided information which suggests that the wealth accumulated by ancient Egyptian pharaohs was greater than <u>believed</u>.

 (A) is believed

 (B) was believed

 (C) they have believed before

 (D) had been believed

13. Malnutrition is the most serious health problem still facing many developing countries, but <u>it has or soon will</u> be greatly reduced in many others.

 (A) they have or soon will

 (B) that it would or soon could

 (C) it has or will soon

 (D) it has been or soon will

14. <u>Having discovered the Roman aristocrats to be suffering from lead poisoning</u>, it is now thought that this was a major cause of their inability to reproduce.

 (A) To have discovered the Roman aristocrats to be suffering from lead poisoning,

 (B) Since scientists have discovered that the Roman aristocrats suffered from lead poisoning,

 (C) Since the suffering of lead poisoning by Roman aristocrats was discovered by scientists,

 (D) Due to the fact Roman aristocrats were suffering from lead poisoning was discovered by scientists,

15. It is characteristic of the Metropolitan Opera, <u>as of every major international company, that the casting is based more on the availability of singers as it is</u> on the tastes of the music director and the public.

 (A) as it is of every major international company, that the casting is based more on the availability of singers than it is

 (B) as it is of every major international company, that the casting had been based more on the availability of singers as

 (C) as about every major international company, that casting is based more on the availability of singers than it was

 (D) as it is of every major international company, where the casting is based more on the availability of singers than it is

ANSWER KEY AND EXPLANATIONS

Exercise 1

1.	A	6.	A	11.	A	16.	D	21.	A
2.	D	7.	A	12.	A	17.	C	22.	D
3.	C	8.	B	13.	C	18.	A	23.	B
4.	A	9.	D	14.	C	19.	A	24.	D
5.	B	10.	C	15.	D	20.	C	25.	B

1. **The correct answer is (A).** The original sentence is incorrect because the subject and verb do not agree. Further, it is incorrect to use *as* to mean *because*. (B) is incorrect because the resulting sentence lacks a main verb. (C) is incorrect because the *it* has no clear and unambiguous antecedent. (D) is not technically wrong, but it is too wordy. It's better to write sentences that are simple in structure and state ideas directly.

2. **The correct answer is (D).** The correct construction for this sentence is *not only x but y*. (A) introduces an incorrect verb tense, *it had been believed*, and a construction, *not x but rather y*, which is incorrect. (B) uses the proper construction but fails to make the verbs parallel. In (C), the pronoun *their* does not agree with *student*.

3. **The correct answer is (C).** The phrase *but also* implies a contrast between two ideas, but no such contrast is supported by the original. (C), by using the simple conjunction *and*, makes it clear that the two ideas are parallel. (A) and (B) use superfluous *alsos* and *toos*. Try to avoid packing your sentences with unnecessary words. Finally, the *their* in (D) does not have a clear antecedent.

4. **The correct answer is (A).** The original sentence commits the error of faulty parallelism. The *this rather than that* construction requires two elements of the same form: *join rather than continue*. (C) and (D) fail on the grounds of parallel-

ism. As for (B), the phrase *convince about* is not idiomatic English.

5. **The correct answer is (B).** The first part of the original sentence (from *although* to *colleagues*) is correct. The comparison is logical and properly completed. So (A), (C), and (D), which makes changes in that part of the original, are incorrect. The second part of the original, however, contains a logical error. The *and* fails to specify the nature of the connection between the person's modesty and the fact that the poetry is unpublished. (B) correctly supplies the connection. In general, stay away from awkward constructions. If a sentence doesn't mean to say what you want it to clearly and directly, then you should rewrite it for the benefit of your reader, plus the lack of clarity may be tied to an outright error.

6. **The correct answer is (A).** In the original sentence, the verb *knows* does not agree with the plural subject *both management and labor*. (B) is incorrect because the verb *knew* does not correctly reflect the fact that the requirement of posting is an ongoing one. (C) and (D) are both incorrect because the use of the verb *would* implies a condition that is not mentioned or suggested by the sentence.

7. **The correct answer is (A).** The original sentence contains a misplaced modifier. As a rule, a modifier should be placed as close to the element modified as possible. (A), therefore, is better than the original. (B), (C), and (D) all make

unneeded changes and result in awkward sentences. In general, building a sentence is like building a house: the pieces have to fit together in a solid, meaning logical, way. For example, in (B), sticking the phrase *sketching them* on to the end of the sentence would be like putting a toilet, as an afterthought, into the corner of the living room.

8. **The correct answer is (B).** The element of the sentence following the introductory descriptor or modifier must apply to the first noun after the comma. The researchers were not *primarily accomplished* through the use of electron microscopes, so (A) is out. (C) and (D) use locutions that are either meaningless or wordy. (B) keeps everything in order.

9. **The correct answer is (D).** The first part of the sentence speaks of the cuisine, so we do not want to shift suddenly to the peoples themselves as the original does. (A) and (B) fail for the same reason. (C) fails to mention the French cuisine, which is an error. The resulting sentence seems to generalize, making the claim that all cuisines are distinguished from one another in the way they utilize garlic. (D) is correct, because then the word *cookery* can be carried forward in the reader's mind to yield French cookery being compared to Italian cookery.

10. **The correct answer is (C).** The original errs in its use of *that*, which is singular, while *powers*, for which it stands, is plural. This eliminates (A). (B) fails because it is comparing our powers of communication with other animals, rather than with the powers of communication of the other animals. (D) is inferior to (C) because it changes the tense to *have been* without cause. (C)'s change to *far greater*, while not strictly necessary, does leave the meaning intact and even improves the sentence.

11. **The correct answer is (A).** *Healthy* refers to the state of health of some organism. *Healthful* is the proper way to describe something that promotes health. *Tasty* refers to the quality of having a good taste when eaten. *Tasteful* refers to being in accord with good aesthetic taste, or having such taste. In addition, the original erred in having *neither . . . or*, when *neither . . . nor* is required. Only (A) conveys the intended meaning of the original.

12. **The correct answer is (A).** The *they* in the original refers to *plan* and not to *schools*, so you need the singular pronoun *it*. (B) completely disrupts the logical flow of the sentence, and (C) and (D) result in very awkward sentences.

13. **The correct answer is (C).** The part of the sentence after *in* is surplus. (C) correctly dispenses with that part and preserves the rest.

14. **The correct answer is (C).** The *them* is unclear, so (A) and (B) are not good alternatives. (C)'s use of the present tense is acceptable since the classification presumably still does what the third phylum was set up to do. (D)'s use of the *would* construction is not acceptable since there is no doubt about what is included.

15. **The correct answer is (D).** The original sentence has the lions playing with lenses while in the trees. This is clearly unacceptable. Only (D) corrects the situation to make it clear that the visitor is the one concerned with telephoto lenses, not the lions.

16. **The correct answer is (D).** *That* is used here to set up a relative clause, and a relative clause must have both a subject and a conjugated or main verb. The problem is that *ignoring* is not a main verb. (D) solves the problem by using *they ignored*. (B) doesn't address this issue, and (A) and (C) use verb tenses that are not consistent with the rest of the sentence.

17. **The correct answer is (C).** *Returning* has no clear function in the original. Sometimes an *-ing* participle is used as an adjective: Returning to work early, Bob found that his office had been vandalized. But *returning* here doesn't serve that function. And sometimes *returning* can be a part of a main verb: They were returning from the movies when the car ran out of gas. But that is not the case here either. (C) solves the problem by using the infinitive form: to return.

18. **The correct answer is (A).** The original confuses two sources of punishment, the *referee's lack* and the referee himself, resulting in awkward use of *who* and needless use of both *punished* and *penalized*. (B) better manages to link *referee* and *who*, but it still requires both *punished* and *penalized*. (C) and (D) change the meaning, (C) by implying that the referee is conscious of his *lack*, (D) by adding *brutality*.

19. **The correct answer is (A).** The original and (D) suffer from faulty parallelism. When two or more phrases/clauses branch off from the same word, that word should come first and they should be in parallel structure (*responsible not only for . . . but also for . . .*).

20. **The correct answer is (C).** The original, (B), and (D) are marred by faulty parallelism: ancient Greek literature is compared with today's Greek people. (B) even leaves *literature* to be inferred, and (D) compares the ancient *Greek* with modern *Greeks*. (A) does achieve parallelism, but errs in using the plural (and here unidiomatic) verb *are containing* with the singular noun *literature*. Only (C) lines up the ideas correctly.

21. **The correct answer is (A).** In the original, (B), and (C), the phrases about the *brothers* are parenthetical; they are not part of the subject. Steve, the true subject, is singular, requiring not *are* but *is*, as in (A). In (D), *his brothers* is linked with *Steve* by *and*, thus creating a plural subject requiring not *is* but *are*.

22. **The correct answer is (D).** In standard written English, *looked like* and *looked as if* are not synonyms for *appeared that*, eliminating (A) and (B). *Appearances were that* and *would be crossing* make (C) wordier than the succinct, and correct, (D).

23. **The correct answer is (B).** The original incorrectly uses *inferred* to mean *implied*. Also, the original uses *it* to refer to *the poor*, a plural noun.

24. **The correct answer is (D).** The original creates ambiguity through faulty parallelism: are streets being compared with streets or with cities? (D) eliminates confusion by using strict parallel structure: *the streets in Paris* is balanced by *the streets in any other city*.

25. **The correct answer is (B).** The phrase about the *aides* simply supplies extra, parenthetical information. It is not part of the subject, which remains the singular *media advisor*.

Exercise 2

1.	D	4.	B	7.	B	10.	A	13.	D
2.	A	5.	B	8.	B	11.	A	14.	B
3.	A	6.	B	9.	C	12.	D	15.	A

1. **The correct answer is (D).** The original is repetitious: if *Lawyers and doctors . . . agree*, then *alike* and *both* are superfluous; if there's a *rise in . . . suits*, the clause *which are on the increase* is redundant. Only (D) avoids all these errors.

2. **The correct answer is (A).** The original is wrong because the "if" clause, stating a past condition contrary to fact, requires a past-perfect subjunctive ("had known"). Additionally, the "possible conclusion" clause requires the perfect form of a modal auxiliary ("would have run"). Finally, "if" is already implicit in the *had . . . known* construction.

3. **The correct answer is (A).** In the original, the verb *is* does not agree with its subject *findings*. Also, do not confuse *from* with *than*: things differ from one another. (D) uses the singular that instead of the plural *those* to refer back to the plural antecedent *findings*.

4. **The correct answer is (B).** The original does not include a conjugated or main verb. As written, the *was* in the original is relegated to the status of a verb in a relative clause introduced by *that*. (B) solves this problem by creating a main clause: *Graf was . . . .* (A) makes it sound as though Graf were *entered into* tennis, as a horse is entered into a race. And the placement of the phrase *for eight years* in both (C) and (D) creates confusion.

5. **The correct answer is (B).** The original is faulty because *that thing* refers to a diffuse idea in the sentence better expressed by (B). (A) doesn't solve the problem because the pronoun *it* doesn't have an antecedent. (C) winds up creating a clause (introduced by *because*) without a conjugated verb. (D) is awkward.

6. **The correct answer is (B).** In Standard Written English, the pattern is *less . . . than* and of course the two parts thus introduced should be in parallel structure. The original's use of *as* is totally unacceptable. (A)'s use of *and more on* might be acceptable in informal speech but not Standard Written English. (C) is illiterate. (D) uses the correct adverb, *than*, but omits the *on* that cinches the parallelism.

7. **The correct answer is (B).** As originally written, the sentence is a mess. First, we have the unacceptable construction *The reason why . . . .* Second, *because* should not be used to introduce a noun clause; that is, you should not use the structure *is because*. (B) corrects the sentence by eliminating unnecessary words and stating directly the meaning of the sentence.

8. **The correct answer is (B).** The original contains two mistakes. First, there is a failure of subject-verb agreement: *order . . . were generally ignored.* Second, *their job* wrongly implies that all of the workers have a single position. What the sentence means to say is *their jobs*.

9. **The correct answer is (C).** The difficulty with the sentence is that *it* doesn't refer to anything. (C) solves the problem by simply eliminating the unnecessary wording. Then, when you compare (C) with (B), you'll note that (C) is more direct—and directness in writing is a virtue.

10. **The correct answer is (A).** The original includes a subject-verb error: *officers . . . was*. (A) corrects the error. (B) adds unneeded words, making the sentence awkward.

11. **The correct answer is (A).** The difficulty with the sentence is a failure of parallelism. The subject of the sentence is the infinitive *to consider*, but the complement is the gerund *is neglecting*. One or the other must be changed so that they both have the same form. (A) does this. (C) changes both, so it commits the mirror image of the original error. (B) introduces wording that makes the sentence illogical. (D) introduces a new error—the unacceptable usage of *amounts to*.

12. **The correct answer is (D).** There is a problem here with verb tense. To express correctly the thought of the sentence, it must be made clear that the erroneous belief preceded the discovery of the new information and that it was ended by that discovery. (D), by using the past perfect *had*, correctly places the *belief* as a completed act in the past.

13. **The correct answer is (D).** The original contains a fractured construction. You have two verb tenses: *has been* and *will be*. But the *been* is missing. (D) adds *been* where it is needed.

14. **The correct answer is (B).** The original sentence contains an error that might best be described as the mirror image of the error of the dangling modifier. The introductory phrase is properly placed to modify a subject that is the person or persons who made the discovery. Unfortunately, the impersonal *it* is the wrong subject. (B) corrects this error. (A) fails to correct the original mistake and compounds the problem by substituting an illogical verb tense. (C) is awkward. Finally, (D) uses the phrase *due to*, which cannot be used as a conjunction in standard written English.

15. **The correct answer is (A).** It is not idiomatic English to say *more on x as on y*. (A) uses the correct idiom, *more on x than on y*. (B) repeats the original error and adds an incorrect verb form, *had been based*. (C) corrects the original error but does not follow the sequence of events. It switches from the present tense (is) to the past tense (was). (D) repeats the original error and introduces a new one, using *where* to mean *in which*.

EXERCISE 1: ISSUE TASK

ISSUE TASK: Present Your Perspective on an Issue

Time: 45 Minutes

You have 45 minutes to plan and write an essay that presents your views on an assigned topic.

The topic is summarized in a brief quotation that states or suggests a position. You can accept, reject, or modify the position. Support your views with reasons and examples drawn from your experience, observation, reading, or study.

Trained graders will score your response, taking into account how well you:

- Understand the complexities and ramifications of the issue
- Organize, develop, and express your ideas
- Deploy the elements of standard written English

You may wish to spend a few minutes thinking about your response before you begin writing and to leave time to reread what you have written in order to make any revisions you think necessary.

Present your point of view on the following issue:

> "Hierarchical structures such as corporations and governments are neither moral nor immoral. The decisions made on behalf of such entities are made by individuals who ultimately bear the ethical responsibilities for the effects of the policies of the hierarchies."

exercises

SAMPLE RESPONSE AND COMMENTARY

Note: The sample answers contain spelling and grammatical errors. This is done to simulate a first draft written under time pressure.

Whether one wants to ascribe moral responsibility to a hierarchical structure depends on the ontological status given to the structure, that is, whether the structure really exists. In one sense, hierarchical structures do not exist at all: take away the people, and you're left with nothing. In another sense, however, hierarchical structures are treated as actual individuals, both by the law (corporations can be fined) and by opinion (governments are censured).

In one sense, hierarchical structures do not exist in the same way that individual people exist, so it doesn't make sense to talk about them as being moral or immoral. If you take a company like General Motors, dissolve the Board of Directors, remove all of management, and then dismiss all of the workers, you're left with an inert organizational table, that is, the company can't make any decisions or take any actions. So in what sense could it be moral or immoral? The same is true of government: recall all of the sitting legislators and don't elect or appoint new ones, impeach all sitting judges and don't fill the vacancies, remove all members of the executive. The "government" would continue to exist in the sense of a Constitutional scheme, but it would be incapable of any act at all and so neither moral nor immoral.

Yet, we do ascribe notions of morality to companies and to governments. We speak of "corporate culture;" and when we recall the collapse of Enron (the huge Houston-based energy trading company that collapsed in 2001), we are likely to define the corporate culture as one of "greed." And companies, while they cannot be imprisoned, are subject to financial and other punishments. The company that commits securities fraud can be fined; a monopolist can be broken up; a company that rigs bids can be barred from further participation in the business. And, importantly, these sanctions have real effects on real people including management, workers, and the shareholders. Additionally, governments can be the object of economic and military sanctions. Governments sometimes even take moral responsibility for their own actions. The government of modern Germany, for example, has accepted some moral responsibility for World War II, the Japanese government for atrocities committed in China and Korea during that same conflict, and the Belgian government for colonialism in Africa. Importantly, these are examples of where officials of the current government are blaming not previous officeholders but the institutions themselves.

What these considerations suggest is that the topic is based upon a flawed assumption. The topic assumes that it is possible to have a corporation or government without people, but once you've have removed the people, the hierarchcal organization no longer exists—except as a theory, and, of course, a theory is neither moral nor immoral. Instead, people and structure are like two sides of the same coin, the heads and the tails, you can talk about them as though they exist independently but you never find them separately. Therefore, it makes just as much sense to ascribe moral responsibility to orgnizations as it does to ascribed those characteristics to people.

COMMENTARY

This is an excellent essay. Notice that the writer has chosen the fourth approach suggested to the issue topic: say that the topic is *faulty* in some respect. And you should also note that the writer has quite a lot to say about the topic itself and, as the directions suggest, explores some of the implications of the topic. The essay makes good use of examples: Enron, Germany, Japan, and Belgium, and also the analogy with a coin. Beyond that, you should be able to see that the response is well organized. And finally, it is very forcefully written in substantially correct prose with a rich vocabulary. This is the kind of essay that gets a 6.

EXERCISE 2: ARGUMENT TASK

ARGUMENT TASK: Analyze an Argument

Time: 30 Minutes

You have 30 minutes to plan and write an essay that presents your views on an assigned topic. Consider the logic of the argument and the soundness of its conclusion.

Trained graders will score your response, taking into account how well you:

- Identify and analyze the structure of the argument
- Organize, develop, and express your ideas
- Deploy the elements of standard written English

You may wish to spend a few minutes thinking about your response before you begin writing and to leave time to reread what you have written in order to make any revisions you think necessary.

Read the following argument and discuss whether it is well-reasoned. You are not being asked to agree or disagree with the conclusion of the argument; you are being asked to analyze the reasoning in the argument. Consider what, if any, assumptions the argument makes and whether they are justified, what evidence is offered for the conclusion and whether it is reliable, as well as any other factors or information that would strengthen or weaken the argument.

Discuss how well-reasoned you find the following argument:

> "The government makes available guarantees of loans not only for students attending college but for students enrolled in training schools for trades such as cosmetology and automotive repairs. It was recently found that a computer repair school located in a large city encouraged unqualified students to enroll in their training programs and take out government loans for tuition but then did little to ensure that they would learn a trade. Once the government-backed tuition loan was paid to the school, its operators didn't care whether the students failed or graduated. This is a waste of taxpayer money and does a disservice to the students themselves. If we discontinued government guarantees for tuition loans for trade schools, the government could save taxpayers a lot of money."

exercises

_____

_____

_____

_____

_____

_____

_____

_____

_____

_____

_____

_____

_____

_____

_____

_____

_____

_____

_____

_____

_____

_____

_____

_____

_____

_____

SAMPLE RESPONSE AND COMMENTARY

Note: The sample answers contain spelling and grammatical errors. This is done to simulate a first draft written under time pressure.

Just as it's often difficult to see the forest for the trees, so too it is easy to magnify a small problem to such a great extent that its elimination seems to be the solution to all of our ills. The speaker above cites a single example of abuse of the government-guaranteed loan program for students and calls not just for a modest reform but the complete elimination of the program and claims, as a result, that the taxpayers will save a lot of money. At best, the speaker overstates the case.

First, it should be noted that the speaker cites only a single example and that in the computer-repair business. Before such a sweeping reform could be justified, we would need to be certain that this example is typical of the trade school industry, and there are good reasons to believe that it is not. Computer-repair, while not a new service, is something quite different from cosmetology and auto-repair, businesses with established structures and long records of providing service and jobs. And it is not clear from what the speaker says that this one school is typical of all computer-repair schools. In other words, we really don't know the extent of the problem.

Second, the speaker, to put it tritely, proposes to throw out the baby with the bath water. Even assuming that this one computer-repair school is typical of all computer-repair schools, then it would make more sense to discontinue loans to this particular kind of school. It makes no sense, without some evidence of widespread abuse, to discontinue the programs to schools that teach cosmetology and auto-repair. And even assuming that fraud is rife in the computer-repair schools, it might even be better just to monitor those business more carefully, audit them more frequently, rather than discontinue aid categorically.

Third, the speaker surely overstates the outcome. Waste is, of course, waste no matter the dollar amount, but in the overall scheme of things, surely the waste caused by the fraudulent practices of one computer-repair training school is not terribly significant. And such drastic action might actually have the effect of costing the taxpayers money. Discontinuing all loans would obviously mean that many people who previously got training in the trades would no longer get that training. These people would likely enter the workforce in lower-paying jobs or might not enter at all. As a result, they would pay less or even no taxes, and that would be the remaining taxpayers would wind up paying more, not to mention that the unemployed and unemployable workers would be eligible for benefits funded by those taxpayers.

COMMENTARY

This is an above-average essay. Notice how the writer uses several of the techniques discussed above to analyze the argument topic: does the evidence prove the claim, is there a less drastic alternative, what would be the cost? The argument is well organized into three paragraphs, each making a particular point. And it is well written and forcefully argued.

Both of the essays presented as responses to the exercises in this chapter are excellent. Now, the point of presenting above-average samples is not to suggest that everyone can start off writing a top essay. Rather, the idea is to show you what you should be working toward. You'll have a lot of opportunity to practice writing as you take the tests in this book. And later, you'll be reviewing examples of bad as well as good essays. As you read both good and bad examples, consciously ask yourself how your essays match up and work to eliminate the weaknesses and introduce new strengths.

SUMMING IT UP

- The writing assessment requires essay responses to two topics (prompts): an issue topic and an argument topic.

- Essays are graded on a scale of 0 to 6 for content, organization, and execution.

- These steps can help you handle the writing assessment:

  1. Read the topic and decide what position you want to take.

  2. Outline your thinking using the scratch paper that is provided.

  3. Type or hand-write your essay.

  4. Proofread your essay.

- You should always write on the given topic.

- You should illustrate your ideas with examples.

- You should organize each essay by using the "three main points" approach.

PART VI

FIVE PRACTICE TESTS

PRACTICE TEST 2 ANSWER SHEET

Verbal Section

1. Ⓐ Ⓑ Ⓒ Ⓓ Ⓔ   7. Ⓐ Ⓑ Ⓒ Ⓓ Ⓔ   13. Ⓐ Ⓑ Ⓒ Ⓓ Ⓔ   19. Ⓐ Ⓑ Ⓒ Ⓓ Ⓔ   25. Ⓐ Ⓑ Ⓒ Ⓓ Ⓔ

2. Ⓐ Ⓑ Ⓒ Ⓓ Ⓔ   8. Ⓐ Ⓑ Ⓒ Ⓓ Ⓔ   14. Ⓐ Ⓑ Ⓒ Ⓓ Ⓔ   20. Ⓐ Ⓑ Ⓒ Ⓓ Ⓔ   26. Ⓐ Ⓑ Ⓒ Ⓓ Ⓔ

3. Ⓐ Ⓑ Ⓒ Ⓓ Ⓔ   9. Ⓐ Ⓑ Ⓒ Ⓓ Ⓔ   15. Ⓐ Ⓑ Ⓒ Ⓓ Ⓔ   21. Ⓐ Ⓑ Ⓒ Ⓓ Ⓔ   27. Ⓐ Ⓑ Ⓒ Ⓓ Ⓔ

4. Ⓐ Ⓑ Ⓒ Ⓓ Ⓔ   10. Ⓐ Ⓑ Ⓒ Ⓓ Ⓔ   16. Ⓐ Ⓑ Ⓒ Ⓓ Ⓔ   22. Ⓐ Ⓑ Ⓒ Ⓓ Ⓔ   28. Ⓐ Ⓑ Ⓒ Ⓓ Ⓔ

5. Ⓐ Ⓑ Ⓒ Ⓓ Ⓔ   11. Ⓐ Ⓑ Ⓒ Ⓓ Ⓔ   17. Ⓐ Ⓑ Ⓒ Ⓓ Ⓔ   23. Ⓐ Ⓑ Ⓒ Ⓓ Ⓔ   29. Ⓐ Ⓑ Ⓒ Ⓓ Ⓔ

6. Ⓐ Ⓑ Ⓒ Ⓓ Ⓔ   12. Ⓐ Ⓑ Ⓒ Ⓓ Ⓔ   18. Ⓐ Ⓑ Ⓒ Ⓓ Ⓔ   24. Ⓐ Ⓑ Ⓒ Ⓓ Ⓔ   30. Ⓐ Ⓑ Ⓒ Ⓓ Ⓔ

Math Section

1. Ⓐ Ⓑ Ⓒ Ⓓ Ⓔ   7. Ⓐ Ⓑ Ⓒ Ⓓ Ⓔ   13. Ⓐ Ⓑ Ⓒ Ⓓ Ⓔ   19. Ⓐ Ⓑ Ⓒ Ⓓ Ⓔ   25. Ⓐ Ⓑ Ⓒ Ⓓ Ⓔ

2. Ⓐ Ⓑ Ⓒ Ⓓ Ⓔ   8. Ⓐ Ⓑ Ⓒ Ⓓ Ⓔ   14. Ⓐ Ⓑ Ⓒ Ⓓ Ⓔ   20. Ⓐ Ⓑ Ⓒ Ⓓ Ⓔ   26. Ⓐ Ⓑ Ⓒ Ⓓ Ⓔ

3. Ⓐ Ⓑ Ⓒ Ⓓ Ⓔ   9. Ⓐ Ⓑ Ⓒ Ⓓ Ⓔ   15. Ⓐ Ⓑ Ⓒ Ⓓ Ⓔ   21. Ⓐ Ⓑ Ⓒ Ⓓ Ⓔ   27. Ⓐ Ⓑ Ⓒ Ⓓ Ⓔ

4. Ⓐ Ⓑ Ⓒ Ⓓ Ⓔ   10. Ⓐ Ⓑ Ⓒ Ⓓ Ⓔ   16. Ⓐ Ⓑ Ⓒ Ⓓ Ⓔ   22. Ⓐ Ⓑ Ⓒ Ⓓ Ⓔ   28. Ⓐ Ⓑ Ⓒ Ⓓ Ⓔ

5. Ⓐ Ⓑ Ⓒ Ⓓ Ⓔ   11. Ⓐ Ⓑ Ⓒ Ⓓ Ⓔ   17. Ⓐ Ⓑ Ⓒ Ⓓ Ⓔ   23. Ⓐ Ⓑ Ⓒ Ⓓ Ⓔ

6. Ⓐ Ⓑ Ⓒ Ⓓ Ⓔ   12. Ⓐ Ⓑ Ⓒ Ⓓ Ⓔ   18. Ⓐ Ⓑ Ⓒ Ⓓ Ⓔ   24. Ⓐ Ⓑ Ⓒ Ⓓ Ⓔ

Analytical Writing—Issue Topic

_____

_____

_____

_____

_____

_____

_____

_____

_____

_____

_____

_____

_____

_____

_____

_____

_____

_____

_____

_____

_____

_____

Analytical Writing—Argument Topic

_____

_____

_____

_____

_____

_____

_____

_____

_____

_____

_____

_____

_____

_____

_____

_____

_____

_____

_____

_____

_____

_____

_____

Practice Test 2

ANALYTICAL WRITING

Issue Topic • 45 Minutes

Present Your Perspective on an Issue

In this part, two topics appear as brief quotations. Each states, either explicitly or implicitly, an issue of broad interest. You are to choose one of the two topics. You will then use the remainder of the 45 minutes to write an essay in which you take a position on the issue.

You may agree with the quotation, disagree with it, or challenge the statement in any way, so long as the ideas that you present are clearly relevant to the topic. You should provide reasons and examples to support your position. In doing so, you may want to draw on your reading of various sources, your personal experience and observations, or your academic studies.

It is a good idea to begin by reading the topic carefully. Then you should decide what position you want to take, after which you will probably want to outline your answer before you begin to write. Your essay will be graded on how well you:

- Assess the implications of the issue, including various complexities implicit in the topic
- Organize, develop, and express your thoughts on the issue
- Provide supporting reasons and examples
- Demonstrate your mastery of the elements of standard written English

You should leave yourself sufficient time to read what you have written and to make any revisions to your essay that you think are needed.

For this exercise, you may choose to use an editing program on a computer (word processor) or write your response by hand using the space provided.

Issue Topics

Choose <u>one</u> of the following two topics to write on.

"Urban landmark commissions serve the useful function of preserving a cultural heritage, but they are often overly protective of existing spaces and structures. A clear-cut demonstration that modernization or development would provide a significant economic advantage to the community should be allowed to override the protection afforded by landmark status."

"With the creation of the Internet and the World Wide Web, books are no longer as important as they once were. Today, it is possible to learn just as much by surfing the Web as by reading books."

Argument Topic • 30 Minutes

Analyze an Argument

In this part, you will be given an argument and have 30 minutes within which to write a critique of the argument. Your essay must address the argument given.

You are to <u>analyze</u> the reasoning of the argument. You should consider whether any of its assumptions are questionable and whether the evidence presented supports the conclusion. You might also discuss what changes in the line of reasoning or additional evidence would strengthen or weaken the conclusion.

Importantly, you are **NOT** being asked to state your own views on the underlying subject.

It is a good idea to begin by reading the argument carefully. Then you should evaluate the argument and consider what response you want to make, after which you will probably want to outline your answer before you begin to write.

Your essay response will be graded on how well you:

- Identify and analyze the important elements of the argument
- Organize, develop, and state your analysis
- Support your analysis with relevant reasons and examples
- Demonstrate your mastery of the elements of Standard Written English

You should leave yourself sufficient time to read what you have written and to make any revisions to your essay that you think are needed.

Timing for this part begins when you click on the "Dismiss the Directions" icon.

Argument Topic

The following was included in a memorandum from the office of the mayor of Culver City to the head of the city's water department:

> "At present, water usage for residential properties in Culver City is based on frontage, that is, the size of the lot. Our neighbor, Merkton, meters usage, and their per capita consumption of water each year is 25% less than ours. Implementing a metering system would enable Culver City to reduce per capita consumption by about 25%."

VERBAL SECTION

30 Questions • 30 Minutes

> **Directions:** Each of the questions below contains one or more blank spaces, each blank indicating that something has been omitted. Each sentence is followed by five (5) words or sets of words. Read and determine the general sense of each sentence. Then choose the word, or set of words that, when inserted in the sentence, best fits the meaning of the sentence.

1. Although —— continues on minor points, the —— themes of the General's plan have been accepted.

   (A) discussion . . peripheral

   (B) debate . . central

   (C) dissension . . cultural

   (D) discovery . . main

   (E) agreement . . basic

2. Recent advances in research methodologies in neuroscience have created excitement in academic circles and have —— greater interest in funding new research projects in the field.

   (A) stymied

   (B) intensified

   (C) magnified

   (D) engendered

   (E) multiplied

3. Although the boom appeared to still be in full swing, in the latter years of the decade, most economic indicators pointed to —— times ahead.

   (A) leaner

   (B) profitable

   (C) healthy

   (D) daring

   (E) aberrant

Directions: In each of the following questions, you are given a related pair of words or phrases in capital letters. Each capitalized pair is followed by five (5) pairs of words or phrases. Choose the pair that best expresses a relationship similar to that expressed by the original pair.

4. PROHIBITED : REFRAIN ::
   (A) innocuous : forbid
   (B) deleterious : embark
   (C) required : decide
   (D) compulsory : comply
   (E) ridiculous : laugh

5. OVERTURE : OPERA ::
   (A) epilogue : movie
   (B) preface : book
   (C) concerto : piano
   (D) footnote : paragraph
   (E) singer : aria

6. RESOLVED : DOUBT ::
   (A) confirmed : suspicion
   (B) announced : candidacy
   (C) included : guest
   (D) suggested : idea
   (E) demolished : opponent

Directions: The passage below is followed by questions based on its content. Choose the best answer to each question.

Desertification in the arid United States is flagrant. Groundwater supplies beneath vast stretches of land are dropping precipitously. Whole river sys-
(5) tems have dried up; others are choked with sediment washed from denuded land. Hundreds of thousands of acres of previously irrigated cropland have been abandoned to wind or weeds. Several
(10) million acres of natural grassland are eroding at unnaturally high rates as a result of cultivation or overgrazing. All told, about 225 million acres of land are undergoing severe desertification.
(15) Federal subsidies encourage the exploitation of arid land resources. Low-interest loans for irrigation and other water delivery systems encourage farmers, industry, and municipalities to mine
(20) groundwater. Federal disaster relief and commodity programs encourage arid-land farmers to plow up natural grassland to plant crops such as wheat and, especially, cotton. Federal grazing fees
(25) that are well below the free market price encourage overgrazing of the commons. The market, too, provides powerful incentives to exploit arid-land resources beyond their carrying capacity. When
(30) commodity prices are high relative to the farmer's or rancher's operating costs, the return on a production-enhancing investment is invariably greater than the return on a conservation investment.
(35) And when commodity prices are relatively low, arid-land ranchers and farmers often have to use all their available financial resources to stay solvent.

If the United States is, as it appears,
(40) well on its way toward overdrawing the arid-land resources, then the policy choice is simply to pay now for the appropriate remedies or pay far more later, when productive benefits from arid-land
(45) resources have been both realized and largely terminated.

7. The author is primarily concerned with
   (A) discussing a solution
   (B) describing a problem
   (C) replying to a detractor
   (D) finding a contradiction
   (E) defining a term

8. The passage mentions all of the following as effects of desertification EXCEPT
   (A) increased sediment in rivers
   (B) erosion of land
   (C) overcultivation of land
   (D) decreasing groundwater supplies
   (E) loss of land to wind or weeds

9. The author's attitude toward desertification can best be described as one of
   (A) alarm
   (B) optimism
   (C) understanding
   (D) conciliation
   (E) concern

Directions: Each of the following questions consists of a word printed in capital letters, followed by five (5) words or phrases. Choose the word or phrase that is most nearly opposite in meaning to the word in capital letters. Consider all the choices before deciding which one is best.

10. COVERT :
   (A) protracted
   (B) insensitive
   (C) reclining
   (D) open
   (E) taxing

11. SALIENT :
   (A) insignificant
   (B) climactic
   (C) worrisome
   (D) awesome
   (E) radical

12. MORIBUND :
   (A) contentious
   (B) malignant
   (C) pretentious
   (D) detestable
   (E) vital

13. PLIANT :
   (A) humble
   (B) rigid
   (C) tactful
   (D) earnest
   (E) solemn

Directions: The passage below is followed by questions based on its content. Choose the best answer to each question.

Reverse discrimination, minority recruitment, racial quotas, and, more generally, affirmative action are phrases that carry powerful emotional charges. But
(5) why should affirmative action, of all government policies, be so controversial? In a sense, affirmative action is like other governmental programs, e.g., defense, conservation, and public schools. Affir-
(10) mative action programs are designed to achieve legitimate government objectives such as improved economic efficiency, reduced social tension, and general betterment of the public wel-
(15) fare. While it cannot be denied that there is no guarantee that affirmative action will achieve these results, neither can it be denied that there are plausible, even powerful, sociological and economic ar-
(20) guments pointing to its likely success.

Government programs, however, entail a cost, that is, the expenditure of social or economic resources. Setting aside cases in which the specific user is
(25) charged a fee for service (toll roads and tuition at state institutions), the burdens and benefits of publicly funded or mandated programs are widely shared.

When an individual benefits person-
(30) ally from a government program, it is only because she or he is one member of a larger beneficiary class, e.g., a farmer; and most government revenue is obtained through a scheme of general taxa-
(35) tion to which all are subject.

Affirmative action programs are exceptions to this general rule, though not, as might at first seem, because the beneficiaries of the programs are spe-
(40) cific individuals. It is still the case that those who ultimately benefit from affirmative action do so only by virtue of their status as members of a larger group, a particular minority. Rather,
(45) the difference is the location of the burden. In affirmative action, the burden of "funding" the program is not shared

universally, and that is inherent in the nature of the case, as can be seen clearly
(50) in the case of affirmative action in employment. Often job promotions are allocated along a single dimension, seniority; and when an employer promotes a less senior worker from a mi-
(55) nority group, the person disadvantaged by the move is easily identified: the worker with greatest seniority on a combined minority-nonminority list passed over for promotion.
(60) Now we are confronted with two competing moral sentiments. On the one hand, there is the idea that those who have been unfairly disadvantaged by past discriminatory practices are en-
(65) titled to some kind of assistance. On the other, there is the feeling that no person ought to be deprived of what is rightfully his or hers, even for the worthwhile service of fellow humans. In this respect,
(70) disability due to past racial discrimination, at least insofar as there is no connection to the passed-over worker, is like a natural evil. When a villainous man willfully and without provocation
(75) strikes and injures another, there is not only the feeling that the injured person ought to be compensated, but there is consensus that the appropriate party to bear the cost is the one who inflicted the
(80) injury. Yet, if the same innocent man stumbled and injured himself, it would be surprising to hear someone argue that the villainous man ought to be taxed for the injury simply because he might
(85) have tripped the victim had he been given the opportunity. There may very well be agreement that he should be aided in his recovery with money and personal assistance, and many will give
(90) willingly; but there is also agreement that no one individual ought to be singled out and forced to do what must ultimately be considered an act of charity.

14. The passage is primarily concerned with
    (A) comparing affirmative action programs to other government programs
    (B) arguing that affirmative action programs are morally justified
    (C) analyzing the basis for moral judgments about affirmative action programs
    (D) introducing the reader to the importance of affirmative action as a social issue
    (E) describing the benefits that can be obtained through affirmative action programs

15. The author mentions toll roads and tuition at state institutions (lines 25–26) in order to
    (A) anticipate a possible objection based on counterexamples
    (B) avoid a contradiction between moral sentiments
    (C) provide illustrations of common government programs
    (D) voice doubts about the social and economic value of affirmative action
    (E) offer examples of government programs that are too costly

16. With which of the following statements would the author most likely agree?
    (A) Affirmative action programs should be discontinued because they place an unfair burden on nonminority persons who bear the cost of the programs.
    (B) Affirmative action programs may be able to achieve legitimate social and economic goals such as improved efficiency.
    (C) Affirmative action programs are justified because they are the only way of correcting injustices created by past discrimination.
    (D) Affirmative action programs must be redesigned so that society as a whole rather than particular individuals bears the cost of the programs.
    (E) Affirmative action programs should be abandoned because they serve no useful social function and place unfair burdens on particular individuals.

17. The author most likely places *funding* in quotation marks (line 47) in order to remind the reader that
    (A) affirmative action programs are costly in terms of government revenues
    (B) particular individuals may bear a disproportionate share of the burden of affirmative action
    (C) the cost of most government programs is shared by society at large
    (D) the beneficiaries of affirmative action are members of larger groups
    (E) the cost of affirmative action is not only a monetary expenditure

18. The *villainous man* discussed in lines 73–93 functions primarily as a(n)
    (A) illustration
    (B) counterexample
    (C) authority
    (D) analogy
    (E) disclaimer

19. According to the passage, affirmative action programs are different from most other government programs in the
    (A) legitimacy of the goals the programs are designed to achieve
    (B) ways in which costs of the programs are distributed
    (C) methods for allocating the benefits of the programs
    (D) legal structures that are enacted to achieve the objectives
    (E) discretion granted to the executive for implementing the programs

Directions: In each of the following questions, you are given a related pair of words or phrases in capital letters. Each capitalized pair is followed by five (5) pairs of words or phrases. Choose the pair that best expresses a relationship similar to that expressed by the original pair.

20. EXEMPLARY : REPROACH ::
    (A) erroneous : correction
    (B) accomplished : praise
    (C) fulfilling : control
    (D) planned : implementation
    (E) unimpeachable : criticism

21. MENDICANT : BEGGING ::
    (A) competitor : joining
    (B) legislator : funding
    (C) miser : donating
    (D) prevaricator : lying
    (E) mechanic : selling

22. RAIN : DELUGE ::
    (A) pond : ocean
    (B) desert : camel
    (C) ore : iron
    (D) street : road
    (E) wheat : crop

23. LUBRICANT : FRICTION ::
    (A) balm : pain
    (B) eraser : correction
    (C) solvent : paint
    (D) reagent : chemical
    (E) merchant : business

Directions: Each of the questions below contains one or more blank spaces, each blank indicating that something has been omitted. Each sentence is followed by five (5) words or sets of words. Read and determine the general sense of each sentence. Then choose the word, or set of words that, when inserted in the sentence, best fits the meaning of the sentence.

24. Despite the fact that she was much ——, the scientist continued to present her controversial theories to the —— of the Royal Academy, whose members repeatedly denounced her research.
    (A) admired . . chagrin
    (B) revered . . benefit
    (C) imitated . . foreboding
    (D) chastened . . temerity
    (E) maligned . . consternation

25. Washington Irving, the father of American literature and creator of such delightful characters as Ichabod Crane and Rip Van Winkle, will be remembered more for the —— of his prose than for the originality of his tales, which were —— from popular folklore.
    (A) density . . obtained
    (B) vulgarity . . stolen
    (C) mediocrity . . descended
    (D) charm . . borrowed
    (E) pomposity . . reduced

26. Although alcoholism has long been regarded as a personality disorder, there is evidence to suggest that alcoholics are often the children of alcoholics and that they are born with a —— the disease.

(A) respect for

(B) predisposition to

(C) liability for

(D) deterioration of

(E) misunderstanding of

Directions: Each of the following questions consists of a word printed in capital letters, followed by five (5) words or phrases. Choose the word or phrase that is most nearly opposite in meaning to the word in capital letters. Be sure to consider all the choices before deciding which one is best.

27. DORMANT :

(A) authoritative

(B) elastic

(C) active

(D) uninteresting

(E) endearing

28. PLACATE :

(A) abet

(B) enrage

(C) invite

(D) witness

(E) repent

29. EXTRANEOUS :

(A) outlandish

(B) tumultuous

(C) impetuous

(D) central

(E) guarded

30. RENOWN :

(A) suggestiveness

(B) superficiality

(C) anonymity

(D) deviousness

(E) valor

MATH SECTION

28 Questions • 45 Minutes

Numbers: All numbers used are real numbers.

Figures: The position of points, angles, regions, and so forth are in the order shown. Figures are assumed to lie in a plane unless otherwise indicated. Figures are drawn as accurately as possible for problem-solving questions, unless otherwise indicated. Figures are NOT drawn to scale for quantitative analysis problem, unless otherwise indicated. You should solve the problems by using your knowledge of mathematics and not by estimating sizes by sight or measurement.

Lines: Assume that lines shown as straight are indeed straight.

Directions: For each of the following questions, select the best of the answer choices. For quantitative comparison questions, two quantities are given, one in Column A and one in Column B. Compare the two quantities and choose

(A) if the quantity in Column A is greater
(B) if the quantity in Column B is greater
(C) if the two quantities are equal
(D) if the relationship cannot be determined from the information given

Information applying to both columns is centered between the columns and above the quantities in columns A and B. Symbols that appear in both columns represent the same idea or quantity in each column.

	Column A	**Column B**
1.	$16 \div 4$	$\frac{4}{11} \times 11$

$$x = \frac{1}{3} \text{ of } 12$$
$$y = \frac{4}{3} \text{ of } 9$$

2.	x	y

When n is divided by 49,
the remainder is 0.

3.	The remainder when n is divided by 7	7

4.	$\left(\frac{101}{202}\right)^{11}$	$\left(\frac{-101}{202}\right)^{11}$

An apartment building has 5 floors,
one of which has only 2 apartments.
Each of the other floors has 4 apartments.

5.	3 times the number of floors in the building	The number of apartments in the building

Directions: For each of the following questions, select the best of the answer choices given.

6. Which of the following is equal to 0.00127?

(A) 1.27×10

(B) 1.27×0.10

(C) 1.27×0.01

(D) 1.27×0.001

(E) 1.27×0.0001

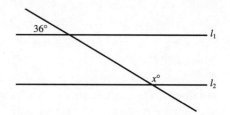

7. A prize of $240 is divided between two persons. If one person receives $180, then what is the difference between the amounts received by the two persons?

(A) $30

(B) $60

(C) $120

(D) $210

(E) $420

8. If $3x - 4y = 5$ and $\frac{y}{x} = \frac{1}{3}$, then what is x?

(A) $-5y$

(B) $-5x$

(C) 1

(D) 3

(E) 4

9. In the figure above, if $l_1 \parallel l_2$, what is the value of x?

(A) 36

(B) 54

(C) 90

(D) 144

(E) 154

10. If $\frac{x-1}{x+1} = \frac{4}{5}$, then $x =$

(A) 3

(B) 4

(C) 5

(D) 9

(E) 12

Directions: For each of the following questions, select the best of the answer choices. For quantitative comparison questions, two quantities are given, one in Column A and one in Column B. Compare the two quantities and choose

(A) if the quantity in Column A is greater
(B) if the quantity in Column B is greater
(C) if the two quantities are equal
(D) if the relationship cannot be determined from the information given

Information applying to both columns is centered between the columns and above the quantities in columns A and B. Symbols that appear in both columns represent the same idea or quantity in each column.

<u>**Column A**</u>   <u>**Column B**</u>

$$x^2 - 3x - 4 = (x + m)(x - n)$$

11. m n

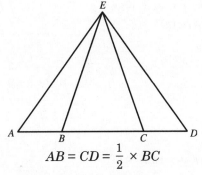

$$AB = CD = \frac{1}{2} \times BC$$

12.   Area of triangle BEC Sum of the areas of triangles AEB and CED

13. $\sqrt{\dfrac{3}{16}} + \sqrt{\dfrac{3}{16}} + \sqrt{\dfrac{3}{16}}$ $\sqrt{\dfrac{9}{16}}$

14. $5\left(\dfrac{x}{5} + \dfrac{y}{5} - \dfrac{7}{5}\right)$ $x + y - 7$

Point P has coordinates (x, y);
point Q has coordinates $(x - 1, y - 1)$.

15.   The distance from P The distance from Q
                    to the origin   to the origin

Directions: For each of these questions, select the best of the answer choices given.

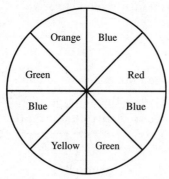

16. The figure above shows a wheel of fortune divided into sections of equal size and painted with the colors indicated. If the wheel has a diameter of 64 centimeters, what is the total area of the wheel that is painted blue (expressed in square centimeters)?

(A) 3π

(B) 24π

(C) 40π

(D) 128π

(E) 384π

17. Right circular cylinder P has a radius of 3 and a height of 4. If the volume of P is equal to the volume of right circular cylinder Q, which has a radius of 2, what is the height of Q?

(A) 6

(B) 9

(C) 12

(D) 18

(E) 36

18. If $\frac{1}{x} - \frac{1}{y} = \frac{1}{z}$, then z is equal to which of the following?

(A) $\dfrac{y-x}{xy}$

(B) $\dfrac{x-y}{xy}$

(C) xy

(D) $\dfrac{xy}{x} - y$

(E) $\dfrac{xy}{y-x}$

19. In a certain company, the ratio of the number of female employees to the number of male employees is 3 to 2. If the total number of employees is 240, how many of the employees are men?

(A) 40

(B) 48

(C) 96

(D) 144

(E) 160

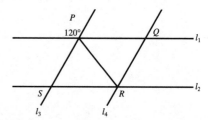

20. In the figure above, $l_1 \parallel l_2$, and $l_3 \parallel l_4$. If $PQ = 3$ and $QR = 3$, then what is the length of PR?

(A) 6

(B) $3\dfrac{\sqrt{3}}{2}$

(C) 3

(D) $9\sqrt{5}$

(E) $\dfrac{\sqrt{3}}{2}$

21. In a certain group of people, $\frac{3}{8}$ of the people are men, and $\frac{2}{3}$ of the men have brown eyes. If $\frac{3}{4}$ of the people have brown eyes, then what fraction of the group are women who do not have brown eyes?

(A) $\dfrac{1}{8}$

(B) $\dfrac{3}{16}$

(C) $\dfrac{1}{4}$

(D) $\dfrac{5}{16}$

(E) $\dfrac{3}{8}$

BUDGET INFORMATION FOR
COLLEGE M IN YEAR N

Outlays*

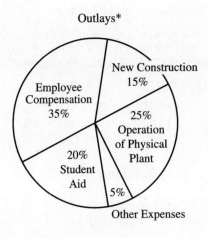

Income**
(Millions of Dollars)

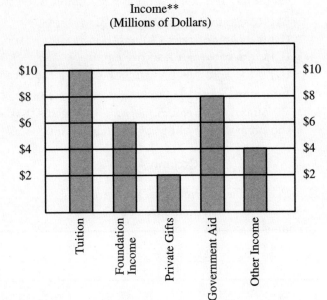

* Includes all expenditures

** Includes all sources of income

Note: Outlays = Income

QUESTIONS 22–24 ARE BASED ON THE GRAPHS ABOVE.

22. For the year shown, College M spent how much money on the operation of its physical plant?

   (A) $2,500,000

   (B) $4,000,000

   (C) $7,500,000

   (D) $8,000,000

   (E) $9,500,000

23. For the year shown, what percentage of College M's income came from foundation income?

   (A) 6%

   (B) 20%

   (C) 25%

   (D) 33%

   (E) 60%

24. For the year shown, how much more money was spent by College M on employee compensation than on student aid?

   (A) $16,500,000

   (B) $10,500,000

   (C) $6,000,000

   (D) $4,500,000

   (E) $2,500,000

Directions: For each of the following questions, select the best of the answer choices. For quantitative comparison questions, two quantities are given, one in Column A and one in Column B. Compare the two quantities and choose

(A) if the quantity in Column A is greater
(B) if the quantity in Column B is greater
(C) if the two quantities are equal
(D) if the relationship cannot be determined from the information given

Information applying to both columns is centered between the columns and above the quantities in columns A and B. Symbols that appear in both columns represent the same idea or quantity in each column.

	Column A	Column B
25.	The perimeter of a square with an an area of 16	The perimeter of a square with a diagonal of $4\sqrt{2}$
26.	$\dfrac{1}{3} \times \dfrac{2}{3}$	$(.333)(.666)$

When $x + 5$ is divided by 3, the remainder is 2.

	Column A	Column B
27.	The remainder when x is divided by 2	1
28.	The least number greater than 12 that is divisible by 12 but not by 8	48

ANSWER KEY AND EXPLANATIONS

Analytical Writing

Issue Topics

TOPIC 1

As you read the following sample response, try to judge for yourself how well it meets the criteria that will be applied by graders:

Category	Below Avg.	Avg.	Above Avg.
Analysis of the Topic			
Organization and Development			
Use of Reasons and Examples			
Use of Standard Written English			
OVERALL SCORE*			

*Below Average = 1–2; Average = 3–4; Above Average = 5–6

SAMPLE RESPONSE AND COMMENTARY FOR ISSUE TOPIC 1

Note: The sample answers contain spelling and grammatical errors. This is done to simulate a first draft written under time pressure.

> The speaker makes several valid points. It is true that landmark commissions tend to be protective of existing structures, for that is, after all, their *raison d'etre*. And it is true that development often (though not always) brings economic advantage to a community, though sometimes at the expense of its cultural store. A conflict between the two points of view is inherent, and it is usually—and rightly—resolved by the political process rather than some universal metric that measures "heritage" against "economic advantage." And therein lies the weakness of the position. It would be a mistake to establish a rule that presumptively favors economic development over cultural heritage.
>
> In the first place, landmark commissions naturally weigh more heavily the cultural value of an existing structure, so much so that outcomes are sometimes amusing. There was a small, multi-family residential structure in the Greenwich Village neighborhood of New York City which comprises many older structure, quite a few of which have been designated as landmarks. This architecture of this particular structure was not particularly noteworthy, and it had been given landmark status largely because of its location on an otherwise historic block. As part of his renovation plan, the owner of the property wanted to move the main entryway from the center of the building to one side. The proposed change would result in more rental units in an area where housing is scarce, but the landmarks commission refused to approve the change, though, they said, he was welcome add a new door in addition to the existing one. When asked for clarification, the commission said "There must be a door located

at the center of the building." The owner took them at their word: at the center of the building is mounted a "door" without a "doorway" behind it.

On the other hand, it would be dangerous to assume that this example proves the point. Such outcomes are usually humorous because they are fairly rare. Just as often, the developer would either ignore or pay only lip service to the value of a cultural treasure. Also in the Greenwich Village area is the Jefferson Market building with its ornate façade and a clock tower that is unique. Once an actual market that had been unused for several years, it was slated for demolition in the sixties but was fortunately save by its landmark status. It now houses a branch of the New York City public library.

Importantly, these conflicts are inherent in the nature of the matter. In an urban setting where vacant land is scarce, often new structures cannot be erected without the destruction of existing ones. Developers, encouraged by the profit motive, often would prefer to raze buildings; landmark commissions and their allies naturally prefer protection. It is necessary to strike a balance, and there is no single measure that will decide all outcomes because "cultural heritage" cannot be reduced to dollars and cents. It would be a mistake to presumptively give preference to economic advantage. Instead, the outcome is usually, as it should be in a pluralistic society, determined by balancing considerations.

COMMENTARY

This essay is very well written with robust language: *raison d'etre*, universal metric, pluralistic society. And the sentence structure is quite sophisticated. In addition, it uses two examples from the same neighborhood to illustrate the conflict between "heritage" and "development." The first is quite effective because of the amusing nature of the anecdote. The second example might have been presented more effectively if the author had offered the reader more detail about the architecture or other cultural value of the structure, but it serves its purpose. The overall point that it would be a mistake to automatically give preference to one side or the other in striking a balance between "heritage" and "development" is a fairly sophisticated way of treating the topic. This essay would probably receive a 6, though some readers, noting the weaknesses mentioned above, might give it only a 5.

TOPIC 2

As you read the following sample response, try to judge for yourself how well it meets the criteria that will be applied by graders:

Category	Below Avg.	Avg.	Above Avg.
Analysis of the Topic			
Organization and Development			
Use of Reasons and Examples			
Use of Standard Written English			
OVERALL SCORE*			

*Below Average = 1–2; Average = 3–4; Above Average = 5–6

SAMPLE RESPONSE AND COMMENTARY FOR ISSUE TOPIC 2

Note: The sample answers contain spelling and grammatical errors. This is done to simulate a first draft written under time pressure.

The internet is replacing books almost every day because you can get as much information from the world wide web as you can get from your local library. Plus it is more convenient. If you want a book, you have to go to your local library, look for the book, check it out, and then take it home to read. With the web, you can find information instantly. Also, there is more information on the web than on books. You can go to a search engine like Yahho! or Lycos and just put in the name of the topic that you want to learn about and, presto, there will be a long list of things for you to read.

Some people don't have access to the web, but most people do. And even thouse who don't will soon get it. Eventually, no one will bother books because the web will be so convenient.

COMMENTARY

This is a fairly weak essay response. The writer does take a clear position and seems to offer some arguments supported by example. But the arguments don't really prove the point. The comparison between the Web and a library is superficial. It overlooks the fact that lending out books is not the only function of the library. Libraries also contain references works and other resources. In addition, the comparison overlooks the fact that libraries are not the only means of obtaining books; bookstores, for example, provide reading material. The reference to search engines is likewise superficial because it fails to take account of the difficulties involved in researching some topics and the problem of sifting through listings to find resources that are both relevant and reliable. In the second paragraph, it looks as though the author is going to consider a counterargument to the topic, but it never gets developed. The language is also fairly simplistic, though generally correct. This essay would likely receive a 2, though a few readers might think it should get a 1.

Argument Topic

As you read the following sample response, try to judge for yourself how well it meets the criteria that will be applied by graders:

Category	Below Avg.	Avg.	Above Avg.
Analysis of the Topic			
Organization and Development			
Use of Reasons and Examples			
Use of Standard Written English			
OVERALL SCORE*			

*Below Average = 1–2; Average = 3–4; Above Average = 5–6

SAMPLE RESPONSE AND COMMENTARY FOR THE ARGUMENT TOPIC

Note: The sample answers contain spelling and grammatical errors. This is done to simulate a first draft written under time pressure.

The question presented is whether implementing a metering system would enable Culver City to reduce its average per capita consumption of water to levels comparable to its neighbor Merkton. The argument makes at least three questionable assumptions.

First, the argument moves from a suggestion about metering residential water usage to a much broader conclusion that seems to be about total per capita consumption for the city as a hole. Whether that is a valid inference would require further information, e.g., data on the differences in billing for commercial properties versus residential units. Depending on the ratio of commercial consumption to residential usage and on how the commercial usage is billed, Culver City may or may not achieve the same result as Merkton.

Second, it assumes, without any proof, that conditions in the two cities are sufficiently similar that a policy in the one would have the same results as a similar policy in the other. But there are many possible variables that would prevent Culver City from achieving the same result. Since many buisiness and industrial properties are high users of water, the mix of commercial and residential properties in the two cities will say a lot abot whether Culver City can expect to achieve the goal of a 25% reduction.

Third, the argument rests on the presupposition that metered usage will encourage conservation in residential properties. But that may depend on who lives on the property. For example, a tenant whose water usage is included in the rent will have little incentive to conserve. Additionally, the charge for metered usage will have to be significantly higher the charge for frontage usage in order to provide a reason to conserve.

The argument has some appeal because generally the law of supply-and-demand predicts that less of a scarce resource will be consumed at a higher price, but whether that principal of economics is applicable here depends on several unexamined variables.

COMMENTARY

The essay is fairly well written and forcefully argued. It has good organization and raises some interesting points. The main weakness is that the second and third paragraphs seem to discuss pretty much the same point: residential versus commercial users. Of course, the writer may have intended two very different points; but, as presented, the essay doesn't make the difference clear to the reader. To the extent that points one and two are really the same, the essay has only two main features and is therefore less effective than if there were three main features. This essay would likely get a 4 or perhaps a 3 from some readers.

Verbal Section

1. B	7. B	13. B	19. B	25. D
2. D	8. C	14. C	20. E	26. B
3. A	9. E	15. A	21. D	27. C
4. D	10. D	16. B	22. A	28. B
5. B	11. A	17. E	23. A	29. D
6. A	12. E	18. D	24. E	30. C

1. **The correct answer is (B).** On two-blank questions, it's easiest to consider one blank at a time. Attacking the second blank first makes most sense since you know that it is in contrast to *minor points* (the trigger word *Although* should tip your hand). What is a contrast to a *minor point*? A major one. You should go look for something like *major* or *important*. That eliminates (A) and (C). Into the first blank, *debate* clearly fits best of the remaining choices, as a debate is more likely to have *themes* than an agreement or discovery. So, (B) is the answer.

2. **The correct answer is (D).** The blank is a word that goes along with *created excitement*, and so it is definitely positive. What is a positive verb that flows with greater interest? *Created* is a good pre-guess. Check the answer choices, and (D), *engendered*, fits your pre-guess quite well.

3. **The correct answer is (A).** The *although* at the beginning of the sentence clues you into the fact that this is a contrast sentence. The good times spoken of in the present are contrasted with what is in the blank. What is a contrast with good times? Tough times. Choice (A) works well.

4. **The correct answer is (D).** A good attack strategy is to formulate a sentence expressing the relationship between the stem words. Remember that you can take some liberties here, changing the parts of speech if you wish or reversing the word order. Here you might have used the sentence "One should REFRAIN from doing that which is PROHIBITED." Similarly, "One should comply with that which is compulsory." Notice also that there is a confirming "echo" between first elements of each pair and the second elements of each pair. Compulsory is the opposite of prohibited and comply is somewhat opposite to refrain.

5. **The correct answer is (B).** The relationship here is one of order of elements. The OVERTURE is the opening portion of an OPERA and the *preface* is the opening portion of a *book*.

6. **The correct answer is (A).** To RESOLVE a DOUBT is to eliminate it, just as to *confirm* a *suspicion* eliminates it by making it a certainty. There is also an "echo" here, since *resolve* and *confirm* are similar, and *doubt* and *suspicion* are similar.

7. **The correct answer is (B).** This is a main idea question. The author's primary concern is to discuss the problem of desertification. So choice (B) is correct. A natural extension of the discussion would be a proposal to slow the process of desertification, but that is not included in the passage as written, so (A) must be incorrect. (C), (D), and (E) are each incorrect because we find no elements in the passage to support those choices. Even admitting that the author intends to define, implicitly, the term "desertification," that is surely not the main point of the passage. The author also dwells at length on the causes of the problem.

8. **The correct answer is (C).** This is an explicit idea question. In the first paragraph, the author mentions (A), (B), (D), and (E) as features of desertification. (C), however, is one of the causes of desertification.

9. **The correct answer is (E).** This is a tone question. We can surely eliminate (B), (C), and (D) as not expressing the appropriate element of worry. Then, in choosing between (A) and (E), we find that (A) overstates the case. The author says we solve the problem now or we can solve it later (at a higher cost). But that is an expression of concern, not alarm.

10. **The correct answer is (D).** *Covert* means "undercover" or "concealed," so a good opposite would be *open*.

11. **The correct answer is (A).** The literal meaning of *salient* is "projecting forward" or "jutting out," and it has come to have the related (and more figurative) meaning of standing out from the rest as obvious or important. A good opposite, then, would be *insignificant*.

12. **The correct answer is (E).** *Moribund* means "dying," so a good opposite would be a word referring to life or good health, such as *vital*.

13. **The correct answer is (B).** *Pliant* means "bending," as found in the composite word "compliant." A good opposite, therefore, is *rigid*.

14. **The correct answer is (C).** This is a main idea question. The passage begins by posing the question: Why are affirmative action programs so controversial? It then argues that affirmative action is unlike ordinary government programs in the way the burden of the program is allocated. Because of this, the passage concludes, we are torn between supporting the programs (because they have legitimate goals) and condemning the programs (because of the way the cost is

allocated). (C) neatly describes this development. The author analyzes the structure of the moral dilemma. (A) is incorrect since the comparison is but a subpart of the overall development and is used in the service of the larger analysis. (B) is incorrect since the author reaches no such clear-cut decision. Rather, we are left with the question posed by the dilemma. (D) is incorrect since the author presupposes that the reader already understands the importance of the issue. Finally, (E) is incorrect since the advantages of the programs are mentioned only in passing.

15. **The correct answer is (A).** This is a logical structure question. In the second paragraph, the author will describe the general structure of government programs in order to set up the contrast with affirmative action. The discussion begins with *Setting aside . . .*, indicating that the author recognizes such cases and does not wish to discuss them in detail. Tolls and tuition are exceptions to the general rule, so the author explicitly sets them aside in order to preempt a possible objection to the analysis based on claimed counterexamples. (B) is incorrect since the overall point of the passage is to discuss this dilemma, but the main point of the passage will not answer the question about the logical substructure of the argument. (C) is incorrect since tolls and tuition are not ordinary government programs. (D) is incorrect since the author never raises such doubts. Finally, (E) misses the point of the examples. The point is not that they are costly but that the cost is borne by the specific user.

16. **The correct answer is (B).** This is an application question. In the first paragraph, the author states that affirmative action is designed to achieve social and economic objectives. Although this claim is qualified, the author seems to believe that those arguments are in favor of

affirmative action. So (B) is clearly supported by the text. (A) is not supported by the text since the author leaves us with a question; the issue is not resolved. (C) can be eliminated on the same ground. The author neither embraces nor rejects affirmative action. (D) goes beyond the scope of the argument. While the author might wish that this were possible, nothing in the passage indicates such restructuring is possible. Indeed, in paragraph 3, the author remarks that the *funding* problem seems to be inherent. Finally, (E) can be eliminated on the same ground as (A). The author recognizes the unfairness of affirmative action, but also believes that the programs are valuable.

17. **The correct answer is (E).** In paragraph 2, the author mentions that government programs entail both social and economic costs. Then the cost of the specific example, the passed-over worker, is not a government expenditure in the sense that money is laid out to purchase something. So the author is using the term *funding* in a nonstandard way and wishes to call the reader's attention to this usage. (E) parallels this explanation. (A) is incorrect since it is inconsistent with the reasoning just provided. (B) is incorrect, for though the author may believe that individuals bear a disproportionate share of the burden, this is not a response to the question asked. (C) is incorrect for the same reason: It is a true but nonresponsive statement. Finally, (D) fails for the same reason. Though the author notes that affirmative action programs are similar to other government programs in this respect, this is not an explanation for the author's placing *funding* in quotation marks.

18. **The correct answer is (D).** This is a logical structure question. In the final paragraph, the author analyzes another, similar situation. This technique is called "arguing from analogy." The strength of

the argument depends on our seeing the similarity and accepting the conclusion of the one argument (*the villainous man*) as applicable to the other argument (affirmative action). (A) is perhaps the second best response, but the author is not offering an illustration, e.g., an example of affirmative action. To be sure, the author is attempting to prove a point, but attempting to prove a conclusion is not equivalent to illustrating a contention. (B) is incorrect since the author adduces the situation to support his contention. (C) is incorrect because the author cites no authority. Finally, (E) can be eliminated since the author uses the case of the villainous man to support, not to weaken, the case.

19. **The correct answer is (B).** This is an explicit idea question. In paragraph 1, the author mentions that affirmative action is like other government programs in that it is designed to achieve certain social and economic goals. (A) cites a similarity rather than a difference. (C) can also be eliminated. In paragraph 3, the author states that the relevant difference is not the method of allocating benefits. The salient difference is set forth in the same paragraph, and it is the difference described by (B). (D) and (E) are simply not mentioned anywhere in the selection.

20. **The correct answer is (E).** This relationship might be expressed as "That which is EXEMPLARY is beyond REPROACH." So, too, is that which is *unimpeachable* not subject to *criticism*.

21. **The correct answer is (D).** Here the relationship is one of defining characteristic. The MENDICANT is a BEGGAR and the *prevaricator* is a *liar*.

22. **The correct answer is (A).** This relationship is simply one of degree: A DELUGE is a big RAIN and an *ocean* is a big *pond*.

23. The correct answer is (A). The relationship here is that of agent to effect. The effect of a LUBRICANT is to reduce FRICTION, and the effect of a *balm* is to reduce *pain*. Notice also that there is an "echo" here. *Friction* and *pain* are somewhat similar in that *friction* is something that "afflicts" a machine as *pain* afflicts a body. And a *lubricant* is something like a "medicine" or *balm* that solves the problem.

24. The correct answer is (E). You can eliminate (B), (C), and (D) on the basis of their second elements. They really make no sense when substituted into the second blank. And you can probably see that (E) is a good answer because it both provides the needed contrast indicated by the introductory word *despite* and supplies a second element that could be used to describe the feeling of the academy. (A), perhaps, is an arguably correct choice, yet if you examine (A) closely, you will see that it fails. Although *admired* is syntactically acceptable for the first blank, it really does not make a meaningful statement. It does not explain the perseverance of the scientist.

25. The correct answer is (D). All but one of the choices can be eliminated on the basis of the first substitution. Notice that the question refers to the *delightful* characters of Irving. Only *charm* is consistent with such a judgment. Additionally, only *borrowed*, of all the possible second elements, provides the logical contrast required by the second part of the sentence: more for this than for that.

26. The correct answer is (B). The *although* that introduces the sentence requires a contrast in the second portion of the sentence; only (B) provides this. The contrast between personality disorder and physical disease must be established.

27. The correct answer is (C). *Dormant* means "sleeping" or "inactive," and a fairly clear opposite is *active*.

28. The correct answer is (B). *Placate* is related to *placid,* and to *placate* means to *calm down*. So a good opposite would be a word meaning to stir up—as here to stir up anger is to *enrage*.

29. The correct answer is (D). *Extraneous* means "coming from outside, foreign or alien to something else." The word is also used to mean "not pertinent," so a good opposite would be *central*: That which is extraneous to an inquiry is surely not central to it.

30. The correct answer is (C). *Renown* means "fame," so a good opposite would be a word describing the complete lack of fame, *anonymity*.

Math Section

1.	C	7.	C	13.	A	19.	C	25.	C
2.	B	8.	D	14.	C	20.	C	26.	A
3.	B	9.	D	15.	D	21.	A	27.	D
4.	A	10.	D	16.	E	22.	C	28.	B
5.	B	11.	B	17.	B	23.	B		
6.	D	12.	C	18.	E	24.	D		

1. **The correct answer is (C).** The arithmetic operations indicated here are very simple, so the best approach to the comparison is to perform the indicated operations. For Column A, 16 divided by 4 is 4. For Column B, $\frac{4}{11}$ multiplied by 11 is 4. So the two columns are equal.

2. **The correct answer is (B).** Again, performing the indicated operations may be the best attack strategy. In this case, the operation is to solve for the variables in the equations in the centered information. In the first equation, $x = 4$; in the second, $y = 12$. So Column B is greater.

3. **The correct answer is (B).** This type of question appears with some regularity in various guises. The heart of the question is the centered information that 49 is one of the factors of n. Then the key to the comparison is recognizing that since 7 is a factor of 49, 7 must also be a factor of n. Thus, when n is divided by 7 (just as when it is divided by 49), there is no remainder. So Column A is 0 while Column B is 7. So Column B is greater.

4. **The correct answer is (A).** Since the operations indicated here are much too cumbersome to be performed, you should look for a shortcut. The key is to recognize that since the fraction in Column A is positive, the final result of performing the operation indicated would also be a positive number. Since the fraction in Column B is negative, the final result of raising the fraction to an odd power will be negative. Thus, the positive quantity in Column A must be greater.

5. **The correct answer is (B).** This question is really not so much a matter of mathematics as just common sense. Indeed, you can probably solve it easily just by counting on your fingers (or multiplying and adding). First, Column A must be 15 since $5 \times 3 = 15$. As for Column B, since there is 1 floor with 2 apartments and 4 floors with 4 apartments, the total number of apartments in the building is 18. So Column B is greater.

6. **The correct answer is (D).** This question is nothing more than a test of your ability to move decimal points. All of the answer choices are expressed as variations of 1.27. To rename 0.00127 as 1.27 times some number, you must move the decimal point three places to the right. In "official" notation, $0.00127 = 1.27 \times 10^{-3}$. $10^{-3} = 0.001$, so $0.00127 = 1.27 \times 0.001$.

7. **The correct answer is (C).** The key to this question is careful reading. If the $240 prize is divided between two people, and if one person receives $180, then the other person receives $60. The difference in the amounts received is $180 - 60 = 120$.

8. The correct answer is (D). One way of solving this problem is to treat the equations as simultaneous equations, isolating a variable in one, substituting it into the other, and then solving for that variable. One way of doing this is to isolate y in the second equation. Since $\frac{y}{x} = \frac{1}{3}$, $y = \frac{x}{3}$. Substitute this value of y into the other equation:

$$3x - 4\left(\frac{x}{3}\right) = 5$$

$$3x - 4\frac{x}{3} = 5$$

$$\frac{9x - 4x}{3} = 5$$

$$5x = 15$$

$$x = 3$$

9. The correct answer is (D). Once it is established that the two lines are parallel, it is possible to calculate the value of all the angles in the figure. The 36° angle and angle x are supplementary angles, that is, they total 180°, so angle x must be 144°.

10. The correct answer is (D). With a question of this type, a good strategy is to cross-multiply:

$$5(x - 1) = 4(x + 1)$$

Multiply: $5x - 5 = 4x + 4$

Solve for x: $x = 9$

11. The correct answer is (B). When you look at the centered information, you should have the strong suspicion that the solution to the entire comparison will be found by factoring the expression on the left side of the centered equation. This is a correct intuition. If we factor $x^2 - 3x - 4$, we get $(x + 1)(x - 4)$. [You can check this by multiplying $(x + 1)(x - 4)$.] Since one of the factors uses addition $(x + 1)$ and the other uses subtraction $(x - 4)$, we can match them up with m and n in the expression to the right of the equals sign in the centered equation: m must be 1 while n must be 4. So Column B is larger.

12. The correct answer is (C). The key to the question is the realization that all three triangles share a common altitude. Drop a line from point E, perpendicular to $ABCD$:

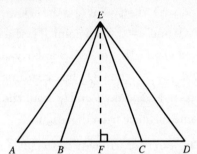

Since the three triangles have a common altitude, whatever difference there might be in their areas must be solely a function of the lengths of their bases. Since AB and CD are half of BC, triangles AEB and CED must have areas equal to half that of BEC. Consequently, the area of triangle BEC is equal to the sum of the areas of triangles AEB and CED.

13. The correct answer is (A). Here the key is the proper manipulation of the radicals. Column B is easily manipulated, for you need only to extract the square root, which is $\frac{3}{4}$. In Column A, do not make the mistake of adding the fractions beneath the radicals as you would ordinary fractions. Column A is not equal to Column B; instead, Column A is equal to $3\sqrt{\frac{3}{16}}$. We can extract the square root of $\frac{1}{16}$, which is $\frac{1}{4}$, giving us $\frac{3}{4}\sqrt{3}$ in Column A. Now we can see that Column A is larger, since $\sqrt{3}$ is about 1.7.

14. The correct answer is (C). The easiest approach to this question is to do the multiplication indicated in Column A. The 5s divide out, so the result is $x + y - 7$ and the two columns are equal.

15. The correct answer is (D). This question is a little tricky, but it can be answered using a principle we have used several times earlier: With a variable such as x or y, be alert for possible values such as zero or negative numbers. For example, if $x = 1$ and $y = 1$, then point Q is the origin. But if $x = 0$ and $y = 0$, then point P is the origin (and Q is farther away). Similarly, if $x = \frac{1}{2}$ and $y = \frac{1}{2}$, then Q has coordinates of $\left(-\frac{1}{2}, -\frac{1}{2}\right)$, and points P and Q would be at the same distance from the origin.

16. **The correct answer is (E).** The wheel is divided into eight equal sectors, 3 of which are painted blue. So $\frac{3}{8}$ of the wheel's area is blue. What is the area of the wheel? Since it is a circle with a diameter of 64 centimeters, it has a radius of 32 centimeters and an area of $\pi \times 32 \times 32 = 1{,}024\pi$ square centimeters. And $\frac{3}{8}$ of $1{,}024\pi$ is 384π.

17. **The correct answer is (B).** The formula for finding the volume of a right circular cylinder is πr^2 times the height of the cylinder. Here we have cylinders of equal volume so πr^2 times the height of the one must be equal to the other:

$$\pi\,(3^2) \times 4 = \pi\,(2^2) \times h$$
$$36\pi = 4\pi \times h$$
$$h = 9$$

18. **The correct answer is (E).** With a question like this, you should perform the indicated operations. First subtract $\frac{1}{y}$ from $\frac{1}{x}$, using the common denominator of xy. The result is $\frac{y-x}{xy} = \frac{1}{z}$. Now cross-multiply and divide. The result is $z = \frac{xy}{y-x}$.

19. **The correct answer is (C).** Here is a question involving ratio parts. Since the ratio of women to men employed by the company is 3 to 2, there are five $(3 + 2)$ ratio parts; that is, the total number of employees is divisible by 5, of which 3 parts, or $\frac{3}{5}$, are women and 2 parts, or $\frac{2}{5}$, are men. And $\frac{2}{5}$ of 240 = 96.

20. **The correct answer is (C).** When you look at this question and see the 120° angle, one of the first things that should come to mind is the possibility that the other angles will be 60° or 30°. If that is correct, then the key to the question will either be an equilateral triangle or the special case of the right triangle, the 30°-60°-90° triangle. As it turns out, the key here is a simple equilateral triangle. The information given is sufficient to establish that all sides are parallel and equal. This means that the measures of angles S and Q are 60°. Then the line PR divides angles P and R, which both measure 120°, into 60° angles. As a result, $\triangle PRS$ turns out to be an equilateral triangle with side 3, so $PR = 3$.

21. **The correct answer is (A).** A table will help us organize the information:

	Brown	Not-Brown	Total
Men			
Women			
Total			

Filling in the information given:

	Brown	Not-Brown	Total
Men	$\frac{1}{4}$		$\frac{3}{8}$
Women			
Total	$\frac{3}{4}$		

Notice that we enter $\frac{1}{4}$ in the square for men with brown eyes. This is because $\frac{2}{3}$ of the $\frac{3}{8}$ of the people who are men have brown eyes. Finally, we complete the table:

	Brown	Not-Brown	Total
Men	$\frac{1}{4}$	$\frac{1}{8}$	$\frac{3}{8}$
Women	$\frac{1}{2}$	$\frac{1}{8}$	$\frac{5}{8}$
Total	$\frac{3}{4}$	$\frac{1}{4}$	1

22. The correct answer is (C). To answer this question, you must first determine the total number of dollars in the budget. This can be done by adding together the various sources of income shown in the bar graph: $10 + $6 + $2 + $8 + $4 = $30 (millions of dollars). From the pie chart, we learn that 25%, or $\frac{1}{4}$, of this $30 million was allocated to operation of the physical plant; $\frac{1}{4}$ of $30 million is $7,500,000.

23. The correct answer is (B). We already have a start on this question given what we learned in the previous explanation. Income from the foundation accounted for $6 million of the total of $30 million, and $\frac{6}{30} = \frac{1}{5} = 20\%$.

24. The correct answer is (D). Given a total budget of $30 million and the distribution shown in the pie chart, the question is answered: 35% of $30 million minus 20% of $30 million = $4,500,000.

25. The correct answer is (C). Whenever you have a question dealing with a square, remember that a number of special relationships exist. First, since a square has four equal sides, you can find the length of each side if you know the perimeter. Also, if you know the length of a side, you know the area. In Column A, a square with an area of 16 has a side of 4 and therefore has a perimeter of 16. In Column B, the diagonal of the square cuts the square into two isosceles right triangles: 45°-45°-90°. In such triangles, the hypotenuse is equal to the length of either of the two shorter sides multiplied by $\sqrt{2}$. Conversely, the shorter sides are each equal to one half the length of the hypotenuse multiplied by $\sqrt{2}$. So if the diagonal of a square (the hypotenuse of the right triangle) is $4\sqrt{2}$, the side of the triangle (which is also the side of the square) is $\frac{1}{2} = \left(4\sqrt{2}\right)\left(\sqrt{2}\right) = 4$. And a side of 4 means a perimeter of 16, so the two squares have the same perimeter.

26. The correct answer is (A). You might get away with doing the manipulation indicated here. After all, multiplying .333 by .666 is not too unmanageable; and multiplying $\frac{1}{3}$ by $\frac{2}{3}$ and renaming that as a decimal will not take forever. The results will show that Column A is greater. But there is an easier approach: .333 and .666 are approximately, but not exactly, $\frac{1}{3}$ and $\frac{2}{3}$, respectively. But how do they differ from the exact decimal equivalents for $\frac{1}{3}$ and $\frac{2}{3}$? The answer is that the actual decimals obtained by dividing 1 by 3 and 2 by 3 are repeating decimals. In other words, $\frac{1}{3}$ is really .3333 . . . and $\frac{2}{3}$ is really .6666 . . . , which is to say that $\frac{1}{3}$ is really larger than just .333 and $\frac{2}{3}$ is really larger than just .666. So Column A must be larger than Column B.

27. The correct answer is (D). Sometimes just substituting numbers is enough to find the pattern needed to answer the question. For example, possible values of x are 6 (6 + 5 ÷ 3 = 3, remainder 2) and 9 (9 + 5 ÷ 3 = 4, remainder of 2). One of these is even and the other odd, which means that when x is divided by 2, you might get a remainder of 0 (in which case Column A is greater) or you might get a remainder of 1 (in which case the columns are equal).

28. The correct answer is (B). Here again, trial and error is probably faster than trying to devise an elaborate mathematical proof. What are the first few numbers divisible by 12? 12, 24, 36, 48, 60, etc. And which is the first one greater than 12 that is not divisible by 8? The answer, as you can see by checking our list, is 36.

PRACTICE TEST 3 ANSWER SHEET

Verbal Section

1. Ⓐ Ⓑ Ⓒ Ⓓ Ⓔ   7. Ⓐ Ⓑ Ⓒ Ⓓ Ⓔ   13. Ⓐ Ⓑ Ⓒ Ⓓ Ⓔ   19. Ⓐ Ⓑ Ⓒ Ⓓ Ⓔ   25. Ⓐ Ⓑ Ⓒ Ⓓ Ⓔ

2. Ⓐ Ⓑ Ⓒ Ⓓ Ⓔ   8. Ⓐ Ⓑ Ⓒ Ⓓ Ⓔ   14. Ⓐ Ⓑ Ⓒ Ⓓ Ⓔ   20. Ⓐ Ⓑ Ⓒ Ⓓ Ⓔ   26. Ⓐ Ⓑ Ⓒ Ⓓ Ⓔ

3. Ⓐ Ⓑ Ⓒ Ⓓ Ⓔ   9. Ⓐ Ⓑ Ⓒ Ⓓ Ⓔ   15. Ⓐ Ⓑ Ⓒ Ⓓ Ⓔ   21. Ⓐ Ⓑ Ⓒ Ⓓ Ⓔ   27. Ⓐ Ⓑ Ⓒ Ⓓ Ⓔ

4. Ⓐ Ⓑ Ⓒ Ⓓ Ⓔ   10. Ⓐ Ⓑ Ⓒ Ⓓ Ⓔ   16. Ⓐ Ⓑ Ⓒ Ⓓ Ⓔ   22. Ⓐ Ⓑ Ⓒ Ⓓ Ⓔ   28. Ⓐ Ⓑ Ⓒ Ⓓ Ⓔ

5. Ⓐ Ⓑ Ⓒ Ⓓ Ⓔ   11. Ⓐ Ⓑ Ⓒ Ⓓ Ⓔ   17. Ⓐ Ⓑ Ⓒ Ⓓ Ⓔ   23. Ⓐ Ⓑ Ⓒ Ⓓ Ⓔ   29. Ⓐ Ⓑ Ⓒ Ⓓ Ⓔ

6. Ⓐ Ⓑ Ⓒ Ⓓ Ⓔ   12. Ⓐ Ⓑ Ⓒ Ⓓ Ⓔ   18. Ⓐ Ⓑ Ⓒ Ⓓ Ⓔ   24. Ⓐ Ⓑ Ⓒ Ⓓ Ⓔ   30. Ⓐ Ⓑ Ⓒ Ⓓ Ⓔ

Math Section

1. Ⓐ Ⓑ Ⓒ Ⓓ Ⓔ   7. Ⓐ Ⓑ Ⓒ Ⓓ Ⓔ   13. Ⓐ Ⓑ Ⓒ Ⓓ Ⓔ   19. Ⓐ Ⓑ Ⓒ Ⓓ Ⓔ   25. Ⓐ Ⓑ Ⓒ Ⓓ Ⓔ

2. Ⓐ Ⓑ Ⓒ Ⓓ Ⓔ   8. Ⓐ Ⓑ Ⓒ Ⓓ Ⓔ   14. Ⓐ Ⓑ Ⓒ Ⓓ Ⓔ   20. Ⓐ Ⓑ Ⓒ Ⓓ Ⓔ   26. Ⓐ Ⓑ Ⓒ Ⓓ Ⓔ

3. Ⓐ Ⓑ Ⓒ Ⓓ Ⓔ   9. Ⓐ Ⓑ Ⓒ Ⓓ Ⓔ   15. Ⓐ Ⓑ Ⓒ Ⓓ Ⓔ   21. Ⓐ Ⓑ Ⓒ Ⓓ Ⓔ   27. Ⓐ Ⓑ Ⓒ Ⓓ Ⓔ

4. Ⓐ Ⓑ Ⓒ Ⓓ Ⓔ   10. Ⓐ Ⓑ Ⓒ Ⓓ Ⓔ   16. Ⓐ Ⓑ Ⓒ Ⓓ Ⓔ   22. Ⓐ Ⓑ Ⓒ Ⓓ Ⓔ   28. Ⓐ Ⓑ Ⓒ Ⓓ Ⓔ

5. Ⓐ Ⓑ Ⓒ Ⓓ Ⓔ   11. Ⓐ Ⓑ Ⓒ Ⓓ Ⓔ   17. Ⓐ Ⓑ Ⓒ Ⓓ Ⓔ   23. Ⓐ Ⓑ Ⓒ Ⓓ Ⓔ

6. Ⓐ Ⓑ Ⓒ Ⓓ Ⓔ   12. Ⓐ Ⓑ Ⓒ Ⓓ Ⓔ   18. Ⓐ Ⓑ Ⓒ Ⓓ Ⓔ   24. Ⓐ Ⓑ Ⓒ Ⓓ Ⓔ

Analytical Writing—Issue Topic

_____

_____

_____

_____

_____

_____

_____

_____

_____

_____

_____

_____

_____

_____

_____

_____

_____

_____

_____

_____

_____

_____

_____

_____

_____

_____

_____

_____

_____

_____

_____

_____

_____

_____

_____

_____

_____

_____

_____

_____

_____

_____

_____

Analytical Writing—Argument Topic

_____

_____

_____

_____

_____

_____

_____

_____

_____

_____

_____

_____

_____

_____

_____

_____

_____

_____

_____

_____

_____

_____

_____

_____

Practice Test 3

ANALYTICAL WRITING

Issue Topic • 45 Minutes

Present Your Perspective on an Issue

In this part, two topics appear as brief quotations. Each states, either explicitly or implicitly, an issue of broad interest. You are to choose one of the two topics. You will then use the remainder of the 45 minutes to write an essay in which you take a position on the issue.

You may agree with the quotation, disagree with it, or challenge the statement in any way, so long as the ideas that you present are clearly relevant to the topic. You should provide reasons and examples to support your position. In doing so, you may want to draw on your reading of various sources, your personal experience and observations, or your academic studies.

It is a good idea to begin by reading the topic carefully. Then you should decide what position you want to take, after which you will probably want to outline your answer before you begin to write. Your essay will be graded on how well you:

- Assess the implications of the issue, including various complexities implicit in the topic
- Organize, develop, and express your thoughts on the issue
- Provide supporting reasons and examples
- Demonstrate your mastery of the elements of standard written English

You should leave yourself sufficient time to read what you have written and to make any revisions to your essay that you think are needed.

For this exercise, you may choose to use an editing program on a computer (word processor) or write your response by hand using the space provided.

Issue Topics

Choose <u>one</u> of the following two topics to write on.

"Although we live in the scientific age, most people are still somewhat superstitious. Otherwise, there would not be such an interest in daily horoscopes, lottery results, and psychic readings."

"The significance of important historical events cannot be assessed by those who live through them, but only by those who are sufficiently removed from them in time."

Argument Topic • 30 Minutes

Analyze an Argument

In this part, you will be given an argument and have 30 minutes within which to write a critique of the argument. Your essay must address the argument given.

You are to <u>analyze</u> the reasoning of the argument. You should consider whether any of its assumptions are questionable and whether the evidence presented supports the conclusion. You might also discuss what changes in the line of reasoning or additional evidence would strengthen or weaken the conclusion.

Importantly, you are **NOT** being asked to state your own views on the underlying subject.

It is a good idea to begin by reading the argument carefully. Then you should evaluate the argument and consider what response you want to make, after which you will probably want to outline your answer before you begin to write.

Your essay response will be graded on how well you:

• Identify and analyze the important elements of the argument

• Organize, develop, and state your analysis

• Support your analysis with relevant reasons and examples

• Demonstrate your mastery of the elements of standard written English

You should leave yourself sufficient time to read what you have written and to make any revisions to your essay that you think are needed.

Timing for this part begins when you click on the "Dismiss the Directions" icon.

Argument Topic

"Twenty-five years ago, the depiction of violence in film was rare in the country of Edonia, because the Decency Commission, a quasi-governmental body appointed by the President of Edonia, had the authority to prohibit the showing of violent movies. The authority of the Decency Commission steadily eroded with the result that the incidence of the depiction of violence increased. Two years ago, the Commission was abolished. During this same time, the incidence of crime among Edonia teenagers has increased dramatically. Over 90% of the parents surveyed by the Independent Inquiry Poll stated that they believe that movies are too violent. Therefore, the Decency Commission should be reestablished with a mandate to preclude the showing of violent movies in order to solve the problem of teenage crime in Edonia."

VERBAL SECTION

30 Questions • 30 Minutes

> **Directions:** Each of the questions below contains one or more blank spaces, each blank indicating that something has been omitted. Each sentence is followed by five (5) words or sets of words. Read and determine the general sense of each sentence. Then choose the word, or set of words that, when inserted in the sentence, best fits the meaning of the sentence.

1. Despite the millions of dollars spent on improvements, the telephone system in India remains —— and continues to —— the citizens who depend on it.

    (A) primitive . . inconvenience

    (B) bombastic . . upset

    (C) suspicious . . connect

    (D) outdated . . elate

    (E) impartial . . vex

2. Contrary to popular opinion, bats are not generally aggressive and rabid; most are shy and ——.

    (A) turgid

    (B) disfigured

    (C) punctual

    (D) innocuous

    (E) depraved

3. Unlike the images in symbolist poetry which are often vague and ——, the images of surrealist poetry are startlingly —— and bold.

    (A) extraneous . . furtive

    (B) trivial . . inadvertent

    (C) obscure . . concrete

    (D) spectacular . . pallid

    (E) symmetrical . . virulent

Directions: In each of the following questions, you are given a related pair of words or phrases in capital letters. Each capitalized pair is followed by five (5) pairs of words or phrases. Choose the pair that best expresses a relationship similar to that expressed by the original pair.

4. CHAPTER : NOVEL ::
   (A) piano : orchestra
   (B) diamond : gem
   (C) scene : drama
   (D) poetry : prose
   (E) fraction : portion

5. IMPLY : AVER ::
   (A) reject : announce
   (B) hint : proclaim
   (C) encourage : absolve
   (D) remind : contradict
   (E) embolden : accept

6. DETENTION : RELEASE ::
   (A) viciousness : attack
   (B) calamity : repair
   (C) qualification : employ
   (D) induction : discharge
   (E) therapy : confuse

7. PONDEROUS : WEIGHT ::
   (A) eternal : temporality
   (B) convincing : decision
   (C) gargantuan : size
   (D) ancient : value
   (E) prototypical : affection

Directions: Each of the following questions consists of a word printed in capital letters, followed by five (5) words or phrases. Choose the word or phrase that is most nearly opposite in meaning to the word in capital letters. Be sure to consider all the choices before deciding which one is best.

8. REVERE :
   (A) collide
   (B) succumb
   (C) threaten
   (D) divide
   (E) despise

9. BOORISH :
   (A) juvenile
   (B) well-mannered
   (C) weak-minded
   (D) unique
   (E) concealed

10. WHIMSICAL :
    (A) chivalrous
    (B) perfect
    (C) predictable
    (D) hidden
    (E) backward

11. NASCENT :
    (A) fully developed
    (B) extremely valuable
    (C) well-regarded
    (D) informative
    (E) measurable

Directions: The passage below is followed by questions based on its content. Choose the best answer to each question.

Art, like words, is a form of communication. Words, spoken and written, render accessible to humans of the latest generations all the knowledge discovered by
(5) the experience and reflection, both of preceding generations and of the best and foremost minds of their own times. Art renders accessible to people of the latest generations all the feelings expe-
(10) rienced by their predecessors, and those already felt by their best and foremost contemporaries. Just as the evolution of knowledge proceeds by dislodging and replacing that which is mistaken, so too
(15) the evolution of feeling proceeds through art. Feelings less kind and less necessary for the well-being of humankind are replaced by others kinder and more essential to that end. This is the purpose
(20) of art, and the more art fulfills that purpose the better the art; the less it fulfills it, the worse the art.

12. The author develops the passage primarily by
   (A) theory and refutation
   (B) example and generalization
   (C) comparison and contrast
   (D) question and answer
   (E) inference and deduction

13. According to the author, knowledge is
   (A) evolutionary and emotional
   (B) cumulative and progressive
   (C) static and unmoving
   (D) dynamic and cyclical
   (E) practical and directionless

14. According to the passage, all of the following are true EXCEPT
   (A) art is a form of communication
   (B) art helps to refine sensibilities
   (C) art is a repository of experience
   (D) real art can never be bad
   (E) art is a progressive human endeavor

Directions: In each of the following questions, you are given a related pair of words or phrases in capital letters. Each capitalized pair is followed by five (5) pairs of words or phrases. Choose the pair that best expresses a relationship similar to that expressed by the original pair.

15. FEBRILE : ILLNESS ::
   (A) tenacious : astonishment
   (B) juvenile : maturity
   (C) classic : cultivation
   (D) eccentric : discrimination
   (E) delusional : insanity

16. INCOMMUNICADO : CONTACT ::
   (A) sequestered : company
   (B) pretentious : affectation
   (C) submissive : compromise
   (D) perpetual : adventure
   (E) severed : replacement

17. EQUIVOCATION : MEANING ::
   (A) feint : intention
   (B) secrecy : stealth
   (C) geniality : amiability
   (D) travesty : insight
   (E) refinement : innovation

Directions: The passage below is followed by questions based on its content. Choose the best answer to each question.

The most damning thing that can be said about the world's best-endowed and richest country is that it is not only not the leader in health status, but that it is so (5) low in the ranks of the nations. The United States ranks 18th among nations of the world in male life expectancy at birth, 9th in female life expectancy at birth, and 12th in infant mortality. More (10) importantly, huge variations are evident in health status in the United States from one place to the next and from one group to the next.

The forces that affect health can be (15) aggregated into four groupings that lend themselves to analysis of all health problems. Clearly the largest aggregate of forces resides in the person's environment. His own behavior, in part derived (20) from his experiences with his environment, is the next greatest force affecting his health. Medical care services, treated as separate from other environmental factors because of the special interest we (25) have in them, make a modest contribution to health status. Finally, the contributions of heredity to health are difficult to judge. We are templated at conception as to our basic weaknesses and strengths; (30) but many hereditary attributes never become manifest because of environmental and behavioral forces that act before the genetic forces come to maturity, and other hereditary attributes are increas-(35) ingly being palliated by medical care.

No other country spends what we do per capita for medical care. The care available is among the best technically, even if used too lavishly and thus dan-(40) gerously, but none of the countries that stand above us in health status have such a high proportion of medically disenfranchised persons. Given the evidence that medical care is not that valu-(45) able and access to care not that bad, it seems most unlikely that our bad showing is caused by the significant propor-

tion who are poorly served. Other hypotheses have greater explanatory (50) power: excessive poverty, both actual and relative, and excessive affluence.

Excessive poverty is probably more prevalent in the U.S. than in any of the countries that have a better infant mor-(55) tality rate and female life expectancy at birth. This is probably true also for all but four or five of the countries with a longer male life expectancy. In the notably poor countries that exceed us in male (60) survival, difficult living conditions are a more accepted way of life and in several of them, a good basic diet, basic medical care and basic education, and lifelong employment opportunities are an every-(65) day fact of life. In the U.S., a national unemployment level of 10 percent may be 40 percent in the ghetto, while less than 4 percent elsewhere. The countries that have surpassed us in health do not (70) have such severe or entrenched problems. Nor are such a high proportion of their people involved in them.

Excessive affluence is not so obvious a cause of ill health, but, at least until (75) recently, few other nations could afford such unhealthful ways of living. Excessive intake of animal protein and fats, dangerous imbibing of alcohol and use of tobacco and drugs (prescribed and pro-(80) scribed), and dangerous recreational sports and driving habits are all possible only because of affluence. Our heritage, desires, opportunities, and our machismo, combined with the relatively (85) low cost of bad foods and speedy vehicles, make us particularly vulnerable to our affluence. And those who are not affluent try harder. Our unacceptable health status, then, will not be improved (90) appreciably by expanded medical resources nor by their redistribution so much as by a general attempt to improve the quality of life for all.

18. Which of the following would be the most logical continuation of the passage?

    (A) Suggestions for specific proposals to improve the quality of life in America

    (B) A listing of the most common causes of death among male and female adults

    (C) An explanation of the causes of poverty in America, both absolute and relative

    (D) A proposal to ensure that residents of central cities receive more and better medical care

    (E) A study of the overcrowding in urban hospitals serving primarily the poor

19. All of the following are mentioned in the passage as factors affecting the health of the population EXCEPT

    (A) the availability of medical care services

    (B) the genetic endowment of individuals

    (C) overall environmental factors

    (D) the nation's relative position in health status

    (E) an individual's own behavior

20. The author is primarily concerned with

    (A) condemning the U.S. for its failure to provide better medical care to the poor

    (B) evaluating the relative significance of factors contributing to the poor health status in the U.S.

    (C) providing information the reader can use to improve his or her personal health

    (D) comparing the general health of the U.S. population with world averages

    (E) advocating specific measures designed to improve the health of the U.S. population

21. The passage best supports which of the following conclusions about the relationship between per capita expenditures for medical care and the health of a population?

    (A) The per capita expenditure for medical care has relatively little effect on the total amount of medical care available to a population.

    (B) The genetic makeup of a population is a more powerful determinant of the health of a population than the per capita expenditure for medical care.

    (C) A population may have very high per capita expenditures for medical care and yet have a lower health status than other populations with lower per capita expenditures.

    (D) The higher the per capita expenditure on medical care, the more advanced is the medical technology; and the more advanced the technology, the better is the health of the population.

    (E) Per capita outlays for medical care devoted to adults are likely to have a greater effect on the status of the population than outlays devoted to infants.

22. The author refers to the excessive intake of alcohol and tobacco and drug use in order to

    (A) show that some health problems cannot be attacked by better medical care

    (B) demonstrate that use of tobacco and intoxicants is detrimental to health

    (C) cite examples of individual behavior that have adverse consequences for health status

    (D) refute the contention that poor health is related to access to medical care

    (E) illustrate ways in which affluence may contribute to poor health status

23. The passage provides information to answer which of the following questions?

    (A) What is the most powerful influence on the health status of a population?

    (B) Which nation in the world leads in health status?

    (C) Is the life expectancy of males in the U.S. longer than that of females?

    (D) What are the most important genetic factors influencing the health of an individual?

    (E) How can the U.S. reduce the incidence of unemployment in the ghetto?

Directions: Each of the following questions consists of a word printed in capital letters, followed by five (5) words or phrases. Choose the word or phrase that is most nearly opposite in meaning to the word in capital letters. Be sure to consider all the choices before deciding which one is best.

24. INURED :
    (A) authoritative
    (B) dissolute
    (C) bereft
    (D) sensitive
    (E) taxing

25. IRASCIBLE :
    (A) even-tempered
    (B) well-informed
    (C) repetitious
    (D) motionless
    (E) synchronous

26. EXONERATE :
    (A) testify
    (B) engender
    (C) accuse
    (D) inundate
    (E) abrogate

27. ALACRITY :
    (A) skullduggery
    (B) reluctance
    (C) interment
    (D) bellicosity
    (E) specificity

Directions: Each of the questions below contains one or more blank spaces, each blank indicating that something has been omitted. Each sentence is followed by five (5) words or sets of words. Read and determine the general sense of each sentence. Then choose the word, or set of words that, when inserted in the sentence, best fits the meaning of the sentence.

28. A good trial lawyer will argue only what is central to an issue, eliminating —— information or anything else that might —— the client.

    (A) seminal . . amuse

    (B) extraneous . . jeopardize

    (C) erratic . . enhance

    (D) prodigious . . extol

    (E) reprehensible . . initiate

29. Psychologists and science fiction writers argue that people persist in believing in extraterrestrial life, even though the Federal government —— all such beliefs, because people need to feel a personal sense of —— in a godless universe.

    (A) decries . . morbidity

    (B) endorses . . despair

    (C) creates . . guilt

    (D) discourages . . spirituality

    (E) debunks . . alienation

30. Pollen grains and spores that are 200 million years old are now being extracted from shale and are —— the theory that the breakup of the continents occurred in stages; in fact, it seems that the breakups occurred almost ——.

    (A) refining . . blatantly

    (B) reshaping . . simultaneously

    (C) countermanding . . imperceptibly

    (D) forging . . vicariously

    (E) supporting . . haphazardly

MATH SECTION

28 Questions • 45 Minutes

Numbers: All numbers used are real numbers.

Figures: The position of points, angles, regions, and so forth are in the order shown. Figures are assumed to lie in a plane unless otherwise indicated. Figures are drawn as accurately as possible for problem-solving questions, unless otherwise indicated. Figures are NOT drawn to scale for quantitative analysis problem, unless otherwise indicated. You should solve the problems by using your knowledge of mathematics and not by estimating sizes by sight or measurement.

Lines: Assume that lines shown as straight are indeed straight.

Directions: For each of the following questions, select the best of the answer choices. For quantitative comparison questions, two quantities are given, one in Column A and one in Column B. Compare the two quantities and choose

(A) if the quantity in Column A is greater
(B) if the quantity in Column B is greater
(C) if the two quantities are equal
(D) if the relationship cannot be determined from the information given

Information applying to both columns is centered between the columns and above the quantities in columns A and B. Symbols that appear in both columns represent the same idea or quantity in each column.

	Column A	**Column B**
1.	5% of 36	36% of 5
2.	$\sqrt{15}$	$\sqrt{5} + \sqrt{10}$

$$(346 \times 23) + p = 34{,}731$$
$$(346 \times 23) + q = 35{,}124$$

3.	p	q

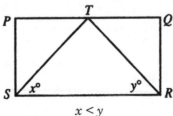

$x < y$
$PQRS$ is a rectangle

4.	PT	TQ

$x > 0$

5.	x^2	$2x$

Directions: For each of the following questions, select the best of the answer choices given.

6. From the time 6:15 p.m. to the time 7:45 p.m. of the same day, the minute hand of a standard clock describes an arc of

   (A) 30°

   (B) 90°

   (C) 180°

   (D) 540°

   (E) 910°

7. Which of the following fractions is the LEAST?

   (A) $\dfrac{8}{9}$

   (B) $\dfrac{7}{8}$

   (C) $\dfrac{7}{12}$

   (D) $\dfrac{1}{2}$

   (E) $\dfrac{6}{17}$

8. The length of each side of a square is $\dfrac{3x}{4} + 1$. What is the perimeter of the square?

   (A) $x + 1$

   (B) $3x + 1$

   (C) $3x + 4$

   (D) $\dfrac{9x^2}{16} + \dfrac{3x}{2} + 1$

   (E) It cannot be determined from the information given.

9. A truck departed from Newton at 11:53 a.m. and arrived in Far City, 240 miles away, at 4:41 p.m. on the same day. What was the approximate average speed of the truck on this trip?

   (A) $\dfrac{16}{1,200}$ mph

   (B) $\dfrac{240}{288}$ mph

   (C) $\dfrac{1,494}{240}$ mph

   (D) 50 mph

   (E) $\dfrac{5,640}{5}$ mph

10. If m, n, o, and p are real numbers, each of the following expressions equals $m(nop)$ EXCEPT

    (A) $(op)(mn)$

    (B) $ponm$

    (C) $p(onm)$

    (D) $(mp)(no)$

    (E) $(mn)(mo)(mp)$

Directions: For each of the following questions, select the best of the answer choices. For quantitative comparison questions, two quantities are given, one in Column A and one in Column B. Compare the two quantities and choose

(A) if the quantity in Column A is greater
(B) if the quantity in Column B is greater
(C) if the two quantities are equal
(D) if the relationship cannot be determined from the information given

Information applying to both columns is centered between the columns and above the quantities in columns A and B. Symbols that appear in both columns represent the same idea or quantity in each column.

	Column A	**Column B**
11.	$\dfrac{4}{5} - \dfrac{3}{4}$	$\dfrac{1}{20}$
12.	the ratio 3:13	the ratio 13:51

Let S_n be defined by the equation: $S_n = 3n + 2$

13.	$S_5 + S_4$	$S_9 + S_8$

Directions: For each of the following questions, select the best of the answer choices given.

14. Which of the following fractions expressed in the form $\frac{p}{q}$ is most nearly approximated by the decimal $.PQ$, where P is the tenths' digit and Q is the hundredths' digit?

   (A) $\dfrac{1}{8}$

   (B) $\dfrac{2}{9}$

   (C) $\dfrac{3}{4}$

   (D) $\dfrac{4}{5}$

   (E) $\dfrac{8}{9}$

15. If b books can be purchased for d dollars, how many books can be purchased for m dollars?

   (A) $\dfrac{bm}{d}$

   (B) bdm

   (C) $\dfrac{d}{bm}$

   (D) $\dfrac{b+m}{d}$

   (E) $\dfrac{b-m}{d}$

Directions: For each of the following questions, select the best of the answer choices. For quantitative comparison questions, two quantities are given, one in Column A and one in Column B. Compare the two quantities and choose

(A) if the quantity in Column A is greater
(B) if the quantity in Column B is greater
(C) if the two quantities are equal
(D) if the relationship cannot be determined from the information given

Information applying to both columns is centered between the columns and above the quantities in columns A and B. Symbols that appear in both columns represent the same idea or quantity in each column.

	Column A	**Column B**
16.	The cost of ten pounds of meat at $2.50 per pound.	The cost of five kilograms of meat at $5.00 per kilogram.
17.	$\dfrac{10}{10,000}$	$\dfrac{1,000}{1,000,000}$
18.	The number of pears in a cubical box with a side of 24 inches.	The number of potatoes in a cubical box with a side of 36 inches.

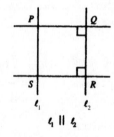

$\ell_1 \parallel \ell_2$

19.	PQ	QR

$$4x^2 + 3x + 2x^2 + 2x = 3x^2 + 2x + 3x^2 + 2x + 3$$

20.	x^2	9

Directions: For each of the following questions, select the best of the answer choices given.

QUESTIONS 21–25 ARE BASED ON THE FOLLOWING GRAPHS.

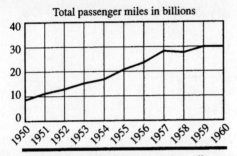

Total passenger miles in billions

Deaths per 100 million passenger-miles

21. All of the following statements can be inferred from the information provided in the graphs EXCEPT

(A) the highest rate of passenger deaths per mile traveled during the period covered by the graphs occurred in 1951

(B) the largest yearly increase in deaths per mile traveled occurred in the period 1954 to 1955

(C) the rate of passenger deaths per mile traveled was approximately the same in both 1954 and 1957

(D) total passenger miles traveled approximately tripled between 1951 and 1959

(E) the percentage increase in deaths per 100 million passenger miles was constant for 1958, 1959, and 1960

22. In which year did the longest uninterrupted period of increase in the rate of passenger deaths per mile traveled finally end?

(A) 1951

(B) 1953

(C) 1955

(D) 1957

(E) 1960

23. How many fatalities were reported in the year 1955?

(A) 20 billion

(B) 1.2 million

(C) 240,000

(D) 2,000

(E) 240

24. The greatest number of fatalities were recorded in which year?

(A) 1960

(B) 1957

(C) 1955

(D) 1953

(E) 1951

25. In which year did the greatest number of passengers travel?

(A) 1960

(B) 1955

(C) 1953

(D) 1951

(E) It cannot be determined from the information given.

ABCD is a square.

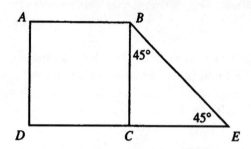

26. If the area of the triangle *BCE* is 8, what is the area of the square *ABCD*?

(A) 4 sq. feet

(B) 8 sq. feet

(C) 16 sq. feet

(D) 22 sq. feet

(E) 82 sq. feet

27. The diagonal of the floor of a rectangular closet is $7\frac{1}{2}$ feet. The shorter side of the closet is $4\frac{1}{2}$ feet. What is the area of the closet in square feet?

(A) 37

(B) 27

(C) $\dfrac{54}{4}$

(D) $\dfrac{21}{4}$

(E) 5

28. If the ratio of women to men in a meeting is 4 to 1, what percent of the persons in the meeting are men?

(A) 20%

(B) 25%

(C) $33\frac{1}{3}$ %

(D) 80%

(E) 100%

ANSWER KEY AND EXPLANATIONS

Analytical Writing

Issue Topics

Topic 1

As you read the following sample response, try to judge for yourself how well it meets the criteria that will be applied by graders:

Category	Below Avg.	Avg.	Above Avg.
Analysis of the Topic			
Organization and Development			
Use of Reasons and Examples			
Use of Standard Written English			
OVERALL SCORE*			

*Below Average = 1–2; Average = 3–4; Above Average = 5–6

SAMPLE RESPONSE AND COMMENTARY FOR ISSUE TOPIC 1

Note: The sample answers contain spelling and grammatical errors. This is done to simulate a first draft written under time pressure.

When we distinguish between science and superstition, we must be careful because the science of era may be the superstition of another. For example, alchemy was once regarded as a science but is today seen by chemistry as superstition, and astrology was once viewed as means of obtaining knowledge but is now regarded by astronomy as superstition. The change, however, is gradual. As a result, one would expect elements of the earlier science, now condemned by today's science as mere superstition, to survive and even thrive right along side more modern conceptions. Certainly this is true of the three examples given by the speaker.

First, almost every newspaper carries a daily horoscopes in which advice is dispense to people based upon their astrological signs. It's difficult to believe that the daily horoscopes would be such a popular feature (as evidenced by the fact that it is almost universal) unless many if not most people were interested in their horoscopes. Or it is not unusual for people to make generalizations such as "He's a Virgo and so meticulous," or "She's a Leo an not very systematic."

Second, the lottery results in the daily paper almost always include a list of "hot" and "cold" numbers. Of course, anyone familiar with probability theory knows that lottery numbers are produced at random. But again, many if not most people still accept, at some deep level, the gamblers' fallacy: number 23 hasn't come up in a while, so it's due. And many people seem to think that some numbers are luckier for them than others because they play their spouse's birthdate or their children's ages.

Third, advertisings for psychic readings frequently appear in newspapers and upon television. These ads are almost always accompanied by a disclaimer that the service is "for amusement purposes only," but it is hard to believe that so many people could be so easily amused. There must be quite a few who truly accept the psychic's ability to see things.

Does this mean that most people are superstitious in a very crude sense. Not at all, for at a certain level, these are harmless diversions. To really label someone as superstitious, we'd want to see some evidence of an elaborate ritual such as dancing under the full moon prior to animal sacrifice. Reading a daily horoscope, playing lucky numbers, or dialing the psychic hotline doesn't seem to compare with that. On the other, there must be some element of superstition that still servives even it's very deeply subconscious. After all, what should we think of someone who says "I'm not superstitious" even while knocking on wood?

COMMENTARY

This essay has a lot to recommend it, but it falls short of being an outstanding essay. It is fairly well written with relatively few errors, but then the prose is not really outstanding. The essay is well organized, and it's easy to follow the three points that the writer develops internally: horoscopes, numbers, and readings. But the first and the last paragraphs don't hang together quite as well. The author begins by distinguishing superstition and science and noting that what was once science may now be merely superstition, but along the way, the author seems to lose track of that point. In the concluding paragraph, the author makes a nice case for the point that superstition may still be a component of the modern mind but doesn't tie that back to the distinction drawn in the first paragraph. Consequently, this essay would probably be graded a 5 by many readers and perhaps even a 4 by some. Had the author been able to develop the last point more thoroughly and tie it back to the first paragraph, it would likely have been an easy 5 and maybe even a 6.

Topic 2

As you read the following sample response, try to judge for yourself how well it meets the criteria that will be applied by graders:

Category	Below Avg.	Avg.	Above Avg.
Analysis of the Topic			
Organization and Development			
Use of Reasons and Examples			
Use of Standard Written English			
OVERALL SCORE*			

*Below Average = 1–2; Average = 3–4; Above Average = 5–6

SAMPLE RESPONSE AND COMMENTARY FOR ISSUE TOPIC 2

Note: The sample answers contain spelling and grammatical errors. This is done to simulate a first draft written under time pressure.

Read for its obvious content, the statement seems difficult to reject. After all, if history shows anything, it is that the people who are caught up in the events of the moment often only partly appreciate their significance. When Abraham Lincoln delivered his address at Gettyburg, he stated "The world will little note no longer remember" his speech though it would the events that occasioned the address. Lincoln understood full well that Gettysburg was an important battle, but did he recognize it as a turning point of the Civil War? He certainly underestimated his own contribution.

That sort of observation, however, seems not to do the topic justice because it is so obvious. Instead, the fundamental weakness with the statement is that is says too little rather than too much. We should say instead that the statement is wrong because it implies that there will be a point, sufficiently removed in time from an actual event, at which historians will be able to describe unequivocally and definitely, the final significance of the events. But this is an oversimplied view of the job of historians.

The history of history teaches us that we are not likely to find a final resting point. It seems that there will always be room for yet another revision. The consensus following the end of World War II is that the decision to drop the atomic bomb on Hiroshima and Nagasaki saved countless American lives because the Japanese surrender avoided the necessity of mounting an island to island invasion of the Japanese homeland. Later revisionists questioned whether Truman's decision had, in fact, been necessary, suggesting that it was made hastily and resulted in needless loss of civilian life. Revisionists of the revisionist history argue that Truman's decision actually, on balance, saved the lives of countless Japanese civilians as well as those of soldiers on both side because the Japanese leadership was committed to an all-out defense of the homeland even though it new that massive starvation was likely.

What is the final truth of the history of that event? The answer is that there is not one final truth. An evaluation of the historical significance of an event is always open to reassessment by the next wave of revisionists.

COMMENTARY

This is certainly an above-average response, probably even a 5; but it doesn't quite make it to the highest grade. The writing is strong with few errors, and the statement of the writer's position (history is always open to revision) is intriguing. The problem is that the main example (developed in paragraph 2) doesn't quite prove what the speaker claims. The example proves that the decision to drop the atomic bomb has been interpreted, reinterpreted, and reinterpreted again, but it doesn't demonstrate the possibility of yet another revision. The essay would have been stronger had the writer offered some argument to support the claim that history is open-ended (rather than just making the assertion) or if the writer had used the example to suggest this, e.g., by showing how the next wave of revisionists might view the event. Because the argument is not fully developed, the essay would not likely get a 6 but would be given a 5 by many readers.

Argument Topic

As you read the following sample response, try to judge for yourself how well it meets the criteria that will be applied by graders:

Category	Below Avg.	Avg.	Above Avg.
Analysis of the Topic			
Organization and Development			
Use of Reasons and Examples			
Use of Standard Written English			
OVERALL SCORE*			

*Below Average = 1–2; Average = 3–4; Above Average = 5–6

SAMPLE RESPONSE AND COMMENTARY FOR THE ARGUMENT TOPIC

Note: The sample answers contain spelling and grammatical errors. This is done to simulate a first draft written under time pressure.

The argument fails to prove that reestablishing the Decency Commission would solve Edonia's teenaged crime problem for three reasons. One, the evidence brought forth doesn't support such a drastic plan. Two, the course of action may not solve the problem. Three, the social side-effects of the plan could be devastating.

First, the evidence given in the argument doesn't support such a drastic plan. Consider too points. One, the problem sited is "teenage" crime, but the evidence talks about violence in the movies. Perhaps the rise in teenage crime is in areas like shoplifting or joyriding. If so, then the link between violence in the movies and crime in general has not been clearly proven. Two, the suggestion that most parents worry about violence really doesn't prove anything. It would be necessary to find out who is the Independent Inquiry Poll, whether it has a political agenda, and more generally what the survey asked. And even if it should turn out that the survey proves that most parents want to curtail violence because they see a link between it and crime, that doesn't prove such a link. After all, public opinion has often been wrong.

Second, the plan fails to consider some other factors. For example, it may be that the decline in the authority of the Commission was the result of some more systemic problem in Edonia, for example, maybe a war or extended economic depression caused people to lose faith in the Commission's judgment. Then, perhaps, it was these greater events that caused the rise in crime. The breakdown of the Commission itself might have been a result rather than a cause. Just reinstating the Commision won't solve the problem.

Third, it is necessary to consider the effect of censorship. In essence, the plan is saying that the government can tell the citizens of Edonia that they can't watch certain movies.

COMMENTARY

This appears to be an average essay. The writer does clearly state a position with supporting reasons and then signals the reader with transitional clues. So the argument is easy to follow. The language is not brilliant, but neither is it weak. The development of the second paragraph raises two fairly persuasive points, questioning whether the evidence provided proves what is claimed. The third paragraph introduces what might otherwise have been a very good point but the development seems truncated. And the final paragraph really makes an assertion rather than providing an analysis. To make the third point useful, the writer would need to have explored the consequences of censorship in the context of Edonian society rather than just make a blanket assertion that censorship is wrong. Had the third and fourth paragraphs lived up to the promise of the second, then this might have been an above-average essay even though the prose is somewhat dry. Readers would probably tend to give the response a 4.

Verbal Section

1.	A	7.	C	13.	B	19.	D	25.	A
2.	D	8.	E	14.	D	20.	B	26.	C
3.	C	9.	B	15.	E	21.	C	27.	B
4.	C	10.	C	16.	A	22.	E	28.	B
5.	B	11.	A	17.	A	23.	A	29.	D
6.	D	12.	C	18.	A	24.	D	30.	B

1. **The correct answer is (A).** The sentence starts with a thought-reverser, so we know that the correct choice will describe something unexpected given the amount of money invested. The second blank will be a logical continuation of the first blank as the verb *continues* indicates. (B), (C), and (E) can be eliminated immediately because they do not create meaningful phrases when substituted into the first blank. (A) and (D) are possibilities because a phone system can be both primitive and outdated. Next, we eliminate (D) because an outdated phone system would hardly elate those who depend on it. (A) creates a logical sentence. The system is primitive, despite the money spent on it, and it continues to inconvenience those who use it.

2. **The correct answer is (D).** This sentence starts with a thought-reverser, so we know that bats are going to be something that is the opposite of aggressive and rabid. The item is basically a vocabulary question. We can eliminate (A), (B), and (C) because they are not things one could say about bats and are not opposites of *aggressive* and *rabid*. We can also eliminate (E) because bats would probably not be described as *depraved*. (D), *innocuous*, which means "harmless," is the opposite of *rabid* and goes nicely with *shy*.

3. **The correct answer is (C).** In this sentence a thought-extender and a thought-reverser are the logical keys. The first blank needs a word that continues the idea of "vagueness"; the second blank is unlike the first and must therefore be something close to an opposite. All of the choices make sense since they can all be used to describe images, but only one parallels *vague* and that is *obscure*. The second element, *concrete*, is an opposite of *obscure* and completes the sentence nicely. The second elements of (A), (B), (D), and (E) are not things that could be said of images and make no sense when substituted in the sentence.

4. **The correct answer is (C).** This is clearly a part-to-whole analogy. A CHAPTER is part of a NOVEL and a *scene* is part of a *drama*. Don't be deceived by the mention of other literary terms such as *poetry* and *prose* or by other words such as *fraction* and *portion*, which mean "part."

5. **The correct answer is (B).** This analogy is one of degree. To IMPLY is to indicate indirectly; to AVER is to affirm with confidence. To *hint* is to suggest; to *proclaim* is to announce officially.

6. **The correct answer is (D).** This is an analogy based on sequence of events. After DETENTION one may be RELEASED, and after *induction* one may be *discharged*.

7. **The correct answer is (C).** This analogy is based on a defining characteristic. By definition, something that is PONDEROUS has a lot of WEIGHT, and something *gargantuan* is large in *size*.

8. **The correct answer is (E).** To REVERE is to regard with deep awe or respect. A straightforward opposite is *despise*.

9. **The correct answer is (B).** BOORISH means "rude or ill-mannered." A precise opposite, then, is *well-mannered*.

10. **The correct answer is (C).** WHIMSICAL means "fanciful or capricious"; therefore, *predictable* is a good antonym.

11. **The correct answer is (A).** NASCENT means "coming into being" or "beginning to form." A clear opposite, then, is *fully developed*.

12. **The correct answer is (C).** This is a logical structure question that asks about the overall development of the selection. The main organizational principle of the passage is the comparison and contrast of art and knowledge. The author points to both similarities and differences between the two. (A) is incorrect. Though the author proposes a theory of the purpose of art, there is no refutation of anything in the passage. As for (B), the author offers some general conclusions, but makes no generalizations based on examples. As for (D), though the passage can be viewed as an answer to the question "What is art for?" the author does not make question and answer the organizational principle of the selection. Finally, as for (E), the author states bold conclusions, but does not deduce or infer those conclusions from other premises or information.

13. **The correct answer is (B).** This is a specific detail question, so the correct answer will be explicitly stated in the selection. (B) is specifically stated. The author states that the knowledge of prior generations is preserved in speech. So knowledge is cumulative. Later, the author states that knowledge is self-correcting; that is, that errors are, during the passing of time, eliminated. So knowledge is also progressive. Since knowledge progresses, you can eliminate (C), (D), and (E). As for (A), though knowledge is evolutionary, it is art, not knowledge, that treats emotions.

14. **The correct answer is (D).** This is a specific detail question. The author specifically says that art is communication (like words), so (A) is mentioned. The author also states that art has the function of producing loftier emotions, so (B) and (E) are mentioned. And the author says that art renders the experience of previous generations accessible to the present, so (C) is mentioned. (D), however, is not said by the author to be true of art. In fact, in the last sentence, the author strongly implies that art can be bad as well as good.

15. **The correct answer is (E).** This analogy is based on the "sign of" relationship. To be FEBRILE is a sign of ILLNESS and to be *delusional* is a sign of *insanity*.

16. **The correct answer is (A).** This analogy is based on the "lack of" relationship. Lack of CONTACT is a defining characteristic of INCOMMUNICADO, and lack of *company* is a defining characteristic of *sequestered*.

17. **The correct answer is (A).** This analogy doesn't belong to any specific category, but you might create diagnostic sentences such as "EQUIVOCATION is ambiguous speech that hides MEANING" and "*Feint* is a deceptive act or sham that serves to hide *intention*." Do not be misled by *secrecy* and *stealth*, which are related to the key words and to each other.

18. **The correct answer is (A).** This is an application question. As we have noted before, application questions tend to be difficult because the correct answer can be understood as correct only in context. With a question such as this, the most logical continuation depends upon the choices available. Here the best answer is (A). The author concludes the discussion of the causes of our poor showing on the health status index by asserting that the best way to improve this showing is a

general improvement in the quality of life. This is an intriguing suggestion, and an appropriate follow-up would be a list of proposals that might accomplish this. As for (B), this could be part of such a discussion, but a listing of the most common causes of death would not, in and of itself, represent an extension of the development of the argument. (C), too, has some merit. The author might want to talk about the causes of poverty as a way of learning how to improve the quality of life by eliminating the causes of poverty. But this argument actually cuts in favor of (A), for the justification for (C) then depends on (A)—that is, it depends on the assumption that the author should discuss the idea raised in (A). (D) is incorrect because the author specifically states in his closing remarks that redistribution of medical resources is not a high priority. (E) can be eliminated on the same ground.

19. **The correct answer is (D).** This is an explicit idea question, and we find mention of (A), (B), (C), and (E) in the second paragraph. (D), too, is mentioned, but (D) is not a factor *affecting the health of the population*. (D) is a measure of, or an effect of, the health of the population, not a factor causing it.

20. **The correct answer is (B).** This is a main idea question. (A) can be eliminated because the author actually minimizes the importance of medical care as a factor affecting the health of a population. (C) can be eliminated because this is not the author's objective. To be sure, an individual may use information supplied in the passage to improve in some way his or her health, but that is not why the author wrote the passage. (D) is incorrect because this is a small part of the argument, a part that is used to advance the major objective outlined in (B). Finally, (E) is incorrect since the author leaves us with a pregnant suggestion but no specific recommendations. (B), however,

describes the development of the passage. The author wishes to explain the causes of the poor health status of the U.S. It is not, he argues, lack of medical care or even poor distribution of medical care, hypotheses that, we can infer from the text, are often proposed. He then goes on to give two alternative explanations: affluence and poverty.

21. **The correct answer is (C).** This is an application question. (C) is strongly supported by the text. In paragraph 3, the author specifically states that we have the highest per capita expenditure for medical care in the world. Yet, as he notes in the first paragraph, we rank rather low in terms of health. (A) is not supported by the arguments given in the passage. Though medical care may not be the most important determinant of health, the author never suggests that expenditure is not correlated with overall availability. (B) is incorrect and specifically contradicted by the second paragraph, where the author states that genetic problems may be covered over by medical care. (D) is incorrect since the author minimizes the importance of technology in improving health. Finally, (E) is simply not supported by any data or argument given in the passage.

22. **The correct answer is (E).** This is a logical detail question. The author refers to excess consumption to illustrate the way in which affluence, one of his two hypotheses, could undermine an individual's health. As for (A), while it is true that such problems may not be susceptible to medical treatment, the author does not introduce them to prove that. He introduces them at the particular point in the argument to prove that affluence can undermine health. (B) is incorrect for a similar reason. The author does not introduce the examples to prove that drinking and smoking are unhealthful activities. He presupposes his readers

know that already. Then, on the assumption that the reader already believes that, the author can say, "See, affluence causes smoking and drinking-which we all know to be bad." (C) must fail for the same reason. Finally (D) is incorrect since this is not the reason for introducing the examples. Although the author does argue that medical care and health are not as tightly linked as some people might think, this is not the point he is working on when he introduces smoking and drinking. With a logical detail question of this sort, we must be careful to select an answer that explains why the author makes the move he does at the particular juncture in the argument. Neither general reference to the overall idea of the passage (e.g., to prove his main point) nor a reference to a collateral argument will turn the trick.

23. **The correct answer is (A).** The answer to the question posed in answer choice (A) is explicitly provided in the second paragraph: environment. As for (B), though some information is given about the health status of the U.S., no other country is mentioned by name. As for (C), though some statistics are given about life expectancies in the U.S., no comparison of male and female life expectancies is given. As for (D), though genetic factors are mentioned generally in paragraph 2, no such factors are ever specified. Finally, the author offers no recommendations, so (E) must be incorrect.

24. **The correct answer is (D).** To be IN-URED is to become accustomed to something painful. *Sensitive* is an opposite.

25. **The correct answer is (A).** Since IRAS-CIBLE means "irritable" or "easily provoked to anger," *even-tempered* is a perfect antonym.

26. **The correct answer is (C).** EXONER-ATE means "to relieve of blame" or "to clear of guilt." *Accuse* is the best opposite.

27. **The correct answer is (B).** ALACRITY is a cheerful willingness to act or serve, so *reluctance* is a good opposite.

28. **The correct answer is (B).** This sentence has a thought-reverser and a thought-extender as its logical structure. The sentence says that the lawyer argues only what is central, eliminating something. Logically, what is eliminated is what is not central, so you should look for a word that means not central. (B) is the best answer. A lawyer would seek to eliminate *extraneous* (irrelevant) information or anything that might *jeopardize* (endanger) the client.

29. **The correct answer is (D).** This sentence contains a thought-reverser and a thought-extender. The thought-reverser is signaled by the phrase *even though*. Since people persist, even though the government does something, the government must be trying to stop the belief in extra-terrestrial life. The second blank requires a thought-extender, something that extends the idea of *personal*, and reverses the idea of *godless*. Although (A) might seem correct at first glance, since *decry* means "to condemn," the second word of the pair disqualifies it as the correct choice. To say that people need a personal sense of *morbidity* makes little sense. (B) is not correct because it fails to reverse the idea that people persist. To say that they persist even though the government *endorses* their actions is not logical. (C) is not correct for the same reason. If the government *creates* all such theories, it would not be surprising for people to believe in them. (E) appears to be a possibility since *debunk* has the right negative overtones and it explains why the persistent belief is surprising. The second word of (E), however, does not create a logical thought. People would not need a personal sense of *alienation* in a godless universe—in fact, that is what this sentence suggests they are trying to avoid.

30. **The correct answer is (B).** This sentence contains a thought-reverser and a thought-extender. The *in fact* in the second part of the sentence is the clue that tells you that the theory of the breakup of the continents is somehow changed. We are therefore looking for the opposite of "occurring in stages" or something close to it. The second blank requires an extension of that idea. (A) is not correct because although *refining* suggests a change in the theory, the second word, *blatantly*, does not reverse the idea of occurring in stages. (C) certainly suggests a strong reversal of the theory, but the second word is practically synonymous with "in stages." (D) appears plausible, since the idea of *forging* a theory might suggest something new, but the second word does not make a meaningful sentence. (E) is wrong because it does not reverse the theory, but rather supports it; and the idea that the breakup was *haphazard* does not reverse the idea of gradual. (B) is correct because the theory is *reshaped* and the word *simultaneously* reverses the idea that the continents broke up in stages.

Math Section

1.	C	7.	E	13.	B	19.	D	25.	E
2.	B	8.	C	14.	E	20.	C	26.	C
3.	B	9.	D	15.	A	21.	E	27.	B
4.	A	10.	E	16.	C	22.	E	28.	A
5.	D	11.	C	17.	C	23.	E		
6.	D	12.	B	18.	D	24.	A		

1. **The correct answer is (C).** "Of" in this case indicates multiplication. The product of 5 and 36 will be equal to the product of 36 and 5, and .05 and .36 will have the same number of decimal places; therefore, the two quantities must be equal. You do not need to actually do the multiplication in full.

2. **The correct answer is (B).** It is not possible to combine the two radicals of the right column. Although $\sqrt{5} \times \sqrt{10} = \sqrt{50}$, $\sqrt{5} + \sqrt{10} \neq \sqrt{15}$. The operation works only for multiplication. Since $\sqrt{15} < \sqrt{16}$, $\sqrt{15}$ must be less than 4. Since $\sqrt{5} > \sqrt{4}$, $\sqrt{5}$ must be greater than 2; and since $\sqrt{10}$ is greater than $\sqrt{9}$, $\sqrt{10}$ must be greater than 3. The two terms of the right column are slightly greater than 2 and 3, respectively, so their sum must be greater than 5. Column B is slightly greater than 5. Column A is less than 4.

3. **The correct answer is (B).** The (346 × 23) is only a distraction. It does not point to any difference between p and q. Since the first term of both equations is the same, we can assign it the constant value k. The given information can now be simplified:

$$k + p = 34{,}731$$

$$k + q = 35{,}124$$

Since 35,124 is greater than 34,731, q must be greater than p.

4. **The correct answer is (A).** Remember that the drawings in this subsection are not necessarily drawn to scale. Thus, you should not solve problems on the basis of a visual estimate of size or shape alone. However, manipulating the diagram in your mind—seeing what the possibilities are if some line is lengthened or shortened or some angle varied—can often help you to see the answer to a quantitative comparison problem without computation, or at least will reduce your difficulties.

In this case, exploring what it means to say that $x < y$ can start with seeing what it would mean if $x = y$. As the first diagram shows, $x = y$ means that ΔSRT has two equal legs, $\overline{ST}$ and $\overline{TR}$. T will be in the middle of $\overline{PQ}$, hence $\overline{PT} = \overline{QT}$. But as y gets larger, it will result in the line $\overline{RT}$ hitting the line $\overline{PQ}$ closer and closer to Q, thus making $\overline{TQ}$ less and $\overline{PT}$ greater. Therefore $\overline{PT}$ is always greater than $\overline{TQ}$ when $y > x$.

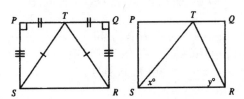

5. **The correct answer is (D).** Since x might be a fraction, it is not possible to determine which of the columns is greater. If x is $\frac{1}{2}$, then Column A is $\frac{1}{4}$ while Column B is 1, making Column B greater. But if x is 2, Column A is 4 and Column B is 4, making the two columns

equal. Finally, if x is greater than 2, say 3, then Column A is 9 and Column B is 6, making A greater.

6. **The correct answer is (D).** The minute hand will make one complete circle of the dial by 7:15. Then it will complete another half circle by 7:45. Since there are 360° in a circle, the arc traveled by the minute hand will be one full 360° plus half of another full 360° yielding 360° + 180° = 540°.

7. **The correct answer is (E).** One way of solving this problem would be to rename each of the fractions as a decimal. Or you could find a common denominator so that a direct comparison can be made. This is too time-consuming. Instead, anytime the GRE asks a question similar to this one, you can be confident that there is very likely some shortcut available. Here the shortcut is to recognize that every answer choice, except for (E), is either equal to or greater than $\frac{1}{2}$. $\frac{7}{8}$ and $\frac{8}{9}$ are clearly much greater than $\frac{1}{2}$. $\frac{7}{12}$ must be greater than $\frac{1}{2}$ since $\frac{6}{12}$ is equal to $\frac{1}{2}$. But $\frac{6}{17}$ is less than $\frac{1}{2}$. So (E) is the least of the fractions. Even if the shortcut had eliminated only two or three answers, your effort would have been worthwhile.

8. **The correct answer is (C).** Even though it is not absolutely necessary to draw a figure to solve this problem, anyone finding the solution elusive will likely profit from a "return to basics":

$$\frac{3x}{4}+1$$

$$\frac{3x}{4}+1 \quad \boxed{} \quad \frac{3x}{4}+1 \qquad P = 4\left(\frac{3x}{4}+1\right)$$

$$\frac{3x}{4}+1$$

Quickly sketching the figure may help you avoid the mistake of multiplying the side of the square by another side, giving the area, answer (D), not the perimeter. The perimeter will be $4s$, not s^2:

$$4\left(\frac{3x}{4}+1\right) = \frac{12x}{4}+4 = 3x+4$$

9. **The correct answer is (D).** Average speed is nothing more than miles traveled divided by the time taken: rate (speed) = $\frac{\text{distance}}{\text{time}}$. The elapsed time here is 4 hours and 48 minutes. 48 minutes is $\frac{4}{5}$ hours. Our formula then will be: $\frac{240 \text{ miles}}{4\frac{4}{5} \text{ miles}}$. We attack the problem by renaming the denominator as an improper fraction: $4\frac{4}{5} = \frac{24}{5}$, and then we multiply by the reciprocal of the divisor:

$$\frac{240}{4\frac{4}{5}} = \frac{240}{\frac{24}{5}} = \frac{5}{24} \times 240 = 50 \text{ mph}$$

Notice that setting up the problem in this way avoids a lot of needless arithmetic. This is characteristic of the GRE. Most problems do not require a lengthy calculation. Usually the numbers used in constructing the questions are selected in a way that will allow for dividing factors, factoring, or other shortcut devices. On the test, fractions are usually easier to work with than decimals.

10. **The correct answer is (E).** Multiplication is both associative and commutative. By associative, we mean that the grouping of the elements is not important—for example, $(5 \times 6) \times 7 = 5 \times (6 \times 7)$. By commutative we mean that the order of the elements is unimportant—for example, $5 \times 6 = 6 \times 5$. So (A), (B), (C), and (D) are all alternative forms for $m(nop)$, but (E) is not: $(mn)(mo)(mp) = m^3nop$.

11. **The correct answer is (C).** Since the numbers here are relatively manageable, the easiest solution to this problem is to do the indicated arithmetic operation:

$$\frac{4}{5} - \frac{3}{4} = \frac{16-15}{20} = \frac{1}{20}$$

You might also notice that $\frac{4}{5} = 80\%$ and $\frac{3}{4} = 75\%$, with their difference being 5%, which is $\frac{1}{20}$.

12. **The correct answer is (B).** We can see that the fraction $\frac{3}{13} < \frac{3}{12}$, thus $\frac{3}{13} < \frac{1}{4}$; but $\frac{13}{51} > \frac{13}{52}$, thus $\frac{13}{51} > \frac{1}{4}$. Therefore, $\frac{3}{13} < \frac{1}{4} < \frac{13}{51}$, answer (B). We look for reference points. For example, the 52 cards in a deck are in four suits of 13 cards each.

13. **The correct answer is (B).** This problem uses the term S_n to indicate that whatever n may be, the S_n value will be found by multiplying n by 3 and adding 2 to the result. One way of solving this problem would be to do the actual work indicated for 5, 4, 9, and 8, finding that S_n for 5 is $S_5 = 3(5) + 2 = 17$ and $S_4 = 14$, $S_9 = 29$, $S_8 = 26$, with $17 + 14$ being smaller than $29 + 26$. But there is really no reason to do the actual work. Since the issue is which column is bigger, we always pay attention to how things get bigger or smaller. S_n will get bigger as n gets bigger because it is just multiplying n by 3. Since Column A has two smaller numbers, the sum is smaller.

14. **The correct answer is (E).** This is an unusual problem, one that requires careful reading rather than some clever mathematical insight. The question asks us to compare the fractions in the form $\frac{p}{q}$ with the decimal $.PQ$. For example, we convert the fraction $\frac{1}{8}$ into the decimal $.18$ for purposes of comparison and ask how closely the second approximates the first. Since $\frac{1}{8}$ is $.125$, we see that the fit is not a very precise one. Similarly, with $\frac{2}{9}$, the corresponding decimal we are to compare is $.29$, but the actual

decimal equivalent of $\frac{2}{9}$ is $.2\bar{2}$. The equivalent for $\frac{3}{4}$ is $.34$, not even close to the actual decimal equivalent of $.75$. Similarly, for $\frac{4}{5}$, the artificially derived $.45$ is not very close to the actual decimal equivalent of $.80$; but for $\frac{8}{9}$ we use the decimal $.89$, and this is fairly close—the closest of all the fractions listed—to the actual decimal equivalent of $\frac{8}{9}$, which is $.88\bar{8}$. If you have difficulties in finding the decimals for fractions, try to relate the fractions to percentages, which are in hundredths, or to other, more common decimal-fraction equivalencies. For example, one third is probably known to you as approximately $.33$ or 33%. A ninth is one-third of a third; hence a ninth is approximately $\frac{33\%}{3} = 11\%$ or $.11$. Eight-ninths is thus $8(11\%) = 88\%$.

15. **The correct answer is (A).** If a problem seems a bit too abstract to handle using algebraic notation, a sometimes useful technique is to try to find a similar, more familiar situation. For example, virtually everyone could answer the following question: Books cost $5 each; how many books can be bought for $100? The calculation goes: $\frac{1 \text{ book}}{\$5} \times \$100 = 20$ books. So, too, here the number of books that can be purchased per d dollars must be multiplied by the number of dollars to be spent, m: $\frac{b}{d} \times m$, or $\frac{bm}{d}$. Pursuing this line of attack, it might be worthwhile to point out that substitution of real numbers in problems like this is often an effective way of solving the problem. Since the variables and the formulas are general—that is, they do not depend upon any given number of books or dollars—the correct answer choice must work for all possible values. Suppose we assume, therefore, 2 books (b) can be purchased for $5 ($d$), and that the amount to be

spent is $50(m)$. Most people can fall back onto common sense to calculate the number of books that can be purchased with $50: 20 books. But of the five formulas offered as answer choices, only (A) gives the number 20 when the values are substituted: For $b = 2$, $d = 5$, and $m = 50$,

(A) $\dfrac{(2)(50)}{5} = 20$

(B) $(2)(5)(50) = 500$

(C) $\dfrac{5}{(2)(50)} = \dfrac{1}{20}$

(D) $\dfrac{2+50}{5} = \dfrac{52}{5}$

(E) $\dfrac{2-50}{5} = \dfrac{-48}{5}$

Substitution will take longer than a direct algebraic approach, but it is much better than simply guessing, if you have the time and can't get the algebra to work right.

16. **The correct answer is (C).** The problem does not presuppose that you're familiar with the metric system. The cost of the meat in Column A is: 10 lbs. × $2.50/lb. = $25.00. The cost of the meat in Column B is: 5 kilos × $5.00/kilo = $25.00.

17. **The correct answer is (C).** The problem is most easily solved by dividing by 10 in each fraction:

$$\dfrac{1\cancel{0}}{10,00\cancel{0}} = \dfrac{1}{1,000} \qquad \dfrac{1,00\cancel{0}}{1,000,00\cancel{0}} = \dfrac{1}{1,000}$$

So Column A and Column B are both $\frac{1}{1,000}$ and equal.

18. **The correct answer is (D).** The information supplied in the two columns is sufficient only to allow us to compute the capacities or volumes of the boxes described. We have no information regarding the size of pears or the size of potatoes,

and we are not even told what part of each box's capacity is being used.

19. **The correct answer is (D).** Do not try to solve a quantitative comparison by visually estimating lengths of lines. In this case, there is not sufficient information to deduce that $PQRS$ is or is not a square—even though it is drawn as one. The following group of drawings will show that no conclusion regarding the relative lengths of $\overline{PQ}$ and $\overline{QR}$ is possible. $\overline{PQ}$ could be congruent to $\overline{QR}$, but it doesn't have to be.

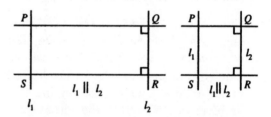

20. **The correct answer is (C).** The problem is most easily solved by grouping like terms and simplifying. We want the x-terms on one side, pure numbers on the other.

$$4x^2 + 2x^2 + 3x + 2x = 3x^2 + 3x^2 + 2x + 2x + 3$$

$$6x^2 + 5x = 6x^2 + 4x + 3$$

$$x = 3$$

Since $x = 3$, x^2 must be 9 and the two columns are equal.

21. **The correct answer is (E).** Looking at the two charts, we see that the upper one, representing the total passenger miles, shows a smooth increase, generally speaking, while the lower one shows large changes. Since the lower one is deaths per passenger-mile, the sharp changes in the rate must be from sharp changes in the number of deaths. (A) is inferable since the highest level reached by the line on the lower graph was approximately 1.3, in 1951. (B) is also inferable. The largest jump in the line on the lower graph, for a one-year period, occurred in the period 1954–1955. (C) is also inferable. The two low points on the line of the

lower graph occurred in 1954 and 1957; both were approximately .1. (D) is inferable: 10 to 30. But (E) is not inferable. Remember not to confuse absolute numbers and percent increase.

22. **The correct answer is (E).** The question stem asks about the *longest*, not the most severe or greatest increase. Although the *largest* increase ended in 1955, the *longest* increase lasted from 1956 until 1960. The word *finally* is also a clue.

23. **The correct answer is (E).** In 1955, total passenger-miles were 20 billion, and the fatality rate was 1.2 per 100 million miles. To compute the actual number of fatalities, we must multiply the total miles by the rate of fatalities (just as one multiplies 5 gallons by 25 miles per gallon to compute the total miles traveled as 125 miles): $20,000,000,000 \times \frac{1.2}{100,000,000} =$ (to make matters easier, we divide by 10) $20,0\cancel{0}0,0\cancel{0}0,0\cancel{0}0 \frac{1.2}{1\cancel{0}0,0\cancel{0}0,0\cancel{0}0} = 240$.

24. **The correct answer is (A).** Problem 23 shows how the number of fatalities can be found. But it would be counterproductive to spend a lot of time computing the actual number of deaths for each of the five years mentioned. Instead, a rough estimate will suffice. At first glance, it appears that the only reasonable possibilities are 1951, 1955, and 1960, since the fatality rate (lower graph) is at least approximately equal in those years. Now, it is absolutely critical to realize that, though the fatality rate in 1951 was higher than the fatality rate in 1960 (1.3 compared with 1.0), there were three times as many miles traveled in 1960 as in 1951. Similarly, though the fatality rate was higher in 1955 than it was in 1960 (1.2 compared with 1.0), there were 50% more miles traveled in 1960 than in 1955. This reasoning shows that the greatest numbers of fatalities occurred in 1960. Even though the fatal-

ity rate that year was not as high as those for 1955 and 1951, this was more than offset by the greater number of passenger-miles traveled. Of course, a longer method of attack is to actually do a rough calculation for each:

(A) 1960: $\frac{1}{100 \text{ million}} \times 30$ billion = 300

(B) 1957: $\frac{.1}{100 \text{ million}} \times 25$ billion = 25

(C) 1955: $\frac{1.2}{100 \text{ million}} \times 20$ billion = 240

(D) 1953: $\frac{.6}{100 \text{ million}} \times 15$ billion = 90

(E) 1951: $\frac{1.3}{100 \text{ million}} \times 10$ billion = 130

25. **The correct answer is (E).** This problem is at once both easy and difficult. It is easily solved if the key word, *passenger*, is not overlooked. The upper graph records passenger-miles traveled, but it tells us nothing about the number of different passengers who traveled those miles. The real-world likelihood that more passenger-miles *probably* means more passengers is only a probability and not a basis for a certain calculation.

26. **The correct answer is (C).** There is an easy and a more complicated way to handle this question. The more complex method is to begin with the formula for the area of a triangle: Area = $\frac{1}{2}$ (altitude)(base). Since angle *CBE* is congruent to angle *E*, $\overline{BC}$ must be congruent to $\overline{CE}$, and it is possible to reduce the altitude to the base (or vice versa). So, Area = $\frac{1}{2}$ (side)^2. The area is 8, so $8 = \frac{1}{2} s^2$, and $s = 4$. Of course, s is also the side of the square, so the area of the square *ABCD* is s^2, or 16. Now, an easier method of solving the problem is to recognize that $\overline{BC}$ and $\overline{CE}$ are congruent to the sides of the

square *ABCD*, so the area of triangle *BCE* is simply half that of the square. So the square must be double the triangle, or 16. A 45-45-90 right triangle is half of a square, and its hypotenuse is the diagonal of the square.

27. **The correct answer is (B).** Although some students will be able to solve this problem without the use of a diagram, for most drawing the floor plan of the closet is the logical starting point:

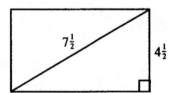

Now it becomes clear that the Pythagorean Theorem is the key to solving this problem. Once the dimensions are renamed as fractions, the problem is simplified further: the triangle is a 3-4-5 right triangle $\left(\frac{9}{12}, \frac{12}{2}, \frac{15}{2}\right)$. The two legs of the right triangle are simultaneously the width and length of the rectangle. So the area of the closet is: $\frac{9}{2} \times 6 = \frac{54}{2} = 27$.

28. **The correct answer is (A).** There are four times as many women as there are men, so if there are x men in the meeting, there are $4x$ women. This means that there is a total of $5x$ persons in the meeting ($x + 4x$). Since the men are x out of a total of $5x$, the men constitute one fifth, or 20%. Choices (D) and (E) can be avoided by noting that there are more women than men in the room and men thus come to less than 50%.

PRACTICE TEST 4 ANSWER SHEET

Verbal Section

1. Ⓐ Ⓑ Ⓒ Ⓓ Ⓔ 7. Ⓐ Ⓑ Ⓒ Ⓓ Ⓔ 13. Ⓐ Ⓑ Ⓒ Ⓓ Ⓔ 19. Ⓐ Ⓑ Ⓒ Ⓓ Ⓔ 25. Ⓐ Ⓑ Ⓒ Ⓓ Ⓔ
2. Ⓐ Ⓑ Ⓒ Ⓓ Ⓔ 8. Ⓐ Ⓑ Ⓒ Ⓓ Ⓔ 14. Ⓐ Ⓑ Ⓒ Ⓓ Ⓔ 20. Ⓐ Ⓑ Ⓒ Ⓓ Ⓔ 26. Ⓐ Ⓑ Ⓒ Ⓓ Ⓔ
3. Ⓐ Ⓑ Ⓒ Ⓓ Ⓔ 9. Ⓐ Ⓑ Ⓒ Ⓓ Ⓔ 15. Ⓐ Ⓑ Ⓒ Ⓓ Ⓔ 21. Ⓐ Ⓑ Ⓒ Ⓓ Ⓔ 27. Ⓐ Ⓑ Ⓒ Ⓓ Ⓔ
4. Ⓐ Ⓑ Ⓒ Ⓓ Ⓔ 10. Ⓐ Ⓑ Ⓒ Ⓓ Ⓔ 16. Ⓐ Ⓑ Ⓒ Ⓓ Ⓔ 22. Ⓐ Ⓑ Ⓒ Ⓓ Ⓔ 28. Ⓐ Ⓑ Ⓒ Ⓓ Ⓔ
5. Ⓐ Ⓑ Ⓒ Ⓓ Ⓔ 11. Ⓐ Ⓑ Ⓒ Ⓓ Ⓔ 17. Ⓐ Ⓑ Ⓒ Ⓓ Ⓔ 23. Ⓐ Ⓑ Ⓒ Ⓓ Ⓔ 29. Ⓐ Ⓑ Ⓒ Ⓓ Ⓔ
6. Ⓐ Ⓑ Ⓒ Ⓓ Ⓔ 12. Ⓐ Ⓑ Ⓒ Ⓓ Ⓔ 18. Ⓐ Ⓑ Ⓒ Ⓓ Ⓔ 24. Ⓐ Ⓑ Ⓒ Ⓓ Ⓔ 30. Ⓐ Ⓑ Ⓒ Ⓓ Ⓔ

Math Section

1. Ⓐ Ⓑ Ⓒ Ⓓ Ⓔ 7. Ⓐ Ⓑ Ⓒ Ⓓ Ⓔ 13. Ⓐ Ⓑ Ⓒ Ⓓ Ⓔ 19. Ⓐ Ⓑ Ⓒ Ⓓ Ⓔ 25. Ⓐ Ⓑ Ⓒ Ⓓ Ⓔ
2. Ⓐ Ⓑ Ⓒ Ⓓ Ⓔ 8. Ⓐ Ⓑ Ⓒ Ⓓ Ⓔ 14. Ⓐ Ⓑ Ⓒ Ⓓ Ⓔ 20. Ⓐ Ⓑ Ⓒ Ⓓ Ⓔ 26. Ⓐ Ⓑ Ⓒ Ⓓ Ⓔ
3. Ⓐ Ⓑ Ⓒ Ⓓ Ⓔ 9. Ⓐ Ⓑ Ⓒ Ⓓ Ⓔ 15. Ⓐ Ⓑ Ⓒ Ⓓ Ⓔ 21. Ⓐ Ⓑ Ⓒ Ⓓ Ⓔ 27. Ⓐ Ⓑ Ⓒ Ⓓ Ⓔ
4. Ⓐ Ⓑ Ⓒ Ⓓ Ⓔ 10. Ⓐ Ⓑ Ⓒ Ⓓ Ⓔ 16. Ⓐ Ⓑ Ⓒ Ⓓ Ⓔ 22. Ⓐ Ⓑ Ⓒ Ⓓ Ⓔ 28. Ⓐ Ⓑ Ⓒ Ⓓ Ⓔ
5. Ⓐ Ⓑ Ⓒ Ⓓ Ⓔ 11. Ⓐ Ⓑ Ⓒ Ⓓ Ⓔ 17. Ⓐ Ⓑ Ⓒ Ⓓ Ⓔ 23. Ⓐ Ⓑ Ⓒ Ⓓ Ⓔ
6. Ⓐ Ⓑ Ⓒ Ⓓ Ⓔ 12. Ⓐ Ⓑ Ⓒ Ⓓ Ⓔ 18. Ⓐ Ⓑ Ⓒ Ⓓ Ⓔ 24. Ⓐ Ⓑ Ⓒ Ⓓ Ⓔ

Analytical Writing—Issue Topic

_____

_____

_____

_____

_____

_____

_____

_____

_____

_____

_____

_____

_____

_____

_____

_____

_____

_____

_____

_____

_____

_____

_____

_____

Analytical Writing—Argument Topic

_____

_____

_____

_____

_____

_____

_____

_____

_____

_____

_____

_____

_____

_____

_____

_____

_____

_____

_____

_____

_____

_____

_____

_____

_____

Practice Test 4

ANALYTICAL WRITING

Issue Topic • 45 Minutes

Present Your Perspective on an Issue

In this part, two topics appear as brief quotations. Each states, either explicitly or implicitly, an issue of broad interest. You are to choose one of the two topics. You will then use the remainder of the 45 minutes to write an essay in which you take a position on the issue.

You may agree with the quotation, disagree with it, or challenge the statement in any way, so long as the ideas that you present are clearly relevant to the topic. You should provide reasons and examples to support your position. In doing so, you may want to draw on your reading of various sources, your personal experience and observations, or your academic studies.

It is a good idea to begin by reading the topic carefully. Then you should decide what position you want to take, after which you will probably want to outline your answer before you begin to write. Your essay will be graded on how well you:

- Assess the implications of the issue, including various complexities implicit in the topic
- Organize, develop, and express your thoughts on the issue
- Provide supporting reasons and examples
- Demonstrate your mastery of the elements of standard written English

You should leave yourself sufficient time to read what you have written and to make any revisions to your essay that you think are needed.

For this exercise, you may choose to use an editing program on a computer (word processor) or write your response by hand using the space provided.

Issue Topics

Choose <u>one</u> of the following two topics to write on.

> "Football* is the quintessential American sport. Its rough and tumble style and aggressive play on a large field, reminiscent of the pioneer era of America's history, represent better than any other sport the nation's unique character."
>
> *American football as opposed to soccer

> "Aristotle wrote that it is not possible to say that a person is happy until that person is dead because a person, no matter how well-off, could always suffer a reversal of fortune that would result in profound unhappiness."

Argument Topic • 30 Minutes

Analyze an Argument

In this part, you will be given an argument and have 30 minutes within which to write a critique of the argument. Your essay must address the argument given.

You are to <u>analyze</u> the reasoning of the argument. You should consider whether any of its assumptions are questionable and whether the evidence presented supports the conclusion. You might also discuss what changes in the line of reasoning or additional evidence would strengthen or weaken the conclusion.

Importantly, you are **NOT** being asked to state your own views on the underlying subject.

It is a good idea to begin by reading the argument carefully. Then you should evaluate the argument and consider what response you want to make, after which you will probably want to outline your answer before you begin to write.

Your essay response will be graded on how well you:

- Identify and analyze the important elements of the argument
- Organize, develop, and state your analysis
- Support your analysis with relevant reasons and examples
- Demonstrate your mastery of the elements of standard written English

You should leave yourself sufficient time to read what you have written and to make any revisions to your essay that you think are needed.

Timing for this part begins when you click on the "Dismiss the Directions" icon.

Argument Topic

"There are several unique pieces of sculpture in the Old Quad. Because they stand out-of-doors, it is not possible to secure them at night, and they could be targets for thieves or vandals. A comprehensive security system in the area, including motion detectors and surveillance cameras, would guarantee that these works of art will come to no harm."

VERBAL SECTION

30 Questions • 30 Minutes

Directions: Each of the following questions consists of a word printed in capital letters, followed by five (5) words or phrases. Choose the word or phrase that is most nearly opposite in meaning to the word in capital letters. Be sure to consider all the choices before deciding which one is best.

1. MUTINOUS :
   (A) routine
   (B) clever
   (C) obedient
   (D) helpful
   (E) pitiful

2. TEMERITY :
   (A) fortitude
   (B) capacity
   (C) interest
   (D) caution
   (E) relevance

3. TRACTABLE :
   (A) incoherent
   (B) advisable
   (C) simplistic
   (D) influential
   (E) uncooperative

4. INSOUCIANT :
   (A) amiable
   (B) fretful
   (C) swift
   (D) inferior
   (E) formidable

Directions: Each of the questions below contains one or more blank spaces, each blank indicating that something has been omitted. Each sentence is followed by five (5) words or sets of words. Read and determine the general sense of each sentence. Then choose the word, or set of words that, when inserted in the sentence, best fits the meaning of the sentence.

5. Because he was —— and the life of the party, his friends thought that he was happy; but his wife was —— and shy and was thought to be unhappy.

   (A) melancholy . . sympathetic
   (B) philanthrophic . . conciliatory
   (C) vitriolic . . sophomoric
   (D) garrulous . . taciturn
   (E) inimical . . gregarious

6. His offhand, rather —— remarks —— a character that was really rather serious and not at all superficial.

   (A) flippant . . masked
   (B) pernicious . . betrayed
   (C) bellicose . . belied
   (D) controversial . . revealed
   (E) shallow . . enlivened

7. Although the faculty did not always agree with the chairperson of the department, they —— her ideas, mostly in —— her seniority and out of respect for her previous achievements.

   (A) scoffed at . . fear of
   (B) harbored . . defense of
   (C) implemented . . deference to
   (D) marveled at . . lieu of
   (E) ignored . . honor of

Directions: The passage below is followed by questions based on its content. Choose the best answer to each question.

In the art of the Middle Ages, we never encounter the personality of the artist as an individual; rather, it is diffused through the artistic genius of centuries
(5) embodied in the rules of religious art. Art of the Middle Ages is a sacred script, the symbols and meanings of which were well settled. The circular halo placed vertically behind the head signifies saint-
(10) hood, while the halo impressed with a cross signifies divinity. By bare feet, we recognize God, the angels, Jesus Christ, and the apostles, but for an artist to have depicted the Virgin Mary with bare feet
(15) would have been tantamount to heresy. Several concentric, wavy lines represent the sky, while parallel lines represent water or the sea. A tree, which is to say a single stalk with two or three
(20) stylized leaves, informs us that the scene is laid on earth. A tower with a window indicates a village; and should an angel be watching from the battlements, that city is thereby identified as Jerusalem.
(25) Saint Peter is always depicted with curly hair, a short beard and a tonsure, while Saint Paul always has a bald head and a long beard.

Through this system, even the most
(30) mediocre talent is elevated by the genius of the centuries. The artists of the early Renaissance break with tradition at their own peril. When they are not outstanding, they are scarcely able to avoid insig-
(35) nificance and banality in their religious works; and even when they are great, they are no more than the equals of the old masters who passively followed the sacred rules.

8. The primary purpose of the passage is to
(A) theorize about the immediate influences on art of the Middle Ages
(B) explain why artists of the Middle Ages followed the rules of a sacred script
(C) discuss some of the important features of art of the Middle Ages
(D) contrast the art of the Middle Ages with that of the Renaissance
(E) explain why the Middle Ages had a passion for religious art

9. All of the following are mentioned in the passage as elements of the sacred script EXCEPT
(A) abstract symbols such as lines to represent physical features
(B) symbols such as halos and crosses
(C) clothing used to characterize individuals
(D) symmetrical juxtaposition of figures
(E) use of figures to identify locations

10. The passage would most likely be found in a
(A) sociological analysis of the Middle Ages
(B) treatise on the influence of the Church in the Middle Ages
(C) scholarly analysis of art in the Middle Ages
(D) preface to a biography of a Renaissance artist
(E) pamphlet discussing religious beliefs

11. By the phrase *diffused through the artistic genius of centuries* (lines 3–4) the author most likely means

    (A) the individual artists of the Middle Ages did not have serious talent

    (B) great works of art from the Middle Ages have survived until now

    (C) an artist who faithfully followed the rules of religious art was not recognized during his lifetime

    (D) the rules of religious art, developed over time, left little freedom for the artist

    (E) religious art has greater value than the secular art of the Renaissance

Directions: In each of the following questions, you are given a related pair of words or phrases in capital letters. Each capitalized pair is followed by five (5) pairs of words or phrases. Choose the pair that best expresses a relationship similar to that expressed by the original pair.

12. WEB : ENTANGLE ::

    (A) spider : spin

    (B) trap : ensnare

    (C) treason : betray

    (D) ransom : kidnap

    (E) grid : delineate

13. LETHARGY : ENERGY ::

    (A) appetite : hunger

    (B) redemption : sacrament

    (C) sorrow : pity

    (D) merit : remuneration

    (E) apathy : interest

14. THWART : ACHIEVE ::

    (A) retain : submit

    (B) couch : conceal

    (C) silence : speak

    (D) pretend : inherit

    (E) permeate : infiltrate

15. APOCRYPHAL : GENUINE ::

    (A) spurious : authentic

    (B) labored : relieved

    (C) fragmented : riddled

    (D) enigmatic : rambunctious

    (E) credulous : flagrant

16. BALEFUL : EVIL ::

    (A) fulsome : refinement

    (B) disjointed : compatibility

    (C) mandatory : requirement

    (D) literacy : obstreperousness

    (E) dogmatic : hostility

Directions: The passage below is followed by questions based on its content. Choose the best answer to each question.

Our current system of unemployment compensation has increased nearly all sources of adult unemployment: seasonal and cyclical variations in the demand for
(5) labor, weak labor force attachment, and unnecessarily long durations of unemployment. First, for those who are already unemployed, the system greatly reduces the cost of extending the period of unem-
(10) ployment. Second, for all types of unsteady work—seasonal, cyclical, and casual—it raises the net wage to the employee, relative to the cost of the employer.

As for the first, consider a worker who
(15) earns $500 per month or $6,000 per year if she experiences no unemployment. If she is unemployed for one month, she loses $500 in gross earnings but only $116 in net income. How does this occur?
(20) A reduction of $500 in annual earnings reduces her federal, payroll, and state tax liability by $134. Unemployment compensation consists of 50 percent of her wage, or $250. Her net income therefore
(25) falls from $366 if she is employed, to $250 paid as unemployment compensation. Moreover, part of the higher income from employment is offset by the cost of transportation to work and other expenses
(30) associated with employment; and in some industries, the cost of unemployment is reduced further or even made negative by the supplementary unemployment benefits paid by employers under collec-
(35) tive bargaining agreements. The overall effect is to increase the duration of a typical spell of unemployment and to increase the frequency with which individuals lose jobs and become unemployed.
(40) The more general effect of unemployment compensation is to increase the seasonal and cyclical fluctuations in the demand for labor and the relative number of short-lived casual jobs. A worker who
(45) accepts such work knows she will be laid off when the season ends. If there were no unemployment compensation, workers could be induced to accept such unstable

jobs only if the wage rate were sufficiently
(50) higher in those jobs than in the more stable alternative. The higher cost of labor, then, would induce employers to reduce the instability of employment by smoothing production through increased
(55) variation in inventories and delivery lags, by additional development of off-season work and by the introduction of new production techniques, e.g., new methods of outdoor work in bad weather.
(60) Employers contribute to the state unemployment compensation fund on the basis of the unemployment experience of their own previous employees. Within limits, the more benefits that those former
(65) employees draw, the higher is the employer's tax rate. The theory of experience rating is clear. If an employer paid the full cost of the unemployment benefits that his former employees received,
(70) unemployment compensation would provide no incentive to an excess use of unstable employment. In practice, however, experience rating is limited by a maximum rate of employer contribution.
(75) For any firm which pays the maximum rate, there is no cost for additional unemployment and no gain from a small reduction in unemployment.

The challenge at this time is to restruc-
(80) ture the unemployment system in a way that strengthens its good features while reducing the harmful disincentive effects. Some gains can be achieved by removing the ceiling on the employer's rate of con-
(85) tribution and by lowering the minimum rate to zero. Employers would then pay the full price of unemployment insurance benefits and this would encourage employers to stabilize employment and pro-
(90) duction. Further improvement could be achieved if unemployment insurance benefits were taxed in the same way as other earnings. This would eliminate the anomalous situations in which a worker's
(95) net income is actually reduced when he returns to work.

17. The author's primary concern is to

    (A) defend the system of unemployment compensation against criticism

    (B) advocate expanding the benefits and scope of coverage of unemployment compensation

    (C) point to weaknesses inherent in government programs that subsidize individuals

    (D) suggest reforms to eliminate inefficiencies in unemployment compensation

    (E) propose methods of increasing the effectiveness of government programs to reduce unemployment

18. The author cites the example of a worker earning $500 per month in order to

    (A) show the disincentive created by unemployment compensation for that worker to return to work

    (B) demonstrate that employers do not bear the full cost of worker compensation

    (C) prove that unemployed workers would not be able to survive without unemployment compensation

    (D) explain why employers prefer to hire seasonal workers instead of permanent workers for short-term jobs

    (E) condemn workers who prefer to live on unemployment compensation to taking a job

19. The author recommends which of the following changes be made to the unemployment compensation system?

    (A) Eliminating taxes on benefits paid to workers

    (B) Shortening the time during which a worker can draw benefits

    (C) Removing any cap on the maximum rate of employer contribution

    (D) Providing workers with job retraining as a condition of benefits

    (E) Requiring unemployed workers to accept public works positions

20. The author mentions all of the following as ways by which employers might reduce seasonal and cyclical unemployment EXCEPT

    (A) developing new techniques of production not affected by weather

    (B) slowing delivery schedules to provide work during slow seasons

    (C) adopting a system of supplementary benefits for workers laid off in slow periods

    (D) manipulating inventory supplies to require year-round rather than short-term employment

    (E) finding new jobs to be done by workers during the off-season

21. With which of the following statements about experience rating would the author most likely agree?

    (A) Experience rating is theoretically sound but its effectiveness in practice is undermined by maximum contribution ceilings.

    (B) Experience rating is an inefficient method of computing employer contribution because an employer has no control over the length of an employee's unemployment.

    (C) Experience rating is theoretically invalid and should be replaced by a system in which the employee contributes the full amount of benefits he will later receive.

    (D) Experience rating is basically fair, but its performance could be improved by requiring large firms to pay more than small firms.

    (E) Experience rating requires an employer to pay a contribution that is completely unrelated to the amount his employees draw in unemployment compensation benefits.

Directions: In each of the following questions, you are given a related pair of words or phrases in capital letters. Each capitalized pair is followed by five (5) pairs of words or phrases. Choose the pair that best expresses a relationship similar to that expressed by the original pair.

22. WATERFALL : CASCADE ::
    (A) snow : freeze
    (B) missile : launch
    (C) tree : exfoliate
    (D) wave : undulate
    (E) monarch : reign

23. INFLATE : MAGNITUDE ::
    (A) measure : weight
    (B) extend : duration
    (C) magnify : coin
    (D) limit : speed
    (E) legislate : crime

24. MOCK : DERISION ::
    (A) despise : contempt
    (B) reject : account
    (C) repair : corruption
    (D) inspire : muse
    (E) observe : refinement

Directions: Each of the questions below contains one or more blank spaces, each blank indicating that something has been omitted. Each sentence is followed by five (5) words or sets of words. Read and determine the general sense of each sentence. Then choose the word, or set of words that, when inserted in the sentence, best fits the meaning of the sentence.

25. Psychologists agree that human beings have a strong need to —— their time; having too much idle time can be as stressful as having none at all.
    (A) threaten
    (B) annihilate
    (C) structure
    (D) punctuate
    (E) remand

26. While scientists continue to make advances in the field of ——, some members of the clergy continue to oppose the research, arguing that it is —— for human beings to tamper with life.
    (A) psychology . . imperative
    (B) astronomy . . fallacious
    (C) genetics . . immoral
    (D) geology . . erroneous
    (E) botany . . unethical

27. Although for centuries literature was considered something that would instruct as well as entertain, the modern reader has little patience with —— works and seeks only to be ——.
    (A) epic . . demoralized
    (B) didactic . . distracted
    (C) bawdy . . absorbed
    (D) superficial . . enlightened
    (E) ambiguous . . misled

> **Directions:** Each of the following questions consists of a word printed in capital letters, followed by five (5) words or phrases. Choose the word or phrase that is most nearly opposite in meaning to the word in capital letters. Be sure to consider all the choices before deciding which one is best.

28. DIFFIDENCE :
    (A) strong attraction
    (B) violent disagreement
    (C) haughty arrogance
    (D) grievous error
    (E) temporary suspension

29. SEDULOUS :
    (A) tangential
    (B) rampant
    (C) esoteric
    (D) morose
    (E) indolent

30. OBDURATE :
    (A) ambiguous
    (B) demoralized
    (C) vitriolic
    (D) malleable
    (E) inimitable

MATH SECTION

28 Questions • 45 Minutes

Numbers: All numbers used are real numbers.

Figures: The position of points, angles, regions, and so forth are in the order shown. Figures are assumed to lie in a plane unless otherwise indicated. Figures are drawn as accurately as possible for problem-solving questions, unless otherwise indicated. Figures are NOT drawn to scale for quantitative analysis problem, unless otherwise indicated. You should solve the problems by using your knowledge of mathematics and not by estimating sizes by sight or measurement.

Lines: Assume that lines shown as straight are indeed straight.

Directions: For each of the following questions, select the best of the answer choices. For quantitative comparison questions, two quantities are given, one in Column A and one in Column B. Compare the two quantities and choose

(A) if the quantity in Column A is greater
(B) if the quantity in Column B is greater
(C) if the two quantities are equal
(D) if the relationship cannot be determined from the information given

Information applying to both columns is centered between the columns and above the quantities in columns A and B. Symbols that appear in both columns represent the same idea or quantity in each column.

	Column A	Column B
1.	The number of hours in 7 days	The number of days in 24 weeks
2.	35% of 60	60% of 35

PLAYER	AGE
Juanita	35
Brooke	28
Glenda	40
Marcia	22
Dwight	24
Tom	30

	Column A	Column B
3.	Tom's age	Average (arithmetic mean) age of the six players

$$4 < m < 6$$
$$5 < n < 7$$

	Column A	Column B
4.	m	n

A square region, P, and a rectangular region, Q, both have areas of 64.

	Column A	Column B
5.	Length of a side of P	Length of Q if its width is 4

Directions: For each of the following questions, select the best of the answer choices given.

6. If $x = 3$ and $y = 2$, then $2x + 3y =$

(A) 5
(B) 10
(C) 12
(D) 14
(E) 15

7. If the profit on an item is $4 and the sum of the cost and the profit is $20, what is the cost of the item?

(A) $24
(B) $20
(C) $16
(D) $12
(E) It cannot be determined from the information given.

8. In 1960, the number of students enrolled at a college was 500. In 1980, the number of students enrolled at the college was $2\frac{1}{2}$ times as great as that in 1960. What was the number of students enrolled at the college in 1980?

(A) 1,750
(B) 1,250
(C) 1,000
(D) 500
(E) 250

Directions: For each of the following questions, select the best of the answer choices. For quantitative comparison questions, two quantities are given, one in Column A and one in Column B. Compare the two quantities and choose

(A) if the quantity in Column A is greater
(B) if the quantity in Column B is greater
(C) if the two quantities are equal
(D) if the relationship cannot be determined from the information given

Information applying to both columns is centered between the columns and above the quantities in columns A and B. Symbols that appear in both columns represent the same idea or quantity in each column.

	Column A	Column B
		$x > 0$	
9.	$3x^3$	$(3x)^3$

$x \cdot y = 1$
$x \neq 0, y \neq 0$

10.	x	y

11.	The number of primes of which 11 is an integer multiple	The number of primes of which 13 is an integer multiple

x, y, and z are consecutive positive integers, not necessarily in that order, and x and z are odd

12.	xy	yz

Directions: For each of the following questions, select the best of the answer choices given.

13. If n is an integer between 0 and 100, then any of the following could be $3n + 3$ EXCEPT

(A) 300

(B) 297

(C) 208

(D) 63

(E) 6

14. A figure that can be folded over along a straight line so that the result is two equal halves which are then lying on top of one another with no overlap is said to have a line of symmetry. Which of the following figures has only one line of symmetry?

(A) Square

(B) Circle

(C) Equilateral triangle

(D) Isosceles triangle

(E) Rectangle

Directions: For each of the following questions, select the best of the answer choices. For quantitative comparison questions, two quantities are given, one in Column A and one in Column B. Compare the two quantities and choose

(A) if the quantity in Column A is greater

(B) if the quantity in Column B is greater

(C) if the two quantities are equal

(D) if the relationship cannot be determined from the information given

Information applying to both columns is centered between the columns and above the quantities in columns A and B. Symbols that appear in both columns represent the same idea or quantity in each column.

<u>**Column A**</u>   <u>**Column B**</u>

$\overline{AD}$ is a transmitter tower held up by support wires $\overline{AB}$ and $\overline{AC}$.

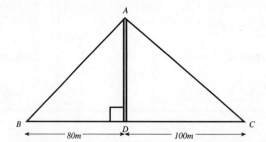

15.   Length of support wire $\overline{AB}$ Length of support wire $\overline{AC}$

16.   2,468 $8 + 6 \cdot 10 + 4 \cdot 10^2 + 2 \cdot 10^3$

$$a^2 = b$$
$$a > 0$$

17. $\dfrac{2a}{b}$ $a \cdot a$

Directions: For each of the following questions, select the best of the answer choices given.

18. A laborer is paid $8 per hour for an 8-hour day and $1\frac{1}{2}$ times that rate for each hour in excess of 8 hours in a single day. If the laborer received $80 for a single day's work, how long did he work on that day?

    (A) 6 hr. 40 min.
    (B) 9 hr. 20 min.
    (C) 9 hr. 30 min.
    (D) 9 hr. 40 min.
    (E) 10 hr.

Directions: For each of the following questions, select the best of the answer choices. For quantitative comparison questions, two quantities are given, one in Column A and one in Column B. Compare the two quantities and choose

(A) if the quantity in Column A is greater
(B) if the quantity in Column B is greater
(C) if the two quantities are equal
(D) if the relationship cannot be determined from the information given

Information applying to both columns is centered between the columns and above the quantities in columns A and B. Symbols that appear in both columns represent the same idea or quantity in each column.

Column A	Column B

19. $\qquad$ x $\qquad$ 10

A family-size box of cereal contain 10 ounces more and costs 80¢ more than the regular size box of cereal.

20. Cost per ounce of the cereal in the family-size box $\qquad$ 8¢

21. The number of different duos that can be formed from a group of 5 people $\qquad$ The number of different trios that can be formed from a group of 5 people

> **Directions:** For each of the following questions, select the best of the answer choices given.

QUESTIONS 22–25 ARE BASED ON THE FOLLOWING GRAPHS.

INVESTMENT PORTFOLIO

Total Investment Profile
$1,080,192 = 100\%$

17.9%
Blue-chip
Stocks

24.9%
Mutual
Funds

48.3%
Government Bonds
and Securities

8.9%

High-risk Stocks

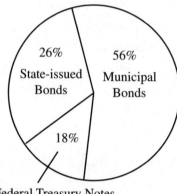

Government Bonds and Securities

26%
State-issued
Bonds

56%
Municipal
Bonds

18%

Federal Treasury Notes

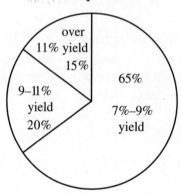

Municipal Bonds

over
11% yield
15%

9–11%
yield
20%

65%

7%–9%
yield

22. According to the graphs, approximately how much money belonging to the investment portfolio was invested in high-risk stocks?

(A) $95,000

(B) $89,000

(C) $50,000

(D) $42,000

(E) $36,000

23. Approximately how much money belonging to the investment portfolio was invested in state-issued bonds?

(A) $260,000

(B) $125,000

(C) $34,000

(D) $26,000

(E) $500

24. Which of the following was the greatest?

    (A) The amount of money invested in municipal bonds that yielded between 7% and 9%

    (B) The amount of money invested in municipal bonds that yielded over 9%

    (C) The amount of money invested in federal treasury notes

    (D) The amount of money invested in state-issued bonds

    (E) The amount of money invested in high-risk stocks

25. Which of the following earned the least amount of money for the investment portfolio?

    (A) Municipal bonds

    (B) State-issued bonds

    (C) Government bonds and securities

    (D) Mutual funds

    (E) It cannot be determined from the information given.

26. A vertex of square *MNOP* is located at the center of circle *O*. If arc *NP* is 4 units long, then the perimeter of the square *MNOP* is

    (A) $\dfrac{32}{\pi}$

    (B) 32π

    (C) 64

    (D) 64π

    (E) It cannot be determined from the information given.

27. How many minutes will it take to completely fill a water tank with a capacity of 3750 cubic feet if the water is being pumped into the tank at the rate of 800 cubic feet per minute and is being drained out of the tank at the rate of 300 cubic feet per minute?

    (A) 3 min. 36 sec.

    (B) 6 minutes

    (C) 7 min. 30 sec.

    (D) 8 minutes

    (E) 1875 minutes

28. Paul is standing 180 yards due north of point *P*. Franny is standing 240 yards due west of point *P*. What is the shortest distance between Franny and Paul?

    (A) 60 yards

    (B) 300 yards

    (C) 420 yards

    (D) 900 yards

    (E) 9000 yards

ANSWER KEY AND EXPLANATIONS

Analytical Writing

Issue Topics

Topic 1

As you read the following sample response, try to judge for yourself how well it meets the criteria that will be applied by graders:

Category	Below Avg.	Avg.	Above Avg.
Analysis of the Topic			
Organization and Development			
Use of Reasons and Examples			
Use of Standard Written English			
OVERALL SCORE*			

*Below Average = 1–2; Average = 3–4; Above Average = 5–6

SAMPLE RESPONSE AND COMMENTARY FOR ISSUE TOPIC 1

Note: The sample answers contain spelling and grammatical errors. This is done to simulate a first draft written under time pressure.

The interesting question raised by the topic is not so much whether football is the quintessential American sport but whether it can truly be said that a sport, any sport, embodies the quintessence of a national character. The comedian George Carlin, in one of his routines, sheds some interesting light on differences between football and that other contender for the quintessential American sport: baseball. Here are some of his observations mixed in with original ones.

Baseball originated as a pastoral game and is even today played on a diamond, while football is a battle that takes place on a gridiron. When technology (often thought of in contrast to nature) is discussed in the context of baseball, it is usually to bemoan how advances in technology have changed the game for the worse, e.g., the ball more lively this year resulting in too many home runs. For football, the question is how to apply the latest technological innovation to the game, including body building medications and painkillers. Football players wear helmets, they blitz, the offense throws the long bomb in an effort to drive into the endzone, and participants get penalized for behavior such as unnecessary roughness. Baseball players wear caps, batters sacrifice to advance other players, pitchers come on in relief of one another, players get charged with an error for making a mistake, and the object of the game (for the offense) is simply to get to home safe. Football is played in the most severe weather, but baseball games get called on account of rain. Football has cheerleaders who exhort the fans to scream for blood; after a few innings of baseball everyone stretches and sings a song.

It is difficult to imagine a more striking contrast. Yet which game better represents the American character? To be sure, the American character is often associated with cowboys and cavalry and an image of a rough-and-tumble western frontier, but it is important to remember that most of the nineteenth century settlers were immigrants who came to America and moved westward looking for a peaceful place to settle, farm or start a business, and raise a family. Which better represents the true spirit of America, the warrior-hunter or the farmer-gatherer? And if there are indeed character differences rooted in gender differences (as many would argue), which set of traits better embodies the national character, the fighter or the keeper of the hearth?

COMMENTARY

This is both an unusual and an excellent essay. It is unusual in that the author chose to cite examples suggested by a comedian and use those to develop an extended contrast between football and baseball. This is indeed one of the features that makes the essay interesting and highly readable (and therefore contributes to its appeal), but it would be wrong to say that the essay is excellent simply because the writer happened across a clever literary device. Instead, the essay also shares important characteristics with other excellent essays. The language is colorful and robust—and not just in the second paragraph. In the third paragraph, the author uses *rough-and-tumble, the warrior-hunter or the farmer-gatherer,* and *the fighter or the keeper of the hearth.* In addition, the essay is well organized. For example, in the second paragraph, the author uses the technique of order to compare and contrast the various features of football and baseball. This organizational principle extends to the third paragraph where the first element of each of the contrasting pairs just mentioned echoes football and the second element baseball. Finally, the humor, the language, and the organization are all used in the service of making a sophisticated point: both games represent aspects of the national character, so it is not possible to say which is quintessential. It would be hard to imagine that this essay would not receive a 6 from many readers, though a few might give it only a 5.

Topic 2

As you read the following sample response, try to judge for yourself how well it meets the criteria that will be applied by graders:

Category	Below Avg.	Avg.	Above Avg.
Analysis of the Topic			
Organization and Development			
Use of Reasons and Examples			
Use of Standard Written English			
OVERALL SCORE*			

*Below Average = 1–2; Average = 3–4; Above Average = 5–6

SAMPLE RESPONSE AND COMMENTARY FOR ISSUE TOPIC 2

Note: The sample answers contain spelling and grammatical errors. This is done to simulate a first draft written under time pressure.

For Aristotle an important question is whether or not a person can ever be truly happy. According to Aristotle, a person might seem to be happy but not really be so because he/she would not know what was coming in the future. For example, a person could be very rich and have a good family but then go bankrupt lose it all.

It follows also that a person might be unhappy but then later become happy, for example, hitting the lottery or inheriting a million dollars. But of course that would not be a permanent state.

On balance, then, it seems that we should wait. If a person is happy when he/she dies, then it is safe to say that person was truly happy, otherwise not.

COMMENTARY

This essay is fundamentally deficient, and not just because there are some weaknesses in the grammar and other mechanics. It is fundamentally flawed because it doesn't engage the topic. In the first place, the writer seems to misunderstand Aristotle's point, because it is not that the person cannot know the future but that happiness is a state of mind that may be transitory. In addition, the writer seems to want to use a "compare and contrast" organization scheme but winds up simply repeating what is already stated in the topic: a person might be happy at one point but unhappy at another. Finally, the examples are hardly examples at all because they are never developed. It is hard to imagine that this essay would be given anything better than a 2, and it is not unlikely that it would get a 1.

Argument Topic

As you read the following sample response, try to judge for yourself how well it meets the criteria that will be applied by graders:

Category	Below Avg.	Avg.	Above Avg.
Analysis of the Topic			
Organization and Development			
Use of Reasons and Examples			
Use of Standard Written English			
OVERALL SCORE*			

*Below Average = 1–2; Average = 3–4; Above Average = 5–6

SAMPLE RESPONSE AND COMMENTARY FOR THE ARGUMENT TOPIC

Note: The sample answers contain spelling and grammatical errors. This is done to simulate a first draft written under time pressure.

In assessing the desirability of implementing the proposed security system, it would be helpful to have answers to four questions. First, is there a serious danger that the sculptures will damaged or stolen? Second, can that danger be minimized by measures short of installing the security system? Third, what would be the cost of the security system? And fourth, would the installation of the security have any unwanted consequences?

First, the argument makes no attempt to quantify the extent of the risk, and it would be wrong to assume that there is a significant risk just from the fact that a university officials seems to have identified a potential problem. In assessing the risk, it would be helpful to know how well lit and traveled the area is now, and whether or not it is patrolled by campus security. It would also be useful to know whether these outdoor sculptures be easily moved and whether they have been the targets of vandalism in the past.

Second, even assuming that there is a significant risk, the security head ought to determine whether any less ambitious alternatives are on hand. Perhaps simply increasing the frequency of foot patrols through the Old Quad would provide all the deterrence the college needs, or providing for additional security only during times of highest risk as during vacations when fewer students are on campus.

Third, the cost of the security system ought to be considered and weighed against the potential monetary loss. After all, if the sculptures are not particularly valuable, say a total of $1,000, then it is probably not advisable to spend $50,000 on an elaborate security system. It might be cheaper to insure their replacement value or to set aside a reserve for repainting if they are vandalized.

Fourth, and finally, it is important to remember that this is a college campus. While security is an important issue, so too is spontenaity and freedom. It is hard to asses (without more details) what effect "surveillance cameras" might have, it is not inconceivable that students and faculty would find them intrusive. There is certainly something ominous about walking around a college knowing that you are under the intense scrutiny of the campus security system.

Answers to these and perhaps other questions would be needed before accepted the conclusion of the argument. Only if, on balance, the advantages of the system would outweigh all of the costs is it a good idea.

COMMENTARY

This essay is perhaps a bit dry (maybe owing to the topic), but it is certainly well organized, easy to follow, and written in understandable prose in substantially correct English. It is, in short, utilitarian and serviceable. It should receive an above-average grade, say a 5, though maybe a half point more or less.

Verbal Section

1.	C	7.	C	13.	E	19.	C	25.	C
2.	D	8.	C	14.	C	20.	C	26.	C
3.	E	9.	D	15.	A	21.	A	27.	B
4.	B	10.	C	16.	C	22.	D	28.	C
5.	D	11.	D	17.	D	23.	B	29.	E
6.	A	12.	B	18.	A	24.	A	30.	D

1. **The correct answer is (C).** MUTINOUS is "rebellious" or "insubordinate," so *obedient* is a straightforward opposite.

2. **The correct answer is (D).** TEMERITY means "foolish boldness" or "recklessness," so an opposite is *caution*.

3. **The correct answer is (E).** TRACTABLE means "easily led" or "docile." *Uncooperative* is a good opposite.

4. **The correct answer is (B).** Since INSOUCIANT means "gay and careless," *fretful* is the best opposite.

5. **The correct answer is (D).** This question contains a thought-extender and a thought-reverser as its logical elements. The first blank must parallel the idea that someone was the life of the party. We can immediately eliminate (A), because someone who is *melancholy* is not likely to be the life of a party. (B), (C), and (E) make no logical sense. This is largely a matter of vocabulary since you must know that *garrulous* means "talkative," *inimical* means "hostile," and *vitriolic* means "nasty." Only (D) makes any sense. His wife must be the opposite of fun and talkative. The second element of (D), *taciturn*, which means "silent," works very nicely.

6. **The correct answer is (A).** This sentence begins with a thought-extender and then reverses the idea. The first blank needs an adjective related to *offhand* that could be applied to *remarks*. This becomes a vocabulary question because you must know the meanings of

all five of the first elements. All five answers make some sense, so it is a matter of substituting each pair to make sure that the logic of the sentence is maintained. If you know the meaning of *flippant*, you don't have to look any further. He was flippant, but this attitude masked a serious nature. This works very well. The logic of "he seemed x but was really y" is maintained.

7. **The correct answer is (C).** This question starts with a thought-reverser, *Although*. (A) does not reverse the idea. The same is true of (D) and (E). (B) and (C) remain possibilities, so test the second elements. The faculty might harbor her ideas, but they can't be doing it in defense of her seniority. That makes no sense. (C) works well. The faculty implements her ideas although they do not agree with her. This makes a perfectly logical and idiomatic sentence.

8. **The correct answer is (C).** This is obviously a main idea question. The author discusses the sacred script. The author mentions the Renaissance primarily as a way of praising the art of the Middle Ages. (C) is the best statement of the author's purpose.

9. **The correct answer is (D).** This is an explicit idea question. Each of the incorrect answers is mentioned as an element of the sacred script. As for (A), lines may be used to represent water or the sky. As for (B), these indicate sainthood or divinity. As for (C), shoes are mentioned as an identifying characteristic. And (E) also is

mentioned (a tree represents earth). (D), however, is not mentioned as an element of the sacred script.

10. **The correct answer is (C).** This is an application question. Of course, we do not know where the passage actually appeared, and the task is to pick the most likely source. We stress this because it is always possible to make an argument for any of the answer choices to a question of this sort. But the fact that a justification is possible does not make that choice correct; the strongest possible justification makes the choice correct. (C) is the most likely source. The passage focuses on art and is scholarly in tone. (A) can be eliminated, for the passage casts no light on social conditions of the period. (B) can be eliminated for a similar reason. The author treats art in and of itself—not as a social force. And we certainly cannot conclude that by discussing religious art the author wants to discuss the church. (D) is incorrect because the selection focuses on art of the Middle Ages. (E) is incorrect because it is inconsistent with the scholarly and objective tone of the passage.

11. **The correct answer is (D).** This is an inferred idea question, one asking for an interpretation of a phrase. The rules of art in the Middle Ages placed constraints on the artist, so that his artistic effort had to be made within certain conventions. As a result, painting was not individualistic. This is most clearly expressed by (D). (A) is incorrect since the author is saying that the artist's talent just did not show as individual talent. (B) is incorrect, for though this is a true statement, it is not a response to the question. (C) is perhaps the second best answer because it at least hints at what (D) says more clearly. But the author does not mean to say the artist was not recognized in his lifetime. Perhaps he was. What the au-

thor means to say is that we do not now see the personality of the artist. Finally, (E) is just a confused reading of the last paragraph.

12. **The correct answer is (B).** A WEB may be used to ENTANGLE and a *trap* is used to *ensnare*. Do not be distracted by (A) because *spider* and *spin* seem related to WEB.

13. **The correct answer is (E).** This analogy is based on a "lack of" relationship. LETHARGY is a lack of ENERGY, and *apathy* is a lack of *interest*.

14. **The correct answer is (C).** This analogy is a twist on the defining characteristic analogy. It is characteristic of THWART that one does not ACHIEVE and of *silence* that one does not *speak*.

15. **The correct answer is (A).** This is a type of "lack of" analogy. Something that is APOCRYPHAL is not GENUINE, and what is *spurious* is not *authentic*.

16. **The correct answer is (C).** This is a defining characteristic analogy. That which is BALEFUL is an EVIL, and that which is *mandatory* is a *requirement*. Note that EVIL in the original pair is a noun and not an adjective.

17. **The correct answer is (D).** This is a main idea question. The main idea of the passage is fairly clear: suggest reforms to correct the problems discussed. Choice (D) is a very good description of this development. (A) is incorrect since the author criticizes the system. (B) is incorrect since no recommendation for expanding benefits and scope is made by the author. (C) overstates the case. The author indicts only unemployment compensation, and indicates a belief that the shortcomings of the system can be remedied. (E) is incorrect because the author is discussing unemployment compensation, not government programs designed to achieve full employment generally.

We may infer from the passage that unemployment compensation is not a program designed to achieve full employment, but a program designed to alleviate the hardship of unemployment. On balance, (D) is the most precise description given of the development of the passage.

18. **The correct answer is (A).** This is a logical detail question. In the second paragraph the author introduces the example of a worker who loses surprisingly little by being unemployed. The author does this to show that unemployment insurance encourages people to remain unemployed by reducing the net cost of unemployment. (A) makes this point. (B) is incorrect, for the author does not discuss the problem of employer contribution until the fourth paragraph. (C) is incorrect, for this is not the reason that the author introduces the point. (D) is incorrect because this topic is not taken up until the third paragraph. Finally, (E) is incorrect since the author analyzes the situation in a neutral fashion; there is no hint of condemnation.

19. **The correct answer is (C).** This is an explicit idea, or specific detail, question. (C) is a recommendation made by the author in the final paragraph. (A) is actually inconsistent with statements made in that paragraph, for the author proposes taxing benefits in the same way as wages. (B), (D), and (E) are interesting ideas, but they are mentioned nowhere in the passage—so they cannot possibly be answers to an explicit idea question.

20. **The correct answer is (C).** Here, too, we have an explicit idea question. (A), (B), (D), and (E) are all mentioned in the third paragraph as ways by which an employer might reduce seasonal and cyclical fluctuations in labor needs. (C), however, was not mentioned as a way to minimize unemployment. Indeed, we may infer from other information supplied by the passage that supplementary benefits actually increase unemployment.

21. **The correct answer is (A).** This is an application question. We are asked to apply the author's analysis of the rating system to conclusions given in the answer choices. The author is critical of the rating system because it does not place the full burden of unemployment on the employer. This is because there is a maximum contribution limit, and in the final paragraph the author recommends the ceiling be eliminated. From these remarks, we may infer that the author believes the rating system is, in theory, sound, but that practically it needs to be adjusted. Choice (A) neatly describes this judgment. (B) can be eliminated since the author implies that the system is, in principle, sound. Moreover, the author implies that the employer does have some control over the time his former employees remain out of work. The maximum limit on employer contribution allows the employer to exploit this control. As for (C), this is contradicted by our analysis thus far and for the further reason that the passage never suggests employee contribution should replace employer contribution. Indeed, the author implies the system serves a useful and necessary social function. (D) can be eliminated because the author never draws a distinction between contributions by large firms and contributions by small firms. Finally, (E) is incorrect since the experience rating system is theoretically tied to the amount drawn by employees. The difficulty is not with the theory of the system, but with its implementation.

22. **The correct answer is (D).** This analogy is a type of defining characteristic. By its nature, a WATERFALL CASCADES and a *wave undulates*. You might be attracted to answer choice (A). But you can eliminate it by trying to improve

it. (A) would be more nearly correct if it were *snow : fall.*

23. **The correct answer is (B).** Although this does not fit into any category, the relationship is clear. To INFLATE something means "to increase its MAGNITUDE," and to *extend* something means "to increase its *duration.*"

24. **The correct answer is (A).** This analogy is a defining characteristic. To MOCK is to show DERISION or scorn. Similarly, to *despise* is to show *contempt* or disdain.

25. **The correct answer is (C).** This question contains a type of thought-reversal. Before looking at the choices, you already know that you need a word that prevents time from being *idle.* All choices except for (C) can be eliminated because they not only say nothing useful about time, they create meaningless sentences.

26. **The correct answer is (C).** You cannot eliminate any of the choices on the grounds of usage, since each when substituted into the sentence will create phrases. The key to the sentence is the word *life.* The field of study that completes the first blank must be a science that not only studies but directs the course of life, as indicated by the word *tamper.* This eliminates (B), (D), and (E). As for (A), although some members of the clergy might oppose research in psychology, those who do so would not argue that it is *imperative* to tamper with life. By the process of elimination, this leaves only (C).

27. **The correct answer is (B).** The logical key to this question is a double-reversal. *Although* sets up a contrast between the idea in the first clause and the idea in the second clause. But the second clause contains the word *little,* which functions as a negative. So the blanks will actually extend the thought expressed in the first clause. The first blank is an extender of the concept of literature that instructs as well as entertains, so you should look for an adjective that describes this type of literature. All of the first choices might describe literature, so you must know that *didactic* means "instructive."

28. **The correct answer is (C).** Since DIFFIDENCE means "self-doubt" or "modesty," *haughty arrogance* makes a nice antonym.

29. **The correct answer is (E).** SEDULOUS means "diligent" or "persevering," so *indolent,* which means "lazy," is a good opposite.

30. **The correct answer is (D).** OBDURATE means "stubborn" or "inflexible," so *malleable* is a fine antonym.

Math Section

1.	C	7.	C	13.	C	19.	C	25.	E
2.	C	8.	B	14.	D	20.	D	26.	A
3.	A	9.	B	15.	B	21.	C	27.	C
4.	D	10.	D	16.	C	22.	A	28.	B
5.	B	11.	C	17.	D	23.	B		
6.	C	12.	D	18.	B	24.	A		

1. **The correct answer is (C).** It would be a mistake to start multiplying before setting up the two quantities:

   24 hours/day × 7 days

   7 days/week × 24 weeks

   Both quantities are 24 × 7, and it is not necessary to multiply them out to see that they are equal.

2. **The correct answer is (C).** As in question 1, it is not necessary to actually carry out the indicated multiplication. Remembering that a % sign indicates that the number is to be divided by 100, each side becomes $\frac{(35)(60)}{100}$. Thus, (C) is correct. Always keep in mind that a percentage is just a number like any other number. The % sign is equivalent to the fraction $\frac{1}{100}$.

3. **The correct answer is (A).** Although the most direct way to solve this problem is to add the column of ages and divide by 6 (average = 29.8), you may find it quicker to do a "running average." Assume that the average is 30 (Tom's age). If that is correct, then the sum of ages above 30 must balance exactly the sum of the ages below 30. Juanita makes the balance +5 (above 30). Brooke brings it down by 2, for a total of +3. Glenda adds 10, for +13. Marcia brings it down by 8, for +5. Finally Dwight's age is 6 below 30, which brings the figure down to −1. This shows that the average will be slightly below 30.

4. **The correct answer is (D).** Since m ranges between 4 and 6, and n ranges between 5 and 7, it is impossible to determine the relationship between m and n. For example, m and n might both be 5.5, or m might be 4.1 and n 6.9, or m might be 5.9 and n 5.1. Neither m nor n is restricted to integers.

5. **The correct answer is (B).** The side of the square must be 8, since $s^2 = 64$. The length of the rectangle Q must be 16, since $W \times L = 64$.

6. **The correct answer is (C).** This problem simply requires finding the value of the expression $2x + 3y$, when $x = 3$ and $y = 2$: $2(3) + 3(2) = 12$.

7. **The correct answer is (C).** You do not need a course in business arithmetic to solve this problem, only the common-sense notion that profit is equal to gross revenue less cost. Expressed algebraically, we have $P = GR - C$; then, transposing the C term, we have $C + P = GR$, which is read: cost plus profit (or markup) is equal to gross revenue (or selling price). In this case, $P = \$4$, $GR = \$20$: $C + 4 = 20$, so $C = \$16$.

8. **The correct answer is (B).** The information given says that the 1980 student population is $2\frac{1}{2}$ times as great as the 1960 student population. So: '80SP = '60SP $\times 2\frac{1}{2}$, or '80SP = $500 \times 2\frac{1}{2}$ = $500 \times \frac{5}{2}$ = 1,250.

9. **The correct answer is (B).** The simplest way to solve this problem is first to perform the indicated operation for Column B: $(3x)^3 = 27x^3$. Now, since $x > 0$, x^3 must be positive, and it is permissible to divide both columns by x^3. The result is that Column A becomes 3, while column B becomes 27, so (B) is correct.

10. **The correct answer is (D).** Since it is not specified that x and y are equal to one another, the relationship is indeterminate. You can see this by visualizing x and y varying inversely with one another, e.g., when x is 2, y is $\frac{1}{2}$, when x is 3, y is $\frac{1}{3}$, etc. Also if you use substitution: if $x = 2$, then y must be $\frac{1}{2}$. On the other hand, x might be $\frac{1}{2}$, in which case y is 2.

11. **The correct answer is (C).** Since 11 is itself a prime number, it is factorable only by itself and 1, and that is one instance in which 11 is an integer multiple of a prime number. But it is also the only one. Any other number that is factorable by 11—say, 22—cannot, by definition, be a prime number (it would be factorable by 11 and some other number, as well as by itself and 1). Thirteen is also a prime number, which means that the only prime number of which it is an integer multiple is itself. So both 11 and 13 are each integer factors of only one prime number—themselves.

12. **The correct answer is (D).** Although we know that y is the even integer and that, of x and z, one is the next-greatest and the other is the next-least integer from y, we do not know which is which. If x is the lesser and z the greater, then Column B may be greater, but if x is the greater and z the lesser, Column A may be greater. Consequently, the correct answer here must be (D).

13. **The correct answer is (C).** We must test each of the answer choices. The question asks for the one choice in which the answer is not equal to $3n + 3$. In (A), for example, does $300 = 3n + 3$? A quick manipulation will show that there is an integer, n, that solves the equation: $297 = 3n$, so $n = 99$. For (C), however, no integral n exists: $3n + 3 = 208$, $3n = 205$, $n = 68\frac{1}{3}$. So (C) is the answer we want. Another approach is to test each of the answer choices for being divisible by 3 since $3n + 3$ is divisible by 3 when n is an integer. If the sum of all the single digits in a number add to a number divisible by 3, the number is itself divisible by 3; if not, the number isn't (208, for example: $2 + 0 + 8 = 10$, is not divisible by 3). Being divisible by 3 does not mean an answer fits the conditions, but not being divisible by 3 means that it doesn't.

14. **The correct answer is (D).** The easiest approach to this problem is to draw the figures.

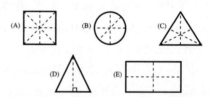

The dotted lines show possible lines of symmetry—that is, these are lines along which a paper cut-out of the figure could be folded and the result will be that the two halves exactly match one another. (D) must be our answer, since it is the only figure with but one line of symmetry.

15. **The correct answer is (B).** Of course, the problem is really about right triangles, not about transmitter towers, and the actual height of the tower is not important. The tower forms the common leg of two right triangles, so our triangles will have one leg of, say, length t. Then, the triangle on the left has a second leg that is shorter than the second leg of the triangle on the right (80 m vs. 100 m). Consequently, the hypotenuse (the support wire) of the triangle on the left ($\overline{AB}$) must be shorter than that of the triangle on the right ($\overline{AC}$).

16. **The correct answer is (C).** Notice that the number in Column A can be understood to be the sum of 2 times 1,000 (the 2 is in the thousands position), 4 times 100 (the 4 is in the hundreds position), 6 times 10 (the 6 is in the tens position), and 8 (the eight is in the units position). This is equivalent to the expression in Column B. The only differences are that the ordering of the elements is reversed in Column B and the hundreds and thousands are expressed in powers of ten.

17. **The correct answer is (D).** Since $a^2 = b$, we can substitute a^2 wherever b appears. Thus, Column A can be rewritten as: $\frac{2a}{a^2}$, which is equal to $\frac{2}{a}$. Since a is positive, we can multiply both columns by a. Thus, Column A becomes 2, and Column B becomes $(a)(a)(a)$, or a^3. Now it is easy to see that the relationship must be indeterminate. If a is a fraction, then Column A is greater. If a is a number like 2, then Column B is larger.

18. **The correct answer is (B).** This problem can, of course, be solved using an equation. We know that the laborer worked 8 hours @ $8 per hour, but what we need to know is how much overtime he worked. We let x be the number of overtime hours: (8 hrs. × $8/hr.) + ($x$ hrs. × $12/hr) = $80. The $12/hr. is the laborer's overtime rate—that is, $8 × 1\frac{1}{2}$ = $12. Now it is a fairly simple matter to manipulate the equation:

$$64 + 12x = 80$$
$$12x = 16$$
$$x = \frac{16}{12}$$
$$x = 1\frac{1}{3}$$

Since $\frac{1}{3}$ of an hour is 20 minutes, the laborer worked 1 hour and 20 minutes of overtime, which, when added to the standard 8 hours, gives a total work day of 9 hours and 20 minutes. Now, it is not absolutely necessary to use an equation.

The equation is just a way of formalizing common-sense reasoning, which might have gone like this: Well, I know he made $64 in a regular day. If he made $80 on a given day, $16 must have been overtime pay. His overtime rate is time-and-a-half, that is $1\frac{1}{2}$ times $8/hr, or $12/hr. In the first hour of overtime he made $12, that leaves $4 more. Since $4 is one third of $12, he had to work another one third of an hour to make that, which is twenty minutes. So he worked 8 hours at standard rates for $64, one full hour of overtime for another $12, and another $\frac{1}{3}$ of an overtime hour for $4. So $80 represents 9 hours and 20 minutes of work.

19. **The correct answer is (C).** Since vertical or opposite angles are equal, we know that $4x = x + 30$. Solving for x: $3x = 30$, $x = 10$; so the two columns are equal.

20. **The correct answer is (D).** To find the cost per ounce of the family-size box, we need to know both its size in ounces and its cost. While we know the relationship between the regular and family sizes for both of those items, we do not know the actual size or cost of the regular size and thus cannot use our knowledge of the relationship between the two sizes to any advantage. We wouldn't even know whether the family size or the regular size had the higher cost per ounce of cereal.

21. **The correct answer is (C).** One direct and simple way of solving this problem would be to count on your fingers the actual number of different duos and trios that could be formed from a group of five. The result is ten. A more elegant way of solving the problem is to recognize that $2 + 3 = 5$. In other words, each time a pair is selected to form a duo, three persons from the group have been left behind, and they form a trio. Or each time a different group of three is selected to form a trio, a pair of persons is left behind, and they constitute a duo. So even

without calculating the actual number of different trios and duos that could be made, you can reach the conclusion that the number of possible combinations for each is the same.

22. **The correct answer is (A).** This problem is both easy and difficult. Conceptually, the problem is easy to set up. High-risk stocks constitute 8.9% of the total investment of $1,080,192. To find the value of the high-risk stocks we just take 8.9% of $1,080,192. Then the problem becomes slightly difficult because it requires a tedious calculation—or at least it seems to. We say "seems to" because you do not actually have to do the arithmetic. The answer choices are spread fairly far apart; that is, they differ from one another by several thousands of dollars. Round 8.9% off to an even 9%, and $1,080,192 to 1,080,000. Then do the arithmetic in your head: 9% of one million is 90,000, then 9% of 80,000 is 7,200, so you need an answer choice that is close to $97,000—slightly less since you rounded your percentage (8.9%) in an upward direction. With a bit of practice, you will find that this technique is more efficient than actually doing arithmetic.

23. **The correct answer is (B).** In this problem, the technique of rounding off and estimating is even more useful. The problem is easy enough to set up: Since state-issued bonds constituted 26% of all government bonds and securities, and since government bonds and securities constituted 48.3% of the total investment fund, state-issued bonds must constitute 26% of 48.3% of the total fund. To compute the dollar value of state-issued bonds, we need to find 26% of 48.3% of $1,080,192, but that will require substantial calculation. You can attack it in this way: 26% is close to one fourth, and one fourth of 48% would be 12%, so state-issued bonds are 12% of the total. Now, 10% of the total of $1,080,000 (rounded

off), would be $108,000, and one fifth of that (since 2% is one fifth of 10%) is approximately $20,000. So 12% must be approximately $128,000, answer (B).

24. **The correct answer is (A).** In this problem you can use the method of pairing. Make a rough comparison of answers (A) and (B). If you find that one of the two is clearly the greater, strike the lesser and proceed to compare answer (C) with the greater of (A) and (B). Again, this calculation will be a rough one, and if you find that one of the two is clearly greater, strike the lesser and proceed to compare the greater with (D). Follow this procedure until you have exhausted the list, and one answer remains as the greatest. Now, if it turns out that any two answers are too close for a rough estimate to tell them apart, keep them both and compare them to the other answers before actually committing yourself to a detailed calculation, which is unlikely to be necessary. When there are two close answers, it is likely that a later one will supersede both of them.

In this problem we compare (A) and (B) first. Since both figures are shares of the same pie, we can compare their shares directly. Since the amount invested in municipal bonds with a 7–9% yield is 65%, (A) must be greater than (B) (the other two combined could account for only 35% of the pie), so we strike (B) and hold on to (A). Municipal bonds yielding 7–9% are 65% of all municipal bonds, and since municipal bonds account for 56% of all government bonds and securities, we can determine that the 7–9% yield municipal bonds account for roughly $\frac{2}{3}$ of the 56% of all government bonds and securities, or slightly less than 40%. This shows that (B) must be greater than (C), since (C) accounts for only 18% of all government bonds and securities—nowhere near 40%. Similarly, we can eliminate (D) from consideration because state-issued bonds account for only 26% of all government bonds and securities—again, that is not even close to 40%. Finally, we compare (A) with (E). Since municipal bonds with a 7–9% yield constitute slightly less than 40% of all government bonds and securities, and since government bonds and securities account for approximately 48% of the entire investment fund, municipal bonds yielding 7–9% must account for 40% of that 48%, or approximately 19% of the total fund. High-risk stocks account for only 8.9% of the total fund, so (E) must be less than (A), and (A) is our answer.

25. **The correct answer is (E).** This question requires a careful reading of the stem. It asks which kind of investment earned the least amount of money, but this group of graphs shows the amount *invested* in types of investment. It cannot be assumed that each type of investment was equally profitable, so we have no way of determining which of the types of investment generated the least income.

26. **The correct answer is (A).** Since *MNOP* is a square, we know that angle *O* must be a right angle, that is, 90°. From that we can conclude that arc *NP* is one fourth of the entire circle. If arc *NP* is 4 units long, then the circumference of the circle must be 4 times that long, or 16 units. We are now in a position to find the length of the radius of circle *O*, and once we have the radius, we will also know the length of the sides of square *MNOP*, since $\overline{ON}$ and $\overline{OP}$ are both radii. The formula for the circumference of a circle is $C = 2\pi r$, so:

$$2\pi r = 16$$
$$r = \frac{8}{\pi}$$

So the side of the square *MNOP* must be $\frac{8}{\pi}$, and its perimeter must be $s + s + s + s$, or $4\left(\frac{8}{\pi}\right) = \frac{32}{\pi}$.

27. **The correct answer is (C).** The most direct way to solve this problem is first to compute the rate at which the water is filling the tank. Water is flowing into the tank at 800 cu. ft. per minute, but it is also draining out at the rate of 300 cu. ft. per minute. The net gain each minute, then, is 500 cu. ft. We then divide 3,750 cu. ft. by 500 cu. ft./min., which equals 7.5 minutes. We convert the .5 minutes to 30 seconds, so our answer is 7 min. 30 sec.

28. **The correct answer is (B).** A quick sketch of the information provided in the problem shows that we need to employ the Pythagorean Theorem:

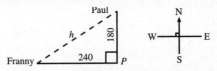

The shortest distance from Paul to Franny is the hypotenuse of this right triangle:

$$180^2 + 240^2 = h^2$$

It is extremely unlikely that the GRE would present a problem requiring such a lengthy calculation. So there must be a shortcut available. The key is to recognize that 180 and 240 are multiples of 60: 3×60 and 4×60, respectively. This must be a 3,4,5 right triangle, so our hypotenuse must be $5 \times 60 = 300$.

PRACTICE TEST 5 ANSWER SHEET

Verbal Section

1. Ⓐ Ⓑ Ⓒ Ⓓ Ⓔ   7. Ⓐ Ⓑ Ⓒ Ⓓ Ⓔ   13. Ⓐ Ⓑ Ⓒ Ⓓ Ⓔ   19. Ⓐ Ⓑ Ⓒ Ⓓ Ⓔ   25. Ⓐ Ⓑ Ⓒ Ⓓ Ⓔ
2. Ⓐ Ⓑ Ⓒ Ⓓ Ⓔ   8. Ⓐ Ⓑ Ⓒ Ⓓ Ⓔ   14. Ⓐ Ⓑ Ⓒ Ⓓ Ⓔ   20. Ⓐ Ⓑ Ⓒ Ⓓ Ⓔ   26. Ⓐ Ⓑ Ⓒ Ⓓ Ⓔ
3. Ⓐ Ⓑ Ⓒ Ⓓ Ⓔ   9. Ⓐ Ⓑ Ⓒ Ⓓ Ⓔ   15. Ⓐ Ⓑ Ⓒ Ⓓ Ⓔ   21. Ⓐ Ⓑ Ⓒ Ⓓ Ⓔ   27. Ⓐ Ⓑ Ⓒ Ⓓ Ⓔ
4. Ⓐ Ⓑ Ⓒ Ⓓ Ⓔ   10. Ⓐ Ⓑ Ⓒ Ⓓ Ⓔ   16. Ⓐ Ⓑ Ⓒ Ⓓ Ⓔ   22. Ⓐ Ⓑ Ⓒ Ⓓ Ⓔ   28. Ⓐ Ⓑ Ⓒ Ⓓ Ⓔ
5. Ⓐ Ⓑ Ⓒ Ⓓ Ⓔ   11. Ⓐ Ⓑ Ⓒ Ⓓ Ⓔ   17. Ⓐ Ⓑ Ⓒ Ⓓ Ⓔ   23. Ⓐ Ⓑ Ⓒ Ⓓ Ⓔ   29. Ⓐ Ⓑ Ⓒ Ⓓ Ⓔ
6. Ⓐ Ⓑ Ⓒ Ⓓ Ⓔ   12. Ⓐ Ⓑ Ⓒ Ⓓ Ⓔ   18. Ⓐ Ⓑ Ⓒ Ⓓ Ⓔ   24. Ⓐ Ⓑ Ⓒ Ⓓ Ⓔ   30. Ⓐ Ⓑ Ⓒ Ⓓ Ⓔ

Math Section

1. Ⓐ Ⓑ Ⓒ Ⓓ Ⓔ   7. Ⓐ Ⓑ Ⓒ Ⓓ Ⓔ   13. Ⓐ Ⓑ Ⓒ Ⓓ Ⓔ   19. Ⓐ Ⓑ Ⓒ Ⓓ Ⓔ   25. Ⓐ Ⓑ Ⓒ Ⓓ Ⓔ
2. Ⓐ Ⓑ Ⓒ Ⓓ Ⓔ   8. Ⓐ Ⓑ Ⓒ Ⓓ Ⓔ   14. Ⓐ Ⓑ Ⓒ Ⓓ Ⓔ   20. Ⓐ Ⓑ Ⓒ Ⓓ Ⓔ   26. Ⓐ Ⓑ Ⓒ Ⓓ Ⓔ
3. Ⓐ Ⓑ Ⓒ Ⓓ Ⓔ   9. Ⓐ Ⓑ Ⓒ Ⓓ Ⓔ   15. Ⓐ Ⓑ Ⓒ Ⓓ Ⓔ   21. Ⓐ Ⓑ Ⓒ Ⓓ Ⓔ   27. Ⓐ Ⓑ Ⓒ Ⓓ Ⓔ
4. Ⓐ Ⓑ Ⓒ Ⓓ Ⓔ   10. Ⓐ Ⓑ Ⓒ Ⓓ Ⓔ   16. Ⓐ Ⓑ Ⓒ Ⓓ Ⓔ   22. Ⓐ Ⓑ Ⓒ Ⓓ Ⓔ   28. Ⓐ Ⓑ Ⓒ Ⓓ Ⓔ
5. Ⓐ Ⓑ Ⓒ Ⓓ Ⓔ   11. Ⓐ Ⓑ Ⓒ Ⓓ Ⓔ   17. Ⓐ Ⓑ Ⓒ Ⓓ Ⓔ   23. Ⓐ Ⓑ Ⓒ Ⓓ Ⓔ
6. Ⓐ Ⓑ Ⓒ Ⓓ Ⓔ   12. Ⓐ Ⓑ Ⓒ Ⓓ Ⓔ   18. Ⓐ Ⓑ Ⓒ Ⓓ Ⓔ   24. Ⓐ Ⓑ Ⓒ Ⓓ Ⓔ

Analytical Writing—Issue Topic

_____
_____
_____
_____
_____
_____
_____
_____
_____
_____
_____
_____
_____
_____
_____
_____
_____
_____
_____
_____
_____

Analytical Writing—Argument Topic

_____

_____

_____

_____

_____

_____

_____

_____

_____

_____

_____

_____

_____

_____

_____

_____

_____

_____

_____

_____

_____

_____

_____

_____

_____

_____

_____

Practice Test 5

ANALYTICAL WRITING

Issue Topic • 45 Minutes

Present Your Perspective on an Issue

In this part, two topics appear as brief quotations. Each states, either explicitly or implicitly, an issue of broad interest. You are to choose one of the two topics. You will then use the remainder of the 45 minutes to write an essay in which you take a position on the issue.

You may agree with the quotation, disagree with it, or challenge the statement in any way, so long as the ideas that you present are clearly relevant to the topic. You should provide reasons and examples to support your position. In doing so, you may want to draw on your reading of various sources, your personal experience and observations, or your academic studies.

It is a good idea to begin by reading the topic carefully. Then you should decide what position you want to take, after which you will probably want to outline your answer before you begin to write. Your essay will be graded on how well you:

- Assess the implications of the issue, including various complexities implicit in the topic

- Organize, develop, and express your thoughts on the issue

- Provide supporting reasons and examples

- Demonstrate your mastery of the elements of standard written English

You should leave yourself sufficient time to read what you have written and to make any revisions to your essay that you think are needed.

For this exercise, you may choose to use an editing program on a computer (word processor) or write your response by hand using the space provided.

Issue Topics

Choose <u>one</u> of the following two topics to write on.

> "When a painter creates a canvas, a dramatist a play, or a musician a composition that is too abstruse, the artist is open to allegations of elitism and may even be justly accused of outright charlatanism. Truly great works of art, however, are readily accessible to ordinary people."

> "There is a distinction between negative freedom and positive freedom. Negative freedom is freedom from external rules and regulations; positive freedom is the ability to act in accordance with one's own conscience and other dictates. Positive freedom is more important than negative freedom."

Argument Topic • 30 Minutes

Analyze an Argument

In this part, you will be given an argument and have 30 minutes within which to write a critique of the argument. Your essay must address the argument given.

You are to <u>analyze</u> the reasoning of the argument. You should consider whether any of its assumptions are questionable and whether the evidence presented supports the conclusion. You might also discuss what changes in the line of reasoning or additional evidence would strengthen or weaken the conclusion.

Importantly, you are **NOT** being asked to state your own views on the underlying subject.

It is a good idea to begin by reading the argument carefully. Then you should evaluate the argument and consider what response you want to make, after which you will probably want to outline your answer before you begin to write.

Your essay response will be graded on how well you:

- Identify and analyze the important elements of the argument
- Organize, develop, and state your analysis
- Support your analysis with relevant reasons and examples
- Demonstrate your mastery of the elements of standard written English

You should leave yourself sufficient time to read what you have written and to make any revisions to your essay that you think are needed.

Timing for this part begins when you click on the "Dismiss the Directions" icon.

Argument Topic

The following is an excerpt from a memo written by the superintendent of the Fort Ann school district:

> "So that we can improve the quality of education for our students, we should merge the Fort Ann school district with the Hudson Falls school district. Scores on standardized tests for students in the Hudson Falls district rose an average of 25 percent in the past six years. Hudson Falls has five times the number of students as Fort Ann and four times the number of teachers, so they're able to field more athletic teams and offer more enrichment programs, such as music and art. Three times as many graduates of Hudson Falls High go on immediately to four-year colleges as Fort Ann. Plus, the state aid reimbursement ratio for Hudson Falls is higher than that for Fort Ann."

VERBAL SECTION

30 Questions • 30 Minutes

> **Directions:** Each of the questions below contains one or more blank spaces, each blank indicating that something has been omitted. Each sentence is followed by five (5) words or sets of words. Read and determine the general sense of each sentence. Then choose the word, or set of words that, when inserted in the sentence, best fits the meaning of the sentence.

1. Because of the —— of acupuncture therapy in China, Western physicians are starting to learn the procedure.

    (A) veracity

    (B) manipulation

    (C) liquidity

    (D) effectiveness

    (E) inflation

2. The conclusion of the program was a modern symphony with chords so —— that the piece produced sound similar to the —— one hears as the individual orchestra members tune their instruments before a concert.

    (A) superfluous . . melody

    (B) pretentious . . roar

    (C) melodious . . applause

    (D) versatile . . harmony

    (E) discordant . . cacophony

3. Black comedy is the combination of that which is humorous with that which would seem —— to humor: the ——.

    (A) apathetic . . ignoble

    (B) heretical . . salacious

    (C) inferior . . grandiose

    (D) extraneous . . innocuous

    (E) antithetical . . macabre

Directions: Each of the following questions consists of a word printed in capital letters, followed by five (5) words or phrases. Choose the word or phrase that is most nearly opposite in meaning to the word in capital letters. Be sure to consider all the choices before deciding which one is best.

4. PARSIMONY :
   (A) contraband
   (B) stealth
   (C) torpor
   (D) generosity
   (E) defoliation

5. ASPERITY :
   (A) smoothness
   (B) fabrication
   (C) duplicity
   (D) indolence
   (E) intercession

6. IGNOMINIOUS :
   (A) melancholy
   (B) cantankerous
   (C) symmetrical
   (D) honorable
   (E) calamitous

7. EVANESCENT :
   (A) indulgent
   (B) obsequious
   (C) permanent
   (D) illimitable
   (E) serendipitous

Directions: In each of the following questions, you are given a related pair of words or phrases in capital letters. Each capitalized pair is followed by five (5) pairs of words or phrases. Choose the pair that best expresses a relationship similar to that expressed by the original pair.

8. SINGER : CHORUS ::
   (A) architect : blueprint
   (B) teacher : student
   (C) author : publisher
   (D) driver : highway
   (E) actor : cast

9. INCISION : SCALPEL ::
   (A) hospital : patient
   (B) playground : swing
   (C) kitchen : knife
   (D) electricity : wire
   (E) cut : saw

10. ALTIMETER : HEIGHT ::
   (A) speedometer : velocity
   (B) observatory : constellation
   (C) racetrack : furlong
   (D) vessel : knots
   (E) metronome : tempo

Directions: The passage below is followed by questions based on its content. Choose the best answer to each question.

It would be enormously convenient to have a single, generally accepted index of the economic and social welfare of the people of the United States. A glance at
(5) it would tell us how much better or worse off we had become each year, and we would judge the desirability of any proposed action by asking whether it would raise or lower this index. Some recent
(10) discussion implies that such an index could be constructed. Articles in the popular press even criticize the Gross National Product (GNP) because it is not such a complete index of welfare, ignor-
(15) ing, on the one hand, that it was never intended to be, and suggesting, on the other, that with appropriate changes it could be converted into one.

The output available to satisfy our
(20) wants and needs is one important determinant of welfare. Whatever want, need, or social problem engages our attention, we ordinarily can more easily find resources to deal with it when output is
(25) large and growing than when it is not. GNP measures output fairly well, but to evaluate welfare we would need additional measures that would be far more difficult to construct. We would need an
(30) index of real costs incurred in production, because we are better off if we get the same output at less cost. Use of just man-hours for welfare evaluation would unreasonably imply that to increase to-
(35) tal hours by raising the hours of eight women from 60 to 65 a week imposes no more burden than raising the hours of eight men from 40 to 45 a week, or even than hiring one involuntarily unem-
(40) ployed person for 40 hours a week. A measure of real costs of labor would also have to consider working conditions. Most of us spend almost half our waking hours on the job and our welfare is vi-
(45) tally affected by the circumstances in which we spend those hours.

To measure welfare we would need a measure of changes in the need our output must satisfy. One aspect, population
(50) change, is now handled by converting output to a per capita basis on the assumption that, other things equal, twice as many people need twice as many goods and services to be equally well off. But an
(55) index of needs would also account for differences in the requirements for living as the population becomes more urbanized and suburbanized; for the changes in national defense requirements; and for
(60) changes in the effect of weather on our needs. The index would have to tell us the cost of meeting our needs in a base year compared with the cost of meeting them equally well under the circumstances
(65) prevailing in every other year.

Measures of "needs" shade into measures of the human and physical environment in which we live. We all are enormously affected by the people around
(70) us. Can we go where we like without fear of attack? We are also affected by the physical environment—purity of water and air, accessibility of park land and other conditions. To measure this re-
(75) quires accurate data, but such data are generally deficient. Moreover, weighting is required: to combine robberies and murders in a crime index; to combine pollution of the Potomac and pollution of
(80) Lake Erie into a water pollution index; and then to combine crime and water pollution into some general index. But there is no basis for weighting these beyond individual preference.

(85) There are further problems. To measure welfare we would need an index of the "goodness" of the distribution of income. There is surely consensus that given the same total income and output, a distribu-
(90) tion with fewer families in poverty would be the better, but what is the ideal distribution? Even if we could construct indexes of output, real costs, needs, and state of the environment, we could not compute a
(95) welfare index because we have no system of weights to combine them.

11. The author's primary concern is to

    (A) refute arguments for a position

    (B) make a proposal and defend it

    (C) attack the sincerity of an opponent

    (D) show defects in a proposal

    (E) review literature relevant to a problem

12. The author implies that man-hours is not an appropriate measure of real cost because it

    (A) ignores the conditions under which the output is generated

    (B) fails to take into consideration the environmental costs of production

    (C) overemphasizes the output of real goods as opposed to services

    (D) is not an effective method for reducing unemployment

    (E) was never intended to be a general measure of welfare

13. It can be inferred from the passage that the most important reason a single index of welfare cannot be designed is

    (A) the cost associated with producing the index would be prohibitive

    (B) considerable empirical research would have to be done regarding output and needs

    (C) any weighting of various measures into a general index would be inherently subjective and arbitrary

    (D) production of the relevant data would require time, thus the index would be only a reflection of past welfare

    (E) accurate statistics on crime and pollution are not yet available

14. The author regards the idea of a general index of welfare as a(n)

    (A) unrealistic dream

    (B) scientific reality

    (C) important contribution

    (D) future necessity

    (E) desirable change

15. According to the passage, the GNP is a(n)

    (A) fairly accurate measure of output

    (B) reliable estimate of needs

    (C) accurate forecaster of welfare

    (D) precise measure of welfare

    (E) potential measure of general welfare

16. According to the passage, an adequate measure of need must take into account all of the following EXCEPT

    (A) changing size of the population

    (B) changing effects on people of the weather

    (C) differences in needs of urban and suburban populations

    (D) changing requirements for governmental programs such as defense

    (E) accessibility of park land and other amenities

Directions: Each of the questions below contains one or more blank spaces, each blank indicating that something has been omitted. Each sentence is followed by five (5) words or sets of words. Read and determine the general sense of each sentence. Then choose the word, or set of words that, when inserted in the sentence, best fits the meaning of the sentence.

17. The press conference did not clarify many issues since the president responded with —— and —— rather than clarity and precision.
    (A) sincerity . . humor
    (B) incongruity . . candor
    (C) fervor . . lucidity
    (D) animation . . formality
    (E) obfuscation . . vagueness

18. It is difficult for a modern audience, accustomed to the —— of film and television, to appreciate opera with its grand spectacle and —— gestures.
    (A) irreverence . . hapless
    (B) sophistication . . monotonous
    (C) minutiae . . extravagant
    (D) plurality . . subtle
    (E) flamboyance . . inane

19. The sonatas of Beethoven represent the —— of classicism, but they also contain the seed of its destruction, romanticism, which —— the sonata form by allowing emotion rather than tradition to shape the music.
    (A) denigration . . perpetuates
    (B) pinnacle . . shatters
    (C) plethora . . heightens
    (D) fruition . . restores
    (E) ignorance . . encumbers

Directions: In each of the following questions, you are given a related pair of words or phrases in capital letters. Each capitalized pair is followed by five (5) pairs of words or phrases. Choose the pair that best expresses a relationship similar to that expressed by the original pair.

20. UNGAINLY : ELEGANCE ::
    (A) stately : majesty
    (B) suitable : propriety
    (C) vacuous : temerity
    (D) feckless : sobriety
    (E) perfunctory : attention

21. CONSERVATOR : WASTE ::
    (A) sentinel : vigilance
    (B) monarch : subject
    (C) demagogue : benevolence
    (D) chaperon : transgression
    (E) minister : profanity

22. POLEMICIST : CONTROVERSY ::
    (A) dilettante : virtuosity
    (B) visionary : dream
    (C) pundit : sophistry
    (D) zealot : benevolence
    (E) bigot : equanimity

23. PROSELYTIZE : CONVERT ::
    (A) argue : persuade
    (B) digress : disturb
    (C) abide : forego
    (D) deflect : condone
    (E) dissemble : abet

Directions: The passage below is followed by questions based on its content. Choose the best answer to each question.

In a sense the university has failed. It has stored great quantities of knowledge; it teaches more people; and despite its failures, it teaches them better. It is in the
(5) application of this knowledge that the failure has come. Of the great branches of knowledge—the sciences, the social sciences, and humanities—the sciences are applied. Strenuous and occasionally suc-
(10) cessful efforts are made to apply the social sciences, but almost never are the humanities well applied. We do not use philosophy in defining our conduct. We do not use literature as a source of real
(15) and vicarious experience. The great task of the university in the next generation is to learn to use the knowledge we have for the questions that come before us. The university should organize courses around
(20) primary problems. The difference between a primary problem and a secondary or even tertiary problem is that primary problems tend to be around for a long time, whereas the less important
(25) ones get solved.

One primary problem is that of interfering with biological development. The next generation, and perhaps this one, will be able to interfere chemically with
(30) the actual development of an individual and perhaps biologically by interfering with an individual's genes. Obviously, there are benefits both to individuals and to society from eliminating, or at least
(35) improving, mentally and physically deformed persons. On the other hand, there could be very serious consequences if this knowledge were used with premeditation to produce superior and subordinate
(40) classes, each genetically prepared to carry out a predetermined mission. This can be done, but what happens to free will and the rights of the individual? Here we have a primary problem that will still
(45) exist when we are all dead. Of course, the traditional faculty members would say, "But the students won't learn enough to

go to graduate school." And certainly they would not learn everything we are in the
(50) habit of making them learn, but they would learn some other things.

24. The author suggests that the university's greatest shortcoming is its failure to
(A) attempt to provide equal opportunity for all
(B) offer courses in philosophy and the humanities
(C) prepare students adequately for professional studies
(D) help students see the relevance of the humanities to real problems
(E) require students to include in their curricula liberal arts courses

25. It can be inferred that the author presupposes that the reader will regard a course in literature as a course
(A) with little or no practical value
(B) of interest only to academic scholars
(C) required by most universities for graduation
(D) uniquely relevant to today's primary problems
(E) used to teach students good writing skills

26. Which of the following questions would the author most likely consider a primary question?
(A) Should Congress increase the level of Social Security benefits?
(B) Is it appropriate for the state to use capital punishment?
(C) Who is the best candidate for president in the next presidential election?
(D) At what month can the fetus be considered medically viable outside the mother's womb?
(E) What measures should be taken to solve the problem of world hunger?

Directions: Each of the following questions consists of a word printed in capital letters, followed by five (5) words or phrases. Choose the word or phrase that is most nearly opposite in meaning to the word in capital letters. Be sure to consider all the choices before deciding which one is best.

27. VILIFY :
    (A) thwart
    (B) purport
    (C) abound
    (D) circumscribe
    (E) laud

28. TENDER :
    (A) demote
    (B) truncate
    (C) retract
    (D) emancipate
    (E) besiege

29. FUNGIBLE :
    (A) corrosive
    (B) iridescent
    (C) unique
    (D) retrograde
    (E) discursive

30. SPLENETIC :
    (A) taciturn
    (B) enigmatic
    (C) complacent
    (D) contrite
    (E) mischievous

MATH SECTION

28 Questions • 45 Minutes

Numbers: All numbers used are real numbers.

Figures: The position of points, angles, regions, and so forth are in the order shown. Figures are assumed to lie in a plane unless otherwise indicated. Figures are drawn as accurately as possible for problem-solving questions, unless otherwise indicated. Figures are NOT drawn to scale for quantitative analysis problem, unless otherwise indicated. You should solve the problems by using your knowledge of mathematics and not by estimating sizes by sight or measurement.

Lines: Assume that lines shown as straight are indeed straight.

Directions: For each of the following questions, select the best of the answer choices. For quantitative comparison questions, two quantities are given, one in Column A and one in Column B. Compare the two quantities and choose

(A) if the quantity in Column A is greater
(B) if the quantity in Column B is greater
(C) if the two quantities are equal
(D) if the relationship cannot be determined from the information given

Information applying to both columns is centered between the columns and above the quantities in columns A and B. Symbols that appear in both columns represent the same idea or quantity in each column.

Column A	Column B
$x = -y$	
1. x	y
2. $\dfrac{1}{100}$	.01%
The price of paper increased from $1.23 per ream to $1.48 per ream.	
3. The percent increase in the price of paper	20%
M is the average (arithmetic mean) of x and y.	
4. $\dfrac{M + x + y}{3}$	$\dfrac{x + y}{2}$
5. $(a + 2)(b + 3)$	$(a + 3)(b + 2)$

Directions: For each of the following questions, select the best of the answer choices given.

6. $\dfrac{3}{4} + \dfrac{4}{5} =$

   (A) $\dfrac{7}{20}$

   (B) $\dfrac{3}{5}$

   (C) $\dfrac{7}{9}$

   (D) $\dfrac{12}{9}$

   (E) $\dfrac{31}{20}$

7. If $x + 6 = 3$, then $x + 3 =$

   (A) -9

   (B) -3

   (C) 0

   (D) 3

   (E) 9

8. A person is standing on a staircase. He walks down 4 steps, up 3 steps, down 6 steps, up 2 steps, up 9 steps, and down 2 steps. Where is he standing in relation to the step on which he started?

   (A) 2 steps above

   (B) 1 step above

   (C) the same place

   (D) 1 step below

   (E) 2 steps below

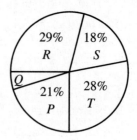

9. What portion of the circle graph above belongs to sector Q?

   (A) 4%

   (B) 5%

   (C) 6%

   (D) 75%

   (E) 96%

10. $326(31) - 326(19) =$

   (A) 3,912

   (B) 704

   (C) 100

   (D) 32.6

   (E) 10

Directions: For each of the following questions, select the best of the answer choices. For quantitative comparison questions, two quantities are given, one in Column A and one in Column B. Compare the two quantities and choose

(A) if the quantity in Column A is greater
(B) if the quantity in Column B is greater
(C) if the two quantities are equal
(D) if the relationship cannot be determined from the information given

Information applying to both columns is centered between the columns and above the quantities in columns A and B. Symbols that appear in both columns represent the same idea or quantity in each column.

Column A	**Column B**

11. The average (arithmetic mean) of the number of degrees in the angles of a pentagon. | The average (arithmetic mean) of the number of degrees in the angles of a hexagon.

A bookshelf contains 16 books written in French and 8 books written in Italian and no other books. 75% of the books written in French and 50% of the books written in Italian are removed from the bookshelf.

12. The proportion of the original number of books remaining on the shelf | $\dfrac{2}{3}$

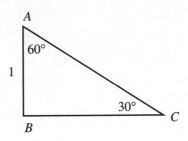

13. $\sqrt{3}$ | BC

$$x^2 - 1 = 0$$

14. x | 1

Tickets to a concert cost $25 and $13.
An agent sells 11 tickets for a total price of $227.

15. The number of $25 tickets sold | The number of $13 tickets sold

Directions: For each of the following questions, select the best of the answer choices given.

QUESTIONS 16–20 ARE BASED ON THE FOLLOWING GRAPHS.

Sales and Earnings of Company *K*

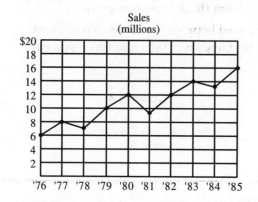

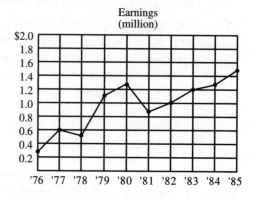

16. From 1977 to 1983, inclusive, what was the amount of the greatest increase in earnings from one year to the next?

    (A) $300,000

    (B) $600,000

    (C) $750,000

    (D) $1,000,000

    (E) $1,200,000

17. From 1980 to 1984, inclusive, in which year did sales change by the greatest percent over the previous year?

    (A) 1980

    (B) 1981

    (C) 1982

    (D) 1983

    (E) 1984

18. For the years 1981 to 1985, inclusive, the average earnings of Company K were approximately

    (A) $1,180,000

    (B) $998,000

    (C) $920,000

    (D) $880,000

    (E) $720,000

19. From 1976 to 1985, the earnings of Company K increased by what percent?

    (A) 150%

    (B) 200%

    (C) $233\frac{1}{3}$%

    (D) 400%

    (E) 500%

20. In how many of the years shown were earnings equal to or greater than 10 percent of sales?

    (A) 3

    (B) 4

    (C) 5

    (D) 6

    (E) 7

Directions: For each of the following questions, select the best of the answer choices. For quantitative comparison questions, two quantities are given, one in Column A and one in Column B. Compare the two quantities and choose

(A) if the quantity in Column A is greater
(B) if the quantity in Column B is greater
(C) if the two quantities are equal
(D) if the relationship cannot be determined from the information given

Information applying to both columns is centered between the columns and above the quantities in columns A and B. Symbols that appear in both columns represent the same idea or quantity in each column.

<u>Column A</u>	<u>Column B</u>

$$x - y \neq 0$$

21. $\dfrac{x^2 - y^2}{x - y}$ $x + y$

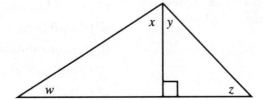

22. $w + x$ $y + z$

Planes X and Y are 300 miles apart and flying toward each other
on a direct course and at constant speeds.
X is flying at 150 miles per hour. After 40 minutes, they pass one another.

23.   Speed of plane Y 150 miles per hour

Directions: For each of the following questions, select the best of the answer choices given.

24. A child withdraws from his piggy bank 10% of the original sum in the bank. If he must add 90¢ to bring the amount in the bank back up to the original sum, what was the original sum in the bank?

(A) $1.00

(B) $1.90

(C) $8.10

(D) $9.00

(E) $9.90

25. If cylinder P has a height twice that of cylinder Q and a radius half that of cylinder Q, what is the ratio between the volume of cylinder P and the volume of cylinder Q?

(A) 1:8

(B) 1:4

(C) 1:2

(D) 1:1

(E) 2:1

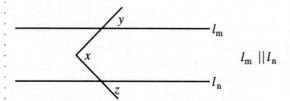

$l_m \| l_n$

26. In the figure above, which of the following is true?

(A) $x = y + z$

(B) $y = 90°$

(C) $x + y + z = 180°$

(D) $y = x + z$

(E) $z = x + y$

27. If the width of a rectangle is increased by 25% while the length remains constant, the resulting area is what percent of the original area?

(A) 25%

(B) 75%

(C) 125%

(D) 225%

(E) It cannot be determined from the information given.

28. The sum of four consecutive odd positive integers is always

(A) an odd number

(B) divisible by 4

(C) a prime number

(D) a multiple of 3

(E) greater than 24

ANSWER KEY AND EXPLANATIONS

Analytical Writing

Issue Topics

Topic 1

As you read the following sample response, try to judge for yourself how well it meets the criteria that will be applied by graders:

Category	Below Avg.	Avg.	Above Avg.
Analysis of the Topic			
Organization and Development			
Use of Reasons and Examples			
Use of Standard Written English			
OVERALL SCORE*			

*Below Average = 1–2; Average = 3–4; Above Average = 5–6

SAMPLE RESPONSE AND COMMENTARY FOR ISSUE TOPIC 1

Note: The sample answers contain spelling and grammatical errors. This is done to simulate a first draft written under time pressure.

It is easy to sympathize with the sentiment expressed in the topic statement. After all, no one wants to feel inadequate to any task, including appreciating art in its various forms. This is perhaps why we've all been in the modern wing of a museum, perhaps looking at a cubist Picasso, and heard someone whisper, "My seven-year old can draw better than that." But surely the fact that not everyone is sufficiently familiar with the artistic concerns that gave rise to cubism doesn't mean that the entire movement was a scam.

The composer Leonard Bernstein, in his popular book on music (the title of which escapes me), wrote that there are three levels of understanding or appreciation of music. The most fundamental of these is the literal level of melody and words; the intermediate level is where we find elements of harmony and structure; and the most abstract level, one which Bernstein says very few are sufficiently trained to appreciate, involves the interaction of purely musical values. Surely, the same taxonomy may be applied to both painting and literature. Everyone can appreciate the subject matter of a realistic landscape, but fewer the techniques such as brush strokes and compositional decision, and still fewer the purely "painterly" consideration such as tonal values. Or in literature, everyone can follow the plot of Shakespeare's "Romeo and Juliet," and many can appreciate the poetic deployment of language, but only those who have given some study will know that the prologue is in sonnet form that is echoed by the speeches of the balcony scene.

The challenge of some works of art, then, is that they address themselves more to the highest, most abstract level of appreciation. A painting that seems to be "nothing more than some painted rectangles" does not appeal to the basic or even the intermediate levels of understanding. The artist's goal is to explore the purely "painterly" values that play on that highest level.

Actually, it doesn't even require so much argument to demonstrate that the statement, at least as written, must be wrong. Just show our whisperer (first paragraph) one of Picasso's more representational paintings. At that point it should become clear that by any measure Picasso was a genius. Instead, we should qualify the statement to say that many great works of art appeal to many people, but some great works of art appeal only to a few.

COMMENTARY

This is an excellent essay. It comes to grips with the topic in a very sophisticated way by describing the three-level analysis of music and then applying that to painting and literature, providing examples for each. Another attractive feature of the essay is that it explores the topic, that is, the writer doesn't start off by simply saying that the topic statement is mistaken. Instead, the writer attempts to give some account as to why some people would regard the statement as plausible. And this sets the stage for the climax of the essay. The writer returns to the "whisperer" to take a final position on the statement: the statement, as written, is wrong, but contains some element of truth that can be salvaged. The language is powerful and correct; the organization is effective; the use of examples is excellent. This essay would almost surely receive a 6.

Topic 2

As you read the following sample response, try to judge for yourself how well it meets the criteria that will be applied by graders:

Category	Below Avg.	Avg.	Above Avg.
Analysis of the Topic			
Organization and Development			
Use of Reasons and Examples			
Use of Standard Written English			
OVERALL SCORE*			

*Below Average = 1–2; Average = 3–4; Above Average = 5–6

SAMPLE RESPONSE AND COMMENTARY FOR ISSUE TOPIC 2

Note: The sample answers contain spelling and grammatical errors. This is done to simulate a first draft written under time pressure.

Freedom is one of the most important things that human beings have. But being free means different things. On the one hand, being free means being free from laws and other rules. On the other hand, being free means having the freedom to do what one chooses.

First, being free means not having law and other rules. If, for example, there is a law saying that we must pay our taxes, then we are not truly free because someone else (the government) is telling us something that we have to do. Or when there is a rule about attending classes, this undermines freedome because someone else is making decisions.

Second, being free means choosing what one wants to do. If I want to become a doctor, and I can, then I am free because I am doing what I want to do.

Of the two kind of freedoms, the second is more important. I can live with some annoying rules. But it would be hard to have a good life if I couldn't do what I choose.

COMMENTARY

This is a below-average essay. It makes an attempt at organization, and the language is not egregiously wrong. On the other hand, the organization is used to do little more than reiterate the points made in the topic statement, and the sentences say so little that there is hardly room for error. Basically, it looks as though the writer of this essay thought it would be sufficient to write something with a superficial structure and simple statements—without the need for coming to grips with the topic. This is a mistake. The very first criterion by which the issue essay is judged is how well it assesses the implications of the issue, including various complexities implicit in the topic. Because of the lack of substantive thought in the essay, it would probably receive a 2.

Argument Topic

As you read the following sample response, try to judge for yourself how well it meets the criteria that will be applied by graders:

Category	Below Avg.	Avg.	Above Avg.
Analysis of the Topic			
Organization and Development			
Use of Reasons and Examples			
Use of Standard Written English			
OVERALL SCORE*			

*Below Average = 1–2; Average = 3–4; Above Average = 5–6

SAMPLE RESPONSE AND COMMENTARY FOR THE ARGUMENT TOPIC

Note: The sample answers contain spelling and grammatical errors. This is done to simulate a first draft written under time pressure.

The conclusion of the superintendent is that a merger with the neighboring district would "improve the quality of education for our students." The evidence presented fails to support that conclusions; additionally, there are factors other than "quality of education" that need to be assessed.

First, the evidence given does not prove that a merger would secure the claimed improvement in education even if that is measured by test scores, programming choices, and college placement. As for test scores, the evidence shows only that scores in the neighboring district "rose an average of 25 percent." For this to be meaningful, it would be necessary to know something about the test scores in Fort Ann (in order to make an inter-district comparison) plus something about the base from which the other district's scores started to rise. After all, a rise from 4 to 5 (on a 100 scale) is a 25 percent increase but hardly noteworthy. Additionally, more programming choices may not translate into better education. Even taking the evidence at face value, it looks as though the faculty-student ratio in the neighboring district is higher than in Fort Ann, so (given that the other district is so much larger) the combined district would have a higher faculty-student ratio that is currently enjoyed by Fort Ann students. Or the availability of more athletics sounds attractive, but will students from the smaller district be competitive for positions on those teams. Finally, the "four year college" data is ambiguous. Perhaps just as many Fort Ann students go to college but opt for a sojourn at a two-year community college for any of the reasons that students make such a choice such as finances or transition.

Second, it is also important to assess extra-educational factors. The argument strongly implies that Fort Ann is a small school district, and there advantages to small schools. Students and parents may feel stronger ties to the school which may constitute a social center for the community. Parents may enjoy greater control over the upbringing of their children in a smaller community. And, perhaps most important, these are choices that, in large measure, should belong to the parents and not to the superintendent of the school district. Even accepting the argument, the merger may be rejected by the parents who feel that the disadvantages more than outweigh the proposed advantages.

COMMENTARY

This is certainly an above-average essay. It takes on the argument head-on. First, it criticizes the argument on its own terms by pointing out three ways in which the proposed merger may fail to achieve the result of better education. Second, it steps outside of the parameters created by the argument to attack the argument as being too limited in its vision. Thus, the essay does a good job of satisfying the important criterion of identifying and analyzing the important elements of the argument. The prose is forceful and almost entirely correct, and the reasoning is persuasive. The argument might receive minor criticism for its organization. The second paragraph perhaps should have been divided into three, but that is a very minor point. Overall, this is at least a 5 and more likely a 6.

answers

Verbal Section

1.	D	7.	C	13.	C	19.	B	25.	A
2.	E	8.	E	14.	A	20.	E	26.	B
3.	E	9.	E	15.	A	21.	D	27.	E
4.	D	10.	A	16.	E	22.	B	28.	C
5.	A	11.	D	17.	E	23.	A	29.	C
6.	D	12.	A	18.	C	24.	D	30.	C

1. **The correct answer is (D).** This is basically a vocabulary question. You do, however, have one clue to the meaning of the sentence. The sentence tells you that Western physicians are learning a procedure. Logically, they are doing this because it is desirable, so you should look for the noun that has a positive connotation. This eliminates (B) and (E). If you substitute (A) or (C), you have a meaningless sentence. So the answer must be (D).

2. **The correct answer is (E).** The second blank is an extension of the first idea. You can eliminate (A) because the idea of hearing a melody does not explain why a chord is superfluous. You can eliminate (B) because the idea of hearing a roar doesn't explain why a chord might be pretentious. You can eliminate (C) because the idea of hearing applause doesn't explain why a chord might be melodious. And you can eliminate (D) because hearing harmony doesn't explain why a chord might be versatile. (E) preserves the sense and logic of the sentence. Hearing *cacophony* indicates that the chord is *discordant*.

3. **The correct answer is (E).** The best way to attack this question is to substitute each pair until you find one that works. You can immediately eliminate (A) on the grounds of usage, as "*apathetic* to humor" makes no sense. Next, the *salacious* is not *heretical* to humor, so eliminate (B). The *grandiose* is not *inferior* to humor, so eliminate (C). The *innocuous* is not *extraneous* to humor, so

eliminate (D). You are left with (E), which does make sense. The *macabre* might be *antithetical* to humor.

4. **The correct answer is (D).** PARSIMONY means "frugality or stinginess," so *generosity* is a good opposite.

5. **The correct answer is (A).** ASPERITY means "roughness or unevenness"; therefore, a good antonym is *smoothness*.

6. **The correct answer is (D).** IGNOMINIOUS means "dishonorable or disgraceful." *Honorable* is a precise antonym.

7. **The correct answer is (C).** EVANESCENT means "vanishing, fleeting, or passing away." A good opposite is *permanent*.

8. **The correct answer is (E).** This is a part-to-whole analogy. A SINGER is part of a CHORUS, and an *actor* is part of a *cast*.

9. **The correct answer is (E).** This analogy falls into the "tool" category. An INCISION is made with a SCALPEL, or a scalpel is the tool used to make an incision. A *cut* is made with a *saw*, or a saw is the tool used to cut.

10. **The correct answer is (A).** This analogy is fairly straightforward. An ALTIMETER measures HEIGHT, and a *speedometer* measures *velocity*.

11. **The correct answer is (D).** This is a main idea question. The author begins by stating that it would be useful to have a general index to measure welfare and notes that some have even suggested the

GNP might be adapted for that purpose. The author then proceeds to demonstrate why such an index cannot be constructed. Generally, then, the author shows the defects in a proposal for a general index of welfare, and (D) nicely describes this development. (A) is incorrect for the author never produces any arguments for the position being attacked. And even when the author raises points such as the suggestion that hours worked might be a measure of cost of production, the author is not citing arguments for that position, but only mentioning the position to attack it. (B) is incorrect since the author is attacking and not defending the proposal discussed. (C) is easily eliminated because the author never attacks the sincerity of opponents. Finally, (E) is wrong, for the author never reviews any literature on the subject being discussed.

12. **The correct answer is (A).** This is an inference question. We turn to the second paragraph. There the author mentions that a general index of welfare would have to include some measure of the cost of producing the output. The author suggests that someone might think hours worked would do the trick, but rejects that position by noting that hours worked, as a statistic, does not take into account the quality of the work time, e.g., long hours versus short hours, working conditions, satisfaction of workers. (A) best describes this argument. (B) is incorrect, for the author discusses environmental costs in connection with another aspect of a general index. (C) is incorrect since this distinction is never used by the author. (D) is incorrect since this is not mentioned as a goal of such a measure. Finally, (E) confuses the GNP, mentioned in the first part of the paragraph, with the index to measure real costs.

13. **The correct answer is (C).** This is an inference question that asks about the main point of the passage. The author

adduces several objections to the idea of a general index of welfare. Then the final blow is delivered in the last paragraph: Even if you could devise measures for these various components of a general index, any combination or weighting of the individual measures would reflect only the judgment (personal preference) of the weighter. For this reason alone, argues the author, the entire idea is unworkable. (C) makes this point. (A) and (D) can be eliminated since the author never uses cost or time as arguments against the index. (B) can be eliminated on similar ground. The author may recognize that considerable research would be needed to attempt such measures, yet does not bother to use that as an objection. (E) can be eliminated for a similar reason. The author may have some arguments against the way such statistics are gathered now, but does not bother to make them. The author's argument has the structure: Even assuming there are such data, we cannot combine these statistics to get a general measure of the quality of the environment.

14. **The correct answer is (A).** This is a tone question, and the justification for (A) is already implicit in the discussion thus far. The author sees fatal theoretical weaknesses inherent in the idea of an index of welfare. So we might say that the author regards such a notion as an unrealistic, that is, unachievable, dream. (B) is incorrect because the author does not believe the idea can ever be implemented. (C), (D), and (E) can be eliminated on substantially the same ground.

15. **The correct answer is (A).** This is an explicit idea question. The second paragraph acknowledges that the GNP is a fairly accurate measure of output. The author never suggests that the GNP can estimate needs, predict welfare, or measure welfare generally. So we can eliminate the remaining choices.

16. **The correct answer is (E).** This is an explicit idea question, with a thought-reverser. (A), (B), (C), and (D) are all mentioned in the third paragraph as aspects of a needs index. The fourth paragraph does not treat the idea of a needs index but the idea of a physical environment index. That is where the author discusses the items mentioned in (E). So the author does mention the items covered by (E), but not as part of a needs index.

17. **The correct answer is (E).** This entire sentence is a thought-reverser. The president responded with something other than clarity and precision. You should immediately look for opposites of these words for the blanks. (E), *obfuscation* and *vagueness*, does the job.

18. **The correct answer is (C).** This sentence contains a thought-reverser and a thought-extender. The first blank requires a word that will reverse the idea of *grand spectacle*, since we know that the modern audience has learned to appreciate the opposite of grand spectacle. The second blank requires a word that extends the idea of grand spectacle. (A) is not possible, since *irreverence* is not the opposite of grand spectacle and *hapless* does not extend that idea. (B) might seem plausible, since one could say that film and television are *sophisticated*, but *monotonous* is hardly the word one would use to describe grand spectacle. (C) is correct because the idea of *minutiae*, or details, is in direct opposition to the idea of something large or grand like opera. The second word also fits nicely, since *extravagant* extends the idea of grand spectacle. As for (D), the first word fails to make a meaningful sentence, and (E) cannot be correct since *flamboyance* extends the idea of grand spectacle instead of reversing it.

19. **The correct answer is (B).** This sentence contains a thought-reverser and a thought-extender. The first blank requires a word that reverses the idea of destruction of classicism and the second blank requires a word that extends the idea of destruction. (A) may appear possible at first, but the second word, *perpetuates*, makes the choice impossible since it does not extend the idea of destruction. (B) is correct because *pinnacle of classicism* is the opposite of the concept of its destruction, and *shatters* perfectly extends the idea of destruction. (C) is wrong because it fails to make a meaningful sentence. (D) appears plausible, because *fruition* certainly reverses the notion of destruction, but *restores* does not extend the idea of destruction. As for (E), if the sonatas represent an *ignorance* of classicism, then they could not also contain the seeds of its destruction.

20. **The correct answer is (E).** This analogy fits into the "lack of " category. That which is UNGAINLY lacks ELEGANCE, and that which is *perfunctory* lacks *attention*.

21. **The correct answer is (D).** This is a variation on the "defining characteristic" analogy. A CONSERVATOR is one who prevents WASTE and a *chaperon* is one who prevents *transgression*.

22. **The correct answer is (B).** This is another "defining characteristic" analogy. A POLEMICIST is involved in CONTROVERSY and a *visionary* in *dreams*.

23. **The correct answer is (A).** To PROSELYTIZE is to try to CONVERT; to *argue* is to try to *persuade*.

24. **The correct answer is (D).** This is a fairly easy inference question. We are asked to determine which of the problems mentioned by the author is the most important. (B) can be eliminated because the author's criticism is not that such

courses are not offered, nor even that such courses are not required. So we eliminate (E) as well. The most important shortcoming, according to the author, is that students have not been encouraged to apply the principles learned in the humanities. As for (C), this is not mentioned by the author as a weakness in the present curriculum structure. Rather, the author anticipates that this is a possible objection to the proposal to require students to devote part of their time to the study of primary problems. Finally, as for (A), the author does not mention the university's failure to achieve complete equality of opportunity as a serious problem.

25. **The correct answer is (A).** This is an inference question as well, though of a greater degree of difficulty. It seems possible to eliminate (C) and (E) as fairly implausible. The author's remarks about literature, addressed to us as readers, do not suggest that we believe literature is required, nor that it is used to teach writing. As for (D), the author apparently presupposes that we, the readers, do not see the relevance of literature to real problems, for that it is relevant is at least part of the burden of the author's argument. (B) is perhaps the second best answer. It may very well be that most people regard literature as something scholarly, but that does not prove that (B) is a presupposition of the argument. The author states that literature is a source of real and vicarious experience. What is the value of that? The author is trying to show that literature has a real, practical value. The crucial question, then, is why the author is attempting to prove that literature has real value. The answer is because the author presupposes that we disagree with this conclusion. There is a subtle but important difference between a presupposition that literature is scholarly and a presupposition that literature has no practical

value. After all, there are many non-scholarly undertakings that may lack practical value.

26. **The correct answer is (B).** This is an application question. The author uses the term "primary problems" to refer to questions of grave importance that are not susceptible to easy answers. Each of the incorrect answers poses a question that can be answered with a short answer. (A) can be answered with a yes or no. (C) can be answered with a name. (D) can be answered with a date. (E) can be answered with a series of proposals. And even if the answers are not absolutely indisputable, the questions will soon become dead issues. The only problem that is likely to still be around after we are all dead is the one of capital punishment.

27. **The correct answer is (E).** To VILIFY is to slander, defile, or defame. *Laud*, which means "praise," is a fine opposite.

28. **The correct answer is (C).** As a verb, TENDER means "to present for acceptance" or "to offer." Therefore, *retract* is a good antonym.

29. **The correct answer is (C).** Since FUNGIBLE means "capable of being used in place of something else," *unique* is a good opposite.

30. **The correct answer is (C).** Since SPLENETIC means "bad-tempered or irritable," *complacent* is the best opposite.

Math Section

1.	D	7.	C	13.	C	19.	D	25.	C
2.	A	8.	A	14.	D	20.	B	26.	A
3.	A	9.	A	15.	A	21.	C	27.	C
4.	C	10.	A	16.	B	22.	C	28.	B
5.	D	11.	B	17.	C	23.	A		
6.	E	12.	B	18.	A	24.	D		

1. **The correct answer is (D).** Since no information is given directly about x or y, we cannot determine the relationship. Do not assume that since $x = -y$, y will be greater than $-y$ and thus greater than x. It is possible that y is a negative number, in which case x is a positive number and greater than y. Also, x and y could both be equal to zero.

2. **The correct answer is (A).** $\frac{1}{100}$ is equal to 1%, so Column A is greater. .01% expressed as a fraction is $\frac{1}{10,000}$.

3. **The correct answer is (A).** To compute a percentage increase, it is necessary to create a fraction: $\frac{\text{difference}}{\text{starting point}}$. In this problem, the price of paper increased from $1.23 to $1.48, for a difference of $0.25. Thus, our fraction is $\frac{.25}{1.23}$. If we actually needed to calculate the percentage increase, we would then divide 0.25 by 1.23 and multiply that quotient by 100 (to rename the decimal as a percent). For purposes of answering the quantitative comparison question, however, a rough estimate will be sufficient. The percentage increase in the price is more than $25 \div 125$, and that would be a $\frac{1}{5}$, or 20%, increase. Thus Column A is slightly greater than 20%, so Column A must be greater.

4. **The correct answer is (C).** The intuitive way of solving this problem is to reason that $\frac{M+x+y}{3}$ is the average of M, x, and y, and that $\frac{x+y}{2}$ is the average of x and y. Since the average of any number and itself is itself—that is, the average of x and x is x—Column A must be equal to Column B. The same conclusion can be more rigorously demonstrated by substituting $\frac{x+y}{2}$ for M in column A:

$$\frac{\frac{x+y}{2}+x+y}{3} = \frac{\frac{x+y+2(x+y)}{2}}{3} = \frac{3x+3y}{6} = \frac{x+y}{2}$$

5. **The correct answer is (D).** The natural starting point for solving this problem is to perform the indicated operations—that is, to multiply the expressions:

$(a + 2)(b + 3)=$ $(a + 3)(b + 2)=$
$ab + 3a + 2b + 6$ $ab + 2a + 3b + 6$

Of course, since ab and 6 are common to both expressions, those terms cannot make any difference in the comparison of the two columns. After we strip away the ab terms and 6, we are left with $3a + 2b$ in Column A and $2a + 3b$ in Column B. Since no information is given about the relative magnitudes of a and b, the answer must be (D).

6. **The correct answer is (E).** A simple method for adding any two fractions is:

Step A: Find the new denominator by multiplying the old ones.

Step B: Multiply the numerator of the first fraction by the denominator of the second.

Step C: Multiply the denominator of the first fraction by the numerator of the second.

Step D: Add the results of B and C.

Step E: Simplify, if necessary.

The process is more easily comprehended when presented in the following way:

$$\frac{a}{b} + \frac{c}{d} = \frac{ad + bc}{bd}$$

Here, we have:

$$\frac{3}{4} + \frac{4}{5} = \frac{15 + 16}{20} = \frac{31}{20}$$

7. **The correct answer is (C).** Since $x + 6 = 3$, $x = -3$. Then, substituting -3 for x in the second expression, $x + 3$ is $-3 + 3 = 0$.

8. **The correct answer is (A).** Probably the easiest way to solve this problem is just to count the steps on your fingers, but the same process can be expressed mathematically. Let those steps he walks down be assigned negative values, and those steps he walks up be positive. We then have: $-4 + 3 - 6 + 2 + 9 - 2 = +2$. So the person comes to rest two steps above where he started.

9. **The correct answer is (A).** In a circle graph such as this, the sectors must total 100%. The sectors P, R, S, and T account for 21%, 29%, 18%, and 28%, respectively, for a total of 96%. So Q must be 4%.

10. **The correct answer is (A).** The easiest way to solve this problem is to factor the 326 from both terms of the expression:

$$326(31 - 19) = 326(12) = 3,912$$

Of course, you might actually do the arithmetic by multiplying first 326 by 31 and then 326 by 19 and then subtracting the lesser total from the greater. That takes quite a bit longer! But if you did not see the first way (factoring) and can manage the arithmetic in thirty or forty seconds, you should proceed with the one way you know to get the correct answer. However, the better approach by far is to find a way of avoiding the calculation.

11. **The correct answer is (B).** The sum of the interior angles of a pentagon is 540°, and that of a hexagon is 720°. If you did not recall this, you could have computed the sum in the following way:

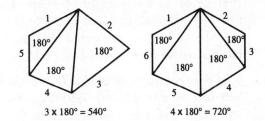

3 x 180° = 540°   4 x 180° = 720°

(Notice that the sum of the interior angles is unrelated to the relative lengths of the sides.)

The average size of the angles of the pentagon, then, is 540 divided by 5, or 108°. And the average size of the angles of the hexagon is 720° divided by 6, or 120°. The general rule is: The average size of the angle grows as the number of sides in the polygon increases.

12. **The correct answer is (B).** The shelf originally contains 24 books. We remove 75% of the 16 French books, or 12, which leaves 4 French books remaining on the shelf. Then we remove 50% of the 8 Italian books, leaving 4 Italian books. Only 8 books remain on the shelf—that is, $\frac{1}{3}$ of the total.

13. **The correct answer is (C).** In a right triangle in which the angles are 90°, 60°, and 30°, the length of the side opposite the 30° angle is one half the length of the hypotenuse, and the length of the side opposite the 60° angle is one half the length of the hypotenuse times $\sqrt{3}$. Since two of the angles of this triangle total 90°, and there are 180° in a triangle, the measure of angle B must equal 90°, and this is a right triangle. Side AB is opposite the 30° angle, and so must be one half the hypotenuse. AB is 1; therefore, AC must be 2. BC, then, will be one half the length of the hypotenuse times $\sqrt{3}$. So BC will be $\sqrt{3}$.

14. **The correct answer is (D).** There are several ways of solving this problem. One way is to manipulate the centered equation so that $x^2 = 1$. Then it should be clear that $x = \pm 1$, and so x might be +1 or –1. Similarly, one might factor $x^2 - 1$ to get $(x + 1)(x - 1) = 0$, showing that there are two values for x, only one of which is +1.

15. **The correct answer is (A).** This problem can be solved using simultaneous equations. Let x be the number of $13 tickets and y the number of $25 tickets.

Then: $\qquad\qquad\qquad\qquad x + y = 11$
And: $\qquad\qquad\qquad\quad 13x + 25y = 227$
By the first equation: $\qquad\quad x = 11 - y$
Substitute: $\qquad 13(11 - y) + 25y = 227$
Then manipulate:
$$143 - 13y + 25y = 227$$
$$12y = 84$$
$$y = 7$$

And if the number of $25 tickets is equal to 7, the number of $13 tickets is only 4, so Column A is greater. An easier and therefore a better way of solving the problem is to recognize that the average value of the tickets must be approximately $20. If an equal number of tickets had been sold (impossible, of course, since an odd number of tickets was sold), the average would have been midway between $13 and $25, or $19. Since the average is above $19, more of the expensive tickets must have been sold.

16. **The correct answer is (B).** The greatest increase occurred from 1978 to 1979. It was:

1979 Earnings – 1978 Earnings =
1.1 – 0.5 = 0.6 million = $600,000

17. **The correct answer is (C).** This question asks about percent change, so use the "change over" strategy. To make the task easier, try to work with the fractions you create directly and avoid changing them to percents.

(A) $\dfrac{1980 - 1979}{1979} = \dfrac{12 - 10}{10} = \dfrac{2}{10} = \dfrac{1}{5}$

(B) $\dfrac{1981 - 1980}{1980} = \dfrac{9 - 12}{12} = -\dfrac{3}{12} = -\dfrac{1}{4}$

(decrease)

(C) $\dfrac{1982 - 1981}{1981} = \dfrac{12 - 9}{9} = \dfrac{3}{9} = \dfrac{1}{3}$

(D) $\dfrac{1983 - 1982}{1982} = \dfrac{14 - 12}{12} = \dfrac{2}{12} = \dfrac{1}{6}$

(E) $\dfrac{1984 - 1983}{1982} = \dfrac{13 - 14}{14} = -\dfrac{1}{14}$

(decrease)

18. **The correct answer is (A).** Just calculate the average:

$(0.9 + 1.0 + 1.2 + 1.3 + 1.5) \div 5 = 5.9 \div 5 = 1.18 = \$1,180,000$

19. **The correct answer is (D).** Since this question asks for percent change, use the "change over" strategy.

$$\frac{1985 - 1976}{1976} = \frac{1.5 - 3.0}{0.3} = \frac{1.2}{0.3} = 4 = 400\%$$

20. **The correct answer is (B).** If you try to solve this problem by writing out a calculation for each of the years, you'll run out of time before you can get halfway through. Instead, you should do the math in your head. You can find 10 percent of a number just by moving the decimal point one place to the left. Take 1976, for example. Ten percent of 6 million is 0.6 million, which is larger than 0.3 million, so in that year earnings were not equal to or greater than 10 percent of sales. Work your way quickly through the other years. You will find that in four years, earnings were either equal to or greater than 10 percent of sales: 1979, 1980, 1981, and 1984.

21. **The correct answer is (C).** This problem requires that the expression in Column A be factored. From basic algebra you will recall that $(x + y)(x - y) = x^2 - y^2$. So the numerator of Column A can be factored into $(x + y)(x - y)$. Then the $x - y$ can be divided, leaving $x + y$ for both columns.

22. **The correct answer is (C).** To make the explanation easier to grasp, we add the following notation:

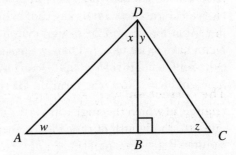

Since BD is perpendicular to AC, both triangle ABD and triangle CBD are right triangles. Consequently:

$w + x + 90° = 180°$ and $y + z + 90° = 180°$

so: $w + x = 90°$ and $y + z = 90°$

23. **The correct answer is (A).** The two planes converge on each other at the rate of 300 miles/40 minutes, or 300 miles/$\frac{2}{3}$ hr. That is a rate of 450 miles per hour—the *sum* of their speeds. Since plane X is flying at 150 mph, plane Y must be flying at 300 mph. Another way of solving the problem would be to reason that *if* plane Y were flying at 150 mph, the two planes would be converging at the rate of 300 mph and it would take a full hour, not 40 minutes, for them to pass. This shows that plane Y must be flying at a speed faster than 150 mph.

24. **The correct answer is (D).** In simple English, the 90¢ the child must replace to bring the amount back up to its original amount is 10% of the original amount. Expressed in notation, that is:

$90¢ = .10$ of x

$\$9 = x$

25. The correct answer is (C). Let us begin by assigning letters to the height and radius of each cylinder. Since most people find it easier to deal with whole numbers instead of fractions, let us say that cylinder Q has a radius of $2r$, so that cylinder P can have a radius of r. Then, we assign cylinder Q a height of h so that P can have a height of $2h$. Now, the formula for the volume of a cylinder is $\pi r^2 \times h$. So P and Q have volumes:

Volume $P = \pi(r)^2 \times 2h$

Volume $Q = (2\pi r)^2 \times h$

$P = 2\pi r^2 h$

$Q = 4\pi r^2 h$

Thus, the ratio of $P{:}Q$ is $\frac{2\pi r^2 h}{4\pi r^2 h} = \frac{2}{4} = \frac{1}{2}$.

26. The correct answer is (A). We begin by extending the lines to give this picture:

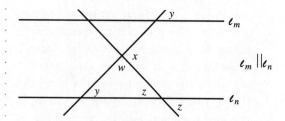

Then we add another angle y (lines l_m and l_n are parallel, so corresponding angles are equal) and another z (vertical angles are equal). We know that $x + w = 180°$, and we know that $y + z + w = 180°$. So, $x + w = y + z + w$, and $x = y + z$.

27. The correct answer is (C). Let us begin by drawing the rectangle:

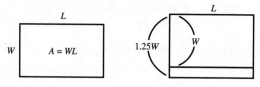

$A = 1.25W \times L = 1.25WL$

The original area is WL. The width of the new rectangle is $W + .25W$ or $1.25W$. So the new area is $1.25WL$. It then follows that the new area is $\frac{1.25WL}{WL}$, or 125% of the old area.

28. The correct answer is (B). Let us take any odd integer, m. The next consecutive odd integer will be two more than m, or $m + 2$. The third integer in the series will be $m + 4$, and the fourth integer in the series will be $m + 6$. The sum of the four is: $(m) + (m + 2) + (m + 4) + (m + 6) = 4m + 12$. And when $(4m + 12)$ is divided by 4, the result is: $\frac{4m+12}{4} = m + 3$. So the sum of four consecutive odd/positive integers is always evenly divisible by 4.

PRACTICE TEST 6 ANSWER SHEET

Verbal Section

1. (A) (B) (C) (D) (E)   7. (A) (B) (C) (D) (E)   13. (A) (B) (C) (D) (E)   19. (A) (B) (C) (D) (E)   25. (A) (B) (C) (D) (E)

2. (A) (B) (C) (D) (E)   8. (A) (B) (C) (D) (E)   14. (A) (B) (C) (D) (E)   20. (A) (B) (C) (D) (E)   26. (A) (B) (C) (D) (E)

3. (A) (B) (C) (D) (E)   9. (A) (B) (C) (D) (E)   15. (A) (B) (C) (D) (E)   21. (A) (B) (C) (D) (E)   27. (A) (B) (C) (D) (E)

4. (A) (B) (C) (D) (E)   10. (A) (B) (C) (D) (E)   16. (A) (B) (C) (D) (E)   22. (A) (B) (C) (D) (E)   28. (A) (B) (C) (D) (E)

5. (A) (B) (C) (D) (E)   11. (A) (B) (C) (D) (E)   17. (A) (B) (C) (D) (E)   23. (A) (B) (C) (D) (E)   29. (A) (B) (C) (D) (E)

6. (A) (B) (C) (D) (E)   12. (A) (B) (C) (D) (E)   18. (A) (B) (C) (D) (E)   24. (A) (B) (C) (D) (E)   30. (A) (B) (C) (D) (E)

Math Section

1. (A) (B) (C) (D) (E)   7. (A) (B) (C) (D) (E)   13. (A) (B) (C) (D) (E)   19. (A) (B) (C) (D) (E)   25. (A) (B) (C) (D) (E)

2. (A) (B) (C) (D) (E)   8. (A) (B) (C) (D) (E)   14. (A) (B) (C) (D) (E)   20. (A) (B) (C) (D) (E)   26. (A) (B) (C) (D) (E)

3. (A) (B) (C) (D) (E)   9. (A) (B) (C) (D) (E)   15. (A) (B) (C) (D) (E)   21. (A) (B) (C) (D) (E)   27. (A) (B) (C) (D) (E)

4. (A) (B) (C) (D) (E)   10. (A) (B) (C) (D) (E)   16. (A) (B) (C) (D) (E)   22. (A) (B) (C) (D) (E)   28. (A) (B) (C) (D) (E)

5. (A) (B) (C) (D) (E)   11. (A) (B) (C) (D) (E)   17. (A) (B) (C) (D) (E)   23. (A) (B) (C) (D) (E)

6. (A) (B) (C) (D) (E)   12. (A) (B) (C) (D) (E)   18. (A) (B) (C) (D) (E)   24. (A) (B) (C) (D) (E)

Analytical Writing—Issue Topic

_____

_____

_____

_____

_____

_____

_____

_____

_____

_____

_____

_____

_____

_____

_____

_____

_____

_____

_____

_____

_____

_____

_____

Analytical Writing—Argument Topic

_____
_____
_____
_____
_____
_____
_____
_____
_____
_____
_____
_____
_____
_____
_____
_____
_____
_____
_____
_____
_____
_____
_____
_____

Practice Test 6

ANALYTICAL WRITING

Issue Topic • 45 Minutes

Present Your Perspective on an Issue

In this part, two topics appear as brief quotations. Each states, either explicitly or implicitly, an issue of broad interest. You are to choose one of the two topics. You will then use the remainder of the 45 minutes to write an essay in which you take a position on the issue.

You may agree with the quotation, disagree with it, or challenge the statement in any way, so long as the ideas that you present are clearly relevant to the topic. You should provide reasons and examples to support your position. In doing so, you may want to draw on your reading of various sources, your personal experience and observations, or your academic studies.

It is a good idea to begin by reading the topic carefully. Then you should decide what position you want to take, after which you will probably want to outline your answer before you begin to write. Your essay will be graded on how well you:

- Assess the implications of the issue, including various complexities implicit in the topic

- Organize, develop, and express your thoughts on the issue

- Provide supporting reasons and examples

- Demonstrate your mastery of the elements of standard written English

You should leave yourself sufficient time to read what you have written and to make any revisions to your essay that you think are needed.

For this exercise, you may choose to use an editing program on a computer (word processor) or write your response by hand using the space provided.

Issue Topics

Choose <u>one</u> of the following two topics to write on.

"Our high schools and colleges place too much emphasis on athletics to the detriment of other enrichment programs and academic achievement."

"Because e-mail places a premium on rapid communication and quick response, it discourages careful thought and well-crafted prose and tends to encourage incivility."

Argument Topic • 30 Minutes

Analyze an Argument

In this part, you will be given an argument and have 30 minutes within which to write a critique of the argument. Your essay must address the argument given.

You are to <u>analyze</u> the reasoning of the argument. You should consider whether any of its assumptions are questionable and whether the evidence presented supports the conclusion. You might also discuss what changes in the line of reasoning or additional evidence would strengthen or weaken the conclusion.

Importantly, you are **NOT** being asked to state your own views on the underlying subject.

It is a good idea to begin by reading the argument carefully. Then you should evaluate the argument and consider what response you want to make, after which you will probably want to outline your answer before you begin to write.

Your essay response will be graded on how well you:

• Identify and analyze the important elements of the argument

• Organize, develop, and state your analysis

• Support your analysis with relevant reasons and examples

• Demonstrate your mastery of the elements of standard written English

You should leave yourself sufficient time to read what you have written and to make any revisions to your essay that you think are needed.

Timing for this part begins when you click on the "Dismiss the Directions" icon.

Argument Topic

The following appeared in a memo written by the manager of the Elm Street store of Home-Style Grocery Company:

> "An important change is taking place in this area that will permit the Elm Street store to attract more business and increase profits. A locally owned grocery store, Ma's Pantry, is permanently closing in two months because its longtime owner is retiring. The store is just one mile away, on the other side of the interstate highway. One feature that has attracted customers to that store is its deli section, where people order sandwiches to take with them. By adding a deli section to this store, we could expect to attract those customers plus others who used to shop for produce and other groceries."

VERBAL SECTION

30 Questions • 30 Minutes

Directions: Each of the questions below contains one or more blank spaces, each blank indicating that something has been omitted. Each sentence is followed by five (5) words or sets of words. Read and determine the general sense of each sentence. Then choose the word, or set of words that, when inserted in the sentence, best fits the meaning of the sentence.

1. The history book, written in 1880, was tremendously ——, unfairly blaming the South for the Civil War.

   (A) biased

   (B) objective

   (C) suppressed

   (D) questionable

   (E) complicated

2. In the Middle Ages, scientists and clergymen thought the universe was well-ordered and ——; today scientists are more likely to see the world as ——.

   (A) baffling . . dogmatic

   (B) harmonious . . chaotic

   (C) transient . . predictable

   (D) emancipated . . intriguing

   (E) divergent . . galling

3. Hot milk has long been a standard cure for insomnia because of its —— quality.

   (A) malevolent

   (B) amorphous

   (C) soporific

   (D) plaintive

   (E) desultory

practice test

Directions: In each of the following questions, you are given a related pair of words or phrases in capital letters. Each capitalized pair is followed by five (5) pairs of words or phrases. Choose the pair that best expresses a relationship similar to that expressed by the original pair.

4. DISLIKABLE : ABHORRENT ::
   (A) trustworthy : helpful
   (B) difficult : arduous
   (C) silly : young
   (D) tender : hard
   (E) ugly : beautiful

5. UNIFORM : SOLDIER ::
   (A) silks : jockey
   (B) leash : dog
   (C) pasture : cow
   (D) farmer : tractor
   (E) costume : scenery

6. MURAL : WALL ::
   (A) pen : letter
   (B) tree : forest
   (C) painting : canvas
   (D) tobacco : smoke
   (E) museum : curator

Directions: The passage below is followed by questions based on its content. Choose the best answer to each question.

One continuing problem in labor-management relations is the "us/them" mentality. In addition to fiscal constraints, continuing problems with the Fair La-
(5) bor Standards Act, bad-faith negotiations, bad management practices, poor union leadership, and a continued loss of management prerogatives will all combine to produce forces that will cause a
(10) significant increase in disruptive job actions in the near future. Neither side is blameless. The tragedy of the situation is that the impact of poor labor-management relations is relatively
(15) predictable and is thus avoidable.
   Since the economic situation will not improve significantly in the next few years, the pressure on the part of union leaders to obtain more benefits for their
(20) members will be frustrating. As a result of the PATCO strike, management has learned that times are conducive to regaining prerogatives lost during the previous decade. The stage for confrontation
(25) between labor and management in the public sector is set, and in many areas, only requires an incident to force disruptive job actions. The only solution to this seemingly intractable problem lies in
(30) the area of skilled negotiations and good-faith bargaining. This requires commitment on the part of management and labor to live up to the terms of existing contracts.

7. It can be inferred that the PATCO strike (line 21)
   (A) was an example of bad-faith negotiations
   (B) lasted only a brief period
   (C) was the fault of incompetent management
   (D) violated the provisions of the Fair Labor Standards Act
   (E) resulted in a victory for management

8. The author's discussion of labor-management relations can best be described as

(A) extremely pro-labor

(B) mildly pro-labor

(C) neutral

(D) mildly pro-management

(E) extremely pro-management

9. The author implies that if the economic conditions improve

(A) management will lose much of its power

(B) labor leaders will not seek more benefits

(C) labor-management tensions will decline

(D) the Fair Labor Standards Act will be repealed

(E) labor will win a voice in management

10. The author mentions all of the following as factors that might contribute to disruptive job actions EXCEPT

(A) unsatisfactory union leadership

(B) loss of management control

(C) bad-faith negotiations

(D) poor management practices

(E) low interest rates

Directions: In each of the following questions, you are given a related pair of words or phrases in capital letters. Each capitalized pair is followed by five (5) pairs of words or phrases. Choose the pair that best expresses a relationship similar to that expressed by the original pair.

11. COMMENCE : PROCRASTINATION ::

(A) terminate : prolongation

(B) show : demonstration

(C) frighten : terror

(D) guarantee : refund

(E) capture : torture

12. BUCOLIC : URBAN ::

(A) dense : sparse

(B) rural : ephemeral

(C) elastic : plastic

(D) mist : smog

(E) rustic : toxic

13. REGRETTABLE : LAMENT ::

(A) praiseworthy : applaud

(B) verbose : rejoice

(C) incongruous : detect

(D) reliable : defend

(E) obnoxious : boast

14. FASTIDIOUS : CLEANLINESS ::

(A) pliant : fabrication

(B) meticulous : detail

(C) timorous : hostility

(D) bereft : animosity

(E) enervated : activity

15. DISAPPROBATION : CONDEMN ::

(A) solvency : deploy

(B) calumny : praise

(C) enigma : enlighten

(D) fallacy : disseminate

(E) exhortation : urge

Directions: Each of the questions below contains one or more blank spaces, each blank indicating that something has been omitted. Each sentence is followed by five (5) words or sets of words. Read and determine the general sense of each sentence. Then choose the word, or set of words that, when inserted in the sentence, best fits the meaning of the sentence.

16. In the Middle Ages, the Benedictine monasteries were often —— of civilization and a refuge for science in an otherwise —— and superstitious world. .

    (A) arbiters . . scholarly
    (B) brethren . . sanctimonious
    (C) forerunners . . erudite
    (D) conservators . . barbarous
    (E) advocates . . rarefied

17. Both coffee and tea have beneficial as well as —— side-effects: while they stimulate the heart and help overcome fatigue, they also —— insomnia and other nervous disorders.

    (A) injurious . . exacerbate
    (B) malignant . . interrupt
    (C) salutary . . heighten
    (D) negligible . . forestall
    (E) specious . . prevent

Directions: Each of the following questions consists of a word printed in capital letters, followed by five (5) words or phrases. Choose the word or phrase that is most nearly opposite in meaning to the word in capital letters. Be sure to consider all the choices before deciding which one is best.

18. GUILE :

    (A) abundance
    (B) forbidden
    (C) treasure
    (D) naïveté
    (E) impression

19. MALIGN :

    (A) refuse
    (B) constrain
    (C) praise
    (D) demand
    (E) reply

20. INCITE :

    (A) forget
    (B) calm
    (C) change
    (D) involve
    (E) produce

Directions: The passage below is followed by questions based on its content. Choose the best answer to each question.

At the present time, 98 percent of the world energy consumption comes from stored sources, such as fossil fuels or nuclear fuel. Only hydroelectric and (5) wood energy represent completely renewable sources on ordinary time scales. Discovery of large additional fossil fuel reserves, solution of the nuclear safety and waste disposal problems, or the (10) development of controlled thermonuclear fusion will provide only a short-term solution to the world's energy crisis. Within about 100 years, the thermal pollution resulting from our in- (15) creased energy consumption will make solar energy a necessity at any cost.

Man's energy consumption is currently about one part in ten thousand that of the energy we receive from the sun. (20) However, it is growing at a 5 percent rate, of which about 2 percent represents a population growth and 3 percent a per capita energy increase. If this growth continues, within 100 years our (25) energy consumption will be about 1 percent of the absorbed solar energy, enough to increase the average temperature of the earth by about 1 degree centigrade if stored energy continues to (30) be our predominant source. This will be the point at which there will be significant effects in our climate, including the melting of the polar ice caps, a phenomenon that will raise the level of (35) the oceans and flood parts of our major cities. There is positive feedback associated with this process, since the polar ice cap contributes to the partial reflectivity of the energy arriving from (40) the sun: As the ice caps begin to melt, the reflectivity will decrease, thus heating the earth still further.

It is often stated that the growth rate will decline or that energy conservation (45) measures will preclude any long-range problem. Instead, this only postpones the problem by a few years. Conservation by a factor of two together with a maintenance of the 5 percent growth (50) rate delays the problem by only fourteen years. Reduction of the growth rate to 4 percent postpones the problem by only twenty-five years; in addition, the inequities in standards of living throughout (55) the world will provide pressure toward an increase in growth rate, particularly if cheap energy is available. The problem of a changing climate will not be evident until perhaps ten years before it (60) becomes critical due to the nature of an exponential growth rate together with the normal annual weather variations. This may be too short a period to circumvent the problem by converting to other (65) energy sources, so advance planning is a necessity.

The only practical means of avoiding the problem of thermal pollution appears to be the use of solar energy. (70) (Schemes to "air-condition" the earth do not appear to be feasible before the twenty-second century.) Using the solar energy before it is dissipated to heat does not increase the earth's energy bal- (75) ance. The cost of solar energy is extremely favorable now, particularly when compared to the cost of relocating many of our major cities.

21. The author is primarily concerned with

    (A) describing a phenomenon and explaining its causes

    (B) outlining a position and supporting it with statistics

    (C) isolating an ambiguity and clarifying it by definition

    (D) presenting a problem and advocating a solution for it

    (E) citing a counter-argument and refuting it

22. According to the passage, all of the following are factors that will tend to increase thermal pollution EXCEPT

(A) the earth's increasing population

(B) melting of the polar ice caps

(C) increase in per capita energy consumption

(D) pressure to redress standard of living inequities by increasing energy consumption

(E) expected anomalies in weather patterns

23. The positive feedback mentioned in lines 36–37 means that the melting of the polar ice caps will

(A) reduce per capita energy consumption

(B) accelerate the transition to solar energy

(C) intensify the effects of thermal pollution

(D) necessitate a shift to alternative energy sources

(E) result in the inundations of major cities

24. The possibility of energy conservation (lines 43–46) is mentioned in order to

(A) preempt and refute a possible objection to the author's position

(B) support directly the central thesis of the passage

(C) minimize the significance of a contradiction in the passage

(D) prove that such measures are ineffective and counterproductive

(E) supply the reader with additional background information

25. It can be inferred that the "air-conditioning" of the earth (line 70) refers to proposals to

(A) distribute frigid air from the polar ice caps to coastal cities as the temperature increases due to thermal pollution

(B) dissipate the surplus of the release of stored solar energy over absorbed solar energy into space

(C) conserve completely renewable energy sources by requiring that industry replace these resources

(D) avoid further thermal pollution by converting to solar energy as opposed to conventional and nuclear sources

(E) utilize hydroelectric and wood energy to replace non-conventional energy sources such as nuclear energy

Directions: Each of the questions below contains one or more blank spaces, each blank indicating that something has been omitted. Each sentence is followed by five (5) words or sets of words. Read and determine the general sense of each sentence. Then choose the word, or set of words that, when inserted in the sentence, best fits the meaning of the sentence.

26. Since the results of the experiment were —— the body of research already completed, the committee considered the results to be ——.

(A) similar to . . speculative

(B) inconsistent with . . anomalous

(C) compounded by . . heretical

(D) dispelled by . . convincing

(E) contradicted by . . redundant

27. Psychologists believe that modern life —— neurosis because of the —— of traditional values that define acceptable behavior.

(A) copes with . . inundation

(B) strives for . . condoning

(C) concentrates on . . plethora

(D) fosters . . disappearance

(E) corroborates . . dispelling

Directions: Each of the following questions consists of a word printed in capital letters, followed by five (5) words or phrases. Choose the word or phrase that is most nearly opposite in meaning to the word in capital letters. Be sure to consider all the choices before deciding which one is best.

28. CONTROVERT :

(A) predict

(B) bemuse

(C) intend

(D) agree

(E) rectify

29. LANGUOROUS :

(A) frenetic

(B) corporeal

(C) explicit

(D) recondite

(E) anomalous

30. PERSPICACIOUS :

(A) of indefinite duration

(B) lacking intrinsic value

(C) insufficiently precise

(D) condemnatory

(E) dull-witted

MATH SECTION

28 Questions • 45 Minutes

Numbers: All numbers used are real numbers.

Figures: The position of points, angles, regions, and so forth are in the order shown. Figures are assumed to lie in a plane unless otherwise indicated. Figures are drawn as accurately as possible for problem-solving questions, unless otherwise indicated. Figures are NOT drawn to scale for quantitative analysis problem, unless otherwise indicated. You should solve the problems by using your knowledge of mathematics and not by estimating sizes by sight or measurement.

Lines: Assume that lines shown as straight are indeed straight.

Directions: For each of the following questions, select the best of the answer choices. For quantitative comparison questions, two quantities are given, one in Column A and one in Column B. Compare the two quantities and choose

(A) if the quantity in Column A is greater
(B) if the quantity in Column B is greater
(C) if the two quantities are equal
(D) if the relationship cannot be determined from the information given

Information applying to both columns is centered between the columns and above the quantities in columns A and B. Symbols that appear in both columns represent the same idea or quantity in each column.

Column A	**Column B**
$h = 6$	

1. The number of minutes in h hours. — The number of degrees in the sum of the angles of a square.

A square has a side that is h inches long.

2. h^2 — The number of inches along the perimeter of the square.

$|x| = 3,\ |y| = 4$

3. $|y - x|$ — 1

---

4. The sum of the three smallest prime numbers. — $\sqrt{49} + \sqrt{8}$

Jackie, Beth, and Allison each have different cars and park in a three-spot parking lot behind their house.

5. The number of possible different arrangements of their cars in the three spots. — 7

Directions: For each of the following questions, select the best of the answer choices given.

6. If $(x-y)^2 = 12$ and $xy = 1$, then $x^2 + y^2 =$

   (A) 14

   (B) 13

   (C) 12

   (D) 11

   (E) 10

7.

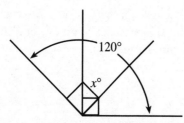

(*Note*: Figure not drawn to scale.)

What is x?

   (A) 30

   (B) 45

   (C) 60

   (D) 90

   (E) 240

8. If n is a positive integer and 95 and 135 are divided by n, and the remainders are 5 and 3 respectively, then $n =$

   (A) 6

   (B) 8

   (C) 10

   (D) 15

   (E) 21

9. A student conducts an experiment in biology lab and discovers that the ratio of the number of insects in a given population having characteristic X to the number of insects in the population not having characteristic X is 5:3, and that $\frac{3}{8}$ of the insects having characteristic X are male insects. What proportion of the total insect population are male insects having the characteristic X?

   (A) 1

   (B) $\frac{5}{8}$

   (C) $\frac{6}{13}$

   (D) $\frac{15}{64}$

   (E) $\frac{1}{5}$

10. If the following were arranged in order of magnitude, which term would be the middle number in the series?

   (A) $\frac{3^8}{3^6}$

   (B) $3^3 - 1$

   (C) 3^0

   (D) 3^{27}

   (E) $3(3^2)$

Directions: For each of the following questions, select the best of the answer choices. For quantitative comparison questions, two quantities are given, one in Column A and one in Column B. Compare the two quantities and choose

(A) if the quantity in Column A is greater
(B) if the quantity in Column B is greater
(C) if the two quantities are equal
(D) if the relationship cannot be determined from the information given

Information applying to both columns is centered between the columns and above the quantities in columns A and B. Symbols that appear in both columns represent the same idea or quantity in each column.

<u>Column A</u>	<u>Column B</u>

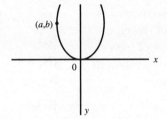

11.	a	b
12.	$3x + 5$	$2x + 3$

$x < 0$

13.	$(x^3)^5$	$x^3 \cdot x^5$

A man buys 16 shirts.
Some of them cost $13 each, while the remainder cost $10 each.
The cost of all 16 shirts is $187.

14.	The number of $13 shirts purchased	The number of $10 shirts purchased
15.	The volume of a sphere with a radius of 5	The volume of a cube with a side of 10

Directions: For each of the following questions, select the best of the answer choices given.

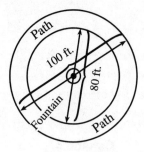

16. The fountain in the above illustration is located exactly at the center of the circular path. How many cubic feet of gravel are required to cover the circular garden path six inches deep with gravel?

(A) 5400π cu. ft.

(B) 4500π cu. ft.

(C) 1250π cu. ft.

(D) 450π cu. ft.

(E) 5π cu. ft.

17. A business firm reduces the number of hours its employees work from 40 hours per week to 36 hours per week while continuing to pay the same amount of money. If an employee earned x dollars per hour before the reduction in hours, how much does he earn per hour under the new system?

(A) $\dfrac{1}{10}$

(B) $\dfrac{x}{9}$

(C) $\dfrac{9x}{10}$

(D) $\dfrac{10x}{9}$

(E) $9x$

18. A ceiling is supported by two parallel columns as shown in the following drawing:

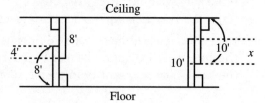

(*Note:* Figure not drawn to scale.)

What is the length of segment x in feet?

(A) 10

(B) 8

(C) 6

(D) 4

(E) It cannot be determined from the information given.

19. A painter has painted one third of a rectangular wall that is ten feet high. When she has painted another 75 square feet of wall, she will be three quarters finished with the job. What is the length (the horizontal dimension) of the wall?

(A) 18 feet

(B) 12 feet

(C) 10 feet

(D) 9 feet

(E) 6 feet

Directions: For each of the following questions, select the best of the answer choices. For quantitative comparison questions, two quantities are given, one in Column A and one in Column B. Compare the two quantities and choose

(A) if the quantity in Column A is greater
(B) if the quantity in Column B is greater
(C) if the two quantities are equal
(D) if the relationship cannot be determined from the information given

Information applying to both columns is centered between the columns and above the quantities in columns A and B. Symbols that appear in both columns represent the same idea or quantity in each column.

	Column A	**Column B**
20.	$-(3^6)$	$(-3)^6$

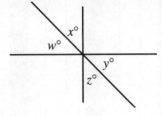

21.	$90 - (w + x)$	$90 - (y + z)$

Directions: For each of the following questions, select the best of the answer choices given.

QUESTIONS 22–25 REFER TO THE GRAPH BELOW.

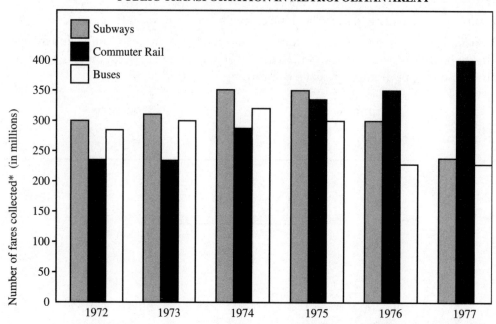

PUBLIC TRANSPORTATION IN METROPOLITAN AREA P

* One passenger paying one fare for one trip

22. From 1972 to 1977, inclusive, the total number of fares collected for subways was approximately how many million?

(A) 1900

(B) 1700

(C) 1500

(D) 1300

(E) 1100

23. From 1975 to 1977, the number of fares collected for subways dropped by approximately what percent?

(A) 90

(B) 35

(C) 25

(D) 15

(E) 9

24. If in 1974 the average subway fare collected was 50¢ and the average bus fare collected was 30¢, then the ratio of the total dollar amount of subway fares collected to the total dollar amount of bus fares was approximately

(A) $\frac{1}{4}$

(B) $\frac{1}{3}$

(C) $\frac{3}{5}$

(D) 1

(E) $\frac{7}{4}$

25. The number of commuter rail fares collected in 1977 accounted for approximately what percent of all fares collected on subways, buses, and commuter rail in that year?

   (A) 200%

   (B) 100%

   (C) 50%

   (D) 28%

   (E) 12%

Directions: For each of the following questions, select the best of the answer choices. For quantitative comparison questions, two quantities are given, one in Column A and one in Column B. Compare the two quantities and choose

(A) if the quantity in Column A is greater
(B) if the quantity in Column B is greater
(C) if the two quantities are equal
(D) if the relationship cannot be determined from the information given

Information applying to both columns is centered between the columns and above the quantities in columns A and B. Symbols that appear in both columns represent the same idea or quantity in each column.

Column A	**Column B**

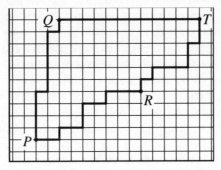

All angles are right angles

26.	Distance from P to T via Q	Distance from P to T via R

27.	The length of the side of any equilateral polygon inscribed in circle O	The length of the diameter of circle O

Peter's grade was higher than that of Victor, and Victor's grade was less than that of Georgette.

28.	Georgette's grade	Peter's grade

ANSWER KEY AND EXPLANATIONS

Analytical Writing
Issue Topics
Topic 1

As you read the following sample response, try to judge for yourself how well it meets the criteria that will be applied by graders:

Category	Below Avg.	Avg.	Above Avg.
Analysis of the Topic			
Organization and Development			
Use of Reasons and Examples			
Use of Standard Written English			
OVERALL SCORE*			

*Below Average = 1–2; Average = 3–4; Above Average = 5–6

SAMPLE RESPONSE AND COMMENTARY FOR ISSUE TOPIC 1

Note: The sample answers contain spelling and grammatical errors. This is done to simulate a first draft written under time pressure.

Whether an academic institution tends to overemphasize its athletics programs at the expense of other extra-curricular activities and academics depends in important ways on the goals of the instutition. At the outset, then, it seems necessary to distinguish secondary from college education.

High school general includes grades 9 through 12 and students in the age group 12 to 18, and the differences between the younger and older students in this range are more pronounced that those at the post-secondary level. A ninth grader may not be able to balance commitments in the same way that a twelfth grader can. Consequently, too great an emphasis on athletics for younger students is more damaging that it might be for older students. Additionally, parents exercise considerable more control over children in this age group. So if a high school is putting too much weight on athletics, a parent is in a position to step in and correct the imbalance.

College students are, of course, older. Still, it may seem to many that colleges overemphasize athletics because the various teams receive so much financial support and publicity. And it is not enough just to point out that athletes are usually held out as "athlete-scholars" because often their academic achievements are not that impressive. On the other hand, college athletic programs are generally not open to all students in the way that junior varsity and even varsity high school athletic programs are. Football players at the large universities, for example, are generally recruited, and the "walk-on" who makes the varsity is a rare exception and the starting unit and even rarer. Additionally, college athletics are in large measure self-funding, receiving monies from boosters and television contracts. So, in a way, the emphasis hardly affects ordinary students.

     While there is a lot of emphasis at both levels on athletics, it is probably not overly great. At the high school level, parents can hold things in check; at the college level, student-athletes are usually athletes first and students on incidentally, but that doesn't affect the great majority of students at the school.

COMMENTARY

This essay does explore some of the implications of the topic, and the writer manages to organize the thoughts pretty well by dividing the points into the "high school" and the "college" levels. The prose is for the most part good with relatively few errors. At the end of the essay, however, one is left wondering "What was the point of the essay anyway?" The writer really does not take a position (is there or is there not too much emphasis on athletics?) but instead wanders through various points and, only at the end, adds almost as an after-thought a conclusion that seems to respond to the topic. This essay would have been much better had the writer started by stating a position such as "While there is too much emphasis on athletics at the high school level, the same cannot be said of colleges." One might also suspect that the writer began the essay before thinking through the issue, that is, the writer started writing and then only late in the day realized it was important to take a position. That is why it is advisable to first think about the issue and decide on a position before writing. In its present form, the essay is probably a 4; with a more specific statement at the beginning and some further support for that position, it could easily become a 5.

Topic 2

As you read the following sample response, try to judge for yourself how well it meets the criteria that will be applied by graders:

Category	Below Avg.	Avg.	Above Avg.
Analysis of the Topic			
Organization and Development			
Use of Reasons and Examples			
Use of Standard Written English			
OVERALL SCORE*			

*Below Average = 1–2; Average = 3–4; Above Average = 5–6

SAMPLE RESPONSE AND COMMENTARY FOR ISSUE TOPIC 2

Note: The sample answers contain spelling and grammatical errors. This is done to simulate a first draft written under time pressure.

     There is no question that e-mail, with its speed-of-light tranmission, is a form of almost instantaneous communication. But, of course, so too is the telephone. Therefore, it seems, at some level, incorrect to blame e-mail on account of its facilitating rapid responses. On the other hand, the telphone is primarily a media for spoken communication, whereas e-mail is designed for the written word (or at least the written word in its electronic form). And there is little doubt that e-mail has introduced some new wrinkles on the tradition of written communication and presents new challenges.

In the first place, e-mail, though usually thought of as asynchronous communications, is now so fast that written exchanges can proceed at almost the same pace as a telephone conversation between parties. This makes e-mail very useful in crisis situations:

"Where is the emergency blood?"

"It will be there in 3 minutes."

And this is especially true where the sender has access to a mailing of people who need the information:

"Because of the snow emergency, all employees should leave the building by noon."

These tend to be situations, however, where careful thought must give way to action, and so the fact that e-mail does not encourage depth at these time is hardly a valid indictment.

Second, it must be admitted that some users act as though there is always a crisis:

"Each sales rep must have they're expense reports in too weeks."

The three errors in the preceding sentence were not the consequence of a crisis but simply carelessness, and standards seems to be somewhat laxer for e-mail than ordinary written communication. But again, it is not clear that this is inherent. E-mail is still relatively new, and one would hope that the community of users will begin to censor this sort of carelessness.

As for incivility, there are always those who speak before they've had a chance to consider their remarks, particularly during a heated exchange; and there is no reason to expect that e-mail should be any different. Of course, unlike a curt response or hurtful remark made verbally, there is a written or electronic record of the e-mail counterpart that's tougher to forgive and forget. Still, there is no reason to believe that this is inherent in e-mail, and one would expect for the community of users to evolve standards governing this sort of behavior as well.

A more serious challenge in this last area is ambiguity. Although telephones do not ordinarily permit face-to-face communication, tone of voice and inflection are very usefully in avoiding ambiguity, ambiguity that may creep into an e-mail:

"Have you received my proposal?"

"Yes, and I'll give it all of the attention it deserves."

A friendly tone of voice says that the proposal will receive serious consideration; a cool tone indicates sarcasm. Which is intended by e-mail?

At bottom, the difficulty with the topic statement is that it wants to say that the problems that users are now experiencing with e-mail, which is still a relatively new medium of communication for most of us, is inherent. Presumably the same thing was true of early telephone. And just as we have become more sophisticated in our use of that instrument (so much so that we hardly give it any thought), so too we will master the techniques of careful, well-crafted, and civil e-mailing.

COMMENTARY

This is an excellent response to the topic. The author does not start out by taking a stance but signals that the essay will explore the "new wrinkles" introduced by e-mail. The essay then explores the three issues suggested by the topic: lack of thought, inadequate prose, and incivility. For each of the three, the author discusses some interesting points and even introduces a sample e-mail exchange to make them more lively. At the end of the essay, the writer unveils the conclusion: the problem with the topic is that it mistakes the current stage of development of e-mail for its inherent nature. That's a fairly sophisticated way of dealing with the topic. Overall, then, the essay engages the topic; it is well organized; the prose is largely correct and interesting to read. This essay would likely receive a 6.

Argument Topic

As you read the following sample response, try to judge for yourself how well it meets the criteria that will be applied by graders:

Category	Below Avg.	Avg.	Above Avg.
Analysis of the Topic			
Organization and Development			
Use of Reasons and Examples			
Use of Standard Written English			
OVERALL SCORE*			

*Below Average = 1–2; Average = 3–4;
Above Average = 5–6

SAMPLE RESPONSE AND COMMENTARY FOR THE ARGUMENT TOPIC

Note: The sample answers contain spelling and grammatical errors. This is done to simulate a first draft written under time pressure.

In the movie "Field of Dreams," the Kevin Costner character hears a voice that tells him "If you build it, they will come." The memo from the manager of the Elm Street store expresses that same sort of blind faith; but whether the outcome will be the same as in the movie seems doubtful. There are three reasons to wonder whether more business and increased profits will follow the addition of a deli section.

First, it seems likely that there are important differences between the business model of Ma's Pantry and the Home-Style Grocery on Elm Street. The one is an independent store; the other is one of a chain. An independent store, particularly if it has deep roots in the community, attracts customers on factors other than price and variety. It may be the knowledge that the owner and family are active in the community; it may be that one's parents and grandparents were regular customers; it may be that the management is responsive to requests for particular items or services; or it may be—as strongly implied by the memo—that the owner and probably staff are well known and liked. A chain store just cannot hope to replicate those factors. A chain store can be a "good neighbor," but it is difficult for a "store" to be active in the community. The store may not have the legacy of the independent. Chain stores strive for efficiency through uniformity. And there is always going to be a turnover in staff, including managers, as people undergo training or receive promotions.

Second, some geographical market research would need to be done. The independent is a mile away, which may be a short distance or a long distance depending on several factors. Is the interstate highway a natural dividing line? Are the deli customers people who work in the immediate area and walk to the store for lunch? And perhaps most importantly, what's within one mile of Ma's Pantry on the other side of the interstate? If there is another independent, say Pa's Pantry, then it may be business that stands to gain the most from Ma's retirement.

Third, more research needs to be done into the nature of the deli business at Ma's Pantry. For an independent, it may be profitable to operate a deli as a deli, that is, just selling sandwiches; but deli customers may not be people who also buy other groceries and produce. Additionally, a deli is food service, an industry with different labor costs, regulatory requirements, and profit margins.

All of this is not to say that if Home-Style builds it, they won't come. But it is to say that if a management is looking for more that a "Field of Dreams," a lot of questions need to be answers.

COMMENTARY

This essay provides an excellent analysis of the argument. It drives three wedges between the evidence provided and the conclusion: the differences between an independent and a chain, the geography of the market, the difference between the grocery and the deli business. For each, the writer raises a number of issues that tend to further attenuate the link between the evidence and the conclusion. All in all, it does as much as one could expect of a 30-minute essay on such a topic in terms of critiquing the argument. Additionally, the essay is well structured, and the analysis is easy to follow. Each of the three main points is developed in its own paragraph, and transitions help to guide the reader through the various points within the paragraphs as well as from paragraph to paragraph. The prose is forceful and accurate, and the author finds a clever way to introduce and to close the analysis ("The Field of Dreams"). This essay would likely receive a 6.

Verbal Section

1.	A	7.	E	13.	A	19.	C	25.	B
2.	B	8.	C	14.	B	20.	B	26.	B
3.	C	9.	C	15.	E	21.	D	27.	D
4.	B	10.	E	16.	D	22.	E	28.	D
5.	A	11.	A	17.	A	23.	C	29.	A
6.	C	12.	D	18.	D	24.	A	30.	E

1. **The correct answer is (A).** The sentence gives you a very strong clue with the word *unfairly*. You can eliminate (B) since something that is unfair could not be objective. You can also eliminate (C) and (D) because they do not create meaningful sentences. (A), *biased*, is the best word to convey the idea that the book blamed the South unfairly.

2. **The correct answer is (B).** This sentence contains both a thought-extender and a thought-reverser. The first blank extends the thought that the universe was well-ordered. You can eliminate (A) since it is not logical that something would be well-ordered and *baffling*. (C), (D), and (E) are not words you would use to describe the universe. This leaves you with (B). There is a *but* or *yet* understood in this sentence, so the word in the next blank will have the opposite meaning of *harmonious*. The second element of (B) works because *chaotic* is the opposite of *harmonious*.

3. **The correct answer is (C).** This is a vocabulary question. You must know that something that cures insomnia is a *soporific*—something that induces sleep.

4. **The correct answer is (B).** To be ABHORRENT is to be extremely DISLIKABLE; to be *arduous* is to be extremely *difficult*.

5. **The correct answer is (A).** This analogy does not fit a category, but the relationship is quite clear. A SOLDIER wears a UNIFORM, and a *jockey* wears *silks*.

6. **The correct answer is (C).** Here there is a clear relationship. A MURAL is painted on a WALL and a *painting* is painted on a *canvas*.

7. **The correct answer is (E).** This is an inference question. The author states that a result of the PATCO strike is that management can now expect to regain some of the power it gave up to labor in earlier decades. So you may infer that the outcome of that strike was favorable to management. This is the description given by (E). As for (A), though the author mentions bad-faith negotiations in the first paragraph, there is nothing to connect that concept with the example mentioned in the second paragraph. As for (B), nothing in the passage supports a conclusion one way or the other about the length of the strike, as opposed to its outcome. (C) and (D) make the same mistake as (A). Though they are ideas mentioned in the passage, there is nothing to connect them with the example of the PATCO strike.

8. **The correct answer is (C).** This is an attitude question, and the choices have already been arranged for you on a spectrum. You can eliminate all but (C) because there is nothing to indicate a preference for one side over the other. In fact, statements such as *neither side is blameless* specifically attest to the author's neutrality.

9. **The correct answer is (C).** This is an implied idea question. The first sentence of the second paragraph states that since

the economic situation will not improve, union leaders will be frustrated. So the stage is set for confrontation. We may infer, therefore, that if economic conditions were better, labor would be happier, and tensions would be lessened. This is choice (C). (A) carries this line of reasoning too far. We can infer that better economic conditions would prevent management from recouping its losses, but we cannot infer that better economic conditions will cause further erosion of management's position. As for (B), the opposite conclusion seems inferable. When economic circumstances are good, labor demands more. As for (E), there is nothing to connect this idea mentioned in the first paragraph with the line of reasoning in the second. Finally, (D) makes the same mistake as (A).

10. **The correct answer is (E).** This is an explicit detail question. The ideas suggested by (A) through (D) are all explicitly mentioned in the selection. At no point, however, does the author mention low interest rates.

11. **The correct answer is (A).** This is a variation on the "lack of" relationship. PROCRASTINATION is a lack of COMMENCEMENT, and *prolongation* is a lack of *termination*. Note that in this analogy it is helpful to change the parts of speech.

12. **The correct answer is (D).** BUCOLIC relates to rural life and suggests the natural; URBAN implies the manufactured. *Mist* is a natural occurrence; *smog* is fog made foul by smoke and chemical fumes.

13. **The correct answer is (A).** This is a "defining characteristic" analogy. By definition, that which is LAMENTED is REGRETTABLE, and that which is *applauded* is *praiseworthy*.

14. **The correct answer is (B).** This is an analogy of degree. To be FASTIDIOUS is

to be extremely preoccupied with CLEANLINESS, and to be *meticulous* is to be extremely preoccupied with *detail*.

15. **The correct answer is (E).** This is a "defining characteristic" analogy. CONDEMNING presupposes DISAPPROBATION, and *urging* presupposes *exhortation*.

16. **The correct answer is (D).** This sentence contains two thought-extenders. The first blank extends the idea of *refuge for science*, and it should also be the reverse of the idea of *superstitious*. The second blank extends the idea of *superstitious*. (A) cannot be correct, for although the first word makes some sense, it makes no sense to say that the world was both *scholarly* and superstitious since that is a contradiction. (B) does not make a meaningful statement, nor does (C). (D) makes sense because the idea that the monks were "*conservators* of civilization" extends the idea that the monasteries were a "*refuge* for science," and the adjective *barbarous* goes well with *superstitious* to produce an idea that is more or less the opposite of *civilized*. (E) looks plausible because one might describe the monks as "*advocates* of civilization," but *rarefied* does not extend the idea of *superstitious*.

17. **The correct answer is (A).** The logical structure of this sentence is fairly clear; the first blank must be a word that is more or less the opposite of *beneficial*. The word *while* gives you the clue that the second blank must be a word with negative overtones since the first example of what coffee and tea do is beneficial. The construction is "while they are (beneficial) they are also (harmful)." (A) looks possible because *injurious* is certainly the opposite of *beneficial*. The second word also works well. Coffee and tea exacerbate problems. This seems to be the correct choice. The best thing to do here is to test the other responses to

make certain that (A) is the best choice. (B) doesn't work because although the first word is possible, if coffee and tea *interrupted* nervous disorders, they would be beneficial, not harmful. (C) is wrong because *salutary* is almost a synonym for *beneficial,* and we are looking for a word that is almost an opposite. (D) is wrong because *negligible* is not the opposite of *beneficial,* and again, if coffee and tea *forestalled* nervous disorders, that would be beneficial. (E) also fails because of the second word. *Preventing* nervous disorders is positive, not negative.

18. **The correct answer is (D).** Since GUILE means "craft or cunning," *naïve* is a good opposite.

19. **The correct answer is (C).** To MALIGN is to speak evil of or to slander; *praise* is a precise opposite.

20. **The correct answer is (B).** To INCITE is to arouse or move to action. *Calm* is an opposite.

21. **The correct answer is (D).** This is a main idea question. This passage does two things: It describes the problem of increasing thermal pollution and it suggests that solar energy will solve the problem. (D) neatly describes this double development. (A) is incorrect, for the author not only describes the phenomenon of thermal pollution and its causes, but also proposes a solution. (B) is incorrect since it fails to make reference to the fact that an important part of the passage is the description of a problem. It can be argued that (B) does make an attempt to describe the development of the passage, but it does not do that as nicely as (D) does. (C) is easily eliminated since no ambiguity is mentioned. Finally, (E) is incorrect since the author never cites and then refutes a counter-argument.

22. **The correct answer is (E).** This is an explicit idea question. (A), (B), and (C) are mentioned in the second paragraph as factors contributing to thermal pollution. (D) is mentioned in the third paragraph as a pressure increasing thermal pollution. (E) is mentioned in the third paragraph—but not as a factor contributing to thermal pollution. Unpredictable weather patterns make it difficult to predict when the thermal pollution problem will reach the critical stage, but the patterns do not contribute to thermal pollution.

23. **The correct answer is (C).** This is an inference question. In discussing the melting of the polar ice caps, the author notes that there is a positive feedback mechanism: Since the ice caps reflect sunlight and therefore dissipate solar energy that would otherwise be absorbed by the earth, the melting of the ice caps increases the amount of energy captured by the earth, which in turn contributes to the melting of the ice caps, and so on. (C) correctly describes this as intensifying the effects of thermal pollution. (A) is easily eliminated since this feedback mechanism has nothing to do with a possible reduction in per capita energy consumption. (B) is incorrect, for though this feedback loop increases the problem, and thereby the urgency for the changeover to solar energy, the loop itself will not cause a change in policy. (D) is incorrect for the same reason. Finally, though the melting of the polar ice caps will result in flooding, this flooding is not an explanation of the feedback loop. Rather it is the result of the general phenomenon of the melting of the ice caps.

24. **The correct answer is (A).** This is a logical detail question. Why does the author discuss energy conservation? Conservation may appear as a possible alternative to solar energy. The author argues, however, that a closer examination shows that conservation cannot avert but only postpone the crisis. In terms of tactics, the author's move is to raise a possible objection and give an answer to

it—as stated in (A). (B) is incorrect, for the refutation of a possible objection does not support the central thesis directly, only indirectly by eliminating a possible counter-argument. (C) is incorrect since the author never acknowledges any contradiction. (D) is incorrect since it overstates the case. The author admits that conservation has a beneficial effect, but denies that conservation obviates the need for solar energy. Finally, (E) is incorrect since the point is argumentative and not merely informational.

25. **The correct answer is (B).** This is an inference question. In the final paragraph the author makes references to the possibility of "air-conditioning" the earth. The quotation marks indicate that the word is being used in a non-standard way. Ordinarily, we use the word "air-condition" to mean to cool, say, a room or an entire building. Obviously, the author is not referring to some gigantic air-conditioning unit mounted, say, on top of the earth. But the general idea of removing heat seems to be what the term means in this context. This is consonant with the passage as well. Thermal pollution is the buildup of energy, and we are showing a positive buildup because fossil fuel and other sources of energy release energy that was only stored. So this, coupled with the sun's energy, which comes in each moment, gives us a positive (though not desirable) balance of energy retention over loss. The idea of air-conditioning the earth, though not feasible according to the passage, must refer to schemes to get rid of this energy, say, into outer space. This is the idea presented in (B). As for (A), redistribution of thermal energy within the earth's energy system will not solve the problem of accumulated energy, so that cannot be what proponents of "air-conditioning" have in mind. (C) is a good definition of conservation, but not "air-conditioning." (D) is the recommendation given by the author, but that is not a response to this question. Finally, (E) is incorrect for the reason that burning wood is not going to cool the earth.

26. **The correct answer is (B).** Given that there is a body of research already existing, the results can only be irrelevant to it, consistent with it, or inconsistent with it. This eliminates choice (C). Then you have to substitute both words of the remaining choices in order to determine the correct answer. (A) cannot be correct, since results would not be *speculative* if they were similar to the research already done. (D) is not possible because the body of research would not be *dispelled by* convincing results. (E) makes no sense because if the results were *redundant*, then they would not contradict the existing research. This leaves you with (B), which works very well. Results might be considered *anomalous* if they were inconsistent with the research already done.

27. **The correct answer is (D).** The logical clue here is a thought-extender. But the order in which the ideas are presented in the sentence makes this difficult to see. The idea that follows the *because* specifies the cause of the first idea: "The —— of traditional values" causes modern life to "—— neurosis." Substitute each of the choices into this new sentence. Only (D) produces a sentence that fits the logical structure.

28. **The correct answer is (D).** To CONTROVERT is to dispute or deny, so *agree* is a good opposite.

29. **The correct answer is (A).** LANGUOROUS means "characterized by lack of vigor or weakness," so frenetic is a good opposite.

30. **The correct answer is (E).** Since PERSPICACIOUS means "having keen insight or understanding," *dull-witted* is a good antonym.

Math Section

1.	C	7.	C	13.	B	19.	A	25.	C
2.	D	8.	A	14.	A	20.	B	26.	C
3.	D	9.	D	15.	B	21.	C	27.	B
4.	A	10.	B	16.	D	22.	A	28.	D
5.	B	11.	B	17.	D	23.	C		
6.	A	12.	D	18.	B	24.	E		

1. **The correct answer is (C).** For Column A, the number of minutes in 6 hours (since $h = 6$) can be found by multiplying: (6)(60 minutes) = 360 minutes, or 360. For Column B, you must know that a square has four right angles, all of which equal ninety degrees. This means Column B works out to: (4)(90) = 360.

   This first problem is fairly straightforward, and even though there was a variable involved, definite real numbers were found for both columns. Be aware that this will change as the questions get harder. On later problems, the use of variables will lead to column quantities that have more than one possible answer, so even though these problems will resemble this earlier one, finding the correct answer will not be as straightforward.

2. **The correct answer is (D).** The perimeter of the square is $4h$, but you do not know how this relates to h^2. If $h = 1$, then Column B is greater, but if $h = 10$, then Column A is greater. Note that if you confuse the area of a square with its perimeter, you will find the two columns are equal, leading you to pick the incorrect answer (C).

3. **The correct answer is (D).** You might jump to saying that the answer is (C), but that would be a little hasty. The absolute value sign (those two bars on either side) means that x could be either 3 or −3, and that y could equal either 4 or −4. Remember that $|y − x| \neq |y| − |x| = 1$. We actually do not know what $|y − x|$ equals. It could be 7, or it could be 1. The answer, then, is (D).

4. **The correct answer is (A).** For people rusty with their math terminology, this question looks much more difficult than it really is. The three smallest prime numbers are 2, 3, and 5, and their sum is 10. As for Column B, the square root of 49 is 7. You probably don't know the square root of 8 off the top of your head, but you do know that the square root of 9 is 3. This means the square root of 8 must be something less than 3. *7 + something less than 3 = something a little less than 10.* Therefore, Column A is greater.

5. **The correct answer is (B).** A good way to attack a problem like this is to sketch it out. If J is space 1 then there are two possibilities: JBA and JAB. If B is in space 1, BJA and BAJ. If A is in space 1, AJB and ABJ. That is six distinct arrangements. Can you get anymore? Try to put J in space 2, AJB or BJA. You already have both of those counted. Try any other arrangement, and you will see that it is a repeat. So, Column B is greater.

6. **The correct answer is (A).** We begin by multiplying $(x − y)^2$:

   $$(x − y)(x − y) = x^2 − 2xy + y^2 = 12$$

   Then we substitute 1 for xy:

   $$x^2 − 2(1) + y^2 = 12$$
   $$x^2 + y^2 = 14$$

7. **The correct answer is (C).** Let us begin by adding the following notation:

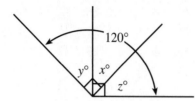

Since the measure of the entire angle is 120°, $y + 90 = 120$, so $y = 30$. Similarly, $z + 90 = 120$, so $z = 30$. Since $x + y + z = 120$, $x + 30 + 30 = 120$, so $x = 60$.

8. **The correct answer is (A).** Certainly the easiest and most direct way to solve this problem is to test each of the integers. There is no reason to try and find some fancy mathematical equation to describe the problem when a simple substitution of answer choices will do. When 95 is divided by 6, 10, and 15—answers (A), (C), and (D)—the remainder in each case is 5. And when 135 is divided by 10, the remainder is 5, not 3; and when 135 is divided by 15 there is a remainder of 0. When 135 is divided by 6, the remainder is 3. So only 6 fits both the conditions for n.

9. **The correct answer is (D).** Since the ratio of insects with X to those without X is 5:3, we know that $\frac{5}{8}$ of the population has X. (There are 8 equal units—$5 + 3$—5 of which are insects with X.) Then, of those $\frac{5}{8}$, $\frac{3}{8}$ are male. So we take $\frac{3}{8}$ of the $\frac{5}{8}$ $\left(\frac{3}{8} \times \frac{5}{8}\right)$, and that tells us that $\frac{15}{64}$ of the total population are male insects with X.

10. **The correct answer is (B).** We can order the elements by clarifying the exponents:

(A) $\dfrac{3^8}{3^6} = 3^{8-6} = 3^2 = 9$

(B) $3^3 - 1 = 27 - 1 = 26$

(C) $3^0 = 1$

(D) 3^{27} is too large to compute here, but is obviously the greatest quantity in the group.

(E) $3(3^2) = 3^3 = 27$

The order is (C), (A), (B), (E), (D); so (B) is the middle term.

11. **The correct answer is (B).** The parabola drawn on the graph actually adds no information needed for solving the problem. Regardless of what figure is drawn through point (a,b), and there are of course an infinite number of different ones, point (a,b) is in the second quadrant—that is, the upper left-hand section of the coordinate system. In that quadrant all x-values are negative and all y-values are positive, so a must be negative and b must be positive. Therefore, b is greater than a.

12. **The correct answer is (D).** We simplify the comparison as much as possible. First we subtract 3 from both sides and then we subtract $2x$ from both sides. This reduces Column A to $x + 2$ and Column B to 0. We can now ask the simpler question: Which is greater, $x + 2$ or 0? This is simpler because we can immediately see that the answer will depend on the value of x, information we lack.

13. **The correct answer is (B).** First, let us perform the indicated operations. In Column A, we find a power raised to a power, and that calls for the multiplication of the two exponents: $(x^3)^5 = x^{3 \cdot 5} = x^{15}$. In Column B, we find multiplication of like bases, so we add the exponents: $x^3 \cdot x^5 = x^{3 + 5} = x^8$.

The centered information states that x is negative. Since a negative number raised to a power that is odd yields a negative number (negative times negative times negative . . . yields a negative number), Column A is negative. Column B, however, must be positive since it is raised to an even power. Consequently, whatever x might be, Column A is negative, Column B is positive; therefore, Column B must be greater than Column A.

14. **The correct answer is (A).** The problem can be worked out using simultaneous equations, but that is not the most efficient way of solving it. For that reason we will set up the equations (for the "aficionados"), but we will not actually solve for x and y. Let x be the number of shirts costing $13 and y the number costing $10.

$$x + y = 16$$
$$13x + 10y = 187$$

Final solution: $x = 9$ and $y = 7$

We have omitted the detailed calculations because there is a simpler method. Let us assume, for the sake of argument, that the two columns are equal—that is, that the man bought equal numbers of both types of shirts. If we are correct in assuming that he bought eight $13 shirts and eight $10 shirts, then $(8 \times 13) + (8 \times 10)$ ought to equal $187. When we do the multiplication, we get the result $184. That tells us our original assumption of equal numbers was incorrect and, further, that the answer to the question is not (C). We should then make a second assumption, but should we assume that he bought more expensive shirts than we first guessed, or fewer? A moment of reflection will show that we should adjust our initial assumption to include a greater number of expensive shirts, for only by increasing that number will we add to the $184 which was the result of our original assumption. So we would

next assume—again for the purposes of argument—that the man bought nine $13 shirts and only seven $10 shirts. But at this point we have already solved the problem! We do not need to know the precise ratio, e.g., whether 9:7, 10:6, 11:5, 12:4, 13:3, 14:2, or 15:1; we have already determined that the ratio is one of those listed, and so it must be the case that Column A is greater.

15. **The correct answer is (B).** This problem, too, can be solved with a little gimmick. It is not necessary to actually calculate the volumes in question. You need only recognize that the sphere will have a diameter of 10 and that this is equal to the side of the cube. This means that the sphere can be placed within the cube, so the cube must have a greater volume.

16. **The correct answer is (D).** The proper way to "visualize" this problem is to imagine that the gravel-covered walk will be a very squat-shaped cylinder with a dough-nut hole removed (the circular region inside the walk). Expressed more abstractly, we need to compute the volume of a cylinder with a radius of 50 feet ($\frac{1}{2}$ of 100 = 50) and a height of 6 inches, or $\frac{1}{2}$ foot. Then we compute the volume of a cylinder with a radius of 40 feet ($\frac{1}{2}$ of 80 = 40) and a height of 6 inches, or $\frac{1}{2}$ foot. Then we subtract the second from the first and what is left is the volume we seek. Now, since both cylinders have the same height, it will be easier to compute the areas of the bases first and subtract before multiplying by $\frac{1}{2}$ foot.

Area of larger circle:
$$\text{Area} = \pi r^2 = \pi (50)^2 = 2500\pi$$

Area of smaller circle:

$$\text{Area} = \pi r^2 = \pi(40)^2 = 1600\pi$$

By subtracting 1600π from 2500π, we determine that the area of the garden path is 900π square feet. To determine the volume of gravel we need, we then multiply that figure by $\frac{1}{2}$ foot (the depth of the gravel), and arrive at our answer: 450π cu. ft.

17. **The correct answer is (D).** Let d stand for the hourly rate under the new system. Since the employee is to make the same amount per week under both systems, it must be the case that:

$$\frac{\$x}{\text{hr.}} \times 40 \text{ hrs.} = \frac{\$d}{\text{hr.}} \times 36 \text{ hrs.}$$

Now we must solve for d:

$$40x = 36d$$
$$d = \frac{10x}{9}$$

The problem can also be solved in an intuitive way. Since the employee is working less time yet making the same weekly total, he must be earning slightly more per hour under the new system than under the old. Answer (A) is just the naked fraction $\frac{1}{10}$, without making reference to monetary units. Answer (B) implies that the employee is making $\frac{1}{9}$ as much per hour under the new system as under the old—that would be a decrease in the hourly rate. Similarly, (C) says that the employee is making only 90% of his old hourly rate and that, too, is a decrease. Finally, (E) says that the employee is making 9 *times* the hourly rate he made under the old system, a figure that is obviously out of line. The only reasonable choice is (D). The moral is: Even if you cannot set up the math in a technically correct way, a little common sense helps you answer the question.

18. **The correct answer is (B).** Since the columns are perpendicular to both ceiling and floor, we know that they are parallel. The left-hand column must be 12 feet long: If the two 8-foot pieces were laid end to end, they would total 16 feet, but there is a 4-foot overlap, so the length of the column is 16 feet minus 4 feet, or 12 feet. The right-hand column must also be 12 feet long. But the two 10-foot pieces, if laid end to end, would form a column 20 feet long. Therefore, the overlap, x, must be 8 feet ($20 - x = 12$).

19. **The correct answer is (A).** This problem must be solved in two stages. First, we need to calculate the total area of the wall. The information given in the problem states that $\frac{1}{3}$ of the job plus another 75 square feet equals $\frac{3}{4}$ of the job. In algebraic notation, this is:

$$\frac{1}{3}x + 75 = \frac{3}{4}x$$
$$75 = \frac{3}{4}x - \frac{1}{3}x$$
$$75 = \frac{5}{12}x$$
$$x = 180$$

So the entire wall is 180 square feet—that is, $W \times L = 180$. We know that the height of the wall is 10 feet; so $10 \times L = 180$, and $L = 18$.

20. **The correct answer is (B).** A quick glance at the two expressions shows that Column A must be negative and Column B positive. Whatever the absolute value of the number 3^6, in Column A it will be negative since it is prefixed with the negative sign. Column B, however, will be positive. The negative sign is enclosed within the parentheses. This indicates that we are raising -3 to the sixth power. Since 6 is an even number, the final result will be positive (negative times negative times negative times negative times negative times negative yields a positive).

21. **The correct answer is (C).** We should notice first that we are definitely not in a position to say that the magnitude of the unlabeled angles is 90°. But we need not make the assumption! We know that $w = y$ and $x = z$ because vertical angles are equal. Therefore, $w + x = y + z$. We can drop these expressions from both sides of our comparison. In effect, we are subtracting equals from both sides of the comparison, a maneuver which, as we have already seen, will neither upset the balance of the original equality nor interfere with the direction of the inequality. This leaves us with 90 on both sides of the comparison, so we conclude that the original comparison must have been an equality.

22. **The correct answer is (A).** This is just a matter of adding up the total fares collected for subways in the six years:

1972:	300	million
1973:	310	million
1974:	350	million
1975:	350	million
1976:	310	million
1977:	250	million
	1,870	

23. **The correct answer is (C).** The number of fares collected in 1975 was 350 million, and the number of fares collected in 1977 was 250 million. The number of fares dropped by 100 million, but we are looking for the rate, or percentage, of decrease. So we set our fraction up, difference over starting amount, $\frac{100}{350} = 28.6\%$, which is closest to 25%.

24. **The correct answer is (E).** The number of subway fares collected in 1974 was 350 million; the number of bus fares collected in that year was 315 million. Our ratio then is $\frac{50 \times 350}{30 \times 315}$, which we then simplify by a factor of 10, $\frac{5 \times 350}{3 \times 315}$, and again

by a factor of 5, $\frac{5 \times 70}{3 \times 63}$; then we can do the arithmetic a little more easily: $\frac{350}{189}$. If we round off 189 to 200 and simplify again by a factor of 10, we get $\frac{35}{20}$, or $\frac{7}{4}$ as a good approximation of the ratio. Actually, we need not do all of this arithmetic. We can see at a glance that more subway fares were collected than bus fares; so, given that the subway fares are more expensive, we can conclude that the revenues derived from subway fares were greater than those for bus fares, and that means our ratio must be greater than 1. Only (E) is possible.

25. **The correct answer is (C).** In 1977, the total number of fares collected was 240 (subways) + 400 (commuter rail) + 235 (bus) = 875 total. Of the 875 million fares collected, 400 were commuter rail fares, so the commuter rail fares accounted for about $\frac{1}{2}$, or 50%, of all the fares collected in that year.

26. **The correct answer is (C).** At first glance, the problem appears to be a difficult one. A closer look, however, shows that it is actually quite simple. Both paths cover the same vertical distance of 10 units and the same horizontal distance of 14 units. Since it makes no difference whether one moves vertically or horizontally first, the two paths are equal. Notice further that each path covers a distance of 24 units. That is equal to the sum of one width and one length of a rectangle with dimension 10 and 14 that could be constructed using points P and T as vertices.

27. **The correct answer is (B).** Let us begin by inscribing an equilateral triangle in a circle:

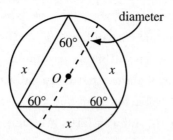

Since the longest chord of any circle is the chord drawn through the center of the circle (that is, the diameter of the circle), and since no side of the triangle can pass through the center, the side of the equilateral triangle must be shorter than the diameter of the circle in which it is inscribed. Having determined that, we then proceed to ask whether the length of the side of a square inscribed in the same circle is longer or shorter than that of the side of the equilateral triangle.

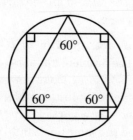

The side of the square is shorter, and we can see that the greater the number of sides, the shorter will be the length of those sides. From this we can conclude that for all equilateral polygons inscribed in circles, the side of the polygon will be shorter than the diameter of the circle.

28. **The correct answer is (D).** Using P, V, and G to represent Peter's, Victor's, and Georgette's grades, respectively, the centered information tells us: P > V and G > V. But we have no information regarding the relationship between P and G.

APPENDICES

GRE Word List

A

abbreviate (verb) To make briefer, to shorten. *Because time was running out, the speaker was forced to abbreviate his remarks.* abbreviation (noun).

aberration (noun) A deviation from what is normal or natural, an abnormality. *Jack's extravagant lunch at Lutece was an aberration from his usual meal, a peanut butter sandwich and a diet soda.* aberrant (adjective).

abeyance (noun) A temporary lapse in activity; suspension. *In the aftermath of the bombing, all normal activities were held in abeyance.*

abjure (verb) To renounce or reject; to officially disclaim. *While being tried by the inquisition in 1633, Galileo abjured all his writings holding that the Earth and other planets revolved around the sun.*

abrade (verb) To irritate by rubbing; to wear down in spirit. *Olga's "conditioning facial" abraded Sabrina's skin so severely that she vowed never to let anyone's hands touch her face again.* abrasion (noun).

abridge (verb) To shorten, to reduce. The Bill of Rights *is designed to prevent Congress from abridging the rights of Americans.* abridgment (noun).

abrogate (verb) To nullify, to abolish. *During World War II, the United States abrogated the rights of Japanese Americans by detaining them in internment camps.* abrogation (noun).

abscond (verb) To make a secret departure, to elope. *Theresa will never forgive her daughter, Elena, for absconding to Miami with Philip when they were only 17.*

accretion (noun) A gradual build-up or enlargement. *My mother's house is a mess due to her steady accretion of bric-a-brac and her inability to throw anything away.*

adjunct (noun) Something added to another thing, but not a part of it; an associate or assistant. *While Felix and Fritz were adjuncts to Professor Himmelman during his experiments in electrodynamics, they did not receive credit when the results were published.*

adroit (adjective) Skillful, adept. *The writer Laurie Colwin was particularly adroit at concocting love stories involving admirable and quirky female heroines and men who deserve them.*

adulterate (verb) To corrupt, to make impure. *Unlike the chickens from the large poultry companies, Murray's free-roaming chickens have not been adulterated with hormones and other additives.*

adversary (noun) An enemy or opponent. *When the former Soviet Union became an American ally, the United States lost its last major international adversary.* adverse (adjective).

aesthete (noun) Someone devoted to beauty and to beautiful things. *A renowned aesthete, Oscar Wilde was the center of a group that glorified beauty and adopted the slogan "art for art's sake."* aesthetic (adjective).

affability (noun) The quality of being easy to talk to and gracious. *Affability is a much-desired trait in any profession that involves dealing with many people on a daily basis.* affable (adjective).

affected (adjective) False, artificial. *At one time, Japanese women were taught to speak in an affected high-pitched voice, which was thought girlishly attractive.* affect (verb), affectation (noun).

affinity (noun) A feeling of shared attraction, kinship; a similarity. *When they first fell in love, Andrew and Tanya marveled over their affinity for bluegrass music, obscure French poetry, and beer taken with a squirt of lemon juice. People often say there is a striking affinity between dogs and their owners (but please don't tell Clara that she and her bassett hound are starting to resemble each other).*

aggrandize (verb) To make bigger or greater; to inflate. *When he was mayor of New York City, Ed Koch was renowned for aggrandizing his accomplishments and strolling through city events shouting, "How'm I doing?"* aggrandizement (noun).

agitation (noun) A disturbance; a disturbing feeling of upheaval and excitement. *After the CEO announced the coming layoffs, the employees' agitation was evident as they remained in the auditorium talking excitedly among themselves.* agitated (adjective), agitate (verb).

alias (noun) An assumed name. *Determined not to reveal his upper-class roots, Harold Steerforth Hetherington III went under the alias of "Hound Dog" when playing trumpet in his blues band.*

allegiance (noun) Loyalty or devotion shown to one's government or to a person, group, or cause. *At the moving naturalization ceremony, forty-three new Americans from twenty-five lands swore allegiance to the United States.*

allocate (verb) To apportion for a specific purpose; to distribute. *The president talked about the importance of education and health care in his State of the Union address, but, in the end, the administration did not allocate enough resources for these pressing concerns.* allocation (noun).

amalgamate (verb) To blend thoroughly. *The tendency of grains to sort when they should mix makes it difficult for manufacturers to create powders that are amalgamated.* amalgamation (noun).

ameliorate (verb) To make something better or more tolerable. *The living conditions of the tenants were certainly ameliorated when the landlord finally installed washing machines and dryers in the basement.* amelioration (noun).

amortize (verb) To pay off or reduce a debt gradually through periodic payments. *If you don't need to take a lump sum tax deduction, it's best to amortize large business expenditures by spreading the cost out over several years.*

amplify (verb) To enlarge, expand, or increase. *Uncertain as to whether they understood, the students asked the teacher to amplify his explanation.* amplification (noun).

anachronistic (adjective) Out of the proper time. *The reference, in Shakespeare's Julius Caesar, to "the clock striking twelve" is anachronistic, since there were no striking timepieces in ancient Rome.* anachronism (noun).

anarchy (noun) Absence of law or order. *For several months after the Nazi government was destroyed, there was no effective government in parts of Germany, and anarchy ruled.* anarchic (adjective).

animosity (noun) Hostility, resentment. *During the last debate, the candidates could no longer disguise their animosity and began to trade accusations and insults.*

anomaly (noun) Something different or irregular. *The tiny planet Pluto, orbiting next to the giants Jupiter, Saturn, and Neptune, has long appeared to be an anomaly.* anomalous (adjective).

antagonism (noun) Hostility, conflict, opposition. *As more and more reporters investigated the Watergate scandal, antagonism between the Nixon administration and the press increased.* antagonistic (adjective), antagonize (verb).

antipathy (noun) A long-held feeling of dislike or aversion. *When asked why he didn't call for help immediately after his wife fell into a coma, the defendant emphasized his wife's utter antipathy to doctors.*

apprehension (noun) A feeling of fear or foreboding; an arrest. *The peculiar feeling of apprehension that Harold Pinter creates in his plays derives as much from the long silences between speeches as from the speeches themselves. The police officer's dramatic apprehension of the gunman took place in full view of the midtown lunch crowd.* apprehend (verb).

arabesque (noun) Intricate decorative patterns involving intertwining lines and sometimes incorporating flowers, animals, and fruits. *Borders of gold and fanciful arabesques surround the Arabic script on every page of this ancient edition of the Koran.*

arbitrary (adjective) Based on random or merely personal preference. *Both computers cost the same and had the same features, so in the end I made an arbitrary decision about which one to buy.*

archaic (adjective) Old-fashioned, obsolete. *Those who believe in "open marriage" often declare that they will not be bound by archaic laws and religious rituals, but state instead that love alone should bring two people together.* archaism (noun).

ardor (noun) A strong feeling of passion, energy, or zeal. *The young revolutionary proclaimed his convictions with an ardor that excited the crowd.* ardent (adjective).

WORD ORIGIN

Greek *chronos* = time. Also found in English *chronic*, *chronicle*, *chronograph*, *chronology*, and *synchronize*.

WORD ORIGIN

Greek *pathos* = suffering. Also found in English *apathy*, *empathy*, *pathetic*, *pathos*, and *sympathy*.

WORD ORIGIN

Latin *arbiter* = judge. Also found in English *arbiter*, *arbitrage*, and *arbitrate*.

WORD ORIGIN

Latin *articulus* = joint, division. Also found in English *arthritis*, *article*, and *inarticulate*.

arid (adjective) Very dry; boring and meaningless. *The arid climate of Arizona makes farming difficult. Some find the law a fascinating topic, but for me it is an arid discipline.* aridity (noun).

articulate (adjective) To express oneself clearly and effectively. *Compared to the elder George Bush, with his stammering and his frequently incomplete sentences, Bill Clinton was considered a highly articulate president.*

asperity (noun) Harshness, severity. *Total silence at the dinner table, baths in icy water, prayers five times a day—these practices all contributed to the asperity of life in the monastery.*

assail (verb) To attack with blows or words. *When the president's cabinet members rose to justify the case for military intervention in Iraq, they were assailed by many audience members who were critical of U.S. policy.* assailant (noun).

assay (verb) To analyze for particular components; to determine weight, quality, etc. *The jeweler assayed the stone pendant Gwyneth inherited from her mother and found it to contain a topaz of high quality.*

assimilate (verb) To absorb into a system or culture. *New York City has assimilated one group of immigrants after another, from the Jewish, German, and Irish immigrants who arrived at the turn of the last century to the waves of Mexican and Latin American immigrants who arrived in the 1980s.* assimilated (adjective).

assuage (verb) To ease, to pacify. *Knowing that the pilot's record was perfect did little to assuage Linnet's fear of flying in the two-seater airplane.*

audacious (adjective) Bold, daring, adventurous. *Her plan to cross the Atlantic single-handed in a twelve-foot sailboat was an audacious, if not reckless one.* audacity (noun).

authoritarian (adjective) Favoring or demanding blind obedience to leaders. *Despite most Americans' strong belief in democracy, the American government has sometimes supported authoritarian regimes in other countries.* authoritarianism (noun).

authoritative (adjective) Official, conclusive. *For more than five decades, American parents regarded Doctor Benjamin Spock as the most authoritative voice on baby and child care.* authority (noun), authorize (verb).

avenge (verb) To exact a punishment for or on behalf of someone. *In Shakespeare's tragedy* Hamlet, *the ghost of the dead king of Denmark visits his son, Prince Hamlet, and urges him to avenge his murder.*

aver (verb) To claim to be true; to avouch. *The fact that the key witness averred the defendant's innocence is what ultimately swayed the jury to deliver a "not guilty" verdict.*

avow (verb) To declare boldly. *Immediately after Cyrus avowed his atheism at our church fund-raiser, there was a long, uncomfortable silence.* avowal (noun), avowed (adjective).

B

barren (adjective) Desolate; infertile. *The subarctic tundra is a barren wasteland inhabited only by lichens and mosses. Women who try to conceive in their 40s are often barren and must turn to artificial means of producing a child.*

belligerent (adjective) Quarrelsome, combative. *Mrs. Juniper was so belligerent toward the clerks at the local stores that they cringed when they saw her coming.*

belligerent (noun) An opposing army, a party waging war. *The Union and Confederate forces were the belligerents in the American Civil War.*

benevolent (adjective) Wishing or doing good. *In old age, Carnegie used his wealth for benevolent purposes, donating large sums to found libraries and schools around the country.* benevolence (noun).

berate (verb) To scold or criticize harshly. *The judge angrily berated the two lawyers for their childish and unprofessional behavior.*

boggle (verb) To overwhelm with amazement. *The ability of physicists to isolate the most infinitesimal particles of matter truly boggles the mind.*

bogus (adjective) Phony, a sham. *Senior citizens are often the target of telemarketing scams pushing bogus investment opportunities.*

bombastic (adjective) Inflated or pompous in style. *Old-fashioned bombastic political speeches don't work on television, which demands a more intimate, personal style of communication.* bombast (noun).

boor (noun) Crude, insensitive and overbearing. *Harold was well-known to be a boor; at parties he horrified people with stories of his past sexual exploits and old, off-color jokes.* boorish (adjective).

brazenly (adverb) Acting with disrespectful boldness. *Some say that the former White House intern brazenly threw herself at the president, but the American public will probably never know the full truth.* brazen (adjective).

broach (verb) To bring up an issue for discussion, to propose. *Knowing my father's strictness about adhering to a budget, I just can't seem to broach the subject of my massive credit-card debt.*

burgeon (verb) To bloom, literally or figuratively. *Due to the extremely mild winter, the forsythia burgeoned as early as March. The story of two prison inmates in Manuel Puig's play* The Kiss of the Spiderwoman *is testimony that tenderness can burgeon in the most unlikely places.*

burnish (verb) To shine by polishing, literally or figuratively. *After stripping seven layers of old paint off the antique door, the carpenter stained the wood and burnished it to a rich hue. When Bill Gates, the wealthiest man in the country, decided to endorse the Big Bertha line of golf cubs, many suggested that he was trying to burnish his image as a "regular guy."*

buttress (noun) Something that supports or strengthens. *The endorsement of the American Medical Association is a powerful buttress for the claims made on behalf of this new medicine.* buttress (verb).

WORD ORIGIN

Latin bene = well.
Also found in English
benediction,
benefactor,
beneficent,
beneficial, benefit,
and benign.

C

cacophony (noun) Discordant sounds; dissonance. *In the minutes before classes start, the high school's halls are filled with a cacophony of shrieks, shouts, banging locker doors, and pounding feet.* cacophonous (adjective).

cadge (verb) To beg for, to sponge. *Few in our crowd want to go out on the town with Piper, since he routinely cadges cigarettes, subway tokens, and drinks.*

calibrate (verb) To determine or mark graduations (of a measuring instrument); to adjust or finely tune. *We tried to calibrate the heating to Rufus's liking, but he still ended up shivering in our living room.* calibration (noun).

castigate (verb) To chastise; to punish severely. *The editor castigated Bob for repeatedly failing to meet his deadlines.* castigation (noun).

catalytic (adjective) Bringing about, causing, or producing some result. *The conditions for revolution existed in America by 1765; the disputes about taxation that arose during the following decade were the catalytic events that sparked the rebellion.* catalyze (verb).

caustic (adjective) Burning, corrosive. *No pretensions were safe when the famous satirist H. L. Mencken unleashed his caustic wit.*

WORD ORIGIN

Greek *kaustikos* = burning. Also found in English *holocaust*.

chaos (noun) Disorder, confusion, chance. *The first few moments after the explosion were pure chaos: no one was sure what had happened, and the area was filled with people running and yelling.* chaotic (adjective).

charisma (noun) Dynamic charm or appeal. *Eva Peron was such a fiery orator and had so much charisma that she commanded an enormous political following.* charismatic (adjective).

chary (adjective) Slow to accept, cautious. *Yuan was chary about going out with Xinhua, since she had been badly hurt in her previous relationship.*

chronology (noun) An arrangement of events by order of occurrence, a list of dates; the science of time. *If you ask Susan about her 2-year-old son, she will give you a chronology of his accomplishments and childhood illnesses, from the day he was born to the present. The village of Copan was where Mayan astronomical learning, as applied to chronology, achieved its most accurate expression in the famous Mayan calendar.* chronological (adjective).

churlish (adjective) Coarse and ill-mannered. *Few journalists were eager to interview the aging film star, since he was reputed to be a churlish, uncooperative subject.* churl (noun).

WORD ORIGIN

Latin *circus* = circle. Also found in English *circumference*, *circumnavigate*, *circumscribe*, and *circumvent*.

circumspect (adjective) Prudent, cautious. *After he had been acquitted of the sexual harassment charge, the sergeant realized he would have to be more circumspect in his dealings with the female cadets.* circumspection (noun).

cleave (verb) NOTE: A tricky verb that can mean either to stick closely together or to split apart. (Pay attention to context.) *The more abusive his father became, the more Timothy cleaved to his mother and refused to let her out of his sight. Sometimes a few words carelessly spoken are enough to cleave a married couple and leave the relationship in shambles.* cleavage (noun).

coagulant (noun) Any material that causes another to thicken or clot. *Hemophilia is characterized by excessive bleeding from even the slightest cut, and is caused by a lack of one of the coagulants necessary for blood clotting.* coagulate (verb).

coalesce (verb) To fuse, to unite. *The music we know as jazz coalesced from diverse elements from many musical cultures, including those of West Africa, America, and Europe.* coalescence (noun).

coerce (verb) To force someone either to do something or to refrain from doing something. *The Miranda ruling prevents police from coercing a confession by forcing them to read criminals their rights.* coercion (noun).

cogent (adjective) Forceful and convincing. *The committee members were won over to the project by the cogent arguments of the chairman.* cogency (noun).

commensurate (adjective) Aligned with, proportional. *Many Ph.D.s in the humanities do not feel their paltry salaries are commensurate with their abilities, their experience, or the heavy workload they are asked to bear.*

WORD ORIGIN

Latin *mensura* = to measure. Also found in English *measure*, *immeasurable*, *immense*, and *mensuration*.

commingle (verb) To blend, to mix. *Just as he had when he was only five years old, Elmer did not allow any of the foods on his plate to commingle: the beans must not merge with the rice nor the chicken rub shoulders with the broccoli!*

complaisant (adjective) Tending to bow to others' wishes; amiable. *Of the two Dashwood sisters, Elinor was the more complaisant, often putting the strictures of society and family above her own desires.* complaisance (noun).

compound (verb) To intensify, to exacerbate. *When you make a faux pas, my father advised me, don't compound the problem by apologizing profusely; just say you're sorry and get on with life!*

conceivable (adjective) Possible, imaginable. *It's possible to find people with every conceivable interest by surfing the World Wide Web—from fans of minor film stars to those who study the mating habits of crustaceans.* conception (noun).

concur (verb) To agree, to approve. *We concur that a toddler functions best on a fairly reliable schedule; however, my husband tends to be a bit more rigid than I am.* concurrence (noun).

condensation (noun) A reduction to a denser form (from steam to water); an abridgment of a literary work. *The condensation of humidity on the car's windshield made it difficult for me to see the road. It seems as though every beach house I've ever rented features a shelf full of* Reader's Digest *condensations of B-grade novels.* condense (verb).

condescending (adjective) Having an attitude of superiority toward another; patronizing. *"What a cute little car!" she remarked in a condescending fashion. "I suppose it's the nicest one someone like you could afford!"* condescension (noun).

condone (verb) To overlook, to permit to happen. *Schools with Zero Tolerance policies do not condone alcohol, drugs, vandalism, or violence on school grounds.*

congruent (adjective) Coinciding; harmonious. *Fortunately, the two employees who had been asked to organize the department had congruent views on the budget.* congruence (noun).

WORD ORIGIN

Latin *jungere* = to join. Also found in English *injunction*, *junction*, and *juncture*.

conjunction (noun) The occurrence of two or more events together in time or space; in astronomy, the point at which two celestial bodies have the least separation. *Low inflation, occurring in conjunction with low unemployment and relatively low interest rates, has enabled the United States to enjoy a long period of sustained economic growth. The moon is in conjunction with the sun when it is new; if the conjunction is perfect, an eclipse of the sun will occur.* conjoin (verb).

consolation (noun) Relief or comfort in sorrow or suffering. *Although we miss our dog very much, it is a consolation to know that she died quickly, without much suffering.* console (verb).

consternation (noun) Shock, amazement, dismay. *When a voice in the back of the church shouted out "I know why they should not be married!" the entire gathering was thrown into consternation.*

WORD ORIGIN

Latin *vivere* = to live. Also found in English *revive*, *vital*, *vivid*, and *vivisection*.

convergence (noun) The act of coming together in unity or similarity. *A remarkable example of evolutionary convergence can be seen in the shark and the dolphin, two sea creatures that developed from different origins to become very similar in form and appearance.* converge (verb).

conviviality (noun) Fond of good company and eating and drinking. *The conviviality of my fellow employees seemed to turn every staff meeting into a party, complete with snacks, drinks, and lots of hearty laughter.* convivial (adjective).

WORD ORIGIN

Latin *volvere* = to roll. Also found in English *devolve*, *involve*, *revolution*, *revolve*, and *voluble*.

convoluted (adjective) Twisting, complicated, intricate. *Income tax law has become so convoluted that it's easy for people to violate it completely by accident.* convolute (verb), convolution (noun).

cordon (verb) To form a protective or restrictive barrier. *Well before the Academy Awards® ceremony began, the police cordoned off the hordes of fans who were desperate to ogle the arriving stars.* cordon (noun).

corral (verb) To enclose, to collect, to gather. *Tyrone couldn't enjoy the wedding at all, since he spent most of his time corralling his two children into the reception room and preventing them from running amok through the Potters' mansion.* corral (noun).

corroborating (adjective) Supporting with evidence; confirming. *A passerby who had witnessed the crime gave corroborating testimony about the presence of the accused person.* corroborate (verb), corroboration (noun).

corrosive (adjective) Eating away, gnawing, or destroying. *Years of poverty and hard work had a corrosive effect on her strength and beauty.* corrode (verb), corrosion (noun).

cosmopolitanism (noun) International sophistication; worldliness. *Budapest is known for its cosmopolitanism, perhaps because it was the first Eastern European city to be more open to capitalism and influences from the West.* cosmopolitan (adjective).

covert (adjective) Secret, clandestine. *The CIA has often been criticized for its covert operations in the domestic policies of foreign countries, such as the failed Bay of Pigs operation in Cuba.*

covetous (adjective) Envious, particularly of another's possessions. *Benita would never admit to being covetous of my new sable jacket, but I found it odd that she couldn't refrain from trying it on each time we met.* covet (verb).

craven (adjective) Cowardly. *Local firefighters were outraged by the craven behavior of a police officer who refused to come to the aid of a hepatitis C-positive accident victim.*

credulous (adjective) Ready to believe; gullible. *Elaine was not very credulous of the explanation Serge gave for his acquisition of the Matisse lithograph.* credulity (noun).

cryptic (adjective) Puzzling, ambiguous. *I was puzzled by the cryptic message left on my answering machine about the arrival of "a shipment of pomegranates from an anonymous donor."*

culmination (noun) The climax. *The Los Angeles riots, in the aftermath of the Rodney King verdict, were the culmination of long-standing racial tensions between the residents of South Central LA and the police.* culminate (verb).

culpable (adjective) Deserving blame, guilty. *Although he committed the crime, because he was mentally ill he should not be considered culpable for his actions.* culpability (noun).

curmudgeon (noun) A crusty, ill-tempered person. *Todd hated to drive with his Uncle Jasper, a notorious curmudgeon, who complained nonstop about the air-conditioning and Todd's driving.* curmudgeonly (adjective).

cursory (adjective) Hasty and superficial. *Detective Martinez was rebuked by his superior officer for drawing conclusions about the murder after only a cursory examination of the crime scene.*

D

debilitating (adjective) Weakening; sapping the strength of. *One can't help but marvel at the courage Steven Hawking displays in the face of such a debilitating disease as ALS.* debilitate (verb).

decelerate (verb) To slow down. *Randall didn't decelerate enough on the winding roads, and he ended up smashing his new sports utility vehicle into a guard rail.* deceleration (noun).

decimation (noun) Almost complete destruction. *Michael Moore's documentary* Roger and Me *chronicles the decimation of the economy of Flint, Michigan, after the closing of a General Motors factory.* decimate (verb).

decry (verb) To criticize or condemn. *Cigarette ads aimed at youngsters have led many to decry the unfair marketing tactics of the tobacco industry.*

defamation (noun) Act of harming someone by libel or slander. *When the article in* The National Enquirer *implied that she was somehow responsible for her husband's untimely death, Renata instructed her lawyer to sue the paper for defamation of character.* defame (verb).

WORD ORIGIN

Latin *celer* = swift.
Also found in English
accelerate and
celerity.

defer (verb) To graciously submit to another's will; to delegate. *In all matters relating to the children's religious education, Joy deferred to her husband, since he clearly cared more about giving them a solid grounding in Judaism.* deference (noun).

deliberate (verb) To think about an issue before reaching a decision. *The legal pundits covering the O.J. Simpson trial were shocked by the short time the jury took to deliberate after a trial that lasted months.* deliberation (noun).

demagogue (noun) A leader who plays dishonestly on the prejudices and emotions of his followers. *Senator Joseph McCarthy was a demagogue who used the paranoia and biases of the anti-Communist 1950s as a way of seizing fame and considerable power in Washington.* demagoguery (noun).

WORD ORIGIN

Greek *demos* = people. Also found in English *democracy*, *demographic*, and *endemic*.

demographic (adjective) Relating to the statistical study of population. *Three demographic groups have been the intense focus of marketing strategy: baby boomers, born between 1946 and 1964; baby busters, or the youth market, born between 1965 and 1976; and a group referred to as tweens, those born between 1977 and 1983.* demography (noun), demographics (noun).

demonstratively (adverb) Openly displaying feeling. *The young congressman demonstratively campaigned for reelection, kissing every baby and hugging every senior citizen at the Saugerties Chrysanthemum festival.* demonstrative (adjective).

derisive (adjective) Expressing ridicule or scorn. *Many women's groups were derisive of Avon's choice of a male CEO, since the company derives its $5.1 billion in sales from an army of female salespeople.* derision (noun).

derivative (adjective) Imitating or borrowed from a particular source. *When a person first writes poetry, her poems are apt to be derivative of whatever poetry she most enjoys reading.* derivation (noun), derive (verb).

desiccate (verb) To dry out, to wither; to drain of vitality. *The long drought thoroughly desiccated our garden; what was once a glorious Eden was now a scorched and hellish wasteland. A recent spate of books has debunked the myth that menopause desiccates women and affirmed, instead, that women often reach heights of creativity in their later years.* desiccant (noun), desiccation (noun).

despotic (adjective) Oppressive and tyrannical. *During the despotic reign of Idi Amin in the 1970s, an estimated 200,000 Ugandans were killed.* despot (noun).

desultory (adjective) Disconnected, aimless. *Tina's few desultory stabs at conversation fell flat as Guy just sat there, stone-faced; it was a disastrous first date.*

deviate (verb) To depart from a standard or norm. *Having agreed upon a spending budget for the company, we mustn't deviate from it; if we do, we may run out of money before the year ends.* deviation (noun).

diatribe (noun) Abusive or bitter speech or writing. *While angry conservatives dismissed Susan Faludi's* Backlash *as a feminist diatribe, it is actually a meticulously researched book.*

diffident (adjective) Hesitant, reserved, shy. *Someone with a diffident personality is most likely to succeed in a career that involves very little public contact.* diffidence (noun).

digress (verb) To wander from the main path or the main topic. *My high school biology teacher loved to digress from science into personal anecdotes about his college adventures.* digression (noun), digressive (adjective).

dirge (noun) Song or hymn of grief. *When Princess Diana was killed in a car crash, Elton John resurrected his hit song "Candle in the Wind," rewrote it as "Good-bye England's Rose," and created one of the most widely heard funeral dirges of all time.*

disabuse (verb) To correct a fallacy, to clarify. *I hated to disabuse Filbert, who is a passionate collector of musical trivia, but I had to tell him that the Monkees had hardly sung a note and had lip-synched their way through almost all of their albums.*

disburse (verb) To pay out or distribute (funds or property). *Jaime was flabbergasted when his father's will disbursed all of the old man's financial assets to Raymundo and left him with only a few sticks of furniture.* disbursement (noun).

discern (verb) To detect, notice, or observe. *With difficulty, I could discern the shape of a whale off the starboard bow, but it was too far away to determine its size or species.* discernment (noun).

discordant (adjective) Characterized by conflict. *Stories and films about discordant relationships that resolve themselves happily are always more interesting than stories about content couples who simply stay content.* discordance (noun).

discourse (noun) Formal and orderly exchange of ideas, a discussion. *In the late twentieth century, cloning and other feats of genetic engineering became popular topics of public discourse.* discursive (adjective).

discredit (verb) To cause disbelief in the accuracy of some statement or the reliability of a person. *Although many people still believe in UFOs, among scientists the reports of "alien encounters" have been thoroughly discredited.*

discreet (adjective) Showing good judgment in speech and behavior. *Be discreet when discussing confidential business matters—don't talk among strangers on the elevator, for example.* discretion (noun).

discrete (adjective) Separate, unconnected. *Canadians get peeved when people can't seem to distinguish between Canada and the United States, forgetting that Canada has its own discrete heritage and culture.*

disparity (noun) Difference in quality or kind. *There is often a disparity between the kind of serious, high-quality television people say they want and the low-brow programs they actually watch.* disparate (adjective).

dissemble (verb) To pretend, to simulate. *When the police asked whether Nancy knew anything about the crime, she dissembled innocence.*

dissipate (verb) To spread out or scatter. *The windows and doors were opened, allowing the smoke that had filled the room to dissipate.* dissipation (noun).

WORD ORIGIN

Latin *credere* = to believe. Also found in English *credential*, *credible*, *credit*, *credo*, *credulous*, and *incredible*.

WORD ORIGIN

Latin *simulare* = to resemble. Also found in English *semblance*, *similarity*, *simulacrum*, *simultaneous*, and *verisimilitude*.

dissonance (noun) Lack of music harmony; lack of agreement between ideas. *Most modern music is characterized by dissonance, which many listeners find hard to enjoy. There is a noticeable dissonance between two common beliefs of most conservatives: their faith in unfettered free markets and their preference for traditional social values.* dissonant (adjective).

distillation (noun) Something distilled, an essence or extract. In chemistry, a process that drives gas or vapor from liquids or solids. *Sharon Olds's poems are powerful distillations of motherhood and other primal experiences. In Mrs. Hornmeister's chemistry class, our first experiment was to create a distillation of carbon gas from wood.* distill (verb).

diverge (verb) To move in different directions. *Frost's poem "The Road Not Taken" tells of the choice he made when "Two roads diverged in a yellow wood."* divergence (noun), divergent (adjective).

diversify (verb) To balance by adding variety. *Any financial manager will recommend that you diversify your stock portfolio by holding some less-volatile blue-chip stocks along with more growth-oriented technology issues.* diversification (noun), diversified (adjective).

divest (verb) To rid (oneself) or be freed of property, authority, or title. *In order to turn around its ailing company and concentrate on imaging, Eastman Kodak divested itself of peripheral businesses in the areas of household products, clinical diagnostics, and pharmaceuticals.* divestiture (noun).

divulge (verb) To reveal. *The people who count the votes for the Oscar® awards are under strict orders not to divulge the names of the winners.*

dogmatic (adjective) Holding firmly to a particular set of beliefs with little or no basis. *Believers in Marxist doctrine tend to be dogmatic, ignoring evidence that contradicts their beliefs or explaining it away.* dogma (noun), dogmatism (noun).

dolt (noun) A stupid or foolish person. *Due to his frequent verbal blunders, politician Dan Quayle was widely considered to be a dolt.*

WORD ORIGIN

Latin *dormire* = to sleep. Also found in English *dormitory*.

dormant (adjective) Temporarily inactive, as if asleep. *An eruption of Mt. Rainier, a dormant volcano in Washington state, would cause massive, life-threatening mud slides in the surrounding area. Bill preferred to think that his math skills were dormant rather than extinct.* dormancy (noun).

dross (noun) Something that is trivial or inferior; an impurity. *As a reader for the* Paris Review, *Julia spent most of her time sifting through piles of manuscripts to separate the extraordinary poems from the dross.*

dubious (adjective) Doubtful, uncertain. *Despite the chairman's attempts to convince the committee members that his plan would succeed, most of them remained dubious.* dubiety (noun).

dupe (noun) Someone who is easily cheated. *My cousin Ravi is such a dupe; he actually gets excited when he receives those envelopes saying "Ravi Murtugudde, you may have won a million dollars," and he even goes so far as to try claiming his prize.*

E

eccentricity (noun) Odd or whimsical behavior. *Rock star Michael Jackson is now better known for his offstage eccentricities—such as sleeping in an oxygen tank, wearing a surgical mask, and building his own theme park—than for his on-stage performances.* eccentric (adjective).

edifying (adjective) Instructive, enlightening. *Ariel would never admit it to her high-brow friends, but she found the latest self-help bestseller edifying and actually helpful.* edification (noun), edify (verb).

efficacy (noun) The power to produce the desired effect. *While teams have been enormously popular in the workplace, there are some who now question their efficacy and say that "one head is better than ten."* efficacious (noun).

effrontery (noun) Shameless boldness. *The sports world was shocked when a pro basketball player had the effrontery to choke the head coach of his team during a practice session.*

elaborate (verb) To expand upon something; develop. *One characteristics of the best essayists is their ability to elaborate ideas through examples, lists, similes, small variations, and even exaggerations.* elaborate (adjective), elaboration (noun).

elegy (noun) A song or poem expressing sorrow. *Thomas Gray's "Elegy Written in a Country Churchyard," one of the most famous elegies in Western literature, mourns the unsung, inglorious lives of the souls buried in an obscure, rustic graveyard.* elegaic (adjective).

embellish (verb) To enhance or exaggerate; to decorate. *The long-married couple told their stories in tandem, with the husband outlining the plot and the wife embellishing it with colorful details.*

embellished (adjective). *Both Salman Rushdie, of India, and Patrick Chamoiseau, of Martinique, emerged from colonized countries and created embellished versions of their colonizers' languages in their novels.*

embezzle (verb) To steal money or property that has been entrusted to your care. *The church treasurer was found to have embezzled thousands of dollars by writing phony checks on the church bank account.* embezzlement (noun).

emollient (noun) Something that softens or soothes. *She used a hand cream as an emollient on her dry, work-roughened hands.* emollient (adjective).

empirical (adjective) Based on experience or personal observation. *Although many people believe in ESP, scientists have found no empirical evidence of its existence.* empiricism (noun).

emulate (verb) To imitate or copy. *The British band Oasis is quite open about their desire to emulate their idols, the Beatles.* emulation (noun).

encomium (noun) A formal expression of praise. *For many filmmakers, winning the Palm d'Or at the Cannes Film Festival is considered the highest encomium.*

enervate (verb) To reduce the energy or strength of someone or something. *The stress of the operation left her feeling enervated for about two weeks.* enervation (noun).

WORD ORIGIN

Latin *facere* = to do. Also found in English *facility, factor, facsimile,* and *faculty.*

engender (verb) To produce, to cause. *Countless disagreements over the proper use of national forests and parklands have engendered feelings of hostility between ranchers and environmentalists.*

enhance (verb) To improve in value or quality. *New kitchen appliances will enhance your house and increase the amount of money you'll make when you sell it.* enhancement (noun).

enigmatic (adjective) Puzzling, mysterious. *Alain Resnais' enigmatic film* Last Year at Marienbad *sets up a puzzle that is never resolved: a man meets a woman at a hotel and believes he once had an affair with her—or did he?* enigma (noun).

enmity (noun) Hatred, hostility, ill will. *Long-standing enmity, like that between the Protestants and Catholics in Northern Ireland, is difficult to overcome.*

ensure (verb) To make certain; to guarantee. *In order to ensure a sufficient crop of programmers and engineers for the future, the United States needs to raise the quality of its math and science schooling.*

epicure (noun) Someone who appreciates fine wine and fine food, a gourmand. *M.F.K. Fisher, a famous epicure, begins her book* The Gastronomical Me *by saying, "There is a communion of more than bodies when bread is broken and wine is drunk."* epicurean (adjective).

epithet (noun) Term or words used to characterize a person or thing, often in a disparaging way. *In her recorded phone conversations with Linda Tripp, Monica Lewinsky is said to have referred to President Clinton by a number of epithets, including "The Creep" and "The Big He."* epithetical (adjective).

WORD ORIGIN

Latin *aequus* = equal.
Also found in English
equality, equanimity,
and *equation.*

equable (adjective) Steady, uniform. *While many people can't see how Helena could possibly be attracted to "Boring Bruno," his equable nature is the perfect complement to her volatile personality.*

WORD ORIGIN

Latin *radix* = root. Also
found in English
radical.

equivocate (verb) To use misleading or intentionally confusing language. *When Pedro pressed Renee for an answer to his marriage proposal, she equivocated by saying, "I've just got to know when your Mercedes will be out of the shop!"* equivocal (adjective), equivocation (noun).

eradicate (verb) To destroy completely. *American society has failed to eradicate racism, although some of its worst effects have been reduced.* eradication (noun).

erudition (noun) Extensive knowledge, usually acquired from books. *When Dorothea first saw Mr. Casaubon's voluminous library she was awed, but after their marriage she quickly realized that erudition is no substitute for originality.* erudite (adjective).

esoterica (noun) Items of interest to a select group. *The fish symposium at St. Antony's College in Oxford explored all manner of esoterica relating to fish, as is evidenced in presentations such as "The Buoyant Slippery Lipids of the Escolar and Orange Roughy," or "Food on Board Whale Ships—from the Inedible to the Incredible."* esoteric (adjective).

espouse (verb) To take up as a cause; to adopt. *No politician in American today will openly espouse racism, although some behave and speak in racially prejudiced ways.*

estimable (adjective) Worthy of esteem and admiration. *After a tragic fire raged through Malden Mills, the estimable mill owner, Aaron Feuerstein, restarted operations and rebuilt the company within just one month.* esteem (noun).

eulogy (noun) A formal tribute usually delivered at a funeral. *Most people in Britain applauded Lord Earl Spencer's eulogy for Princess Diana, not only as a warm tribute to his sister Diana, but also as a biting indictment of the Royal Family.* eulogize (verb).

euphemism (noun) An agreeable expression that is substituted for an offensive one. *Some of the more creative euphemisms for "layoffs" in current use are: "release of resources," "involuntary severance," "strengthening global effectiveness," and "career transition program."* euphemistic (adjective).

exacerbate (verb) To make worse or more severe. *The roads in our town already have too much traffic; building a new shopping mall will exacerbate the problem.*

excoriation (noun) The act of condemning someone with harsh words. *In the small office we shared, it was painful to hear my boss's constant excoriation of his assistant for the smallest faults—a misdirected letter, an unclear phone message, or even a tepid cup of coffee.* excoriate (verb).

exculpate (verb) To free from blame or guilt. *When someone else confessed to the crime, the previous suspect was exculpated.* exculpation (noun), exculpatory (adjective).

executor (noun) The person appointed to execute someone's will. *As the executor of his aunt Ida's will, Phil must deal with squabbling relatives, conniving lawyers, and the ruinous state of Ida's house.*

exigent (adjective) Urgent, requiring immediate attention. *A 2-year-old is likely to behave as if her every demand is exigent, even if it involves simply retrieving a beloved stuffed hedgehog from under the couch.* exigency (noun).

expedient (adjective) Providing an immediate advantage or serving one's immediate self-interest. *When the passenger next to her was hit by a bullet, Sharon chose the most expedient means to stop the bleeding; she whipped off her pantyhose and made an impromptu, but effective, tourniquet.* expediency (noun).

extant (adjective) Currently in existence. *Of the seven ancient "Wonders of the World," only the pyramids of Egypt are still extant.*

extenuate (verb) To make less serious. *Karen's guilt is extenuated by the fact that she was only 12 when she committed the theft.* extenuating (adjective), extenuation (noun).

extol (verb) To greatly praise. *At the party convention, one speaker after another took to the podium to extol the virtues of their candidate for the presidency.*

extraneous (adjective) Irrelevant, nonessential. *One review of the new Chekhov biography said the author had bogged down the book with far too many extraneous details, such as the dates of Chekhov's bouts of diarrhea.*

WORD ORIGIN

Latin *acer* = sharp. Also found in English *acerbity, acrid,* and *acrimonious.*

WORD ORIGIN

Latin *tenere* = to hold. Also found in English *retain, tenable, tenant, tenet,* and *tenure.*

extrapolate (verb) To deduce from something known, to infer. *Meteorologists were able to use old weather records to extrapolate backward and compile lists of El Niño years and their effects over the last century.* extrapolation (noun).

extricate (verb) To free from a difficult or complicated situation. *Much of the humor in the TV show "I Love Lucy" comes in watching Lucy try to extricate herself from the problems she creates by fibbing or trickery.* extricable (adjective).

F

facetious (adjective) Humorous in a mocking way; not serious. *French composer Erik Satie often concealed his serious artistic intent by giving his works facetious titles such as "Three Pieces in the Shape of a Pear."*

facilitate (verb) To make easier or to moderate. *When the issue of racism reared its ugly head, the company brought in a consultant to facilitate a discussion of diversity in the workplace.* facile (adjective), facility (noun).

fallacy (noun) An error in fact or logic. *It's a fallacy to think that "natural" means "healthful"; after all, the deadly poison arsenic is completely natural.* fallacious (adjective).

fatuous (adjective) Inanely foolish; silly. *Once backstage, Elizabeth showered the opera singer with fatuous praise and embarrassing confessions, which he clearly had no interest in hearing.*

fawn (verb) To flatter in a particularly subservient manner. *Mildly disgusted, Pedro stood alone at the bar and watched Renee fawn over the heir to the Fabco Surgical Appliances fortune.*

feckless (adjective) Weak and ineffective; irresponsible. *Our co-op board president is a feckless fellow who has let much-needed repairs go unattended while our maintenance fees continue to rise.*

feint (noun) A bluff; a mock blow. *It didn't take us long to realize that Gaby's tears and stomachaches were all a feint, since they appeared so regularly at her bedtime.*

ferret (verb) To bring to light by an extensive search. *With his repeated probing and questions, Fritz was able to ferret out the location of Myrna's safe deposit box.*

finesse (noun) Skillful maneuvering; delicate workmanship. *With her usual finesse, Charmaine gently persuaded the Duncans not to install a motorized Santa and sleigh on their front lawn.*

florid (adjective) Flowery, fancy; reddish. *The grand ballroom was decorated in a florid style. Years of heavy drinking had given him a florid complexion.*

flourish (noun) An extraneous embellishment; a dramatic gesture. *The napkin rings made out of intertwined ferns and flowers were just the kind of flourish one would expect from Carol, a slavish follower of the home and garden TV show.*

WORD ORIGIN

Latin *fluere* = to flow. Also found in English *affluent, effluvia, fluid,* and *influx.*

fluctuation (noun) A shifting back and forth. *Investment analysts predict fluctuations in the Dow Jones Industrial Average due to the instability of the value of the dollar.* fluctuate (verb).

foil (verb) To thwart or frustrate. *I was certain that Jerry's tendency to insert himself into everyone's conversations would foil my chances to have a private word with Helen.*

foment (verb) To rouse or incite. *The petty tyrannies and indignities inflicted on the workers by upper management helped foment the walkout at the meat-processing plant.*

forestall (verb) To hinder or prevent by taking action in advance. *The pilot's calm, levelheaded demeanor during the turbulence forestalled any hysteria among the passengers of Flight 268.*

fortuitous (adjective) Lucky, fortunate. *Although the mayor claimed credit for the falling crime rate, it was really caused by a series of fortuitous accidents.*

foster (verb) To nurture or encourage. *The white-water rafting trip was supposed to foster creative problem-solving and teamwork between the account executives and the creative staff at Apex Advertising Agency.*

fracas (noun) A noisy fight; a brawl. *As Bill approached the stadium ticket window, he was alarmed to see the fracas that had broken out between a group of Giants fans and a man wearing a Cowboys jersey and helmet.*

functionary (noun) Someone holding office in a political party or government. *The man shaking hands with the governor was a low-ranking Democratic Party functionary who had worked to garner the Hispanic vote.*

G

gainsay (verb) To contradict or oppose; deny, dispute. *Dot would gainsay her married sister's efforts to introduce her to eligible men by refusing to either leave her ailing canary or give up her thrice-weekly bingo nights.*

garble (verb) To distort or slur. *No matter how much money the Metropolitan Transit Authority spends on improving the subway trains, the public address system in almost every station seems to garble each announcement.* garbled (adjective).

garrulous (adjective) Annoyingly talkative. *Claude pretended to be asleep so he could avoid his garrulous seatmate, a self-proclaimed expert on bonsai cultivation.*

generic (adjective) General; having no brand name. *Connie tried to reduce her grocery bills by religiously clipping coupons and buying generic brands of most products.*

gist (noun) The main point, the essence. *Although they felt sympathy for the victim's family, the jurors were won over by the gist of the defense's argument: there was insufficient evidence to convict.*

gouge (verb) To cut out, to scoop out with one's thumbs or a sharp instrument; to overcharge, to cheat. *Instead of picking the lock with a credit card, the clumsy thieves gouged a hole in my door. The consumer watchdog group accused the clothing stores of gouging customers with high prices.*

WORD ORIGIN

Latin *genus* = type or kind; birth. Also found in English *congenital*, *genetic*, *genital*, *genre*, *genuine*, and *genus*.

guile (noun) Deceit, duplicity. *In Margaret Mitchell's* Gone With the Wind, *Scarlett O'Hara uses her guile to manipulate two men and then is matched for wits by a third: Rhett Butler.* guileful (adjective).

gullible (adjective) Easily fooled. *Terry was so gullible she actually believed Robert's stories of his connections to the Czar and Czarina.* gullibility (noun).

H

hackneyed (adjective) Without originality, trite. *When someone invented the phrase "No pain, no gain," it was clever and witty, but now it is so commonly heard that it seems hackneyed.*

harrow (verb) To cultivate with a harrow; to torment or vex. *During grade school, my sister was harrowed mercilessly for being overweight.*

harrowing (adjective) Nerve-wracking, traumatic. *Jon Krakauer's best-selling book* Into Thin Air *chronicles the tragic consequences of leading groups of untrained climbers up Mt. Everest.*

haughty (adjective) Overly proud. *The fashion model strode down the runway, her hips thrust forward and a haughty expression, something like a sneer, on her face.* haughtiness (noun).

hierarchy (noun) A ranking of people, things, or ideas from highest to lowest. *A cabinet secretary ranks just below the president and vice president in the hierarchy of the government's executive branch.* hierarchical (adjective).

WORD ORIGIN

Greek *homos* = same. Also found in English *homologous*, *homonym*, and *homosexual*.

homogeneous (adjective) Uniform, made entirely of one thing. *It's hard to think of a more homogenous group than those eerie children in* Village of the Damned, *who all had perfect features, white-blond hair, and silver, penetrating eyes.*

hone (verb) To improve and make more acute or affective. *While she was a receptionist, Norma honed her skills as a stand-up comic by trying out jokes on the tense crowd in the waiting room.*

hoodwink (verb) To deceive by trickery or false appearances; to dupe. *That was my cousin Ravi calling to say that he's been hoodwinked again, this time by some outfit offering time shares in a desolate tract of land in central Florida.*

I

iconoclast (noun) Someone who attacks traditional beliefs or institutions. *Comedian Dennis Miller relishes his reputation as an iconoclast, though people in power often resent his satirical jabs.* iconoclasm (noun), iconoclastic (adjective).

idolatry (noun) The worship of a person, thing, or institution as a god. *In communist China, admiration for Mao resembled idolatry; his picture was displayed everywhere, and millions of Chinese memorized his sayings and repeated them endlessly.* idolatrous (adjective).

idyll (noun) A rustic, romantic interlude; poetry or prose that celebrates simple pastoral life. *Her picnic with Max at Fahnstock Lake was not the serene idyll she had envisioned; instead, they were surrounded by hundreds of other picnickers blaring music from their boom boxes and cracking open soda cans.* idyllic (adjective).

illicit (adjective) Illegal, wrongful. *When Janet caught her 13-year-old son and his friend downloading illicit pornographic photos from the World Wide Web, she promptly pulled the plug on his computer.*

illuminate (verb) To brighten with light; to enlighten or elucidate; to decorate (a manuscript). *The frosted-glass sconces in the dressing rooms at Le Cirque not only illuminate the rooms but make everyone look like a movie star. Alice Munro is a writer who can illuminate an entire character with a few deft sentences.*

immaculate (adjective) Totally unblemished, spotlessly clean. *The cream-colored upholstery in my new Porsche was immaculate—that is, until a raccoon came in through the window and tracked mud across the seats.*

immaterial (adjective) Of no consequence, unimportant. *"The fact that your travel agent is your best friend's son should be immaterial," I told Rosa, "so, if he keeps putting you on hold and acting nasty, just take your business elsewhere."*

immutable (adjective) Incapable of change. *Does there ever come an age when we realize that our parents' personalities are immutable, when we can relax and stop trying to make them change?*

impartial (adjective) Fair, equal, unbiased. *If a judge is not impartial, then all of her rulings are questionable.* impartiality (noun).

impassivity (noun) Apathy, unresponsiveness. *Dot truly thinks that Mr. Right will magically show up on her doorstep, and her utter impassivity regarding her social life makes me want to shake her!* impassive (adjective).

imperceptible (adjective) Impossible to perceive, inaudible or incomprehensible. *The sound of footsteps was almost imperceptible, but Donald's paranoia had reached such a pitch that he immediately assumed he was being followed.*

imperturbable (adjective) Cannot be disconcerted, disturbed, or excited. *The proper English butler in Kazuo Ishiguro's novel* Remains of the Day *appears completely imperturbable, even when his father dies or when his own heart is breaking.*

impetuous (adjective) Acting hastily or impulsively. *Ben's resignation was an impetuous act; he did it without thinking, and he soon regretted it.* impetuosity (noun).

implacable (adjective) Unbending, resolute. *The state of Israel is implacable in its policy of never negotiating with criminals.*

implosion (noun) To collapse inward from outside pressure. *While it is difficult to know what is going on in North Korea, no one can rule out a violent implosion of the North Korean regime and a subsequent flood of refugees across its borders.* implode (verb).

incessant (adjective) Unceasing. *The incessant blaring of the neighbor's car alarm made it impossible for me to concentrate on my upcoming Bar exam.*

WORD ORIGIN

Latin *mutare* = to change. Also found in English *immutable, mutant,* and *mutation.*

WORD ORIGIN

Latin *placare* = to please. Also found in English *complacent, placate,* and *placid.*

WORD ORIGIN

Latin *caedere* = to cut. Also found in English *concise*, *decide*, *excise*, *incision*, and *precise*.

inchoate (adjective) Only partly formed or formulated. *At editorial meetings, Nancy had a habit of presenting her inchoate book ideas before she had a chance to fully determine their feasibility.*

incise (verb) To carve into, to engrave. *My wife felt nostalgic about the old elm tree since we had incised our initials in it when we were both in high school.*

incisive (adjective) Admirably direct and decisive. *Ted Koppel's incisive questions have made many politicians squirm and stammer.*

incongruous (adjective) Unlikely. *Art makes incongruous alliances, as when punk-rockers, Tibetan folk musicians, gospel singers, and beat poets shared the stage at the Tibet House benefit concert.* incongruity (noun).

incorrigible (adjective) Impossible to manage or reform. *Lou is an incorrigible trickster, constantly playing practical jokes no matter how much his friends complain.*

incursion (noun) A hostile entrance into a territory; a foray into an activity or venture. *It is a little-known fact that the Central Intelligence Agency organized military incursions into China during the 1950s. The comic* Peanuts *was Barbara's first incursion into the world of comic strip artists.*

indefatigable (adjective) Tireless. *Eleanor Roosevelt's indefatigable dedication to the cause of human welfare won her affection and honor throughout the world.* indefatigability (noun).

indelicate (adjective) Blunt, undisguised. *No sooner had we sat down to eat than Mark made an indelicate remark about my high salary.*

inevitable (adjective) Unable to be avoided. *Once the Japanese attacked Pearl Harbor, U.S. involvement in World War II was inevitable.* inevitability (noun).

infer (verb) To conclude, to deduce. *Can I infer from your hostile tone of voice that you are still angry about yesterday's incident?* inference (noun).

inimical (adjective) Unfriendly, hostile; adverse or difficult. *Relations between Greece and Turkey have been inimical for centuries.*

inimitable (adjective) Incapable of being imitated, matchless. *John F. Kennedy's administration dazzled the public, partly because of the inimitable style and elegance of his wife, Jacqueline.*

inopportune (adjective) Awkward, untimely. *When Gus heard raised voices and the crash of breaking china behind the kitchen door, he realized that he'd picked an inopportune moment to visit the Fairlights.*

inscrutability (noun) Quality of being extremely difficult to interpret or understand, mysteriousness. *I am still puzzling over the inscrutability of the package I received yesterday, which contained twenty pomegranates and a note that said simply "Yours."* inscrutable (adjective).

insensible (adjective) Unaware, incognizant; unconscious, out cold. *It's a good thing that Marty was insensible to the titters and laughter that greeted his arrival in the ballroom. In the latest episode of gang brutality, an innocent young man was beaten insensible after two gang members stormed his apartment.*

insinuate (verb) Hint or intimate; to creep in. *During an extremely unusual broadcast, the newscaster insinuated that the Washington bureau chief was having a nervous breakdown. Marla managed to insinuate herself into the Duchess' conversation during the charity event.* insinuation (noun).

insipid (adjective) Flavorless, uninteresting. *Most TV shows are so insipid that you can watch them while reading or chatting without missing a thing.* insipidity (noun).

insolence (noun) An attitude or behavior that is bold and disrespectful. *Some feel that news reporters who shout accusatory questions at the president are behaving with insolence toward his high office.* insolent (adjective).

insoluble (adjective) Unable to be solved, irresolvable; indissoluble. *Fermat's last theorum remained insoluble for over 300 years until a young mathematician from Princeton solved it in 1995. If you are a gum chewer, you probably wouldn't like to know that insoluble plastics are a common ingredient of most popular gums.*

insular (adjective) Narrow or isolated in attitude or viewpoint. *New Yorkers are famous for their insular attitudes; they seem to think that nothing important has ever happened outside of their city.* insularity (noun).

intercede (verb) To step in, to moderate; to mediate or negotiate on behalf of someone else. *After their rejection by the co-op board, Kevin and Sol asked Rachel, another tenant, to intercede for them at the next board meeting.* intercession (noun).

interim (noun) A break or interlude. *In the interim between figure-skating programs, the exhausted skaters retreat to the "kiss and cry" room to wait for their scores.*

interpolate (verb) To interject. *The director's decision to interpolate topical political jokes into his production of Shakespeare's* Twelfth Night *was not viewed kindly by the critics.* interpolation (noun).

intransigent (adjective) Unwilling to compromise. *Despite the mediator's attempts to suggest a fair solution to the disagreement, the two parties were intransigent, forcing a showdown.* intransigence (noun).

intrinsically (adverb) Essentially, inherently. *There is nothing intrinsically difficult about upgrading a computer's microprocessor, yet Al was afraid to even open up the computer's case.* intrinsic (adjective).

inundate (verb) To overwhelm; to flood. *When AOL first announced its flat-rate pricing, the company was inundated with new customers, and thus began the annoying delays in service.* inundation (noun).

invective (noun) Insulting, abusive language. *I remained unscathed by his blistering invective because in my heart I knew I had done the right thing.*

invigorate (verb) To give energy to, to stimulate. *As her car climbed the mountain road, Lucinda felt herself invigorated by the clear air and the cool breezes.* invigoration (noun).

irascible (adjective) Easily provoked into anger, hot-headed. *Soup chef Al Yeganah, the model for* Seinfeld's *"Soup Nazi," is an irascible man who flies into a temper tantrum if his customers don't follow his rigid procedure for purchasing soup.* irascibility (noun).

WORD ORIGIN

Latin *unda* = wave.
Also found in English
undulate.

J

jeopardize (verb) To put in danger. *Terrorist attacks on civilians jeopardize the fragile peace in the Middle East.* jeopardy (noun).

jocular (adjective) Humorous, amusing. *Listening to the CEO launch into yet another uproarious anecdote, Ted was frankly surprised by the jocular nature of the "emergency" board meeting.* jocularity (noun).

L

labyrinthine (adjective) Extremely intricate or involved; circuitous. *Was I the only one who couldn't follow the labyrinthine plot of the movie L.A. Confidential? I was so confused I had to watch it twice to see "who did it."*

laconic (adjective) Concise to the point of terseness; taciturn. *Tall, handsome and laconic, the actor Gary Cooper came to personify the strong, silent American, a man of action and few words.*

lambaste (verb) To give someone a dressing-down; to attack someone verbally; to whip. *Once inside the locker room, the coach thoroughly lambasted the team for their incompetent performance on the football field.*

WORD ORIGIN

Latin *laus* = praise. Also found in English *applaud, laud, laudatory,* and *plaudit.*

laudable (adjective) Commendable, praiseworthy. *The Hunt's Point nonprofit organization has embarked on a series of laudable ventures pairing businesses and disadvantaged youth.*

lethargic (adjective) Lacking energy; sluggish. *Visitors to the zoo are surprised that the lions appear so lethargic, but, in the wild, lions sleep up to 18 hours a day.* lethargy (noun).

levy (verb) To demand payment or collection of a tax or fee. *The environmental activists pushed Congress to levy higher taxes on gasoline, but the auto makers' lobbyists quashed their plans.*

lien (noun) A claim against a property for the satisfaction of a debt. *Nat was in such financial straits when he died that his Fishkill property had several liens against it, and all of his furniture was being repossessed.*

limn (verb) To outline in distinct detail; to delineate. *Like many of her novels, Edith Wharton's* The Age of Innocence *expertly limns the tyranny of New York's upper class society in the 1800s.*

loquacity (noun) Talkativeness, wordiness. *While some people deride his loquacity and his tendency to use outrageous rhymes, no one can doubt that Jesse Jackson is a powerful orator.* loquacious (adjective).

WORD ORIGIN

Latin *lux* = light. Also found in English *elucidate, pellucid,* and *translucent.*

lucid (adjective) Clear and understandable. *Hawking's* A Short History of the Universe *is a lucid explanation of a difficult topic, modern scientific theories of the origin of the universe.* lucidity (noun).

M

magnanimous (adjective) Noble, generous. *When media titan Ted Turner pledged a gift of $1 billion to the United Nations, he challenged other wealthy people to be equally magnanimous.* magnanimity (noun).

maladroit (adjective) Inept, awkward. *It was painful to watch the young congressman's maladroit delivery of the nominating speech.*

malinger (verb) To pretend illness to avoid work. *During the labor dispute, hundreds of employees malingered, forcing the company to slow production and costing it millions in profits.*

malleable (adjective) Able to be changed, shaped, or formed by outside pressures. *Gold is a very useful metal because it is so malleable. A child's personality is malleable, and is often deeply influenced by things her parents say and do.* malleability (noun).

mandate (noun) Order, command. *The new policy on gays in the military went into effect as soon as the president issued his mandate about it.* mandate (verb), mandatory (adjective).

marginal (adjective) At the outer edge or fringe; of minimal quality or acceptability. *In spite of the trend toward greater paternal involvement in child-rearing, most fathers still have a marginal role in their children's lives. Jerry's GRE scores were so marginal that he didn't get accepted into the graduate school of his choice.*

marginalize (verb) To push toward the fringes; to make less consequential. *Hannah argued that the designation of a certain month as "Black History Month" or "Gay and Lesbian Book Month" actually does a disservice to minorities by marginalizing them.*

martial (adjective) Of, relating to, or suited to military life. *My old teacher, Miss Woody, had such a martial demeanor that you'd think she was running a boot camp instead of teaching fifth grade. The military seized control of Myanmar in 1988, and this embattled country has been ruled by martial law since then.*

mediate (verb) To reconcile differences between two parties. *During the baseball strike, both the players and the club owners expressed willingness to have the president mediate the dispute.* mediation (noun).

mercenary (adjective) Doing something only for pay or for personal advantage. *People had criticized the U.S. motives in the Persian Gulf War as mercenary, pointing out that the U.S. would not have come to Kuwait's defense had it grown carrots rather than produced oil.* mercenary (noun).

mercurial (adjective) Changing quickly and unpredictably. *The mercurial personality of Robin Williams, with his many voices and styles, made him a natural choice to play the part of the ever-changing genie in* Aladdin.

WORD ORIGIN

Latin *mandare* = entrust, order. Also found in English *command, demand,* and *remand.*

WORD ORIGIN

Latin *medius* = middle. Also found in English *intermediate, media,* and *medium.*

metamorphose (verb) To undergo a striking transformation. *In just a century, book publishers have metamorphosed from independent, exclusively literary businesses to minor divisions in multimedia entertainment conglomerates.* metamorphosis (noun).

meticulous (adjective) Very careful with details. *Watch repair calls for a craftsperson who is patient and meticulous.*

mettle (noun) Strength of spirit; stamina. *Linda's mettle was severely tested while she served as the only female attorney at Smith, Futterweitt, Houghton, and Dobbs.* mettlesome (adjective).

mimicry (noun) Imitation, aping. *The continued popularity of Elvis Presley has given rise to a class of entertainers who make a living through mimicry of "The King."* mimic (noun and verb).

minatory (adjective) Menacing, threatening. *As soon as she met Mrs. Danforth, the head housemaid at Manderlay, the young bride was cowed by her minatory manner and quickly retreated to the morning room.*

mince (verb) To chop into small pieces; to speak with decorum and restraint. *Malaysia's prime minister Mahathir Mohamad was not a man known to mince words; he had accused satellite TV of poisoning Asia and had denounced the Australian press as "congenital liars."*

WORD ORIGIN

Greek *anthropos* = human. Also found in English *anthropology*, *anthropoid*, *anthropomorphic*, and *philanthropy*.

misanthrope (noun) Someone who hates or distrusts all people. *In the beloved Christmas classic,* It's a Wonderful Life, *Lionel Barrymore plays Potter, the wealthy misanthrope who is determined to make life miserable for everyone, and particularly for the young, idealistic George Bailey.* misanthropic (adjective), misanthropy (noun).

miscreant (adjective) Unbelieving, heretical; evil, villainous. *After a one-year run playing Iago in* Othello, *and then two years playing Bill Sikes in* Oliver, *Sean was tired of being typecast in miscreant roles.* miscreant (noun).

mitigate (verb) To make less severe; to relieve. *There's no doubt that Wallace committed the assault, but the verbal abuse Wallace had received helps to explain his behavior and somewhat mitigates his guilt.* mitigation (noun).

monopoly (noun) A condition in which there is only one seller of a certain commodity. *Wary of Microsoft's seeming monopoly of the computer operating-system business, rivals are asking for government intervention.* **monopolistic** (adjective) *Renowned consumer advocate Ralph Nader once quipped, "The only difference between John D. Rockefeller and Bill Gates is that Gates recognizes no boundaries to his monopolistic drive."*

monotonous (adjective) Tediously uniform, unchanging. *Brian Eno's "Music for Airports" is characterized by minimal melodies, subtle textures, and variable repetition, which I find rather bland and monotonous.* monotony (noun).

morose (adjective) Gloomy, sullen. *After Chuck's girlfriend dumped him, he lay around the house for a couple of days, refusing to come to the phone and feeling morose.*

mutation (noun) A significant change; in biology, a permanent change in hereditary material. *Most genetic mutations are not beneficial, since any change in the delicate balance of an organism tends to be disruptive.* mutate (verb).

N

nadir (noun) Lowest point. *Pedro and Renee's marriage reached a new nadir last Christmas Eve when Pedro locked Renee out of the house upon her return from the supposed "business trip."*

nascent (adjective) Newly born, just beginning. *While her artistry is still nascent, it was 15-year-old Tara Lipinski's technical wizardry that enabled her to win a gold medal in the 1998 Winter Olympics.* nascence (noun).

noisome (adjective) Putrid, fetid, noxious. *We were convinced that the noisome odor infiltrating every corner of our building was evidence of a mouldering corpse.*

notorious (adjective) Famous, especially for evil actions or qualities. *Warner Brothers produced a series of movies about notorious gangsters such as John Dillinger and Al Capone.* notoriety (noun).

O

obdurate (adjective) Unwilling to change; stubborn, inflexible. *Despite the many pleas he received, the governor was obdurate in his refusal to grant clemency to the convicted murderer.*

WORD ORIGIN

Latin *durus* = hard.
Also found in English
durable and *endure*.

oblivious (adjective) Unaware, unconscious. *Karen practiced her oboe solo with complete concentration, oblivious to the noise and activity around her.* oblivion (noun), obliviousness (noun).

obscure (adjective) Little known; hard to understand. *Mendel was an obscure monk until decades after his death, when his scientific work was finally discovered. Most people find the writings of James Joyce obscure; hence the popularity of books that explain the many odd references and tricks of language in his work.* obscure (verb), obscurity (noun).

obsolete (adjective) No longer current; old-fashioned. *W. H. Auden said that his ideal landscape would contain water wheels, grain mills, and other forms of obsolete machinery.* obsolescence (noun).

obstinate (adjective) Stubborn, unyielding. *Despite years of government effort, the problem of drug abuse remains obstinate.* obstinacy (noun).

obtuse (adjective) Dull-witted, insensitive; incomprehensible, unclear, or imprecise. *Amy was so obtuse she didn't realize that Alexi had proposed marriage to her. French psychoanalyst Jacques Lacan's collection of papers, Ecrits, is notoriously obtuse, yet it has still been highly influential in linguistics, film theory, and literary criticism.*

obviate (verb) Preclude, make unnecessary. *Truman Capote's meticulous accuracy and total recall obviated the need for note-taking when he wrote his account of a 1959 murder,* In Cold Blood.

odium (noun) Intense feeling of hatred, abhorrence. *When the neighbors learned that a convicted sex offender was now living in their midst, they could not restrain their odium and began harassing the man whenever he left his house.* odious (adjective).

opprobrium (noun) Dishonor, disapproval. *Switzerland came under public opprobrium when it was revealed that Swiss bankers had hoarded the gold the Nazis had confiscated from their victims.* opprobrious (adjective).

orthodox (adjective) In religion, conforming to a certain doctrine; conventional. *George Eliot's relationship with George Lewes, a married journalist, offended the sensibilities of her more orthodox peers.* orthodoxy (noun).

ossified (adjective) In biology, to turn into bone; to become rigidly conventional and opposed to change. *His harsh view of co-education had ossified over the years, so that he was now the only teacher who sought to bar girls from the venerable boys' school.* ossification (noun).

ostentatious (adjective) Overly showy, pretentious. *To show off his new wealth, the financier threw an ostentatious party featuring a full orchestra, a famous singer, and tens of thousands of dollars' worth of food.* ostentation (noun).

ostracize (verb) To exclude from a group. *In Biblical times, those who suffered from the disease of leprosy were ostracized and forced to live alone.* ostracism (noun).

P

paean (adjective) A joyous expression of praise, gratitude, or triumph. *Choreographer Paul Taylor's dance "Eventide" is a sublime paean to remembered love, with couple after loving couple looking back as they embrace an unknown future.*

parody (noun) An imitation created for comic effect; a caricature. *While the creators of the 1970s comedy series* All in the Family *intended Archie Bunker to be a parody of closed-mindedness in Americans, large numbers of people adopted Bunker as a working-class hero.*

parse (verb) To break a sentence down into grammatical components; to analyze bit by bit. *In the wake of the sex scandal, journalists parsed every utterance by administration officials regarding the president's alleged promiscuity. At $1.25 million a day,* Titanic *is the most expensive movie ever made, but director James Cameron refused to parse the film's enormous budget for inquisitive reporters.*

partisan (adjective) Reflecting strong allegiance to a particular party or cause. *The vote on the president's budget was strictly partisan: every member of the president's party voted yes, and all others voted no.* partisan (noun).

pastoral (adjective) Simple and rustic, bucolic, rural. *While industry grew and the country expanded westward, the Hudson River School of painters depicted the landscape as a pastoral setting where humans and nature could coexist.*

patron (noun) A special guardian or protector; a wealthy or influential supporter of the arts. *Dominique de Menil used her considerable wealth to become a well-known patron of the arts; she and her husband owned a collection of more than 10,000 pieces ranging from cubist paintings to tribal artifacts.* patronize (verb).

peccadillo (noun) A minor offense, a lapse. *What Dr. Sykes saw as a major offense— being addressed as Marge rather than Doctor—Tina saw as a mere peccadillo and one that certainly should not have lost her the job.*

pedantic (adjective) Academic, bookish. *The men Hillary met through personal ads in the* New York Review of Books *were invariably pasty-skinned pedantic types who dropped the names of nineteenth-century writers in every sentence.* pedantry (noun).

pedestrian (adjective) Unimaginative, ordinary. *The new Italian restaurant received a bad review due to its reliance on pedestrian dishes such as pasta with marinara sauce or chicken parmigiana.*

perfidious (adjective) Disloyal, treacherous. *Although he was one of the most talented generals of the American Revolution, Benedict Arnold is remembered today as a perfidious betrayer of the patriot cause.* perfidy (noun).

peripatetic (adjective) Moving or traveling from place to place; always on the go. *In Barbara Wilson's* Trouble in Transylvania, *peripatetic translator Cassandra Reilly is on the road again, this time to China by way of Budapest, where she plans to catch the TransMongolian Express.*

permeate (verb) To spread through or penetrate. *Little by little, the smell of gas from the broken pipe permeated the house.*

personification (noun) The embodiment of a thing or an abstract idea in human form. *Many people view Theodore Kaczynski, the killer known as the Unabomber, as the very personification of evil.* personify (verb).

pervasive (adjective) Spreading throughout. *As news of the disaster reached the town, a pervasive sense of gloom could be felt everywhere.* pervade (verb).

philistine (noun) Someone who is smugly ignorant and uncultured. *A true philistine, Meg claimed she didn't read any book that wasn't either recommended by Oprah Winfrey or on the best-seller list.* philistine (adjective).

pith (noun) The core, the essential part; in biology, the central strand of tissue in the stems of most vascular plants. *After spending seventeen years in psychoanalysis, Frieda had finally come face to face with the pith of her deep-seated anxiety.* pithy (adjective).

placate (verb) To soothe or appease. *The waiter tried to placate the angry customer with the offer of a free dessert.* placatory (adjective).

placid (adjective) Unmarked by disturbance; complacent. *Dr. Kahn was convinced that the placid exterior presented by Frieda in her early analysis sessions masked a deeply disturbed psyche.* placidity (noun).

WORD ORIGIN

Latin *fides* = faith. Also found in English *confide, confidence, fidelity,* and *infidel.*

plaintive (adjective) Expressing suffering or melancholy. *In the beloved children's book The Secret Garden, Mary is disturbed by plaintive cries echoing in the corridors of gloomy Misselthwaite Manor.*

plastic (adjective) Able to be molded or reshaped. *Because it is highly plastic, clay is an easy material for beginning sculptors to use.* plasticity (noun).

platitude (noun) A trite remark or saying; a cliché. *How typical of June to send a sympathy card filled with mindless platitudes like "One day at a time," rather than calling the grieving widow.* platitudinous (adjective).

plausible (adjective) Apparently believable. *The idea that a widespread conspiracy to kill the president has been kept secret by all the participants for more than thirty years hardly seems plausible.* plausibility (noun).

plummet (verb) To dive or plunge. *On October 27, 1997, the stock market plummeted by 554 points, and left us all wondering if the bull market was finally over.*

polarize (adjective) To separate into opposing groups or forces. *For years, the abortion debate polarized the American people, with many people voicing views at either extreme and few people trying to find a middle ground.* polarization (noun).

ponderous (adjective) Unwieldy and bulky; oppressively dull. *Unfortunately, the film director weighed the movie down with a ponderous voice-over narrated by the protagonist as an old man.*

poseur (noun) Someone who pretends to be what he isn't. *Gerald had pretensions for literary stardom with his book proposal on an obscure World War II battle, yet most agents soon realized that the book would never be written and categorized him as a poseur.*

positivism (noun) A philosophy that denies speculation and assumes that the only knowledge is scientific knowledge. *David Hume carried his positivism to an extreme when he argued that our expectation that the sun will rise tomorrow has no basis in reason and is purely a matter of belief.* positivistic (adjective).

pragmatism (noun) A belief in approaching problems through practical rather than theoretical means. *Roosevelt's attitude toward the economic troubles of the Depression was based on pragmatism: "Try something," he said. "If it doesn't work, try something else."* pragmatic (adjective).

precedent (noun) An earlier occurrence that serves as an example for a decision. *In a legal system that reveres precedent, even defining the nature of a completely new type of dispute can seem impossible.* precede (verb).

precept (noun) A general principle or law. *One of the central precepts of Tai Chi Ch'uan is the necessity of allowing ki (cosmic energy) to flow through one's body in slow, graceful movements.*

WORD ORIGIN

Latin *claudere* = to close. Also found in English *conclude*, *include*, *recluse*, and *seclude*.

precipitate (verb) To spur or activate. *In the summer of 1997, the selling off of the Thai baht precipitated a currency crisis that spread throughout Asia.*

preclude (verb) To prevent, to hinder. *Unfortunately, Jasmine's appointment at the New Age Expo precluded her attendance at our weekend* Workshop for Shamans and Psychics. preclusive (adjective), preclusion (noun).

precursor (noun) A forerunner, a predecessor. *The Kodak Brownie camera, a small boxy camera made of jute board and wood, was the precursor to today's sleek digital cameras.* precursory (adjective).

preponderance (noun) A superiority in weight, size, or quantity; a majority. *In Seattle, there is a great preponderance of seasonal affective disorder, or SAD, a malady brought on by light starvation during the dark Northwest winter.* preponderate (verb).

presage (verb) To foretell, to anticipate. *According to folklore, a red sky at dawn presages a day of stormy weather.*

prescience (noun) Foreknowledge or foresight. *When she saw the characteristic eerie yellowish-black light in the sky, Dorothy had the prescience to seek shelter in the storm cellar.* prescient (adjective).

presumptuous (adjective) Going beyond the limits of courtesy or appropriateness. *The senator winced when the presumptuous young staffer addressed him as "Ted."* presume (verb), presumption (noun).

prevaricate (verb) To lie, to equivocate. *When it became clear to the FBI that the mobster had threatened the 12-year-old witness, they could well understand why the youngster had prevaricated during the hearing.*

primacy (noun) State of being the utmost in importance; preeminence. *The anthropologist Ruth Benedict was an inspiration to Margaret Mead for her emphasis on the primacy of culture in the formation of an individual's personality.* primal (adjective).

pristine (adjective) Pure, undefiled. *As climbers who have scaled Mt. Everest can attest, the trails to the summit are hardly in pristine condition and are actually strewn with trash.*

probity (noun) Goodness, integrity. *The vicious editorial attacked the moral probity of the senatorial candidate, saying he had profited handsomely from his pet project, the senior-citizen housing project.*

procure (verb) To obtain by using particular care and effort. *Through partnerships with a large number of specialty wholesalers, W.W. Grainger is able to procure a startling array of products for its customers, from bear repellent for Alaska pipeline workers to fork-lift trucks and toilet paper.* procurement (noun).

prodigality (noun) The condition of being wastefully extravagant. *Richard was ashamed of the prodigality of his bride's parents when he realized that the cost of the wedding reception alone was more than his father earned in one year.* prodigal (adjective).

proliferate (verb) To increase or multiply. *For about fifteen years, high-tech companies had proliferated in northern California, Massachusetts, and other regions.* proliferation (noun).

prolixity (noun) A diffuseness; a rambling and verbose quality. *The prolixity of Sarah's dissertation on Ottoman history defied even her advisor's attempts to read it.* prolix (adjective).

propagate (verb) To cause to grow; to foster. *John Smithson's will left his fortune for the founding of an institution to propagate knowledge, leaving open whether that meant a university, a library, or a museum.* propagation (noun).

prophetic (adjective) Auspicious, predictive of what's to come. *We often look at every event leading up to a new love affair as prophetic—the flat tire that caused us to be late for work, the chance meeting in the elevator, the horoscope that augured "a new beginning."* prophecy (noun), prophesy (verb).

propitiating (adjective) Conciliatory, mollifying or appeasing. *Management's offer of a 5 percent raise was meant as a propitiating gesture, yet the striking workers were unimpressed.* propitiate (verb).

propriety (noun) Appropriateness. *Some people expressed doubts about the propriety of the president discussing his underwear on MTV.*

proximity (noun) Closeness, nearness. *Neighborhood residents were angry over the proximity of the proposed sewage plant to the local elementary school.* proximate (adjective).

pundit (noun) Someone who offers opinions in an authoritative style. *The Sunday morning talk shows are filled with pundits, each with his or her own theory about this week's political news.*

WORD ORIGIN

Latin *poena* = pain.
Also found in English
*impunity, penal,
penalty,* and
punishment.

pungency (noun) Marked by having a sharp, biting quality. *Unfortunately, the pungency of the fresh cilantro overwhelmed the delicate flavor of the poached turbot.* pungent (adjective).

purify (verb) To make pure, clean, or perfect. *The new water-treatment plant is supposed to purify the drinking water provided to everyone in the nearby towns.* purification (noun).

Q

quiescent (adjective) In a state of rest or inactivity; latent. *Polly's ulcer has been quiescent ever since her mother-in-law moved out of the condo, which was well over a year ago.* quiescence (noun).

quixotic (adjective) Foolishly romantic, idealistic to an impractical degree. *In the novel* Shoeless Joe, *Ray Kinsella carries out a quixotic plan to build a baseball field in the hopes that past baseball greats will come to play there.*

quotidian (adjective) Occurring every day; commonplace and ordinary. *Most of the time, we long to escape from quotidian concerns, but in the midst of a crisis we want nothing more than to be plagued by such simple problems as a leaky faucet or a whining child.*

R

raconteur (noun) An excellent storyteller. *A member of the Algonquin Roundtable, Robert Benchley was a natural raconteur with a seemingly endless ability to turn daily life and its irritations into entertaining commentary.*

rancorous (adjective) Marked by deeply embedded bitterness or animosity. *While Ralph and Kishu have been separated for three years, their relationship is so rancorous that they had to hire a professional mediator just to discuss divorce arrangements.* rancor (noun).

rapacious (adjective) Excessively grasping or greedy. *Some see global currency speculators like George Soros as rapacious parasites who destroy economies and then line their pockets with the profits.* rapacity (noun).

rarefied (adjective) Of interest or relating to a small, refined circle; less dense, thinner. *Those whose names dot the society pages live in a rarefied world where it's entirely normal to dine on caviar for breakfast or order a $2,000 bottle of wine at Le Cirque. When she reached the summit of Mt. McKinley, Deborah could hardly breathe in the rarefied air.*

raucous (adjective) Boisterous, unruly, and wild. *Sounds of shouts and raucous laughter drifted out of the hotel room where Felipe's bachelor party was being held.*

reactionary (adjective) Ultra conservative. *Every day, more than twenty million listeners used to tune in to hear Rush Limbaugh spew his reactionary opinions about "Feminazis" and environmental "fanatics."* reactionary (noun).

recede (verb) To draw back, to ebb, to abate. *Once his hairline began to recede, Hap took to wearing bizarre accessories, like velvet ascots, to divert attention from it.* recession (noun).

reclusive (adjective) Withdrawn from society. *During the last years of her life, Garbo led a reclusive existence, rarely appearing in public.* recluse (noun).

recompense (noun) Compensation for a service rendered or to pay for damages. *The 5 percent of the estate, which Phil received as executor of his aunt Ida's will, is small recompense for the headaches he endured in settling her affairs.* recompense (verb).

reconcile (verb) To make consistent or harmonious. *Franklin D. Roosevelt's greatness as a leader can be seen in his ability to reconcile the differing demands and values of the varied groups that supported him.* reconciliation (noun).

recondite (adjective) Profound, deep, abstruse. *Professor Miyaki's recondite knowledge of seventeenth-century Flemish painters made him a prized—if barely understood—member of the art history department.*

redemptive (adjective) Liberating and reforming. *While she doesn't attend formal church services, Carrie is a firm believer in the redemptive power of prayer.* redeem (verb), redemption (noun).

refractory (adjective) Stubbornly resisting control or authority. *Like a refractory child, Jill stomped out of the car, slammed the door, and said she would walk home, even though her house was 10 miles away.*

relevance (noun) Connection to the matter at hand; pertinence. *Testimony in a criminal trial may only be admitted to the extent that it has clear relevance to the question of guilt or innocence.* relevant (adjective).

WORD ORIGIN

Latin *frangere* = to break. Also found in English *fraction*, *fractious*, *fracture*, *frangible*, *infraction*, and *refract*.

reparation (noun) The act of making amends; payment of damages by a defeated nation to the victors. *The Treaty of Versailles, signed in 1919, formally asserted Germany's war guilt and ordered it to pay reparations to the allies.*

reproof (noun) A reprimand, a reproach, or castigation. *Joe thought being grounded for one month was a harsh reproof for coming home late only once.* reprove (verb).

repudiate (verb) To reject, to renounce. *After it became known that the politician had been a leader of the Ku Klux Klan, most Republican leaders repudiated him.* repudiation (noun).

repugnant (adjective) Causing dislike or disgust. *After the news broke about Mad Cow Disease, much of the beef-loving British public began to find the thought of a Sunday roast repugnant.*

requiem (noun) A musical composition or poem written to honor the dead. *Many financial analysts think that the ailing typewriter company should simply say a requiem for itself and shut down; however, the CEO has other plans.*

resilient (adjective) Able to recover from difficulty. *A pro athlete must be mentally resilient, able to lose a game one day and come back the next with renewed enthusiasm and confidence.* resilience (noun).

resonant (adjective) Full of special import or meaning. *I found the speaker's words particularly resonant because I, too, had served in Vietnam and felt the same mixture of shame and pride.* resonance (noun).

resplendent (adjective) Glowing, shining. *In late December, midtown New York is resplendent with holiday lights and decorations.* resplendence (noun).

rite (noun) Ceremony. *From October to May, the Patwin Indians of California's Sacramento Valley held a series of rites and dances designed to bring the tribe health and prosperity.*

rogue (noun) A mischievously dishonest person; a scamp. *In Jane Austen's* Pride and Prejudice, *Wickham, a charming rogue, seduces Darcy's young sister Georgiana and later does the same thing with Kitty Bennett.*

ruffian (noun) A brute, roughneck, or bully. *In Dickens's* Oliver Twist, *Fagin instructs his gang of orphaned ruffians on the arts of picking pockets and shoplifting.*

rumination (noun) The act of engaging in contemplation. *Marcel Proust's semi-autobiographical novel cycle* Remembrance of Things Past *is less a narrative than an extended rumination on the nature of memory.* ruminate (verb).

S

sage (noun) A person of great wisdom, a knowing philosopher. *It was the Chinese sage Confucius who first taught what is now known the world over as "The Golden Rule."* sagacious (adjective), sagacity (noun).

salutary (adjective) Restorative, healthful. *I find a short dip in an icy stream to be extremely salutary, although the health benefits of my bracing swims are, as yet, unclear.*

sanction (verb) Support or authorize. *Even after a bomb exploded on the front porch of his home, the Reverend Martin Luther King Jr. refused to sanction any violent response and urged his angry followers to love their enemies.* sanctify (verb), sanction (noun).

sap (verb) To exhaust, to deplete. *The exhaustive twelve-city reading tour so sapped the novelist's strength that she told her publicist that she hoped her next book would be a flop! While the African nation was making enormous economic strides under its new president, rebel fighting had sapped much of the country's resources.*

satiate (verb) To fulfill to or beyond capacity. *Judging by the current crop of films featuring serial killers, rape, ritual murder, gun-slinging, and plain old-fashioned slugfests, the public appetite for violence has not yet been satiated.* satiation (noun), satiety (noun).

saturate (verb) To drench or suffuse with liquid or anything that permeates or invades. *The hostess's furious dabbing at the tablecloth was in vain, since the spilt wine had already saturated the damask cloth.* saturation (noun), saturated (adjective).

scrutinize (verb) To study closely. *The lawyer scrutinized the contract, searching for any detail that could pose a risk for her client.* scrutiny (noun).

scurvy (adjective) Shabby, low. *I couldn't believe that Farouk was so scurvy as to open up my computer files and read my e-mail.*

sedulous (adjective) Diligent, industrious. *Those who are most sedulous about studying this vocabulary list are likely to breeze through the antonyms sections of their GRE exam.*

sequential (adjective) Arranged in an order or series. *The courses required for the chemistry major are sequential; you must take them in the prescribed order, since each course builds on the previous ones.* sequence (noun).

sidereal (adjective) Relating to the stars or the constellations. *Jacqueline was interested in matters sidereal, and was always begging my father to take the dusty old telescope out of our garage.*

signatory (noun) Someone who signs an official document or petition along with others. *Alex urged me to join the other signatories and add my name to the petition against toxic sludge in organic foods, but I simply did not care enough about the issue. The signatories of the Declaration of Independence included John Adams, Benjamin Franklin, John Hancock, and Thomas Jefferson.*

WORD ORIGIN

Latin *salus* = health. Also found in English *salubrious, salutation,* and *salute*.

WORD ORIGIN

Latin *sequi* = to follow. Also found in English *consequence, sequel,* and *subsequent*.

sinuous (noun) Winding, circuitous, serpentine. *Frank Gehry's sinuous design for the Guggenheim Museum in Bilbao, Spain, has led people to hail the museum as the first great building of the twenty-first century.* sinuosity (noun).

specious (adjective) Deceptively plausible or attractive. *The infomercial for "Fat-Away" offered mainly specious arguments for a product that is, essentially, a heavy-duty girdle.*

splice (verb) To unite by interweaving separate strands or parts. *Amateur filmmaker Duddy Kravitz shocked and angered his clients by splicing footage of tribal rituals into his films of their weddings and bar mitzvahs.*

spontaneous (adjective) Happening without plan or outside cause. *When the news of John F. Kennedy's assassination hit the airwaves, people everywhere gathered in a spontaneous effort to express their shock and grief.* spontaneity (noun).

spurious (adjective) False, fake. *The so-called Piltdown Man, supposed to be the fossil of a primitive human, turned out to be spurious, though who created the hoax is still uncertain.*

squander (verb) To use up carelessly, to waste. *Those who had made donations to the charity were outraged to learn that its director had squandered millions on fancy dinners, first-class travel, and an expensive apartment for entertaining.*

stanch (verb) To stop the flow. *When the patient began to bleed profusely, the doctor stanched the blood flow by applying direct pressure to the wound.*

stint (verb) To limit, to restrain. *The British bed and breakfast certainly did not stint on the breakfast part of the equation; they provided us with fried tomatoes, fried sausages, fried eggs, smoked kippers, fried bread, fried mushrooms, and bowls of a cereal called "Wheatabix" (which tasted like cardboard).* stinting (adjective).

stolid (adjective) Impassive, unemotional. *The popular animated television series* King of the Hill *chronicles the woes of a stolid, conservative Texan confronting changing times.* stolidity (noun).

subordination (noun) The state of being subservient or treated as less valuable. *Heather left the naval academy because she could no longer stand the subordination of every personal whim or desire to the rigorous demands of military life.* subordinate (verb).

subpoena (noun) An order of a court, legislation, or grand jury that compels a witness to be present at a trial or hearing. *The young man's lawyer asked the judge to subpoena a boa constrictor into court on the grounds that the police had used the snake as an "instrument of terror" to coerce his confession.*

subside (verb) To settle or die down. *The celebrated lecturer had to wait ten minutes for the applause to subside before he began his speech.*

subsidization (noun) The state of being financed by a grant from a government or other agency. *Without subsidization, the nation's passenger rail system would probably go bankrupt.* subsidize (verb).

substantiated (adjective) Verified or supported by evidence. *The charge that Nixon had helped to cover up crimes was substantiated by his comments about it on a series of audio tapes.* substantiate (verb), substantiation (noun).

subsume (verb) To encompass or engulf within something larger. *In Alan Dershowitz's Reversal of Fortune, he makes it clear that his work as a lawyer subsumes his personal life.*

subterranean (adjective) Under the surface of the earth. *Subterranean testing of nuclear weapons was permitted under the Nuclear Test Ban Treaty of 1963.*

summarily (adverb) Quickly and concisely. *No sooner had I voiced my concerns about the new ad campaign than my boss put her hand on my elbow and summarily ushered me out of her office.*

superficial (adjective) On the surface only; without depth or substance. *Her wound was only superficial and required no treatment except a light bandage. His superficial attractiveness hides the fact that his personality is lifeless and his mind is dull.* superficiality (noun).

superimpose (verb) To place or lay over or above something. *The artist stirred controversy by superimposing portraits of certain contemporary politicians over images of such reviled historical figures as Hitler and Stalin.*

supersede (verb) To displace, to substitute or supplant. *"I'm sorry," the principal announced, "but today's afternoon classes will be superseded by an assembly on drug and alcohol abuse."*

supine (adjective) Prone. *One always feels rather vulnerable when wearing a flimsy paper gown and lying supine on a doctor's examining table.*

supposition (noun) Assumption, conjecture. *While most climate researchers believe that increasing levels of greenhouse gases will warm the planet, skeptics claim that this theory is mere supposition.* suppose (verb).

surge (noun) A gush; a swelling or sweeping forward. *When Mattel gave the Barbie doll a makeover in the late 1980s, by manufacturing dolls like doctor Barbie and astronaut Barbie, the company experienced a surge in sales.*

T

tangential (adjective) Touching lightly; only slightly connected or related. *Having enrolled in a class on African-American history, the students found the teacher's stories about his travels in South America only of tangential interest.* tangent (noun).

tedium (noun) Boredom. *For most people, watching even a 15-minute broadcast of the earth as seen from space would be an exercise in sheer tedium.* tedious (adjective).

temperance (noun) Moderation or restraint in feelings and behavior. *Most professional athletes practice temperance in their personal habits; too much eating or drinking and too many late nights, they know, can harm their performance.*

WORD ORIGIN

Latin *tangere* = to touch. Also found in English *contact, contiguous, tactile, tangent,* and *tangible.*

temperate (adjective) Moderate, calm. *The warm gulf streams are largely responsible for the temperate climate of the British Isles.*

tenuous (adjective) Lacking in substance; weak, flimsy, very thin. *His tenuous grasp of the Spanish language was evident when he addressed Señor Chavez as "Señora."*

terrestrial (adjective) Of the earth. *The movie* Close Encounters of the Third Kind *tells the story of the first contact between beings from outer space and terrestrial creatures.*

throwback (noun) A reversion to an earlier type; an atavism. *The late-model Volkswagen Beetle, with its familiar bubble shape, looked like a throwback to the 1960s, but it was actually packed with modern high-tech equipment.*

tiff (noun) A small, almost inconsequential quarrel or disagreement. *Megan and Bruce got into a tiff when Bruce criticized her smoking.*

tirade (noun) A long, harshly critical speech. *Reformed smokers, like Bruce, are prone to delivering tirades on the evils of smoking.*

torpor (noun) Apathy, sluggishness. *Stranded in an airless hotel room in Madras after a 27-hour train ride, I felt such overwhelming torpor that I doubted I would make it to Bangalore, the next destination in my journey.* torpid (adjective).

tout (verb) To praise highly, to brag publicly. *A much happier Eileen is now touting the benefits of Prozac, but, to tell you the truth, I miss her witty, self-lacerating commentaries.*

WORD ORIGIN

Latin *tractare* = to handle. Also found in English *intractable*, *tractate*, and *traction*.

tractable (adjective) Obedient, manageable. *When he turned 3, Harrison suddenly became a tractable, well-mannered little boy after being, quite frankly, an unruly little monster!*

tranquillity (noun) Freedom from disturbance or turmoil; calm. *She moved from New York City to rural Vermont seeking the tranquillity of country life.* tranquil (adjective).

transgress (verb) To go past limits; to violate. *If Iraq has developed biological weapons, then it has transgressed the UN's rules against manufacturing weapons of mass destruction.* transgression (noun).

transmute (verb) To change in form or substance. *Practitioners of alchemy, a forebearer of modern chemistry, tried to discover ways to transmute metals such as iron into gold.* transmutation (noun).

treacherous (adjective) Untrustworthy or disloyal; dangerous or unreliable. *Nazi Germany proved to be a treacherous ally, first signing a peace pact with the Soviet Union, then invading. Be careful crossing the rope bridge; parts of the span are badly frayed and treacherous.* treachery (noun).

tremor (noun) An involuntary shaking or trembling. *Brooke felt the first tremors of the 1989 San Francisco earthquake while she was sitting in Candlestick Park watching a Giants baseball game.*

trenchant (adjective) Caustic and incisive. *Essayist H. L. Mencken was known for his trenchant wit and was famed for mercilessly puncturing the American middle class (which he called the "booboisie").*

trepidation (noun) Fear and anxiety. *After the tragedy of TWA flight 800, many previously fearless flyers were filled with trepidation whenever they stepped into an airplane.*

WORD ORIGIN

Latin *trepidus* = alarmed. Also found in English *intrepid*.

turbulent (adjective) Agitated or disturbed. *The night before the championship match, Martina was unable to sleep, her mind turbulent with fears and hopes.* turbulence (noun).

turpitude (noun) Depravity, wickedness. *Radical feminists who contrast women's essential goodness with men's moral turpitude can be likened to religious fundamentalists who make a clear distinction between the saved and the damned.*

tyro (noun) Novice, amateur. *For an absolute tyro on the ski slopes, Gina was surprisingly agile at taking the moguls.*

U

unalloyed (adjective) Unqualified, pure. *Holding his newborn son for the first time, Malik felt an unalloyed happiness that was unlike anything else he had ever experienced in his 45 years.*

undermine (verb) To excavate beneath; to subvert, to weaken. *Dot continued to undermine my efforts to find her a date by showing up at our dinner parties in her ratty old sweat suit.*

unfeigned (adjective) Genuine, sincere. *Lashawn responded with such unfeigned astonishment when we all leapt out of the kitchen that I think she had had no inkling of the surprise party.*

univocal (adjective) With a single voice. *While they came from different backgrounds and classes, the employees were univocal in their demands that the corrupt CEO resign immediately.*

unstinting (adjective) Giving with unrestrained generosity. *Few people will be able to match the unstinting dedication and care which Mother Teresa had lavished on the poor people of Calcutta.*

WORD ORIGIN

Latin *urbs* = city. Also found in English *suburb* and *urban*.

urbanity (noun) Sophistication, suaveness, and polish. *Part of the fun in a Cary Grant movie lies in seeing whether the star can be made to lose his urbanity and elegance in the midst of chaotic or kooky situations.* urbane (adjective).

usurious (adjective) Lending money at an unconscionably high interest rate. *Some people feel that Shakespeare's portrayal of the Jew, Shylock, the usurious money lender in* The Merchant of Venice, *has enflamed prejudice against the Jews.* usury (adjective).

WORD ORIGIN

Latin *validus* = strong.
Also found in English
*invalid, invaluable,
prevail,* and *value.*

V

validate (verb) To officially approve or confirm. *The election of the president is formally validated when the members of the Electoral College meet to confirm the verdict of the voters.* valid (adjective), validity (noun).

vapid (adjective) Flat, flavorless. *Whenever I have insomnia, I just tune the clock radio to Lite FM, and soon those vapid songs from the 1970s have me floating away to dreamland.* vapidity (noun).

venal (adjective) Corrupt, mercenary. *Sese Seko Mobuto was the venal dictator of Zaire who reportedly diverted millions of dollars in foreign aid to his own personal fortune.* venality (noun).

veneer (noun) A superficial or deceptive covering. *Beneath her folksy veneer, Samantha is a shrewd and calculating businessperson just waiting for the right moment to pounce.*

venerate (verb) To admire or honor. *In Communist China, Mao Tse-Tung is venerated as an almost god-like figure.* venerable (adjective), veneration (noun).

veracious (adjective) Truthful, earnest. *Many people still feel that Anita Hill was entirely veracious in her allegations of sexual harassment during the Clarence Thomas confirmation hearings.* veracity (noun).

WORD ORIGIN

Latin *verus* = true.
Also found in English
*verisimilitude,
veritable,* and *verity.*

verify (verb) To prove to be true. *The contents of Robert L. Ripley's syndicated "Believe it or Not" cartoons could not be verified, yet the public still thrilled to reports of "the man with two pupils in each eye," "the human unicorn," and other amazing oddities.* verification (noun).

veritable (adjective) Authentic. *A French antiques dealer recently claimed that a fifteenth-century child-sized suit of armor that he purchased in 1994 is the veritable suit of armor worn by heroine Joan of Arc.*

vindictive (adjective) Spiteful. *Paula embarked on a string of petty, vindictive acts against her philandering boyfriend, such as mixing dry cat food with his cereal and snipping the blooms off his prize African violets.*

viscid (adjective) Sticky. *The 3M company's "Post-It," a simple piece of paper with one viscid side, has become as commonplace—and as indispensable—as the paper clip.*

viscous (adjective) Having a gelatinous or gooey quality. *I put too much liquid in the batter, and so my Black Forest cake turned out to be a viscous, inedible mass.*

vitiate (verb) To pollute, to impair. *When they voted to ban smoking from all bars in California, the public affirmed their belief that smoking vitiates the health of all people, not just smokers.*

vituperative (adjective) Verbally abusive, insulting. *Elizabeth Taylor should have won an award for her harrowing portrayal of Martha, the bitter, vituperative wife of a college professor in Edward Albee's* Who's Afraid of Virginia Woolf? vituperate (verb).

volatile (adjective) Quickly changing; fleeting, transitory; prone to violence. *Public opinion is notoriously volatile; a politician who is very popular one month may be voted out of office the next.* volatility (noun).

volubility (noun) Quality of being overly talkative, glib. *As Lorraine's anxiety increased, her volubility increased in direct proportion, so during her job interview the poor interviewer couldn't get a word in edgewise.* voluble (adjective).

voracious (adjective) Gluttonous, ravenous. *"Are all your appetites so voracious?" Wesley asked Nina as he watched her finish off seven miniature sandwiches and two lamb kabob skewers in a matter of minutes.* voracity (noun).

WORD ORIGIN

Latin *vorare* = to eat. Also found in English *carnivorous*, *devour*, and *omnivorous*.

W

wag (noun) Wit, joker. *Tom was getting tired of his role as the comical wag who injected life into Kathy's otherwise tedious parties.* waggish (adjective).

whimsical (adjective) Based on a capricious, carefree, or sudden impulse or idea; fanciful, playful. *Dave Barry's* Book of Bad Songs *is filled with the kind of goofy jokes that are typical of his whimsical sense of humor.* whim (noun).

X

xenophobia (noun) Fear of foreigners or outsiders. *Slobodan Milosevic's nationalistic talk played on the deep xenophobia of the Serbs, who after 500 years of brutal Ottoman occupation had come to distrust all outsiders.*

Z

zenith (noun) Highest point. *Compiling this vocabulary list was the zenith of my literary career: after this, there was nowhere to go but downhill.*

Financing Your Graduate Education

You have already taken a step toward graduate school because you have in hand a preparation book for a graduate school admission exam. Presumably you are about to take one or more of these exams. A good score on the exam is an important component of the picture of competence and capability that you present to graduate programs and funding sponsors. If your grades and achievements have been impressive, a high score confirms you as an all-around good candidate. If either grades or achievements are mediocre, then high scores are imperative to bolster your cause. If you have not already taken the exam, study hard; prepare well. If you did not achieve a competitive score on a previous exam, it might be worthwhile to prepare further and try again. If you feel you need additional GRE practice, log on to Peterson's GRE CAT® Center at www.petersons.com/testprepchannel/graduate_entrance.asp. Here you'll have access to Peterson's GRE PracticePlus where you can:

- Enjoy 3 hours of real-time GRE tutoring, including essay help
- Take 3 complete, computer-adaptive practice tests with answers and explanations
- Learn strategies and shortcuts from test-prep experts

The next thing to do is to begin to investigate which schools have the right programs for you. If you are still in college or out only a year or two, consult with professors who know you well, who are familiar not only with your interests but with your style of working.

Professors may suggest programs that suit your needs, universities that offer emphasis in your areas of interest, and faculty members with whom you might work especially well. Your professors may have inside information about contemplated changes in program, focus, or personnel at various institutions. This information can supplement the information in university bulletins and help you decide which schools to apply to.

If you have been out of school for several years, you may have to rely more on information bulletins. But do not stop there. Ask for advice and suggestions from people in the field, from present employers if your job is related to your career goals, and from the current faculty and advising staff at your undergraduate school. While the current personnel may not be familiar with you and your

appendix b

learning style, they will have up-to-date information on programs and faculties. Send for university and departmental literature. Read everything you can about programs offered. Then study the statements on aid, both need-based and merit-based. Be sure that you are completely clear as to the process-criteria, forms required, other supporting documents, and deadlines. If any step of the process seems ambiguous, make phone calls. You can't afford to miss out on possible funding because you misinterpreted the application directions.

It's a good idea to prepare a master calendar dedicated to graduate school. Note the deadlines for each step of the process for every school, for every foundation, for every possible source of funds. Consult the master calendar daily. Anticipate deadlines, record actions taken by you and by others, follow up, keep on top of it. Do not just let events happen. Be proactive every step of the way.

The university, graduate school, and departmental bulletins will inform you about need-based aid and about any merit-based funding—teaching assistantships, research assistantships, no-strings fellowships, and private foundation fellowships—administered by the university or any of its divisions. This information will be complete for the funding to which it applies. It will include all deadlines, procedures, and documentation required. None of the literature you receive from the university, however, will tell you about fellowships or other funding for which you must apply directly. You must consult grant directories, foundation directories, the Internet, and other source books to find the prizes, awards, scholarships, grants, and fellowships for which you might qualify.

Education is expensive, and the higher the level of education, the greater the cost. As you contemplate going on to graduate or professional school, you must face the question, "How am I going to pay for this?"

With the possible exceptions of a winning lottery ticket, a windfall inheritance, or a very wealthy family, no single source of funds will be adequate to cover tuition, other educational costs, and living expenses during your years of graduate study. While the funding task is daunting, it is not impossible. With patience and hard work, you can piece together your own financing plan.

CONSIDER DEFERRING YOUR APPLICATION

You might consider putting off applying for a few years while you work at the highest paying job you can find and accumulate some funds. A few years' savings will not cover the entire bill, but they can help. It may also give you a chance to resolve outstanding credit problems. If you cannot find a really high paying job, you might seek a position or series of positions closely related to your field for the years between undergraduate and graduate or professional school. A year or more of exposure and involvement can help you to focus your interest. Experience in the field shows up as an asset on your graduate admissions applications and on your applications for fellowships.

The more crystallized your interests, the better essays and personal statements you can write to support your requests. Another benefit to deferral is the opportunity to establish residence. As you research the various graduate programs, you are likely to discover that some of the most exciting programs in your field of interest are being offered at state universities. State universities tend to have lower tuition rates than do private universities. The tuition charged to in-state residents is considerably lower than that charged to out-of-state residents. The requirements for establishing residence vary from state to state; make it a point to inquire about the possibility of in-state tuition at each state university you are considering.

WORKING PART-TIME

Another possible alternative is to be a part-time student and a full- or part-time wage earner. Again, there are a number of options. You might find a totally unrelated but high paying job. You will have to be creative in your search. The Career Center at your college is the best source of information for off-campus employment opportunities in the local area.

If possible, look for a job in a field related to your studies. Such a job could reinforce your learning and contribute to the job experience section of your resume. If you are earning a degree in computer science, you might find computer-related employment. If you are entering law school, you might work as a paralegal or law clerk in a local firm.

You may be fortunate enough to find an employer who will pay for a part or even all of your graduate education. This option is most viable if the advanced degree is to be in business or law, but some corporations will finance a master's degree or even a doctorate if the further training will make the employee more valuable to them. Employers cannot require that you continue your employment for any specified number of years after earning your degree. Rather they rely on your gratitude and goodwill. The programs under which employers help pay for education are as varied as the number of employers and the graduate programs. Many banks, insurance companies, and brokerage houses offer tuition rebates as part of their benefits packages. These companies rebate part or all of the tuition for courses successfully completed by their employees. Sometimes the rate of reimbursement is tied to the grade earned in the course.

Some large law firms will advance part of the law school tuition for promising paralegals after a number of years of service. If these students successfully complete law school and return to the firm for summers and a certain number of years afterward, the balance of the tuition may be reimbursed. Some industrial corporations will cover the cost of part-time study that enhances the skills of employees, thus making them still more useful to the organization. Such corporations may permit these employees to work a shortened workweek at full-time pay while they study.

Some companies even give the employee a year's leave, without salary but with tuition paid, and with a guarantee that the employee will have a job at the end of the leave. This guaranteed position at the end of the leave is worth a lot. It offers peace of mind and freedom to concentrate on research and writing and assures that you will immediately begin earning money with which to repay supplementary graduate loans and leftover undergraduate loans.

If you have been working for the same employer for a year or more, you might do well to inquire about a tuition rebate program. If you are a valuable employee, your employer may be willing to make an investment in you.

THE MILITARY OPTION

There are a number of military programs that provide some form of tuition assistance and/or a monthly stipend. Many public institutions offer tuition remission to members of the National Guard in their home state. For more information, contact a military recruiter or the Veterans Affairs coordinator at the university.

NEED-BASED FUNDING

The need-based funding picture for graduate studies is quite different from its counterpart at the undergraduate level. Most undergraduate funding is need-based; most graduate funding is not. All universities have a mechanism for distributing graduate need-based funding, in grant/loan/self-help packages similar to undergraduate packages, but the funds are more limited. Your application information packet will tell you how to apply for need-based funding.

All students interested in federal assistance must file the Free Application for Federal Student Aid (FAFSA). The FAFSA is available online at www.fafsa.ed.gov. Students need to have their federal PIN to electronically sign the application. If you do not already have a PIN, you can easily obtain one at www.pin.ed.gov. With the exception of a few federal programs for the health professions, all graduate students are considered "independent" for federal student aid purposes. This means you do not need to provide your parents' financial information. Your eligibility is based solely on your income and assets (and spouse's, if married). Most federal aid at the graduate/professional school level is in the form of student loans. The university will coordinate its need-based package with department-sponsored merit funding and with any outside funding you can gather. Plan to look beyond university need-based funding.

You may be eligible for financial aid if you are enrolled at least half-time (usually five semester hours during the academic year, or three semester hours during the summer session) as a graduate student in a program leading to a degree. Students admitted as Special Non-degree Students may also be eligible for some of the programs listed below.

How to Apply

The FAFSA is the primary application for financial aid. Some colleges and universities may have additional applications to complete. Some schools use the PROFILE® application from the College Scholarship Service or Need Access from the Access Group. Both applications are available online at http://profileonline.collegeboard.com/index.jsp and http://www.needaccess.org and charge a fee based on the number of schools you request. Some colleges have an institutional application form that is usually included with the admission material. Some financial aid programs are subject to the availability of funds (first-come, first-served); others are not. To be considered for all limited funds, be sure to submit your FAFSA as soon as possible after January 1 of the year you plan to enroll. The PROFILE® and Need Access form should be filed in September or October prior to your enrollment for the next fall term.

FEDERAL STUDENT AID PROGRAMS

There are a number of federal student aid programs available to graduate students. Additional information can be found in The Student Guide available from any financial aid office or on the Web at www.studentaid.ed.gov. Here is a brief description of the main federal programs:

- The Federal Work-Study Program is an employment program that provides job opportunities both on and off campus. There is a matching requirement of about 25 percent from the employer. Students should contact the financial aid office or the student employment office for more information. Most jobs are part-time during the academic year, but may be full-time during break periods.

- The Federal Perkins Loan Program provides long-term federal loans based on exceptional need. The interest rate is 5 percent, and there is a nine-month grace period following graduation. Amounts are limited and are determined by the financial aid office.

- Subsidized Federal Stafford Loans are long-term federal loans based on need and arranged either with a financial institution or directly by the college, depending on their method of disbursement. These loans are interest free while you are enrolled in school. The current maximum amount is $8,500 per academic year. The Unsubsidized Federal Stafford Loan program is not based on need, and the current maximum is $18,500 (less any subsidized loan eligibility). Interest accrues on the loan from the date of disbursement. Both loans offer a six-month grace period following graduation.

There are a number of federal income tax programs that provide financial assistance to students who file a return. For additional information on the various educational tax incentive programs, refer to IRS Publication 970, which can be accessed at www.irs.gov/publications/p970/index.html.

FELLOWSHIPS AND ASSISTANTSHIPS

The greatest source of funding for graduate study is the graduate department or program itself. Most departments dispense a mixed bag of fellowships, teaching assistantships, graduate assistantships, and research assistantships. Some of these may be allocated to the department by the university; still others are foundation fellowships for which the department nominates its most promising candidates. In most cases, the amount of money attached to the various fellowships and assistantships varies greatly—from tuition remission alone, to tuition remission plus a stipend (also of varying sums), to a stipend alone. Some of the fellowships and assistantships are specifically earmarked for only the first year of graduate study. Others are annually renewable upon application and evidence of satisfactory work in the previous year. Still others are guaranteed for a specified number of years—through three years of course work, for one year of research or fieldwork, or a stipend to pay living costs during the year of writing a dissertation, for example. This can be confusing, so be sure you clearly understand the specific terms and conditions of the award you are being offered.

Since most assistantship income is classified as "wages," it will not affect your academic year financial aid award (which is usually based on your previous year's income, according to the federal formula for determining financial aid eligibility).

However, fellowship income classified as "scholarship" rather than "wages" will be treated as "scholarship resources" in your financial aid package, and thus may affect your eligibility for other financial aid programs.

The information below describes graduate student funding only at the University of Iowa. It is presented here to illustrate the array of possibilities. The information provided by other universities is similar, but each is unique.

SUPPORT FROM THE INSTITUTION

The following awards and appointments are the primary sources of financial assistance available to graduate students through their department or program.

- Teaching and Research Assistantships available in most departments offer stipends typically ranging from $15,000 to $18,000 for half-time appointments. In accordance with general university policy, assistantship holders (quarter-time or more) are classified as residents for fee purposes for the terms during which their appointments are held and any adjacent summer sessions in which they are enrolled. Students on an appointment of half-time or more may have to carry a reduced academic load.

- Iowa Fellowships for first-year graduate students entering doctoral programs carry a minimum stipend of $15,000 plus full tuition for four years on a year-round basis (academic year and summer session). For two of the four years and all summers, recipients have no assignments and are free to pursue their own studies, research, and writing.

- Graduate College Block Allocation Fellowships carry a stipend of $15,000 for the academic year.

- Graduate Merit Fellowships for first-year doctoral students from underrepresented ethnic minority groups carry a one-year stipend of $18,000 plus tuition and fees for the academic year.

- Scholarships, traineeships, and part-time employment are offered by many graduate departments and programs. Funds are received from both public and private agencies, individuals, corporations, and philanthropic organizations. In general, submission of the Application for Graduate Awards places eligible applicants in consideration for these awards.

How to Apply

Submit your Application for Graduate Awards to your department or program by February if you wish to be considered for the following fall.

These non-need-based awards are made on the basis of academic merit. Only students admitted to a graduate department or program are eligible to apply.

Fellowship and assistantship recipients are also eligible to apply for tuition scholarships awarded in amounts up to full-time tuition and fees. Contact your program or department for more specific information.

Surprisingly, the overall wealth of the institution is not necessarily reflected in the graduate funding it offers. Some universities choose to devote the bulk of their discretionary funds to undergraduate need-based aid. Others offer a greater share to graduate students. Some graduate departments in some universities have separate endowments apart from the university endowment as a whole. A department with its own source of funds can dispense these funds as it wishes, within the restrictions of the endowment, of course.

The case of Clark University in Worcester, Massachusetts, is illustrative of the ways a particular department funds its students. Due to its size and available funds, university-based financial aid for *undergraduates* is very limited.

Yet, every doctoral candidate in the geography department is equally funded; each receives tuition abatement and an equal stipend in return for teaching or research assistance. The funding is guaranteed for three years of course work. How can this be? The geography department at Clark has, over the years, developed an extremely high reputation. It is considered one of the premier geography departments in the United States. The university considers investment in its geography department to be one of its priorities because maintaining the reputation of its flagship department enhances the reputation of the university as a whole. Leading professors are eager to be associated with leading departments, so the Clark geography faculty includes some luminaries in its ranks. These faculty members in turn attract research funds. Research funds are used in part to pay for the services of research assistants.

Publishing the results of research attracts additional grants, which help to cover the educational expenses of a number of graduate students. The reputation of the department also helps to draw the best and brightest among its doctoral candidates. These highly qualified students often are awarded merit-based outside fellowships. Students who employ their own funding allow the university to release funds for other students. And because of its reputation and the reputed caliber of its students, the department is often offered the opportunity to nominate its students to compete for private fellowships.

Money entering the department in this way releases still more of the limited funds for student support. In a good year, there may even be funds to help some students at the beginning of their dissertation research.

The situation at Clark, while it is Clark's alone, indicates that it may be possible to find funding even at a small school. Graduate aid is not monolithic. You must ask about the special features in each department and in each program. Do not limit your research to the overall university bulletin!

Sometimes a university will offer some departments the opportunity to nominate candidates for outside fellowships open to students of certain specified departments or to students of the university at large. For example, the MacArthur Foundation funds a number of interdisciplinary fellowships in peace studies at a few selected universities.

Each participating university is allocated a number of fellowships to dispense at its discretion. The university then opens the competition to appropriate departments, and the departments in turn nominate candidates from among their most promising applicants. The departments choose nominees on the basis of personal statements submitted at the time of application and on the basis of those applicants' credentials and background experiences. They then solicit the nominees to prepare additional application materials and essays and supply additional recommendations to support application for the fellowship. Having MacArthur fellows among its students brings both money and prestige to the department. Each department studies credentials and statements carefully before soliciting applicants. However, the department could overlook someone. If you have not been invited to apply for a fellowship that you think you qualify for, you can suggest to the department— diplomatically, of course—that you consider yourself a likely candidate.

Few individuals are awarded any one fellowship, but each person who does win one is assured a comfortable source of funding. And someone has to win. It might as well be you. Those who win the named fellowships are removed from the competition for other merit-based or need-based funding, thus increasing the chance of other applicants to win any remaining funds.

Most foundation-funded fellowships, especially those for entering graduate students, are channeled through the department or program. To be considered for these fellowships, you must be recommended by the department. There are some fellowships out there, however, for which you must apply as an individual. Some of these are regional, and some are targeted at a specific population. Some are tied to a field, such as economics or philosophy, and others have a specific purpose in mind, such as studies aimed at improving the welfare of the homeless. Of the privately funded fellowships some are for the first year only, some for the full graduate career, some for the last year of course work only, and still others to support the dissertation at a specific stage or throughout research and writing. Some are relatively small awards; others are so generous that they provide total financial security to the student. The sources of these fellowships range from your local Rotary Club to Rotary International, to the American Association of University Women (AAUW) fellowships, to the prestigious Rhodes Scholarships.

FUNDING POSSIBILITIES FROM PRIVATE SOURCES

The names of some of the philanthropic foundations that give grants for graduate study are almost household words—Dana, Mellon, Ford, Sloan, Rockefeller, Guggenheim, MacArthur, Fulbright, and Woodrow Wilson are but a few. These foundations, and others like them, offer funding at many levels of study and for a variety of purposes.

The National Science Foundation offers funding for the full graduate program in science and engineering for minority students as well as for other students. Other National Science Foundation fellowships specifically fund the research and writing of doctoral dissertations. The U.S. Department of Education Jacob K. Javits Fellowships fund full doctoral programs in the arts, humanities, and social sciences.

The National Research Council Howard Hughes Medical Institute Doctoral Fellowships offer individual awards with an $18,000 annual stipend, with an additional $16,000 for tuition and fees for up to five years of doctoral work in biology or the health sciences. The Mellon and Ford Foundations both fund fellowships for Ph.D. candidates.

The AAUW is very active in disbursing funds to women for graduate study. Local units give small gifts to undergraduates.

Larger grants are made by the AAUW through its Educational Foundation Programs office. In some years, the AAUW supports as many as fifty women at the dissertation stage. The Business and Professional Women's Foundation gives scholarships to mature women entering graduate programs. Some of these scholarships are earmarked for women over the age of 35. The American Women in Selected Professions Fellowships fund women in their last year of law or graduate studies in sums ranging from $5,000 to $12,000 to support women in a variety of fields. Other funding for doctoral dissertations comes from the Woodrow Wilson National Fellowship Foundation (in social sciences and humanities), the Social Science Research Council, and the Guggenheim Foundation. Some foundation funding is reserved for study abroad. Rhodes Scholarships, in particular, support students studying at Oxford. Various Fulbright, Wilsons, Marshalls, and MacArthurs, among others, support research in foreign universities and at field sites.

The above listing is far from exhaustive. In fact, this is only a tiny sampling of the funding possibilities from private foundations. Even so, the number of grants available is far exceeded by the number of graduate students who would like to have them. You must work hard to identify and to earn the grants for which you qualify.

FINDING SOURCES OF FINANCIAL AID

There are a number of directories that list these prizes, scholarships, and fellowships one by one. Two excellent resources include *Peterson's Getting Money for Graduate School* and *Peterson's Scholarships, Grants & Prizes*. The directories give the name of the sponsor, contact information, eligibility requirements, and application deadlines. They also describe the grants, the number of grants awarded, and the dollar amounts. If the grants are awarded to support research, the directories may give representative titles of projects funded. One of the most useful features of the directories is their cross-indexing. When you consult a grants directory you can look up sources under academic fields; civic, professional, social, or union affiliation; corporate affiliation; employment experience; military service; ethnic heritage; religious affiliation; talent; residency; etc. These directories are very useful as a starting point in the search for outside funding.

Give yourself plenty of time to research all the possible grants for which you may qualify. Immediately call or write each sponsor requesting application materials. Do not rely on deadlines printed in the directories and put off requesting materials. Deadlines change. Do not discount grants or prizes with low dollar amounts attached. A small grant may not be adequate to see you through even a semester of study, but it will do much to enhance your resume. The fact that you were able to compete successfully for any prize makes you a more attractive candidate for the higher-tagged fellowships you apply for next year. If a grant cannot be combined, you may have to decline it, but the fact of having won is already in your favor. Most often, small grants can be combined with other sources of funding, so even small ones help. Some excellent sources of grant and foundation support information are now available online. One of the most helpful organizations in terms of general assistance in the search for grants is The Foundation Center, which can be found online at http://fdncenter.org.

APPLYING FOR A GRANT

The procedure for applying for grants and fellowships for your coursework years is similar for both university-administered and private foundation sources. The best advice is to start early. Everything takes longer than you expect, and deadlines tend to be inviolate. Everyone with money to give away is besieged by applicants. There is no need to extend deadlines.

Once you receive application material, begin immediately to accumulate the specified documentation. Each sponsor has different requirements, so read carefully. You will probably need official transcripts from every college you ever attended, even if you took only one course over the summer. You are likely to be asked for official copies of test scores, too. Letters of recommendation are always required. Think about them carefully. You want to request letters from people who have known you as a scholar—professors with whom you have worked closely or authors for whom you have done research or fact checking. You want your letters to be written by people whom you believe have admired your work and who express themselves well.

And, consider the reliability of the people from whom you request letters of recommendation. Your application can be seriously jeopardized or even torpedoed if your recommendations do not come through on time. Choose carefully. Consider asking for one extra recommendation just in case someone lets you down. Having recommendations sent to you and then forwarding them in their sealed envelopes is the best way to keep track of what has come in if this procedure is permitted by the sponsor. Many university career offices will keep these letters on file for your use.

You are more in control of the other documents you are likely to be asked for in support of your application. The first of these is a "personal goals statement." This is a carefully reasoned, clear statement of your interests, the reasons for your choice of program, personal growth goals, and career goals. Tailor each statement to the needs and interests of the specific sponsor. Try to tie in your statement with the special strengths of the program and with the advantages offered by a particular sponsor. Be sincere and enthusiastic. Adhere to the page limits or word count specified in the application instructions. And remember, neatness counts.

You may also be asked for your resume, samples of scholarly writing, or summaries of research you have done. If the grant you seek is meant to finance research or dissertation, you may have to go into detail about the scope of your research, methodology, purpose, expected final results, and even proposed budget. Give thought before you write. Then follow the sponsor's instructions, providing all the information that is requested, but not so much more as to overwhelm or bore the reader.

One caveat: Read the requirements carefully before you apply. If you do not fully qualify, do not apply. There are ample qualified applicants for every grant. Requirements will not be waived. The application process is an exacting one and requires you to impose upon others. Do not waste their time or your own.

EMPLOYMENT OPPORTUNITIES ON CAMPUS

Your department is clearly the best university-based source for fellowships, teaching assistantships, and research assistantships. If you are not successful here, look at other departments on campus that can help you, specifically the student employment office, the career counseling center, and the financial aid office. If you have an area of expertise outside of your own graduate department, by all means build upon it. If you are fluent in a language taught at the university, you may be able to teach in the language department. Your best chance for a teaching assistantship outside of your department is in a university with relatively few graduate programs. Departments favor their own graduate students, but if a department has no qualified students of its own, it may be delighted to acquire the services of a graduate student from another department. Some universities even have a formalized mechanism for allocating teaching assistants where they are needed. To return to the example of Clark, where all graduate students must serve as research or teaching assistants, often there are not as many openings for assistants in the undergraduate geography department as there are students. Clark has relatively few graduate programs, and geography students tend to have strong backgrounds in political science, economics, and ecology. The graduate geography department and the undergraduate deans readily cooperate to place geography students where they are most needed. In universities with less-defined needs for teaching assistants, you may have to be your own advocate. Regardless of your current department, if you can document your ability to assist in another department, you should pursue opportunities there. Do not be shy; let your area of special competence be well known.

Another possible source of university employment is as a residence adviser or freshman adviser. If you took peer counseling training while in high school or were successful in a counseling function during your own undergraduate years, consider yourself a candidate. In very large universities with big freshmen dormitories, a few graduate students with experience in residence advising may be taken on to coordinate and supervise the senior undergraduates who serve as floor or wing advisers.

There are a number of possible advantages to being appointed to a major university-based position such as teaching assistant or residence adviser. One is that, at a state university, you may be considered for in-state tuition. Another possibility is that you will be classified as an employee of the university. Policies vary, of course, but at many institutions employees of the university are eligible for reduced tuition or even for total remission of tuition. In addition, assistants generally receive a stipend, which, even if it does not totally cover living expenses, is certainly a big help. Residence hall advisors may get free room along with tuition remission, and they generally get choice accommodations. There are usually a wide range of job possibilities on campus, from the library to food service. Develop some good contacts with faculty and staff to learn the ropes and find these job possibilities.

If you were a member of a fraternity or sorority as an undergraduate, you may fulfill a role similar to that of residence adviser in your fraternity or sorority house. You should contact the Dean of Students office for additional information.

ALL LOANS ARE NOT ALIKE

We previously discussed the federal loan options for graduate students. If you still need additional assistance, the financial aid office can provide you with a number of options for private loans. These are "credit based," meaning you will need to have a good credit score or a co-signer with a good rating. The financial aid office is the best source of information for these loans. We recommend getting a free copy of your credit report as part of planning for graduate school. Try and resolve all reported credit problems before enrolling in graduate school.

Many universities have established private loan programs to assist their students. Some of the higher cost private schools have developed a network of funding sources with attractive terms and conditions. If you need this help, check out the Web site of the university's financial aid page and graduate information page.

After graduation, you will be required to attend an "exit interview" to review your loans and plan for repayment. Be sure to look into the various loan forgiveness programs available from federal, state, and employer-based sources. Loan forgiveness is offered, in many cases, to students who accept teaching positions in low-income school districts. There are programs for health professionals, law enforcement officers, and lawyers who decide to work in lower-income positions in an effort to alleviate shortages. Many students consider the Peace Corps or AmeriCorps programs as an interesting first career step with attractive loan repayment assistance options.

If your ideals encourage using your educational opportunities to help others, you may find that this type of assistance program gives you the best of all possible worlds. The time commitment tends to only be a few years, after which you can move into the private sector with excellent experience to further your applications. Or, you may find that you really enjoy the work you have taken on and build a satisfying career in public service.

There are a number of other loan programs that offer attractive features. The Hattie M. Strong Foundation, for instance, offers interest-free loans for the final year of graduate school or law school on the assumption that without money worries the student can earn higher grades in the final year and obtain a better position after graduation.

Everything that has been said about private foundation funding applies equally to loans as to grants and fellowships. The same directories that can lead you to grants and fellowships can lead you to foundation loans. Again, some of these require evidence of need; others are strictly merit-based. Some apply to the early years of graduate study; others are geared to the dissertation years. Some carry no or low rates of interest, and some have forgiveness provisions if certain conditions are met. In general, foundation loans offer better terms than commercial loans. Do not limit your search through the grant directories to high-paying grants. Give equal attention to the smaller prizes and to the loan programs.

NOTES

NOTES

NOTES

NOTES

NOTES